TERRORISM

Perspectives from the Social Sciences

TERRORISM

Perspectives from the Social Sciences

MURAT HANER

ASSISTANT PROFESSOR, SCHOOL OF CRIMINOLOGY AND CRIMINAL JUSTICE,
ARIZONA STATE UNIVERSITY

MELISSA M. SLOAN

PROFESSOR, DEPARTMENT OF SOCIOLOGY AND INTERDISCIPLINARY
SOCIAL SCIENCES, UNIVERSITY OF SOUTH FLORIDA

OXFORD
UNIVERSITY PRESS

OXFORD
UNIVERSITY PRESS

Oxford University Press is a department of the University of Oxford.
It furthers the University's objective of excellence in research, scholarship,
and education by publishing worldwide. Oxford is a registered trade mark
of Oxford University Press in the UK and in certain other countries.

Published in the United States of America by Oxford University Press
198 Madison Avenue, New York, NY 10016, United States of America.

Library of Congress Control Number: 2024044397

ISBN 978–0–19–759987–7

Printed by Integrated Books International, United States of America

PREFACE

Terrorism is an incredibly complex problem of global concern. As such, a comprehensive understanding of the topic necessitates insights from the theoretical perspectives and empirical research of multiple academic disciplines, research centers, and think tanks. While much remains to be understood, an increasing number of rigorous research programs have furthered our knowledge in many areas of terrorism studies—factors that lead to the radicalization of individuals into terrorist organizations, motivations for different types of terrorism, terrorist group operations and attack planning, and the effects of terrorism on populations.

Drawing on the emerging body of research from the social sciences, this text guides students through an analysis of terrorism and counterterrorism measures. By covering key theoretical perspectives and empirical findings on the diversity of issues related to the phenomenon, utilizing real-world case studies of terrorist groups and attacks, and incorporating an extensive art program of photographs and diagrams, we have provided an accessible and engaging presentation of the essential knowledge in the field.

More specifically, each chapter first provides key content at a general level and follows that overview with case studies and images to demonstrate the severe, wide-ranging, and multifaceted impacts of terrorism and terrorists' actions. The multiple case studies integrated throughout the text facilitate an exploration of the diverse perspectives of individuals labeled as terrorists to gain insight into their motivations and rationales for joining these groups. By examining these perspectives, the reader can uncover the underlying themes and driving factors that influence such decisions. This approach not only provides a balanced understanding of the topic but also encourages critical thinking and the application of academic knowledge as students connect theoretical concepts with real-world scenarios. Our intention is to foster a more engaging and impactful learning experience, grounded in current academic research.

The book contains thirteen chapters, which are divided into five sections as follows:

- **Part I** reviews key concepts and definitions in the field of terrorism studies. This initial section also discusses the experience of living under the threat of terrorism and the psychological impacts of terrorism on its victims and on societies in general.

- **Part II** presents the predominant theoretical explanations of terrorism, including individual and social factors that influence participation in terrorist groups and theories of the radicalization process. This section also includes a chapter on women's engagement in terrorism and political violence, a pressing topic.
- **Part III** covers different types of terrorism including ideological terrorism, nationalistic terrorism, and religious terrorism, and uses case studies of specific groups to illustrate each of the discussed terrorism types.
- **Part IV** covers the operations of terrorist organizations, including factors that influence terrorists' choice of attack strategies and targets, the interrelationships among terrorists, the media, and the public, and how terrorists finance their operations
- **Part V** focuses on combating terrorism. This section covers theoretical and empirical research on deterring terrorism and discusses research-informed strategies and programs for preventing future attacks. The concluding chapter considers the ethical issues raised by counterterrorism measures.

In addition, each chapter includes learning objectives, a list of key words that are defined in the text glossary, and recommended readings.

Finally, a theme emphasized throughout the text is that terrorism is an enduring challenge. Many of the concepts covered in the text—including terrorism itself—have no universal definition, and multiple theories and perspectives can be applied to different aspects of terrorism. A critical analysis of existing knowledge and continued social scientific research are essential to furthering our understanding of the nature, causes, consequences, and prevention of terrorism. It is our hope that the distinctive approach offered in this text inspires the critical thinking needed to address the contemporary threat of terrorism and its impact on societies.

ACKNOWLEDGMENTS

Excerpts from Chapter 5 have appeared in M. M. Sloan & M. Haner, "Women's involvement in terrorist organizations," in S. L. Browning, L. C. Butler, & C. L. Jonson (Eds.), *Gender and crime: Contemporary theoretical perspectives*, Routledge (2024), and excerpts from Case Study 2 in the chapter were originally published in M. Haner, F. T. Cullen, & M. L. Benson, "Women and the PKK: Ideology, gender, and terrorism," *International Criminal Justice Review*, *30*(3), 279–301 (2019).

CONTENTS

Understanding the Basics of Terrorism and Political Violence

CHAPTER 1

Terrorism

Definitions and Classifications

Learning Objectives
1. To understand the extent of terrorism in the world.
2. To discuss the geographical distribution of terrorist violence across the world.
3. To examine the definitional issues regarding terrorism.
4. To explore the history of terrorism.
5. To describe the diverse forms and categories of terrorism.
6. To offer a comprehensive definition of terrorism.

1.1 INTRODUCTION

Terrorism—the use of violence against noncombatants to affect a larger audience and achieve some social or political goal—is a controversial issue of worldwide concern. This chapter will introduce the concept of terrorism and discuss the complexities associated with defining it. For some it may seem like a recent phenomenon, something that emerged with the 2001 attacks on the World Trade Center in New York. But terrorism has existed for hundreds of years. Throughout history, terrorists have carried out devastating attacks to advance diverse sets of political agendas. Leaders have been assassinated, entire cities and nations have been targeted, and thousands of innocent people have lost their lives because of terrorist attacks (Haner 2017). In many countries, including the ones where terrorism is a rare occurrence, the issue of counterterrorism ranks high on national agendas.

According to the Global Terrorism Database kept by the University of Maryland, more than 20,000 people have died as a result of 8,438 terrorist activities globally in 2020 (the most recent year for which data are available) (Global Terrorism Database 2024). That means in 2020 alone, there were on average 700 terrorist attacks worldwide, causing 1,700 deaths per month. That year was the sixth consecutive year of declining terrorist violence since 2014, in which the **global death toll** because of terrorism peaked to more than to 44,490 deaths, including perpetrators. Even though regional trends vary significantly, the total number of deaths from terrorism has decreased more

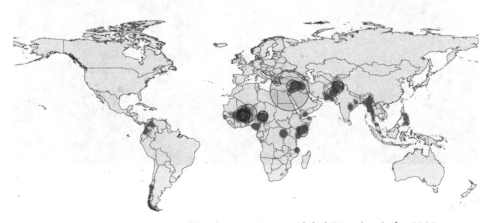

FIGURE 1.1   Terrorist incidents worldwide, 2023. *Source:* Global Terrorism Index 2024.

TABLE 1.1   Top 10 Countries with the Most Terrorist Attacks in 2020

	Total Attacks	Total Deaths
Afghanistan	2,604	10,081
Iraq	764	525
Nigeria	478	2,102
Yemen	474	903
India	450	212
Congo	310	1,356
Philippines	294	280
Pakistan	294	322
Somalia	280	885
Syria	256	973
Worldwide	8,438	22,847

Source: Miller 2022

than 50 percent since 2014 (Institute for Economics and Peace 2020). Yet this statistic is still much higher today compared to the year 2010, at which the global death toll was 7,827 (Miller 2020).

In addition to year-to-year variability in the number of terrorist incidents, there is variation across countries, with some parts of the world considerably more troubled by terrorism than others. If we have a closer look at the exact numbers as shown in Table 1.1, we see that Afghanistan, first on the list, suffered more terrorist attacks than any other country in the world, with more than 10,000 people killed because of terrorist activities in 2020. Nigeria ranked second in deaths from terrorism, with about 2,100 people killed (Miller 2022). The Democratic Republic of the Congo also suffered over a thousand casualties during the year.

What about Western nations, such as the United States and Germany? Table 1.2 indicates that in 2020, a total of 50 people died as a result of terrorist activities in Western Europe and North America (START 2024)—a statistic that is drastically different than for countries such as Afghanistan, Iraq, and Syria. The same holds for the United States; 12 US citizens were killed in terrorist activities in 2020 (Global Terrorism Database 2024).

If we put these numbers on a map of the world, we can see the regional differences in the impact of terrorism during the year 2020. Researchers use choropleth maps, like the one shown in Figure 1.2, to visualize statistical data for a given region or area. These maps use varying shades to visually represent the global distribution and frequency of terrorism-related fatalities. The shading intensity indicates the scale of casualties, with darker shades signifying regions experiencing higher numbers of fatalities linked to terrorist incidents. For instance, in Figure 1.2, the darkest areas highlight the most heavily impacted regions in 2020, emphasizing where terrorist activity resulted in significant loss of life. This map shows where terrorists killed the most people in 2020. The prevalence of terrorist casualties across the world are depicted with a range of colors, from green and yellow for lower numbers of casualties to bright red for the highest number. As is clear here, terrorist violence is heavily concentrated in certain parts of the world. We see **hot spots** in Southeast Asia, the Middle East, and Northern Africa, and we also see that many parts of Asia, America, and Western Europe are relatively less affected by terrorism.

TABLE 1.2   Terrorism in the West, by Country, 2020

	Total Attacks	Total Deaths
United States	103	12
United Kingdom	90	6
Greece	50	0
Netherlands	37	0
Germany	33	14
France	24	11
Canada	14	3
Italy	13	0
Cyprus	11	0
Ireland	10	0
Austria	4	6
Belgium	3	0
Sweden	3	0
Switzerland	2	1
Norway	2	0
Finland	1	0
Total	**400**	**50**

Source: GTD (2024)

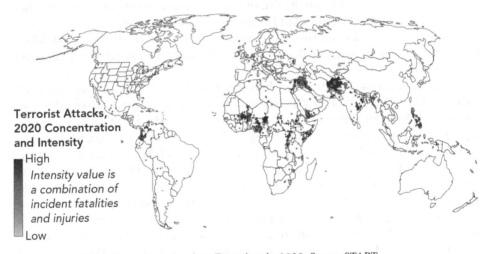

FIGURE 1.2   Global terrorism overview: Terrorism in 2020. *Source:* START.

While terrorism is a worldwide phenomenon, there is enormous regional variation in its prevalence and impact (Miller 2020; START 2024).

It is of course true that the West has experienced many large and devastating terrorist attacks that have claimed the lives of thousands of people, such as the September 11, 2001 attacks in the United States, the coordinated suicide bombing attacks that targeted passengers traveling on London's public transport system in 2005, and the 2004 attacks

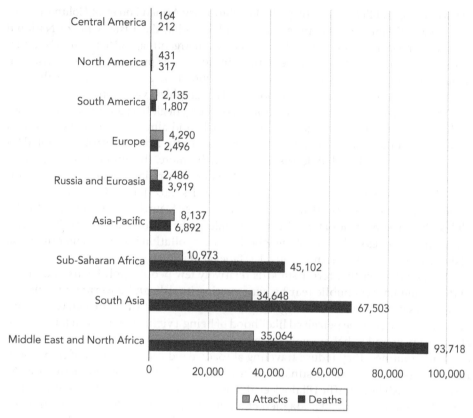

FIGURE 1.3   Attacks and deaths from terrorism by region, 2002–2019. *Source:* Miller (2020).

that targeted four separate commuter trains in Madrid, Spain (Haner 2017). But again, the casualties from these attacks are still extremely low when compared to the toll terrorism has taken in, for example, Afghanistan alone. If we look at the statistics for the past two decades (Figure 1.3), we see that 95 percent of the casualties from terrorism between 2002 and 2019 occurred in the Middle East, North Africa, and Southeast Asia. Only 1.2 percent of the deaths occurred in North America and Europe during the same time (Institute for Economics & Peace 2020). In other words, terrorism and terrorist incidents tend to be strongly geographically focused.

Readers should be cautioned, however, regarding three important facts about the issue of terrorism. First, even the specific regions that are recognized as a hotbed of terrorist activities (the Middle East, North Africa, and Southeast Asia) do not have prevalent terrorism in all countries within said regions. Terrorism is heavily concentrated in only a few specific countries, such as Iraq and Afghanistan. Not all countries in the Middle East or Africa are heavily affected by terrorism.

Second, even though the majority of **terrorism-related deaths** occur in Afghanistan, Iraq, Nigeria, and Syria, this was not always the case. People in South and Central America have been the victims of terrorism for many decades. More specifically, between the 1960s and late 1980s, guerilla movements in Argentina, Bolivia, Chile, Colombia,

Mexico, Peru, and El Salvador (e.g., the Revolutionary Armed Forces of Columbia, Farabundo Marti Liberation People's Forces in El Salvador, Zapatista Army of National Liberation in Mexico, People's Revolutionary Army in Argentina, and Sandinista National Liberation Front in Nicaragua) were responsible for a large proportion of terrorist incidents worldwide (Anderson 1980; Jenkins 2006; Lopez 2020). Historically, the **prevalence of terrorism** has had temporal and geographical variation.

Third, even though the issue of terrorism is an urgent global concern, the actual risk of dying from a terrorist attack is extremely small, and almost nonexistent in several parts of the world (Haner et al. 2020). For example, deaths from terrorism accounted for only .05 percent of all global deaths in 2018. Furthermore, this number is much lower in developed countries such as the United States, Australia, France, and Germany. According to the National Center for Health Statistics (2021), out of an approximately 3.5 million registered deaths that occurred in the United States in 2020, only 12 individuals lost their lives because of terrorist attacks. Indeed, the risk of dying from other threats in the United States such as smoking, obesity, or air pollution is much higher than that of dying from a potential terrorist attack (Haner et al. 2021).

Despite the fact that terrorism kills relatively few people, politicians and media outlets often harness public **fear** by exaggerating its risk, and governments allocate large shares from their annual budgets to counterterrorism efforts. Further, researchers have discovered that the perceived likelihood of being a victim of terrorism (and associated fear) may lead to behavioral changes in which individuals amend their lifestyles and daily routines: they reduce traveling abroad; avoid certain modes of transportation, such as flying; restrict destinations for vacations; limit their outside activities; and avoid peak rush hour traffic (Blalock et al. 2009; Eisenman et al. 2009; Goodwin et al. 2005; Lee and Lemyre 2009; Maguen et al. 2008; Sloan et al. 2020; Torabi and Seo 2004). In Chapter 2, we will examine in more detail the effects this fear has on individuals and society.

1.2 DEFINITIONAL ISSUES REGARDING TERRORISM

It is difficult to define terrorism because there is no agreement on what kind of violence constitutes an act of terrorism. Although nations worldwide grapple with the issue of terrorism, to date, there is no universally accepted definition. Not only do the governments around the world create their own definitions of terrorism, but formal agencies within a single country may develop and adopt their own unique definitions. For example, almost every agency in the United States that deals with the issue of terrorism, such as the FBI, CIA, and State Department, has historically used a different definition of terrorism. In 2004, leading terrorism experts Leonard Weinberg, Ami Pedahzur, and Sivan Hoefler examined the definitions of terrorism used in peer-reviewed journal publications between 1977 and 2001 and discovered 73 different definitions in the top three journals in the field: *Terrorism; Terrorism and Political Violence*; and *Studies in Conflict and Terrorism* (Weinberg et al. 2004). Even in academia, researchers have developed and used dozens of different definitional constructs. As American historian and journalist Walter Laquear observed, "terrorism has appeared in so many different forms and under so many different circumstances that a comprehensive definition is impossible" (Laqueur 2017).

There are several reasons why a unanimously agreed definition has not been adopted during terrorism's centuries-old history. Here, we will discuss the four main issues that prevent this (Schmid 2004):

1) The term "terrorism" has had different meanings at different times.
2) The issue of terrorism is a contested concept (e.g., "One man's terrorist is another man's freedom fighter").
3) There are issues related to the processes of delegitimization and criminalization of certain groups.
4) Similar to other forms of violence (rape, murder, theft, vandalism, etc.), there are several different types of terrorism.

1.2.1 The Term Has Had Different Meanings and Attributions at Different Times

The word "terrorism," from its first use during the **French Revolution** to its application to a recent incident—the insurrection at the United States Capitol Building on January 6, 2021—has had different meanings. Certain violent acts that today we might label as terrorism were called something else in other times. For example, consider the assassination of the 35th President of the United States, John F. Kennedy, on November 22, 1963, as he rode in a motorcade in Dallas, Texas. President Kennedy was killed by a former marine who was known to embrace Marxist-Leninist ideas. Newspaper headlines read "President Slain by Assassin," "Martyred!," or "Kennedy Assassinated." The suspect, Lee Harvey Oswald, was called a fanatic, an anarchist, and an assassin. The news all around the world was shocking and sorrowful. However, if we examine the information produced at that time—the newspapers, journals, TV and radio programs, and the statements delivered by prominent leaders in the US and across the world—we will not find any use of the word "terrorism" to describe this horrific event. Nowhere in these outlets was the incident referred to as terrorism or the assassin described as a terrorist. However, today, the killing of a US president would most certainly raise questions about terrorism, no matter who the perpetrator is. The multifaceted history of terrorism makes any definition problematic and difficult, and the meaning of the word has undergone significant changes between the present day and when it was first used by the Jacobins, from being used to describe "government by intimidation" to "intimidation and coercion of governments."

Reign of Terror, France

The term "terrorism" was first used to describe the violence applied by the French government to protect the French Revolution from its perceived enemies between late 1793 and the summer of 1794 (Shepard 1953). During this time, the revolutionary forces in France—commonly known as the **Jacobins**—believed that the use of indiscriminate terrorism was a necessary means to reshape the society and destroy the remnants of the old regime. Approximately 40,000 people who were perceived as enemies of the newly established government were executed without trials in the name of protecting the order and consolidating power in the country. The term *"terrorisme"* was not used in an anti-government sense when it was first applied by the Jacobins. *"Regime de la terror"* (administration by fear or terrorism) was a means to control society; it was a

FIGURE 1.4   The term *"terrorisme"* was coined to describe the violence applied by the French Jacobins. Remains of guillotine victims from the Reign of Terror can still be found in Paris chapel's walls. *Source:* Paris Musées collections.

method of rule, similar to the "state of emergency" measures employed by governments in modern times (Crawford 2013).

Propaganda By the Deed

The meaning of terrorism drastically changed during the second half of the nineteenth and early twentieth centuries. Unsuccessful at using dialogue and other peaceful methods to distribute their propaganda and achieve their political goals, anarchists and revolutionary groups in Russia, England, Germany, France, and other parts of the world began to employ terrorist tactics such as bombings and assassinations to achieve social change and overthrow the established governments and their institutions (Bantman 2019; Schmid 2004). This was called **propaganda by the deed**. Different from the **reign of terror** of the French government, revolutionaries applied discriminate violence, or **targeted killings**, attacking only the "enemies of the people"—members of the elite and government officials including industrialists, politicians, judges, and police officers. In their eyes, it was justifiable to kill government officials and the symbols of capitalism to destroy and delegitimize the oppressive social and political order and spread fear among its supporters (Fleming 1980).

The State as Terrorist: Red Terror of Soviet Russia and Nazi Germany

Next, the world witnessed the use of terrorism by **totalitarian** states such as the Bolsheviks' Soviet Russia (1917–1922) and the Nazi Party in Germany (1933–1945). Similar to the Jacobins' reign of terror in France, Bolsheviks and Nazis used political repression and executions to eliminate the opposition and other threats to themselves, and to consolidate and maximize their powers (Anderson 1995; Musolff 2010). All aspects of social life were controlled by the governments in both countries. Civil liberties were curtailed, freedom of press abolished, and people were denied the right of assembly. Absolute and unconditional obedience was expected of the public. Police were given extreme powers, such as the ability to detain people indefinitely without charges. Those who were suspected as potential opponents of the system were prosecuted and punished directly by the police (Primoratz 2013). It is estimated that at least two million Russians lost

FIGURE 1.5 Explosions at an opera house in Barcelona by an anarchist (1893). *Source:* BnF Gallica.

their lives under the Bolshevik regime (Timofeychev 2018) and 11 million Germans, Jews, and others (Romani people, intellectually disabled people, political opponents of the Nazi regime, criminals, and LGBTQ+ individuals) became victims of Nazi political, racial, and religious persecution (History.com 2021; Holocaust Encyclopedia 2021).

In both Germany and Russia, Nazi and Bolshevik administrations used terrorism, as they lacked the popular support necessary to stay in power. They employed several measures including genocide, mass murder, large-scale forced labor, starvation, medical experiments, **terror bombings**, and concentration camps under guise of defending the state from "internal enemies" (Sutuurman 2019).

Decolonization and Separation Struggle By Insurgent Groups

During the second half of the twentieth and the early twenty-first centuries, terrorist tactics were mostly employed by insurgent groups. Nations that were colonized by Western powers demanded their independence and self-determination, often via violent clashes with the colonizers (Adams & Mulligan 2012; Collins 2016). Additionally, Jewish-British conflict in Palestine, Arab-Israeli conflict in the Middle East, Latin American insurgency, and the European guerilla warfare (in Italy, Germany, and Ireland) after World War II were all labeled as terrorism. The label became a pejorative such that no one—neither the states nor the separatist groups—intentionally used the word "terrorism" to define their fighting strategy as others had in the past (Schmid 2004).

FIGURE 1.6   After becoming chancellor of Germany in 1933, Adolf Hitler quickly turned Germany into a one-party dictatorship and used the police to enforce Nazi policies. *Source:* IgorGolovniov/Shutterstock.

Even though they were labeled terrorists by foreign and dominant powers, these insurgent groups often argued that they were "freedom fighters," fighting against the oppression and injustice applied by the occupiers.

Islam and Terrorism

After the 1990s, the word "terrorism" has almost exclusively been used for actions carried out by Islamist groups, the perceived link between Islam and terrorism becoming pervasive in American and Western society (D'Orazio & Salehyan 2018; Powell 2018; Saleem & Anderson 2013; Tehranian 2008). Professor of Law Caroline Mala Corbin (2017) argues that this link is supported by two false narratives: first, "all terrorists are Muslim," which is sometimes understood as "all Muslims are terrorists"; and second, "White people are never terrorists." Built on false, discriminatory stereotypes of Muslims as terrorists—and the White privilege of avoiding the terrorist label—these narratives are frequently communicated to the public through media and government propaganda. Chapter 2 discusses in more detail the history and consequences of conflating Islam and terrorism.

1.2.2 Terrorism Is a Contested Concept

The second reason we do not have a universal definition of terrorism is because terrorism is a *contested concept*—in other words, there is a very thin line between engaging in terrorism and the act of freedom fighting. This issue can be best illustrated by the old saying,

FIGURE 1.7 Terrorism is a highly contested and complex concept. Its definition and interpretation can vary significantly depending on the perspective of different individuals, governments, organizations, and scholars. *Source:* Ladislav Faigl, Public domain, via Wikimedia Commons; Anton-Ivanov/Shutterstock; Hamid Mir, CC BY-SA 3.0, via Wikimedia Commons; John Mathew Smith 2001/CC BY-SA 2.0, via Wikimedia Commons.

"one person's terrorist is another person's freedom fighter" (Schmid 2004). The very same act can either be terrorism or freedom fighting, depending on who is defining the action. Figure 1.7 shows four individuals associated with terrorism.

In Figure 1.7, the first face you see is that of Menachem Begin. He was the leader of a Zionist group named Irgun Zvai Leumi in Israel that engaged in bloody terrorist missions against the British rule between the years of 1947 and 1948, before the creation of the state of Israel in 1948. His goal was to force the British army to remove its military presence from Palestine by engaging in a series of guerilla attacks, to diminish the prestige of the British army. Britain and other European countries labeled Begin a terrorist and the British Intelligence Agency MI-5 put a "dead or alive" bounty on his head (Crenshaw 1981; Walton 2014). But Begin became the prime minister of Israel in 1977 and he even won the Nobel Peace Prize in 1979 for signing a peace treaty with Egypt.

Second from the left in Figure 1.7 is Yasser Arafat. He was the cofounder of Fatah in 1950, a Palestinian military organization fighting for the liberation of Palestinians under the Israeli authority. He engaged in terrorist tactics such as roadside bombings and attacks on Israeli civilians. In 1994, he received the Nobel Peace Prize, along with Israeli Prime Minister Yitzhak Rabin. Israel and other states that support Israel often regarded Yasser Arafat as an authoritarian leader and a manipulative terrorist, and he was a persona non grata in the United States and Europe for several years (Chang 2005; Tamimi 2007). However, for Arabs and many others, not only was he a great statesman and peacemaker, but he was also a hero who brought Palestinian concerns into the world's agenda. For example, former French President

FIGURE 1.8 The 1994 Nobel Peace Prize was jointly awarded to Yasser Arafat, Shimon Perez, and Yitzhak Rabin for their peace efforts in the Middle East. *Source:* Government Press Office (Israel), CC BY-SA 3.0, via Wikimedia Commons.

Jacques Chirac (who served between 1995 and 2007) said Arafat was "a man of courage and conviction who for 40 years incarnated the Palestinians' fight for recognition of their national rights" (El Amraoui 2012). Russian President Vladimir Putin described Arafat as "a great political leader of international significance" (Frankel 2004).

Next in Figure 1.7 we have Osama bin Laden—the deceased leader of the militant terrorist organization al-Qaeda, who is regarded as a terrorist throughout most of the world. Bin Laden came from a wealthy family, learned English in Oxford during his teenage years, and later joined the Afghan Mujahideen in 1979, at the age of 22, to fight against the Soviet invasion of Afghanistan (Bergen 2006; Scheuer 2011).

The Afghan **Mujahideen**, which essentially formed the Taliban in the early 1990s, was hosted in the White House in 1983 when another world power, the Soviet Union, regarded them as terrorists. President Ronald Reagan stated at this gathering that "in making mention of freedom fighters, all of us are privileged to have in our midst tonight one of the brave commanders who lead the Afghan freedom fighters—Abdul Haq. Abdul Haq, we are with you. They are our brothers, these freedom fighters, and we owe them our help" (Ingersoll 2013; Reuters 2011). The Mujahideen were considered a close ally of the United States government and fought against the Russians with the backing of the CIA. Operation Cyclone—the longest and the most expensive covert CIA operation ever

FIGURE 1.9 Ronald Reagan meeting with Mujahideen at the White House in 1983. The United States provided substantial military and financial assistance to the Afghan Mujahideen as part of a covert operation known as Operation Cyclone. This support was aimed at weakening the Soviet Union's influence in Afghanistan and the broader region. *Source:* Michael Evans, see stamp and name on roll #C12820, Public domain, via Wikimedia Commons.

undertaken—was the code name for the CIA program to arm, train, and finance the Mujahideen in Afghanistan from the 1980s to the 1990s (Hassan 2013; Marshall 2011). Russia suffered close to 15,000 deaths by the hands of the Mujahideen (Pear 1988; Woody 2018). After four decades, alliances shifted. Today, Russia views the Mujahideen as freedom fighters and provides military and tactical support to them to fight US and coalition forces in Afghanistan. Intelligence reports indicate that Russia was offering bounties to Taliban fighters to kill American soldiers in Afghanistan (Ignatius 2020).

Finally, on the right in Figure 1.7, we see Nelson Mandela. Mandela waged a campaign of terrorism against the South African apartheid to gain independence for his people. He was regarded as a terrorist and incarcerated for 27 years. However, many people sympathetic to his cause hailed him as a freedom fighter (Brookfield 2008). In 1993, he received the Nobel Peace Prize and became the president of the country in 1994. Almost all state representatives worldwide, including the past and current presidents of the United States, attended his funeral in 2013 (Ndlovu-Gatsheni 2014).

Examples come from Europe as well, most notably in the case of Irish Republican Army (IRA). Martin McGuinness, who served as a high-ranking commander within the IRA during the Troubles, was considered a terrorist by British authorities. However, to many Irish people, he was viewed as the Nelson Mandela of Northern Ireland. Beginning in the 1980s, he transitioned to a political role within Sinn Fein, the political wing of the IRA. In 1982, the British authorities banned McGuinness from entering Great Britain under the Prevention of Terrorism Act (Clarke & Johnston 2001).

Throughout his career, McGuinness held significant political positions, including Minister of Education and Deputy First Minister of Northern Ireland. He served as Sinn Fein's chief negotiator, playing a pivotal role in the 1998 Good Friday Agreement (Westcott & Masters 2017). Often acknowledged as one of the main architects of the agreement, alongside US Senator George Mitchell and Sinn Fein leader Gerry Adams, McGuinness helped pave the way for a permanent peace process between the Catholic and Protestant communities.

Despite being labeled a terrorist for much of his life, McGuinness symbolically shook hands with Queen Elizabeth in 2012. At his funeral in 2017, former US President Bill Clinton hailed him as a "courageous" leader, and British Prime Minister Theresa May described him as an important figure who made an "essential and historic contribution to the extraordinary journey of Northern Ireland from conflict to peace" (Smith 2017).

History is replete with many other examples of terrorism as a contested concept. As described in the previous section, terrorism has been practiced by both state and **nonstate actors**. States—both totalitarian and nontotalitarian ones—have applied harsh terrorism practices for conservative reasons such as to strengthen their powers and maintain oppression and injustice. Insurgent and separatist groups have also used terrorism, mainly for revolutionary reasons, such as to gain their national liberation, combat foreign occupations, and establish self-determination. Yet today there is the question of whether the term "terrorism" should apply to the actions of states in the same way it is applied to the actions of **paramilitary** groups. And if the goal of using terrorist tactics is aimed at national liberation from an oppressive dominant power, such as the one in South Africa, should the violence used to reach to this goal be described as terrorism? What about the terrorist tactics used by governments during their official military missions? As Alex Schmid (2004) stated, in many conflicts around the world, governments are the "principal defining agency" and whether it is true or not, government officials and pro-government media tend to depict select insurgent activities as terrorism. From this perspective, a state can apply terrorist violence but can never be guilty of acts of terrorism. Instead, such acts are considered war—in other words, protecting the state from internal enemies and defending innocent citizens. But when the same act is undertaken by an insurgent group, it is often labeled as terrorism without question.

As prominent British sociologist Philip Schlesinger stated, "no commonly agreed definition in principle can be reached, because the very process of definition is in itself part of a wider contestation over ideologies or political objectives" (Schlesinger 1981). Some even go further, arguing that "terrorism is simply the violence that you don't support/like" (Richards 2014, p. 220) because the very issue of terrorist **designation** depends upon who decides what it is or is not.

1.2.3 Issues Related to the Process of Delegitimization and Criminalization of Certain Groups

The third reason it is difficult to define terrorism is related to the process of **delegitimization** and **criminalization** of certain groups. As mentioned, unlike in the past, the term "terrorism" has a strong negative connotation in the present day with which no one, including the insurgent groups, wants to be associated. However, once a group or an entity is officially labeled as a terrorist organization they face a wide range of political, economic, and social consequences. This is why many states and international organizations around the world have publicly available lists of designated terrorist organizations. For example, the United States Department of State has a list of foreign terrorist organizations published on their website. There are currently 72 organizations that are listed as terrorist groups by the Department of State and the list is regularly updated, meaning that new groups may be added and some groups that were previously designated as terrorist organizations may be removed from the list in the future. Not only is the definition of terrorism controversial, but it is also ever-changing. The African National Congress (ANC) in South Africa, Hezbollah in Lebanon, ETA in Spain, and FARC in Columbia are just some examples of organizations once designated with the terrorist label by the international community but later determined to be legitimate political actors recognized by the world and the states they fought against (Kennedy 1999).

Notably, the terrorist designation has significant legal and political ramifications on a group's activities. Once labeled as a terrorist organization a group can experience frozen financial assets, membership arrests, and economic sanctions, and have its members listed as persona non grata. Further, by using these lists, countries put pressure on other nations and international organizations to criminalize a certain group, or to delist another and lift sanctions. Such lists provide significant political power to some countries to put pressure on others.

One organization that has been repeatedly considered for inclusion on the list of designated terrorist organizations in different nations is Hamas, the Palestinian political and military organization. Hamas was established in 1987 in the Israeli-occupied territories of Palestine and has used both political activities and violence to pursue its goals. The group has engaged in terrorist acts, such as suicide bombings and rocket attacks against the Israeli forces, often describing them as reprisal the killings of

Palestinians by Israeli forces (Ganor 2012; Roy 2013). Most recently, on October 7, 2023, Hamas launched multiple coordinated attacks in Israel, killing approximately 1,400 individuals and taking more than 200 hostages (Deeb 2023). Countries including the United States, Canada, and Israel designate Hamas as a terrorist organization, whereas others including Brazil, China, Russia, Turkey, Switzerland, and Norway do not. In October of 2023, the United Nations rejected a resolution by Canada to condemn the October 7 terrorist attacks by Hamas, with 88 member nations in favor, 55 against, and 23 abstentions (UN 2023).

If there was a universally accepted definition of terrorism—or if the world used the same standards for all actors (state or nonstate) that use certain forms of violence—then nations would not have such discretion in designating a group as a terrorist organization. Most importantly, the designation of certain groups as terrorist organizations would not be influenced by geopolitical preferences or the prevailing political landscape.

1.2.4 There Are Several Different Types of Terrorism

The final explanation for the lack of a generally accepted definition of terrorism is the fact that there are many types of terrorism, each with a different form and manifestation. Figure 1.10 provides a categorization of terrorism that distinguishes several different types, based on ideology and actor.

Despite the world's attention to Islamist terrorism since the 1990s, and especially after the 9/11 attacks, there are in fact many forms of terrorism based on the type of

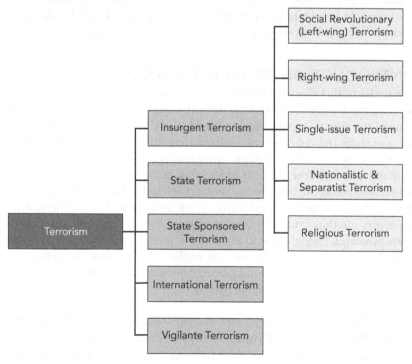

FIGURE 1.10 Types of terrorism.

targets and the identity of the actors. As shown in Figure 1.10, political terrorism has five main domains:

1. **Vigilante terrorism** refers to violence committed by the citizens of a country against other citizens (such as the violence committed by Ku Klux Klan against Black people in the United States).
2. **State terrorism** is violence committed by a government against its own citizens to consolidate its power and scare its opponents (such as the genocide of Jewish people by the Nazis during World War II), or military violence directed against the civilian population of another country.
3. **State-sponsored terrorism** refers to a government's use and support of violent nonstate actors as proxies, which may be done in several ways, including funding terrorist activities, providing training and arms, and protecting them. For example, Iran has been listed by the US State Department as a state sponsor of terrorism for providing funding, training, and supplies to Hezbollah.
4. **International terrorism** occurs when citizens of one country target the citizens and institutions of another country (such as the 9/11 attacks).
5. **Insurgent terrorism** is the most common type of terrorism—violence committed by citizens of a country against their own government, institutions, and other entities to achieve a specific political goal. Insurgent terrorism is divided into five categories, based on ideology. In Figure 1.10 you can see **religious terrorism**, which is distinct from ethno-nationalist and separatist terrorism, and **left-wing** or revolutionary terrorism, as well as **right-wing terrorism**. There is also **single-issue terrorism**, in which certain groups or individuals fight for one cause, such as for animal rights or against abortion access.

1.3 INTRODUCTION TO CASE STUDIES

The remainder of this chapter presents two case studies that illustrate the controversy surrounding the definition of terrorism. In both cases—the British and American aerial bombing of the city of Dresden during World War II and the 1921 **Tulsa massacre**—hundreds of thousands of innocent civilians were killed. Despite meeting the general definition of terrorism outlined earlier, where violence is used to target and kill innocent civilians and achieve some political or social objective, these acts were not generally labeled as terrorism at the time they occurred. Even today, the assignment of the terrorism label to these events is debated. Critics often argue that these acts were committed by state actors and thus cannot be labeled as terrorism. Others argue that because state actors are powerful, they are able to avoid the terrorism label, although their acts may meet this definition. As you read these case studies, consider the four defining features of terrorism contained in the aforementioned definition, and consider the consequences of defining or not defining these cases as such.

1.3.1 Case Study 1: Deliberate Terror Bombings in Germany By the Royal Air Force (RAF) and United States Army Air Force (USAAF)

The British and American bombing of the German city of Dresden between February 13 and 15 of 1945 is one of the most controversial and debated allied actions of World War II. It is estimated that approximately 30,000 German civilians, including women and

FIGURE 1.11 Dresden, after the bombing by England and United States. The bombings resulted in significant destruction and a high number of casualties. The bombings have been the subject of controversy and debate. Some argue that the raids were a necessary military operation aimed at disrupting German transportation and communication networks, while others criticize them as a form of indiscriminate bombing that caused extensive civilian suffering. *Source:* Cassowary Colorizations, CC BY 2.0, via Wikimedia Commons.

children, lost their lives during these aerial bombings, in which more than 3,900 tons of high-explosive bombs were dropped by the Royal Air Force (RAF) and United States Army Air Forces (USAAF) in the city center (Parks 1995; Taylor 2015). German officials called the incident mass murder, whereas both American and British officials defended the operation as justifiable on the grounds that Dresden was a strategic target, hosting a major rail transport center for the German army. Allied forces even called these attacks "deliberate terror bombing" (Willcocks 1998).

Beginning in 1942, the British RAF had started to attack enemy civilian populations and private German property to break enemy morale. The head of the aerial bomber unit at the RAF, Arthur Harris, publicly argued that civilian death and destruction of houses was necessary to disrupt the morale of the German workforce. Accordingly, almost all German industrial cities were destroyed to decrease the German public's support of the Nazi regime and to force Germany to surrender. The effectiveness of this bombing campaign is still debated. However, the toll was too heavy. Not only were almost all major German cities (such as Cologne, Hamburg, Frankfurt, and Dresden) destroyed, with millions of Germans left homeless, but also German civilian deaths had reached almost 400,000 (Grassey 2007).

The attack on the undefended city of Dresden, known for its architecture, was the most tragic. Thousands of civilians died, either under the firestorms or from suffocation as the strong fire sucked almost all the oxygen from the air. The mix of highly explosive bomb materials (called incendiary bombs which contained chemicals such as magnesium, phosphorous, petroleum napalm) not only blasted the schools, churches, houses, and even hospitals apart but also created air currents where civilians fleeing the flames would be sucked down from the streets into the burning buildings (Grayling 2007; Taylor 2015). It is reported that the temperature had reached 1,800 degrees Fahrenheit during the back-to-back bombings of the city by the RAF and USAAF. Hundreds of German civilians were found, their feet burned, as they attempted to flee over the melted roads. Reports also indicate that the firefighting and first aid efforts of the Germans were hampered by American fighter pilots. A British prisoner of war would later state: "While charred adult bodies could be seen throughout the rubble, there was little left of the children because their bones were too tender and they just melted." The scale of death was so high that it would take SS guards two weeks to burn the bodies of dead German citizens (Knight 2020; Luckhurst 2020).

As Allied forces would later accept, the attack on Dresden was a terror campaign. The intent of this massive destruction was to terrorize the German civilian population nationwide and also give approaching forces from Russia, an untrustworthy ally of England and the US at that time, a serious warning—demonstrating the Allies' superior bombing capabilities, should Stalin later turn against them (Jansen 2020).

Russia later described these attacks on the largely unarmed German civilians as "pure Western cruelty." Further, Winston Churchill, the prime minister of England during World War II, who was repeatedly challenged to justify these attacks on civilians, would later question, "Are we beasts? Are we taking this too far?" (Harmon 1991). In 1945, reacting to the airing of the video footage of these attacks in the House of Commons, Churchill says (Luckhurst 2020):

> It seems to me that the moment has come when the question of bombing of German cities simply for the sake of increasing terror, though under other pretexts, should be reviewed. . . . I feel the need for more precise concentration upon military objectives . . . , rather than on mere acts of terror and wanton destruction.

1.3.2 Case Study 2: The 1921 Tulsa Massacre

During and after the First World War, Greenwood, a neighborhood in Tulsa, Oklahoma, was recognized as an affluent African American community. At that time, Tulsa was a growing city with a population of over 100,000 people. Most of the city's Black population (close to 10,000) was segregated from the White population and lived in the Greenwood neighborhood, which included a thriving business district often referred as the "Black Wall Street" (Smith 2021). The area was composed of formerly enslaved Black people who relocated to Greenwood fleeing racial terror and lynch mobs, which were very common in much of the United States during the years following World War I, and were typically carried out by the White supremacist group the KKK (Richardson 2021).

However, in 1921, the entire neighborhood of Greenwood was destroyed during an 18-hour-long race massacre led by a White mob from May 31 to June 1, 1921 (Li 2021). This event would later be recorded as the single worst instance of racial terrorism in the history of the United States (since the emancipation of slaves). According to Human Rights Watch, an estimated 300 Black people were brutally killed, more than 1,000 homes and businesses, including churches, a school, a hospital, and a library, were first looted and then set on fire by the White mob (Richardson 2021).

FIGURE 1.12   Greenwood neighborhood in Tulsa, Oklahoma, after the massacre by the White mobs deputized by local law enforcement and the US National Guard. *Source:* Unknown source, public domain, via Wikimedia Commons.

But what caused this massacre was nothing more than a front-page story based on fabricated reporting by a local newspaper. On May 29, 1921, a young Black shoe polisher (Dick Rowland) was accused of sexually assaulting a White elevator operator, Sarah Page, while riding the elevator at the Drexel Building. Rowland was using the elevator to access one of the few available segregated public restrooms in downtown Tulsa (Sullivan 2021). While it is almost impossible to uncover the details of the incident, the most accepted explanation is that Rowland stepped on the shoe of Page while entering the elevator, which caused her to scream. The description of the incident was exaggerated, and ultimately depicted as a sexual assault, as it was told from one White person to another. The next day, May 30, 1921, the *Tulsa Tribune* published two sensationalist front-page articles, one showing the incident as Rowland attempting to rape Page inside the elevator and the other one calling on the White residents of Tulsa "To Lynch Negro Tonight" (Ellsworth 2021; Hirsch 2002; Verhovek 1996).

Based on the news, the Tulsa Police arrested Dick Rowland to investigate the incident. By the end of the day, however, hundreds of Whites answered the call by *Tulsa Tribune* and gathered in front of the courthouse seeking vigilante justice, demanding that law enforcement release the Black teenager to the crowd for lynching. Upon hearing the news, approximately 25 Black World War I veterans came to the courthouse, offering help to the sheriff to protect Dick Rowland from the White mob. This was a common method of protection at that time when Black people were on trial, as they usually faced lynching. However, the veterans returned to Greenwood after the sheriff dismissed their offer, arguing that the situation was under control and the White crowd would soon disperse (Smith 2021).

Contrary to what the sheriff thought, the White mob grew to more than 2,000 people throughout the night, and the police lost control of the situation. Around 10:00 p.m., the angry crowd attempted to break into the National Guard armory building to steal weapons and ammunition. Approximately 75 Black men from Greenwood rushed to the courthouse, again to protect Rowland from lynching by White people. A bloody massacre ensued when a White man asked a Black veteran to hand over his gun during the encounter in front of the courthouse. Shots were fired and the Black men who came to protect Rowland again retreated to Greenwood. Thousands of White people, frustrated over their failed attempt to lynch Rowland, then invaded Greenwood before dawn, killing men and women and looting and burning down buildings as they advanced. Carloads of White people engaged in drive-by shootings in Black residential neighborhoods. Reports indicate that at least one machine gun and several airplanes from World War I were used during these attacks. The once vibrant Black community was turned into smoldering ashes within a few hours (Perry et al. 2021; Richardson 2021; Li 2021).

Local authorities did little to protect the Black people during this terror rampage. On the contrary, reports indicate that Tulsa Police officers deputized the White men and even distributed firearms and ammunition shortly after the incident at the courthouse.

The Governor of Oklahoma declared martial law and deployed the National Guard troops to Tulsa. However, the guards were placed close to a White neighborhood, protecting the residents from a so-called possible Black counterattack, and giving the White mob enough time to loot and burn down Greenwood. It was not until after the late hours of the morning that the National Guard entered Greenwood to extinguish the fire (by then,

FIGURE 1.13 A group of Black men are being taken to internment camp at the city center. *Source:* SMU Central University Libraries, via Wikimedia Commons.

most of Greenwood was already burned down to ashes). The National Guard then imprisoned the Black people that the White mob had captured, along with the other Black Greenwood men that they found in the neighborhood.

The Black men were held for days at internment camps located at the city center and fairgrounds, allowing the White crowd to further loot and destroy the unprotected Greenwood neighborhood. The White mob stole, damaged, and destroyed the personal property of Greenwood residents, and more than 10,000 Black people were left homeless, forced to live in tents for months until they were able to rebuild their ruined homes and businesses. Black residents were not provided with any kind of financial assistance from the government for their rebuilding efforts. Insurance companies also refused to pay compensation, arguing that the destruction was due to a "Negro uprising." Many of them later left the city and never returned (Perry et. al. 2021; Rolseth 2019).

A trial, which was heard by an all-White jury, later found Dick Rowland not guilty. All of the charges against Rowland were dropped. Nonetheless, not a single White person has ever been charged, prosecuted, or punished by federal or local government for the destruction and loss of life (Smith 2021). This terror and violence were intentionally kept hidden from the world for several decades. The Tulsa police and National Guard reports about this incident went missing, and the newspaper, the *Tulsa Tribune*, removed the May 30, 1921 front-page stories from their archives (Perry et al. 2021). The chief of police in Tulsa ordered the police to confiscate all pictures taken after the incident by the photography studios (Richardson 2021). Researchers who attempted to study the incident had their careers and lives threatened. The state and federal government not only covered up this violence, but also depicted it as a race riot, implying that the violence had been instigated by the Black community of Tulsa, which in turn meant they eschewed the responsibility of rebuilding the district (Sullivan 2021).

1.4 CONCLUSION

Without a definitive consensus on what constitutes an act of terrorism, one significant consequence is the failure to develop effective national and international counterterrorism measures. At a minimum, the fight against terrorism requires a mutual agreement on the definition and characteristics of the problem and how it is different from other forms of violence. If the designation of terrorism continues to be used as a political tool (concerning states' shifting interests), then it will be impossible to mobilize international forces against the sources of terrorism and sign international agreements aimed at curtailing the activities of terrorist organizations.

As explained, having a clear definition of terrorism is not straightforward. However, regardless of when it is used or who uses it, terrorism always involves two common themes: strategic use of violence, and **intimidation** (fear and insecurity) (Schmid 2004). This violence, or threat of violence, is not random. In other words, not all violent acts are terrorism. For a violent act to qualify as terrorism, it must be carried out for some political, ideological, religious, or social reason.

State agencies, international organizations, and some academics prefer to use a narrow definition of terrorism by constraining the domain of terrorism to nonstate actors only. For example, the most comprehensive dataset on terrorism in the world, the Global Terrorism Database—which has been kept by University of Maryland's National

Consortium for the Study of Terrorism and Responses to Terrorism (START) center—defines terrorism as "the threatened or actual use of illegal force and violence by a nonstate actor to attain a political, economic, religious, or social goal through fear, coercion, or intimidation" (GTD 2024). This definition clearly excludes the violence perpetrated by states.

For the purposes of this book, we will use a broader definition of terrorism (as embraced by prominent political scientist Ted Robert Gurr (1989) and the Oxford Dictionary), which encompasses acts perpetrated by both states and nonstate actors, including subnational actors. Terrorism can therefore be defined as: "The use of violence against noncombatants to intimidate or coerce people in the pursuit of political or social objectives."

Our definition includes the four common defining features of terrorism used by academics, government agencies, and international organizations:

1) The use of violence
2) Attacks against noncombatants, civilians, and innocents
3) Designed to affect a larger audience (beyond the immediate victims)
4) To achieve some political or social objectives.

Key Lessons

Lesson 1

Terrorism is not a new phenomenon. Throughout history, terrorists from all over the world have carried out attacks to advance diverse sets of political agendas.

Lesson 2

Not all parts of the world are affected by terrorist violence; it is heavily concentrated in certain regions.

Lesson 3

Historically, the prevalence of terrorism has had temporal and geographical variation.

Lesson 4

Even though the issue of terrorism is an urgent global concern, the actual risk of dying from a terrorist attack is very rare, and almost nonexistent in several parts of the world.

Lesson 5

The word "terrorism" had different meanings and attributions at different times.

Lesson 6

Terrorism is a highly contested concept because "one person's terrorist is another person's freedom fighter."

Lesson 7

It is hard to define terrorism, because there is no agreement on what kind of violence constitutes acts of terrorism.

Lesson 8

As often depicted by the media and articulated by politicians, terrorism is not the monopoly of nonstate actors or Muslims. It has been practiced by states and members of all religions.

Lesson 9

The biggest issue with not having a consensus on what constitutes an act of terrorism is the failure to develop effective national and international counterterrorism measures.

Lesson 10

Regardless of when it is used, or who uses it, terrorism always involves two common themes: (1) strategic use of violence, and (2) intimidation (fear and insecurity).

KEY WORDS

criminalization
delegitimization
designation
fear
French Revolution
global death toll
hot spots
insurgent terrorism
international terrorism
intimidation
Jacobins
left-wing terrorism
Mujahideen
nonstate actors
prevalence of terrorism

paramilitary
propaganda by the deed
reign of terror
religious terrorism
right-wing terrorism
single-issue terrorism
state terrorism
State-sponsored terrorism
targeted killings
terror bombings
terrorism
terrorism-related death
totalitarian
Tulsa massacre
vigilante terrorism

RECOMMENDED SOURCES

Research Articles & Books

Betus, A. E., Kearns, E. M., & Lemieux, A. F. (2020). How perpetrator identity (sometimes) influences media framing attacks as "terrorism" or "mental illness". *Communication Research*, 0093650220971142.

Corbin, C. M. (2017). Terrorists are always Muslim but never white: At the intersection of critical race theory and propaganda. *Fordham L. Rev.*, 86, 455.

D'Orazio, V., & Salehyan, I. (2018). Who is a terrorist? Ethnicity, group affiliation, and understandings of political violence. *International Interactions*, 44(6), 1017–1039.

Ganor, B. (2002). Defining terrorism: Is one man's terrorist another man's freedom fighter? *Police Practice and Research*, 3(4), 287–304.

Gibbs, J. P. (1989). Conceptualization of terrorism. *American sociological review*, 329–340.

Huff, C., & Kertzer, J. D. (2018). How the public defines terrorism. *American Journal of Political Science*, 62(1), 55–71.

Ramsay, G. (2015). Why terrorism can, but should not be defined. *Critical Studies on Terrorism*, 8(2), 211–228.

Ruby, C. L. (2002). The definition of terrorism. *Analyses of social issues and public policy*, 2(1), 9–14.

Schmid, A. (2004). Terrorism-the definitional problem. *Case W. Res. J. Int'l L.*, 36, 375.

Schmid, A. P. (2011). The definition of terrorism. In The Routledge handbook of terrorism research (pp. 39–157). Routledge.

Sutuurman, Z. (2019). Terrorism as controversy: The shifting definition of terrorism in state politics. *E-international Relations*, Sep, 24, 465–80.

Weinberg, L., Pedahzur, A., & Hirsch-Hoefler, S. (2004). The challenges of conceptualizing terrorism. *Terrorism and Policical Violence*, 16(4), 777–794.

News Articles & Government and Think Tank Reports

How we define and use the word terrorism in the Israel-Hamas war matters a lot.
> Author(s): Emilie El Khoury
> Source: The Conversation

The Global Terrorism Database: how do researchers measure terrorism?
> Author(s): Bastian Herre
> Source: Our World In Data

When it comes to defining 'terrorism,' there is no consensus.
> Author(s): Kamala Kelkar
> Source: PBS

'Terrorism': An ambiguous and highly political concept.
> Author(s): Marc Semo
> Source: Le Monde

Documentaries, Videos, and Other Educational Media

How Do You Define Terrorism? The People Speak
> Producer(s)/Director(s): VICE News
> Source: VICE News YouTube Channel

Why is there no definition of domestic terrorism?
> Producer(s)/Director(s): Alexa Liautaud
> Source: NBC News

Can Terrorism be Defined?
> Producer(s)/Director(s): Council on Foreign Affairs
> Source: CFR Education YouTube Channel

The Privileges Afforded To The Nashville Bomber
> Featuring: Mehdi Hassan
> Source: MSNBC YouTube Channel

Terrorism and the United States: An Ironic Perspective
> Featuring: Ron Hirschbein
> Source: California State University Chico webpage

REFERENCES

Adams, W. B., & Mulligan, M. (2012). *Decolonizing nature: Strategies for conservation in a post-colonial era*. Routledge.

Anderson, J. H. (1995). The Neo-Nazi menace in Germany. *Studies in Conflict & Terrorism, 18*(1), 39–46.

Anderson, T. P. (1980). The ambiguities of political terrorism in Central America. *Studies in Conflict & Terrorism, 4*(1–4), 267–276.

Bantman, C. (2019). The Era of Propaganda by the Deed. In C. Levy & M. S. Adams (Eds.), *The Palgrave handbook of anarchism* (pp. 371–387). Palgrave Macmillan.

Bergen, P. L. (2006). *The Osama bin Laden I know: An oral history of al Qaeda's leader*. Simon & Schuster.

Blalock, G., Kadiyali, V., & Simon, D. H. (2009). Driving fatalities after 9/11: A hidden cost of terrorism. *Applied Economics, 41*(14), 1717–1729.

Brookfield, S. (2008). Radical questioning on the long walk to freedom: Nelson Mandela and the practice of critical reflection. *Adult Education Quarterly, 58*(2), 95–109.

Chang, B. O. (2005). Islamic Fundamentalism, Jihad, and Terrorism. *Journal of International Development and Cooperation, 11*(1), 57–67.

Clarke, L., & Johnston, K. (2001). *Martin McGuinness: From guns to government*. Mainstream Publishing Company.

Collins, M. (2016). Decolonization. In J. Mackenzie (Ed.), *The encyclopedia of empire*, 1–15. Oxford: Wiley-Blackwell.

Corbin, C. M. (2017). Terrorists are always Muslim but never white: At the intersection of critical race theory and propaganda. *Fordham Law Review, 86*, 455.

Crawford, J. (2013). *Gothic fiction and the invention of terrorism: The politics and aesthetics of fear in the age of the reign of terror*. Bloomsbury Publishing.

Crenshaw, M. (1981). The causes of terrorism. *Comparative Politics, 13*(4), 379–399.

D'Orazio, V., & Salehyan, I. (2018). Who is a terrorist? Ethnicity, group affiliation, and understandings of political violence. *International Interactions, 44*(6), 1017–1039.

Eisenman, D. P., Glik, D., Ong, M., Zhou, Q., Tseng, C. H., Long, A., Fielding, J., & Asch, S. (2009). Terrorism-related fear and avoidance behavior in a multiethnic urban population. *American Journal of Public Health, 99*(1), 168–174.

El Amraoui, A. (2012). The two sides of Yasser Arafat. Al Jazeera. https://www.aljazeera.com/news/2012/7/3/the-two-sides-of-yasser-arafat

El Deeb, S. (2023). What is Hamas? The group that rules the Gaza Strip has fought several rounds of war with Israel. Associated Press. https://apnews.com/article/hamas-gaza-palestinian-authority-israel-war-ed7018d-baae09b81513daf3bda38109a

Ellsworth, S. (2021). Tulsa race massacre. *The Encyclopedia of Oklahoma History and Culture.* https://www.okhistory.org/publications/enc/entry.php?entry=TU013

Fleming, M. (1980). Propaganda by the deed: Terrorism and anarchist theory in late nineteenth-century Europe. *Studies in Conflict & Terrorism, 4*(1–4), 1–23.

Frankel, G. (2004). World leaders praise courage, conviction. *Washington Post.* https://www.washingtonpost.com/archive/politics/2004/11/12/world-leaders-praise-courage-conviction/756d2b12-103a-4450-8a1f-4c076d58f794/

Ganor, B. (2012). The hybrid terrorist organization and incitement. In A. Baker (Ed.), *The changing forms of incitement to terror and violence: The need for a new international response.* Jerusalem Center for Public Affairs, 13–19.

Goodwin, R., Willson, M., & Stanley Jr, G. (2005). Terror threat perception and its consequences in contemporary Britain. *British Journal of Psychology, 96*(4), 389–406.

Grassey, T. B. (2007). Among the dead cities: The history and moral legacy of the WWII bombing of civilians in Germany and Japan. *Parameters, 37*(3), 118.

Grayling, A. C. (2007). *Among the dead cities: The history and moral legacy of the WWII bombing of civilians in Germany and Japan.* Bloomsbury Publishing.

Gurr, T. R. (Ed.). (1989). *Violence in America: The history of crime* (Vol. 1). Sage.

Haner, M. (2017). *The freedom fighter: A terrorist's own story.* Routledge.

Haner, M., Sloan, M. M., Pickett, J. T., & Cullen, F. T. (2020). Safe haven or dangerous place? Stereotype amplification and Americans' perceived risk of terrorism, violent street crime, and mass shootings. *British Journal of Criminology, 60*(6), 1606–1626.

Haner, M., Sloan, M. M., Pickett, J. T., & Cullen, F. T. (2021). When do Americans "see something, say something"? Experimental evidence on the willingness to report terrorist activity. *Justice Quarterly, 39*(5), 1079–1103.

Harmon, C. C. (1991). *Are we beasts?: Churchill and the moral question of World War II area Bombing* (No. 1). Center for Naval Warfare Studies, Naval War College.

Hassan, M. H. (2013). Mobilization of Muslims for Jihad: Insights from the past and their relevance today. *Counter Terrorist Trends and Analyses, 5*(8), 10–15.

Hirsch, J. (2002). *Riot and remembrance: The Tulsa race war and its legacy.* Houghton Mifflin.

History.com (2021). The Holocaust. https://www.history.com/topics/world-war-ii/the-holocaust

Holocaust Encyclopedia (2021). Documenting numbers of victims of the holocaust and Nazi persecution. Holocaust Encyclopedia. https://encyclopedia.ushmm.org/content/en/article/documenting-numbers-of-victims-of-the-holocaust-and-nazi-persecution

Ignatius, D. (2020). Opinion: Trump doesn't understand that Putin is in the payback business. *Washington Post.* https://www.washingtonpost.com/opinions/2020/06/29/were-trumps-aides-too-afraid-tell-him-about-russian-bounties/

Ingersoll, G. (2013). That time Ronald Reagan hosted those "freedom fighters" at the Oval Office. *Business Insider.* https://www.businessinsider.com/reagan-freedom-fighters-taliban-foreign-policy-2013-2

Institute for Economics & Peace (2020). Global Terrorism Index 2020: Measuring the impact of terrorism, Sydney. Retrived from: https://visionofhumanity.org/reports.

Jansen, V. (2020). Why was Dresden so heavily bombed? History. https://www.history .com/news/dresden-bombing-wwii-allies

Jenkins, B. M. (2006). The new age of terrorism. In D. Kamien (Ed.), *The McGraw-Hill homeland security handbook*, 117–130. McGraw-Hill.

Kennedy, R. (1999). Is one person's terrorist another's freedom fighter? Western and Islamic approaches to "just war" compared. *Terrorism and Political Violence*, 11(1), 1–21.

Knight, B. (2020). Dresden marks WWII bombing in far-right stronghold. Deutsche Welle. https://amp.dw.com/en/dresden-marks-wwii-bombing-in-far-right-strong hold/a-52368359

Laqueur, W. (2017). *A history of terrorism*. Routledge.

Lee, J. E., & Lemyre, L. (2009). A social-cognitive perspective of terrorism risk perception and individual response in Canada. *Risk Analysis: An International Journal*, 29(9), 1265–1280.

Li, Y. (2021) Black Wall Street was shattered 100 years ago. How the Tulsa race massacre was covered up and unearthed. CNBC. https:// www.cnbc.com/2021/05/31/black-wall-street-was-shattered-100-years-ago-how-tulsa-race-massacre-was-covered-up.html

Lopez, G. A. (2020). Terrorism in Latin America. In *The politics of terrorism* (pp. 497–524). CRC Press.

Luckhurst, T. (2020). Dresden: The World War Two bombing 75 years on. BBC. https://www .bbc.com/news/world-europe-51448486

Maguen, S., Papa, A., & Litz, B. T. (2008). Coping with the threat of terrorism: A review. *Anxiety, stress, and coping*, 21(1), 15–35.

Marshall, A. (2011). Terror "blowback" burns CIA. *Independent*. https://www.independent .co.uk/news/terror-blowback-burns-cia-1182087.html

Miller, E. (2020). Background report. Global terrorism overview: Terrorism in 2019. *START*. https://www.start.umd.edu/pubs/ START_GTD_GlobalTerrorismOverview 2019_July2020.pdf

Miller, E. (2022). A look back at 2020: Trends from the Global Terrorism Database (GTD). *START*. https://www.start.umd.edu/look-back-2020-trends-global-terrorism-database-gtd

Musolff, A. (2010). Hitler's children revisited: West German terrorism and the problem of coming to terms with the Nazi Past. *Terrorism and Political Violence*, 23(1), 60–71.

National Center for Health Statistics (2021). Health, United States, 2019. CDC. https:// www.cdc.gov/mmwr/volumes/70/wr/ mm7014e1.htm

Ndlovu-Gatsheni, S. J. (2014). From a "terrorist" to global icon: A critical decolonial ethical tribute to Nelson Rolihlahla Mandela of South Africa. *Third World Quarterly*, 35(6), 905–921.

Parks, W. H. (1995). "Precision" and "area" bombing: Who did which, and when? *Journal of Strategic Studies*, 18(1), 145–174.

Pear, R. (1988). Arming Afghan guerrillas: A huge effort led by U.S. *New York Times*. https://www.nytimes.com/1988/04/18/ world/arming-afghan-guerrillas-a-huge-effort-led-by-us.html

Perry, M., Barr, A., & Romer, C. (2021). The true costs of the Tulsa race massacre, 100 years later. The Brookings. https://www.brookings .edu/research/the-true-costs-of-the-tulsa-race-massacre-100-years-later/

Powell, K. A. (2018). Framing Islam/creating fear: An analysis of US media coverage of terrorism from 2011–2016. *Religions*, 9(9), 257.

Primoratz, I. (2013). *State terrorism and counterterrorism*. In G. Meggle, A. Kemmerling & M. Textor (eds.), Ethics of Terrorism & Counter-Terrorism. De Gruyter. pp. 69–82 (2004).

Reuters (2011). Q+A: Haqqani: From White House guest to staunch U.S. enemy. Reuters. https://www.reuters.com/article/us-kabul-attack-haqqani/qa-haqqani-from-white-house-guest-to-staunch-u-s-enemy-idUST RE78D1UG20110914

Richards, A. (2014). Conceptualizing terrorism. *Studies in Conflict & Terrorism*, 37(3), 213–236.

Richardson, R. (2021). Tulsa race massacre, 100 years later: Why it happened and why it's still relevant today. NBC News. https://www.nbcnews.com/news/nbcblk/ tulsa-race-massacre-100-years-later-why-it-happened-why-n1268877

Rolseth, M. (2019). Let's call the Tulsa race massacre what is it—domestic terrorism. *The*

Tulsa World. https://tulsaworld.com/opinion/columnists/missy-rolseth-lets-call-the-tulsa-race-massacre-what-is-it----domestic/article_c54c98b1-8914-5388-8dce-c78db34afab1.html

Roy, S. (2013). *Hamas and civil society in Gaza.* Princeton University Press.

Saleem, M., & Anderson, C. A. (2013). Arabs as terrorists: Effects of stereotypes within violent contexts on attitudes, perceptions, and affect. *Psychology of Violence, 3*(1), 84.

Scheuer, M. (2011). *Osama bin Laden.* Oxford University Press.

Schlesinger, P. (1981). " Terrorism," the media, and the liberal-democratic state: A critique of the orthodoxy. *Social Research*, 74–99.

Schmid, A. (2004). Terrorism: The definitional problem. *Case Western Reserve Journal of International Law, 36*, 375.

Shepard, W. F. (1953). *Price control and the reign of terror: France, 1793–1795* (Vol. 45). University of California Press.

Sloan, M. M., Haner, M., Cullen, F. T., Graham, A., Aydin, E., Kulig, T. C., & Jonson, C. L. (2020). Using behavioral strategies to cope with the threat of terrorism: A national-level study. *Crime & Delinquency, 67*(2), https://doi.org/10.1177/0011128720940984

Smith, B. R. (2021). Tulsa race massacre at 100: An act of terrorism America tried to forget. *The Guardian.* https://www.theguardian.com/us-news/2021/may/31/tulsa-race-massacre-at-100-act-of-terrorism

Smith, M. (2017). Martin McGuinness was "proud" of his IRA history despite turning to peacemaking and politics. *The Sun.* https://www.mirror.co.uk/news/politics/martin-mcguinness-proud-ira-history-10066190

START (2024). Global Terrorism Database. University of Maryland, National Consortium for the Study of Terrorism and Responses to Terrorism. https://www.start.umd.edu/gtd/

Sullivan, M. (2021). "Black Wall Street" before, during and after the Tulsa race massacre: Photos. History Channel. https://www.history.com/news/tulsa-massacre-black-wall-street-before-and-after-photos

Sutuurman, Z. (2019). Terrorism as controversy: The shifting definition of terrorism in state politics. *E-international Relations, September, 24*, 465–480.

Tamimi, A. (2007). Hamas: A history from within. Northampton, MA.: Olive Branch Press.

Taylor, A. (2015). Remembering Dresden: 70 years after the firebombing. https://www.theatlantic.com/photo/2015/02/remembering-dresden-70-years-after-the-firebombing/385445/

Tehranian, J. (2008). *Whitewashed: America's invisible middle eastern minority* (Vol. 46). NYU Press.

Timofeychev, A. (2018). How many lives did the Red Terror claim? Russia Beyond. https://www.rbth.com/history/329091-how-many-lives-claimed-red-terror

Torabi, M. R., & Seo, D. C. (2004). National study of behavioral and life changes since September 11. *Health Education & Behavior, 31*(2), 179–192.

United Nations. (2023). General Assembly Adopts Resolution Calling for Immediate, Sustained Humanitarian Truce Leading to Cessation of Hostilities between Israel, Hamas Member States Fail to Adopt Amendment Condemning 7 October Terrorist Attacks by Hamas in Israel. https://press.un.org/en/2023/ga12548.doc.htm

Verhovek, S. H. (1996). 75 years later, Tulsa confronts its race riot. *New York Times.* https://www.nytimes.com/1996/05/31/us/75-years-later-tulsa-confronts-its-race-riot.html

Walton, C. (2014). How Zionist extremism became British spies' biggest enemy. *Foreign Policy.* https://foreignpolicy.com/2014/01/01/how-zionist-extremism-became-british-spies-biggest-enemy/

Weinberg, L., Pedahzur, A., & Hirsch-Hoefler, S. (2004). The challenges of conceptualizing terrorism. *Terrorism and Political Violence, 16*(4), 777–794.

Westcott, B., & Masters, J. (2017). Clinton hails "calm and courageous" Martin McGuinness. CNN. https://www.cnn.com/2017/03/21/europe/martin-mcguinness-dead/index.html

Willcocks, R. H. (1998). *The ethics of bombing Dresden.* US Army War College.

Woody, C. (2018). "A fighting war with the main enemy": How the CIA helped land a mortal blow to the Soviets in Afghanistan 32 years ago. *Business Insider.* https://www.businessinsider.com/32-year-anniversary-of-first-stinger-missile-use-in-afghanistan-2018-9

CHAPTER 2

Living with the Terrorist Threat

The Psychosocial Impact of Terrorism

Source: Walter Cicchetti/Shutterstock.

Learning Objectives
1. To define the concept of fear.
2. To describe the direct psychosocial impact of terrorism on its victims and societies.
3. To describe the indirect psychosocial impact of terrorism on its victims and societies.
4. To describe the extents, sources, and patterns in terrorism-related fear.
5. To discuss the consequences of terrorism-related fear.

2.1 INTRODUCTION

As established in Chapter 1, terrorism is an area of urgent global concern. Clearly, the direct impacts of a terrorist attack on human life and physical infrastructure are devastating. A poignant example is the September 11, 2001, attacks on the twin towers of the World Trade Center in New York, which had a shocking effect around the world. The scale of the atrocity committed on that day was unprecedented among the annals of terrorism. In little more than one hour, almost 3,000 people from more than 80 nations were killed (Hoffman 2012). The death toll was equal to the number of deaths caused by global terrorism from 1988 through 2000. Massive property destruction occurred at the Pentagon, the center of US military command, and at the World Trade Center, a symbol of the world's financial markets. As it would require calculations beyond the extent of property damage or summing up the number of dead and injured, it is not even possible to estimate the economic loss. These attacks drew Americans' attention to the reality of globalization. The world was a smaller place and they no longer felt safe.

Over 20 years have passed since 9/11. Enormous resources have been devoted to combat terrorism; international operations have been conducted; wars have been started and countries invaded; and several

FIGURE 2.1 Explosions at the south tower of the World Trade Center as the hijacked United Airlines Flight 175 from Boston crashes into the building. *Source:* Public domain, via Wikimedia Commons.

FIGURE 2.2   On July 7, 2005, 56 people were killed by coordinated assaults in London. *Source:* Francis Tyers, CC BY-SA 3.0, via Wikimedia Commons.

terrorist groups have been annihilated. Osama bin Laden and several other senior al-Qaeda leaders have been captured or killed, their freedom of operation has been severely weakened, and their command, communication, and training systems have been destroyed. Yet al-Qaeda and its affiliates are still able to inspire, plot, and launch regional and transnational attacks on Western targets from their safe havens. In Yemen, al-Qaeda members are using asymmetric tactics in a campaign of bombings and assassinations against government targets, soldiers, civilians, and foreign diplomatic personnel. In Somalia, the militant group al-Shabaab is carrying out attacks against the government and American targets, killing innocent civilians, and causing fear on the streets. There are intelligence reports indicating that the group's members are being trained as airplane pilots to carry out attacks similar to 9/11 around the world (Travers 2019).

The Islamic State of Iraq and Syria (ISIS)—also known as the Islamic State (IS) and the Islamic State of Iraq and the Levant (ISIL)—have been able to regroup its members in those countries after the fall of its so-called caliphate. Despite losing many of its leaders, ISIS is still conducting violent atrocities, storming public avenues and killing and injuring hundreds of innocent people across Iraq and Syria. In Europe, anarchists in Greece and Italy are launching periodic attacks, targeting private businesses, foreign missions, and symbols of state. In Northern Ireland, dissident Republican groups continue their campaign of violence. People of Europe are still feeling the shocks of the Madrid and London bombings, which killed 300 people and injured thousands. Also increasing the perceived threat of terrorism among Europeans is the aforementioned emergence of ISIS. ISIS-inspired individuals have carried out several lethal attacks across Europe, including attacking police officers, driving vehicles into pedestrians, and suicide bombing campaigns (Haner et al. 2020).

While the threat of terrorism persists in the United States, the greater threat comes from domestic terrorism, primarily from people who are inspired by White

FIGURE 2.3   In recent years, White supremacist violence has become a primary national security threat in the United States. *Source:* Evan Nesterak, CC BY 2.0, via Wikimedia Commons.

supremacist ideology. According to the FBI and the Anti-Defamation League, almost 81 percent of the extremist-related murders in 2019 were committed by White supremacists. The American public have been victim to various violent incidents, including the invasion of the US Capitol by White supremacists, domestic terrorist attacks by native-born Americans, and several school shootings and other mass shootings such as the high school shooting in Parkland, Florida and the Orlando nightclub shooting in 2016. These attacks undermine Americans' confidence in the ability of existing security institutions to protect citizenry from the devastating effects of terrorism.

The physical trauma of terrorism on a global scale is undeniable, especially for those living in regions of high terrorist activity. However, the psychosocial effects of terrorism extend well beyond the direct physical casualties and to populations and regions that are not directly affected. The accessibility of news and social media today extends terrorism's reach even further.

Terrorists and terrorist organizations use fear to achieve their social, political, or religious goals. For the most part, terrorist attacks are unpredictable, and terrorists' tactics are unconventional. The uncertainty produced by terrorism can paralyze populations with fear, affecting the everyday activities of civilians with community and society-wide repercussions. Of course, these psychosocial impacts are greatest in regions regularly affected by terrorism, such as Pakistan, Iraq, Afghanistan, Israel, and Palestine. Yet research has shown that the fear generated from terrorism also reaches populations with little likelihood of experiencing an actual attack.

This chapter explores the psychosocial consequences of terrorism. We first discuss the impacts on those directly affected by terrorism. Next, we cover a growing area of research on fear of terrorism in relatively stable nations and its impact on social relations and policy formation, with an emphasis on the US population.

2.2 DIRECT PSYCHOSOCIAL EFFECTS OF TERRORISM

In addition to the human, physical, and economic toll, terrorism exacts a major psychological toll on its victims. One severe consequence of terrorism is **post-traumatic stress disorder (PTSD)**, which includes nightmares, **anxiety**, **depression**, and intrusive memories of the event, among other symptoms. Research on survivors of terrorist attacks consistently reveal elevated levels of PTSD symptoms. For example, in a study of evacuees from the World Trade Center towers during the 9/11 attacks, DiGrande and colleagues (2011) found that nearly all participants reported at least one symptom of PTSD two to three years following the attack, and in a multiyear follow-up study of 9/11 survivors, 13 percent of participants reported symptoms consistent with PTSD almost 15 years following the attacks. A majority of those participants also had symptoms of depression (Adams et al. 2019). Similarly, in a survey implemented just six months after the bombing of the Murrah Federal Building in Oklahoma City, about 34 percent of adult survivors had symptoms of psychiatric disorders (North et al. 1999).

Research conducted in other countries has also revealed elevated **psychological symptoms**. High levels of PTSD and depression were found in Madrid, Spain, after the 2004 terrorist attacks on a commuter railway. Among individuals exposed to the 1995 and 1996 terrorist bombings in France that killed 12 and injured more than 200, 31 percent reported

PTSD symptoms almost a decade later. Similarly, a survey of London residents found elevated **stress** levels a few weeks after the July 7, 2005, attacks (Antonius 2015).

For various reasons—the sensitivity of the issue and vulnerability of attack survivors, the unpredictability of an attack, the difficulty of mobilizing research efforts in response to a tragedy, the dangerousness of traveling to areas most frequently exposed to terrorism, and so on—studying survivors of terrorism is challenging. The evidence that we do have, however, clearly illustrates that terrorist attacks can have considerable psychological effects on survivors and on those in close proximity to them. In addition to the evidence of direct psychological effects of terrorism and at a more general level, a growing body of literature is emerging on terrorism's indirect effects.

2.3 INDIRECT PSYCHOSOCIAL EFFECTS OF TERRORISM: TERRORISM-RELATED FEAR

Fear is a basic emotion that people feel when they experience a decrease in their sense of power (Kemper 1987; 2011). It follows that fear is a primary response to the **powerlessness** people feel when faced with an experience of terrorism, or the threat of terrorism. Fear is important because it has survival value—it signals danger to oneself or one's social group and encourages a **fight-or-flight** response (Barbalet 2001). When people are afraid, they behave in ways that will protect their self-interests. Too much fear, however, can have negative consequences, such as **psychological distress** or depression, interference with thought processes, decreased physical health, increased **avoidance behaviors** and **social isolation**, and an overall lowered quality of life.

At the macro level, fear can become an "emotional climate" (de Rivera 1992). Defined as "collective emotions experienced as a result of a society's response to its sociopolitical conditions" (Bar-Tal et al. 2007, 443), emotional climates can dominate the behaviors of the public (de Rivera 1992). Fear-based emotional climates are common in dictatorships or in regions that experience political violence or frequent terrorist attacks. Fear in these cases serves to isolate individuals; community members restrict their behaviors, avoid social interaction, and may experience psychological distress (de Rivera 1992).

2.3.1 Extent of Terrorism-Related Fear

As suggested by the academic research on fear, the psychosocial consequences of terrorism linger in populations around the world. Much of the data that we have on the extent of terrorism-related fear comes from polling organizations housed in Western nations. The data from these polls are telling, as much of the populations surveyed have very little risk of experiencing a terrorist attack. For example, in the United States, an individual's likelihood of dying in a terrorist attack is about one in 75,000 (Mueller 2009). To place this in context, in a typical year, more Americans are killed by deer than by terrorists (Pinker 2011a). However, despite the small likelihood of experiencing an attack, a recent national survey found that 45 percent of Americans are afraid or very afraid of a terrorist attack (Haner et al. 2019).

Additionally, a 2017 Gallup poll reported that 60 percent of Americans feel that it is either very or somewhat likely that a terrorist attack will occur in the United States in the near future—an increase from the 38 percent of Americans feeling this way in 2011. When asked the question, "How worried are you that you or someone in your family will

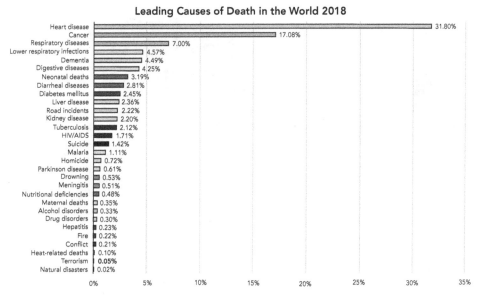

FIGURE 2.4 Terrorism poses a very small threat to people. *Source:* Institute for Health Metrics and Evaluation (IHME), Global Burden of Disease.

become a victim of terrorism?" in 2019, 46 percent of American respondents indicated that they are either very worried or somewhat worried. According to the Gallup polls, worry about terrorism was lowest among Americans in 2000 (24 percent worried) and, perhaps unsurprisingly, highest in 2002 (58 percent worried) (Gallup 2021).

A similar pattern is found in other Western countries. For example, in a 2017 national poll, Australians ranked terrorism (tied with climate change) as the number one most important problem facing the world (Roy Morgan 2017), while 52 percent of Canadians polled indicated that terrorism is a "moderately big" or "very big" problem in the country in 2018 (Anderson & Coletto 2018). In 2020, three weeks after a terrorist murdered French schoolteacher Samuel Paty, a representative survey of over 2,000

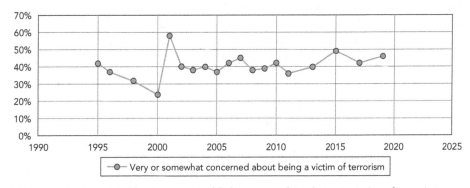

FIGURE 2.5 Trends in the American public's concern about being a victim of terrorism, 1990–2019. *Source:* Adapted from a 2019 Gallup poll about the worry of terrorism in the United States.

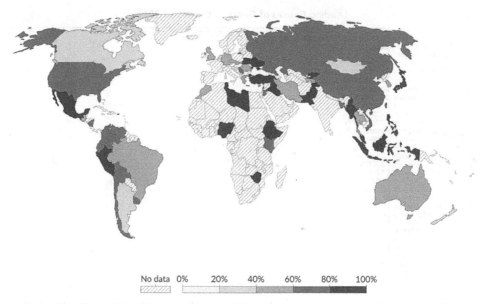

No data 0%   20%   40%   60%   80%   100%

FIGURE 2.6   Share of people who are worried about terrorism. *Source:* World Values Survey (2022) processed by Our World in Data.

participants in France indicated that 96 percent believe the terrorist threat is "high" or "very high." Forty-one percent of the French respondents reported that they think their lives will change in the near future due to the risk of attack (Institut français d'opinion publique 2020).

The World Values Survey is an international longitudinal survey that has been conducted seven times since 1981 with nationally representative samples from almost a hundred countries. It reveals worldwide concern about terrorism. The seventh survey, which interviewed participants between 2017 and 2021 and so far includes data from 48 nations, shows that in some nations—including the Philippines, Indonesia, Ethiopia, Nigeria, Pakistan, Peru, and Turkey—more than 85 percent of those surveyed worried very much or a great deal about terrorism. In the United States, 64 percent of the survey participants reported at least "a great deal" of worry about terrorism. Participants from New Zealand, Canada, and Mongolia are among the least worried about terrorism, reporting 33 percent, 27 percent, and 31 percent, respectively. While countries face varied levels of risk about terrorism and levels of worry tend to correspond to risk, the data from the World Values Survey suggests that terrorism exerts a psychosocial impact on a substantial portion of the world population. In the next section, we examine social patterns in fears about terrorism and its consequences.

2.3.2 Patterns in Terrorism-Related Fear

While we have some current data on the extent of terrorism-related fear, social scientists are only just beginning to examine social patterns in this area. This is an important field of research because identifying factors that may heighten fear of terrorism can provide insight into those most at risk for its psychosocial consequences.

To date, studies of terrorism fear patterns have drawn on the broader criminological literature related to fear of crime. Within this research, the **vulnerability perspective** argues that fear of crime is greatest among individuals who, due to personal characteristics, are believed to face a greater risk of criminal victimization than others (Lane et al. 2014; Wyant 2008). That is, fear stems from the perception of vulnerability to crime. This literature has documented patterns in fear of crime by gender (with women more fearful than men), age (with older individuals more fearful than younger ones), race (with non-Whites more

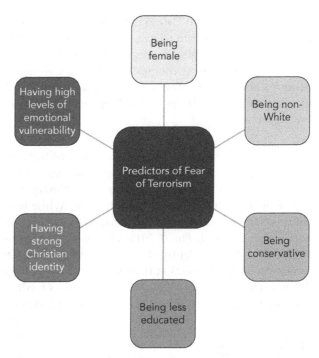

FIGURE 2.7 Predictors of fear of terrorism. *Source:* Adapted from Haner et al. (2019).

fearful than Whites), and socioeconomic status (with individuals of lower socioeconomic status more fearful than those with a higher level) (Hale 1996; Henson & Reyns 2015; Lane et al. 2014; Warr 2000). In an annual survey of fear conducted at Chapman University, Christopher Bader and colleagues (2020) found gender and race to be among the strongest predictors of fear in general, with women and non-Whites being more fearful than men and Whites, respectively.

When applied to the case of terrorism, similar patterns emerge. Continuing with the vulnerability perspective, a 2006 survey of residents of New York City and Washington, DC, found that women reported greater fear of terrorism than men (Nellis 2009). Likewise, in a national survey of Americans, Haner and colleagues (2019) found women to be more fearful of terrorism than men and also that non-Whites reported more fear of terrorism than Whites. In both surveys, age was not associated with terrorism-related fear. However, Haner and coauthors found that fear of terrorism was more prevalent among conservatives, individuals expressing strong Christian religiosity, individuals who were less educated, and those who reported higher levels of emotional vulnerability (Haner et al. 2019).

In addition to these patterns, recent research has identified **stereotypes** about Muslims as a strong influence on the fear of terrorism. In a recent survey of residents of Kaiserslautern, Germany, Andersen and Mayerl (2018) found that respondents' negative attitudes toward Muslims exerted the greatest influence on fear of terrorism, beyond the effects of the demographic characteristics previously noted. Those who more strongly agreed that "the practice of the Islamic faith in Germany should be restricted" and more strongly disagreed that "Islam is compatible with German society" showed elevated levels of fear of terrorism relative to those with more favorable attitudes toward Islam. These findings highlight the way in which terrorism has been conflated with Islam—largely due to political rhetoric and media coverage of terrorism—and this raises concerns about the treatment of Muslims more generally. We discuss the role of the media in shaping public fears as well as the consequences of fear of terrorism in the following section.

2.3.3 The Influence of the Media and Politics on Fear of Terrorism

In addition to the general social patterns in fear discussed previously, the **media** and politicians, often in combination, serve as primary contributors to the level and substance of the public's fears about terrorism. While fear is a universal experience, its sources, extent, and expression are shaped by culture, and the things that worry people change over time (e.g., Furedi 2018; Glassner 1999; Stearns 2006). For example, historian Peter Stearns (2006) identified a shift in American society in which Americans were no longer encouraged to master their fears but instead became socialized to avoid them. Attention to various potential threats in the mass media has led to excessive fear among Americans, and researchers argue that the media and politicians generate and manipulate these fears (Altheide 2017; Best 2018; Glassner 1999; Stearns 2006; 2010). For example, many news stations deliberately use fear-based reporting to build and capture audiences—this can be seen during coverage of major terrorist events, but even during weather reports (Stearns 2010).

In regard to fear of terrorism, Altheide (2017) argues that the American media operate on the **politics of fear**—where fear creates entertainment value, generates profits, and controls audiences. The topic of terrorism, in particular, is notably fear-arousing and generates intense emotional responses in audiences. Even in relatively secure countries, such as the United States, politicians use fear to achieve political goals. Following the 9/11 terrorist attacks, many countries embarked on a racialized war on terror in which Muslims and migrants became

Muslims represent an "extraordinary influx of hatred and danger coming into our country."

President Donald J. Tump
December 7, 2015

"There are thousands of Muslims who proudly call themselves Americans, and they know what I know—that the Muslim faith is based upon peace and love and compassion."

President George W. Bush
September 28, 2001

FIGURE 2.8 Donald Trump's anti-Muslim rhetoric has been associated with an increase in hate crimes against Muslims in the United States. During his 2016 presidential campaign and first term in office, President Trump made various statements and policy proposals related to Muslims and Islam that were criticized by many as being inflammatory and discriminatory. These included proposals to ban Muslims from entering the United States and rhetoric that conflated Islam with terrorism.

suspect populations, assumed to be prone to terrorism because of their "religious extremism and ethnic-separatism" (Nagra & Maurutto 2020; Pantazis & Pemberton 2009, 650). Targeted political rhetoric has been used to ignite a **fear of outsiders** among Americans and to generate support for discriminatory counterterrorism policies, such as the surveilling of mosques and predominantly Muslim neighborhoods (Altheide 2017; Best 2018; Gadarian 2010). Public opinion surveys often show that a substantial portion of Americans believe that immigration will lead to higher levels of crime and violence and that immigrants (i.e., outsiders) have a tendency to engage in violent behavior, despite evidence that immigration actually reduces crime and improves the economy (Chavez 2008; Ousey & Kubrin 2018).

Studies of the media's contribution to fear of terrorism show that greater consumption of news media is associated with higher levels of fear of terrorism (Godefroidt & Langer 2020; Nellis & Savage 2012). The media enables terrorism to reach much broader audiences, even those not directly affected by terrorist attacks (Rashid & Olofsson 2021). Furthermore, data from the World Values Survey illustrate that fear stems from concern about a potential future attack, rather than from actual exposure to attacks (Godefroidt & Langer 2020). The media's impact on fear of terrorism is concerning because, as noted previously, it has the potential to shape the content of public fear and serve political interests.

2.3.4 Consequences of Terrorism-Related Fear: Stereotyping and Prejudice

A major consequence of the media's influence is the proliferation of anti-Muslim stereotypes and **prejudice**. Historically, even prior to the events of 9/11, Muslims have been vilified in the US, and Islamist terrorism, rather than the terrorism of right-wing, left-wing, or other extremist groups, has dominated mass media (Akram et al. 2009; Shaheen 2014; Tehranian 2008). This has contributed to a pervasive perceived link between Islam and terrorism in American society (D'Orazio & Salehyan 2018; Powell 2018; Saleem & Anderson 2013).

For example, in an analysis of over 850,000 US newspaper articles published between 1996 and 2015, Bleich and van der Veen (2018) found that the tone of articles mentioning Muslims was significantly more negative than those referencing other religious minority groups (in this case, Hindus, Jews, and Catholics). Articles including Muslim actors were also more likely than those with non-Muslims to concern issues of extremism and cover locations outside of the United States. This trend in the tone and content of media portrays Muslims as threatening outsiders. A recent analysis of US news article coverage of all terrorist incidents cataloged in the Global Terrorism Database between 2006 and 2015 found that attacks with a Muslim perpetrator received 357 percent more coverage than other attacks (Kearns et al. 2019). Articles about attacks with Muslim perpetrators were five times more likely to mention the term "terrorism" than those about attacks carried out by non-Muslim perpetrators (Betus et al. 2020). Because people get their information about terrorism from the media, this bias against Muslims and emphasis on the threat of Islamist terrorism shapes the public's understanding of terrorism and diverts its attention from the reality of domestic terrorist threats.

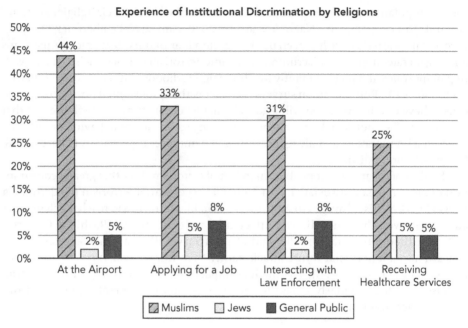

FIGURE 2.9 Institutional religious discrimination is highest among Muslim Americans compared to Jewish people and the general public. *Source:* Institute for Social Policy and Understanding (ISPU) (2020).

Naturally, Muslims experience psychosocial consequences as a result of this emphasis on a perceived Islamist threat. The Institute for Social Policy and Understanding regularly releases its American Muslim Poll, a survey of a nationally representative sample of self-identified Muslims and Jews and a nationally representative sample of the general American public. The survey is from 2020 and polls not only Americans who are Muslim, but also Americans of other faiths in order to understand American Muslims' perspectives within the context of their nation's faith landscape and not in isolation. The data show significant costs to Muslims living in the US. Compared to Americans in general, Muslims were more likely than those of other faiths (with the exception of Jews) to report having experienced **religious discrimination** in the past year—60 percent of Muslims reported discrimination, compared to 58 percent of Jews, 26 percent of Catholics, 29 percent of Protestants, 43 percent of White Evangelicals, 27 percent of the nonaffiliated, and 33 percent of the general public. Muslims were also more likely to experience religious discrimination at airports (44 percent of Muslims vs. 2 percent of Jews and 5 percent of the general public), in job applications (33 percent of Muslims vs. 5 percent of Jews and 8 percent of the general public), in encounters with law enforcement (31 percent of Muslims vs. 2 percent of Jews and 8 percent of the general public), and in healthcare settings (25 percent of Muslims vs. 5 percent of Jews and the general public). In addition, almost half of the Muslims surveyed reported interpersonal discrimination in public places and bullying in school settings, compared to 23 percent and 27 percent of the general public, respectively (Mogahed & Ikramullah 2020).

2.4 CONSEQUENCES OF TERRORISM-RELATED FEAR: PSYCHOLOGICAL, SOCIAL, AND BEHAVIORAL IMPACTS

Beyond the damaging effect that fear of terrorism has on Muslims, fear carries additional social and psychological consequences for the individuals who are afraid and for broader society as well. Psychologically, increases in PTSD and heightened distress and anxiety symptoms have been observed in individuals who are indirectly exposed to terrorist events—through the media, rather than the first-hand experience of an attack (Nellis & Savage 2012; Schuster et al. 2001). Fear of terrorism also impacts **social trust**, which is the general belief that people can be trusted—faith in people, in other words. Belgian and German researchers Amélie Godefroidt and Arnim Langer found that fear about a future terrorist attack is correlated with decreased levels of social trust, particularly for residents of democratic countries. Their analyses, which includes data from 54 countries, shows that fear of terrorism correlates with television news consumption. The authors explain that fear of terrorism has serious consequences that reach beyond the direct impact of terrorism's physical destruction. They argue that "terrorism (that is, the violent acts of terrorists) and terror (that is, the psychological effects of these actions) are two separate phenomena, in which the latter is especially damaging to our social fabric" (1,497). The destruction of social trust limits the ability for societies to function efficiently. It can slow economic progress, decrease the stability of political institutions, and foster corruption and conflict. These indirect effects of terrorism can therefore have large-scale social impacts.

Additional consequences of fear of terrorism are behavioral in nature. The threat of terrorism operates as a **macro-level stressor**—one that exerts its influence on whole societies. As such, people engage in behaviors in attempts to prevent or deal with the harm caused by experience of stress. These **behavioral coping strategies** tend to take two forms: avoidance behaviors (those involving a restriction of what one does), or

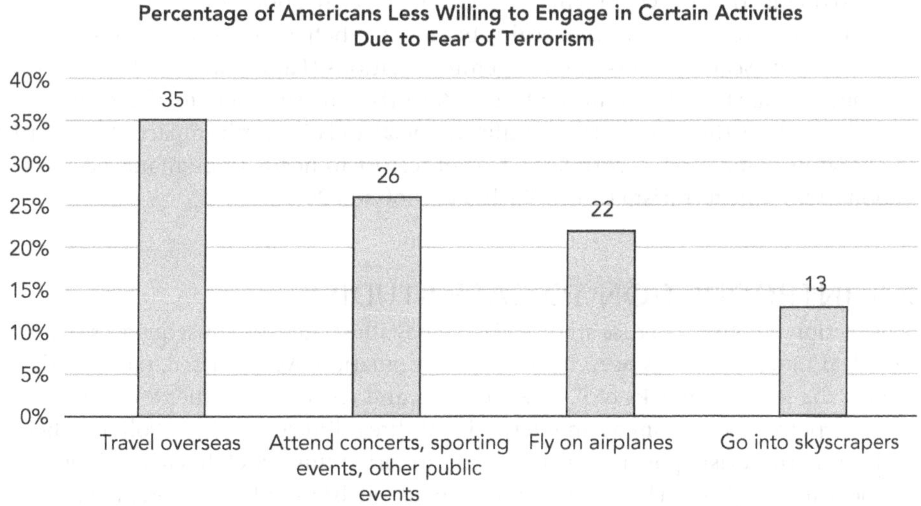

FIGURE 2.10 Percentage of Americans less willing to engage in certain activities due to fear of terrorism. *Source:* Haner et al. (2019).

protective behaviors (those involving actions taken) (Lee & Lemyre 2009; May et al. 2010; Rader & Haynes 2014; Stein et al. 2013). Avoidance behaviors include limiting one's travel, social engagements, and community involvement in response to fear, while protective behaviors include taking actions to secure oneself and significant others, such as installing a security system or purchasing a gun.

The most common behavioral coping strategies in response to terrorism are **behavioral disengagement** (Liverant et al. 2004), reducing travel (Gigerenzer 2006; Greenberg et al. 2004), and avoiding crowds, tall buildings, public transportation, and air travel (Malik et al. 2018; Nellis 2009). This is the case even among those not directly affected by a terrorist attack. For instance, a 2017 Gallup poll conducted after the terrorist attacks in London and Manchester found that the percentage of Americans who are less willing to attend public events due to risk of terrorism (38 percent) was at its highest level since 2001 (Reinhart 2017). The poll also identified heightened levels of other avoidance behaviors, with large percentages of Americans indicating that they were less willing to travel overseas (46 percent), fly on airplanes (32 percent), and go into skyscrapers (26 percent) (Reinhart 2017). In a 2018 survey of Americans, Sloan and colleagues (2020) found that over a quarter of respondents reported being less willing to attend concerts, sporting events, or other public events. Twenty percent reported hesitancy to use public transportation, and more than one in 10 respondents reported that they purchased a gun to address their fears of terrorism (a protective behavior). Likewise, Israelis reported a preference for homebound entertainment (over outside leisure activities), stopped shopping in large malls, traveled more by trains (as terrorists often targeted busses in Israel), and avoided waiting in long lines in public places, which have traditionally been a hot spot for terrorist targeting (Herzenstein et al. 2015; Kirschenbaum 2006; Sheppard 2011).

These behaviors have implications for community engagement, the economy, and psychological well-being on an individual level. In particular, avoidance behaviors such as these can lead to feelings of social isolation, psychological symptoms, and an overall lowered quality of life (Lee & Lemyre 2009; Maguen et al. 2008). Arming oneself as protection from terrorism is also concerning because the behavior of those in possession of a weapon can escalate events into dangerous situations (Lane et al. 2014). Again, these findings indicate that the indirect effects of terrorism are sufficient to affect a nation as a whole and have the potential for significant social and economic impacts. Due to all of the previously mentioned correlates, fear of terrorism needs to be managed, even in nations with little terrorism threat (Rashid & Olofsson 2021).

2.5 INTRODUCTION TO CASE STUDIES

This section presents two case studies. Each study illustrates the consequences that arise once fear of terrorism has been instilled in a population. As discussed, particularly following the terrorist attacks of 9/11, Americans and residents of other Western nations came to perceive terrorism as an international threat linked to Islam. Political rhetoric and counterterrorism policies reflected and supported this belief, having serious consequences for Muslims. These case studies focus on Islamophobia—prejudice against Muslims or the religion of Islam more generally—in the United States. Case Study 1 examines Americans' attitudes toward Muslims and Islam, and Case Study 2 describes recent research on fear of terrorism and support for anti-Muslim counterterrorism policies.

2.5.1 Case Study 1: Fear of International Terrorism and Islamophobia

The United States has experienced many major violent events over the past several decades, including the terrorist attacks of 9/11, domestic terrorist attacks by native-born Americans, and several school and mass shootings that occurred across the country (e.g., Newtown, Parkland, and Las Vegas). September 11 was by far the deadliest terrorist attack recorded on American soil, taking 2,979 lives and causing massive property destruction at the World Trade Center and the Pentagon (Hoffman 2012; Nowrasteh 2019). These attacks shocked Americans and undermined their confidence in the ability of existing security institutions to protect them from terrorism (Pinker 2011b). These international acts of terrorism also ignited an already simmering anti-Muslim sentiment in the United States.

The emergence of ISIS further increased the perceived threat of international terrorism among Americans. Between 2014 and 2019, ISIS-inspired individuals carried out seven deadly attacks in the United States—a beheading of coworkers, an attack on police officers, mass shootings, a vehicle attack on pedestrians, and a suicide bombing that killed over 80 individuals (Haner et al. 2020). The reality, however, is that none of those attacks were directly planned by the ISIS headquarters in Iraq and Syria (Herzenstein et al. 2015; Lyons & Davies, 2015). Excluding the 2,979 deaths that occurred on 9/11, native-born terrorists were responsible for 77 percent (or 413/539) of deaths from terrorism in the United States between 1975 and 2017 (Nowrasteh 2019). Thus, much of the terrorism threat is homegrown, with no direct involvement from abroad. In short, terrorist attacks in the United States are, with the exception of 9/11, mostly in-group violence.

Despite the fact that the majority of terrorist attacks in the United States are committed by Americans, politicians have capitalized on resentments against Muslims and have mobilized Americans against Muslim immigration (Brown 2016; Schmuck et al. 2017). With 80–90 percent of media coverage involving Muslims in the US and UK having a "negative slant or tone," media bias against Muslims reinforces stereotypes communicated in anti-Muslim political discourse (Duffy 2018, 114).

Donald Trump, for example, campaigned on his intention to create a database to track all Muslims within the United States as well as surveil mosques (Saleem et al. 2017; Stephenson & Becker 2016). After the election in 2016, President Trump continued heavily emphasizing threats related to Muslims and terrorism and repeatedly advanced Muslim-specific security measures with the stated intent of reducing terrorism, which garnered tremendous media attention (Haner et. al. 2020).

On January 27, 2017, Donald Trump signed executive order 13769, Protecting the Nation from Foreign Terrorist Entry into the United States, which prohibited foreign nationals from seven majority-Muslim nations, plus North Korea, from entering the country and suspended all refugee arrivals (ACLU 2019). Referred to as the "Muslim ban," the order was revised three times, ultimately prohibiting most residents of Iran, Iraq, Libya, Somalia, Syria, Yemen, Sudan, and North Korea from entering the United States. Immigration lawyers have estimated that because of the ban tens of thousands of people had their visa applications denied or stalled for months, and in some cases years (Hauslohner 2020). Indeed, the ban was wildly unpopular with large numbers of the US public and resulted in numerous protests across the country (Lajevardi et al. 2021). Still, a version of the ban remained in effect for four years until President Joe Biden ended it on his inauguration day, January 20, 2021.

The anti-Muslim sentiment communicated by Donald Trump via his political rhetoric and actions has played a significant role in encouraging these attitudes among the American public (Duffy 2018; Hawley 2019). Shortly after Trump's election, mosques throughout the country received threat letters, explicitly warning genocide against Muslims. One letter read: "There is a new sheriff in town—Donald Trump. He is going to cleanse America and make it shine again. And, he is going to start with you Muslims" (Katirai 2016).

Meanwhile, an academic study conducted by a team of researchers at California State University indicated that there was an almost 80 percent increase in hate crimes against Muslims in the US in 2015, during Trump's candidacy for the presidency (Pitter 2017). The same trend continued during the following years. According to a study published by the Council on American-Islamic Relations (CAIR), recorded hate crimes against Muslims consecutively increased in 2015, 2016, and 2017. In the report, the CAIR director highlighted the fact that not only did anti-Muslim bias incidents increase after Trump took office, but they also became significantly more violent, targeting Muslim American children, youth, and their families (Deutsche Welle 2018). Several additional studies have found a correlation between Donald Trump's speeches against Muslims and fluctuations in hate crimes. A study conducted by researchers from the University of North Texas discovered that Trump's rhetoric and rallies across the country heightened White nationalistic sentiments. More specifically, the researchers found that counties that hosted a Trump rally experienced a 226 percent increase in hate-motivated crimes (Kunzelman & Shear 2019). The suspect of 2019 El-Paso Walmart shooting, Patrick Wood Crusius, who killed more than 20 people and injured dozens of others, simply stated that he was following the orders of Trump and his attack as in response to the Hispanic invasion of Texas (Baker & Shear 2019).

Unfortunately, Trump's divisive rhetoric was not confined to the US. The New Zealand Al Noor Mosque shooting suspect, Brenton Tarrant, who killed more than 50 worshippers, had published a manifesto praising President Trump not only as his inspiration, but also "as a symbol of renewed white identity and common purpose" (Al Jazeera 2019).

In terms of broader public opinions, the 2019 American Muslim Poll found that Islamophobia in the United States increased (on a scale of 0 to 100) from 24 in 2018 to 28 in 2019 (Mogahed & Mahmood 2019). Similarly, another survey on the American public's perceptions of Muslim Americans conducted in November 2018 by New America, a DC-based think tank, and the American Muslim Institution (AMI) found that the

THE ISLAMOPHOBIA INDEX

Please indicate how much you agree or disagree with the following statements, where 1 means you strongly disagree and 5 means you strongly agree in regards to most Muslims living in the United States.

- Most Muslims living in the United States are more prone to violence than other people.
- Most Muslims living in the United States discriminate against women.

- Most Muslims living in the United States are hostile to the United States.
- Most Muslims living in the United States are less civilized than other people.
- Most Muslims living in the United States are partially responsible for acts of violence carried out by other Muslims.

Source: Mogahed and Ikramullah (2020).

demographic profile of respondents and the extent of their news consumption played a role in the increase of negative views toward Muslims. However, the study found that the strongest indicator of negative attitudes toward Muslims was ideological, with Trump supporters showing much higher rates of nonacceptance of Muslims (McKenzie 2018).

Recent experimental research has found that inflammatory political rhetoric (Donald Trump's, in particular) has an "emboldening" effect in that it encourages those who are already prejudiced to express and act on those beliefs. This effect is particularly pronounced when multiple political elites endorse such prejudiced attitudes. Conversely, in the absence of prejudiced speech by political elites, individuals who hold prejudices tend to constrain them (Newman et al. 2021). Research findings such as these demonstrate the power of political messages and suggest that anti-Muslim prejudice may be countered by politicians who vocalize and act in ways that promote justice, equity, and inclusiveness and create an environment in which such expressions are no longer considered acceptable.

2.5.2 Case Study 2: Fear of Terrorism: A National Study of the American Public

Recent polls indicate that Americans are fearful of terrorism to such an extent that they are altering their lifestyles (Reinhart 2017). As discussed, such responses to the threat of terrorism have implications for community engagement, the economy, and psychological well-being on an individual level. Certain coping behaviors have been found to lead to feelings of social isolation, psychological symptoms, and a lowered quality of life (Lee & Lemyre 2009; Maguen et al. 2008).

Sensing these concerns, political leaders often emphasize the threat of violent attack and advance a platform of making public safety a high priority. Fear of terrorism is a salient consideration because elected officials point to Americans' worries to justify a

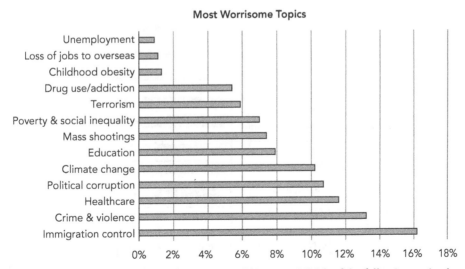

FIGURE 2.11 National Survey of American public, 2018: Which of the following topics do you find the most worrying in the US? *Source:* Haner & Sloan (2019).

range of policies, such as Trump's travel ban or expanding the national security powers of the federal government. For these reasons, it is important that social scientists implement systematic studies that measure the extent of fear of terrorism versus other threats to public safety, identify possible sources of variations in such feelings, and determine whether and under what conditions these fears are (or are not) related to homeland security proposals.

Academics around the world conduct studies (usually through public opinion surveys) to assess the extent to which the people manifest a fear of terrorism, how they experience this threat, and how they manage it. Through these surveys, they ask participants questions to understand various issues such as: (1) the extent to which people are personally fearful of being victimized; (2) which type of terrorism—domestic or foreign—concerns them the most; (3) whether they are more fearful of terrorism or other safety threats (e.g., crime, natural disasters); and (4) what solutions do they favor to reduce the risk of terrorism victimization.

For example, to understand how individuals living in the US experience the fear of terrorism, Haner and Sloan administered a national survey in August 2018. Overall, their results indicated that Americans were less worried about being a victim of a terrorist attack compared to a number of other issues. Among the worrisome topics that ranked higher than being a terrorism victim were immigration control, healthcare, political corruption, climate change, education, and mass shootings. Responses varied by political party, with Republicans ranking the influx of immigrants and crime and violence as the top two concerns and Democrats being most concerned about healthcare and climate change.

In contrast, when asked how afraid they are of a terrorist attack, 45 percent of the sample indicated that they were "afraid" or "very afraid" about the possibility, while 20 percent of Americans reported that they were "not afraid at all." Relative to the other fears considered, fear of terrorism was the second greatest fear among respondents after

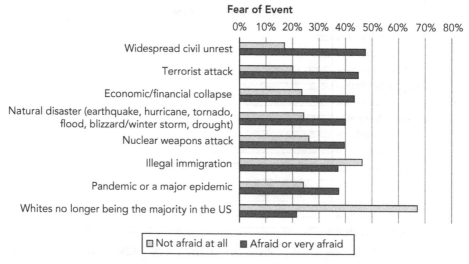

FIGURE 2.12 National Survey of American public, 2018: How afraid are you of the following events? *Source:* Haner & Sloan (2019).

Agreement with Statement

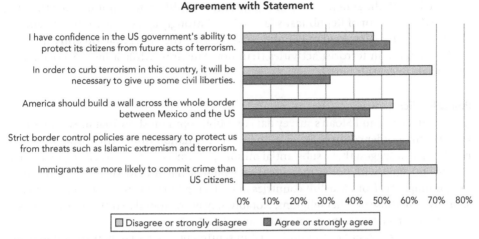

FIGURE 2.13 National Survey of American Public, 2018: American Public Opinion on Counterterrorism Measures. *Source:* Haner & Sloan (2019).

widespread civil unrest. While Americans reported less worry about being a victim of an attack themselves, a substantial portion of respondents indicated a more general fear of a potential terrorist attack.

When it comes to behavioral changes, a minority of Americans reported that they were less willing to engage in certain activities due to fears of terrorism such as attending public events (26 percent), flying on airplanes (23 percent), giving views on certain topics (27 percent), and using public transportation (21 percent). These survey results illustrate the prevalence of avoidance behaviors in response to the perceived threat of terrorism.

Additionally, most Americans felt that the government was not doing enough to combat terrorism. Just half of the sample expressed agreement or strong agreement with the statement "I have confidence in the US government's ability to protect its citizens from future acts of terrorism." And a majority of Americans overwhelmingly approve of several measures to prevent terrorist attacks—including increased security screenings at airports, metal detectors in office buildings and public places, and security screening for mass transit systems. At the same time, most (70 percent) are unwilling to give up civil liberties, even to prevent terrorism. Seventy-five percent of Americans are against government policies that would allow legal authorities to read mail and email, or tap phones.

While Americans appear willing to be personally inconvenienced by measures to prevent terrorist attacks, most "disagree" or "strongly disagree" with measures that would discriminate against Muslims. Over 60 percent of respondents "disagreed" or "strongly disagreed" with ceasing immigration from Muslim countries, subjecting Muslims to more scrutiny than people in other religious groups, and increasing police presence in Muslim neighborhoods.

Again, Haner and Sloan discovered notable partisan cleavages in attitudes. For example, Republicans were much more likely to be concerned about immigrants and Muslims in particular. Whereas 90 percent of Democrats "disagreed" or "strongly disagreed" with the statement, "Immigrants are more likely to commit crime than US citizens," 54 percent of Republicans "agreed" or "strongly agreed" with this statement. Similarly, nearly 70 percent of Republicans endorsed the belief that Muslims are more likely to engage in terrorist activities than non-Muslims, while almost 80 percent of Democrats reject this belief.

Policy Implications

In general, Haner and Sloan's survey data on public opinion show that most Americans want stricter border control measures to protect the nation from extremism and terrorism. They also suggest that a substantial minority of Americans (between 30 percent and 40 percent) agree with policy measures that would be harmful to Muslims, such as banning immigrants from Muslim countries and placing Muslims in the US under greater scrutiny than those of other religions. Notably, however, around two-thirds of Americans reject these practices, perhaps seeing them as "un-American."

Given the existence of this anti-Muslim sentiment, the researchers sought to determine the extent to which emotions underlie support for such policies. Their analyses revealed that feelings about terrorism have real-world policy implications. The strongest predictor of support for anti-Muslim counterterrorism policies was conservative political ideology. It is difficult to know if this association was heightened by Donald Trump's use of anti-Muslim rhetoric during his presidential campaign, but given the other academic research discussed earlier, this possibility is likely (Best 2018).

Next to conservativism, the researchers found that fear and worry about terrorism were the most influential predictors of anti-Muslim Policy support. This finding suggests that what matters is not only political ideology but also emotions. Policies such as the Muslim ban are likely to hold special appeal for those who are conservative and for those who fear and worry about terrorism. Consistent with arguments in the culture of fear literature, these beliefs and emotions may be inviting targets for exploitation by right-wing, nationalist politicians (e.g., Altheide 2017; Saleem et al. 2017, von Sikorski et al. 2017). By contrast, elected officials who ignore this emotional infrastructure and seek to persuade voters only by rational argumentation may be ineffective in reaching a large slice of the voters.

2.6 CONCLUSION

Responsible for tens of thousands of deaths and damage to infrastructure and commerce worth hundreds of billions of dollars worldwide, terrorism can devastate communities and entire nations. Beyond these costs, terrorism can also have substantial psychosocial consequences. This chapter has reviewed recent research on the direct psychosocial effects of terrorism on its victims as well as the indirect effects terrorism has on the general population. Directly, terrorism causes trauma to those impacted—through the death of loved ones, and loss of property and community resources. Indirectly, terrorist attacks instill fear in large swathes of the population, much of which is fueled by the media and political agendas.

The consequences of fear of terrorism are significant. When people are afraid of the potential for a terrorist attack they can become distressed, perceive others as less trustworthy, and engage in socially isolating behaviors. Notably, the erroneous connection made between terrorism and Islam, and its amplification in political rhetoric and the media, has devastating consequences for Muslims. In Western nations, Muslims are stereotyped, discriminated against, and perceived as outsiders. Terrorism's psychosocial impact—on individuals, interpersonal and intergroup relations, and society as a whole—is far-reaching.

In addition, understanding the indirect effects of terrorism is important because public opinion drives political agendas and policy development (Huff & Kertzer 2018; Shamir & Shamir 2000). In particular, the fear and worry about terrorism predicts support for anti-Muslim policies such as ceasing immigration from predominantly Muslim countries and subjecting Muslims to greater scrutiny than members of other religious groups (Haner et al. 2019). As politicians strive to serve their constituents and seek election, these public opinions matter. The media and politicians shape the types of acts that the public considers to be terrorism as well as who the public believes terrorists are; however, public support is ultimately necessary for the successful development and implementation of counterterrorism policies.

Key Lessons

Lesson 1

The uncertainty produced by terrorism can paralyze populations with fear, affecting the everyday activities of civilians with community and society-wide repercussions.

Lesson 2

Terrorists and terrorist organizations use fear as a means to achieve their social, political, or religious goals.

Lesson 3

The evidence indicates that terrorist attacks can have considerable psychological effects not only on survivors but also on those who are not directly affected by a terrorist attack.

Lesson 4

Fear is important because it has survival value. However, too much fear can have negative consequences, such as psychological distress or depression, interference with thought processes, decreased physical health, increased avoidance behaviors and social isolation, and an overall lowered quality of life.

Lesson 5

Despite the very small likelihood of experiencing an actual terrorist attack, a substantial portion of Americans are afraid or very afraid of a terrorist attack.

Lesson 6

Fear of terrorism is more prevalent among women, non-Whites, conservatives, individuals expressing strong Christian religiosity, individuals who are less educated, and those who report higher levels of emotional vulnerability.

Lesson 7

Studies of the media's contribution to fear of terrorism show that greater consumption of news media is associated with higher levels of fear of terrorism.

Lesson 8

A major consequence of the media and politicians' conflation of Islam with terrorism is the proliferation of anti-Muslim stereotypes and prejudice.

Lesson 9

The most common behavioral coping strategies in response to terrorism are avoidance behaviors including behavioral disengagement, reducing travel, and avoiding crowds, tall buildings, public transportation, and air travel.

Lesson 10

The indirect effects of terrorism are sufficient to affect a nation as a whole and have the potential for significant social and economic impacts.

KEY WORDS

anxiety

avoidance behaviors

behavioral coping strategies

behavioral disengagement

depression

fear

fear of outsiders

fight-or-flight

macro-level stressors

media

politics of fear

post-traumatic stress order (PTSD)

powerlessness

prejudice

protective behaviors

psychological distress

psychological symptoms

religious discrimination

social isolation

social trust

stereotyping

stress

vulnerability perspective

RECOMMENDED SOURCES

Research Articles & Books

Akram, S. M., Johnson, K. R., & Martinez, S. (2009). The demonization of persons of Arab and Muslim ancestry in historical perspective. In *International Migration and Human Rights* (pp. 98–114). University of California Press.

Altheide, D. L. (2017). *Terrorism and the politics of fear.* Lanham, MD: Rowman & Littlefield.

Bader, C. D., Baker, J. O. Day, E. & Gordon, A. L. (2020). *Fear itself: The causes and consequences of fear in America.* NYU Press.

Best, J. (2018). *American nightmares: Social problems in an anxious world.* Berkeley, CA: University of California Press.

DiGrande, L., Neria, Y., Brackbill, R. M., Pulliam, P., & Galea, S. (2011). Long-term posttraumatic stress symptoms among 3,271 civilian survivors of the September 11, 2001, terrorist attacks on the World Trade Center. *American Journal of Epidemiology, 173*(3), 271–281.

Gadarian, S. K. (2010). The politics of threat: How terrorism news shapes foreign policy attitudes. *The Journal of Politics, 72*(2), 469–483.

Glassner, B. (1999). *The Culture of Fear: Why Americans Are Afraid of the Wrong Things.* New York: Basic Books.

Godefroidt, A., & Langer, A. (2020). How fear drives us apart: Explaining the relationship between terrorism and social trust. *Terrorism and Political Violence, 32*(7), 1482–1505.

Kearns, E. M., Betus, A. E., & Lemieux, A. F. (2019). Why do some terrorist attacks receive more media attention than others? *Justice Quarterly, 36*(6), 985–1022.

Mueller, J. (2009), Inflating terrorism, in A. T. Thrall and J. K. Cramer, eds. *American Foreign Policy and the Politics of Fear: Threat Inflation Since 9/11,* 192–209. Routledge.

Schmuck, D., Matthes, J., & Paul, F. H. (2017). Negative stereotypical portrayals of Muslims in right-wing populist campaigns: Perceived discrimination, social identity threats, and hostility among young Muslim adults. *Journal of Communication, 67*(4), 610–634.

Stearns, P. N. (2006). *American fear: The causes and consequences of high anxiety.* New York: Routledge.

News Articles & Government and Think Tank Reports

When fear is a weapon: How terror attacks influence mental health.
> Author(s): Daniel Antonius
> Source: The Conversation

Terrorism: The Thing We Have to Fear the Most is Fear Itself.
> Author(s): Anthony H. Cordesman
> Source: Center for Strategic and International Studies (CSIS)

How to Not Be Scared of Terrorism—Or Anything Else.
> Author(s): Joan Cook
> Source: TIME

Why are Americans still so afraid of Islamic terrorism?
> Author(s): John Mueller and Mark G. Stewart
> Source: The Washington Post

How do I... live in the shadow of terrorism?
> Author(s): Kate Lyons and Caroline Davies
> Source: The Guardian

Understanding the Spread of Myths, Misinformation, and Hate Against Muslims in the United States.
> Source: New America

Terrorism fears drive more in U.S. to avoid crowds.
> Author(s): RJ Reinhart
> Source: GALLUP

Fearing fear itself.
> Author(s): Paul Krugman
> Source: The New York Times

Terrorism fears don't justify islamophobia.
> Author(s): W. Paul Smith
> Source: Human Rights Watch (HRW)

Documentaries, Movies, and Other Educational Media Resources

Fear Itself: America's Dysfunctional Relationship with Terrorism
> Featuring: Daniel Snook
> Source: TEDx

Taking the Terror Out of Terrorism
> Featuring: Neal Sideman and Debra Kissen
> Source: Anxiety and Depression Association of America, YouTube channel

We all worry about the threat of terrorism but should we?
> Featuring: Stephen Coleman
> Source: TEDx YouTube channel

World Report 2016: 'Politics of Fear' Threatens Rights
> Featuring: Kenneth Roth
> Source: Human Rights Watch (HRW) webpage

John Mueller discusses the fear of terrorism on The Gary Null Show
> Featuring: John Mueller
> Source: The Gary Null Show (CATO Institute)

REFERENCES

ACLU (2019, May 31). Timeline of the Muslim ban. American Civil Liberties Union of Washington, Inc. [US]. https://www.aclu-wa.org/pages/timeline-muslim-ban

Adams, S. W., Bowler, R. M., Russell, K., Brackbill, R. M., Li, J., & Cone, J. E. (2019). PTSD and comorbid depression: Social support and self-efficacy in World Trade Center tower survivors 14–15 years after 9/11. *Psychological trauma: Theory, research, practice, and policy, 11*(2), 156–164.

Akram, S. M., Johnson, K. R., & Martinez, S. (2009). The demonization of persons of Arab and Muslim ancestry in historical perspective. In S. Martinez (Ed.), *International migration and human rights* (pp. 98–114). University of California Press.

Al-Jazeera (2019). New Zealand mosque attacks suspect praised Trump in manifesto. https://www.aljazeera.com/news/2019/3/16/new-zealand-mosque-attacks-suspect-praised-trump-in-manifesto

Altheide, D. L. (2017). *Terrorism and the politics of fear.* Rowman & Littlefield.

Andersen, H., & Mayerl, J. (2018). Attitudes towards Muslims and fear of terrorism. *Ethnic and Racial Studies, 41*(15), 2634–2655.

Anderson, B., & Coletto, D. (2018). For most Canadians, the world is in trouble. Abacus Data. https://abacusdata.ca/problemsfacing canada_poll/

Antonius, D. (2015, December 4). When fear is a weapon: How terror attacks influence mental health. *The Conversation.* https:// theconversation.com/when-fear-isa-weapon-how-terror-attacks-influence-mental-health-51010

Bader, C. D., Baker, J. O. Day, E. & Gordon, A. L. (2020). *Fear itself: The causes and consequences of fear in America.* NYU Press.

Baker, P., & Shear, M. D. (2019). El Paso shooting suspect's manifesto echoes Trump's language. *New York Times.* https://www.nytimes .com/2019/08/04/us/politics/trump-mass-shootings.html

Barbalet, J. M. (2001). *Emotion, social theory, and social structure: A macrosociological approach.* Cambridge University Press.

Bar-Tal, D., Halperin, E., & De Rivera, J. (2007). Collective emotions in conflict situations: Societal implications. Journal of Social Issues, *63*(2), 441–460.

Best, J. (2018). *American nightmares: Social problems in an anxious world.* University of California Press.

Betus, A. E., Kearns, E. M., & Lemieux, A. F. (2020). How perpetrator identity (sometimes) influences media framing attacks as "terrorism" or "mental illness." *Communication Research, 48*(8), https://doi.org/10.1177/ 0093650220971142.

Bleich, E., Souffrant, J., Stabler, E., & Van der Veen, A. M. (2018). Media coverage of Muslim devotion: A four-country analysis of newspaper articles, 1996–2016. *Religions, 9*(8), 247.

Brown, J. A. (2016). Running on fear: Immigration, race and crime framings in contemporary GOP presidential debate discourse. *Critical Criminology, 24*(3), 315–331.

Chavez, L. R. (2008). *The Latino threat: Constructing immigrants, citizens, and the nation.* Stanford University Press.

de Rivera, J. (1992). Emotional climate: Social structure and emotional dynamics. In K. T. Strongman (Ed.), *International review of studies on emotion, vol. 2* (pp. 197–218). Wiley.

Deutsche Welle (2018, April 23). Anti-Muslim hate crime on the rise in Donald Trump's US—report. https://www.dw.com/en/anti-muslim-hate-crime-on-the-rise-in-donald-trumps-us-report/a-43500942

DiGrande, L., Neria, Y., Brackbill, R. M., Pulliam, P., & Galea, S. (2011). Long-term posttraumatic stress symptoms among 3,271 civilian survivors of the September 11, 2001, terrorist attacks on the World Trade Center. *American Journal of Epidemiology, 173*(3), 271–281.

D'Orazio, V., & Salehyan, I. (2018). Who is a terrorist? Ethnicity, group affiliation, and understandings of political violence. *International Interactions, 44*(6), 1017–1039.

Duffy, B. (2018). *The perils of perception: Why we're wrong about nearly everything.* Atlantic Books.

Furedi, F. (2018). *How fear works: The culture of fear in the 21st century.* Bloomsbury.

Gadarian, S. K. (2010). The politics of threat: How terrorism news shapes foreign policy attitudes. *Journal of Politics, 72*(2), 469–483.

Gallup (2021). Terrorism. https://news.gallup .com/poll/4909/terrorism-united-states.aspx

Gigerenzer, G. (2006). Out of the frying pan into the fire: Behavioral reactions to terrorist attacks. *Risk Analysis: An International Journal, 26*(2), 347–351.

Glassner, B. (1999). *The culture of fear: Why Americans are afraid of the wrong things.* Basic Books.

Godefroidt, A., & Langer, A. (2020). How fear drives us apart: Explaining the relationship between terrorism and social trust. *Terrorism and Political Violence, 32*(7), 1482–1505.

Greenberg, M., Craighill, P., & Greenberg, A. (2004). Trying to understand behavioral responses to terrorism: Personal civil liberties, environmental hazards, and US resident reactions to the September 11, 2001 attacks. *Human Ecology Review, 11*(2), 165–176.

Hale, C. (1996). Fear of crime: A review of the literature. *International review of Victimology, 4*(2), 79–150.

Haner, M., Sloan, M. M., Cullen, F. T., Graham, A., Lero Jonson, C., Kulig, T. C., & Aydın, Ö. (2020). Making America safe again: Public support for policies to reduce terrorism. *Deviant Behavior, 42*(10), 1209–1227.

Haner, M., Sloan, M. M., Cullen, F. T., Kulig, T. C., & Lero Jonson, C. (2019). Public concern about terrorism: Fear, worry, and support for anti-Muslim policies. *Socius, 5*, https://doi.org/10.1177/2378023119856825.

Hauslohner, A. (2020, December 2). Undoing Trump's "Muslim ban" could take minutes, but results could take months or years. *Washington Post*. https://www.washingtonpost.com/politics/2020/12/02/biden-trump-muslim-travel-ban/

Hawley, G. (2019). Are Trump supporters anti-Muslim? Brookings. https://www.brookings.edu/articles/are-trump-supporters-anti-muslim/

Henson, B., & Reyns, B. W. (2015). The only thing we have to fear is fear itself . . . and crime: The current state of the fear of crime literature and where it should go next. *Sociology Compass, 9*(2), 91–103.

Herzenstein, M., Horsky, S., & Posavac, S. S. (2015). Living with terrorism or withdrawing in terror: Perceived control and consumer avoidance. *Journal of Consumer Behaviour, 14*(4), 228–236.

Hoffman, B. (2012). The changing face of al-Qaeda and the global war on terrorism. In J. Horgan & K. Braddock (Eds.), *Terrorism studies: A reader* (pp. 392–413). Routledge.

Huff, C., & Kertzer, J. D. (2018). How the public defines terrorism. *American Journal of Political Science, 62*(1), 55–71.

Institut français d'opinion publique (2020). The view of the French on the terrorist threat and Islamism. https://www.ifop.com/en/

Institute for Social Policy and Understanding. (2020). American Muslim poll 2020: Amid pandemic and protest. Institute for Social Policy and Understanding. https://www.ispu.org/american-muslim-poll-2020

Katirai, N. (2016). Hate toward Muslims is growing and it's Donald Trump's fault. *Times*. https://time.com/4587915/donald-trump-muslim-registry/

Kearns, E. M., Betus, A. E., & Lemieux, A. F. (2019). Why do some terrorist attacks receive more media attention than others? *Justice Quarterly, 36*(6), 985–1022.

Kemper, T. D. (1987). How many emotions are there? Wedding the social and the autonomic components. *American Journal of Sociology 93*(2), 263–289.

Kemper, T. D. (2011). *Status, power and ritual interaction: A relational reading of Durkheim, Goffman, and Collins*. Ashgate Publishing.

Kirschenbaum, A. (2006, March 4). Terror, adaptation and preparedness: A trilogy for survival. *Journal of Homeland Security and Emergency Management, 3*(1), https://doi.org/10.2202/1547-7355.1178.

Kunzelman, M. & Shear, M. D. (2019). Trump words linked to more hate crime? Some experts think so. *AP News*. https://apnews.com/article/az-state-wire-tx-state-wire-race-and-ethnicity-el-paso-caribbean-7d0949974b1648a2bb592cab1f85aa16

Lajevardi, N., Oskooii, K. A. R., & Collingwood, L. (2021, January 27). Biden reverses Trump's "Muslim ban." Americans support the decision. *Washington Post*. https://www.washingtonpost.com/politics/2021/01/27/biden-reversed-trumps-muslim-ban-americans-support-that-decision/

Lane, J., Rader, N. E., Henson, B., Fisher, B. S. and May, D. C. (2014). *Fear of crime in the United States: Causes, consequences, and contradictions*. Carolina Academic Press.

Lee, J. E., & Lemyre, L. (2009). A social-cognitive perspective of terrorism risk perception and individual response in Canada. *Risk Analysis: An International Journal, 29*(9), 1265–1280.

Liverant, G. I., Hofmann, S. G., & Litz, B. T. (2004). Coping and anxiety in college students after the September 11th terrorist attacks. *Anxiety, Stress & Coping, 17*(2), 127–139.

Lyons, K., & Davies, C. (2015, November 20). How do I . . . live in the shadow of terrorism? *The Guardian*. https://www.theguardian.com/uk-news/2015/nov/20/how-do-i-live-in-the-shadow-of-terrorism

Maguen, S., Papa, A., & Litz, B. T. (2008). Coping with the threat of terrorism: A review. *Anxiety, Stress, and Coping, 21*(1), 15–35.

Malik, O. F., Schat, A. C., Raziq, M. M., Shahzad, A., & Khan, M. (2018). Relationships between perceived risk of terrorism, fear, and avoidance behaviors among Pakistani university students: A multigroup study. *Personality and Individual Differences, 124*, 39–44.

May, D. C., Rader, N. E., & Goodrum, S. (2010). A gendered assessment of the "threat of victimization": Examining gender differences in fear of crime, perceived risk, avoidance, and defensive behaviors. *Criminal Justice Review, 35*(2), 159–182.

McKenzie, R. L. (2018). Understanding the spread of myths, misinformation, and hate against Muslims in the United States. New America. https://www.newamerica.org/muslim-diaspora-initiative/press-releases/survey-examines-perceptions-muslim-americans/

Mogahed, D., & Ikramullah, E. (2020). American Muslim poll 2020: Amid pandemic and protest. Institute for Social Policy and Understanding. https://www.ispu.org/american-muslim-poll-2020-amid-pandemic-and-protest/

Mogahed, D., & Mahmood, A. A. (2019). American Muslim poll 2019: Muslims at the crossroads. https://www.ispu.org/american-muslim-poll-2019-predicting-and-preventing-islamophobia/#II

Mueller, J. (2009). Inflating terrorism. In A. T. Thrall & J. K. Cramer (Eds.), *American foreign policy and the politics of fear: Threat inflation since 9/11* (pp. 192–209). Routledge.

Nagra, B., & Maurutto, P. (2020). No-fly lists, national security and race: The experiences of Canadian Muslims. *British Journal of Criminology, 60*(3), 600–619.

Nellis, A. M. (2009). Gender differences in fear of terrorism. *Journal of Contemporary Criminal Justice, 25*(3), 322–340.

Nellis, A. M., & Savage, J. (2012). Does watching the news affect fear of terrorism? The importance of media exposure on terrorism fear. *Crime & Delinquency, 58*(5), 748–768.

Newman, B., Merolla, J. L., Shah, S., Lemi, D. C., Collingwood, L., & Ramakrishnan, S. K. (2021). The trump effect: An experimental investigation of the emboldening effect of racially inflammatory elite communication. *British Journal of Political Science, 51*(3), 1138–1159.

North, C. S., Nixon, S. J., Malionee, S., McMillen, J. C., Spitznagel, E. L., & Smith, E. M. (1999). Psychiatric disorders among survivors of the Oklahoma City bombing. *Journal of the American Medical Association, 282*(8), 755–762.

Nowrasteh, A. (2019). Terrorists by immigration status and nationality: A risk analysis, 1975–2017. CATO Institute. https://www.cato.org/publications/policy-analysis/terrorists-immigration-status-nationality-risk-analysis-1975-2017

Ousey, G. C., & Kubrin, C. E. (2018). Immigration and crime: Assessing a contentious issue. *Annual Review of Criminology, 1*, 63–84.

Pantazis, C., & Pemberton, S. (2009). From the "old" to the "new" suspect community: Examining the impacts of recent UK counter-terrorist legislation. *British Journal of Criminology, 49*(5), 646–666.

Pinker, S. (2011a). *The better angels of our nature: Why violence has declined.* Viking.

Pinker, S. (September 24, 2011b). Violence vanquished. *Wall Street Journal*, 24.

Pitter, L. (2017). Hate crimes against Muslims in US continue to rise in 2016. The Human Rights Watch. https://www.hrw.org/news/2017/05/11/hate-crimes-against-muslims-us-continue-rise-2016

Powell, K. A. (2018). Framing Islam/creating fear: An analysis of US media coverage of terrorism from 2011–2016. *Religions, 9*(9), 257–272.

Rader, N. E., & Haynes, S. H. (2014). Avoidance, protective, and weapons behaviors: An examination of constrained behaviors and their impact on concerns about crime. *Journal of Crime and Justice, 37*(2), 197–213.

Rashid, S., & Olofsson, A. (2021). Worried in Sweden: The effects of terrorism abroad and news media at home on terror-related worry. *Journal of Risk Research, 24*(1), 62–77.

Reinhart, R. J. (2017). Terrorism fears drive more in U.S. to avoid crowds. *Gallup*. https://news.gallup.com/poll/212654/terrorism-fears-drive-avoid-crowds.aspx

Roy Morgan. (2017). Australians' concerns: New in-depth research exploring the concerns of Australians both in Australia and globally found Australians are concerned about war and terrorism on the global front, but at home it's all about the economy—especially unemployment and housing affordability. http://www.roymorgan.com/findings/7249-most-important-problems-facing-australia-the-world-may-2017-201706231630

Saleem, M., & Anderson, C. A. (2013). Arabs as terrorists: Effects of stereotypes within violent contexts on attitudes, perceptions, and affect. *Psychology of Violence, 3*(1), 84–99.

Saleem, M., Prot, S., Anderson, C. A., & Lemieux, A. F. (2017). Exposure to Muslims in media and support for public policies harming Muslims. *Communication Research, 44*, 841–869.

Schmuck, D., Matthes, J., & Paul, F. H. (2017). Negative stereotypical portrayals of Muslims in right-wing populist campaigns: Perceived discrimination, social identity threats, and hostility among young Muslim adults. *Journal of Communication, 67*(4), 610–634.

Schuster, M. A., Stein, B. D., Jaycox, L. H., Collins, R. L., Marshall, G. N., Elliott, M. N., Zhou, A. J., Kanouse, D. E., Morrison, J. L., & Berry, S. H. (2001). A national survey of stress reactions after the September 11, 2001, terrorist attacks. *New England Journal of Medicine, 345*(20), 1507–1512.

Shaheen, J. (2014). *Reel bad Arabs: How Hollywood vilifies a people.* Olive Branch Press.

Shamir, J., & Shamir, M. (2000). *The anatomy of public opinion.* University of Michigan Press.

Sheppard, B. (2011). Mitigating terror and avoidance behavior through the risk perception matrix to augment resilience. *Journal of Homeland Security and Emergency Management, 8*(1), https://doi.org/10.2202/1547-7355.1840.

Sloan, M. M., Haner, M., Cullen, F. T., Graham, A., Aydin, E., Kulig, T. C., & Jonson, C. L. (2020). Using behavioral strategies to cope with the threat of terrorism: A national-level study. *Crime & Delinquency, 67*(12), https://doi.org/10.1177/0011128720940984.

Stearns, P. N. (2006). *American fear: The causes and consequences of high anxiety.* Routledge.

Stearns, P. N. (2010). Dare to compare: The next challenge in assessing emotional cultures. *Emotion Review, 2*(3), 261–264.

Stein, N. R., Schorr, Y., Litz, B. T., King, L. A., King, D. W., Solomon, Z., & Horesh, D. (2013). Development and validation of the coping with terror scale. *Assessment, 20*(5), 597–609.

Stephenson, E. & Becker, A. (2016, June 15). Trump backs surveillance of mosques despite criticism of rhetoric. Reuters. https://www.reuters.com/article/us-usa-election/trump-backs-surveillance-of-mosques-despite-criticism-of-rhetoric-idUSKCN-0Z12AS

Tehranian, J. (2008). *Whitewashed: America's invisible Middle Eastern minority.* NYU Press.

Travers, R. E. (2019, October). Global Terrorism: Threats to the Homeland, Hearing Before the House Committee on Homeland Security, Testimony of Mr. Russell Travers, Acting Director, National Counterterrorism Center, Office of the Director of National Intelligence.

von Sikorski, C., Schmuck, D., Matthes, J., & Binder, A. (2017). "Muslims are not terrorists": Islamic state coverage, journalistic differentiation between terrorism and Islam, fear reactions, and attitudes toward Muslims. *Mass Communication and Society, 20*(6), 825–848.

Warr, M. (2000). Fear of crime in the United States: Avenues for research and policy. *Criminal Justice, 4*(4), 451–489.

Wyant, B. (2008). Multi-level impacts of perceived incivilities and perceptions of crime risk on fear of crime. *Journal of Research in Crime and Delinquency, 45*(1), 39–64.

World Values Survey. (2022). Share of people who are worried about terrorism [Data set]. Processed by Our World in Data. https://ourworldindata.org

Explaining Terrorism and Political Violence

CHAPTER 3

Theories of Terrorism

*Psychological, Sociological,
and Criminological Explanations*

Source: NatBasil/Shutterstock.

Learning Objectives
1. To define the concept of theory.
2. To describe the major explanations of terrorism from the fields of psychology, sociology, and criminology.
3. To illustrate the practical application of theories in understanding terrorism cases.

3.1 INTRODUCTION

Theories are generalized propositions that are connected to existing knowledge and seek to explain how something works and why certain factors are related. Theories are important because they provide us with different lenses through which to view complex social problems, such as terrorism, and frameworks through which we conduct analyses. The theoretical framework specifies the particular variables that influence a phenomenon and under what conditions they operate, and theories offer us a basis upon which we can make predictions about future occurrences. While it is helpful to describe social reality, it is theory that provides the explanations behind the observations and furthers our understanding of an issue. Theories that are well-supported by empirical data are valuable for developing policy, such as counterterrorism measures.

Many of the theories that researchers utilize to explain aspects of terrorism have stemmed from prominent theories in the disciplines of **psychology, sociology**, and **criminology**. We describe these theories and their application to the case of terrorism in the following sections. It is important to keep in mind that social problems such as terrorism are incredibly complex, and therefore no single theory can explain all aspects of a social phenomenon. Multiple theories may be used to provide understandings of different components of terrorism—from **radicalization** and persistence in terrorist organizations to the use of terrorism as a tactic, and intergroup conflict—as well as guidance for the development of homeland security, deradicalization, and disengagement programs.

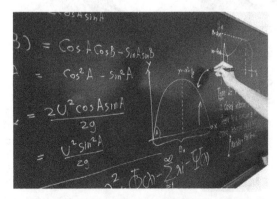

FIGURE 3.1 New evidence should be compatible with a theory. If it isn't, the theory is refined or rejected.

3.2 PSYCHOLOGICAL EXPLANATIONS OF TERRORISM

Psychology can be described as the study of the human mind (e.g., emotions, memories, perceptions) and behaviors (American Psychological Association 2021). According to the American Psychological Association, the scientific discipline of psychology examines all aspects of human behavior, ranging from the functions of the brain to the actions of the nations, from child

FIGURE 3.2   Psychology can be described as the study of the human mind (e.g., emotions, memories, perceptions) and behaviors.

development to care for the elderly. Many psychological theories are derived from the observation of these diverse types of behaviors. There are several different specializations within the discipline of psychology including, but not limited to, cognitive, clinical, forensic, evolutionary, social, and developmental.

The field of psychology is one of the earliest disciplines to examine the issue of radicalization and terrorists' personal and situational characteristics. Like those from other disciplines, psychological explanations of terrorism have their advantages and limitations. For example, for decades much of the **psychological research** and analyses of terrorists have erroneously focused on the search for a terrorist personality. Early theories took a nature as opposed to a nurture argument. In the early 1970s, psychologists first attempted to explain terrorism by diagnosing its perpetrators as having paranoia, schizophrenia, or delusions, or by presenting them as mentally ill, cold-blooded murderers (Silke 2003; Sprang 2003). The belief was that only people who were mentally ill or who possessed a deviant personality would be capable of committing the horrific acts carried out by terrorist groups. Although these claims have never been substantiated by empirical research, scholars argued that participation in a terrorist organization could only be the manifestation of pathology, low intelligence, and egocentrism (Schmid 2012).

As the years passed, however, one of the most robust findings to come from terrorism studies was that terrorists are psychologically normal people and participation in terrorism is not the product of an innate disposition (Borum 2010; Horgan & Braddock 2012; Merari 2005; Pape 2012; Richardson 2006). The extant research does not provide clear evidence of particular or distinctive individual traits that could justify the classification of terrorists as psychotics, neurotics, fanatics, or psychopaths.

Building on these clinical insights, psychological researchers' biggest contribution to the field of terrorism studies came from their findings that terrorists come from a diversity of social backgrounds and have often undergone diverse paths of radicalization (Bjorgo 2011; Borum 2004; Horgan 2005; Schmid 2013; Victoroff & Kruglanski 2009). In other words, there is not a single cause or explanation for radicalization leading to the

FIGURE 3.3   Terrorists come from a diversity of social backgrounds.
From left to right: Ulrike Meinhof, of Red Army Faction; "Unabomber" Ted Kaczynski; Anders Breivik, Norwegian terrorist; and Omar Mateen, Pulse nightclub attacker. *Source:* Permission granted by Werner Meinhof's granddaughter, Bettina Röhl, copyrighted free use, via Wikimedia Commons; George Bergman, GFDL 1.2, via Wikimedia Commons; Wolfmann, CC BY-SA 4.0, via Wikimedia Commons; Florida Department of Highway Safety and Motor Vehicles, Public domain, via Wikimedia Commons.

acts of terrorism (Victoroff 2005). Radicalization is the outcome of complex interactions among a multiplicity of factors, including, but not limited to, poor political and socio-economic conditions, feelings of humiliation, grievances, oppression, inequality, long-standing historical injustices, the experience of discrimination, being obstructed from expressing cultural identities, alienation, identification with the victims, and kinship and social ties to those experiencing similar issues (Gurr 1968; 1970; 2006; Horgan 2005; Schmid 2012). This is true for all kinds of terrorism, including nationalist and separatist, left-wing and right-wing, and ideological and religious terrorism. Depending on the specific circumstances of individuals, these **causal factors** may differ in the extent to which they contribute to radicalization into terrorism (Crenshaw 1986).

To better explain the issue of terrorist violence, contemporary psychological studies of terrorism focus on **vulnerability factors** (motivational factors that push or pull people into terrorism) such as perceived injustice, humiliation, the need for identity, or the need for belonging (Crenshaw 1986; 1992; Hudson 1999; Horgan 2005; Silke 1998). More specifically, these studies have highlighted the need to examine the complex interplay among micro, meso, and macro-level factors over the course of time in order to more fully understand terrorism and develop preventative efforts (LaFree & Miller 2008).

In this context, this section reviews two major psychological theories: (1) frustration-aggression (drive) theory, and (2) group process theory.

3.2.1 Frustration-Aggression (Drive) Theory

The **frustration-aggression theory** was proposed in 1939 by a team of psychologists led by John Dollard from the Yale University Institute of Human Relations. In their famous book *Frustration and Aggression*, Dollard and colleagues (1939, 1) described their theory by two basic principles: (1) the occurrence of aggressive behavior always presupposes the existence of frustration, and (2) the existence of frustration always leads to some form of aggression. The theory basically implies that frustration always leads to aggression, and that aggression is always the consequence of the frustration (in humans and other animals).

More specifically, the researchers argued that if individuals are prevented from achieving a goal because of an **external factor**, they will become frustrated, which will in turn lead to an act of aggression or violence. Dollard and colleagues further argued that if the source of the frustration cannot be challenged, then the aggression may get displaced on other targets. For example, if a man is harassed and humiliated by his bosses at work and he cannot respond to this due to the fear of losing his job, he may displace his aggression onto his friends, or his children or spouse at home.

The biggest criticism of Dollard et al.'s theory came from their sweeping claims that aggression is always a consequence of frustration and that the existence of frustration always leads to some form of aggression (Breuer & Elson 2017). Over time, the frustration-aggression hypothesis was rejected by empirical research because scientists discovered that aggression is not always caused by frustration. According to the social learning and social disorganization theories (discussed later in this chapter), aggressive behavior can be learned by imitating others, especially if these types of behaviors are positively reinforced within peer groups. Contrary to Dollard and colleagues' propositions, aggression can occur in the absence of frustration.

In 1968 and 1989, psychologist Leonard Berkowitz revised Dollard et al.'s (1939) original frustration-aggression theory by arguing that the emotion of frustration does not always lead to aggression, and frustration is just one of the many potential recourses for negative affect or aggressive inclinations. Berkowitz's reformulation of the theory suggests that there are additional antecedents of a "readiness to aggress," such as insults, humiliation, unpleasant environmental stimulants, and anxiety. According to Berkowitz, aggression will only occur in the presence of certain cues, such as the presence of provocative stimuli (unpleasant feelings) or availability of the weapons. For example, in a study with Anthony LePage, Berkowitz (1967) discovered the "weapons effect," by which frustrated individuals showed greater aggression in the presence of guns compared to neutral objects.

Even though the original theory proposed by Dollard and colleagues (1939) has been discredited by contemporary researchers, Berkowitz's (1989) reformulation of the frustration-aggression theory has seen greater success and has been used as a theoretical base by researchers (Gilbert & Bushman 2017). Randy Borum, one of the leading terrorism experts in the

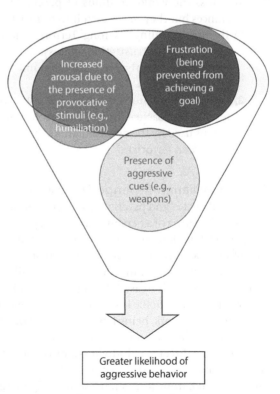

FIGURE 3.4 Frustration-aggression theory.

field of psychology, claims that the frustration-aggression hypothesis can be viewed as a master explanation for understanding the causes of human violence (Borum 2004). Ted Gurr systematically applied Berkowitz's reformulation of frustration-aggression theory to the study of political violence and terrorism, arguing that frustration-aggression is the "primary source of the human capacity for violence" (Gurr 1970, 70). Using a cross-sectional data collected from 114 democratic and autocratic regimes between 1961 and 1965, Gurr (1968) tested whether intense deprivation (the tension between your actual state and what you feel you should be able to achieve) among members of a community can lead to civil strife and turmoil. His data supported the argument that the intensity of the relative deprivation—as measured by economic discrimination, political discrimination, separatism, dependency on foreign capital, religious cleavages, and lack of educational opportunity—had a significant positive relationship with the potential for collective violence: turmoil, conspiracy, or internal war. He further argued that the more intense and prolonged the feeling of frustration, the greater the possibility of aggression.

Despite Gurr's (1968) findings, the application of frustration-aggression theory to the study of terrorism has been criticized by several other researchers. In his seminal article "The Mind of the Terrorist," psychologist Jeff Victoroff (2005) listed three examples why the use of frustration-aggression theory to explain terrorist behavior is erroneous:

1) Across the world, millions of people live in depriving or frustrating circumstances but they never turn into terrorists.
2) Terrorist profiling is wrong. Terrorists do not only come from desperate classes as stated by the frustration-aggression hypothesis. The leftist terrorism in 1970s Europe was mainly perpetrated by individuals who came from privileged lifestyles and classes.
3) Terrorism does not appear to be a last resort for people who have exhausted alternate approaches for conflict resolution. If we view the issue of terrorism as a means used by the deprived groups as a last resort, how can we explain the state-sponsored terrorism?

3.2.2 Humiliation-Revenge Theory

As medical doctor and psychologist Evelin Lindner (2006) describes, humiliation is the "enforced lowering of a person or a group, a process of subjugation that damages or strips away pride, honor, or dignity. To be humiliated is to be placed, mostly against one's will and often in a deeply hurtful way, in a situation that is greatly inferior to what one feels one should expect" (Lindner 2006, 172). Humiliation is felt by individuals whose social status is forcefully decreased through intimidation, physical or mental mistreatment, or by embarrassment. Some instances in which one might experience humiliation include being fired from work, being labeled as a thief or liar, being ostracized, being discredited, and being insulted by someone more powerful. As the definition implies, the feeling of humiliation is directed to individuals by others. Historically, humiliation has been used as a tactic by the powerful to oppress the weak. Many of the public punishments from the medieval Europe (e.g., shame walks, pillories and stock, tarring and feathering) and in the history of the United States (e.g., publishing the names and pictures of prostitutes) were deliberately designed to humiliate with the rationale of "keeping order," "teaching lessons to transgressors," or "driving the violators out of the community" (Burton 2015; Lindner 2001). The purpose of the humiliation is to give a clear message to the victim that they are no longer wanted by a group.

Humiliation is a powerful emotion. Some scholars describe heightened feelings of social humiliation as the strongest force that creates rifts and breaks down relationships (Muenster & Lotto 2010; Lindner 2001). It can have destructive influences in the behaviors of individuals who are subjected to it because it involves abasement of honor and dignity. A person who is humiliated can suffer from several psychological consequences, such as depression, fear, apathy, suspicion and para-

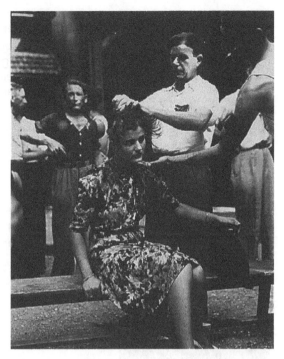

FIGURE 3.5 After D-Day, French women who were accused of collaborating with Germans were publicly humiliated. Their heads were shaved, they were stripped of their clothes, smeared with tar, paraded through towns, stoned, kicked, and beaten.

noia, feelings of worthlessness and helplessness, suicidal thoughts, and anxiety. Recent academic studies indicate that the feeling of humiliation is experienced by our brains as intensely as physical pain (Kross et al. 2011). Scholars have described humiliation as "mental cruelty" (Margalit 1998), "psychological scars" (Baumeister 1999), "excessive overt derogation" (Coleman et al. 2006), and "threat to the core psychological existence of the victim" (Swift 1991).

When turned outward, the feeling of humiliation can also lead to a desire for **revenge**, anger, and violence. It can generate long-lasting negative emotions that fuel violence (Muenster & Lotto 2010). It is this aspect of the feeling of humiliation (the internal pressure for revenge) that is pertinent to terrorism studies.

Applying the insights from **humiliation-revenge theory** to the case of terrorism, scholars hypothesize that like individuals, if a society suffers from collective humiliation by an **out-group** (e.g., ethnic cleansing, genocide, national defeat in a war, mistreatment by an occupying force), if they are denied their humanity, it can result in mass violence against the oppressor or out-group (Gilligan 1996; Juergensmeyer 2000; Scheff 1990). This is because humiliated individuals seek retribution and corrective action, even at the risk of additional cost to themselves. It is the feeling of humiliation that transforms deprivation into the urge to retaliate with violence.

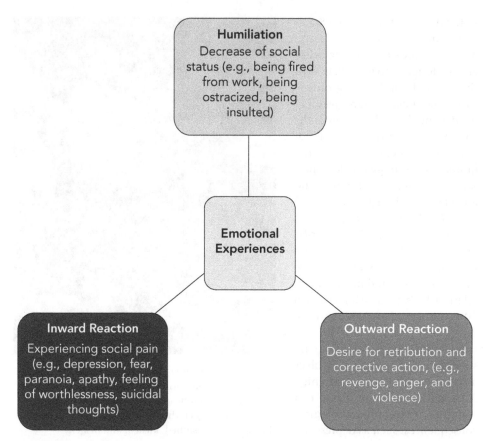

FIGURE 3.6   Humiliation-revenge theory.

Several empirical studies to date have confirmed that humiliation by political oppressors can provoke participation in terrorist acts (Hinton 2002; Jones 2008; Lindner 2006; McCauley 2017; Scheff 2019; Stern 2003; Strozier et al. 2010; Victoroff 2005). In her famous book *Terror in the Name of God*, leading terrorism expert Jessica Stern states the following:

> It is the pernicious effect of repeated, small humiliations that add up to a feeling of nearly unbearable despair and frustration, and a willingness on the part of some to do anything—even commit atrocities—in the belief that attacking the oppressor will restore their sense of dignity. (Stern 2003, 62)

For example, scholars universally accept that it was the harsh social humiliation of Germany at the Treaty of Versailles that gave Hitler his rise to power, which eventually led to World War II and the Holocaust (Kohut 1972; Redles 2010; Strozier & Mart 2017). Hitler attempted to redress this humiliation by inflicting the same on Germany's perceived humiliators (Lindner 2001). Similarly, Lindner suggests that Osama bin Laden would not have had any followers if there were no Muslim victims of humiliation in other parts of the world. She boldly argued that the West is responsible for the rise of terrorism in Muslim countries because, while "the rich and powerful West" has been teaching human rights and equality to its own people, they were inflicting inequality, pain, and poverty on non-Western (non-Christian) people. This inconsistency—in other words, double standard—heightens feelings of humiliation and therefore encourages some Muslims to avenge their humiliations (Lindner 2001; Moisi 2007). She posits that in the terrorist's eyes, violence is easily rationalized because revenge equals exacting justice, thus the vengeful act is considered a moral duty to restore justice (Muenster & Lotto 2010). This may be why violent jihadist leaders such as Bin Laden and Abu Bakr Al-Baghdadi had followers all around the world. They justified violence by citing the humiliation suffered by Muslims around the world (Strozier & Mart 2017).

During her time in Egypt as a psychological counselor (1984–1991), Lindner met with a twenty-year-old Palestinian female patient who despaired at the suffering around her. The patient told Lindner that she would like to give birth to suicide bombers who would avenge the humiliation of Palestinian individuals in Gaza:

> My father wants me to study, get married, and have a life. But I cannot smile and laugh and think of a happy life, when at the same time my aunts and uncles, my nieces and other family members face suffering in Palestine. This suffering is like a heavy burden on me. . . . Sometimes I cannot sleep. Our people are suffering and we should stand by them. If we cannot help them directly, we should at least not be heartless and forget them altogether. I feel that I do not have any right to enjoy life as long as my people suffer. . . . I would go to my homeland, get married and have as many sons as I could have. . . . I would be overjoyed to have a martyr as a son, a son who sacrifices his life for his people. I feel that suicide bombers are heroes, because it is hard to give your life. I want to give my life. I want to do something. I cannot just sit here in Cairo and watch my people suffer. . . . Their suffering eats me up. I feel so powerless, so heavy. The burden crushes me. What shall I do? (Lindner 2001, 60)

Despite this anecdotal evidence that humiliation serves as a justification for rage, violence, and righteous action, the humiliation-revenge theory has not been studied in its entirety (McCauley 2017). The theory still awaits better substantiation; to date, no comprehensive dataset has been compiled or academic work undertaken to analyze the issue of retribution in terrorist groups.

3.3 SOCIOLOGICAL EXPLANATIONS OF TERRORISM

Sociology is the study of social life, including the social causes and consequences of human behavior (American Sociological Association 2021). Sociologists study groups and group interactions, from small personal groups to large complex organizations and entire societies, and the interests of sociologists span a range of topics including, but certainly not limited to, childhood and family, the environment, social inequalities, **collective behavior** and social movements, and crime and social control. With an emphasis on external (social) influences on human behavior, a sociological approach provides insight into the formation of terrorist groups, the sources of intergroup conflict, and the radicalization of individual terrorist group members.

As with many other disciplines, it was not until after the events of September 11, 2001 that sociologists deepened their interest in the study of terrorism (Turk 2004). However,

FIGURE 3.7 Sociology is the study of social life, including the social causes and consequences of human behavior. *Source:* By blvdone/Shutterstock.

because terrorism falls within the domain of sociological interest (as a social phenomenon), researchers have recognized the contribution of existing prominent sociological theories to our understanding of terrorism. In particular, we discuss the relevance and insights of three theories in the following sections: (1) social learning theory, (2) social movements theory, and (3) social identity theory.

3.3.1 Social Learning Theory

In the 1930s and 1940s, Edwin Sutherland developed the **differential association** theory of criminal behavior, in which he argued that criminal behavior is learned rather than innate (Sutherland 1947). Sutherland explained that people commit criminal acts because they have learned definitions—including values, perspectives, attitudes, motivations, and techniques—that favor criminal behaviors over conventional behaviors through their interactions with others who share those definitions. In other words, an individual learns to be a criminal by interacting with others, such as family members and peers, who hold definitions that support criminality. The greater the frequency, duration, and intensity of these associations with criminal others, the more likely the individual will become a criminal themself.

Although the idea of learning criminal behavior through differential association is critical because it emphasizes social influences rather than inherited traits, differential association theory does not specify the mechanisms by which the learning of criminal behavior occurs. It simply states that people learn definitions favorable to crime through association with others. Subsequently, in an attempt to specify how this learning happens, Ronald Akers (1973) incorporated the arguments of differential association theory into his **social learning theory** of crime (SLT). SLT includes four key elements: (1) definitions, (2) imitation, (3) differential **reinforcement**, and (4) differential association.

Like Sutherland, Akers argued that individuals learn beliefs that define crime as desirable, justifiable, or excusable in certain situations. However, Akers elaborated this model and more precisely described the beliefs that lead to crime. He explained that approving *definitions* favorable to the commission of criminal or deviant behaviors are basically positive or neutralizing. Positive definitions are beliefs or attitudes which make the behavior morally desirable or permissible. Neutralizing definitions favor the commission of crime by justifying or excusing it. Neutralizing attitudes include "I can't help myself; I was born this way," "He deserved it," and other excuses and justifications for committing deviant acts and victimizing others.

Akers further argued that crime may be learned through *imitation* and *differential reinforcement*. He noted that in addition to definitions, people can become involved in crime through imitation—that is, they imitate the criminal behaviors of others, especially valued others whose own criminal behavior is reinforced. When imitating behavior, the individual may not quite understand the behavior's importance or whether it will be rewarded. It is through a second process, differential reinforcement, that individuals will continue to commit illegal acts. Borrowing from operant psychology, Akers argued that people continue to offend because they are differentially reinforced for criminal behavior. Through *differential reinforcement*, individuals learn whether behaviors will be rewarded or punished—whether an individual will continue or cease a behavior depends upon previous, present, and anticipated rewards and punishments for that behavior. It is when criminal behaviors are reinforced (rewarded, either through actual or anticipated rewards by others or through fulfilling a goal) that they are likely to continue (Akers & Silverman 2004).

Finally, the fourth element, *differential association*, recognizes that social interactions with close network members (i.e., primary groups) as well as more peripheral contacts serve as important sources of learning. Differential association includes the total influence of an individual's associates, from family and friends to teachers, neighbors, and public and religious figures.

Recognizing the role of **social context**, Akers later suggested that a person's structural location in society will affect their social learning and therefore criminal involvement. Akers (1998) identified four dimensions of social structure that affect the four elements of SLT (definitions, imitation, differential reinforcement, and differential reinforcement) and, in turn, have an indirect impact on the individual's likelihood of committing crime:

1. differential social organization (society, community)
2. differential location in the social structure (age, gender, race, class)
3. theoretically defined structural variables (anomie, social disorganization, conflict); and
4. differential social location (family, peers, school, leisure groups).

Scholars argue that SLT has direct relevance to the case of terrorism. As an example, Lauren Shapiro and Marie-Helen Maras (2019) applied SLT to understand the radicalization of US women into ISIS to serve as foreign fighters. Through an analysis of court documents, the researchers found that social networks were key to women's entry into and continuation in the terrorist organization.

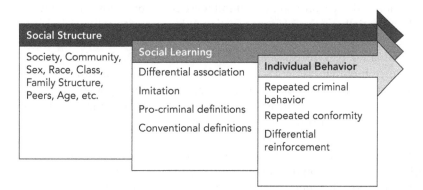

FIGURE 3.8   Social learning theory.

More specifically, ISIS utilizes online and in-person contacts to create a community of supporters and sympathizers to indoctrinate the women in their extremist beliefs. Through exposure to propaganda, strategic narratives, and images of violence, ISIS encourages the development of criminal (terrorist) definitions, and reinforces the espousal of these beliefs, compliance with the group's rules, actions in support of the group, and punishes their failures. The recruited women were praised for their beliefs and promised "a place in paradise." Some were rewarded with a house, while those who failed to comply with expectations were subjected to severe punishment such as disfigurement for failing to wear a face covering (Shapiro & Maras 2019). As with crime, terrorism is learned; individuals must internalize definitions that support the use of terrorism as a means to achieve a social, political, or religious goal, feel rewarded for their attitudes and actions, and associate with others who are familiar with the terrorist mindset, motivations, strategies, and techniques.

3.3.2 Social Movement Theory

Social movement theory (SMT) is a relatively recent approach to the study of terrorism. It is not a singular theory, but rather a combination of insights from research primarily based in sociology and political science. Social movements involve collective behavior that is purposeful and organized, and dedicated to achieving a common social goal. Some examples of contemporary social movements include Black Lives Matter, #MeToo, and various environmental movements, such as Extinction Rebellion. Although social movements rarely advocate the use of violence, they frequently use unconventional means, such as disruptive protests, which have the potential to escalate (della Porta 2018).

Although scholarly research has tended to examine progressive social movements, such as the previous examples, insights from SMT can be applied to the case of terrorism as well. Importantly, terrorism frequently stems from organizations seeking to achieve a social or political goal, and thus terrorist organizations are subject to dynamics and challenges similar to those of other social movement organizations (Beck 2008). A key contribution of SMT to understanding terrorism is its integrative tripartite (or threefold) model that includes (1) political opportunities, (2) **resource mobilization**, and (3) **framing**.

Political opportunities refer to the structure of political prospects and limitations external to the social movement organization. The extent to which organizations have access to political decision-making will influence their ability for contention and determine the potentially successful forms of action. When access to political decision-making is limited or blocked, groups may turn to more extreme forms of action, such as violent protest, militancy, or terrorism (McAdam 1982; Ravndal 2018).

Resource mobilization recognizes that resources, such as funding, knowledge, communication abilities, labor, and member and community support, must be available for movements to advance. Like formal organizations, many terrorist groups have sophisticated central control units that direct members, coordinate attacks, accumulate and manage resources, provide general leadership for members, and navigate broader community relations. As such, like social movement organizations, terrorist groups are rational actors that seek to maximize the utility of the resources available to them. In general, the use of violence as a tactic tends to be more likely when resources are limited.

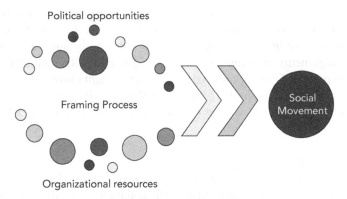

FIGURE 3.9 Social movement theory.

As the third component of the tripartite model, framing refers to the ways in which social movement organizations communicate their positions and goals in order to generate commitment and support. Frames are worldviews that guide individual and collective behaviors, and *frame alignment* refers to linkage of individual and organizational frames such that values, beliefs, and goals of individual members are congruent with those of the social movement organization. Frame alignment is necessary to generate participation in social movements (Snow et al. 1986).

Social movement leaders create frames through ideological manifestos, speeches, propaganda, and social media representations to identify the social problem of concern (the diagnosis), develop strategies for dealing with the problem (the prognosis), and create incentives for acting to address the problem (the motivation). The process of frame alignment is illustrated through ISIS's use of the internet to mobilize foreign fighters from Western nations. ISIS uses its e-magazine, *Dabiq*, to admonish the immorality of Western values, emphasize the solution of creating an Islamist caliphate, and highlight the potential contributions of ISIS, such as healthcare and assistance to people in need as well as its military success (Andersen & Sandberg 2020).

In another example of the applicability of social movement insights to terrorism, Jacob Aasland Ravndal (2018) utilized SMT to explain why, between 1990 and 2015, right-wing terrorism was far more prevalent in Sweden relative to other Nordic nations. According to a dataset that documented incidences of right-wing terrorism and violence in Western Europe from 1990 to 2015, Sweden ranked first in deadly right-wing terrorist attacks per capita.

In a detailed comparative analysis of the history and social and political context of the Nordic countries—Denmark, Norway, Finland, and Sweden—the research illustrates how the case of Sweden, and the Swedish Resistance Movement in particular, differs in terms of the tripartite classification of social movements. First, in terms of political opportunities, Sweden has a higher rate of immigration and lower electoral support for anti-immigration (far-right) parties than other Nordic countries. To a greater extent than in Denmark, Norway, and Finland, Sweden's right wing had limited access to political decision-making, leaving the radical right to resort to violent protest.

Second, in terms of resources that may be maximized, due to its uniquely limited (neutral) role in World War II, Sweden was able to maintain a larger and more organized mass of active militants (or "mobilized activists") (Hewitt 2003, 46). Finally, compared to the other Nordic countries, Sweden can be characterized as having a "more restrictive public debate on immigration," where political elites flatly reject to consider anti-immigration arguments and stigmatize radical right actors (Ravndal 2018, 787). This context "resonates with frames produced by the extreme right movement, portraying the political elite as traitors unwilling to protect the cultural heritage of its own people (diagnosis), and thus the need for violent revolution (prognosis) to create a better future (motivation)" (Ravndal 2018, 786).

3.3.3 Social Identity Theory

Social identity theory is a social psychological theory that was developed in the 1970s and 1980s by Henri Tajfel and John Turner, who sought to emphasize the *social* aspects of psychology and explain intergroup relations. The theory is psychological in that it concerns the mechanisms through which **intergroup processes** such as stereotyping, cooperation, ethnocentrism, and collective behavior occur, while its emphasis on socially constructed categories and group-based identities have made the theory influential among sociologists.

The basic premise of the theory is that individuals have, as a part of their self-conceptions, *group-based* social identities. According to Tajfel (1981, 255), social identities are the "part of an individual's self-concept which derives from his knowledge of his membership of a social group (or groups) together with the value and emotional significance attached to that membership." Social identities can be based on any number of socially constructed categories, including national origin, ethnicity, gender, religion, age cohort, occupation, sports team, and so on. The existence of social groups from which social identities are formed depends on the extent to which people identify with the social group and are seen by others as members of that group (Tajfel 1981). The group's reality is not dependent on its size or function; what matters is that certain individuals are consistently categorized by themselves and others as group members. These social groups provide individuals with a sense of identity based on the defining characteristics of the group, and individuals have varying sets of social identities that differ in their level of importance to their self-concepts. Importantly, social identities operate at the collective level. In contrast to individual-level personal identities, according to which individuals think as "me" (who *I* am, e.g., a textbook writer), collective-level social identities are understood as "we" (who *we* are, e.g., professors) and characterized by the features of the group as a whole (Thoits & Virshup 1997).

According to the theory, intergroup processes come into play because social groups are differentially valued in society, and individuals are motivated to have positive group identities. To do so, people assess the status of their own group (in-group) through a process of social comparison to a relevant reference group (out-group), and highlight positive stereotypical characteristics that favor their own group while emphasizing negative stereotypical characteristics that devalue the out-group.

Through the process of categorization, individuals come to view their own group as better than the out-group, which is viewed in terms of negative stereotypes—a prototype of the group. Categorization also involves the **depersonalization** of both in-group and out-group members, a process by which individual group members are seen only as the

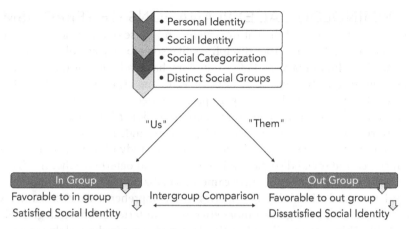

FIGURE 3.10   Social identity theory.

stereotypical group prototype and not as unique individual actors. Depersonalization contributes to group cohesiveness and conformity because group members assume that they are alike and that they are distinct from out-group members. Hence, an "us versus them" mentality is established.

Stability and change come from a group's relative positioning in society. Driven by a desire for self-enhancement, individuals strive to feel positively about their group memberships and will act in ways that can enhance their self-concepts. For example, if an individual believes a group's lower status is illegitimate and boundaries between groups are relatively permeable, there will be little cohesion among group members, and the individual may seek to gain entrance into the higher status group, thus achieving social mobility. However, if a group believes that its lower status position is illegitimate and boundaries between groups cannot be trespassed, group members will act collectively and engage in intergroup conflict in an attempt to change the social order (Hogg et al. 1995). Consistent with the conflict theoretical approach within sociology, the higher-status group is likely to resist the change and intergroup competition will ensue.

In addition, social identity theory implies that terrorist groups may appeal to susceptible individuals because they provide members with a group-level identity that enables them to feel a sense of community with similar others. This may be especially the case when individuals experience self-uncertainty. Terrorist groups tend to have very clear expectations for the attitudes and behavior of members (a prototype) and clear boundaries of group membership (Haner 2018). Social psychologist Michael Hogg (2012, 19) argues that extremism is an example of what can occur when social identities "turn dark—specifically when social identity reduces or protects from profound self-uncertainty." The strong social identity associated with terrorism groups includes a rigid contrast between the in-group's principles and those of the out-group, which, through categorization and self-enhancement processes, can lead to moral absolutism, zealotry, ethnocentrism, intolerance, and violence against the out-group. The group becomes more likely to engage in conflict against the out-group when members feel their security and lifestyle are threatened.

3.4 CRIMINOLOGICAL EXPLANATIONS OF TERRORISM

Criminology is the study of the nature, extent, and cause of crime, and the control of criminal behavior. As with other disciplines like sociology, psychology, and political science, the interdisciplinary field of criminology has made significant theoretical and methodological contributions to the issue of terrorism, especially after 9/11 (LaFree & Dugan 2015). More specifically, during the past three decades, terrorism-related research and academic courses became core components of major criminology programs. Funding for terrorism-related research in criminology has expanded, and several criminological theories and perspectives have been applied to the study of terrorism, ranging from rational choice and social disorganization to strain and deterrence theories (Freilich & LaFree 2015). Research on terrorism became a specialization among criminologists, and scholars have tested criminological theories with comprehensive datasets and revealed unique insights that have guided more effective counterterrorism strategies (Fisher & Dugan 2019). This section will explore the three main criminological theories of crime: (1) rational choice and deterrence, (2) strain, and (3) social disorganization—and their application to terrorism and counterterrorism.

3.4.1 Rational Choice and Deterrence Theory

The origin of rational choice theory dates back to the seventeenth century, to a movement commonly known as the Enlightenment. The classical school of criminology was established during this period. Defenders of this school of thought argued that people make choices to commit crimes and that punishment should be about preventing future crimes from being committed (i.e., deterrence). According to this school, people weigh pros (potential benefits) and cons (possible costs) when they make a decision. Rational choice theory argues that this process works in the same way for the decision of whether or not to commit a crime. People will decide to commit crime if they believe that their acts can provide immediate benefit without the threat of long-term risks. This is known as hedonistic calculus. **Hedonism** is the seeking of pleasure and avoidance of pain—if the rewards of criminal behavior are great and the perceived risks are small, the likelihood of committing a crime increases. From this perspective, criminal behavior is rational; people choose to commit crime after weighing the potential benefits and consequences of their criminal act.

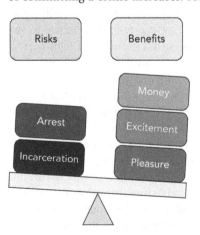

FIGURE 3.11 Rational choice theory.

For example, imagine that your car was broken into and the burglar stole valuable items from the backseat—a bag, laptop, and watch. You are angry about this incident, but you also want to understand why the burglar chose your car to burglarize. The rational choice theory of criminology says that people make logical choices regarding the circumstances under which they commit crimes. Perhaps the burglar noticed that you did not lock the doors of your car. If the car doors were locked the burglar might have moved on, looking for an easier target. But the unlocked doors gave them an opportunity to rationally consider options and to realize that their job was made easier by your behavior. So before breaking into your car, the burglar did some hedonistic calculus. They figured that if they steal the items from the backseat of your car, they can sell them. This will let them buy things that will bring pleasure. But if caught they might go to jail, which would cause pain. In this instance, the burglar weighed the possibility of getting caught against the possible pleasure derived from eluding consequences and determined that the benefits outweighed the potential costs.

Several scholars applied the **rational choice and deterrence** perspective to understand issues related to terrorism, including, but not limited to, the occurrence of worldwide aerial hijackings; the actions of radical eco-groups; the protection of abortion clinics, staff, and patients from terrorist violence; and the deterrent effects of counterterrorism laws (Carson 2014; Dugan et al. 2005; Dugan & Chenoweth 2012; Pridemore & Freilich 2007; LaFree et al. 2009).

For example, in line with the logic of rational choice theory, Dugan et al. (2005) discovered that increased security measures at airports, such as use of metal detectors and enhanced body screening tools, significantly reduced the risk of aerial hijackings by terrorists. In this case, these security measures increase the probability of foiling a terrorism attempt, making the potential costs of the criminal act weigh more heavily in hedonistic calculus.

One critique of rational choice theory, however, is its use to justify punitive policies, which have been shown to be dismal failures. For example, Dugan and Chenoweth (2012) applied the rational choice framework to understand the effect of increased punishment measures on the level of terrorist activities in Israel. Contrary to the expectations of rational choice theory, the authors discovered repressive measures (increased level of punishment) were not associated with a decrease in terrorist activity. Rather, the findings indicated that conciliatory actions by Israeli government were significantly associated with a decrease in the terrorist activities of Palestinian groups. Similarly, Pridemore and Freilich (2007) found that increasing the severity of punishments for engaging in terrorism has no effect on dissuading the terrorist from terrorist activities.

3.4.2 Strain Theory

The origin of the **strain theory** can be traced back to well-known sociologist Robert Merton, who proposed his theory of "social structure and anomie" in 1938, and subsequently added clarifications and revisions until the late 1960s. The logical flow of Merton's work suggests two theories within it: a macro-level anomie theory and a micro-level strain theory.

At the macro (societal) level, anomie theory attempted to explain why some groups in the US exhibited higher rates of crime compared to others. Merton (1938) proposed that the goal of achieving the monetary success was very important within the US. However, there was a weak emphasis on how to achieve this goal in a legitimate way. As a consequence, individuals used whatever means necessary, including criminal behaviors to pursue monetary success. Merton (1938) thus described **anomie** as the inability of a state to adequately regulate goal seeking behaviors and the acts of its people. Generally, societal-level goals (e.g., wealth) are not achievable by the readily available means (e.g., poor job opportunities).

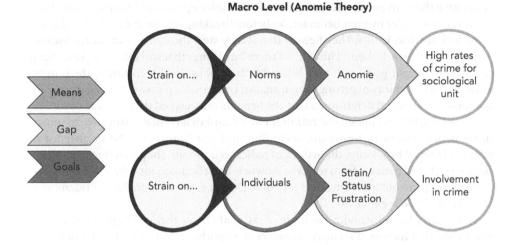

FIGURE 3.12 Anomie and strain theories.

At the micro level, Merton (1938) suggested that individuals are especially pressured to commit crimes when they are prevented from achieving monetary goals. He observed that everyone in the US is encouraged to achieve monetary goals. However, middle- and lower-class individuals can be prevented from achieving such goals in legitimate ways because they may not have enough money for a college education or to live in nontroubled neighborhoods, thus leading to strain and an involvement in various crimes, such as theft, drug-dealing, and prostitution, in order to achieve the so-called American Dream.

Merton (1938) detailed several adaptations to the experience of this strain. These include:

1) **conformity**—individual acceptance of both the goals and means of society;
2) **innovation**—individual acceptance of the goals, but rejection of the means;
3) **rebellion**—individual rejection of both the goals and means of society, and substitution of other goals and means;
4) **ritualism**—individual rejection of the goals, but with overconformity to the means; and
5) **retreatism**—individual rejection of both the goals and means, by withdrawing from society. The rejection of the institutional (culturally approved) means for goal achievement may result in a turn to criminal behaviors.

TABLE 3.1 Merton's Modes of Adaptation to Anomie and Strain

Modes of Adaptation	Cultural Goals	Institutional Means
Conformity	Accept	Accept
Innovation	Accept	Reject
Ritualism	Reject	Accept
Retreatism	Reject	Reject
Rebellion	Reject/Replace	Reject/Replace

source: Merton, R. (1938). Social structure and anomie. *American Sociological Review, 3*(5), 672–682.

After the 1970s, strain theory lost its effect on public policies because a number of empirical studies failed to support it. A growing amount of evidence showed that crime was highest among the people with low aspirations and low expectations, not among the people with high aspirations and low expectations as the strain theorists predicted (Hirschi 1979).

Subsequently, Robert Agnew (1992) contended that strain was a more general phenomena, rather than the simple discrepancy between aspirations and expectations, and developed a more comprehensive version of the classic strain theory. He suggested that the failure to achieve positively valued goals was one of several types of strain, and more broadly that strain was the consequence of negative relationships with others. Individuals developed strain because they were not treated by other individuals as they would like to be treated. Agnew called his new theory "general" strain because he sought to explain a diverse range of delinquent behavior.

According to Agnew (1992), strain is a necessary cause of delinquency, but it is not sufficient. He introduced the intervening variable of negative affect (a psychological state), including disappointment, anger, and frustration. In his view, negative emotions create pressure for corrective action; individuals feel bad and want to do something about it. When individuals face strain they will experience increased levels of negative emotions, such as anger, and may use crime as one possible solution to escape from the strain. For example, they might assault the ones who insulted or mistreated them, seek some sort of revenge, or use drugs to manage the negative emotions. According to Agnew (1992), anger is the most important reaction to strain because it increases the likelihood that the individual will deal with strain in a criminal manner.

Agnew also detailed three types of negative relationships that produce strain on individuals. In the first type, individuals may develop strain when they are prevented or threatened from achievement of positively valued goals, such as monetary success. In the second type, individuals may develop strain when their positively valued stimuli are removed. For instance, the death of a family member can produce strain on individuals. Finally, individuals may develop strain when their relationships with other individuals present or threaten to present negatively valued stimuli, such as insult or physical assault

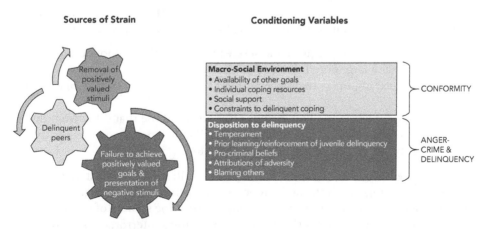

FIGURE 3.13 Agnew's general strain theory.

(Agnew 1992). As a result of these negative relationships, individuals will have increased levels of negative emotions, such as anger, and may use crime as a possible solution to escape from the strain. Consequently, strain leads to crime because it increases negative emotions, which in the end create pressure for corrective action.

In 2001, based on an examination of empirical research from several areas, Agnew argued that strains are more likely to result in crime when individuals see these strains as unjust (e.g., occurring as voluntary and intentional behaviors to cause harm), high in magnitude (e.g., involving a large financial loss, a long duration, or being threatening to one's core identity), the strained individual has low social control (e.g., they are impulsive and insensitive to others), and when they create pressure for criminal coping (e.g., criminal forms of coping are normative among one's social groups). Under these types of strains, individuals often lose their ability to engage in conventional forms of coping and cannot see the perceived cost of crime.

Furthermore, Agnew (2001) argued that vicarious and anticipated strains can be the source of criminal behaviors, as individuals may seek revenge against those who victimized their family and friends or those living in neighborhoods with high rates of criminal activity may carry weapons in an effort to prevent future victimization. Agnew also suggested that not every source of strain has the same effect on an individual. He proposed that intense, more recent, and enduring strains have more powerful effects on the individuals. Moreover, the clustering of straining events (e.g., the occurrence of multiple stressors at once) has an impact beyond the sum of their individual effects.

Agnew made it clear, however, that not all strains that meet this criteria result in criminal behaviors. Some individuals cope with strain in conventional ways because they have cognitive, behavioral, and emotional adaptations that enable them to cope successfully in culturally approved manners. Such individuals usually have access to social support, strong moral restraint, and are high in self-efficacy.

Using this general strain theory framework, Agnew (2016) developed a theory of terrorism which proposes that collective strains (presentation of negative stimuli, failure to achieve positively valued goals at the group or societal-level) increase the likelihood of engaging in terrorist acts because they increase the negative emotions (anger, frustration, humiliation, and disappointment) and foster the social learning of terrorism as a coping strategy. More specifically, Agnew's **general strain theory of terrorism (GSTT)** suggests that engagement in terrorism is more likely when "collective strains" are:

1) high in magnitude (frequent and severe physical, social, economic, and mental harms), with large populations of civilians affected;
2) perceived as unjust (so they generate moral outrage against the external agents); and
3) inflicted by substantially more powerful others (those that differ from the repressed group by their superior numbers, religion, language, race/ethnicity, nationality, or political ideology). (Agnew 2016)

According to Agnew, these collective strains will produce negative emotions (frustration and anger) and the desire for corrective action. Repressed groups may be likely to engage in terrorism to obtain revenge against the sources of strain. As with the GST of crime, Agnew notes that the effect of strains on terrorism is conditioned by several mediating factors, such as coping skills and resources, social support, individual traits, and the rational calculation of costs and benefits of engagement in terrorism.

Researchers from several fields have attempted to explain terrorism in terms of strains, such as harsh state repression, human right violations, and ethnic, territorial, and religious disputes. A majority of the case studies (qualitative studies) of terrorist groups have provided strong support for the notion that strains do in fact contribute to terrorism (Agnew 2010; Bjorgo 2005; Forst 2009; Gurr & Moore 1997; Haner 2018; LaFree & Ackerman 2009; Piazza 2007). Quantitative studies, on the other hand, have provided weak or mixed support for the propositions of the strain theory of terrorism. For example, the relationship between material deprivation (being poor) and engagement in terrorism is weak or absent in most empirical research on the topic; economically disadvantaged individuals are not more likely to engage in terrorism. The only exception to this finding came from Gruenewald et al. (2013), who analyzed the crimes committed by far-right terrorist groups in the United States and found that approximately half of the far-right extremists who committed homicide between the years of 1990 and 2010 were unemployed (Gruenewald et al. 2013). More quantitative research with comprehensive datasets is needed to fully test the status of the GSTT.

3.4.3 Social Disorganization Theory

Another mainstream criminological theory that has guided terrorism research is **social disorganization theory** (SDT). To date, several studies of terrorism have drawn on SDT.

The origin of the SDT goes back to the early phases of the 1940s, to Clifford R. Shaw and Henry D. McKay, both prominent members of the Chicago School of criminology. During the 1940s, Shaw and McKay (1942) used crime mapping techniques in an attempt to explain the high juvenile delinquency rates in certain areas of Chicago neighborhoods between 1900 and 1933. By analyzing juvenile court records, truancy, and recidivism rates, Shaw and McKay mapped crimes according to the addresses of the delinquents. The major finding was that crime was highest in a zone in transition (e.g., impoverished areas with high residential turnover), no matter which ethnic group resided there. Therefore, Shaw and McKay proposed that the key element to understanding criminal behaviors might not lay in individual traits (which was a popular view at that time) but in the social context in which people lived.

During this time, as Chicago's population grew, the business and industrial areas remained in the center of cities. Outside this area was known as the "zone in transition." Within this zone was the intersection of poverty, heterogeneity, rapid population growth, transiency, and family disruption. The dwellings in this area were often undesirable and were frequently left to deteriorate, since further investments were not profitable. Eventually, the physical undesirability of these areas reduced the rents and prompted people with high and moderate incomes to move to the outer boundaries of the cities. On the other hand, the low prices and proximity to work areas forced a mixture of immigrants from diverse cultures and African Americans to be concentrated in these areas of physical deterioration, which were previously owned by White Protestant populations.

Shaw and McKay argued that this structural density (large social forces resulting from transiency, poverty, heterogeneity, and urbanism) or intersection of large social forces created stress in the zone in transition. According to the 1920 federal census,

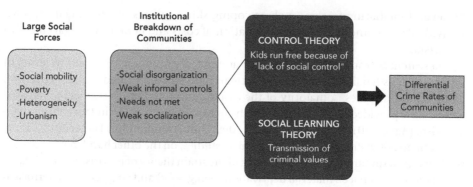

FIGURE 3.14   Social disorganization theory.

more than 30 foreign groups—with divergent definitions of behaviors and cultural standards—were living in the area (Shaw & Moore 1931, 15). The existence of conflicting cultural standards and the continuous change in the composition of the area had prevented the establishment of a neighborhood tradition. For example, what was approved in some groups was condemned in other groups. In some groups, personal status could be enhanced by manifestations of criminal skills, whereas in other groups the commission of such as acts would definitely result in ostracism. There was a confusion of standards in the zone in transition. Children living in this community were exposed to a variety of interests, forms of behavior, and stimulations, rather than a consistent pattern of conventional standards and values (Shaw & Moore 1931). It is important to note that Shaw and McKay's findings did not imply that conventional values were not existent; instead, it indicated that these values were in competition with unconventional values.

Shaw and McKay also found that crime rates progressively decreased among the immigrant groups themselves as they moved away from the zone in transition (as they got wealthier) and into the outer zones. These findings simply indicated that it was the characteristics of the areas, not the characteristics of the individuals, that influenced the crime rates in Chicago. Based on these findings, the researchers defined social disorganization as the institutional breakdown of the social institutions in a community. As described earlier, in the "zone in transition," conventional institutions such as churches, schools, and voluntary associations were affected by the rapid population growth, the different ethnic and racial groups, and poverty, which eventually resulted in social disorganization. In turn, social disorganization weakened the community's ability to provide informal social control and socialize youth, thereby leading to higher levels of crime.

Researchers in the field of criminology have tested the application of SDT to terrorism to understand whether the causal mechanisms highlighted by Shaw and McKay operate in the same way to explain ideologically motivated violence (Gruenewald et al. 2013; Johnson & Braithwaite 2009, LaFree et al. 2012). For example, using a dataset that included approximately 600 terrorist attacks in US counties between 1990 to 2011, LaFree and Bersani (2014) developed a set of hypotheses informed by social disorganization theory. In line with the arguments of SDT, the researchers discovered that terrorist attacks in the United States were most common in counties that were characterized by **population heterogeneity** (greater language diversity and larger proportion of foreign-born residents), greater residential instability, and a higher percentage of urban residents. Contrary to SDT, however, the authors also found that terrorist attacks were less common in counties marked by high levels of **concentrated disadvantage** (e.g., families below the poverty line, unemployed individuals, individuals receiving public assistance). Despite this contradiction—that the concentrated disadvantage is associated with lower levels of terrorist attacks—this finding is in line with the conclusions of decades of terrorism research: that terrorists are not drawn from the poor communities.

Similarly, analyzing data from United States Extremist Crime Database, Freilich et al. (2015) tested the principles of the SDT (along with other macro-level criminology frameworks) to understand whether social disorganization is associated with the locations of far-right extremist homicides by comparing them with the locations of regular homicide incidents occurring between the years of 1990 and 2012. Their findings were complex, but generally offered support for SDT in that social disorganization measures (e.g., racial and ethnic diversity, availability of Jewish or Muslim congregations, residential instability, percentage divorced) were strong predictors of having a far-right extremist homicide within the county.

3.5 CONCLUSION

Theories offer explanations of social phenomena. They help us to define and categorize observations and relationships and to predict future occurrences. By proposing the reasons why individuals, social groups, and societies behave in the ways they do, theories provide guidance for data collection and furthering knowledge on a topic. Theories that are well-supported by empirical data are essential to the development of effective counterterrorism measures. We need to understand why individuals join terrorist organizations if we want to prevent radicalization. Policies designed to deter or prevent radicalization into terrorism will depend on the proposed causes of radicalization. Theories provide the rationale for policy development.

Importantly, terrorism is a multifaceted social problem that exerts its influence on a global scale, and scholars have developed several theories in attempts to understand it. Due to its complexity, no single theory can explain all issues related to terrorism. Multiple theories can be used together to provide different lenses through which to view the many aspects of terrorism. In this chapter, we reviewed key theoretical contributions from the social science disciplines of psychology, sociology, and criminology. As these disciplines have long-studied issues relevant to terrorism—individual cognitions, mental processes, and behaviors (psychology); social influences, group-based identities, and intergroup conflict (sociology); and criminal behaviors (criminology)—many classic theories from these disciplines have been applied to the case of terrorism. The theories discussed in this chapter thus highlight different features of terrorism of interest to scholars in these areas and offer guidance for future research and further theory development.

Key Lessons

Lesson 1

Theories are generalized propositions that are connected to existing knowledge and seek to explain how something works and why certain factors are related. Multiple theories can be used to understand different aspects of terrorism.

Lesson 2

Psychology is the study of the human mind, mental processes, and behaviors and how they influence behavior.

Lesson 3

Early psychological theories that sought to identify a single terrorist profile, based on psychological abnormality, have been discredited. However, the knowledge that terrorists, in general, do not suffer from some mental abnormality has been a major contribution to the study of terrorism.

Lesson 4

Contemporary psychological theories of terrorism focus on vulnerability factors and the role of emotions in terrorism, including frustration-aggression and humiliation-revenge.

Lesson 5

Sociology is the study of social life, including the social causes and consequences of human behavior, with a particular focus on groups and group interactions.

Lesson 6

Sociological theories of terrorism examine how social factors, such as socialization and family or peer influence, political context and organizational resources, and group-based identities relate to involvement in terrorism.

Lesson 7

Influential theories that utilize a sociological perspective include social learning theory, social movements theory, and social identity theory.

Lesson 8

Criminology is the study of the nature, extent, and cause of crime and the control of criminal behavior. It is an interdisciplinary field of study, with its emphasis focused on crime and criminal justice.

Lesson 9

As terrorism involves criminal behaviors, research on terrorism, and the application of criminological theories to the case of terrorism, has become a growing area of focus within the field of criminology.

Lesson 10

Prominent criminological theories that have been utilized to understand terrorism emphasize the issue of rational choice, the experience of strain, and the problem of social disorganization.

KEY WORDS

anomie
causal factors
collective behavior
concentrated disadvantage
criminology
depersonalization
differential association
external factors
framing
frustration-aggression (drive) theory
general strain theory of terrorism (GSTT)
hedonism
humiliation-revenge theory
intergroup processes
out-groups
population heterogeneity

psychology
psychological research
radicalization
rational choice and deterrence
reinforcement
resource mobilization
revenge
social context
social disorganization theory
social identity theory
social learning theory
social movement theory (SMT)
sociology
strain theory
vulnerability factors

RECOMMENDED SOURCES

Research Articles & Books

Bjørgo, Tore (2005) 'Introduction', in Tore Bjorgo (ed.) *Root Causes of Terrorism*, pp. 1–15. London: Routledge.

Crenshaw, M. (1987). Theories of terrorism: Instrumental and organizational approaches. *The Journal of Strategic Studies, 10*(4), 13–31.

Crenshaw, M. (1992). How terrorists think: what psychology can contribute to understanding terrorism. In L. Howard (Ed.), *Terrorism: Roots, Impact, Responses* (pp. 71–80), London: Praeger.

della Porta, D. (2018). Radicalization: A relational perspective. *Annual Review of Political Science, 21*, 461–474.

Fisher, D. G., & Dugan, L. (2019). Sociological and criminological explanations of terrorism. *The Oxford Handbook of Terrorism*, 163.

Fisher, D., & Kearns, E. M. (2024). The theorizing of terrorism within criminology. *Journal of Research in Crime and Delinquency, 61*(4), 487–520.

Freilich, J. D., & LaFree, G. (Eds.). (2017). *Criminology theory and terrorism: New applications and approaches*. Routledge.

Horgan, J. (2005). *The psychology of terrorism*. London: Routledge.

Hudson, R. (1999). *The Sociology and Psychology of Terrorism: Who Becomes a Terrorist and Why?* Washington, DC: Library of Congress, Federal Research Division.

Kruglanski, A. W., Molinario, E., Ellenberg, M., & Di Cicco, G. (2022). Terrorism and conspiracy theories: A view from the 3N model of radicalization. *Current Opinion in Psychology, 47*, 101396.

LaFree, G., & Dugan, L. (2015). "How Has Criminology Contributed to the Study of Terrorism since 9/11?" *Sociology of Crime, Law and Deviance* 20 (September): 1–23. http://www.emeraldinsight.com/doi/abs/10.1108/S1521-613620150000020002

Victoroff, J. (2005). The mind of the terrorist: A review and critique of psychological approaches. *Journal of Conflict Resolution, 49*(1), 3–42.

REFERENCES

American Psychological Association (2021). About APA. https://www.apa.org/support/about-apa?item=7

American Sociological Association (2021). About ASA. https://www.asanet.org/about/what-sociology

Agnew, R. (1992). Foundation for a general strain theory of crime and delinquency. *Criminology, 30*(1), 47–88.

Agnew, R. (2001). Building on the foundation of general strain theory: Specifying the types of strain most likely to lead to crime and delinquency. *Journal of Research in Crime and Delinquency, 38*(4), 319–361.

Agnew, R. (2010). A general strain theory of terrorism. *Theoretical Criminology, 14*(2), 131–153.

Agnew, R. (2016). General strain theory and terrorism. In G. LaFree & J. D. Freilich (Eds.), *The handbook of the criminology of terrorism* (pp. 119–132). Wiley.

Akers, R. (1973). *Deviant behavior: A social learning approach*. Wadsworth.

Akers, R. (1998). *Social learning and social structure: A general theory of crime and deviance*. Northeastern University Press.

Akers, R. L., & Silverman, A. (2004). Toward a social learning model of violence and terrorism. In M. A. Zahn, H. H. Brownstein, & S. L. Jackson (Eds.), *Violence: From theory to research*. Lexis-Nexis-Anderson Publishing.

Andersen, J. C., & Sandberg, S. (2020). Islamic State propaganda: Between social movement framing and subcultural provocation. *Terrorism and Political Violence, 32*(7), 1506–1526.

Baumeister, R. F. (1999). *Evil: Inside human violence and cruelty*. Macmillan.

Beck, C. J. (2008). The contribution of social movement theory to understanding terrorism. *Sociology Compass, 2*(5), 1565–1581.

Berkowitz, L. (1968). The study of urban violence: Some implications of laboratory studies of frustration and aggression. *American Behavioral Scientist, 11*(4), 14–17.

Berkowitz, L. (1989). Frustration-aggression hypothesis: Examination and reformulation. *Psychological Bulletin, 106*(1), 59.

Berkowitz, L., & LePage, A. (1967). Weapons as aggression-eliciting stimuli. *Journal of Personality and Social Psychology, 7*(2p1), 202.

Bjørgo, T. (2005). Introduction. In Tore Bjørgo (Ed.), *Root Causes of Terrorism* (pp. 1–15). Routledge.

Bjørgo, T. (2011). Dreams and disillusionment: Engagement in and disengagement from militant extremist groups. *Crime, Law and Social Change, 55*, 277–285.

Borum, R. (2004). *Psychology of terrorism. Mental Health Law & Policy Faculty Publications*, 571. https://digitalcommons.usf.edu/mhlp_facpub/571

Borum, R. (2010). Understanding terrorist psychology. In A. Silke (Ed.), *The psychology of counter-terrorism* (pp. 19–33). Routledge.

Breuer, J., & Elson, M. (2017). Frustration-aggression theory. In P. Sturmey (Ed.), *The Wiley handbook of violence and aggression*, 1–12. Wiley.

Burton, N. L. (2015). *Heaven and hell: The psychology of the emotions*. Acheron Press.

Carson, J. V. (2014). Counterterrorism and radical eco-groups: A context for exploring the series hazard model. *Journal of Quantitative Criminology, 30*, 485–504.

Coleman, P. T., Goldman, J. S., & Kugler, K. G. (2006). Emotional intractability: The effects of perceptions of emotional roles on immediate and delayed conflict outcomes. IACM Meetings Paper. http://dx.doi.org/10.2139/ssrn.915947

Crenshaw, M. (1986). The psychology of political terrorism. In M. G. Hermann (Ed.), *Political psychology: Contemporary problems and issues* (pp. 379–413). Josey-Bass.

Crenshaw, M. (1992). How terrorists think: What psychology can contribute to understanding terrorism. In L. Howard (Ed.), *Terrorism: Roots, Impact, Responses* (pp. 71–80). Praeger.

della Porta, D. (2018). Radicalization: A relational perspective. *Annual Review of Political Science, 21*, 461–474.

Dollard, J., Miller, N. E., Doob, L. W., Mowrer, O. H., & Sears, R. R. (1939). *Frustration and aggression*. Yale University Press. https://doi.org/10.1037/10022-000

Dugan, L., & Chenoweth, E. (2012). Moving beyond deterrence: The effectiveness of raising the expected utility of abstaining from terrorism in Israel. *American Sociological Review, 77*, 597–624.

Dugan, L., LaFree, G., & Piquero, A. R. (2005). Testing a rational choice model of airline hijackings. *Criminology, 43*, 1031–1065.

Fisher, D. G., & Dugan, L. (2019). Sociological and criminological explanations of terrorism. In E. Chenoweth, R. English, A. Gofas, & S. N. Kalyvas (Eds.), *The Oxford handbook of terrorism*, 163. Oxford University Press.

Forst, Brian (2009) *Terrorism, crime, and public policy*. Cambridge University Press.

Freilich, J. D., Adamczyk, A., Chermak, S. M., Boyd, K. A., & Parkin, W. S. (2015). Investigating the applicability of macro-level criminology theory to terrorism: A county-level analysis. *Journal of Quantitative Criminology, 31*(3), 383–411.

Freilich, J. D., & LaFree, G. (Eds.). (2015). *Criminology theory and terrorism: New applications and approaches*. Routledge.

Gilbert, M. A., & Bushman, B. J. (2017). Frustration-aggression hypothesis. In V. Zeigler-Hill & T. K. Shackelford (Eds.), *Encyclopedia of personality and individual differences*. Springer.

Gilligan, J. (1996).*Violence: Our deadly epidemic and how to treat it*. Putnam.

Gruenewald, J., Chermack, S., & Freilich, J. D. (2013). Distinguishing "loner" attacks from other domestic extremist violence. *Criminology and Public Policy, 12*(1), 65–91.

Gurr, T. (1968). A causal model of civil strife: A comparative analysis using new indices. *American Political Science Review, 62*(4), 1104–1124.

Gurr, T. R. (1970). *Why men rebel*. Princeton University Press.

Gurr, T. R. (2017). Sources of rebellion in Western societies: Some quantitative evidence. In J. F., Jr. Short & M. E. Wolfgang (Eds.), *Collective violence* (pp. 132–148). Routledge.

Gurr, T. R., & Moore, W. H. (1997) Ethnopolitical rebellion: A cross-sectional analysis of the 1980s with risk assessment for the 1990s.

American Journal of Political Science, 41(4), 1079–1103.

Haner, M. (2018). *The freedom fighter: A terrorist's own story.* Routledge.

Hewitt, C. (2003). *Understanding terrorism in America.* Routledge.

Hinton, A. L. (2002). *Annihilating difference: The anthropology of genocide.* University of California Press.

Hirschi, T. (1979). Separate and unequal is better. *Journal of Research in Crime and Delinquency, 16*(1), 34–38.

Hogg, M. A. (2012). Self-uncertainty, social identity, and the solace of extremism. In M. A. Hogg & D. L. Blaylock (Eds.), *Extremism and the psychology of uncertainty* (pp. 19–35). Wiley.

Hogg, M. A., Terry, D. J., & White, K. M. (1995). A tale of two theories: A critical comparison of identity theory with social identity theory. *Social Psychology Quarterly, 58*(4), 255–269.

Horgan, J. (2005). *The psychology of terrorism.* Routledge.

Horgan, J., & Braddock, K. (2013). *Terrorism studies.* Taylor & Francis.

Hudson, R. (1999). *The sociology and psychology of terrorism: Who becomes a terrorist and why?* Library of Congress, Federal Research Division.

Johnson, S. D., Braithwaite, A., Freilich, J. D., & Newman, G. R. (2009). *Reducing terrorism through situational crime prevention.* Criminal Justice Press.

Jones, J. (2008). *Blood that cries out from the earth: The psychology of religious terrorism.* Oxford University Press.

Juergensmeyer, M. (2000). Responding to religious terrorism. *Georgetown Journal of International Affairs, 1*(1), 27–33.

Kohut, H. (1972). Thoughts on narcissism and narcissistic rage. *The Psychoanalytic Study of the Child, 27*(1), 360–400.

Kross, E., Berman, M. G., Mischel, W., Smith, E. E., & Wager, T. D. (2011). Social rejection shares somatosensory representations with physical pain. *Proceedings of the National Academy of Sciences, 108*(15), 6270–6275.

LaFree, G., & Ackerman, G. (2009). The empirical study of terrorism: Social and legal research. *Annual Review of Law and Social Science, 5*, 347–374.

LaFree, G., & Bersani, B. E. (2014). County-level correlates of terrorist attacks in the United States. *Criminology & Public Policy, 13*(3), 455–481.

LaFree, G., & Dugan, L. (2015). How. 2015. How has criminology contributed to the study of terrorism since 9/11? *Sociology of Crime, Law and Deviance* 20 (September): 1–23.

LaFree, G., Dugan, L., & Korte, R. (2009). The impact of British counterterrorist strategies on political violence in Northern Ireland: Comparing deterrence and backlash models. *Criminology, 47*, 17–45.

LaFree, G., Dugan, L., Xie, M., & Singh, P. (2012). Spatial and temporal patterns of terrorist attacks by ETA 1970 to 2007. *Journal of Quantitative Criminology, 28*(1), 7–29.

LaFree, G., & Miller, E. (2008). Desistance from terrorism: What can we learn from criminology? *Dynamics of asymmetric conflict, 1*(3), 203–230.

Lindner, E. G. (2001). Humiliation as the source of terrorism: A new paradigm. *Peace Research, 33*(2), 59–68.

Lindner, E. (2006). *Making enemies: Humiliation and international conflict.* Greenwood Publishing Group.

Lotto, D., & Muenster, B. (2010). The social psychology of humiliation and revenge: The origin of the fundamentalist mindset. In C. B. Strozier, D. M. Terman, & J. W. Jones (Eds.). *The fundamentalist mindset: Psychological perspectives on religion, violence, and history.* Oxford University Press.

Margalit, A. (1998). *The decent society.* Harvard University Press.

McAdam, Doug 1982. *Political process and the development of black insurgency, 1930–1970.* University of Chicago Press.

McCauley, C. (2017). Toward a psychology of humiliation in asymmetric conflict. *American Psychologist, 72*(3), 255.

Merari, A. (2005). Social, organizational and psychological factors in suicide terrorism. In T. Bjørgo (Ed). *Root causes of terrorism* (pp. 88–104). Routledge.

Merton, R. (1938). Social structure and anomie. *American Sociological Review, 3*(5), 672–682.

Moisi, D. (2007). The clash of emotions: Fear, humiliation, hope, and the new world order. *Foreign Affairs,* Jan./Feb. https://www

.foreignaffairs.com/articles/2007-01-01/clash-emotions

Muenster, B., & Lotto, D. (2010). The social psychology of humiliation and revenge: The origins of the fundamentalist mindset. *The Fundamentalist Mindset*, 71–79.

Pape, R. A. (2012). The strategic logic of suicide terrorism. In J. Horgan & K. Braddock (Ed). *Terrorism studies: A reader* (pp. 260–289). Routledge.

Piazza, James A. (2007). Draining the swamp: Democracy promotion, state failure, and terrorism in 19 Middle Eastern countries. *Studies in Conflict & Terrorism*, 30(6): 521–39.

Pridemore, W. A., & Freilich, J. D. (2007). The impact of state laws protecting abortion clinics and reproductive rights: Deterrence, backlash, or neither? *Law and Human Behavior*, 31, 611–627.

Ravndal, J. A. (2018). Right-wing terrorism and militancy in the Nordic countries: A comparative case study. *Terrorism and Political Violence*, 30(5), 772–792.

Redles, D. (2010). The Nazi old guard: Identity formation during apocalyptic times. *Nova Religio*, 14(1), 24–44.

Richardson, L. (2006). The roots of terrorism. In L. Richardson (Ed). *The roots of terrorism: An overview*. Routledge.

Scheff, T. J. (2015). Runaway nationalism: Alienation, shame, and anger. In B. S. Phillips (Ed). *Understanding terrorism: Building on the sociological imagination* (pp. 93–114). Routledge.

Scheff, T. J. (2019). *Bloody revenge: Emotions, nationalism, and war*. Routledge.

Schmid, A. P. (2012). Terrorism and democracy. In A. Schmid & R. D. Crelinsten (Eds). *Western responses to terrorism* (pp. 14–25). Routledge.

Schmid, A. P. (2013). Radicalisation, deradicalisation, counter-radicalisation: A conceptual discussion and literature review. *ICCT Research Paper*, 97(1), 22.

Shapiro, L. R., & Maras, M. H. (2019). Women's radicalization to religious terrorism: An examination of ISIS cases in the United States. *Studies in Conflict & Terrorism*, 42(1–2), 88–119.

Shaw, C. R., & McKay, H. D. (1942). *Juvenile delinquency and urban areas*. University of Chicago Press.

Shaw, C. R., & Moore, M. E. (1931). *The natural history of a delinquent career*. University of Chicago Press.

Silke, A. (1998). Cheshire-cat logic: The recurring theme of terrorist abnormality in psychological research. *Psychology, Crime & Law*, 41, 51–69.

Silke, A. (2003). Deindividuation, anonymity, and violence: Findings from Northern Ireland. *The Journal of Social Psychology*, 143(4), 493–499.

Snow, D. A., Rochford Jr, E. B., Worden, S. K., & Benford, R. D. (1986). Frame alignment processes, micromobilization, and movement participation. *American Sociological Review*, 51(4), 464–481.

Sprang, G. (2003). The psychological impact of isolated acts of terrorism. In A. Silke (Ed). *Terrorists, victims and society: Psychological perspectives on terrorism and its consequences* (pp. 133–159). Wiley.

Stern, J. (2003). *Terror in the name of God: Why religious militants kill*. Ecco.

Strozier, C. B., & Mart, D. (2017). The politics of constructed humiliation. *Research in Psychoanalysis*, 1, 27–36.

Strozier, C. B., Terman, D. M., Jones, J. W., & Boyd, K. (2010). *The fundamentalist mindset: Psychological perspectives on religion, violence, and history*. Oxford University Press.

Sutherland, E. H. (1947). *Principles of criminology* (4th ed.). J. B. Lippincott.

Swift, C. F. (1991). Some issues in inter-gender humiliation. *Journal of Primary Prevention*, 12(2), 123–147.

Tajfel, H. (1981). *Human groups and social categories: Studies in social psychology*. Cambridge University Press.

Thoits, P. A., & Virshup, L. K. (1997). Me's and we's. In R. D. Ashmore & J. Lee (Eds). *Self and identity: Fundamental issues* (pp. 106–133). Oxford University Press.

Turk, A. T. (2004). Sociology of terrorism. *Annual Review of Sociology*, 30(1), 271–286.

Victoroff, J. (2005). The mind of the terrorist: A review and critique of psychological approaches. *Journal of Conflict Resolution*, 49(1), 3–42.

Victoroff, J. & Kruglanski, A. (Eds.). (2009). *Psychology of terrorism: Classic and contemporary insights*. Psychology Press.

CHAPTER 4

Why People Join Terrorist Groups

The Radicalization Process

Source: Getmilitaryphotos/Shutterstock.

Learning Objectives
1. To define the concept of radicalization.
2. To describe the well-established knowledge in the area of radicalization.
3. To explain the different models of radicalization.
4. To explain the process of deradicalization.

4.1 INTRODUCTION

Knowing what makes people turn to terrorism or why groups employ terrorist tactics can inform the development of prevention efforts. However, because our understanding of factors that lead to terrorism has policy implications, careful research is critical. Some counterterrorism policies have been criticized for being discriminatory toward certain groups of people, based on assumptions about terrorists' characteristics (e.g., the surveilling of mosques). Without rigorous research, we risk making misguided accusations and developing ineffective policies. With the recognition that empirical data are limited, this chapter covers the current state of knowledge about why people become terrorists.

The process of becoming a terrorist is typically referred to as **radicalization**. By its root word, this term seems appropriate for labeling the path to terrorism. A radical idea or behavior advocates for fundamental change to some aspect of the social order. Terrorists' actions attempt to do this. However, as with the definition of terrorism discussed in Chapter 1, the definition and usage of the term "radicalization" has generated controversy, largely stemming from the distinction between the radicalization of beliefs and the radicalization of behaviors. Individuals can hold radical beliefs and not act on them; they can hold radical beliefs and act on them in a nonviolent manner; they can hold radical beliefs and employ violence to initiate change; or they can engage in radical behavior without a corresponding radical ideology.

In other words, an individual can undergo the process of radicalization but not engage in terrorism. In relative terms, terrorism is exceptionally rare. Researchers estimate that there may be a few hundred terrorists in the United States compared to tens of thousands of individuals with radical opinions (McCauley & Moskalenko 2017). Throughout history, numerous leaders who advocated what were, at the time, radical agendas used peaceful means to achieve their campaigns for change. For example, Mohandas Karamchand Gandhi, Martin Luther King Jr., and Malala Yousafzai led nonviolent efforts that resulted in significant societal change.

Conversely, many terrorists have come to participate in terrorism for reasons other than radical views; for example, personal revenge, because of love or connections with others in a terrorist group, or in order to escape an undesirable situation. These instances of radicalism without terrorism or terrorism without radical beliefs reflect the well-known inconsistency of the link between attitudes and behavior identified by social psychologists. Attitudes are not strong or reliable predictors of behaviors, and whether or not an attitude will lead to overt behaviors depends on a number of factors such as the social acceptability of the behavior, the accessibility of alternative actions, and perceived ability to act successfully (Ajzen 2001).

The examples given earlier imply a process of radicalization into terrorism that occurs at the individual level. However, groups may undergo a collective process of radicalization into terrorism as well. Social movements—purposeful and organized group-level behavior that is aimed toward instigating social change—can experience an intensification in their use of tactics to the point of engaging in terrorism. The strategies of action that a group may employ depend on factors such as the resources available to them, the extent of competition with other groups, social and cultural contexts of the movement, and the responses of law enforcement. The complex interaction of these factors may cause a group's actions to escalate into violence (della Porta 2018). With a recognition of the caveats associated with the use of the term "radicalization" to describe the process of becoming a terrorist, we will use the following definition of radicalization for the purposes of this text, offered by Italian Sociologist Donatella della Porta (2018, 462):

> Radicalization is a process of escalation from nonviolent to increasing violent repertoires of action that develop through a complex set of interactions unfolding over time.

Here, violence refers to interactions that result in seizure or damage of objects despite resistance from others. With this definition in mind, we consider what we know about radicalization in the following section.

4.2 WHAT WE KNOW ABOUT RADICALIZATION

Terrorists come from an array of social backgrounds and have often undergone diverse paths of radicalization (Bjørgo 2011; Horgan 2008; Schmid 2013). There is not a single cause or explanation for radicalization that leads to terrorism (Victoroff 2005). Radicalization is the outcome of complex interactions among a multiplicity of factors, which may include but are not limited to: poor political and socioeconomic conditions, feelings of humiliation, grievances, oppression, inequality, long-standing historical injustices, the experience of discrimination, being obstructed from expressing cultural identities, alienation, identification with the victims, and kinship and social ties to those experiencing similar issues, to name a few (Alonso et al. 2008; Gurr 1970; 2006; Horgan 2008; NIJ 2015; Schmid 2013). **Violent extremism** does not have one inciting incident. To date, no **terrorist profile** has been found, "not only between members of different terrorist movements, but also among members of the same particular movements" (Horgan 2008). This is true for all kinds of terrorism, including nationalist and separatist, left-wing and right-wing, ideologist and religious. Also, depending on the specific circumstances of individuals, these causal factors may differ in the extent to which they contribute to radicalization into terrorism (Crenshaw 1981).

Despite this uncertainty of how and why someone becomes a terrorist, the search for the cause of radicalization is important in all disciplines in order to understand the occurrence or beginnings of a particular terrorism campaign. While the complexity of the issue of radicalization makes it almost impossible to develop a single explanatory model, scholars have agreed on number of points that are now considered well-established knowledge about radicalization into terrorism (Schmid 2013):

- While early speculation about radicalization blamed psychological abnormalities for an individual's entry into terrorism, research has widely discredited the idea that terrorists suffer from **mental illness**. Histories of the lives of terrorists often describe a mental toughness and stability that is required to withstand the rigors of life underground, to commit fully to a cause or organization, and to be trusted to carry out attacks.

- There is no single terrorist profile. There is no single course or set of life experiences that will put a person on a path to terrorism. Even though scholars have identified factors that may be associated with radicalization into terrorism, not all individuals exposed to those factors become terrorists. As we note, radicalization into terrorism is a very rare occurrence, and most individuals who have the experiences or characteristics identified as risk factors for terrorism will not become terrorists. This fact must be acknowledged when studying such risk factors and utilizing knowledge of risk factors in the creation of counterterrorism policies.
- Radicalization occurs gradually. One's attitudes and behaviors do not go from normative to radical overnight. As indicated by the definition provided previously, radicalization into terrorism is a *process* and involves a period of *escalation* to violence.
- Economic factors do not cause terrorism. Radicalization into terrorism involves a complex set of processes that occur at the micro, meso, and macro levels. Socioeconomic deprivation alone does not cause individuals to turn to terrorism.
- Social networks play a vital role in an individual's recruitment and entry into a terrorist organization. Connections to terrorist groups through family, friends, romantic partners, social groups, and so on can provide the gateway into terrorism through introduction and initial **socialization**.
- The expansion and worldwide reach of the internet has facilitated the spread of terrorism. The internet has enhanced terrorist organizations' opportunities for fundraising and recruitment and increased the means available for planning and carrying out attacks.
- Islam does not cause terrorism. Despite a tendency of the media to portray Muslims as terrorists, and publicize attacks committed by Islamist groups, terrorists come from diverse religious and nonreligious backgrounds and fight for social and political causes as well as religious ones.

We consider these points in detail in the following sections.

4.2.1 Terrorists Are Not Mentally Ill

For decades, terrorists have carried out attacks against noncombatant targets, causing massive destruction. But why do these people participate in these brutal attacks? Much of the psychological research and analysis on terrorists of previous decades revolved around the search for a terrorist personality. As noted in Chapter 3, in the 1960s and 1970s, scholars first attempted to explain acts of terrorism by diagnosing their perpetrators as having paranoia, schizophrenia, or delusions or some other psychiatric condition, and portraying terrorists as cold-blooded murderers (Schmid 2013; Silke 2003; Sprang 2003). Early analysts showed little interest in meso- or macro-level explanations for individual motivations, considering them as irrelevant for explaining terrorist acts.

In contrast to this early perspective, subsequent empirical research has shown that it is the state of "normalcy" that is the outstanding characteristic of individuals who engage in terrorism (Cottee & Hayward 2011; Horgan & Braddock 2012; Pape 2012;

Crenshaw 1981). Terrorists do not have any psychological disorders or psychopathic tendencies that reliably distinguish them from the general population. The evidence suggests that terrorists are equally or more educated than the populations from which they come (Atran 2003; Pape 2008; Webber & Kruglanski 2017).

The idea of terrorism as the product of mental disorder or psychopathology has been discredited by empirical examinations (Della Porta 2018). Individuals who join terrorist groups like ISIS, Irish Republican Army (IRA), or Euskadi Ta Askatasuna (ETA) are not distinguishable from other ordinary people—they have no psychological traits that would predict their risk of involvement in terrorism. The current state of terrorism research indicates that terrorist groups tend to purposefully exclude individuals who show signs of psychopathology or who are undisciplined and unreliable (Crenshaw 1995; Della Porta 2018; Horgan 2008).

For the most part, people who become involved in terrorist activity do so by intention. Therefore, it is now more useful to see terrorists as rational and intentional actors who develop deliberate

FIGURE 4.1 The Las Vegas shooting occurred on October 1, 2017, at the Route 91 Harvest music festival on the Las Vegas Strip in Nevada. A shooter named Stephen Paddock opened fire from the 32nd floor of the Mandalay Bay Resort and Casino onto the crowd attending the festival. Paddock's attack resulted in the deaths of 60 individuals, including himself, and left hundreds more injured, making it the deadliest mass shooting committed by an individual in US history at that time. In the aftermath, public debate occurred around whether Paddock suffered from mental disorder. *Source:* Rmvisuals, CC BY-SA 4.0, via Wikimedia Commons.

strategies to achieve certain objectives. Similar to normal people, terrorists make their choices between different options and tactics on the basis of the limitations and possibilities of the situation.

4.2.2 There Is No Single Terrorist Profile

Involvement in terrorism is a complex process of accommodation and assimilation that occurs throughout life (Crenshaw 2012; Della Porta 2012). Terrorists come from all parts of the world, from a diversity of social backgrounds, and they fight for a range of different causes. Terrorism has been practiced by those on the political right as well as the left, by atheists and by Christians, Jews, Muslims, and members of most other religions

FIGURE 4.2 Upper row: Ulrike Meinhoff, Ted Kaczynski, Timoth McVeigh, Brenton Tarrant. Lower row: Carlos the Jackal, Osama bin Laden, Yitzhak Shamir, Eric Rudolph.
There is no consensus about what makes a terrorist. The factors contributing to terrorism are multifaceted and complex, and they can vary significantly from one case to another. Scholars and experts in the field of terrorism studies have identified a wide range of potential factors that can play a role in the radicalization and recruitment of individuals into terrorist organizations. Some of the key factors include political grievances, religious or ideological beliefs, social and peer influence, psychological factors, propaganda and **online radicalization**, trauma and personal experiences, political instability and conflict, and cultural and identity factors. *Source:* Permission granted by Werner Meinhof's granddaughter, Bettina Röhl, copyrighted free use, via Wikimedia Commons; Federal Bureau of Investigation, public domain, via Wikimedia Commons; United States Federal Government, public domain, via Wikimedia Commons; Automated biometric entry camera at Istanbul Airport, public domain, via Wikimedia Commons; unknown author, public domain, via Wikimedia Commons; Hamid Mir, CC BY-SA 3.0, via Wikimedia Commons; Marcel Antonisse/Anefo, CC BY-SA 3.0 NL, via Wikimedia Commons; FBI, image recadrée, public domain, via Wikimedia Commons.

(Rapoport 2012; Vertigans 2011). People get pulled into terrorism through a socialization process that is facilitated by personal, emotional, and psychological factors (UNDP 2016); there is no single terrorist profile (Bjørgo 2011) and there is no single pathway to terrorism. The process by which individuals come to embrace violent acts is an outcome of the interaction between a complex set of factors and is highly individualized (Patel 2011).

These findings have led many researchers to conclude that profiling, in order to capture actual or potential terrorists, does not work as an effective **counterterrorism** strategy (Alonso et al. 2008). For example, a House of Commons report prepared by a collaboration between the police and intelligence and security agencies in London after the July 7, 2005, suicide bombings indicated that:

> What we know of previous extremists in the UK shows that there is not a consistent profile to help identify who may be vulnerable to radicalisation. Of the 4 individuals here, 3 were second generation British citizens whose parents were of Pakistani origin and one whose parents were of Jamaican origin; Kamel Bourgass, convicted of the Ricin plot, was an Algerian failed asylum seeker; Richard Reid, the failed shoe bomber, had an English mother and Jamaican father. Others of interest have been white converts. Some have been well-educated, some less so. Some genuinely poor, some less so. Some apparently well integrated in the UK, others not. Most single, but some family men with children. Some previously law-abiding, others with a history of petty crime. In a few cases there is evidence of abuse or other trauma in early life, but in others their upbringing has been stable and loving. (House of Commons Report, Annex B 2005, 31)

Due to the complexity of factors that may push people into terrorism, it is almost impossible to predict who will transition from an otherwise normal person to a radical one willing to commit violent acts (Patel 2011). As a result, it is difficult to develop strategies to identify potential terrorists before they join terrorist organizations. As political scientist Tore Bjørgo indicates, doing so may produce many false positives—innocent individuals being identified as terrorists just because they fit into a specific profile—as well as many false negatives: terrorists who go undetected because they do not fit into a profile developed by security agencies (Bjørgo 2011). This reality has also been described by psychologist John Horgan, who stated that even though there are millions of Muslims who live in Britain, an extreme few commits acts of terrorism, despite the fact that many of these individuals are exposed to the same social conditions and come from similar social and familial backgrounds (Horgan 2008). Similarly, an MI5 report published in 2008 indicated that it is not possible to draw up a typical profile of the "British terrorist," as most are "demographically unremarkable" and simply reflect the communities in which they live (Travis 2008). In a nutshell, while several studies have identified some factors that may influence the radicalization process, few people in the population who have these risk factors actually commit violent acts.

FIGURE 4.3   Being a terrorist requires an incremental progression of socialization and cognitive restructuring. *Source:* Maisei Raman/Shutterstock.

4.2.3 Radicalization Is a Gradual Process

Consensus among counterterrorism scholars indicates that being a terrorist often requires an incremental progression of socialization and **cognitive restructuring**; there is a gradual learning process that appears to encourage involvement in terrorism (Crenshaw 2012; Schmid 2013). An individual seeking revenge does not become a terrorist in a vacuum; becoming a terrorist is a phased process. It is not something that happens overnight—quickly or easily.

Participation in terrorism is often the outcome of a complexity of preconditions (root causes) that set the stage for terrorism in the long run—these can include historical, cultural, economic, and sociopolitical characteristics that create an enabling environment for a terrorist group to capitalize on—and also of precipitants, or "triggers": the specific events that occur immediately before an act of terrorism (Crenshaw 1981). Scholars argue that preconditions such as religious or ethnic grievances by themselves are not enough for the outbreak of violence. A trigger mechanism or a catalyst event is needed, such as the personal experience of discrimination, harassment, the death of a loved one, alienation, identification with victims, or anger that may turn an individual onto the path to terrorism (Wiktorowicz 2004). For example, in the case of the IRA, ETA, and Partîya Karkerên Kurdistanê (PKK), recruits often explained their rationale for joining terrorist groups as an act of revenge after the killings of their fathers, brothers, or relatives by state agencies. Precipitants are usually unpredictable. Gupta (2005) argues that a charismatic leader is necessary to give voice to the frustration that individuals are experiencing; the leader mixes an individual's feelings with their desire for revenge and therefore propels them into action (Della Porta 2012). The leader not only provides an ideology, but also identifies the enemy and creates an us-versus-them paradigm. A charismatic leader also serves as a source of legitimacy and provides the justification for the use of violent actions against the enemy.

Individuals are often introduced to the fringes of violent extremist groups by friends, family members, or authority figures in their communities. Involvement follows a trajectory that may become noticeable through attendance at demonstrations and meetings, and these initial activities often sustain further involvement. Participation in these activities also connects individuals to like-minded others, and as their relationships with those who support terrorism become stronger, they start to separate themselves from conventional society (Smith 2018). Radicalized individuals acquire commitment to the cause gradually, as they gain membership in a group (Post et al. 2003). By belonging to a group, otherwise powerless individuals become powerful (Horgan 2003). Increased association with an extremist group causes them to dismiss all ties with outsiders (Della Porta 2012; Gupta 2008). Over time, intensive ideological, religious, and political trainings, combined with peer pressure, strengthens their involvement in violent acts (Bjørgo 2005).

Even though scholars now agree that radicalization is a gradual process, the actual process may include different pathways and mechanisms for different people. Today, there are many models depicting this process of change—the slow incremental marginalization from conventional society to an extremist one (Muro 2016). The most well-known of these models are 1) the four-stage model, 2) the staircase to terrorism, and 3) the pyramid model of radicalization.

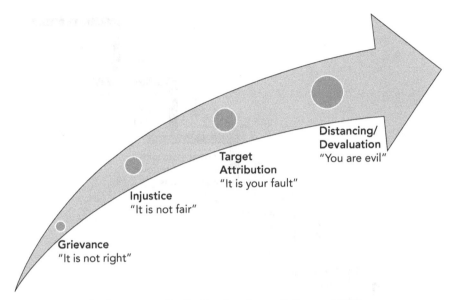

FIGURE 4.4 The four stages of radicalization. *Source:* R. Borum (2011).

The Four-Stage Model of Radicalization

Proposed by psychologist and intelligence studies expert Randy Borum (2003), the **four-stage model of radicalization** explains the emergence of a terrorist mindset through incremental stages. Borum created this model by analyzing violent extremist groups with diverse ideologies. According to this model, the birth of radicalization starts with an unsatisfying event or grievance among a subgroup (such as an ethic minority) of a larger population. In the second and third steps, individuals who experience this injustice or unjust event define a target that is responsible for their emotional vulnerability. In the final stage, de-humanization of the enemy is undertaken. Individuals begin to believe that violence is absolutely necessary and that engaging in violence against the enemy is not immoral, but instead a justifiable defense against an enemy who humiliated or sub-jugated them. They view their engagement in terrorist action as a provoked reaction and as an effective means to their pursued goal.

The Staircase Model of Radicalization

In 2005, Fathali Moghaddam proposed a psychological explanation for the gradual pro-gression of a small minority group into violent radicalization out of a large number of disgruntled people in society. In this model, which includes a metaphorical **staircase model of terrorism**, fewer and fewer individuals ascend to higher floors, and only an extreme few eventually arrive at the fifth floor, where applying terrorist violence is the only option. With five floors (and a ground floor), each step is influenced by a specific psychological process, and each floor must be passed, in order, before moving to a higher floor. According to the researcher, a large number of people in society exist on the ground floor. For people who live here, the concern is in regard to their perception of fairness. Individuals will prefer to stay on the ground floor as long as they feel that they are justly treated and content.

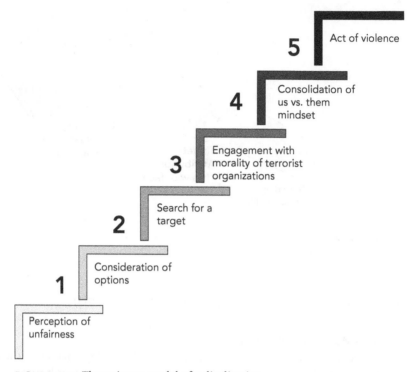

FIGURE 4.5 The staircase model of radicalization.

However, those who feel distressed and unjustly treated will seek alternatives and eventually march to the first floor in an effort to seek justice. Here, individuals will explore their options for improving their conditions. They may leave the staircase at this floor if they find legitimate opportunities to make their voices heard and if they believe that their personal efforts will be fairly rewarded. However, they will oppose authority figures if they believe they are still not being treated fairly and if there are no options for them to participate in decision-making.

The second floor is composed of people who have found no solution to their problems via legitimate means at the first floor. On the second floor, individuals displace their anger onto a target, who is often perceived as evil. This target may be a government entity, or a religious or ethnic group. Here, people go through an educational transformation where they are trained in us-versus-them thinking and some of them embrace the idea that they should direct their aggression directly to the enemy. Ascending to the third floor are individuals who are morally ready to commit violent atrocities against a perceived enemy. On this floor, individuals search for dedicated organizations to change their current situation by any means available. Factors like isolation, affiliation, secrecy, and fear can be effective at this stage to persuade individuals to see the perceived enemy as morally disengaged.

Recruitment into a terrorist organization occurs at the fourth floor. Moghaddam argues that once individuals reach this floor they rarely withdraw from terrorism or exit this floor alive because now they are a part of a very tight-knit, secretive group. As a new recruit, they are socialized to the military operations, interpersonal relationships, organizational ideology and structure. As a result, their commitment to terrorism increases.

Finally, on the fifth floor, recruits are trained to treat the out-group, including civilians, as the enemy. According to their mentality, anyone who is not actively resisting the perceived enemy is a legitimate target for violence. Acts of violence against civilians are justified because they are part of the enemy. On this floor, recruits are fully prepared and psychologically motivated to commit indiscriminate acts of violence against the enemy as a whole.

Moghaddam states, "as individuals climb the staircase, they see fewer and fewer choices, until the only possible outcome is the destruction of others, or oneself, or both." Prevention strategies should focus on identifying and removing the conditions that channel individuals into the paths of radicalization rather than creating a profile of terrorists: "Only by reforming conditions on the ground floor can societies end terrorism" (2005, 167).

The Two-Pyramids Model of Radicalization

Developed by psychologists Clark McCauley and Sophia Moskalensko in 2017, this model consists of two models that separate the notion of radicalization into extreme opinions (attitudes) and extremist actions (behaviors). The **two-pyramids model of terrorism** distinguishes the types of individuals that occupy each level from neutral individuals to radicals. Although the processes by which individuals move from locations in the pyramids are not specified, this model illustrates the different roles an individual can occupy from their initial engagement in extremism to later stages of terrorist activities.

From the pyramid perspective, the higher the level reached by an individual, the higher their commitment to terrorism. Unlike the staircase model, individuals do not need to traverse each level of the pyramid to reach the apex. As depicted by the model, fewer and fewer individuals are located at each section as one moves higher in the pyramid, which is to say that within populations, only very few individuals actually become terrorists.

The *opinion pyramid* consists of four levels within which individuals can move up or down freely. People who do not care about a political cause (or who are basically content with their lives) occupy the first level, which is described by McCauley and Moskalenko as neutral.

Sympathizers, who believe in a cause but do not justify or engage in violence, are located in the second level. *Justifiers*, who are the occupants of the third level, condone the use of violence in defense of a legitimate cause. Finally, individuals who feel a personal moral obligation to fight against the perceived enemy occupy the apex of the pyramid. Again, this pyramid represents the attitudinal (cognitive) restructuring of individuals. According to the authors, an individual's location in the opinion pyramid does not necessarily correspond to their

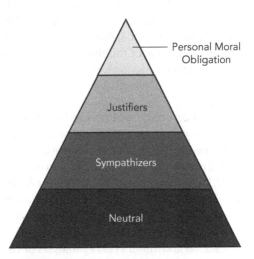

FIGURE 4.6 The opinion pyramid.

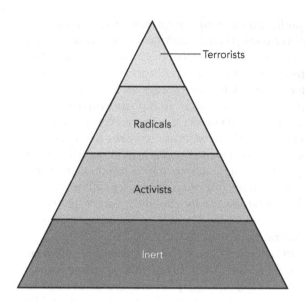

FIGURE 4.7   The action pyramid.

location in the action pyramid. Even though one may be located at the apex of the opinion pyramid, they may not engage in radical actions. In support of this argument, the current state of radicalization research also indicates that most people who hold radical ideas do not engage in terrorism (Della Porta 2018).

Similar to the opinion pyramid, individuals who are not associated with a political cause occupy the base of the *action pyramid*, and they are described as inert by McCauley and Moskalenko (2017). The authors explain that this group is the section of the society that terrorists claim to represent. **Activists**, or the people who are engaged in legal political action, are located in the second level. While the activities that activists carry out are not illegal in their nature, the actions of activists whose goals align with terrorist organizations serve vital functions in the operation and sustenance of those organizations. For example, activists may generate publicity or provide some other kind of support for the cause. Radicals who defend the idea of illegal action for their political agenda occupy the third level. They do not yet engage in violent acts themselves but provide the individuals at the next level with support activities (e.g., housing terrorists, providing intelligence, raising funds). Finally, the small area at the apex of the pyramid represents active terrorists who engage in military action against the perceived enemy, including civilians. Only a very small number of individuals engage in terrorist action. Most radicals are not visible and they use nonviolent methods to achieve their goals. As Horgan (2008, 86) explains, "the person we think of as 'the terrorist' is therefore fulfilling only one of multiple functions in the movement, albeit the most dramatic in terms of direct consequences."

4.2.4 Economic Factors Do Not Cause Terrorism

Terrorists come from all socioeconomic backgrounds (Stern 2003). Scholars who have examined the waves of radicalization that lead to terrorism have concluded that individual **poverty** or **unemployment** do not cause terrorism (UNDP 2016; Russell & Miller 1977; Taylor 1988; Stern 2003; Krueger & Maleckova 2003). While economic conditions are clearly a prominent factor in individuals' lives, the relationship between poverty, unemployment, and people's willingness to engage in terrorism is most often weak or absent (Krueger & Maleckova 2003).

Russel and Miller's (1977) analyses of 18 revolutionary groups in Europe, the Middle East, Latin America, and Asia indicated that individuals who engaged in terrorism were quite well educated, and approximately 70 percent of them came from the middle and upper classes. Similarly, through the examination and analyses of data from extensive fieldwork studies in eight Middle Eastern countries (Turkey, Lebanon, Israel, Syria, Egypt, Iraq, Iran, Jordan), Daniel Lerner (1958) concluded that extremists are not the poor people—they are not the "have-nots," but middle- and upper-class individuals who can be thought of as the "want-mores."

More recently, several public opinion polls conducted between 2001 and 2015 by independent think tanks in Palestine indicated that support for armed attacks against Israeli targets is strong among merchants, professionals, and farmers. Contrary to common perception, the researchers discovered that unemployed or poor people were less likely to support attacks against Israeli forces, including civilian targets, and that Palestinian suicide bombers usually hailed from well-educated and economically advantaged families (PCPSR, 2001–2015). Research indicates that all members of the Makhteret (Jewish Underground), the radical right-wing terrorist organization who terrorized Palestinian civilians by attacking college students, planting bombs in city administrators' cars, and blowing up public busses in the early 1980s, were well educated and worked in high-level professions (Krueger & Maleckova 2003).

From surveying the literature on radicalization, we can conclude that participation in terrorism is not based on an individuals' income or education level. As Maxwell Taylor (1988) put it: "Neither social background, educational opportunity or attainment seem to be particularly associated with terrorism." If we review terrorist events from recent decades— for example the 9/11 attacks—we see that none of the perpetrators suffered from poverty. They were well educated and came from comfortable middle-class Saudi and Egyptian families. Osama bin Laden himself was a son of a multibillionaire Saudi businessman, who had a special relationship with the Saudi royal family (Horgan 2005; Krueger & Maleckova 2003). Mohamed Atta, the leader of the 9/11 team, was the son of an Egyptian lawyer and had earned a PhD in urban planning (Mohammad 2005).

4.2.5 Connections with Other Terrorists Are Often Necessary

As previously covered, a combination of several factors gives rise to terrorism and other forms of violent struggle. A recurrent finding in radicalization research is that direct contact with persons involved in terrorism is a critical influence on an individual's radicalization (Schmid 2013; Doosje et al. 2016; Horgan 2008; Patel 2011; Sageman 2011; Webber & Kruglanski 2016). Furthermore, a review of the existing literature conducted by the US National

FIGURE 4.8 Increased access to the internet and social media has significantly facilitated the ability of extremists to connect with like-minded individuals and promote their ideologies. *Source:* Blogtrepreneur, CC BY 2.0, via Wikimedia Commons.

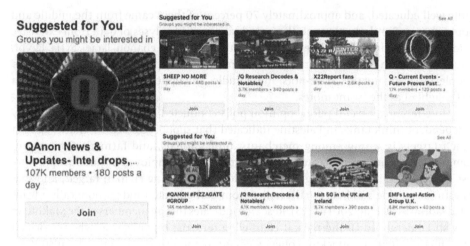

FIGURE 4.9 Social media platforms have become significant incubators for radicalization and extremist content dissemination in recent years.

Institute of Justice in 2015 indicated that connections with violent **extremists** (family members, friends, and other acquaintances) are the most frequently cited facilitator of individuals' radicalization into violent extremism (NIJ 2015).

These findings hold true in more recent studies of individuals' engagement in foreign fighting, especially for Islamic State fighters. For example, Fishman (2009) and Dragon (2015) asserted that face-to-face social connections were more influential in the process of radicalization into violence than other factors, including the use of social media and the internet. More specifically, Fishman's research indicated that personal social networks were important in the development of extremism, radicalization, and recruitment—approximately 65 percent of the foreign fighters who traveled to Iraq to join IS were recruited through the members of local extremist groups and other personal networks (friends, family, and relatives). By analyzing 20 profiles of Western foreign fighters, Dragon (2015) also discovered that approximately 80 percent of Western foreign fighters were recruited into IS via traditional social networks (i.e., family, friends, occupational and religious groups). Further, results of a more recent study conducted by Reynolds and Hafez (2019) suggest that the group pressure and social influence that occurs within the individuals' social networks were the most important influential factors for the mobilization of German foreign fighters into Syria.

Based on their analysis of hundreds of case studies, the British Intelligence Agency MI5 concluded that radicalization into violence is always driven by contact with others (Patel 2011). Through this socialization process—which may occur in person, via audio or video recordings posted on the internet, and by a variety of other sources—not only do these extremist individuals find role models, but they also become dedicated to a cause that justifies and advocates the use of violence.

4.2.6 The Internet Facilitates Radicalization

The internet has become a prominent domain for terrorist activities—from marketing and recruitment to fundraising, to planning and carrying out attacks. Online radicalization into terrorism, whereby individuals are introduced to an extremist ideology that supports the use of violence through websites and social networking applications such as Facebook, X, and YouTube, is a growing national security threat (Neumann 2013). Many extremist groups have public social media profiles where users can find a substantial amount of information regarding violent extremist perspectives and even educational videos on how to construct weapons and explosives. With over half of the world's population—and over 85 percent of Americans—having internet access, such messages have the potential to reach a considerable number of people, including those for whom radicalization may have otherwise been inaccessible. Whereas physical terrorist training camps and meeting locations are difficult to sustain because they are subject to surveillance and attack, online communications provide terrorist organizations with a safer and farther-reaching venue for recruitment methods, radicalization, and training.

Of particular concern is the increased ability of extremist groups to appeal to marginalized individuals, especially the youth. Once an individual is drawn in by extremist content, online forums provide a space for like-minded individuals to make connections and reinforce their developing beliefs, serving as "echo chambers" for extremist attitudes (O'Hara & Stevens 2015). This fosters group polarization—whereby group ideas and actions become more extreme than they would be otherwise—and the development of an us-versus-them mentality, where violence becomes the only solution (Torok 2013). Upon radicalizing individuals, terrorist groups can then provide virtual opportunities to participate in the group. Such activities may involve fundraising and distributing propaganda or even implementing cyberattacks. Individuals recruited into terrorism via online methods may even travel internationally to become foreign fighters for the terrorist group.

In addition to recruitment and radicalization, the internet has fostered the development of "lone wolves"—radicalized individuals who act alone and are unaffiliated with any particular group. Indeed, the extent of resources available online, including extremist manifestos, details of successful attacks, and weapon-making tutorials, provide a kind of handbook for self-radicalization (Koehler 2014). Between 2014 and 2019, individuals inspired by ISIS (i.e., not ISIS members) carried out seven deadly attacks within the United States, including an attack on police officers, a beheading, a mass shooting, vehicular homicide, and a suicide bombing (Haner et al. 2020). Not only does the internet provide opportunities for terrorist organizations to recruit and carry out attacks, but the persuasiveness of online extremist narratives and the availability of information needed to commit acts of terrorism also provides opportunities for self-radicalization and lone-wolf terrorism.

4.2.7 Islam Does Not Cause Terrorism

Despite the popular emphasis on the connection between Islam and terrorism, terrorists come from all religions (Henderson & Tucker 2001; Henne 2019; Pearce 2005). One may argue that religious Islamist groups like al-Qaeda, ISIS, and Hezbollah have been historically responsible for the majority of suicide attacks against Western democracies, and hence there *must* be a link between terrorism and Islam. However, as Robert Pape (2003; 2005) indicated, it is not the religion (here, Islam specifically) but the presence of the foreign combat forces that causes individuals to engage in suicide terrorism. Pape's analyses show that foreign combat forces explained about 95 percent of all suicide attacks in the world, and that suicide attacks (especially the ones that occurred in predominantly Muslim regions) often stopped after the withdrawal of the foreign occupying forces. For example, Hezbollah emerged only after Israeli forces invaded Lebanon in 1982, and engaged in suicide attacks against Israeli, French, and American forces during the invasion of their territories. The suicide attacks stopped once foreign combat forces withdrew from Lebanon in 1983, after truck bombs struck buildings at Beirut Airport housing American and French marines.

Scholars argue that the focus on Islam when explaining terrorism causes is the result of controversial political agendas (Corbin 2017). In her article "Terrorists Are Always Muslim But Never White," law professor Caroline Marla Corbin states that there are two false narratives that are pervasive in American society: first, that terrorists are always Muslims (which is sometimes viewed as "all Muslims are terrorists"); and second, that White people are never terrorists. According to Corbin, these two perceptions are communicated to the American public through movies, news coverage, and government policies. For example, a comprehensive analysis of 900 Hollywood movies demonstrated that Muslim men frequently played roles as terrorists or uncivilized and dangerous characters (Akram 2002).

Similarly, studies analyzing the media coverage of minorities in Western nations found that major news outlets continuously link Muslims with the issue of terrorism. For example, in September 2019, the Media Portrayals of Minorities Project (MpoMP) Lab found that Muslims were by far the most negatively portrayed minority group in the United States. The study found that the coverage of Muslims was not about their culture, education, or other positive aspects of social life but instead heavily focused on politics and crime, specifically their engagement in terrorism, which ultimately made it harder for American people to see Muslims as part of general society. Another study discovered that terrorist attacks carried out by Muslims received 357 percent more media coverage than attacks carried out by members of other religious groups. The authors concluded that the disparities in news coverage based on perpetrators' religion explained why the American public tends to fear Muslims more than other religious groups and unconsciously associates them with terrorism (Kearns et al. 2019).

If a terrorist suspect is Muslim, there is a widespread presumption that Islam has engendered their terrorism. In contrast, terrorist acts committed by Christian extremists are often considered exceptions, carried out by individuals who are psychologically deficient. As Corbin and others indicate, terrorist acts committed by White supremacists against women's health clinics, police officers, Jewish community centers, and Mosques are categorized as "hate crimes" but not as terrorism. The term "terrorist" has historically not been applied to White supremacists; for example, Anders Behring Breivik, who carried out the 2011 Norway massacre and killed almost 80 people; Canadian Alexandre Bissonnette, who killed six Muslim worshippers in a Quebec Mosque in 2017; or Dylan Roof, an American White supremacist who killed nine people in an African American Church in South Carolina in 2015. Instead, the mainstream media identified background issues, mental illness, or other psychological problems as the explanation for these individuals' violence, rather than concluding that they acted because of their religion or ideology, as is typically the case for Muslims. When the suspect in question is not a Muslim, there is a presumption that there must be a psychological problem (paranoia or schizophrenia) driving the individual into terrorism. As the 83rd Attorney General of United States, Loretta Lynch, noted, "the terrorist label is usually reserved for when violence is perpetrated by a Muslim" (Corbin 2017, p. 462).

In short, terrorism is not unique to Islam. It has taken place in rich and poor countries, under authoritarian and democratic regimes, and has been practiced by Christians,

Jews, Hindus, Muslims, and atheists (Rapoport 2012; Vertigans 2011). Overemphasis on Islam is misleading, a point to which we will return in Chapter 8.

4.3 WHAT WE KNOW ABOUT THE EXIT FROM TERRORISM

Just as the process of radicalization into terrorism is varied and complex, so too is the exit from terrorism and the conclusion of terrorist campaigns. Two distinct processes are associated with the exit from terrorism: **deradicalization** and **disengagement**. Deradicalization occurs when an individual rejects the terrorist mindset or experiences a change in the values or attitudes that led them to support terrorism. In comparison, disengagement involves refraining from terrorist actions and thus requires a change in behavior. As with radicalization, both deradicalization and disengagement can happen at the individual level (i.e., a single terrorist rejects the terrorist ideology or leaves the group) or at the collective level (i.e., a terrorist organization stops using violence).

It is important to note that deradicalization and disengagement are independent; the occurrence of one is not necessary for the occurrence of the other. As noted, attitudes do not correspond to behaviors as well as we might expect. For example, an individual may stop using terrorist violence but may still believe in the cause and that the use of violence is appropriate, or one may question prior radical beliefs but feel compelled or forced to continue their violent actions. It is therefore essential to understand the antecedents of both processes in order to develop comprehensive counterterrorism efforts. In the following section, we will consider the factors that have been identified as precursors to both deradicalization and disengagement.

4.3.1 Deradicalization

For deradicalization to occur at both the individual and group levels, those engaging in terrorism must experience a change in the mindset that justifies the use of violence. According to psychologist Arie Kruglanski and colleagues (2014, 84):

> Radicalization reflects (1) a high-level commitment to the ideologically suggested goal (e.g., liberating one's land from occupation, bringing about the return of the caliphate) and to violence as a means to its attainment, coupled with (2) a reduced commitment to alternative goals and values. Its obverse, deradicalization, represents (1) a restoration of the latter concerns and/or (2) a reduction of commitment to the focal, ideological goal, or to the recommended means (of violence and terrorism) to that goal. For instance, one may grow disenchanted with one's leaders' and comrades' conduct and begin to doubt that the organization's activities (the means) indeed serve the lofty ideological objectives they were alleged to serve.

Doubting the radical beliefs that supported violence in the past is thus key to the deradicalization process. Many factors may cause this, though commonly deradicalized individuals now feel that the use of violence for the cause is either immoral (e.g., against newly formed or realized religious beliefs), ineffective (e.g., failing to accomplish one's goals), or both (Kruglanski et al. 2014). In addition, just as interpersonal relationships may contribute to one's radicalization, close contacts may also encourage the rejection of the terrorist ideology that the terrorist previously embraced. For example, if a fellow comrade becomes disillusioned with a group's terrorist means, they may convince others of the same. Whatever the cause, deradicalization is not a sufficient or necessary precondition for disengagement from terrorism (Horgan 2009).

4.3.2 Disengagement at the Individual Level

Disengagement from terrorism occurs when one ceases involvement in terrorist activities. It may be voluntary or involuntary and can result from psychological or physical processes. A variety of experiences related to push-and-pull factors contribute to disengagement. Push forces are negative experiences that repel an individual from their current circumstances while pull forces are positive factors that make involvement in a terrorist group seem like a better alternative (Bjørgo 2018).

While there is no single path to disengagement from terrorism, psychologist John Horgan (2009, 22, 25) identified five key causes of **psychological disengagement** and six causes of **physical disengagement** at the individual level.

Psychologically, the reality of being involved in a terrorist organization may depart severely from one's initial expectations: disagreements may arise within the group, or an individual may become burned out and overwhelmed from the rigors of terrorist life. Or, an individual may experience a change in priorities—goals that are incompatible with life as a terrorist (e.g., having a family or professional career) may become more important.

Physically, an individual may voluntarily disengage from terrorism—by leaving the movement or transitioning into another role within the movement (i.e., to serve support **functions**). For example, through the documentation of a life history of a PKK terrorist,

PSYCHOLOGICAL AND PHYSICAL DISENGAGEMENT FROM TERRORISM

Psychological Disengagement

1. Disillusionment arising from incongruence between the initial ideals and fantasies that shaped a person's initial involvement and their subsequent experiences with the reality of what is entailed by involvement—in other words, the mismatch between the fantasy and the reality
2. Disillusionment arising from disagreement over tactical issues
3. Disillusionment arising from strategic, political, or ideological differences
4. Becoming burned out
5. Changing personal priorities

Physical Disengagement

1. Voluntary exit from the movement
2. Involuntary exit from the movement
3. Involuntary movement into another role
4. Voluntary movement into another role
5. Involuntary exit from the movement altogether
6. Experiences stemming from psychological disengagement that act as a catalyst for physical disengagement across factors 1 to 4

Source: Horgan (2009).

criminologist Murat Haner (coauthor of this text) revealed that guerrillas often could not withstand the harshness of life underground and opted for a nonphysical support role in the organization. Haner also revealed incidents whereby individuals disengaged out of fear of retaliation following a disagreement with leadership or wrongdoing—a combination of psychological and physical disengagement. Terrorists also face the risk of involuntary disengagement through imprisonment, injury, or death. In many cases, particularly with involuntary disengagement, disengagement does not coincide with deradicalization. Those who disengage from terrorism may still hold radical beliefs that validate the use of violence.

4.3.3 Disengagement at the Group Level

Group-level or collective disengagement from terrorism also occurs, and does so frequently, despite a common misconception that terrorist groups are likely to persist for long periods of time. In an analysis of the 1,500 distinct terrorist groups included in National Consortium for the Study of Terrorism and Responses to Terrorism's Global Terrorism Database, about three-quarters of terrorist groups cease activities within one year of their first attack. In contrast, only 6 percent of groups have been active for more than 10 years (LaFree 2012).

A variety of factors have been associated with disengagement from terrorism at the collective or group level. In a report on how terrorism ends, political scientist Martha Crenshaw notes five categories of reasons, as shown in Table 4.1.

TABLE 4.1   Reasons for Collective Disengagement from Terrorism

Reason for Disengagement	Explanation
Success	The terrorists may have accomplished their objectives, such as the overthrow of a government or the end of an occupation. Terrorism per se cannot achieve long-term goals such as revolution or independence, but it can sometimes do so in conjunction with less violent political action.
Preliminary success	A corollary to achieving objectives is having at least achieved public recognition for an organization and the cause it espouses. In this case, continued terrorist actions may alienate supporters, sponsors, or key third-country actors for whom continued violence is unacceptable.
Organizational breakdown	Terrorist organizations, like any organizations, must constantly work to maintain themselves. If recruiting dries up, or if funding becomes unavailable, the organization may be unable to sustain itself. On the other hand, self-preservation may in fact force organizations to continue terrorist activities even if the leadership otherwise wishes to give them up. It may be that the only way for the organization to continue to attract new recruits and financial support is to continue to gain publicity for its terrorist actions.
Dwindling support	Organizations may lose the support of their various constituencies—the populations they seek to represent or the governments or other organizations that support them. They can do so for reasons of ideological or strategic differences, personality clashes, or simple fatigue. Terrorist actions can also provoke moral outrage and undermine support.
New alternatives	At times, other options for political change emerge. They can include more traditional forms of warfare or revolution, mass protests, or political negotiations.

Source: Alterman (1999).

As these reasons for collective-level disengagement show, the causes of disengagement may be internal or external to the terrorist organization. The type of grievance against which the group is fighting is important to consider too. Movements that are concerned with ethnically based issues typically have broad support from the populations they aim to serve and are therefore less likely to disengage due to external pressures than those that are politically motivated (Alterman 1999).

Continued study of collective-level disengagement from terrorism is essential. Indeed, political scientist Tore Bjørgo (2018, 4) explains that "the most effective way of preventing terroristic violence in the long term is to get entire terrorist groups to lay down their arms." Understanding disengagement at the individual level is also critical because this knowledge can inform the efforts to identify vulnerabilities in terrorist organizations (Cronin 2009). Knowing why individuals leave a particular group provides insight into the overall operation and structure of the group, and may reveal weaknesses within the group for counterterrorism programs to target.

4.4 INTRODUCTION TO CASE STUDIES

We conclude this chapter with three case studies focused on radicalization into terrorism. The first, the case of Mrs. Terror, demonstrates the power of the internet in radicalization. The second case, a White nationalist attack on a Jewish community, speaks to the seventh point about terrorism that we discuss in this chapter—the inaccurate tendency to think of terrorists as Muslim. Finally, the third case study is a story of radicalization that illustrates the complexity of factors that can shape the path to terrorism.

4.4.1 Case Study 1: Mrs. Terror

The Islamic State of Iraq and Syria has been successful in the recruitment of tens of thousands of people through social media (Craig 2019). The group is considered to be the most adept terrorist organization at using the internet and social media for the recruitment of new members (Alfifi et al. 2018). It is estimated that ISIS operates in 25 different languages to recruit sympathizers from around the world solely online, through one-on-one video chats, internet calling, and personal text messaging with potential recruits (Speckhard & Ellenberg 2020; Prajuli 2017).

We know that ISIS utilizes social media to spread its ideology to potential foreign fighters, and it is believed that ISIS's strategic use of high-quality and professionally produced propaganda videos depicting the large-scale destruction and loss of human lives by the Western coalition forces in Iraq and Syria was successful in mobilizing more than 45,000 foreign nationals from about 110 countries to travel to conflict zones and fight for the caliphate (Speckhard & Ellenberg 2020; Ward 2018). Through these videos, ISIS promised its followers the opportunity to seek revenge on those who destroyed Muslim lands (Haner et al. 2018). Interestingly, Haner et al.'s 2018 research indicated that none of the foreign fighters who traveled to Syria to join ISIS suffered directly from these tragedies. However, their statements revealed that feelings of hatred and revenge were elicited by watching highly graphic videos and images posted by ISIS—which included the destruction of homes; the murders of children, women, and the elderly; cruel treatment measures applied to people in the conflict zone; and the mutilated bodies of Muslims killed and

FIGURE 4.10 Sally Jones, often referred to as "Mrs. Terror," gained notoriety as a British woman who joined the Islamic State (ISIS) in Syria and became one of the most prominent female members of the terrorist organization. Her journey from ordinary British citizen to jihadist highlights the complexities of radicalization and the allure of extremist ideologies. *Source:* Screenshot from YouTube; video since taken down.

wounded by Western forces—coupled with the continuous discussion of these issues within their online networks.

Another reason that people from all over the world have joined ISIS is because of the living conditions promised by the organization. ISIS was able to attract a significant number of foreign fighters online by citing the existence of cozy lifestyles, job opportunities, and monthly payments (Haner et al. 2018). Using its online magazines *Dabiq* (later renamed to *Rumiyah*) and *Inspire*, which are published in English as well as several other languages, ISIS encouraged people across the globe to come and live for the Caliphate in Iraq and Syria (Mullen & Todd 2014). These publications emphasized personal benefits such as getting a free home, finding a spouse, and free public services including food, water, electricity, and health (Craig 2019; Prajuli 2017). Official statements from incarcerated ISIS fighters indicate that they were presented with the comfort of living in houses and apartments previously owned by the Syrians, and were assured that they would also be provided with opportunities to further their education and occupational experiences if they fought for and lived under the caliphate (Haner et al. 2018).

In addition to recruitment tactics, ISIS has also used its superior social media aptitude to further an atmosphere of terror and fear among Western societies. Use of social media platforms such as Twitter, YouTube, Facebook, Telegram, and Surespot has allowed ISIS to spread terror by showing disturbing execution content including Western people being burned and beheaded (Alfifi et al. 2018; Craig 2019, Haner et al. 2018). Additionally, through its online magazine *Inspire*, ISIS has published numerous articles showing Western sympathizers how to plan and execute terrorist attacks in European capitals by describing how to make bombs and sneak them into crowded public areas such as planes, concert arenas, and sporting events (Mullen & Todd 2014).

A notable example of ISIS's internet tactics can be seen in the case of Sally-Anne Frances Jones, a single mother of three and former punk musician (Diyab 2019). It is believed that Sally (also known as Umma Hussain al-Britani, white widow, and Mrs. Terror) played an important role in recruiting hundreds of British people to ISIS before she was killed in a 2017 drone strike (BBC 2018; Weaver 2017). Jones was born in Greenwich, in London, and had a troubled upbringing due to her parents' divorce at an early age and her father's suicide when she was 10 years old. She was raised Catholic and attended Christian youth groups when she was a teenager (Asharq Al-Awsat 2018). She dropped out of school at the age of 16 and played as the lead guitarist in an all-girl rock band called Krunch in the 1990s (Cockburn 2017; Tomlinson 2015). Her radicalization into terrorism started in 2013, at the age of 45, when she met twenty-year-old Hussain Junaid, a British-Pakistani computer hacker who eventually became her husband, on an online dating platform (Cockburn 2017). At that time, Jones was working in perfume sales for L'Oréal cosmetics in Chatham and living on state benefits. She converted to Islam the same year and traveled to Syria during the winter of 2013 with her nine-year-old son, JoJo, to fight for the caliphate and unite with her husband (Fruen 2019). Soon after her relocation to Syria, Jones became a leading propagandist and recruiter for ISIS on social media. Using 20 different Twitter accounts, she managed to recruit individuals from the West and offered practical guidance for planning safe travel to Syria. She also promoted life in the Islamic State and provided tips to female sympathizers who wanted to join the caliphate. Her social media accounts soon accrued thousands of followers. She became the commander of the female wing of Anwar al-Awlaki battalion, a unit composed of foreign fighters who traveled to Syria (Sengupta 2017). With her husband Junaid's help, she retrieved more than 1,300 US soldiers' home addresses and personal information and published them online as a "kill list" for ISIS militants to target (Cockburn 2017; Fruen 2019). She also encouraged Muslims living in London, Glasgow, and Wales to carry out terror attacks in London by offering them guidance on how to construct homemade bombs (Weaver 2017).

In addition to encouraging attacks in the West, Jones also threatened to kill non-Muslims by posting tweets such as "You Christians all need beheading with a nice blunt knife and stuck on the railings at Raqqa . . . Come here I'll do it for you" (Diyab 2019). She was reported to be killed in June 2017 by a drone strike carried out by US military forces.

FIGURE 4.11 Tweets made by Sally Jones in 2015.

This case illustrates the power of the internet to engage people in terrorism. Jones became engaged with ISIS through an online connection that led to her using social media to make further recruitments for the organization and encourage violence.

4.4.2 Case Study 2: Robert Bowers

On October 27, 2018, forty-six-year-old Robert Gregory Bowers entered the Tree of Life Synagogue in Pittsburgh, Pennsylvania, during the Sabbath morning service and opened fire on its congregants, yelling "All Jews must die" (Dobuzinskis 2019). The synagogue is located in the Squirrel Hill neighborhood, which is considered to be the center of Jewish life in Pittsburgh; more than 40 percent of its population identifies as Jewish. Armed with an assault rifle and three handguns, Bowers brutally murdered 11 people and injured six, including four police officers, in the shooting spree (Saldivia et al. 2018), which was investigated as a hate crime (BBC 2018). The event is considered the deadliest terrorist attack against the Jewish community in United States history (Robertson et al. 2018; Turkewitz & Roose 2018).

The assailant fired for more than 20 minutes at congregants and was leaving the synagogue when he encountered SWAT officers at the door. Bowers eventually surrendered to the police, after retreating into the synagogue and briefly exchanging fire with the officers (Saldivia et al. 2018). While in custody, he reportedly made anti-Semitic statements to the police, including, "They are committing genocide to my people. I just want to kill Jews" (Ahmed & Murphy 2018; BBC 2018; Chavez et al. 2018).

FIGURE 4.12 The Pittsburgh synagogue shooting was the deadliest attack on the Jewish community in the United States. *Source:* Official White House Photo by Andrea Hanks, Public domain, via Wikimedia Commons.

Robert Bowers @onedingo
2 hours ago

HIAS likes to bring invaders in that kill our people.

I can't sit by and watch my people get slaughtered.

Screw your optics, I'm going in.

∧   ● Comments   ○ Repost   ❝❝ Quote

FIGURE 4.13 Robert Bowers regularly posted anti-Semitic and xenophobic messages on social media.

According to law enforcement, Bowers had an active license to carry firearms and owned 21 guns, legally purchased and registered to his name. He had no criminal record and was unknown to law enforcement (Robertson et al. 2018). Bowers did, however, have a history of posting hateful and violent messages on various social media platforms, including Facebook, Twitter, and Gab, a microblogging service known for its prominence of far-right users (Roose 2018). His posts were reported to be full of extreme anti-Semitic and xenophobic comments. He called immigrants "invaders" and referred to Jews as the "enemy of white people," "the children of Satan," "filthy," "an infestation," and "evil" (BBC 2018; Salehvan 2018; Turkewitz & Roose 2018).

The authorities also discovered that weeks before his terrorist attack, Bowers targeted some Jewish organizations in other ways—by claiming that Jews were helping to transport thousands of undocumented immigrants from Latin American countries into the US. For example, he accused Jewish nonprofit organization HIAS, the Hebrew Immigrant Aid Society, which has been organizing aid for refugees around the country, of helping Central Americans move toward the border of United States (May & Hafner 2018). He described HIAS as "sugar-coated evil" (Ahmed & Murphy 2018). His Gab caption read: "Why hello there HIAS! You like to bring in hostile invaders to dwell among us?" (Robertson et al. 2018). Horrifically, hours before his Synagogue attack, he posted the following message: "HIAS likes to bring invaders in that kill our people. I can't sit by and watch my people get slaughtered. Screw your optics, I'm going in."

Bowers lived in an apartment in the suburbs of Pittsburgh and his neighbors described him as a normal and quiet person. He rarely interacted with others and his neighbors never saw anyone visiting him (BBC 2018). The only time he was seen was when he was smoking a cigarette in front of his door.

Official accounts indicate that Bowers's parents had a divorce when he was one year old. His father committed suicide in 1979, when Bowers was seven years old, while pending trial for a rape charge in Squirrel Hill (Lord 2018). His maternal grandparents raised Bowers because his mother had serious health issues. He dropped out of high school during his senior year and started to work as a delivery driver for a baked goods company in the early 1990s. His coworkers from Dormont's Potomac Bakery described him as a happy person who liked beer, Hooters, action films, and guns (Lord 2018). They also noted that Bowers had some paranoid theories and violent thoughts. According to his best friend from adolescence, Robert Walters, Bowers's radicalization into White nationalism started when he began listening to Jim Quinn's radio show, *The WarRoom*, an ultra-conservative program. Another coworker of Bowers stated of Jim Quinn: "Oh, my God, that was his [Bowers'] God!"

Bowers quit his delivery job in 2002 and began working as a truck driver. He became very active in online platforms by reposting tweets from other White nationalist extremists such as Jack Corbin, targeting anti-fascist and left-wing groups in the United States

(BBC 2018). He is reported to have subscribed to an online software that allows encrypted messages to be sent between its members. In 2018, as Twitter and Facebook began to implement policies to prevent hate speech and abuse, Bowers—along with other prominent White nationalists and neo-Nazis—switched to Gab, a fringe social media platform that describes itself as "the free speech social network" (Chavez et al. 2018; May & Hafner 2018). His account's introductory statement read: "Jews are the children of Satan." His profile picture included the number 1488, which is widely used by White nationalists and refers to the 14-word slogan coined by David Lane, a founding member of the terrorist organization The Order: "We must secure the existence of our people and a future for white children" (Michael, 2009).

Since its launch, Gab has been described as "extremist friendly," with almost no user guidelines, and has been very popular among White nationalists, neo-Nazis, and other far-right extremists (Roose 2018; Turkewitz & Roose 2018) who have been expelled from the mainstream social networks. Unlike other platforms, Gab allows extremists to congregate and converse freely. Bowers was able to get in touch with likeminded individuals, and actively posted offensive remarks against immigrants and Jews, often reposting content from other Nazi advocates. He alleged that "Jews control the United States" and wrote: "Open your eyes! It is filthy EVIL Jews bringing the filthy evil Muslims into the country!" He also criticized President Trump for not being nationalist enough and for accommodating Jewish influence in the White House (Chavez et al. 2018; Roose 2018), and disparaged White women who have relationships with Black men.

Following the attack, a debate ensued: the FBI considered Bowers's attack on the Tree of Life Synagogue a hate crime rather than a terrorist attack, despite the fact that leading terrorism experts, such as Peter Simi and John Horgan, argued that Bowers should be classified as a terrorist, his act of violence motivated by a political ideology and carried out to intimidate the community (Lord 2018). Some argued that the term "terrorism" is applied inconsistently and discriminately, depending on the race and religion of the person responsible for the violence. Even though far-right groups have killed more Americans than Islamist militants during the last two decades, Americans are often quick to label Muslim perpetrators as terrorists but Whites as mentally ill or outliers (Salehyan 2018). John Horgan, director of the Violent Extremism Research Group at Georgia State University, addressed this unfortunate situation, stating, "We have been so obsessed with Muslim-related terrorism that we have completely taken our eyes off the ball of domestic threats" (Lord 2018).

4.4.3 Case Study 3: Radicalization into Terrorism: The Fight for Land and Identity

The Kurdistan Workers' Party, or the Partiya Karkeren Kurdistan (PKK), is one of the oldest armed groups in the Middle East. The PKK has fought for autonomy for the Kurdish people within Turkey since 1978 and was designated as a foreign terrorist organization by the US Department of State in 1997 (Haner 2017). In 2015, Haner, coauthor of this book, conducted intensive interviews with an incarcerated PKK member over a five-month period. The life history provided by this individual, named Deniz, provides us with unique, first-hand insight into the radicalization process, which will be summarized here. In his early forties at the time of the interviews, Deniz had been a member of

FIGURE 4.14 The PKK, or the Kurdistan Workers' Party (Partiya Karkerên Kurdistanê in Kurdish), is a Kurdish militant and political organization. The group was founded in 1978 with the goal of achieving greater autonomy and rights for the Kurdish population in Turkey. The PKK has been involved in a long-running armed conflict with the Turkish government, which has resulted in violence and instability in southeastern Turkey. *Source:* Kurdishstruggle, CC BY 2.0, via Wikimedia Commons.

the PKK for nearly 20 years and had accelerated through the ranks of the organization into key leadership positions. Haner's analyses of the interviews with Deniz revealed that a complex set of factors combined to entrench him on a pathway to terrorism, including (1) a sense of injustice, (2) opportunity structures, (3) sense of duty and honor, and (4) personality traits.

The first key factor that led Deniz to join the PKK was a feeling of injustice and resentment caused by agents of the Turkish state. Deniz and his siblings became exposed to discrimination and alienation during their early childhood. For example, as part of its historic policy of forced assimilation, the Turkish security forces replaced Kurdish place names with Turkish names, prohibited the use of the Kurdish language, and mandated that only the Turkish language could be used in the courts, schools, and other venues (Haner 2017). Thousands of Kurds had little choice but to forgo formal education because they could not understand the language used, even though the local Kurdish population was required to pay an education tax. This situation caused great resentment among the Kurds.

Additionally, as Deniz described, every two days, Turkish soldiers would round up every male in the village and beat them with rifle butts or boots, smashing their heads until they lost consciousness. The women and the children were forced to watch this cruelty. Over time, Deniz became increasingly resentful of the unjust practices of the agents of the Turkish state. Eventually, Deniz developed the us-versus-them paradigm. He cited his prime motivation for joining the PKK was the Turkish government's actions that sought to rob the Kurds of their identity, dignity, and security.

As he grew older, Deniz increasingly encountered opportunities to become familiar with the PKK. He began joining mass protests and meetings organized by Kurdish activists in the city. Deniz was impressed with the Kurdish politicians, who were resourceful, educated, and well-integrated—and considered them to be role models in the context of the Kurdish community. It was these speeches, he recalled, that made him realize that there was an oppressed ethnic minority population in Turkey, the Kurds, and that he was a member of this population.

Through his participation in demonstrations, Deniz met and developed close relationships with new friends who shared similar opinions and beliefs. Soon he felt a part of this small group of like-minded individuals. They engaged in various activities, including field trips to learn more about the history of the Kurds and possible solutions to overcome their oppression and discrimination. By talking to each other and meeting with ideologues at nearby locations, these friends reinforced and transmitted radical ideas and attitudes. It was through these events and social networks that Deniz had the opportunity to learn the values and skills necessary to join a terrorist organization. Deniz was able to become a terrorist because he learned the ideology, had the network support, and was sufficiently close to the mountains (training camps). He became socialized into a cultural value system that celebrated revenge and hatred of the enemy, which in turn increased his readiness to support violent acts.

FIGURE 4.15   Deniz in Northern Iraq. *Source:* Author.

Concurrent with these opportunity structures was Deniz's growing sense of duty and honor, our third key factor on his path to terrorism: Deniz and his associates felt obliged to participate in the organization because they would be disloyal to their Kurdish community if they did not do so. They embraced the idea of radicalization because of their experience with ethnic discrimination. In Deniz's eyes, his ethic group had been systematically deprived of their rights to equal social and political opportunities, prevented from expressing their cultural identities, forbidden to use their language, and excluded from the legitimate opportunities to make their voices heard. He strongly believed that it was his duty to fight on behalf of the Kurdish people's future—even though participating in the war against Turkey would likely cost them their lives.

Finally, Haner's analyses revealed that Deniz's personality characteristics contributed to his radicalization. Notably, Deniz held strong ethical values. His parents always reinforced two principles: (1) always telling the truth no matter what the consequences would be, and (2) not stealing from the others. These teachings were influential, as even when Deniz experienced serious events that had the potential to cause him trouble and engender punishment, he refused to lie to disguise his responsibility. Deniz's history revealed no signs of aggressive or violent proclivities. He was intelligent and motivated to learn new things. For example, even though he had no formal education, he taught himself how to read and write.

Nor did Deniz appear to suffer from any psychological, mental, or personality disorders that would predispose him to violence. On the contrary, he had high moral values, empathy for the others around him, and was a valued member of his community. He thus chose to join the PKK not due to an underlying pathology but because he possessed the traits of moral conviction, attachment to others, and physical courage, including a willingness to use firearms if necessary.

In sum, the social and political context in which Deniz went through childhood and adolescence helped solidify his social identity as a Kurd and his desire for revenge against an oppressive Turkish state. However, consistent with the research findings discussed earlier in this chapter, it was not this context alone that led Deniz to terrorism. Via engagement in political events, he developed peer networks, gained an awareness of the PKK and its mission, connected with likeminded peers, and learned of the requirements of fighters and opportunities to become involved. He also possessed personal characteristics that influenced how he responded to his circumstances. It was not a predisposition to violence or mental illness that facilitated his radicalization; Deniz felt a strong sense of duty to defend his ethnic group and was guided by deep-rooted ethical values.

4.5 CONCLUSION

Radicalization is the process by which people come to engage in terrorism. It occurs gradually, has a complexity of antecedents, and is characterized by an escalation from nonviolent to increasingly violent behaviors over time. When we discuss radicalization into terrorism we are really referring to the radicalization of behaviors—to the point where one commits acts of terrorism. As we explained previously, one can experience a radicalization of attitudes, behaviors, or both. While the development of a radical ideology may precede radical behaviors, it is not a necessary precondition, and most individuals who hold radical beliefs do not become terrorists.

While there are no reliable predictors of terrorism and no single terrorist profile, empirical research has provided us with several key insights regarding radicalization into terrorism. We know that terrorists, in general, are not mentally ill, that radicalization is a complex and gradual process, that the internet is increasingly involved in the radicalization process, and that neither poverty nor Islam cause terrorism.

Additionally, as with radicalization, deradicalization and disengagement from terrorism have varied antecedents at the individual and group levels. They are complex processes, and they can occur independently from each other. As we note, many who disengage from terrorism—who are no longer committing terrorist acts—still hold radical views. Identifying the reasons why people leave terrorism may lead to the detection of vulnerabilities in terrorist organizations that can be targeted to facilitate disengagement from terrorism at the collective level.

Key Lessons

Lesson 1

There are multiple pathways to terrorism and these pathways may vary according to the extremist ideologies and narratives an individual embraces, as well as the time periods in which they radicalize, the groups or movements they join, and their characteristics and experiences.

Lesson 2

Engagement in terrorism is exceptionally rare. An individual can undergo the process of radicalization but not engage in terrorism.

Lesson 3

Being a terrorist often requires an incremental progression of socialization and cognitive restructuring. An individual seeking revenge does not become a terrorist overnight.

Lesson 4

Terrorists are psychologically normal people. There is no clear evidence that personality traits, psychological disorders, or psychopathic tendencies distinguish terrorists from the general population.

Lesson 5

Terrorists come from all socioeconomic backgrounds. Individual poverty or unemployment do not cause terrorism.

Lesson 6

Radicalization into violence is often driven by contact with other extremists.

Lesson 7

Muslims are not more prone to violence than members of other religious groups. Despite the popular emphasis on the connection of Islam to terrorism, terrorists come from all religions.

Lesson 8

The internet and social media have become a prominent domain for terrorist activities—from marketing and recruitment to fundraising, to planning and carrying out attacks.

Lesson 9

Deradicalization and disengagement are independent phenomena. An individual may stop using terrorist violence but may still believe in the cause and that the use of such violence is appropriate, or one may question prior radical beliefs but feel compelled or forced to continue violent actions.

Lesson 10

Empirical research on radicalization into and disengagement from terrorism is critical to identify vulnerabilities in terrorist organizations and inform the development of nondiscriminatory counterterrorism measures.

KEY WORDS

activists

cognitive restructuring

counterterrorism

deradicalization

disengagement

extremists

four-stage model of radicalization

mental illness

online radicalization

physical disengagement

poverty

psychological disengagement

radicalization

socialization

staircase model of terrorism

terrorist profiling

two-pyramids model of terrorism

unemployment

violent extremism

RECOMMENDED SOURCES

Research Articles & Books

Alonso, R., Bjorgo, T., Della Porta, D., Coolsaet, R., Khosrokhavar, F., Lohker, R., . . . & Taarnby, M. (2008). Radicalisation Processes Leading to Acts of Terrorism. A concise Report prepared by the European Commission's Expert Group on Violent Radicalisation.

Bjørgo, T. (2005). *Root causes of terrorism: Myths, reality and ways forward*. New York, NY: Routledge.

Borum, R. (2003). Understanding the terrorist mind-set. *FBI L. Enforcement Bull.*, 72, 7.

Crenshaw, M. (1981). The causes of terrorism. *Comparative politics*, 13(4), 379–399.

della Porta, D. (2012). 15 On individual motivations in underground political organizations. *Terrorism studies: A reader, 231*.

della Porta, D. (2018). Radicalization: A relational perspective. *Annual Review of Political Science*, 21, 461–474.

Gupta, D. K. (2005). Exploring roots of terrorism. *Root causes of terrorism: Myths, reality and ways forward*, 16.

Horgan, J. (2003). The search for the terrorist personality. *Terrorists, victims and society*, 3–27.

LaFree, G. (2012). Countering Myths about Terrorism: Some Lessons Learned from the Global Terrorism Database. In *What do we Expect from our Government?* eds. Beryl A. Radin and Joshua M. Chanin. Lanham, MD: Lexington Books, 71–98.

McCauley, C., & Moskalenko, S. (2017). Understanding political radicalization: The two-pyramids model. *American Psychologist*, 72(3), 205.

Richardson, L. (2007). *What terrorists want: Understanding the enemy, containing the threat*. Random House Incorporated.

Russell, C. A., & Miller, B. H. (1977). Profile of a Terrorist. *Studies in conflict & terrorism*, 1(1), 17–34.

Schmid, A. P. (2013). Radicalisation, deradicalisation, counter-radicalisation: A conceptual discussion and literature review. *ICCT Research Paper*, 97(1), 22.

Stern, J. (2003). *Terror in the name of god: Why religious militants kill*. New York, NY: Ecco

Victoroff, J. (2005). The mind of the terrorist: A review and critique of psychological approaches. *Journal of Conflict Resolution*, 49(1), 3–42.

News Articles & Government and Think Tank Reports

What Drives an Individual to Join a Terrorist Group?
Mapping the connection between mental health and membership in a terrorist group.
    Author(s): Fablana Franco
    Source: Psychology Today
Why People Join Terrorist Groups
Scholar debunks common beliefs in why individuals become terrorists
    Author(s): Marc Sageman and Steve Hartsoe
    Source: Duke Today
What Motivates Terrorists?
It's an important question. But is it the best one to be asking?
    Author(s): Simon Cottee
    Source: The Atlantic

Why average people decide to become terrorists
    Author(s): Jennifer Williams
    Source: Vox
The Psychology of Radicalization: How Terrorist Groups Attract Young Followers
    Author(s): Maggie Penman & Shankar Vedantam
    Source: NPR
How ordinary people decide to become terrorists
    Author(s): Jennifer Williams
    Source: Vox
What we've learned about radicalisation since 7/7 bombings a decade ago
    Author(s): Matthew Francis
    Source: The Conversation

Documentaries, Videos, and Other Educational Media

Terrorism and Counterterrorism, a Discussion by Martha Creenshaw
    Featuring: Martha Crenshaw
    Source: Stanford Program on International and Cross-Cultural Education (SPICE) YouTube Channel
How young people join violent extremist groups—and how to stop them
    Featuring: Erin Marie Saltman
    Source: TEDx
Extremism, ISIS and the Doomsday Cults of the 1970s | Retro Report
    Producer(s)/Director(s): Geoffrey O'Connor
    Source: PBS Learning Media

'Against All Enemies' explores why some vets join extremist groups
    Producer(s)/Director(s): MSNBC Morning Joe
    Source: MSNBC YouTube Channel
American Terror: The Military's Problem With Extremism in the Ranks
    Producer(s)/Director(s): VICE News
    Source: VICE News YouTube Channel
The Mind of the Terrorist
    Featuring: Jerold Post
    Source: C-Span

REFERENCES

Ahmed, S., & Murphy, P. P. (2018). Here's what we know so far about Robert Bowers, the Pittsburgh synagogue shooting suspect. CNN. https://www.cnn.com/2018/10/27/us/synagogue-attack-suspect-robert-bowers-profile/index.html

Ajzen, I. (2001). Nature and operation of attitudes. *Annual Review of Psychology, 52*(1), 27–58.

Akram, S. M. (2002). The aftermath of September 11, 2001: The targeting of Arabs and Muslims in America. *Arab Studies Quarterly*, 61–118.

Alfifi, M., Kaghazgaran, P., Caverlee, J., & Morstatter, F. (2018). Measuring the impact of ISIS social media strategy. Stanford Network Analysis Project, Misinformation and Misbehavior Mining on the Web MIS2.

Alonso, R., Bjorgo, T., Della Porta, D., Coolsaet, R., Khosrokhavar, F., Lohker, R., Ranstorp, M., Reinares, F., Schmid, A. P., Silke, A., Taarnby, M., & De Vries, G. (2008). Radicalisation processes leading to acts of terrorism: A concise report prepared by the European Commission's Expert Group on Violent Radicalisation. European Commission.

Alterman, D. (1999). *How terrorism ends*. Special Report. United States Institute of Peace.

Asharq al-Awsat (2018). Sally Jones, the most dangerous ISIS operative alive. *Asharq al-Awsat*. https://english.aawsat.com/home/article/1441726/sally-jones-most-dangerous-isis-operative-alive

Atran, S. (2003). Genesis of suicide terrorism. *Science*, 299(5612), 1534–1539.

BBC (2018). Pittsburgh synagogue gunman suspect: Who is Robert Bowers? *BBC*. https://www.bbc.com/news/world-us-canada-46022930

Bjørgo, T. (2005). *Root causes of terrorism: Myths, reality and ways forward*. Routledge.

Bjørgo, T. (2011). Dreams and disillusionment: Engagement in and disengagement from militant extremist groups. *Crime, Law and Social Change*, 55(4), 277–285.

Bjørgo, T. (2018). Disengagement from terrorism. In G. Overland, A. J. Andersen, & K. E. Førde (Eds.). *Violent extremism in the 21st century: International perspectives*. Cambridge Scholars Publishing.

Borum, R. (2003). Understanding the terrorist mind-set. *FBI Law Enforcement Bulletin*, 72, 7.

Borum, R. (2011). Radicalization into violent extremism I: A review of social science theories. *Journal of Strategic Security*, 4(4), 7–36.

Chavez, N., Grinberg, E., & McLaughlin, E. C. (2018). Pittsburgh synagogue gunman said he wanted all Jews to die, criminal complaint says. *CNN*. https://www.cnn.com/2018/10/28/us/pittsburgh-synagogue-shooting/index.html

Cockburn, P. (2017). The IS Caliphate and the West's Wars in Syria and Iraq: A challenge to religious pluralism in the middle east. In J. Eibner (Ed). *The future of religious minorities in the middle east*, (pp. 87–96). Lexington Books.

Corbin, C. M. (2017). Terrorists are always Muslim but never white: At the intersection of critical race theory and propaganda. *Fordham Law Review*, 86, 455.

Cottee, S., & Hayward, K. (2011). Terrorist (e)motives: The existential attractions of terrorism. *Studies in Conflict & Terrorism*, 34(12), 963–986.

Craig, D. (2019). How ISIS really recruits its members. *Columbia Magazine*. https://magazine.columbia.edu/article/how-isis-really-recruits-its-members

Crenshaw, M. (1981). The causes of terrorism. *Comparative Politics*, 13(4), 379–399.

Crenshaw, M. (1995). Thoughts on relating terrorism to historical contexts. *Terrorism in Context*, 4, 7.

Crenshaw, M. (2012). The causes of terrorism. In J. Horgan & K. Braddock (Eds.), *Terrorism studies: A reader* (pp. 99–114). Routledge.

Cronin, A. K. (2009). How terrorism ends: Understanding the decline and demise of terrorist campaigns. Princeton University Press.

della Porta, D. (2012). On individual motivations in underground political organizations. In J. Horgan & K. Braddock (Eds.), *Terrorism studies: A reader* (pp. 231–250). Routledge.

della Porta, D. (2018). Radicalization: A relational perspective. *Annual Review of Political Science*, 21, 461–474.

Diyab, H. (2019). Women in jihad: Militant leadership monitor special report: Personalities behind the insurgency. Jamestown Foundation Report. https://jamestown.org/wp-content/uploads/2019/03/Special-Report-Women-in-Jihad-2.pdf?x59415

Dobuzinskis, A. (2019). U.S. to seek death penalty for accused Pittsburgh synagogue shooter. Reuters. https://www.reuters.com/article/us-pennsylvania-shooting/u-s-to-seek-death-penalty-for-accused-pittsburgh-synagogue-shooter-idUSKCN1VG27B

Doosje, B., Moghaddam, F. M., Kruglanski, A. W., De Wolf, A., Mann, L., & Feddes, A. R. (2016). Terrorism, radicalization and deradicalization. *Current Opinion in Psychology*, 11, 79–84.

Dragon, J. D. (2015). *Western foreign fighters in Syria: An empirical analysis of recruitment and mobilization mechanisms*. Naval Postgraduate School.

Fishman, B. (Ed.). (2009). *Bombers, bank accounts, and bleedout: Al-Qa-ida's road in and out of Iraq.* Diane Publishing.

Fruen, L. (2019). The Kent Jihadist who was Sally Anne Jones, when was the "White Widow" terrorist killed and how did she become an ISIS recruiter? *The Sun.* https://www.thesun.co.uk/news/3506926/sally-jones-dead-isis-recruiter-syria-white-widow-drone-strike/

Gupta, D. K. (2005). Exploring roots of terrorism. In T. Bjørgo (Ed.), *Root causes of terrorism: Myths, reality and ways forward* (pp. 34–50). Routledge.

Gupta, D. K. (2008). Accounting for the waves of international terrorism. *Perspectives on Terrorism, 2*(11), 3–9.

Gurr, T. R. (1970). Sources of rebellion in Western societies: Some quantitative evidence. *The Annals of the American Academy of Political and Social Science, 391*(1), 128–144.

Gurr, T. R. (2006). Economic factors. In L. Richardson (Ed.), *The roots of terrorism* (pp. 85–101). Routledge.

Haner, M. (2017). *The freedom fighter: A terrorist's own story.* Routledge.

Haner, M., Sloan, M. M., Cullen, F. T., Graham, A., Jonson, C. L., and Kulig, T. C. (2020). Making America safe again: Public support for policies to reduce terrorism. *Deviant Behavior, 42*(10), 1209–1227.

Haner, M., Wichern, A., & Fleenor, M. (2018). The Turkish foreign fighters and the dynamics behind their flow into Syria and Iraq. *Terrorism and Political Violence, 32*(6), 1329–1347.

Henderson, E. A., & Tucker, R. (2001). Clear and present strangers: The clash of civilizations and international conflict. *International Studies Quarterly, 45*(2), 317–338.

Henne, P. (2019). Terrorism and religion: An overview. In W. R. Thompson (Ed.), *Oxford research encyclopedia of politics.* Oxford University Press.

Horgan, J. (2003). The search for the terrorist personality. In A. Silke (Ed.), *Terrorists, victims and society,* 3–27. Wiley.

Horgan, J. (2005). The social and psychological characteristics of terrorism and terrorists. In T. Bjørgo (Ed.), *Root causes of terrorism,* *myths reality and ways forward* (pp. 62–71). Routledge.

Horgan, J. (2008). From profiles to pathways and roots to routes: Perspectives from psychology on radicalization into terrorism. *The ANNALS of the American Academy of Political and Social Science, 618*(1), 80–94.

Horgan, J. (2009). *Walking away from terrorism: Accounts of disengagement from radical and extremist movements.* Routledge.

Horgan, J., & Braddock, K. (Eds.). (2012). *Terrorism studies: A reader.* Routledge.

House of Commons Report of the official account of the bombings in London on 7th July 2005. (2005). Her Majesty's Stationery Office https://assets.publishing.service.gov.uk/government/uploads/system/uploads/attachment_data/file/228837/1087.pdf

Kearns, E. M., Betus, A. E., & Lemieux, A. F. (2019). Why do some terrorist attacks receive more media attention than others? *Justice Quarterly, 36*(6), 985–1022.

Koehler, D. (2014). The radical online: Individual radicalization processes and the role of the Internet. *Journal for Deradicalization, 1,* 116–134.

Krueger, A. B., & Malečková, J. (2003). Education, poverty and terrorism: Is there a causal connection? *Journal of Economic Perspectives, 17*(4), 119–144.

Kruglanski, A. W., Gelfand, M. J., Bélanger, J. J., Sheveland, A., Hetiarachchi, M., & Gunaratna, R. (2014). The psychology of radicalization and deradicalization: How significance quest impacts violent extremism. *Political Psychology, 35,* 69–93.

LaFree, G. (2012). Countering myths about terrorism: Some lessons learned from the Global Terrorism Database. In B. W. Radin & J. M. Chanin (Eds.), *What do we expect from our government?* (pp. 71–98). Lexington Books.

Lerner, D. (1958). *The passing of traditional society: Modernizing the Middle East.* Free Press.

Lord, R. (2018). How Robert Bowers went from conservative to White nationalist. *Pittsburgh Post-Gazette.* https://www.post-gazette.com/news/crime-courts/2018/11/10/Robert-Bowers-extremism-Tree-of-Life-massacre-shooting-pittsburgh-Gab-Warroom/stories/201811080165

May, A., & Hafner, J. (2018). Pittsburgh synagogue shooting: What we know, questions that remain. *USA Today.* https://www.usatoday.com/story/news/nation-now/2018/10/29/pittsburgh-synagogue-shooting-what-we-know/1804878002/

McCauley, C., & Moskalenko, S. (2017). Understanding political radicalization: The two-pyramids model. *American Psychologist, 72*(3), 205.

Merari, A. (2005). Social, organizational and psychological factors in suicide terrorism. In T. Bjørgo (Ed.), *Root causes of terrorism: Myths, reality and ways forward* (pp. 70–86). Routledge.

Michael, G. (2009). David Lane and the fourteen words. *Totalitarian Movements and Political Religions, 10*(1), 43–61.

Moghaddam, F. M. (2005). The staircase to terrorism: A psychological exploration. *American Psychologist, 60*(2), 161.

Mohammad, A. Y. S. (2005). Roots of terrorism in the Middle east: Internal pressures and international constraints. In T. Bjorgo (Ed.), *Root causes of terrorism: Myths, reality and ways forward* (pp. 103–119). Routledge.

Mullen, J., & Todd, B. (2014). Battling "crusaders": ISIS turns to glossy magazine for propaganda. CNN. https://edition.cnn.com/2014/09/17/world/meast/isis-magazine/index.html

Muro, D. (2016). What does radicalisation look like? Four visualisations of socialisation into violent extremism. *Notes Internacionals, 162*(2). https://www.cidob.org/en/publication/what-does-radicalisation-look-four-visualisations-socialisation-violent-extremism

Neumann, P. R. (2013). Options and strategies for countering online radicalization in the United States. *Studies in Conflict & Terrorism, 36*(6), 431–459.

NIJ (2015). Radicalization and violent extremism-lessons learned from Canada, the UK and the US meeting summary, July 28–30.

O'Hara, K., & Stevens, D. (2015). Echo chambers and online radicalism: Assessing the Internet's complicity in violent extremism. *Policy & Internet, 7*(4), 401–422.

Pape, R. A. (2003). The strategic logic of suicide terrorism. *American Political Science Review, 97*(3), 343–361.

Pape, R. A. (2008). Dying to win: The strategic logic of suicide terrorism. In M. Perry & H. E. Negrin (Eds.), *The theory and practice of Islamic terrorism* (pp. 129–132). Palgrave Macmillan.

Pape, R. A. (2012). The strategic logic of suicide terrorism. In J. Horgan & K. Braddock (Ed.). *Terrorism Studies: A Reader* (pp. 260–289). Routledge.

Patel, F. (2011). *Rethinking radicalization.* Brennan Center for Justice.

PCPSR (2001–2015). Palestinian Center for Policy and Survey Research polls. https://www.pcpsr.org/

Pearce, S. (2005). Religious rage: A quantitative analysis of the intensity of religious conflicts. *Terrorism and Political Violence, 17*(3), 333–352.

Post, J., Sprinzak, E., & Denny, L. (2003). The terrorists in their own words: Interviews with 35 incarcerated Middle Eastern terrorists. *Terrorism and Political Violence, 15*(1), 171–184.

Prajuli, W. A. (2017). On social media, ISIS uses fantastical propaganda to recruit members. *The Conversation, 4.* https://theconversation.com/on-social-media-isis-uses-fantastical-propaganda-to-recruit-members-86626

Rapoport, D. (2012). Fear and trembling: Terrorism in three religious traditions. In J. Horgan & K. Braddock (Eds.), *Terrorism studies: A reader* (pp. 3–27). Routledge.

Reynolds, S. C., & Hafez, M. M. (2019). Social network analysis of German foreign fighters in Syria and Iraq. *Terrorism and Political Violence, 31*(4), 661–686.

Robertson, C., Mele, C., & Tavernise, S. (2018). 11 killed in synagogue massacre; suspect charged with 29 counts. *New York Times.* https://www.nytimes.com/2018/10/27/us/active-shooter-pittsburgh-synagogue-shooting.html

Roose, K. (2018). On gab, an extremist-friendly site, Pittsburgh shooting suspect aired his hatred in full. *New York Times.* https://www.nytimes.com/2018/10/28/us/gab-robert-bowers-pittsburgh-synagogue-shootings.html

Russell, C. A., & Miller, B. H. (1977). Profile of a terrorist. *Studies in Conflict & Terrorism, 1*(1), 17–34.

Sageman, M. (2011). *Leaderless jihad: Terror networks in the twenty-first century.* University of Pennsylvania Press.

Saldivia, G., Van Sant, S., Bowman, E. (2018). Suspect charged with 29 federal counts in Pittsburgh synagogue massacre. *NPR*. https://www.npr.org/2018/10/27/661347236/multiple-casualties-in-shooting-near-pittsburgh-synagogue

Salehyan, I. (2018). Should Robert Bowers, the Pittsburgh synagogue shooting suspect, be called a terrorist? *Washington Post*. https://www.washingtonpost.com/news/monkey-cage/wp/2018/11/01/should-robert-bowers-the-pittsburgh-synagogue-shooting-suspect-be-called-a-terrorist/

Schmid, A. P. (2013). Radicalisation, de-radicalisation, counter-radicalisation: A conceptual discussion and literature review. *ICCT Research Paper*, *97*(1), 22.

Sengupta, K. (2017). Sally Jones: How did a woman from Kent join ISIS and became the "White Widow"? *The Independent*. https://www.independent.co.uk/news/world/middle-east/sally-jones-white-widow-dead-uk-isis-jihadi-kent-junaid-hussein-drone-strike-syria-a7997251.html

Silke, A. (Ed.). (2003). *Terrorists, victims and society: Psychological perspectives on terrorism and its consequences*. Wiley.

Smith, A. G. (2018). *How radicalization to terrorism occurs in the United States: What research sponsored by the National Institute of Justice tells us*. US Department of Justice, Office of Justice Programs, National Institute of Justice.

Speckhard, A., & Ellenberg, M. (2020). Is internet recruitment enough to seduce a vulnerable individual into terrorism? *Homeland Security Today*. https://www.hstoday.us/subject-matter-areas/counterterrorism/is-internet-recruitment-enough-to-seduce-a-vulnerable-individual-into-terrorism/

Sprang, G. (2003). The psychological impact of isolated acts of terrorism. In A. Silke (Ed.), *Terrorists, victims and society* (pp. 133–159). Wiley.

Stern, J. (2003). *Terror in the name of god: Why religious militants kill*. Ecco.

Taylor, M. (1988). *The terrorist*. Brassey's Defence Publishers.

Tomlinson, S. (2015). 'White Widow' jihadi Sally-Anne Jones warns she will "expose more U.S. military" and "prove social media will be your downfall" in latest Twitter threat. *Daily Mail*. https://www.dailymail.co.uk/news/article-3289726/White-Widow-jihadi-Sally-Anne-Jones-warns-expose-U-S-military-prove-social-media-downfall-latest-Twitter-threat.html

Torok, R. (2013). Developing an explanatory model for the process of online radicalisation and terrorism. *Security Informatics*, *2*, 1–10.

Travis, A. (2008). MI5 report challenges views on terrorism in Britain. *The Guardian*. http://www.guardian.co.uk/uk/2008/aug/20/uksecurity.terrorism1

Turkewitz, J., & Roose, K. (2018). Who is Robert Bowers, the suspect in the Pittsburgh synagogue shooting? *New York Times*. https://www.nytimes.com/2018/10/27/us/robert-bowers-pittsburgh-synagogue-shooter.html

UNDP (2016). Preventing violent extremism through promoting inclusive development, tolerance, and respect for diversity: A development response to addressing radicalization and violent extremism. United Nations Development Programme.

Vertigans, S. (2011). *The sociology of terrorism: peoples, places and processes*. Routledge.

Victoroff, J. (2005). The mind of the terrorist: A review and critique of psychological approaches. *Journal of Conflict Resolution*, *49*(1), 3–42.

Ward, A. (2018). ISIS's use of social media still poses a threat to stability in the Middle East and Africa. *Georgetown Security Studies Review*. https://georgetownsecuritystudiesreview.org/author/ahw42/

Weaver, M. (2017). Sally Jones: UK punk singer who became leading ISIS recruiter. *The Guardian*. https://www.theguardian.com/world/2017/oct/12/sally-jones-the-uk-punk-singer-who-became-isiss-white-widow

Webber, D., & Kruglanski, A. W. (2016). Psychological factors in radicalization: A "3 N" approach. In G. LaFree & J. D. Freilich (Eds.), *The handbook of the criminology of terrorism*, 33–46. Wiley.

Wiktorowicz, Q. (Ed.). (2004). *Islamic activism: A social movement theory approach*. Indiana University Press.

CHAPTER 5

Women, Gender, and Terrorism

Exploring Gendered Pathways and Experiences

Learning Objectives
1. To understand women's motivation and recruitment into terrorist groups.
2. To outline the diverse roles women assume within violent groups.
3. To analyze the strategic advantages associated with the recruitment of women in terrorist organizations.
4. To appreciate the role of women's agency in their involvement with terrorism.

5.1 INTRODUCTION

In popular media and in many academic studies, terrorists in the United States are typically portrayed as males (Annan et al. 2009; Haner et al. 2020). There is some justification for this stereotype given that recent domestic and international terrorist attacks in the United States have been perpetrated predominantly by males. Domestically, the Oklahoma City bombing (1995), the Virginia Tech massacre (2007), the DC sniper incident (2009), the Aurora movie theatre shooting (2012), the Boston Marathon bombing (2013), and the Orlando nightclub shooting (2016) were all carried out by men. Internationally inspired terrorism, such as the September 11 tragedy, sees a similar pattern: that event involved 11 male terrorists. Indeed, the most recent example of a female perpetrating a terrorist act in the United States is Tashfeen Malik, one of the shooters in the 2015 San Bernardino attack. While no recent attacks have been carried out by women on US soil, several American women have been indicted for terrorism-related offenses such as providing material support, traveling overseas to join ISIS, training recruits, and financing terrorism (Barr 2022; Katersky 2023; Nesi 2024; Rabinowitz 2024).

The United States is far from the only country to suffer at the hands of male terrorists. Terrorist groups predominated by men can be found throughout Europe, the Middle East, Africa, Central America, and Asia. For example, the 2011 shooting spree in Norway and the relatively recent Islamic State attacks in France (Nice and Paris), Germany (Bavaria and Munich), Afghanistan (Kabul), Turkey (Ankara, Urfa, Gaziantep), Russia (Naurskaya), and the United Kingdom (Manchester) were all committed by male terrorists.

It is therefore unsurprising that descriptions of men appear in news reports whenever terrorism occurs. But although certainly understandable, this focus on male terrorists obscures the reality—that women have played important, though little understood, roles in many terrorist groups and movements. For example, National Liberation Front in Algeria, which defeated and drove out the French colonizers, assigned women direct roles in carrying out violence as well as serving as message bearers, spies, and transporters of assault weaponry (Benson et al. 1982; Weinberg & Eubank 2011). In the Middle East, women in the Palestinian Liberation Organization engaged in several hijacking incidents that captured the world's attention (Ness 2005).

In Israel, women played important roles in clandestine operations by Irgun and the Lehi in the Zionist fight against British rule (Weinberg & Eubank 2011). In Europe, women served in various operational capacities in the Red Army Faction, Red Brigades, Irish Republican Army, and Euskadi Ta Askatasuna. In Latin America, women of the

FIGURE 5.1   Leila Khaled, the first woman to hijack an airplane, was a member of the Popular Front of the Liberation of Palestine and came to public attention for her role in the flight hijacking in 1969. *Source:* Public domain, via Wikimedia Commons.

Tupamaros and the Shining Path organizations played active roles by planning and executing deadly missions (Benson et al. 1982). In Russia and Sri Lanka, the women of People's Will and the Liberation Tigers of Tamil Eelam assassinated state leaders (Sutten 2009). Because of the ongoing involvement of women in terrorist groups and movements, it is important to understand how they are recruited, the roles that they play, and the activities in which they are involved. Failure to investigate the role of women in terrorism will inevitably lead to an incomplete understanding of the structure of terrorist groups and undermine our ability to confront the menace that terrorism poses to the world.

The goal of this chapter is to extend the understanding of women as terrorists through an analysis of their participation in past and modern-day terrorist organizations. We explore three themes regarding female involvement in terrorist groups: (1) women's motivation and recruitment; (2) the roles of women in violent groups; and (3) the strategic benefits of female recruitment in terrorist groups. We then present four case studies: Chechen Black Widows, Red Army Faction (RAF), Kurdistan Workers' Party (PKK), and Islamic State of Iraq and Syria (ISIS). These will provide an in-depth study of women's involvement in terrorism and political violence.

FIGURE 5.2 Women of the Provisional Irish Republican Army (IRA) on active service in West Belfast with assault rifles.

FIGURE 5.3 Three female members of the Official Irish Republican Army (OIRA) at a checkpoint in the Bogside area of Derry. Women have played significant roles in the Irish Republican Army (IRA). While traditionally the IRA was male-dominated, women contributed in various ways, including intelligence gathering, logistics, fundraising, and even combat. Some notable female figures in the IRA's history include Mairead Farrell, who was involved in the Balcombe Street Siege and later killed by British special forces in Gibraltar in 1988, and Dolours Price, who was involved in the Old Bailey bombing in London in 1973. *Source:* Eamon Melaugh (cain .ulster.ac.uk/melaugh).

5.2 WHY DO WOMEN BECOME TERRORISTS?

In order to understand why women become terrorists, it is helpful to consider the factors that contribute to our perception of women and political violence. As a social construction—an idea that is socially created—gender carries with it expectations for behavior and stereotypes about what is masculine and what is feminine. While masculinity is typically associated with agentive and aggressive characteristics, **femininity** can be associated with more passive, peaceful behaviors (Ridgeway 2011). Our beliefs about gender contribute to our collective shock when we learn about women's acts of violence. Terrorist activities—opposition, aggression, and violence—fall under the domain of masculine behaviors. Indeed, in a study of Palestinian women who were incarcerated for security violations, all interviewees acknowledged that their actions placed them in violation of gender expectations and reported that they are now rejected by others because they did not carry out the roles expected of women in Palestinian society (Berko & Erez 2007). In order to appreciate the full complexity of factors that contribute to women's participation in political violence, therefore, we must consider the influence of gender and the expectations of women and men in patriarchal societies (Agara 2015; Bhattacharya 2019).

Given the strength of gender expectations, particularly in traditional patriarchal cultures with deep-rooted cultural, religious, and legal structures that perpetuate male dominance, why do women become terrorists? For obvious reasons—such as the challenges involved in reaching the population of interest—empirical research on female members of terrorist organizations has historically been limited (compared to other areas of research in the field of terrorism). However, empirical investigations of women in terrorism have grown in recent years, especially after 9/11 (Davis et al. 2021; Margolin & Cook 2024). For example, Margolin and Cook (2024) found that on average, there were less than two studies on women's engagement in terrorism published per year between 1997 and 2003. For the most part, existing studies have examined biographical accounts of individuals engaged in terrorist activities from archival sources (e.g., secondary data sources such as literature reviews, film analysis, news outlets, and court documents) or have included interviews with individuals who have been incarcerated (i.e., inactive) or otherwise defected from terrorist organizations. Much of the data examines women's motivations to engage in suicide bombing in particular. From this existing research, scholars have identified several factors that contribute to women's participation in political violence. These are typically grouped as personal factors and structural factors. Personal factors reflect experiences or life events that while perhaps common in a given population, affect women on an individual level. Structural factors are those that affect women on a collective level, by holding the status of "female" in a society. We discuss these different types of motivations in detail in the following section.

5.2.1 Personal Motivators: The Five Rs

Based on ethnographic research, including interviews with female suicide bombers whose acts were unsuccessful, professor of communication and Middle East studies Mia Bloom (2011a) identified the Five Rs of motivations behind women's involvement in political violence. These include (1) revenge, (2) redemption, (3) relationship, (4) respect, and (5) rape.

In Bloom's study, the most frequently cited motive for terrorism was **revenge** for the death of a family member, typically a husband or father. In nations such as Iraq, Afghanistan, and Syria, where political violence is commonplace, many women are subjected to the loss of a loved one due to armed conflict. Terrorism, in these cases, provides an outlet for revenging the loss.

Redemption, in this case, refers to the belief that a voluntary act of martyrdom (in the case of suicide bombing) will atone for past misdeeds or accusations. The literature on terrorism contains many reports about "fallen women" who believe their efforts will cleanse them of past sins, such as illicit relationships with men or familial disgraces. In a culture that dictates women be held accountable for their transgressions, terrorism—even martyrdom—often seems like a better alternative.

The motivation of *relationship* includes the networks that connect women to terrorist organizations. Bloom notes that "the best predictor that a woman will engage in terrorist violence is if she is related to a known insurgent or Jihadi" (2011b, 12). Having a family member who is engaged in a terrorist group provides women with insight into the structure and mission of the organization as well as a gateway to membership. Women may also marry into a terrorist group, either by choice or through an arrangement made by their families. Strategic marriages are frequently formed between sisters and daughters of group leaders and their colleagues, thus strengthening close network connections within the organization. The relationship motive encompasses women's participation in terrorism that may be either voluntary or coerced.

Bloom (2011b) notes that the motivation of *respect* typically occurs in conjunction with other motives. The female suicide bombers in her study reported seeking to earn respect from their communities for being as capable as men at supporting the group's cause. The women felt that their choice to sacrifice themselves would demonstrate their commitment and make them role models for the younger generations in a society where parks and streets are named after women who become suicide bombers.

The fifth R, *rape*, was added to the first four in response to the widespread **sexual exploitation** of women. Terrorist groups, particularly in Iraq and Chechnya, use sexual violence to coerce women into supporting the organization. The trauma of rape makes women vulnerable to transformation into terrorist operatives.

Although these motivations may occur at the individual level, with the experience of a particular negative event, stressful situation, or personal trauma, the frequency with which these motivations are reported represents a theme in women's participation in terrorism. In an analysis of academic articles about female involvement in terrorism published between 1983 and 2006, Jaques and Taylor (2009) identified personal reasons for participating in terrorist activity—such as personal distress, monetary worries, and feeling like a social outsider—among the most frequently cited motivations, second to social and structural factors, which we discuss in the next section. While these motivations reflect personal experiences, these women are not alone in their circumstances.

5.2.2 Additional Motivators

In addition to the personal motivations behind women's engagement in terrorism, scholars have identified several social and structural influences on women's involvement. They may be motivated to join terrorist movements due to a lack of political access, oppressive political regimes, social discrimination, and economic influences (Jahanbani & Willis 2019). In contexts where women have little power, they may feel that using unconventional means such as political violence is the only way to initiate change.

Women may also join terrorist groups for idealistic reasons such as religious beliefs or nationalism, though empirical research suggests that these factors are more influential among men than among women (Jacques & Taylor 2009). In their 2008 review of female motivations for engaging in terrorism, Jacques and Taylor identified five different categories of motivations. The most frequently noted type of motivation in the research was categorized as "social." This includes issues related to structural inequality in society, such as a desire for gender equality, a lack of career or educational opportunities, and family problems. Personal factors were the second most frequently cited motivations, followed by idealistic factors, including religious and nationalistic reasons, and then negative key events and a desire for revenge. Table 5.1 is a replication of a table from their analysis. It shows how frequently each of the aforementioned motivators was cited in the academic research.

In sum, many factors contribute to women's involvement in terrorist groups. Of course, not all women who experience traumatic events or personal difficulties turn to terrorism. The existing research on the topic suggests that along with a group's ideological appeal, the subordination of women under **patriarchy** gives rise to both personal and

FIGURE 5.4 The Japanese Red Army, with Fusako Shigenobu as its head, grew out of Japan's radical student movement of the 1960s to become one of the world's most feared guerrilla groups, with a stated goal of overthrowing the Japanese government and monarchy and bringing about world revolution.

TABLE 5.1   Female Motivations and Their Frequency within the Literature

Motivation Category	Example Motivations	Frequency of Motivations
Social	Gender equality	34
	Education/career needs	
	Humiliation and repression	
	Family problems	
Personal	Personal distress	18
	Monetary worries	
	Social outsider	
Idealistic	Religion	15
	Nationalism	
	Commitment to cause	
	Wish for martyrdom	
Key event	Loss of a loved one	12
	Specific humiliating instances	
	Displacement	
	Other negative uncontrollable event	
Revenge	Vengeance	4
	Anger	

Source: Adapted from Jacques & Taylor (2009).

structural factors that may push women toward terrorism. At the same time, most terrorist groups recognize the value of female members and actively engage in recruitment efforts that target women in particular, thus creating pull factors as well.

5.3 WHY TERRORIST GROUPS WANT FEMALE MEMBERS

For numerous reasons, terrorist organizations seek female recruits. At a practical level, women's participation leads to a greater number of group members. The nature of terrorism places members at a high risk of being captured or killed. Casualties within groups can necessitate the recruitment of women simply to sustain the organization (Bhattacharya 2019; Wood 2019).

An additional appeal of female recruits relates to gendered expectations for the behavior of women in society. The perception of women as peaceful and nurturing means that they are less likely than men to be suspected as terrorists. In male-dominated societies, women are not considered to pose a security threat in the way that men are (Cunningham 2003; Jahanbani & Willis 2019). This perception enables women to gain access to restricted areas and get close to targets in ways that men could not. Women can also use their gender to facilitate an attack. For example, in 2006, a woman disguised herself as pregnant in order to hide explosives under her clothes, gain entry to a Sri Lankan army hospital, and complete a suicide bomb attack, killing eight people (BBC 2006). Social norms that prohibit scrutinizing women's bodies enable women to hide weaponry in their garments without detection. Women can use gendered assumptions

FIGURE 5.5   Example of a female recruitment poster: Popular Front for the Liberation of Palestine (1981). *Source:* Palestinian Youth Movement.

about female behavior and female bodies in acts of terrorism.

The public shock value of women's successful suicide missions and the concurrent media attention serves the terrorist organization: it calls attention to the depths of its commitment to resistance (Bloom 2005). Based on gendered expectations for behavior, many people find it difficult to believe that a woman would be capable of such aggressive and violent actions, and news of such acts generates great interest among the public. This is the very reason why the media accounts and government documents often referred to women who joined terrorism as crazy, psychologically impaired, or seduced by men (Bigio & Vogelstein 2019b; Haner et al. 2020). This understanding ignores women's agency.

In addition to grabbing the public's attention, the participation of female fighters in an organization can increase the public's sympathy for the group and its cause and may increase the amount of support the group receives from international organizations (Wood 2019). Research also suggests that women's successful missions can encourage men to do the same—if women can do it, men might reason, then they are just as capable, if not more (Berko & Erez 2007; Hasso 2005). Women's participation in political violence can therefore generate even greater participation among men.

Due to the value of female members, terrorist groups utilize several methods of recruitment. These include ideological appeal, internet-based recruiting tactics (e.g., social media and chat rooms where men may form relationships with women), and coercion—both physical and emotional (Bhattacharya 2019). Ideologically, women tend to have greater representation in left-wing terrorist groups than right-wing ones due to their emphasis on equality as well as increased opportunities for leadership roles within the organizations (Cunningham 2003; Henshaw et al. 2019; Wood 2019). Groups such as the PKK have been recognized for promoting gender equality to an extent that may generate change in the greater patriarchal Kurdish society (Haner et al. 2020). These groups may provide women with opportunities to experience gender equality, to hold roles and responsibilities they could not otherwise access.

In contrast to the pull quality of progressive ideology, terrorist groups also engage in coercive recruiting measures. Blackmail, **forced marriage**, sexual servitude, and other methods of forced recruitment are frequently used to make women participate in terrorist groups (Raghavan & Balasubramaniyan 2014). ISIS in Syria and Iraq, Boko Haram and al-Shabaab in Africa, the Lord's Resistance Army in Uganda, and the Communist Party of Nepal-Maoist in Nepal are notorious for targeting females for forced marriages (Darden 2019). In 2019, Human Rights Watch reported systematic rape, sexual slavery, and forced marriages of Yezidi women and girls by ISIS militants (Human Rights Watch 2019). These marriages not only served to bind members through indoctrination but also provided a means of recruiting new members through the children born from these unions. For example, Annan et al. (2009) found that the Lord's Resis-

FIGURE 5.6 Example of a female recruitment poster: Provisional Irish Republican Army (IRA), 1970s. *Source:* Reddit.

tance Army preferred to abduct younger girls because they were less likely to escape, more susceptible to indoctrination, and more likely to remain loyal to the LRA cause.

In sum, a host of both push and pull factors influence women's participation in terrorism. Terrorist groups' use of coercion, deliberate recruiting tactics that target women, structural factors related to gender inequality, and the perception that involvement in terrorism may alleviate the effects of life events and personal struggles to which women tend to be vulnerable all lead to engagement in political violence.

As Karla Cunningham (2003, 172) explains, women's participation in terrorism has been increasing due to a confluence of factors:

> Increasing contextual pressures (e.g., domestic/international enforcement, conflict, social dislocation) creates a mutually reinforcing process driving terrorist organizations to recruit women at the same time women's motivations to join these groups increases; contextual pressures impact societal controls over women thereby facilitating, if not necessitating, more overt political participation up to, and including, political violence.

5.4 NEGATIVE STEREOTYPES: THE ROLES OF WOMEN IN VIOLENT GROUPS

As noted, terrorist groups have often utilized stereotypes of women to achieve their goals. These gendered conceptions of women's engagement in violence, or lack thereof, have been reinforced in media accounts of women's roles in terrorist activities. Political scientist Brigitte Nacos (2005) likens the portrayal of female terrorists in the media to that of female politicians and identifies several frames that have been used to construct images of women in both legitimate and illegitimate (i.e., terrorist) political acts. For example, media reports of female terrorists tend to focus on their appearance and their familial connections to terrorism and describe their choices as acts of love, activities initiated to escape from boredom in their lives, or attempts to express gender equality—topics and motivations that would be unlikely to appear in reports about male terrorists. Nacos (2005) suggests that this misrepresentation by the media contributes to the success of terrorist groups' deliberate use of gender in missions. Public perception is influenced by the media, creating a disconnect between our understanding of women's involvement in terrorism and the roles that they actually serve (Cruise 2016).

Public perceptions of women's involvement in political violence have generally followed gendered notions of women's roles. Women are assumed to carry out auxiliary or less important functions in terrorist attacks (Cunningham 2003; Hearne 2009), and are frequently depicted as victims and innocent bystanders rather than perpetrators of violence (Weinberg & Eubank 2011). Consequently, their participation in terrorist organizations has not been regarded as a serious problem that merits policy considerations (Bigio & Vogelstein 2019a; Cunningham 2007; Jacques & Taylor 2008).

Although women's involvement in terrorist organizations might have followed traditional **gender roles** historically, with women serving supportive functions for their male counterparts by gathering intelligence and providing healthcare (Hearne 2009), beginning in the 1960s, women began to hold more active roles in notable terrorist groups (Cruise 2016). A small body of research on women's involvement in terrorist activities shows that the reality of women's participation is quite complex and often does not follow traditional notions of gender-appropriate behavior (Benson et. al 1982; Berko & Erez 2007; Bigio & Vogelstein 2019b; Bloom 2011a; Cruise 2016; Cunningham 2003; 2007; Dalton & Asal 2011; Jacques & Taylor 2009; Nacos 2005; Ness 2005; Margolin 2016; Parashar 2011; Raghavan & Balasubramaniyan 2014; Sutten 2009; White 2022; Von Knop 2007).

Importantly, this research has revealed that there is considerable variation in the roles that women play across different terrorist groups, reflecting in part the diversity of terrorist organizations. Terrorist groups may be characterized by a variety of motives, demands, organizational structures, and methods of operation (Ganor 2008). In some groups, women have a wide range of duties from the dissemination of propaganda to the execution of terrorist attacks; however, in other groups, women's duties are limited to providing logistical and moral support, and first aid to members (Berko & Erez 2007; Hearne 2009; Ness 2005; Sutten 2009).

For example, in leftist groups such as the Red Brigades of Italy and the Red Army Faction of Germany, women's work extended well beyond the traditional roles of housekeeping, caring for the sick and wounded, cooking, or running errands (Benson et al. 1982; Hearne 2009; Martin 2014; Raghavan & Balasubramaniyan 2014). Women in these

FIGURE 5.7 Ulrike Meinhof (left) and Gudrun Ensslin (right) were the leaders of the Red Army Faction, popularly known as the Baader–Meinhof Gang. *Source:* Permission granted by Werner Meinhof's granddaughter, Bettina Röhl, copyrighted free use, via Wikimedia Commons; and dpa picture alliance/Alamy Stock Photo.

groups became key figures in almost every aspect of the group's terrorist activities and advanced to important leadership positions (Sutten 2009).

In other organizations, however, women are often assigned secondary roles with duties dictated by tradition-bound patriarchal social systems (Margolin 2016). For example, in Palestinian terrorist organizations, women are not allowed to rise into important leadership positions (Sutten 2009). The term "female terrorist" must be used with caution, because its meaning can vary considerably depending on the context.

In a recent analysis of data on women's roles in nonstate armed groups from 1979 to 2009, Henshaw and colleagues (2019) identify having a leftist ideology as the strongest predictor of the inclusion of women in leadership positions. Left-wing groups that fight for social change tend to be more attractive to women and provide greater opportunities for active participation and a better quality of life. Women in these groups may serve various roles ranging from those of support to warrior (fighting in battle) to warrior leader (actively involved in group leadership). In contrast, groups that identify strictly with religious or cultural norms or do not seek to instigate change in society itself tend to be less likely to permit women to serve in roles in which they would not be able to engage in the larger society. Women's roles in these organizations are often limited to support functions, or sometimes gathering intelligence (Davis 2017; Jaques & Taylor 2009).

Despite the tendency of conservative groups to adhere to traditional gender roles, research has demonstrated that the roles women play in terrorist groups, even in strictly patriarchal societies, can evolve over time. For example, during the Algerian uprising against the French, women's involvement in the National Liberation Front (FLN) changed from being confined to the mountains, caring for guerrillas, to being permitted to deliver explosives or weapons to men at the scene of an attack (Benson et al. 1982). Similarly, in the Liberation Tigers of Tamil Eelam, women began participating in support roles but from the mid-1980s onward were involved as fighters, ultimately being recognized among the most experienced members (Allison 2003). Even in religious fundamentalist groups such as the Islamic Revival Movement (Hamas) of Palestine, women have been employed as skilled operatives (Bloom 2011b).

In an analysis of the research on female participation in major terrorist organizations, Raghavan and Balasubramaniyan (2014) clearly illustrate the changing roles that women have played. Prior to the 1980s women often performed only supportive functions, which were consistent with traditional gender roles. As time passed, frequently due to external pressures and the changing needs of the group, women took on more active roles, even in the more traditionally conservative groups. Table 5.2 is adapted from the study and shows the evolution of women's roles in different terrorist organizations.

TABLE 5.2   Examples of the Changing Roles of Women in Major Terrorist Groups

Name	Country	Ideology	Original Role	Later Roles
Fatah	Palestine	Religious	Logistics Recruitment	Suicide bombing
ETA	Spain	Nationalist	Logistics Administration Front-line roles	More prominent front-line roles
FARC	Columbia	Marxist-Leninist	Front-line roles	Intelligence gathering Operational roles Access to leadership positions
LTTE	Sri Lanka	Nationalist	Logistics	Front-line roles Suicide bombing Access to leadership positions
FLN	Algeria	Nationalist	Logistics	Operational roles
PKK	Turkey	Nationalist	Logistics	Operational roles Suicide bombing Recruitment Access to leadership positions
HAMAS	Palestine	Religious	Logistics Recruitment	Suicide bombing
Black Widows	Russia	Nationalist	Logistics	Operational roles Suicide bombing
al-Qaeda	Afghanistan & Iraq	Religious	Logistics Child-bearing Education Facilitators	Suicide bombing
ISIS	Middle East	Religious	Child-bearing Education Logistics	Operational roles Suicide bombing

Source: Adapted from Raghavan & Balasubramaniyan (2014).

5.5 INTRODUCTION TO THE CASE STUDIES

Overall, the existing research on women's roles in terrorist groups illustrates that female terrorism takes various forms that depend on social and cultural factors as well as organizational contexts. In the sections that follow, we present five case studies that provide further insight into women's participation in terrorism. We selected these particular case studies because they depict the diversity of women's involvement and experiences in terrorism and political violence. Each case connects with the themes of gender equality, women's roles in terrorist groups, and the framing of women's violent behaviors.

5.5.1 Case Study 1: Behind the Veil: The Evolving Role of Women in the Islamic State of Iraq and Syria

Women played a key role in the rise of the one of the most feared and deadly contemporary terrorist organizations, the **Islamic State of Iraq and Syria (ISIS)**. During the past decade ISIS achieved control of an area the size of the United Kingdom, committed mass atrocities, and launched terror attacks all over the world. Thousands of Muslims, mostly from the Middle East and Europe, flocked to join the group. By 2016, ISIS recruited around 43,000 fighters from 130 countries to the so-called caliphate in Iraq and Syria (Cruickshank 2017; Radicalization Awareness Network 2017; Speckhard & Ellenberg 2020). The group not only called for fighters but also for doctors, engineers, and regular citizens, including women and children. By 2019, experts estimate that adult females represented approximately 16 percent of the foreigners who traveled to Iraq and Syria to join the IS (Vale 2019). The Western media, government officials, and academics have called the thousands of women and girls who joined ISIS "jihadi brides," implying they were motivated by love or marriage with male fighters (Jackson 2021; Jacoby 2015; Martini 2018; Milton & Dodwell 2018). In one particular case of a wife of an ISIS fighter, who was repatriated to Germany in 2019, German journalist Claudia Dantschke stated:

> We believe that the woman mainly travelled to Syria out of love for her partner and not because she is deeply immersed in Islamist ideology. (Oltermann 2019)

Despite this mainstream perception that women are naïve, passive followers rather than active supporters, many academics discovered that female participation in ISIS was driven by a complex combination of factors, both personal and structural. Factors such as social exclusion, the appeal of sisterhood, female empowerment, ideological commitment to the group's teachings, revenge for past atrocities, experiences of discrimination, the desire to be part of something big, marriage, and love have all been found to affect women's participation in ISIS (Vale 2019).

In ISIS, women's roles have varied significantly and they were crucial to the initial success of the Islamic State's caliphate (Margolin 2019). Foreign women who joined the group from the United States and Europe played significant roles in the recruitment of female fighters online by spreading radical propaganda of the group and by fundraising for the caliphate (Darden 2019). They have been active in various jihadist platforms on social media and convinced several women and teenage girls to join ISIS and marry its members (Ozeren et al. 2018; Radicalization Awareness Network 2022).

Women have been deployed as foot soldiers and have executed terrorist operations planned by ISIS. For example, in 2016, a group of women radicalized by ISIS propaganda were arrested with gas cylinders and bomb-making materials. Investigations revealed that they were plotting to attack the Gare de Lyon train station in Paris (Chrisafis 2016). Similarly, in 2019, a female member of the Abu Sayyaf Group (which has pledged allegiance to ISIS) participated in a bombing with her husband at a cathedral in Jolo, Philippines, killing over 20 individuals Al-Jazeera 2021. ISIS women have served in the all-female religious police force (**Al-Khansaa Brigade**) and monitored women in the ISIS territories to make sure that they adhered to groups' rules and guidelines (such as dress code for women) by punishing the violators (Khelghat-Doost 2017). Some, on the other hand, played traditional roles as mothers, wives, and educators of the next generation of the Islamic State. They also served as nurses and caretakers to help the wounded members of the group (Davis 2017).

Notably, research indicates that the more active roles of women in ISIS that we see today have evolved over time (Biswas & Deylami 2019). Whereas the women in ISIS ranks started out primarily in subordinate supporting roles, over time, in response to changing strategic conditions, they assumed greater equality with men (Gan et al. 2019). During the rise of the group, women were not allowed to take part in military missions. ISIS leaders ordered that women stay at home, take care of children, and raise as many children as possible for the caliphate. In its official magazine, *Dabiq*, ISIS declared that the essential role of women was to build the caliphate by being a wife and the bearer of the next generation of jihadists rather than fighting at the front lines (Margolin 2019).

While ISIS also allowed women to serve in its online propaganda and recruitment strategies, the role of women in ISIS was still largely domestic in nature. Women had to adhere to strict conservative gender norms in ISIS territories. For example, women were required to follow the group's clothing policy, and they were prohibited from interacting with men who were not their close relatives. Their mobility was highly restricted (Spencer 2016). All but the few women who were fulfilling educational and medical roles were ordered to stay in their homes. These rules were strictly enforced by the Al-Khansaa Brigade. Reports indicate that several women and girls have been tortured and killed by these "morality police" simply because they did not follow the rules of clothing or public behavior (Human Rights Watch 2016; Kafanov 2016).

However, as the group suffered increasing military and territorial losses in 2015, ISIS became willing to place women in front-line roles and urged them to prepare for jihad, as the women of Iraq and Chechnya did in the past (Winter & Margolin 2017). In 2016, ISIS established an all-female sniper team, and women began to appear in various battles, fighting alongside the men. In 2017, the ISIS online magazine *Rumiya* published a manifesto telling all of the women of ISIS to take up arms. By then, serving on the military fronts had become an obligation.

For many, the group's shift from a very strict gender hierarchy to forcing women's participation in military roles may be interpreted as a response of necessity or desperation. To replenish its fighting force, ISIS was simply citing inadequate resources to encourage women to take up arms. This shift in roles illustrates that even terrorist organizations with strict gender restrictive ideologies can override their teachings and rules under external pressure. In other words, the change in women's engagement from supportive roles to participation in actual combat was just a tactical advantage for the group.

The Issue of Returnees

During the last decade, as ISIS has lost many of its territories and most of its male fighters (including its leader) have been killed or arrested, hundreds of women who were once married to these Islamic State militants, often with children, are seeking to return to their home countries in the West, including the United States. Several nations far from the battlefield face an increasingly urgent challenge: what to do with the children and wives of foreign fighters who were captured or killed (Eriksson 2024).

Many European countries (as well as the US and Australia) generally rejected responsibility for the women and children detained in the closed confines of camps in Syria and Iraq (Cook & Vale 2019). For example, a young British woman, Shamima Begum, who left the UK in 2015 at the age of 15, married an ISIS fighter, and spent four years with the group, was denied re-entry into England. British authorities stripped her of her citizenship and declared that Begum would never be allowed to return to England (Pylas 2024).

Similarly, Hoda Muthana, a young woman in her early twenties who was born in New Jersey and left the United States in 2014 to marry a jihadist and join ISIS, was denied reentry into the US to rejoin her family in Alabama (Laughland 2023). In 2019, President Trump said that he had directed the State Department to refuse the return of Muthana into the US (Morin 2019).

Some argue that the ISIS women who are detained in the camps are the women who truly believed in ISIS's ideology, and therefore they are the group's strongest supporters. Following this logic, there is a potential that they can be used as the group's next generation of fighters, facilitators, martyrs, and sources of income if they are brought back to Western countries. There is also the potential risk that once repatriated, these women can recruit new members by spreading extremist ideology, as Western women were especially active in the online recruitment activities of ISIS (Hassan 2021). Another major concern mentioned by policymakers was that these women would raise their children (who were fathered by members of ISIS) as soldiers, to launch an attack someday in the future (Weine 2019). They strictly reject the idea of **repatriation**, and if repatriation is necessary, argue that these women and children should be treated as a significant terrorist threat (Hoffman & Furlan 2020).

On the other hand, others view the matter of bringing back mothers and children as a humanitarian issue. These people, who are often called **new humanitarians**, not only support the repatriation of these women and children into their home countries, but also argue that the children and their mothers should be regarded as victims (even though some were taught extremist ideology and received military training) and provided with extensive social and psychological assistance (Weine 2019).

According to them, theologians should also work with the mothers and children to provide

FIGURE 5.8 Examples of public comments on an article published at *Washington Post* titled "How ISIS women and their children are being left stranded in the desert," December 23, 2019.

rehabilitation that focuses on the re-education of moderate religious texts to protect them from falling prey to extremism and violence in the future. For example, Elena Pokalova (2019) from the National Defense University in Washington, DC, opposes the idea of leaving these people behind at the detention camps in Syria because ISIS can radicalize them and make them even more dangerous in the future. If they are left behind, these widows—many with children and no sources of income, living under terrible conditions—will have no choice but to turn back to ISIS in order to survive.

Between 2019 and 2023, at least 38 countries have repatriated approximately 7,000 of their citizens (Asetta 2023). However, a March 2024 report from the United Nations Human Rights Council reveals that despite ISIS's complete defeat, over 44,000 women and children still remain unlawfully detained in al-Hawl and Roj camps in Kurdish-controlled parts of Syria due to their alleged links to ISIS (United Nations Human Rights Council 2024). Independent human rights experts and international organizations report that these camps are plagued by insecurity and violent incidents, including murder, assault, and sexual abuse (Eriksson 2024).

5.5.2 Case Study 2: The Women of the Kurdistan Workers' Party (PKK)—The Rise of Feminism

Women have been integral to the success and long-term maintenance of the **Kurdistan Workers' Party (PKK)**. Even though the PKK is situated in a traditional and deeply paternalistic society, women in the PKK are not as constrained by the patriarchal hegemony that typifies the experiences of women involved in other nationalistic or religious struggles in the Middle East (see Berko & Erez 2007; Haner et al. 2020). Indeed, because of the ideology on which it was founded, the PKK may be unique among the armed organizations located in the region in terms of the roles that women play. While there is no reliable information on the exact numbers, it is estimated that at the time of writing, around 40–50 percent of the PKK cadre (approximately 25,000 personnel) is composed of female fighters (Foreign Affairs 2015; Khezri 2018). In this specific geographic region, such a high rate of female participation in a militant political organization is unusual.

As a group founded within a patriarchal and Kurdish religious culture, the PKK might well have

FIGURE 5.9 Western media has often highlighted the remarkable resilience and contributions of Kurdish women and freedom fighters in the battle against ISIS (Islamic State of Iraq and Syria) in the Middle East. While Western media has highlighted the resilience of Kurdish women and freedom fighters, it's crucial to remember that the conflict in the region has been multifaceted, with various actors and complexities. *Source:* Kurdishstruggle, CC BY 2.0, via Wikimedia Commons.

been informed by those values, which would have resulted in a subordinate role for women. In the 1970s—but even today, especially in rural areas—Kurdish women were subjected to genital mutilation, child marriages, and honor killings (Khezri 2018; Kurdish Women in Culture, 2018). But a different contingency has shaped the organization's culture and gender relationships. Emerging in the mid-1970s in the shadow of groups such as the Palestinian Liberation Organization (PLO), the PKK embraced Marxist-Leninist ideology and trained its recruits in the teachings of Mao Zedong and other revolutionary groups in Russia, China, and Vietnam (McDowall 2000). Its most influential leader is Abdullah Öcalan, popularly known as Apo. Apo rejected the traditional systems of authority and gender restrictions to forge a new Kurdish identity (White 2000). Although imprisoned for the past two decades, he has continued to write about the centrality of gender equality to Kurdish nationalism (see Öcalan 2013). Öcalan's (2013) vision for gender equality is summarized passionately in his book *Liberating*

FIGURE 5.10 Abdullah Öcalan is a highly controversial and polarizing figure, and opinions about him are deeply divided. The controversy surrounding Abdullah Öcalan reflects the complex nature of the Kurdish issue in Turkey and the broader region. It's important to acknowledge that perspectives on Öcalan are often shaped by political, cultural, and historical factors, and discussions about him are deeply sensitive and emotionally charged for many individuals and communities. *Source:* Halil Uysal, CC BY-SA 3.0, via Wikimedia Commons.

Life: Women's Revolution. According to Öcalan, true freedom and liberation in life are "impossible without a radical women's revolution which would change man's mentality and life" (Ocalan 2013, 51). Society's social problems, he claims, will only be solved by "a movement for women's freedom, equality, and democracy" (56). And the consequences of a true revolution are profound, for "the level of women's freedom and equality determines the freedom and equality of all sections of society" (57).

The PKK has managed to transcend the historical and cultural constraints of its region and grant to its female members a level of equality they would likely never attain as civilians in Kurdistan (West 2015). This organizational characteristic may help explain some of the PKK's longevity and success, as it expands the talent pool that the organization has at its disposal.

The Ideology of Equality

Öcalan integrated ideas from Marx and Mao and challenged the existing social hierarchies that restricted women's freedom by applying gender inclusive policies to end discrimination against women. This included assigning women to positions of authority and leadership, establishing women's own military units, prohibiting domestic and sexual violence, and banning forced marriage. The PKK cadre, especially men, complete an intensive ideological training to become socialized with these new basic values and goals of the organization.

This ideology soon became central to the trainings of the PKK members and affected various aspects of life in the PKK, including how women are viewed and the role they play. This facilitated social integration and provided high participation rates from Kurdish women. In the PKK, Kurdish women discovered that they were able to challenge the cultural and traditional prescriptions ascribed to them in the society (e.g., childbirth, caregiving, and other domestic duties). The PKK not only offered women an opportunity to defy the patriarchal and gender hierarchies, but it also enabled them to obtain (informal) schooling and training, and then fill positions of authority in the group's political and military wings. This educational attainment and participation in activities (which were traditionally reserved for men) served as a precursor to increasing numbers of Kurdish female recruits into the PKK cadres.

The great importance given by the PKK leadership to fostering gender equality and the greater socialization and interaction between men and women in the group eventually changed the beliefs (stereotypes) of men about women's ability to participate in nontraditional roles and increased their willingness to accept female militants as their equals in carrying out tasks and duties and filling positions of responsibility and authority. Respect for women increased as they became more active in important missions, such as raids, attacks, and ambushes. Affirmative action was used to further increase their status—special rules were brought into action regarding the appointment of women into important leadership positions, new codes of behaviors were developed on the treatment of women, and auxiliary roles and duties once filled only by women were eventually assigned to men so that women could focus on professional development activities.

Even though the appeal of the PKK to women originated from the rights granted to them, it is important to note that the notion of equality extended into every aspect of life, including punishment and the division of labor. Women are treated the same as men in these matters. Male and female recruits who violate the codes of the organization are subjected to the same consequences. In the same way, the division of labor recognized no gender. Women in the PKK are required to do the same tasks as men.

These findings are consistent with the recent scholarship emerging in political science and political sociology, especially in studies on women's participation in Latin American rebellions in 1970s and 1980s. Several other researchers also discovered that organizations that espouse Marxist-Leninist and egalitarian ideologies are more likely to recruit female combatants than other groups such as those guided by Islamist and nationalist ideologies (Israelsen 2018; Thomas & Bond 2015; Wood & Thomas 2017). Thomas and Bond's (2015) analysis of data on women's combat participation in rebel movements from 1979 to 2009 indicated that expressing an egalitarian gender ideology is the largest determinant of women's participation in violent political organizations. More specifically, the Farabundo Martí National Liberation Front in El Salvador (FMLN), the Sandinistas in Nicaragua, and Zapatista Army of National Liberation of Mexico (EZLN) all benefitted from increased levels of female recruitment by changing long-established gender norms and creating new opportunities for women to engage in social and political life (Kampwirth 2002; Luciak 2001; Mason 1992; Reif 1986; Thomas & Wood 2018; Viterna 2013).

Is Gender Equality the Sole Motivation?

The promise of equality is an important reason why women join the PKK. Women are typically motivated by the desire to achieve gender equity and improve their status in society (where the traditional values dictate gender inequality and view women primarily as homemakers and child-bearers). This insight is echoed by Meral Düzgün (2016, 284), who observes that Kurdish women join the fighting ranks "because they offer a possibility of achieving freedom and equality . . . Many Kurdish women demand gender justice."

Still, it is important to highlight that the motivations of women for participating in insurgencies are complex and the issue of the female empowerment is often multifaceted and nuanced. As Viterna (2006, 2) notes, even within the same structural contexts, there may be "multiple, conjuncturel causes of mobilization" that arise from individual-level biography, networks, and situational context.

As explained in the previous sections, the literature on women in terrorism suggests that their participation in violence can be shaped by a variety of contributing factors at the individual and collective levels, rather than being driven only by an explicit feminist agenda (Ali 2006; Alison 2003; Blee 1991; Dalton & Asal 2011; Herrera & Porch 2008; Jacques & Taylor 2009; MacDonald 1991; Margolin 2016; Ness 2005; O'Rourke 2008; Reif 1986; Schweitzer 2006; Speckhard & Akhmedova 2006; Victor 2003; Wang 2011). As in the case of the women of PKK, factors such as depression, personal tragedy, peer pressure, coercion, commitment to an ideological cause, a desire to improve social status, familial connections, desire to avenge personal suffering or loss of a significant other, opposition to perceived oppression, and a desire for national independence have all served as important considerations affecting Kurdish women's participation in the PKK. For example, Bejan Matur, an author and columnist who interviewed PKK members in Kandil Mountain for her book *Looking Beyond the Mountain*, found that even though the Kurdish women often cited gender equality as their main motivation for joining the PKK, several other factors were also at play. These included such experiences as witnessing loved ones being imprisoned or killed by the security forces, being prohibited from speaking their own language, and wanting to escape from forced marriages (Matur 2011).

Training and Fighting

In the PKK, women and men are required to complete the same curricula for both political and practical military training. Training is usually held in mixed-gender classrooms, and guerillas are not segregated except when covering a few certain topics (e.g., women's history, gynecology, gender constructs) that are unique to women (which we will return to later). In general, the PKK provides women a level of training and combat experience that is equivalent with that of men. This equality of opportunity separates the PKK from other terrorist groups (e.g., Palestinian groups such as Al-Aqsa Martyrs Brigades, Palestinian Islamic Jihad, Hamas, The Fatah, and Tamil women in Sri Lanka) in which women are recruited or sometimes forced to participate and then trained to surprise the enemy with new forms of combat tactics, which are often suicide missions (Beyler 2006; Bloom 2007; Israeli Ministry of Foreign Affairs 2002; Ness 2005; Page 2004; Von Knop 2007).

Besides mixed-gender training, female guerillas are required to participate in classes that are limited to them. In these lessons, women are given lectures by female instructors on gender constructs, sexuality, identity, diversity of women's lives, and the existing social and institutional power structures that represent inequality between the genders. They are lectured on the lived experiences of revolutionary women and the key figures in the struggle for women's rights so that they become familiar with the leadership roles that women have played in history. Through this training, women are able to deconstruct the stereotypes associated with being female (e.g., that women are weak and should submit to patriarchy) and are also encouraged to assume key positions in the organization (Haner et al. 2020).

In sum, women in the PKK are trained to assume leadership positions and given important roles in the planning and execution of guerilla missions. Unlike many other groups in the Middle East, they are not recruited because of the tactical advantages that they bring as perpetrators of violence (e.g., because they are less likely to arouse suspicion, able to conceal bombs under their clothing or by appearing pregnant).

Notably, the impact of Kurdish female fighters in Syria has been chronicled by *New York Times* reporter Rod Nordland (2018) in "Women Are Free, and Armed, in Kurdish-Controlled Northern Syria." Nordland explains that in this region, the Kurds govern and are a prime force, supported by the United States, in combating ISIS. The Kurds employ all-women fighting units called Women's Protections Units, or the YPJ. It is instructive that when the Syrian Democratic Forces captured Raqqa from ISIS, "the overall commander was a YPJ woman, Rojda Felat" (Nordland 2018; see also Khezri 2018). As one commentator noted: "There are always men thinking that women are slaves, but when women are an armed force, men are scared of them" (quoted in Nordland 2018). More consequential, according to Nordland (2018), "the authority wielded by women here—in the police, the courts, and the militias—is patterned on the gender egalitarian philosophy of the Kurd's ideological leader, Abdullah Öcalan," whose "philosophy is widely popular among Kurds."

FIGURE 5.11 The PKK has placed significant importance on women's roles within its organization. Women have been actively involved in combat, leadership, and decision-making processes, challenging traditional gender roles and advocating for gender equality. This emphasis on women's participation is a distinctive feature of the PKK's ideology and has had a profound impact on the group's structure and operations. *Source:* Kurdish PKK Guerillas, CC BY 2.0, Via, Wikimedia Commons.

Leadership

Access to leadership positions for women is one of the most striking features of the PKK that separates it from the other terrorist groups. Women in the PKK have had a prominent role in the administration of the organization due to the insistence of its founders, especially Abdullah Öcalan.

Today, the PKK has a certain number of guaranteed seat allocations for women in all executive positions: in the Union of Kurdish Communities (KCK), the Headquarters Command Management (HPG), the Guerilla Parliament, and the Defense Committee. For example, similar to the Baader–Meinhof Group in Germany (1970–1998), the regulations of the PKK require the application of the cochair model for the highest administrative structure after President Apo, the KCK. According to this model, the KCK needs to appoint two leaders, a man and a woman, who are jointly in charge of the PKK and share equal leadership responsibilities on the governance and oversight of the organization. The PKK also requires women to serve as cochairs in committees, including those that concern appointment, nomination, investigation, discipline, promotion, and several others that are essential to the proper functioning of the organization. Women serve in the judicial committees and render verdicts in important cases. They play key roles during the assignment of guerillas to their duty stations. They serve as senior advisors and supervisors to men in various leadership positions (Haner et al. 2020).

Another significant step taken by the PKK to raise gender awareness in power structures is the right given to female guerillas to establish their own autonomous units within the organization. Women in the PKK have their own headquarters, administrative units, political branches, and even separate congressional meetings—all independent from the men's. Within this system, women are in charge of decisions and have their own decision-making processes regarding their own lives without the worry of male intervention (Haner et al. 2020).

Kurdish women within the PKK now have a strong foothold in the political, military, and administrative arena due to this autonomous power structure. The strategies implemented by senior executives not only narrowed down the gender leadership gap within the PKK, but also empowered women to be an independent source of power—which is able to transform the organization's military and political agendas. Again, this inclusiveness departs significantly from conceptions of gender roles in other armed groups in the Middle East such as al-Qaeda, ISIS, Boko Haram, and al-Shabaab (as well as some religious Palestinian groups) where women's activities are heavily dictated by the patriarchal hierarchy and where they are not allowed to become leaders or provide input into policy formation—and where many are prompted to carry out deadly suicide missions rather than be recruited as traditional fighters (Berko & Erez 2007; Cunningham 2003; 2007; Haner & Lee 2017; Margolin 2016; Myers 2004; Raghavan & Balasubramaniyan 2014; Weinberg & Eubank 2011).

5.5.3 Case Study 3: Chechen Black Widows

The **Black Widows** is the Russian nickname for the Chechen all-female battalion of suicide bombers dedicated to spreading terror in Russia. The history of the Black Widows dates back to 2000, when the first Chechen female suicide bombers (Khava Barayeva and Luisa Magomadova) drove a truck filled with explosives into a building, temporarily housing the Russian Special Forces in Chechnya. Since then, the Black Widows have been involved in more than 26 suicide attacks (Jamali 2017; Keating 2013; Speckhard & Akhmedova 2006), resulting in more than 900 casualties (Gillespie 2010; Speckhard &

Akhmedova 2007). Initiating bloody hostage-takings at schools and theaters, driving trucks filled with explosives, and blowing up planes and subway stations, the Black Widows' presence has made them the most feared militants in Russia, convincing Russians that there is no safe place in the country (Ward 2010).

The "Black Widow" Label

The nickname "Black Widow" highlights the loss of male relatives and the type of dress that these women wear. "Black" refers to the black traditional Muslim dress—the head-to-toe **niqāb**, which covers all parts of the body except for the eyes—worn by the Chechen women (Niyat 2005). The "widow" is used because it is widely believed that the group is composed of women who have lost their husbands, brothers, fathers, or other close relatives to the fight with Russians, and that they now seek revenge against their oppressors in the form of suicide attacks (Elder 2010; Jamali 2017).

Prior to the Chechen female fighters, the Black Widow label was used for women who killed their husbands or lovers or who were accused of serial murders. It was also used in the reporting of terrorist events that were committed by female perpetrators. For example, in 1994, British security officials referred to the Palestinian woman, Samar Alami, who bombed the Israeli Embassy in London as "the Black Widow" (Zimmer 2014).

However, with the 2002 Dubrovko theater incident, in which 18 Chechen females, each dressed in long black niqābs with explosives strapped to their bodies, threatened to blow up a theater in Moscow in the middle of a musical, the Russian and Western media began to use the term "Black Widows" for the group (Shaikh 2010; Stephen 2003; Zimmer 2014). The first usage of the name Black Widows appeared in the *London Daily Mail*: "Held by Black Widows: Faces Frozen in Fear, the Women Hostages Await Their Destiny" (Banner 2009). After the incident in which more than 130 civilians lost their lives, the Black Widows became known as grieving mothers or wives who are willing to sacrifice their lives as suicide bombers for the independence of Chechnya (Curry 2013).

Motivations of Chechen Female Suicide Bombers

Scholarly research has identified several historical, social, and political factors that inspire the Black Widows to engage in suicide attacks. Studies of the Chechen female **suicide terrorists** have found that many of them experienced serious personal trauma—many lost their men and had nothing left behind to care about. These women were then exposed to the recruitment efforts of jihadist groups (Keating 2013). For example, a 2006 study based on 45 interviews with family members, friends, or former hostages of 34 suicide bombers by psychologists Anne Speckhard and Khapta Akhmedova discovered that all individuals within their sample had experienced deep personal traumatization and then were attracted to radical groups to seek revenge. Their desire for revenge, combined with continuous harassment by Russian security officials after the death of their loved ones, facilitated their recruitment and training by radical Islamic extremists to carry out terrorist attacks (Kostro & Riba 2014). Many have also argued that the majority of these women were poorly educated, which made it easy for radical extremists to recruit them into their ranks.

However, the presentation of Black Widows solely as grieving mothers or wives is problematic in several ways. Importantly, the portrayal of women acting out of despair over the loss of the men in their lives implies that they lack agency and control of their own actions: in other words, that they do not engage in their own decision-making (Sjoberg & Gentry 2007). The idea that these women were drugged or zombified by male terrorists also implies that these women are subjugated and do not have control over their destiny. This view diminishes the recognition of the deep motivations that drive women militants into suicide terrorism. During an interview with BBC World Service, Mia Bloom, a well-known academic in the area of women and terrorism, argued that portraying the issue as a pure visceral reaction by women who were mourning to lash out was just a tactic used by Russians to downgrade the decades long conflict and undermine the political aspects of it (Porzucki, 2013). Bloom further argues that the women's motivations for engaging in terrorism are not necessarily different from those of men—they simply wanted to get the Russians out of their country.

It is correct that many women may have experienced the cruel execution of their relatives by Russian troops in Chechnya, but not all women who become suicide bombers have experienced this loss (Stephen 2003). When we look at the Chechen women who have been suicide bombers in the last two decades, it is clear that not all of them have been widows or have been married.

For example, Naida Asiyalova, the female suicide bomber who killed six and injured 37 in a bus attack in southern Russia, does not fit the common pattern attributed to Chechen female suicide bombers by the media and Russian official sources. Nadia had no apparent motive. She had lived and studied in Moscow for years, worked in good jobs, and did not lose any of her relatives to the fight with the Russians (Keating 2013). Her suicide mission was not an act of revenge for the loss of her home, property, relatives, or dignity. She was not an instrument of controlling men and had not been manipulated by extremists due to a state of emotional weakness (Yuzik 2013). Nadia had become a suicide bomber because she saw few alternatives for pursuing justice, had no trust in the Russian government, and wanted to achieve her goals through violent means.

Calling these women Black Widows is misleading because this label not only obscures Chechen women's motivations but also makes the experiences of the Chechen people invisible (Zimmer 2014). To understand these female suicide bombers, we need to look at the tragic history of the region because the answer to female participation in suicide terrorism lies in Russia's historic mistreatment of the Chechen people (Jamali 2017).

The origin of the problem goes back to the Stalin era and the fall of the Soviet Republic in the early 1990s (Shaikh 2010). During the 1940s, thousands of Chechens, who were forcibly displaced to Siberia, died in harsh living conditions (Pohl 2002). In the 1960s, when they were allowed to return to Chechnya, they found that their homes and jobs had been taken by Russian settlers, and they were treated as second-class citizens. After the fall of the Soviet Union, Chechens waged two uprisings for their independence, one in 1994 and another one in 1999 (Curry 2013). Even though they were partly successful in 1994, Russia invaded Chechnya that winter and destroyed the capital, Grozny, with bombardments at a scale that had not been seen since World War II. Thousands were killed; hundreds of thousands were forced to leave their homes to shelter in the Caucasus Mountains.

Upon invasion, the Russian officials carried out cleansing operations (*zachistkas*) all over Chechnya to capture the Chechen rebels. Heavy brutal tactics were used against the civilian population, including women, to flush out the rebels. Thousands of men were caught, sent to filtration camps, and faced heavy torture and execution. Arrest, torture,

FIGURE 5.12 Russian troops burying corpses in a trench in Chechnya during the Second Chechen War. *Source:* Natalia Medvedeva, CC BY-SA 3.0, via Wikimedia Commons.

and disappearance had become a common experience for young male Chechens (The Economist 2003). The majority of the men who entered these camps were never seen again. Some were later found with hands and faces cut off in garbage dumps and mass graves (Williams 2014). Agence France-Presse (2008) reported that 57 mass graves of Chechens were found during postwar reconstruction projects.

In the second Chechen uprising, torture, humiliation, and sexual violence became part of the daily life in Chechnya. The extent of sexual violence among women was so great that the saying "It is better to have a dead daughter than a sullied one" had become commonplace (Ward 2010). Yusik (2007) notes that "daughters and sisters who have experienced shame or trauma in war are often sent away to relatives and many times not heard from again." Russian security forces had targeted the women in a way that had not been seen anywhere else in the world. Reports state that women were sexually abused by the security forces, kept for weeks under custody, and then returned to their families in exchange for large bribes. The security forces were also allowed to strip search women who were wearing traditional clothes, requiring them to be fully naked, which humiliated and pushed these women to their limits (Rousseva, 2004).

This trauma—the extreme human rights violations combined with the grief of losing close family members in air raids, bombings, and cleansing operations—plus a desire for national independence, led to feelings of anger, grief, and eventually action (Ward 2010). It was in this context that the Chechen women began to deploy themselves as what Russians called "living bombs" (Williams 2014). The deadly suicide attacks were followed by other suicide attacks on military and soft civilian targets, blowing up buses, planes, trains, underground stations, schools, and public entertainment avenues such as theaters (Williams 2014).

The most publicized of these attacks was the Dubrovka theater siege, which occurred on October 23, 2002. Approximately 1,000 civilians, including audience members and actors, were held hostage for 57 hours (Ward 2010). The Black Widows, who made up roughly half of the attacking group, demanded that the Russian government withdraw all of its troops from Chechnya and stop the human rights abuses. Rejecting their offer, the Russian security forces pumped lethal gas into the theater that knocked everyone unconscious in order to prevent the Black Widows from setting off the bombs on their bodies. The incident ended in tragedy, however, as 129 civilians lost their lives inhaling the gas.

Political Framing of Female Suicide Bombings

Russian officials insisted that the use of women in suicide bombings was purely a religious phenomenon, indicating ties between Chechen fighters and fundamentalist Saudi terrorists worldwide (Stephen 2003). According to them, the increasing engagement of women as suicide bombers was clear evidence of the "Palestinization" of the Chechen conflict with the presence of radical Islamists (Alvanou, 2008). They argued that the women were simply brainwashed to engage in suicide terrorism by the ideology of the extremism. This was a false logic as women in several other secular groups, such as Tamil Tigers in Sri Lanka and the Kurdish Workers' party (PKK), had also used this tactic.

The Russian state propaganda went further by portraying the women militants as pawns of the male terrorists, arguing that Islamic extremists had used psychotropic drugs to coerce the Chechen women into becoming suicide bombers. For example, sociologist Francine Banner (2009) presents claims by the media and Russian officials that Chechen rebels targeted women who have lost their husbands and brothers and simply confused and brainwashed them to become willing to kill themselves in revenge. President Putin's senior advisor, Sergei Yastrzhemsbky, issued a press release telling the world that the girls had been raped and then forced into participating in suicide missions due to the fear of bringing shame on their families: "I have heard that they rape these women and record the rapes on video. After that, such Chechen girls have no chance at all of resuming a normal life in Chechnya. They have only one option: to blow themselves up with a bomb full of nails and ball bearings" (Banner 2009).

The emergence of female suicide bombers in a highly paternalistic society (in which women were not allowed to take combat roles previously) is a serious departure from Chechen cultural norms. The women's participation as suicide bombers does not suggest gender equality, as no Chechen females have played significant leadership roles in their originations (Speckhard & Akhmedova 2007). As several scholars stated, this was just an asymmetric strike against the powerful Russian military. With the introduction of women into suicide terrorism, the outgunned Chechens had acquired a new guerilla tactic that could inflict pain on the enemy targets. Many women appeared to volunteer for suicide bombing not for revenge or because of a specific trauma, but to be a part of a larger organization working to get Russians out of Chechnya.

In these circumstances, suicide bombing was the most effective way of carrying out a terrorist attack—a single mission with many victims that has a traumatizing impact on the Russian public and gains the attention of media outlets around the world (Abdullaev 2013; Keating 2013; Yuzik 2013). The strategy had proved itself as a powerful and tactically successful weapon because immediately after each attack, Russian people confined themselves to their homes, avoided outside entertainment activities, and refused to travel on planes if there were veiled female passengers (Abdullaev 2013; Elder 2010; Kostro & Riba 2014).

Speckhard and Akhmedova (2006) found no evidence to support the Kremlin's claims—that the Black Widows were the victims of rape and molestation or that they had been brainwashed or drugged into suicide missions by religious fanatics. As human rights groups repeatedly reported, this was a problem of Russia's own making (Osborn 2010). The Chechen women suicide bombers were just one manifestation of a population which had gone through collective trauma. The West and the media, solely focusing on the depiction of the terrorists, had ignored the background realities of life in Chechnya. As indicated by Professor of Islamic History, Brian Glyn Williams, "Black Widows are victims who are transformed into victimizers" (Williams 2014).

5.5.4 Case Study 4: Gudrun Ensslin and Ulrike Meinhof—The Red Army Faction

The **Red Army Faction (Rote Armee Fraktion, or RAF)**, popularly known as the Baader–Meinhof Gang, was a West German far-left militant organization founded in the late 1960s (Horchem 1974; Stuchbery 2019). Its origins go back to German university protests of the 1960s, where the United States was viewed as an imperialist power and the West German capitalist establishment as the reincarnation of Nazi Germany (Jenkins 1998). During this era, radical student groups in West Germany condemned the US involvement in the Vietnam War and organized a large campaign against the use of nuclear weapons with violent protests (Schenck 2006).

The group was formed as a radical socialist and revolutionary organization and engaged in a wide variety of terrorist activities (BBC 2016; Dugdale-Pointon 2007a). Their primary targets were the US military establishments in Germany and the business places of West German corporations. While bank robberies were carried out to fund the groups' military activities, US soldiers and German police were also targeted for killings, as they were representatives of the so-called corrupt system (Stuchbery 2019). The RAF launched massive bomb attacks against the headquarters of the Fifth US Army Corps in Frankfurt and the US Army European Headquarters in Heidelberg, killing four US soldiers and wounding more than 20 as a demonstration of support for the "liberation struggle of the Vietnamese people" (Horchem 1974).

The group also engaged in kidnappings, murder, and assassinations of the prominent financial, political, and governmental figures in West Germany, planted bombs at police stations, and hijacked two airplanes (Graham 2002). It is estimated that at least 40 people, including prominent industrialists, government officials, and businessmen, were killed in RAF attacks (Deutsche Welle 2006).

The group members opposed fascist tendencies not only in Germany but also in other Western European states. Even though the group started with only 25 members, their ultimate goal was to spark a mass revolutionary movement led by the working class, which would topple the existing government structures in the Federal Republic of Germany, where former Nazi officials enjoyed prominent roles (BBC 2016). To achieve this goal, they set out to establish an urban guerilla force similar to Black Panthers of the United States and the Tupamaros of Latin America (Schenck 2006).

For them, the concept of urban guerilla was far from the definition

FIGURE 5.13   Logo of the 1970s German underground terrorist organization Red Army Faction (RAF): a red star (similar to that of the Red Army of the Soviet Union) and a submachine gun Heckler & Koch MP5. *Source:* Ratatosk, Public domain, via Wikimedia Commons.

of terrorism. Ulrike Meinhof, who has been characterized as the brain of the group, explained the difference between terrorism and the guerilla movement:

> Terrorism is the destruction of utilities such as dykes, waterworks, hospitals, power stations. All the targets at which the American bomb attacks in North Vietnam were systemically aimed from 1965 onwards. Terrorism operates amidst fear of the masses. The city guerilla movement, on the other hand, carries fear into the machinery of the state . . . The actions of the guerillas are never, never directed against people. They are always directed against the imperialist machine. The urban guerilla fights the terrorism of the state. (Holmes 2002, 26)

It is estimated that approximately one quarter of West Germany and the majority of the West German political left expressed sympathy and support for the group during its initial years. However, the group lost much of their support as its tactics became more violent (Jenkins 1998). Propaganda created by mainstream media outlets and government officials denounced the RAF members as murderous nihilists who had no real political goals in the creation of dangerous propaganda by the (Stuchbery 2019).

The RAF formally dissolved itself with a five-page-long manifesto sent to Reuters news agency on April 20, 1998 (Graham 2002; Stuchbery 2019). The letter read: "Nearly 28 years ago, on May 14, 1970, the RAF was born in a liberation action. Today, we end this project. The urban guerilla battle of the RAF is now history" (Gambetta 2010).

Women of the RAF
The RAF cadres involved a disproportionately large number of women (Bielby 2006). Two of the three most influential members of the RAF fulfilling leadership roles were women: Ulrike Meinhof and Gudrun Ennslin (Schenck 2006).

Ulrike Meinhof was known as the most influential thinker of the German left in the 1960s. She was the younger of two sisters from a middle-class family. Her father was an art historian, and her mother was a schoolteacher. After losing both of her parents to cancer at a relatively young age, Meinhof and her sister were raised by Renate Riemeck, a well-known historian and a peace activist (Williams 2016). It is believed that the young Meinhof was strongly influenced by the political attitudes of her foster mother (Horchem 1974).

Meinhof was recognized as an extremely talented and intelligent student by her teachers during her early school years. Later, she would obtain one of the most prestigious scholarships in Germany, the Study Foundation of Germany, to study educational science and psychology. During her university education, Meinhof joined the German Socialist Student Union and she took part in anti-nuclear weapon and anti-rearmament protests (Dugdale-Pointon 2007b; Horchem 1974). In 1956, she began to work for *Konkret*, a radical leftist political magazine funded by the East German Communist party, and became its chief editor in 1960. At the same time, she worked as the editor of the *Das Argument*, a magazine that published articles on German rearmament and the world peace (Gless 2020).

During her time at *Konkret*, Meinhof became publicly known in Germany and gained a reputation for being a critically minded journalist, mainly because of her writings on social problems, including gender inequality and foreign workers. Her writings, increasingly radical in political tone, became famed in Germany (Williams 2016). *Der Spiegel* would later refer to her as "the courageous columnist of *Konkret*" (Gless 2020). This reputation would allow her to occupy a prominent position in the outlawed German Communist Party, the APO (extraparliamentary movement).

Gudrun Ensslin was also a well-behaved and exemplary child during her early education years. She was the daughter of an evangelical pastor and an active member of the Protestant Girl Scouts (Sontheimer 2019). Until the end of her high school years, she organized Bible studies as parish work. Similar to Ulrike Meinhof, she received a very prestigious scholarship from the German National Academic Foundation (Dugdale-Pointon 2007a). During her university years, she was a politically active student (Huffman 2011).

Ensslin's transition into violent political struggle began immediately following the Shah of Iran's visit to Berlin on June 2, 1967. During a peaceful demonstration against the brutal Shah, a young political activist, Benno Ohnesburg, was fatally shot in the back of his head by a police officer (BBC 2016). That same night, Ensslin, a twenty-seven-year-old student with a month-old baby, delivered an influential speech at a meeting of the local Socialist German Student Union (SDS), denouncing West Germany as a fascist state and arguing that violence was the only way to fight the state oppression. In this speech, she stated: "This fascist state means to kill us all. Violence is the only answer to violence" (Karpel 2009). This event marked the birth of the Red Army Faction (Becker 1978).

During this period, Ensslin met and fell in love with Andreas Baader (who already had a long career as a petty criminal) and left her husband and young son in pursuit of a more radical fight (Huffman 2011). Together with Baader, in response to the police killing of Ohnesburg, she decided to escalate her actions from political activism to urban guerilla violence by setting two large department stores in Frankfurt on fire using homemade bombs (BBC 2016; Dugdale-Pointon 2007a). After serving a year in jail, both Ensslin and Baader were temporarily released, pending an appeal. However, they escaped to France after their appeal was rejected (Huffman 2011). Meinhof, who was then a well-known activist, publicly acknowledged and showed sympathy for Baader and Ensslin's protest in her column at *Konkret*. With Ennslin, she shared the view that after years-long theoretical debates and verbal protests with no significant success, the only viable option to change the existing political structures was through violence (Horchem 1974; Stuchbery 2019).

RAF and the Start of the Fight

After writing this column, Meinhof became close friends with Baader and Ensslin. When both returned to Berlin from France, it was Meinhof who hid and supported them in her apartment when they were both wanted by the police. Despite the help from Meinhof, Baader was soon recaptured by the police. Ensslin then convinced Meinhof to help her rescue her boyfriend from jail (Horchem 1974). They planned a scheme in which journalist Meinhof would pretend to write a book on Baader, allowing her to interview him outside of the jail environment. The plan worked. In May of 1970, Ulrike Meinhof was allowed to interview Baader in an institute outside of prison. Ensslin, Meinhof, and two others, all armed, liberated Baader through a window by wounding an employee of the institute (BBC 2016; Gless 2020; New York Times 1976).

After this incident, Meinhof, Baader, and Ensslin went into hiding and organized the Red Army Faction, which would terrorize West Germany for the next few years (New York Times 1976; Sontheimer 2019). Meinhof not only came up with the name of the group, but also wrote the first manifesto of the RAF (Horchem 1974). Over the next two years she produced many articles and the doctrines for the RAF, including the most famous one: "The Concept of Urban Guerilla" (Dugdale-Pointon 2007b). Ensslin, on the other hand, was considered the intellectual head and moral authority of the RAF.

The media dubbed the group the Baader–Meinhof Gang, despite Ensslin being the mastermind behind the rescue plan and the one who convinced her friend Meinhof to be part of this plan (Huffman 2011). A month later, in June, all three traveled to Jordon to obtain arms training, including shooting

FIGURE 5.14   Wanted poster for the members of the Red Army Faction. *Source:* INTERFOTO/Alamy Stock Photo.

with Kalashnikovs, throwing hand grenades, and robbing banks, at a military camp run by Palestinian insurgent groups (BBC 2016; Schenck 2006).

When they returned to Berlin, the group started an underground struggle, which would last for the next two years. Between 1970 and 1972 the RAF engaged in various terrorist activities, including bank robberies, car thefts, shoot-outs with the police, and bomb attacks against the US military establishments in Germany. Eventually, the members became Germany's most wanted fugitives (Dugdale-Pointon 2007a; Gless 2020).

Prison Life

Efforts to capture the group members intensified after a police officer was killed by the RAF during a bank robbery in 1971 and the group targeted a judge in 1972 who was issuing search warrants against RAF members, but mistakenly killed his wife. Meinhof, Baader, and Ensslin were all captured by the authorities in the summer of 1972 and were charged with murder, attempted murder, robbery, and forming a criminal association (Colvin 2009; Horchem 1974; Jenkins 1998; Stuchbery 2019). They were incarcerated at **Stammheim Prison**, a specially constructed maximum-security prison for the Baader–Meinhof trial (New York Times 1976). The prison conditions were extremely inhumane—specifically designed to deconstruct the personality of the defendants through absolute isolation from the world outside the prison; this would later be known as the "Stammheim Model" (Gless 2020). The intent was not only the complete isolation of the prisoners, both from each other and from the outside world, but also psychological torture through sensory deprivation. Psychologist Sief Teuns would later describe this isolation and sensory deprivation as state programmed torture. The cofounder and the leader of the group, Ulrike Meinhof, was placed in a cell called "dead wing," which was soundproofed, painted bright white, and lit 24 hours a day with a single neon light. She was forbidden from hanging any kind of picture, photographs, or anything else on the walls. All other cells above, below, and to the left and the right were intentionally kept vacant so she would not hear any kind of human voice. She was prohibited from participating in all group activities, including church services. The only contact she had with another human being was when food was delivered to her cell (German Guerilla 2010). After some time of this torture, prisoners would be so damaged, both physically and mentally, that they would be unable to walk.

For example, Astrid Proll, another female member of the RAF who was also placed in the dead wing, would later describe her experiences: "The shocking experience was that I could not hear any noises apart from the ones that I generated myself. Nothing. Absolute silence. I went through states of excitements, I was haunted by visual and acoustic hallucinations. There were extreme disturbances of concentration and attacks of weakness. I had no idea how long this would go on for. I was terrified that I would go mad" (Sales 2016, 182).

Totally isolated, Meinhof and other members of the RAF went through several hunger strikes to improve their imprisonment conditions, demanding access to independent doctors and a transfer to the general prison population. A committee organized by the European Commission of Human Rights had observed that the RAF prisoners were suffering from problems of concentration, instability, reduced mental capacity, disorders of speech and vision, and depression due to their incapacitation in these cells (Sales 2016; Schenck 2006). Many European intellectuals, including Jean-Paul Sartre, Simone de Beauvoir, and Michel Foucault, signed an open letter (which was later published in major French newspapers) condemning the mistreatment of the RAF prisoners in Germany (Gless 2020).

German Autumn

On May 8, 1976, after four years of troublesome prison life, Ulrike Meinhof hung herself in her cell using a rope made of towels (Gless 2020; New York Times 1976; Williams 2016). The prison officials argued that she killed herself because the other members of the Baader–Meinhof Gang had isolated her.

A second generation of the RAF emerged due to Meinhof's suicide and in an effort to stop the mistreatment of the remaining imprisoned RAF members. They carried out high-profile attacks in the autumn of 1977, which would later be recognized as **German Autumn**, to secure the release of the first-generation RAF members (BBC 2006; Schenck 2006; Stutchbery 2019).

During this time, RAF members engaged in various terrorist activities to liberate the incarcerated members, including hijacking and kidnapping. In 1976, after Meinhof killed herself, they seized the German embassy in Sweden and killed the attachés when the Chancellor of Germany refused to release the prisoners. Later in 1977, they killed the

German Attorney General and then the chief executive of Dresdner Bank (Stuchbery 2019). In September of 1972 they kidnapped a wealthy businessperson, the head of the Federation of German Industry and German Association of Employees, and offered to release him in exchange for the relocation of the leading members of the RAF to a safe country. When the German government refused to release the prisoners, the RAF, in cooperation with the Palestinian insurgents, hijacked a Lufthansa plane full of tourists bound for Switzerland and threatened to blow it up if

FIGURE 5.15 Aftermath of the 1981 Red Army Faction bombing of US Air Forces Europe headquarters at Ramstein Air Base, Germany. *Source:* US Air Force photo, public domain, via Wikimedia Commons.

their demands were not met (Horchem 1974). However, German Special Forces intervened successfully and released the hostages by killing all of the hijackers (BBC 2016).

During the same night, shortly after the storming of the plane, the remaining RAF members at Stammheim Prison allegedly committed suicide: Ensslin was found hanging in her cell while three others, including Baader, were found shot in their cells (Stuchbery 2019). Many claimed that they were murdered by the German authorities, as the circumstances surrounding the deaths were suspicious. Not only was it highly questionable to smuggle guns into a maximum-security prison, but also the prisoners were shot in the backs of their heads (BBC 2016; Jenkins 1998).

Political Framing of the RAF Women

The media accounts and government documents often referred to the women of the RAF as crazy, psychologically impaired, or abused and seduced by men into joining the armed struggle (Melzer 2016; Bonisch 2015). For example, an article published in *Der Spiegel* suggested that Meinhof had turned to violence after the failure of her marriage (Bielby 2006). Similarly, both Meinhof and Ensslin were often depicted as bad mother figures—Meinhof had left her twins to found the Red Army Faction, and Ensslin had left her son and husband behind in order to pursue the struggle against the state (Williams 2016). Based on this, some argued that Ensslin and Meinhof were not real women because a normal mother would never choose political violence over her own children (Nacos 2005). Rejection of motherhood and their desire to live an underground life for the RAF's ideology was seen as strong evidence of their abnormality (Melzer 2016).

Other accounts explained Meinhof's unusual development from a prestigious left-wing journalist into a terrorist and revolutionary fighter by the theory that her brain had been damaged during an operation. In 1962, Meinhof had surgery because a tumor was suspected in her brain. Some scientists later claimed that she had abandoned her career as a journalist and turned to violence because her emotional control center was damaged during the surgery. Six days after her death, her brain was removed (without her family's knowledge) by pathologist Jurgen Peiffer. Meinhof's brain was later given to psychologist Berhard Bogerts in 1997 and would travel from laboratory to laboratory in an effort by psychologists to identify a neurological cause for her acts (Bonisch 2015). After five years of research, Bogerts claimed that Meinhof's brain had pathological modifications (resulting in increased aggression), which could have precipitated her behavioral changes and her move into radicalization—from an aspiring journalist to become a cofounder of a violent organization (Schenck 2006; Williams 2016).

Bogert's report was intentionally circulated among the members and sympathizers of the RAF to discredit the group by Meinhof's alleged pathology. The goal was to destroy the credibility of the movement and embarrass the followers by showing them that their leader was a mad woman from the very beginning (German Guerilla 2010; Sales 2016; Schenck 2006). However, while some narratives depicted Meinhof as a psychologically troubled person, others viewed her as a talented student, a respected journalist, and a dedicated political activist. She focused on poverty alleviation and social justice. Especially the RAF sympathizers saw her as a courageous individual willing to take significant risks to challenge the German state (Schenck 2006).

Only a small minority of scholars have argued that the women of the RAF made conscious and politically motivated decisions to join this violent movement (Bonisch 2015). Ulrike Meinhof and Gudrun Ensslin had taken part in this armed struggle because they were frustrated with the system, they wanted to fight against the existing political institutions, there were few alternatives for pursuing political justice, and they had little to no trust in government institutions (Schenck 2006). They had established this left-wing group because they were highly concerned about the potential outbreak of a nuclear war on a global scale and had a hatred for the existing capitalist and imperialist structures and a desire for long-term peace in the world. As former member Inge Viett indicated: "None of us came from the feminist movement. We simply took the decision to join, and then fought and did all the same things as men" (Williams 2016). Like the other women fighters discussed in earlier case studies in this chapter, the women of the RAF were fighting for a cause that came from conviction. They were just pushing their political goals with violent means, just as men do.

5.5.5 Case Study 5: The Growing Presence of American Women in Far-Right Extremist Organizations

Although women's involvement in far-right groups is not unprecedented and has been well-documented in various organizations like the Ku Klux Klan (KKK) (Blee 2008), the last two decades has seen a significant rise in the participation of women in modern-day right-wing extremist groups (Blee 2003; Blee 2020; Blee & Creasap 2010; Bradatan 2023; Daymon & Margolin 2022; Matfess & Margolin 2022; Miller-Idriss 2022b; Ness 2008a; Saarijärvi & Siafaka 2021). Scholars often find it surprising that women are attracted to groups that are generally associated with masculinist, anti-feminist, and misogynistic characteristics that have historically viewed them as sexual objects, child-bearers, and caretakers for their husbands (Blee & Creasap 2010; Bradatan 2023; Latif et al. 2020; Vertigans 2007). This case study will explore the factors that draw women to far-right organizations and the roles that they play in these groups by providing notable examples.

A thorough review of the literature reveals that a key factor driving women's radicalization into far-right groups is the appeal of far-right conspiracy theories and the fear they ignite. As will be elaborated on in Chapter 8, far-right groups' grievances in the United States and globally often revolve around increasing immigration rates, the influx of refugees, crimes committed by immigrants, perceived economic threats to White individuals from minorities, and notably, the great replacement theory (e.g., White genocide)—a right-wing conspiracy theory that the White race is under the risk of extinction due to the immigration of non-White individuals into Western societies (Bauder 2022).

FIGURE 5.16   Female members of the Ku Klux Klan marching down Pennsylvania Avenue in Washington, DC, in 1928, with the Capitol in the background. Grouped under the name Women of the Ku Klux Klan (WKKK), these women initially served in backstage roles for the KKK. Over time they engaged in more active roles, such as education and social reforms with a very strict racist and intolerant agenda against immigrants, Jews, Catholics, and Black people. *Source:* NAID: 541885, Public Domain.

Existing research indicates that these groups consistently promote racist, xenophobic, fascist, authoritarian, anti-LGBTQ+, and anti-democratic rhetoric through social media platforms and various internet forums and blogs (Blee 2020). Experts argue that these groups' fear-mongering about foreigners and immigrants, such as allegations of child sex trafficking and sexual violence by non-White men toward White women, makes women more susceptible to extremist narratives (Ebner & Davey 2019; Gutsche 2018). For instance, female far-right blogger Cecilia Davenport and Wolfie James provide guidance to men on convincing their partners to join these groups by exploiting fears of rape and sexual assault by immigrants, suggesting that "women are more emotional than rational" (Ebner & Davey 2019; E. W. 2017). These women position far-right extremism as a necessary mechanism to protect the "vulnerable and endangered" (Blee 2020, 419) White, heterosexual, Christian women, who are deemed essential for the American nation's future, from the perceived threats posed by sexually and economically predatory races (Koronaiou & Sakellariou 2020).

By manipulating women's (and mothers') fears about children, community safety, school quality, and loved ones, far-right groups garner support for their causes and mobilize crowds toward violent action (Blee 2003; Miller-Idriss 2022a). A prime example is QAnon, a far-right group that propagates the conspiracy theory that the world is controlled by a group of Satan-worshipping pedophiles. Today, the majority of QAnon supporters are women, drawn to the group by misinformation on sensitive issues such as child sex trafficking and the alleged killing of children by a secret, Democrat-led political faction (Pandith et al. 2020).

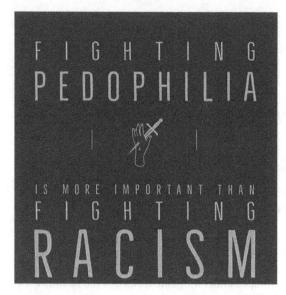

FIGURE 5.17 A QAnon post argues that the fight against pedophilia, as they perceive it, holds greater significance than the struggle against racism, as advocated by the Black Lives Matter movement. The post suggests that the eradication of pedophilia should take precedence because in their view, it addresses a more immediate and severe threat to children's safety and well-being. Supporters of QAnon believe that there exists a widespread, clandestine network of powerful individuals involved in child trafficking and abuse. *Source:* Image compiled by Pastel QAnon researcher Marc-André Argentino in September 2020, Public domain, via Wikimedia Commons.

Through their online platforms, QAnon members share information claiming that children are molested by high-level government officials and Hollywood celebrities, who then kill and consume these children to extract a life-extending chemical called adrenochrome (Roose 2021; Santucci et al. 2021). These conspiracy theories appeal to women by exploiting their fears and concerns about children's safety, encouraging them to join groups purportedly fighting to protect children from horrific abuse (Matfess & Margolin 2022; Saarijärvi & Siafaka 2021).

Why Do Far-Right Groups Recruit Women?

Far-right groups benefit from women's participation in several ways. As with other conservative extremist groups, women in far-right groups, such as the Ku Klux Klan (KKK), primarily served in supportive roles. They carried out tasks like sewing hoods and robes, cooking meals for gatherings, disseminating tips on raising a "pure" White Aryan race, and homeschooling children (Miller-Idriss 2022a; 2022b). Although there were exceptions, with some women participating in activities like spreading rumors and organizing boycotts, their roles were largely confined to the background (Blee 2008).

In contemporary society, however, the impact of women's participation in far-right groups is far more significant than is often recognized. Women now contribute to far-right extremism in various capacities, including as violent actors, facilitators, promoters, fundraisers, recruiters, activists, and exemplars (Champion 2020). Despite the far right's sexist practices, research indicates that women play active and important roles in these groups ranging from engaging in actual violence to being a public face in right-wing media platforms and making inroads in politics (e.g., into US Congress), to working behind the scenes in various social media outlets to increase membership in these groups (Blee 2020; Bradatan 2023; Matfess & Margolin 2022; Ryan 2023).

Softening of Public Image and Increased Publicity and Media Attention

Women's enrollment in these groups attracts increased publicity and media attention (often due to biased gender expectations), which then helps them spread their message to broader segments of society (Saarijärvi & Siafaka 2021). Relatedly, the participation of women in these extreme organizations, which are generally acknowledged as hostile and violent toward minority groups, can help to soften their image in the eyes of the public and serve to legitimize the groups' activities (Leidig 2021; Miller-Idriss 2022). Through the influence of women, particularly social media influencers, right-wing extremist groups have been able to normalize and popularize their hateful rhetoric—such as White nationalism, anti-immigration stances, and anti-democratic ideologies—to millions worldwide (Ebner & Davey 2019).

Active Participation in Violence

Women, alongside men, actively engage in acts of violence to further their groups' causes. This was starkly evident during the January 6, 2021 insurrection at the US Capitol, where women—from housewives to highly trained military veterans—took prominent front-line roles in rioting, assaulting security personnel, conspiring, and damaging government property (Miller-Idriss 2022a; Ryan 2023; Santucci et al. 2021). As of March 2022, women accounted for approximately 13–14 percent of federal cases related to the storming (Matfess & Margolin 2022). To date, 104 women from 28 US states have been arrested in connection with the Capitol attacks, with ongoing investigations by the intelligence community to identify their direct involvement in the violence (Miller-Idriss 2022b; Santucci et al. 2021).

For example, Jessica Watkins, a member of the Oath Keepers—an extremist group describing itself as "a non-partisan association of current and former military, police, and first responders dedicated to defending the Constitution" (US Library of Congress 2024)—organized the transportation of 40 heavily armed militias to the January 6 rally. Using encrypted communication via Zello, she coordinated their storming of the Capitol building (Ryan 2023). Similarly, Rachel Powell, known as the "bullhorn lady," assaulted officers, used an ice axe and large pipe to break Capitol windows, and issued instructions to fellow rioters through a bullhorn, urging them to "coordinate together if

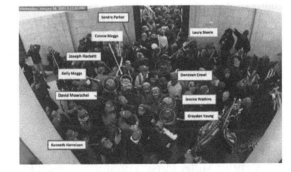

FIGURE 5.18 The US Department of Justice has released various images and videos related to the January 6 insurrection cases, providing evidence of the involvement of numerous individuals and groups. One particular image shows men and women associated with the Oath Keepers, a far-right militia group, forcibly entering the Capitol and then congregating inside the north section of the Rotunda. This evidence, captured by surveillance video from inside the Capitol, has been crucial in the ongoing investigations and prosecutions. *Source:* United States Department of Justice, Public domain, via Wikimedia Commons.

FIGURE 5.19 Jessica Watkins, a member of the Oath Keepers, was prominently involved in the January 6 Capitol riot. Watkins, a former Army Ranger and bar owner from Ohio, became a key figure in the planning and execution of activities related to the Capitol breach. On January 6, Watkins and other Oath Keepers members traveled to Washington, DC, with the explicit intention of participating in the rally and subsequent actions that led to the storming of the Capitol. Watkins and her fellow Oath Keepers were seen in tactical gear, moving in a military-style stack formation as they entered the Capitol building.

you are going to take this building." A subsequent FBI search of her home and vehicle uncovered smashed cellphones, an AK-47, ammunition, lighters, and kidnapping tools such as ropes, duct tape, zip ties, and knives (CBS News 2021).

Two other women from Pennsylvania, Dawn Bancroft and Diana Santos-Smith, recorded a selfie video inside the US Capitol during the attack, wearing "Make America Great Again" hats. In the video, they expressed intentions to locate House Speaker Nancy Pelosi, stating they wanted to "shoot her in the fricking brain" (Helsel 2022).

Recruitment and Propaganda

Researchers and experts argue that women not only play a significant role in disseminating hateful and anti-democratic right-wing views to larger audiences but also in recruiting other women (and men) to extremist causes through online propaganda on mainstream social media platforms such as TikTok, Instagram, YouTube, and Facebook, as well as through fringe outlets like Parler, Gab, and Discord (Bigio & Vogelstein 2019b; Bradatan 2023; Ebner & Davey 2019; Leidig 2021). Studies indicate that women's involvement in online propaganda for right-wing extremism has significantly enhanced the capabilities and outreach of these groups (Matfess & Margolin 2022). By strategically targeting audiences through platforms like lifestyle blogs or parenting groups, far-right women have mainstreamed fringe extremist ideas, aiming to cultivate a sense of community and belonging within the far-right movement (Santucci et al. 2021).

Cynthia Miller-Idriss, a prominent expert in this field, notes that extremist women often leverage their identities as mothers to justify their engagement and to recruit and mobilize others on these platforms (Miller-Idriss 2022a). She further argues that right-wing groups deliberately employ rhetoric around motherhood to de-politicize their actions and portray their violent activities as efforts to protect children and families.

The proliferation of conspiracy theories surrounding trafficking, torture, rape, and murder of children by alleged Satan-worshipping global elite pedophilia rings has drawn millions of women worldwide into extremism (Miller-Idriss 2022b). Influential right-wing women in the online arena, often referred to as "QAnon Moms," command large online followings through platforms focused on health, food, cooking, home decorating, and child-rearing—spaces traditionally free of extremist content—and regularly disseminate content alleging child trafficking under hashtags like #SaveTheChildren, mobilizing thousands of individuals into extremism (Miller-Idriss 2022a).

Similarly, female influencers played pivotal roles in the global spread of the #DefendEurope campaign, an online initiative aimed at galvanizing White Europeans to obstruct civil society organizations from rescuing drowning migrants in the Mediterranean Sea (Ebner & Davey 2019). By disseminating narratives of victimhood through various platforms, such as reports of migrant rape crimes, the campaign garnered over 300,000 female followers within five months in 2017.

Far-right extremist women frequently use the motherhood rhetoric in online platforms to radicalize women into their cause, positing a rejection of modernity and promoting anti-feminist content and traditional values (Bradatan 2023; Matfess & Margolin 2022). Livestreaming from the confines of their homes through webcams, these women share their personal "lightening"

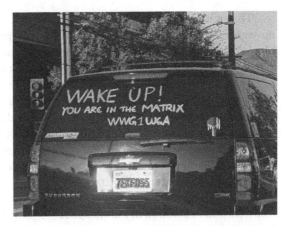

FIGURE 5.20 The concept of the "red pill" and the "awakening" has been appropriated by various groups, including QAnon supporters, drawing on the imagery from the 1999 film *The Matrix*. In *The Matrix*, taking the red pill symbolizes the acceptance of harsh truths and awakening to a new, often unsettling reality. QAnon supporters use the "red pill" metaphor to describe their own perceived awakening to what they believe is a hidden truth about global conspiracies involving elite figures. They see themselves as having awakened from the "matrix" of mainstream media and societal norms, believing they have uncovered the truth behind global events and the actions of powerful individuals. *Source:* Cory Doctorow, CC BY-SA 2.0, via Wikimedia Commons.

stories (often described as "red pill awakening") to millions of viewers in a conversational setting (Ebner & Davey 2019). They talk about the alleged danger posed by Marxists, socialists, liberals, and feminists and encourage their followers to adopt a simpler life by embracing traditional roles as caretakers and homemakers as daughters, mothers, and wives who need the protection of men. They perceive feminism to be a dangerous idea created by liberals to destroy the Western civilization (e.g., by making women unnaturally competitive), and the only way to fix the issues in today's society is to go back to traditionalism, a society in which men and women have a clear division of roles based on their gender (Leidig 2021).

One example of such a group is the "tradwife" (traditional wife) movement, a popular TikTok community among Gen Zers. This movement views feminism and gender equality initiatives as challenges to traditional femininity. It advocates for Christian women to "de-program" themselves by embracing traditional roles: staying at home, upholding religious values, and prioritizing the upbringing of children within their ingroup (Leidig 2021; Matfess & Margolin 2022). The movement argues that societal pressures, influenced by feminist ideals, have led many women—particularly White women—to feel dissatisfied by diverting from their innate desires to nurture and manage households in favor of pursuing professional careers.

Through various social media platforms such as TikTok, proponents of the tradwife movement caution their followers about demographic shifts, often referencing concerns like "White genocide." They highlight perceived threats posed by immigration policies and multiculturalism, promoting initiatives like the "White baby challenge" proposed by figures such as Ayla Sytewart from the far right, aimed at countering declining birth rates among White populations (Darby 2020; Ryan 2023). These groups encourage followers to undergo a process of "unlearning" liberal indoctrination, particularly feminist ideologies, in order to alleviate perceived suffering and victimization. They advocate for the restoration of traditional gender roles, asserting that this will allow men to express their natural masculinity—characterized by dominance and leadership—without obstruction (Blee 2020; Leidig 2021).

Activism and Promotion in Public Space

Women also play significant roles as activists and promoters of ideas within the public sphere. A notable example is the Florida-originated far-right anti-government organization Moms for Liberty—a group that self-identifies as a modern parental rights movement and is considered as an extremist organization by the Southern Law and Poverty Center (Ryan 2023; Yousef 2023). Established in 2021 by a group of conservative mothers, the Moms for Liberty gained more than 110,000 members across 42 states to promote book bans (e.g., for books they believe to be anti-American and anti-White) in school libraries against what they consider as "woke indoctrination" (SPLC 2024).

Moms for Liberty are also known for organizing protests against the public health regulations that were put in place during the COVID-19 pandemic (e.g., mask use requirements), acceptance and inclusion of the LGBTQ+ community in public schools, and the school curriculums that incorporate racially inclusive educational resources (e.g., Black history and literature, and critical race theory).

Group members frequently accompany members of the Proud Boys, target teachers and other school staff, ask members to apply for available positions on school boards, and encourage them to attend school board meetings as watchdogs (e.g., to question student textbook selections). Moms

FIGURE 5.21   Tina Descovich is a cofounder of Moms for Liberty, an organization established in January 2021. The group focuses on parental rights and advocacy, particularly in relation to education, such as opposing certain educational curricula and school policies they view as infringing on parental rights. *Source:* ReasonTV, CC BY 3.0, via Wikimedia Commons.

for Liberty also advocates for the elimination of the US Department of Education, which they perceive as a government indoctrination mechanism that subjects their kids to a progressive Marxist ideology. They label teachers and librarians, who have or assign books that they deem inappropriate, as "groomers" and request separate classrooms for students who identify themselves as a member of the LGBTQ+ community (Yousef 2023).

Gender Roles in Modern Far-Right Groups

Despite the benefits that male-dominated far-right groups gain from women's participation, it is important to note that women's roles in far-right groups vary from group to group, as do gender-based expectations (Blee 2020; Blee & Creasap 2010). Modern far-right groups are not homogeneous and are composed of several different groups and subgroups with different goals and activities (e.g., QAnon, Oath Keepers, Proud Boys, Three Percenters, involuntary celibates) (Matfess & Margolin 2022). Some of these groups still maintain strict traditional gender views which resign women to backstage roles, whereas others have adopted more gender inclusive perspectives where women are encouraged to take various public facing leadership roles (Matfess & Margolin 2022).

For example, even though both the Oath Keepers and QAnon have a large percent of women in violent roles and leadership positions and value gender inclusivity and operate under gender neutral guidelines (Amarasingam et al. 2020; Moskalenko et al. 2021), a similar group, **Proud Boys,** strictly opposes the participation of women in their cadres (Ross 2020). Instead, the group recommends women to take backstage roles, such as raising children and hosting group gatherings, and taking care of family members. On December 21, 2021, the group ostracized longtime supporter Tara LaRosa, a former Mixed

Martial Arts fighter, who participated in the group's protests and activities all around the country, for establishing a Telegram channel named "ProudGirlsUSA." In response to this, the ProudBoys-USA channel made a post telling her "Don't ride our coattails": "Want to support us? Get married, have babies, and take care of your family" (Ross 2020).

Similarly, other right-wing groups, such as the Neo-Nazi National Alliance, The Order, and the Covenant, the Sword, and the Arm of the Lord (CSA), also ask their women followers to take up auxiliary roles (e.g., help with the day-to-day logistics) and further their groups' cause by giving birth to White babies and nurturing them (Matfess & Margolin 2022).

FIGURE 5.22   The Proud Boys' membership and leadership are predominantly male. Women are not typically members of the Proud Boys, as the organization is explicitly designed for men. However, women can be supporters or involved in activities related to the Proud Boys. The women of Proud Boys participate in rallies, events, and online discussions, expressing alignment with the Proud Boys' views on nationalism, traditional gender roles, and other conservative values.
Source: Anthony Crider, CC BY 2.0, via Wikimedia Commons.

5.6 CONCLUSION

When most people think of a terrorist, the image of a dangerous-looking man may come to mind. There has been a tendency in both the academic literature and the popular media to portray terrorists as men. When women are considered as participants in terrorism, they are typically assumed to have only minor, supportive roles that are consistent with traditional understandings of women's responsibilities in patriarchal societies (i.e., conservative societies as explained by Ness [2008b]). Women's affiliations with terrorist groups are thought to be limited to that of wife, mother (raising the next generation of male fighters), or caretaker. However, throughout history women have had important roles in the formation, sustenance, and lethality of major terrorist organizations worldwide. Women have initiated terrorist organizations, recruited members, completed suicide missions, planned attacks, fought alongside men, and held leadership positions with independent decision-making responsibilities. In many organizations—even strictly religious, conservative ones—women's roles have evolved over time to include activities previously performed only by men. In ISIS, women's position changed from being a wife, educator, and child-bearer to fighting alongside men. For ISIS and other religious or conservative groups, the use of women in traditionally male roles is a strategic response to dwindling resources and power—a choice made to support the organization despite its stark contradiction of the group's gender ideology.

In addition, academic research has revealed that women's motivations for engaging in terrorism and political violence are varied and complex. Studies of female terrorists, including interviews with women who have been incarcerated or who have left terrorist groups and analyses of biographies and other archival sources, have revealed a number of influences including those that are personal in nature (e.g., psychological distress) and those experienced at a collective level (e.g., gender-based oppression). Issues related to gender inequality often precipitate the experiences that lead women to engage in terrorism. However, not all women who join terrorist groups are motivated by feminist concerns. Ultimately, women's reasons for joining violent movements may be no different from men's—they are fighting for a cause that they believe in, to initiate change in society.

Finally, the media and government institutions have shown a pattern of presenting female terrorists as crazy, psychologically impaired, or abused and seduced by men into joining armed struggles. This depiction of violent women enables the public to understand their actions while still maintaining traditional notions of feminine behavior—it leads people to believe that these women failed to adhere to traditional gender roles because something was wrong with them on an individual level. Seeing these women as unfit to make rational decisions or as victims of controlling men denies their agency and thwarts efforts to prevent terrorism more generally. Although coercion through sexual exploitation and forced marriages certainly exists, research suggests that many women who engage in terrorism and political violence make conscious decisions to do so. Policymakers must recognize this phenomenon, as well as the extent of women's roles in terrorism, in order to develop comprehensive and effective counterterrorism strategies.

Key Lessons

Lesson 1

Despite the common perception that terrorists are men, throughout history women have played important roles in many terrorist groups and movements around the world.

Lesson 2

The literature on women in terrorism suggests that women's participation in violence is influenced by a variety of contributing factors at both the individual and collective levels.

Lesson 3

Ideologically, women tend to have greater representation in left-wing terrorist groups than right-wing ones due to their emphasis on equality as well as increased opportunities for leadership roles within the organizations.

Lesson 4

Women's roles in terrorist groups vary and often do not follow traditional notions of gendered behavior. In some groups, women have a wide range of duties from the dissemination of propaganda to the execution of actual terrorist attacks; however, in other groups women's duties are limited to providing logistical and moral support and first aid to members.

Lesson 5

Women's roles within a terrorist group can evolve over time. Even terrorist organizations with strict gender restrictive ideologies can override their teachings and rules under external pressure and assign women positions typically held by men (e.g., combat).

Lesson 6

Although female-specific rationales are often attributed to women's participation in political violence, women's motivations for joining terrorist movements are not necessarily different from those of men.

Lesson 7

Media accounts and government documents often present female terrorists as crazy, psychologically impaired, or abused and seduced by men into joining the armed struggle. Academic research suggests that these depictions are often inaccurate.

Lesson 8

This tendency to explain women's participation in terrorism using gendered notions of women's behavior (seeing them as psychologically abnormal or as victims for failing to adhere to traditional gender roles) denies agency from the female fighters and thwarts efforts to develop effective counterterrorism strategies.

KEY WORDS

Al-Khansaa Brigade
Black Widows
femininity
forced marriage
gender roles
German Autumn
Islamic State of Iraq and Syria (ISIS)
Kurdistan Workers' Party (PKK)
new humanitarians

niqāb
patriarchy
Red Army Fraction (RAF)
redemption
repatriation
revenge
sexual exploitation
Stammheim Prison
suicide terrorism

RECOMMENDED SOURCES

Research Articles & Books

Bhattacharya, S. (2019) Gender, insurgency, and terrorism: Introduction to the special issue. *Small Wars & Insurgencies, 30*(6–7), 1077–1088.

Bigio, J., & Vogelstein, R. (2019). Women and Terrorism-Hidden Threats, Forgotten Partners. Council on Foreign Relations. https://cdn.cfr.org/sites/default/files/report_pdf/Discussion_Paper_Bigio_Vogelstein_Terrorism_OR.pdf.

Blee, K. (2020). Where do we go from here? Positioning gender in studies of the far right. *Politics, Religion & Ideology, 21*(4), 416–431

Bloom, M. (2007). Women as victims and victimizers. *Countering the Terrorist Mentality. US Department of State, 12*(5).

Bloom, M. (2011b). Bombshells: Women and terror. *Gender Issues, 28*(1–2), 1–21.

Cunningham, K. J. (2003). Cross-regional trends in female terrorism. *Studies in Conflict and Terrorism, 26*, 171–195.

Davis, J. (2017). *Women in modern terrorism: from liberation wars to global jihad and the Islamic State.* Rowman & Littlefield.

Davis, J., West, L., & Amarasingam, A. (2021). Measuring impact, uncovering bias? Citation analysis of literature on women in terrorism. *Perspectives on Terrorism, 15*(2), 58–76.

Jacques, K., & Taylor, P. J. (2009). Female terrorism: A review. *Terrorism and Political Violence, 21*(3), 499–515.

Margolin, D., & Cook, J. (2024). Five Decades of Research on Women and Terrorism. *Studies in Conflict & Terrorism*, 1–29.

Nacos, B. L. (2005). The portrayal of female terrorists in the media: Similar framing patterns in the news coverage of women in politics and in terrorism. *Studies in Conflict & Terrorism, 28*, 435–451.

Ness, C. D. (2005). In the name of the cause: Women's work in secular and religious terrorism. *Studies in Conflict and Terrorism, 28*, 353–373.

Sjoberg, L., & Gentry, C. E. (2007). *Mothers, monsters, whores: Women's violence in global politics.* Zed Books: London, UK.

Weinberg, L., & Eubank, W. (2011). Women's involvement in terrorism. *Gender issues, 28*, 22–49.

Wood, R. M., & Thomas, J. L. (2017). Women on the frontline: Rebel group ideology and women's participation in violent rebellion. *Journal of Peace Research, 54*, 31–46.

News Articles & Government and Think Tank Reports

Why understanding the role of women is vital in the fight against terrorism.
    Author(s): Jamille Bigio Rachel Vogelstein
    Source: The Washington Post.
When Women Become Terrorists
    Author(s): Jayne Huckerby
    Source: The New York Times
My mother, the terrorist.
    Author(s): DW staff and Bettina Röhl
    Source: Deutsche Welle
Behind the woman, behind the bomb.
    Author(s): Linsey O'Rourke
    Source: The New York Times
'White Widow', 'Black Widow': why do female terrorists perplex us?
    Author(s): Alexandra Phelan

    Source: The Conversation
How right-wing extremists weaponize the idea of motherhood.
    Author(s): Cynthia Miller-Idriss
    Source: MSNBC.
Women and Terrorism: *Hidden Threats, Forgotten Partners*
    Author(s): Jamille Bigio & Rachel B. Vogelstein
    Source: Council on Foreign Affairs
Gender and Right-Wing Extremism in America: Why Understanding Women's Roles is Key to Preventing Future Acts of Domestic Terrorism
    Author(s): Julia Santucci, Regina Waugh, & Hallie Schneir
    Source: Just Security

Behind the Instagram Posts: The Role of Female Influencers on the Far-Right
Author(s): Jordan Chapman
Source: Global Network on Extremism & Technology

"We Are Worth Fighting for": Women in Far-Right Extremism
Author(s): Eviane Leidig
Source: The International Centre for Counter-Terrorism (ICCT)

Female Veterans and Right-Wing Extremism: Becoming 'One of the Boys'
Author(s): Hanna Rigault Arkhis & Jessica White
Source: The International Centre for Counter-Terrorism (ICCT)

Female terrorists and their role in jihadi groups
Author(s): Beverley Milton-Edwards & Sumaya Attia
Source: The Brookings Institution

Why Do We Underestimate The Role Of Women In Terrorist Organizations?
Author(s): Nikita Malik
Source: Forbes

Why do women become terrorists?
Author(s): Candida Moss
Source: The Daily Beast

Documentaries, Videos, and Other Educational Media

Women & Terrorism: Perpetrators and Peacemakers
Featuring: Brice Hoffman, Naureen Chowdhury Fink, Edit Schlaffer
Source: Georgetown Institute for Women, Peace, & Security YouTube channel

Women Suicide Bombers
Featuring: Farhana Ali
Source: C-Span

Terrorism and Women
Featuring: Lori Poloni-Staudinger
Source: C-Span

Seeing the New Face of Terrorism
Featuring: Mia Bloom
Source: TEDx Talks

Saints Talk: Women and Terrorism by Professor Caron Gentry
Featuring: Caron Gentry
Source: University of St. Andrews Alumni YouTube channel

Everywoman - Women and terrorism
Featuring: Farhana Ali
Source: Al Jazeera English YouTube Channel

Gender equality and counter-terrorism
Featuring: Jessica White
Source: France 24 English

REFERENCES

Abdullaev, N. (2013). Russia's "Black Widows": Organization behind sensation. Harvard Kennedy School Belfer Center. https://www.belfercenter.org/publication/russias-black-widows-organization-behind-sensation

Agara, T. (2015). Gendering terrorism: Women, gender, terrorism and suicide bombers. *International Journal of Humanities and Social Science, 5*(6), 115–125.

Agence France-Presse. (21 June, 2008). Russia: Chechen Mass Graves Found. www.nytimes.com/2008/06/21/world/europe/21briefs-CHECHENMASSG_BRF.html

Al Jazeera (2021). Two people linked to Philippine church blast killed in Indonesia. Al-Jazeera. https://www.aljazeera.com/news/2021/1/6/indonesia-two-people-linked-to-philippine-church-bombing-killed

Ali, F. (2006). Rocking the cradle to rocking the world: The role of Muslim female fighters. *Journal of International Women's Studies, 8*, 21–35.

Alison, M. (2003). Cogs in the wheel: Women in the liberation tigers of Tamil Eelam. *Civil Wars 6*, 37–54.

Alvanou, M. (2008). Palestinian women suicide bombers: The interplaying effects of Islam, nationalism and honor culture. *Homeland Security Review, 2*, 1.

Amarasingam, A., & Argentino, M. A. (2020). The QAnon conspiracy theory: A security threat in the making. *CTC Sentinel*, *13*(7), 37–44.

Annan, J., Blattman, C., Mazurana, D., & Carlson, K. (2009). Women and girls at war: "Wives," mothers and fighters in the Lord's Resistance Army. Households in Conflict Network Working Paper, 63.

Asetta, C. (2023). Progress in repatriations: How foreign assistance is addressing the humanitarian and security crises in Northeast Syria: Part 1 of 2. US Department of State. https://www.state.gov/progress-in-repatriations-how-foreign-assistance-is-addressing-the-humanitarian-and-security-crises-in-northeast-syria-part-1-of-2/

Banner, F. (2009). *Making death visible: Chechen female suicide bombers in an era of globalization.* Dissertation. Arizona State University.

Barr, L. (2022). American woman arrested, allegedly trained women of ISIS. ABC News. https://abcnews.go.com/US/american-woman-arrested-allegedly-trained-women-isis/story?id=82566924

Bauder, D. (2022). What is "great replacement theory" and how does it fuel racist violence? *PBS News.* https://www.pbs.org/newshour/politics/what-is-great-replacement-theory-and-how-does-it-fuel-racist-violence

BBC (2006, April 25). Bomb targets Sri Lanka army chief. BBC. http://news.bbc.co.uk/1/hi/world/south_asia/4941744.stm.

BBC (2016). Who were Germany's Red Army Faction Militants? BBC. https://www.bbc.com/news/world-europe-35354812

Becker, J. (1978). *Hitler's children.* Panther.

Benson, M., Evans, M., & Simon, R. (1982). Women as political terrorists. *Research in Law, Deviance, and Social Control, 4,* 121–130.

Berko, A., & Erez, E. (2007). Gender, Palestinian women, and terrorism: Women's liberation or oppression? *Studies in Conflict and Terrorism, 30,* 493–519.

Beyler, C. (2006, November 15). Using Palestinian women as bombs. *New York Sun*, p. 15.

Bhattacharya, S. (2019) Gender, insurgency, and terrorism: Introduction to the special issue.

Bielby, C. (2006). "Bonnie und Kleid": Female Terrorists and the Hysterical Feminine. *Forum: University of Edinburgh Postgraduate Journal of Culture & The Arts, 2.* https://journals.ed.ac.uk

Bigio, J. & Vogelstein, R. (2019a). Why understanding the role of women is vital in the fight against terrorism. *Washington Post.* https://www.washingtonpost.com/opinions/2019/09/10/why-understanding-role-women-is-vital-fight-against-terrorism/

Bigio, J., & Vogelstein, R. (2019b). *Women and terrorism: Hidden threats, forgotten partners.* Council on Foreign Relations. https://cdn.cfr.org/sites/default/files/report_pdf/Discussion_Paper_Bigio_Vogelstein_Terrorism_OR.pdf?_gl=1*bxxtsw*_gcl_au*MTA4NDY4MTUwNi4xNzIwNjIxMTQ0*_ga*MTM1OTE5Mzg4My4xNzIwNjIxMTQ1*_ga_24W5E70YKH*MTcyMDczMjAyOC4zLjAuMTcyMDczMjA0NC40NC4wLjA.

Biswas, B., & Deylami, S. (2019). Radicalizing female empowerment: Gender, agency, and affective appeals in Islamic State propaganda. *Small Wars & Insurgencies, 30*(6–7), 1193–1213.

Blee, K. (2020). Where do we go from here? Positioning gender in studies of the far right. *Politics, Religion & Ideology, 21*(4), 416–431.

Blee, K. M. (1991). Women in the 1920s' Ku Klux Klan movement. *Feminist Studies, 17,* 57–77.

Blee, K. M. (2003). *Inside organized racism: Women in the hate movement.* University of California Press.

Blee, K. M. (2008). *Women of the Klan: Racism and gender in the 1920s.* University of California Press.

Blee, K. M., & Creasap, K. A. (2010). Conservative and right-wing movements. *Annual Review of Sociology, 36*(1), 269–286.

Bloom, M. (2005). *Dying to kill: The allure of suicide terror.* Columbia University Press.

Bloom, M. (2007). Women as victims and victimizers. *Countering the Terrorist Mentality: US Department of State, 12*(5). https://www.hsdl.org/c/view?docid=474005

Bloom, M. (2011a). *Bombshell: Women and terrorism.* Hurst.

Bloom, M. (2011b). Bombshells: Women and terror. *Gender Issues, 28*(1–2), 1–21.

Bonisch, D. (2015). How explaining female terrorism can only fail: Terror brides and jihadi poster girls. Kaput. https://kaput-mag.com/stories_en/how-explaining-female-terrorism-can-only-fail/

Bradatan, A. (2023). The overlooked roles of women in far-right extremist organizations and how to prevent their further radicalization. Fordham Democracy Project. https://fordhamdemocracyproject.com/2023/04/26/the-overlooked-roles-of-women-in-far-right-extremist-organizations/

CBS News (2021). Federal prosecutors fight release of Rachel Powell, mercer county mother arrested in capitol riots. https://www.cbsnews.com/pittsburgh/news/federal-prosecutors-fight-release-rachel-powel-capitol-riots/

Champion, K. (2020). Women in the extreme and radical right: Forms of participation and their implications. *Social Sciences, 9*(9), 149. https://doi.org/10.3390/socsci9090149

Chrisafis, A. (2016). Women arrested in Paris had planned "imminent" attack on Gare de Lyon, say officials. *The Guardian.* https://www.theguardian.com/world/2016/sep/09/paris-women-arrested-had-planned-imminent-attack-gare-de-lyon-say-officials

Colvin, S. (2009). *Ulrike Meinhof and West German terrorism: Language, violence, and identity.* Camden House.

Cook, J., & Vale, G. (2019). From Daesh to 'Diaspora' II: The challenges posed by women and minors after the fall of the caliphate. *CTC Sentinel, 12*(6), 30–45.

Cruickshank, P. (2017). A view from the CT foxhole: Lisa Monaco, former assistant to President Barack Obama for Homeland Security and Counterterrorism. *CTC Sentinel West Point, 10*(9). https://ctc.westpoint.edu/a-view-from-the-ct-foxhole-lisa-monaco-former-assistant-to-president-barack-obama-for-homeland-security-and-counterterrorism/

Cruise, R. S. (2016). Enough with the stereotypes: Representations of women in terrorist organizations. *Social Science Quarterly, 97*(1), 33–43.

Cunningham, K. J. (2003). Cross-regional trends in female terrorism. *Studies in Conflict and Terrorism, 26,* 171–195.

Cunningham, K. J. (2007). Countering female terrorism. *Studies in Conflict and Terrorism, 30,* 113–129.

Curry, C. (2013). Chechens' violent history includes "Black Widows," attacks on school, theater. ABC News. https://abcnews.go.com/US/chechens-violent-history-includes-black-widows-attacks-school/story?id=18997035

Dalton, A., & Asal, V. (2011). Is it ideology or desperation: Why do organizations deploy women in violent terrorist attacks? *Studies in Conflict and Terrorism, 34,* 802–819.

Darby, S. (2020). *Sisters in hate: American women on the front lines of white nationalism.* Hachette.

Darden, J. T. (2019). *Tackling terrorists' exploitation of youth.* American Enterprise Institute.

Davis, J. (2017). *Women in modern terrorism: From liberation wars to global jihad and the Islamic State.* Rowman & Littlefield.

Davis, J., West, L., & Amarasingam, A. (2021). Measuring impact, uncovering bias? Citation analysis of literature on women in terrorism. *Perspectives on Terrorism, 15*(2), 58–76.

Daymon, C., & Margolin, D. (2022). Women in American violent extremism: An examination of far-right and Salafi-Jihadist movements. *Reports, Projects, and Research.* https://digitalcommons.unomaha.edu/ncitereportsresearch/8/

Deutsche Welle (2006). My mother, the terrorist. Deutsche Welle. https://www.dw.com/en/my-mother-the-terrorist/a-1933629

Dugdale-Pointon, T. (2007a). Gudrun Ensslin (1940–1977). History of War. http://www.historyofwar.org/articles/people_ensslin.html

Dugdale-Pointon, T. (2007b). Ulrike Meinhof (1934–1972). History of War. http://www.historyofwar.org/articles/people_meinhof_ulrike.html

Düzgün, M. (2016). Jineology: The Kurdish women's movement. *Journal of Middle East, 12,* 284–287.

E. W. (2017). Women and the alt-right. *The Economist.* https://www.economist.com/democracy-in-america/2017/02/01/women-and-the-alt-right

Ebner, J., & Davey, J. (2019). How women advance the internationalization of the far-right. About the Program on Extremism. George Washington University. https://extremism.gwu.edu/sites/g/files/zaxdzs5746/files/How%20Women%20Advance%20the%20Internationalization%20of%20the%20Far-Right.pdf

Elder, M. (2010). Moscow bombings blamed on Chechnya's Black Widows. *The Guardian.* https://www.theguardian.com/world/2010/mar/29/black-widows-women-moscow-bombings

Eriksson, B. (2024). Lost childhoods: The on-going plight of children in detention camps in Northeast Syria. ICCT. https://www.icct.nl/publication/lost-childhoods-ongoing-plight-children-detention-camps-northeast-syria

Foreign Affairs. (2015, June 3). Women of the PKK. https://www.foreignaffairs.com/photo-galleries/2015-06-03/women-pkk

Gambetta, D. (2010). Heroic impatience. *The Nation*. https://www.thenation.com/article/archive/heroic-impatience/

Gan, R., Neo, L. S., Chin, J., & Khader, M. (2019). Change is the only constant: The evolving role of women in the Islamic State in Iraq and Syria (ISIS). *Women & Criminal Justice, 29*(4–5), 204–220.

Ganor, B. (2008). Terrorist organization typologies and the probability of a boomerang effect. *Studies in Conflict & Terrorism, 31*, 269–283.

German Guerilla (2010). Staying alive: Sensory deprivation, torture, and the struggle behind bars. German Guerilla. http://germanguerilla.com/2010/09/13/staying-alive-sensory-deprivation-torture-and-the-struggle-behind-bars/

Gillespie, B. (2010). The avenging Black Widows. CBC News. https://www.cbc.ca/news/world/the-avenging-black-widows-1.866287

Gless, S. (2020). Meihof, Ulrike (1934–1972). Women in world history: A biographical encyclopedia. https://www.encyclopedia.com/women/encyclopedias-almanacs-transcripts-and-maps/meinhof-ulrike-1934-1972

Graham, S. (2002). Terrorism goes trendy in Germany. *Los Angeles Times*. https://www.latimes.com/archives/la-xpm-2002-dec-22-adfg-terror22-story.html

Gutsche, E. (Ed.). (2018). Triumph of the women? The female face of the populist & far right in Europe. Friedrich Ebert Stiftung, Forum Politik und Gesellschaft.

Haner, M., Cullen, F. T., & Benson, M. L. (2020). Women and the PKK: Ideology, gender, and terrorism. *International Criminal Justice Review, 30*(3), 279–301.

Haner, M., & Lee, H. (2017). Placing school victimization in a global context. *Victims and Offenders, 12*, 845–867.

Hassan, L. (2021). Repatriating ISIS foreign fighters is key to stemming radicalization, experts say, but many countries don't want their citizens back. PBS Frontline. https://www.pbs.org/wgbh/frontline/article/repatriating-isis-foreign-fighters-key-to-stemming-radicalization-experts-say-but-many-countries-dont-want-citizens-back/

Hasso, F. H. (2005). Discursive and political deployments by/of the 2002 Palestinian women suicide bombers/martyrs. *Feminist Review 81*, 23–51.

Hearne, E. B. (2009, December). *Participants, enablers, and preventers: The roles of women in terrorism*. Paper presented at the 35th Annual Meeting of the British International Studies Association, Leicester, England.

Helsel, P. (2022). Jan. 6 rioter who talked of shooting Nancy Pelosi is sentenced to 60 days. NBC News. https://www.nbcnews.com/news/us-news/jan-6-rioter-talked-shooting-nancy-pelosi-was-sentenced-60-days-rcna39484

Henshaw, A., Eric-Udorie, J., Godefa, H., Howley, K., Jeon, C., Sweezy, E., & Zhao, K. (2019). Understanding women at war: A mixed-methods exploration of leadership in non-state armed groups. *Small Wars & Insurgencies, 30*(6–7), 1089–1116.

Herrera, N., & Porch, D. (2008). "Like going to a fiesta": The role of female fighters in Colombia's FARC-EP. *Small Wars & Insurgencies, 19*, 609–634.

Hoffman, A., & Furlan, M. (2020). Challenges posed by returning foreign fighters. CW Program on Extremism.

Holmes, D. (2002). *Terrorism: A Marxist perspective*. Resistance Books.

Horchem, H. J. (1974). West Germany's Red Army anarchists. Institute for the Study of Conflict.

Huffman, R. (2011). The Baader–Meinhof Gang. http://www.baader-meinhof.com/gudrun-ensslin/

Human Rights Watch (2016). Iraq: Women suffer under ISIS. https://www.hrw.org/news/2016/04/06/iraq-women-suffer-under-isis

Human Rights Watch (2019). Human Rights Watch Submission to the Committee on the Elimination of All Forms of Discrimination

Against Women (CEDAW) of Iraq's periodic report for the 74th CEDAW Session. https://www.hrw.org/sites/default/files/supporting_resources/hrw_submission_cedaw_iraq.pdf

Israelsen, S. (2018). Why now? Timing rebel recruitment of female combatants. *Studies in Conflict & Terrorism, 43*(2), 123–144.

Jackson, L. B. (2021). Framing British "jihadi brides": Metaphor and the social construction of IS women. *Terrorism and Political Violence, 33*(8), 1733–1751.

Jacoby, T. A. (2015). Jihadi brides at the intersections of contemporary feminism. *New Political Science, 37*(4), 525–542.

Jacques, K., & Taylor, P. J. (2008). Male and female suicide bombers: Different sexes, different reasons? *Studies in Conflict and Terrorism, 31*, 304–326.

Jacques, K., & Taylor, P. J. (2009). Female terrorism: A review. *Terrorism and Political Violence, 21*(3), 499–515.

Jahanbani, N. P., & Willis, C. N. (2019). The ballot or the bomb belt: The roots of female suicide terrorism before and after 9/11. *Small Wars & Insurgencies, 30*(6–7), 1117–1150.

Jamali, A. B. (2017). Chechnya's Black Widows have nothing left to lose. *International Policy Digest.* https://intpolicydigest.org/2017/07/06/chechnya-s-black-widows-have-nothing-left-to-lose/

Jenkins, J. P. (1998). Red Army Faction: German radical leftist group. Britannica. https://www.britannica.com/topic/Red-Army-Faction

Kafanov, L. (2016). How all-female ISIS morality police "Khansaa Brigade" terrorized Mosul. NBC News. https://www.nbcnews.com/storyline/isis-uncovered/how-all-female-isis-morality-police-khansaa-brigade-terrorized-mosul-n685926

Kampwirth, K. (2002). *Women and guerrilla movements: Nicaragua, El Salvador, Chiapas, Cuba.* Pennsylvania State University Press.

Karpel, D. (2009). Child of the revolution. Haaretz. https://www.haaretz.com/1.5035405

Katersky, A. (2023). New York City woman charged with financing terrorist groups in Syria through cryptocurrency. ABC News. https://abcnews.go.com/US/new-york-city-woman-charged-financing-terrorist-groups/story?id=96818461

Keating, J. (2013). What motivates Russia's "Black Widows"? *Slate.* https://slate.com/news-and-politics/2013/12/why-are-so-many-of-russias-suicide-bombers-women.html

Khelghat-Doost, H. (2017). Women of the caliphate: The mechanism for women's incorporation into the Islamic State (IS). *Perspectives on Terrorism, 11*(1), 17–25.

Khezri, H. (2018, March 20). The complex gender politics of Kurdistan. *Pacific Standard.* https://psmag.com/social-justice/the-complex-gender-politics-of-kurdistan

Koronaiou, A., & Sakellariou, A. (2020). Women and Golden Dawn: Reproducing the nationalist habitus. In C. Miller-Idriss & H. Pilkington (Eds.), *Gender and the Radical and Extreme Right* (pp. 126–143). Routledge.

Kostro, S. S., & Riba, G. (2014). 2014 Olympics terror threat: The hunt for Black Widows. Center for Strategic & International Studies. https://www.csis.org/analysis/2014-olympics-terror-threat-hunt-black-widows

Kurdish Women in Culture (2018, May 26). *The Kurdish Project.* https://thekurdishproject.org/history-and-culture/kurdish-women/kurdish-women-in-culture/

Latif, M., Blee, K., DeMichele, M., & Simi, P. (2020). Do white supremacist women adopt movement archetypes of mother, whore, and fighter? In A. Phelan (Ed.), *Terrorism, gender and women* (pp. 63–80). Routledge.

Laughland, O. (2023). Alabama woman who joined Islamic State says she still hopes to return to US. *The Guardian.* https://www.theguardian.com/world/2023/jan/09/hoda-muthana-alabama-woman-islamic-state-hopes-return-us

Leidig, E. (2021). "We are worth fighting for": Women in far-right extremism. ICCT. https://www.icct.nl/publication/we-are-worth-fighting-women-far-right-extremism

Luciak, I. A. (2001). *After the revolution: Gender and democracy in El Salvador, Nicaragua, and Guatemala.* Johns Hopkins University Press.

MacDonald, E. (1991). *Shoot the women first.* Random House.

Margolin, D. (2016). A Palestinian woman's place in terrorism: Organized perpetrators or individual actors? *Studies in Conflict and Terrorism, 39*, 912–934.

Margolin, D. (2019). The changing roles of women in violent Islamist groups. In A. Alexander (Ed.), *Perspectives on the future of women, gender, & violent extremism* (pp. 40–49). George Washington University Program on Extremism.

Margolin, D., & Cook, J. (2024). Five decades of research on women and terrorism. *Studies in Conflict & Terrorism*, 1–29.

Martin, M. (2014, March). *Women's participation in terrorism, conflict and violent extremism: Gender equality or pure pragmatism*. Annual University of Nottingham PhD Student Conference. http://www.nottingham.ac.uk/hrlc/documents/student-conference-2014/m-martin-ms-nottinghamstudentconference.pdf.

Martini, A. (2018). Making women terrorists into "Jihadi brides": An analysis of media narratives on women joining ISIS. *Critical Studies on Terrorism*, 11(3), 458–477.

Mason, T. D. (1992). Women's participation in Central American revolutions: A theoretical perspective. *Comparative Political Studies*, 25, 63–89.

Matfess, H., & Margolin, D. (2022). The women of January 6th: A gendered analysis of the 21st century American far-right. Report. George Washington University Program on Extremism.

Matur, B. (2011). *Dağın ardına bakmak*. Timas.

McDowall, D. (2000). *A modern history of the Kurds*. I. B. Tauris.

Melzer, P. (2016). Death in the shape of a young girl: Women's political violence in the Red Army Faction. Wellesley Centers for Women. https://www.wcwonline.org/Women-s-Review-of-Books-Mar/Apr-2016/feminism-and-terrorism

Miller-Idriss, C. (2022a). How right-wing extremists weaponize the idea of motherhood. MSNBC News. https://www.msnbc.com/opinion/msnbc-opinion/how-far-right-uses-motherhood-manipulate-recruit-women-n1294922

Miller-Idriss, C. (2022b). Women among the Jan. 6 attackers are the new normal of right-wing extremism: Women are increasingly ditching their backstage role in right-wing extremist movements. MSNBC News. https://www.msnbc.com/opinion/women-among-jan-6-attackers-are-new-normal-right-wing-n1287163

Milton, D., & Dodwell, B. (2018). Jihadi brides? Examining a female guesthouse registry from the Islamic State's Caliphate. *CTC Sentinel*, 11(5), 16–22.

Morin, R. (2019). Trump says he directed Pompeo not to let ISIS bride back in U.S. *Politico*. https://www.politico.com/story/2019/02/20/trump-hoda-muthana-isis-1176678

Moskalenko, S., & McCauley, C. (2021). QAnon. *Perspectives on Terrorism*, 15(2), 142–146.

Myers, S. (2004, September 10). From dismal Chechnya, women turn to bombs. *New York Times*. https://www.nytimes.com/2004/09/10/world/europe/from-dismal-chechnya-women-turn-to-bombs.html

Nacos, B. L. (2005). The portrayal of female terrorists in the media: Similar framing patterns in the news coverage of women in politics and in terrorism. *Studies in Conflict & Terrorism*, 28, 435–451.

Nesi, C. (2024). Repatriated NYC woman charged with completing ISIS terror training in Syria, using AK-47: Feds. *New York Post*. https://nypost.com/2024/05/09/us-news/repatriated-nyc-woman-charged-with-completing-isis-training-in-syria-feds/

Ness, C. D. (2005). In the name of the cause: Women's work in secular and religious terrorism. *Studies in Conflict and Terrorism*, 28, 353–373.

Ness, C. D. (2008). In the name of the cause: Women's work in secular and religious terrorism. In C. D. Ness (Ed.), *Female terrorism and militancy: Agency, utility, and organization* (pp. 25–50). Routledge.

New York Times (1976). Ulrike Meinhof, an anarchist leader In Germany, is found hanged in cell. https://www.nytimes.com/1976/05/10/archives/ulrike-meinhof-an-anarchist-leader-in-germany-is-found-hanged-in.html

Nivat, A. (2005). The black widows: Chechen women join the fight for independence—and Allah. *Studies in Conflict & Terrorism*, 28(5), 413–419.

Nordland, R. (2018, February 24). Women are free, and armed, in Kurdish-controlled northern Syria. *New York Times.* https://www.nytimes.com/2018/02/24/world/middleeast/syria-kurds-womens-rights-gender-equality.html

Öcalan, A. (2013). *Liberating life: Women's revolution.* International Initiative Edition and Mesopotamian Publishers.

Oltermann, P. (2019). Women married to ISIS fighters due to land in Germany from Turkey. *The Guardian.* https://www.theguardian.com/world/2019/nov/15/women-married-to-isis-fighters-due-to-land-in-germany-from-turkey

O'Rourke, L. (2008, August 2). Behind the woman, behind the bomb. *New York Times.* https://www.nytimes.com/2008/08/02/opinion/02orourke.html

Osborn, A. (2010). Moscow bombing: Who are the Black Widows. *The Telegraph.* https://www.telegraph.co.uk/news/worldnews/europe/russia/7534464/Moscow-bombing-who-are-the-Black-Widows.html

Ozeren, S., Hekim, H., Elmas, M. S., & Canbegi, H. I. (2018). An analysis of ISIS propaganda and recruitment activities targeting the Turkish-speaking population. *International Annals of Criminology, 56*(1–2), 105–121.

Page, J. (2004, February 7). Spectre of the Chechen "black widows." *The Times.* https://www.thetimes.co.uk/article/spectre-of-the-chechen-black-widows-gjscp5gthjg

Pandith, F., Ware, J., & Bloom, M. (2020). Female extremists in QAnon and ISIS are on the rise. We need a new strategy to combat them. NBC News. https://www.nbcnews.com/think/opinion/female-extremists-qanon-isis-are-rise-we-need-new-strategy-ncna1250619

Parashar, S. (2011). Gender, jihad, and jingoism: Women as perpetrators, planners, and patrons of militancy in Kashmir. *Studies in Conflict & Terrorism, 34*(4), 295–317.

Pohl, M. (2002). "It cannot be that our graves will be here": The survival of Chechen and Ingush deportees in Kazakhstan, 1944–1957. *Journal of Genocide Research, 4*(3), 401–430.

Pokalova, E. (2019). Pay more attention to the women of ISIS. *Defense One.* https://www.defenseone.com/ideas/2019/10/pay-more-attention-women-isis/161012/ Press.

Porzucki, N. (2013). What motivates women to commit acts of terror? The World. https://www.pri.org/node/62440/popout

Pylas, P. (2024). IS bride stuck in Syrian refugee camp loses her appeal over the removal of her UK citizenship. Associated Press. https://apnews.com/article/britain-shamima-begum-appeal-citizenship-5d6de3ac785ecb7d3a2b46f79e037777

Rabinowitz, H. (2024). American woman repatriated from Syria accused of training with ISIS. CNN. https://www.cnn.com/2024/05/07/politics/repatriated-american-accused-isis-training/index.html

Raghavan, S. V., & Balasubramaniyan, V. (2014). Evolving role of women in terror groups: Progression or regression? *Journal of International Women's Studies, 15,* 197–211.

Reif, L. L. (1986). Women in Latin American guerrilla movements: A comparative perspective. *Comparative Politics, 18,* 147–169.

Ridgeway, C. L. (2011). *Framed by gender: How gender inequality persists in the modern world.* Oxford University Press.

Roose, K. (2021). What is QAnon, the viral pro-Trump conspiracy theory? *New York Times.* https://www.nytimes.com/article/what-is-qanon.html

Ross, R. A. (2020). Proud Boys are at war with their female extremist wing. *The Daily Beast.* https://www.thedailybeast.com/proud-boys-are-at-war-with-their-proud-girls-female-extremist-wing

Rousseva, V. (2004). Rape and Sexual Assault in Chechnya. *Culture, Society, & Praxis, 3*(1), 1–4

Ryan, M. (2023). "Better martyrs": The growing role of women in the far-right movement. *The Guardian.* https://www.theguardian.com/world/2023/aug/12/conservative-women-tradwife-republican

Saarijärvi, J & Siafaka, A. (2021). The role of women in far-right extremism. Counterterrorism Group. https://www.counterterrorismgroup.com/post/the-role-of-women-in-far-right-extremism

Sales, P. P. (2016). *Psychological torture: Definition, evaluation and measurement.* Routledge.

Santucci, J., Waugh, R., & Schneir, H. (2021). Gender and right-wing extremism in America: Why understanding women's roles is key to preventing future acts of domestic terrorism. *Just Security*. https://www.justsecurity.org/75068/gender-and-right-wing-extremism-in-america-why-understanding-womens-roles-is-key-to-preventing-future-acts-of-domestic-terrorism/

Schenck, M. C. (2006). The birth of the Baader–Meinhof Group. https://www.dw.com/en/germanys-raf-terrorism-anunresolved-story/a-68474099

Schweitzer, Y. (2006). Palestinian female suicide bombers: Reality vs. myth. In Y. Schweitzer (Ed.), *Female suicide bombers: Dying for equality*. Jaffee Center for Strategic Studies. https://www.files.ethz.ch/isn/91112/2006-08_Female%20Suicide%20Bombers_complete%20document.pdf

Shaikh, T. (2010). Attacks bear hallmarks of Chechen "Black Widows." *CNN*. https://www.theguardian.com/world/2010/mar/29/moscow-metro-bombs-explosions-terror

Sjoberg, L., & Gentry, C. E. (2007). *Mothers, monsters, whores: Women's violence in global politics*. Zed Books.

Sloan, M. M., & Haner, M. (2024). Women's involvement in terrorist organizations. In S. L. Browning, L. C. Butler, & C. L. Jonson (Eds.), *Gender and crime: Contemporary theoretical perspectives* (pp. 281–298). Routledge.

Sontheimer, M. (2019). RAF prisoners in Stuttgart-Stammheim: On life and death. Spiegel. https://www.spiegel.de/plus/raf-gefaengnis-stammheim-die-gefangenen-der-roten-armee-fraktion-a-d3dcbf4e-9136-4556-875a-201eaa3a3f99

Speckhard, A. & Akhmedova, K. (2006). Black Widows: The Chechen female suicide terrorists. Jaffe Center for Strategic Studies. https://www.inss.org.il/publication/black-widows-chechen-female-suicide-terrorists/

Speckhard, A., & Akhmedova, K. (2007). Black widows and beyond: Understanding the motivations and life trajectories of Chechen female terrorists. In C. D. Ness (Ed.), *Female terrorism and militancy* (pp. 114–135). Routledge

Speckhard, A., & Ellenberg, M. D. (2020). ISIS in their own words. *Journal of Strategic Security, 13*(1), 82–127.

Spencer, A. N. (2016). The hidden face of terrorism: An analysis of the women in Islamic State. *Journal of Strategic Security, 9*(3), 74–98.

SPLC (2024). Moms for Liberty. Southern Poverty Law Center. https://www.splcenter.org/fighting-hate/extremist-files/group/moms-liberty

Stephen, C. (2003). Moscow concert suicide bombers linked to Chechen "Black Widows." *Irish Times*. https://www.irishtimes.com/news/moscow-concert-suicide-bombers-linked-to-chechen-black-widows-1.365476

Stuchbery, M. (2019). What Germany's Red Army Faction can tell the world about terror. *The Local*. https://www.thelocal.de/20190405/what-germanys-red-army-faction-can-tell-the-world-about-terror

Sutten, M. L. (2009). *The rising importance of women in terrorism and the need to reform counterterrorism strategy*. Army Command and General Staff Coll Fort Leavenworth School of Advanced Military Studies.

The Economist (2003). The Black Widows' revenge. *The Economist*. https://www.economist.com/europe/2003/07/10/the-black-widows-revenge

Thomas, J. L., & Bond, K. D. (2015). Women's participation in violent political organizations. *American Political Science Review, 109*(3), 488–506.

Thomas, J. L., & Wood, R. M. (2018). The social origins of female combatants. *Conflict Management and Peace Science, 35*, 215–232.

United Nations Human Rights Council (2024). Punishing the innocent: Ending violations against children in the north-east of the Syrian Arab Republic. Independent International Commission of Inquiry on the Syrian Arab Republic. https://reliefweb.int/report/syrian-arab-republic/punishing-innocent-ending-violations-against-children-north-east-syrian-arab-republic-independent-international-commission-inquiry-syrian-arab-republic-ahrc55crp8

US Library of Congress (2024). Oath Keepers: Guardians of the Republic. https://www.loc.gov/item/lcwaN0003728/

Vale, G. (2019). *Women in Islamic State: From caliphate to camps*. International Center for Counter-Terrorism.

Vertigans, S. (2007). Beyond the fringe? Radicalisation within the American far-right.

Totalitarian Movements and Political Religions, 8(3–4), 641–659.

Victor, B. (2003). *Army of roses: Inside the world of Palestinian women suicide bombers.* Rodale.

Viterna, J. S. (2006). Pulled, pushed, and persuaded: Explaining women's mobilization into the Salvadoran guerrilla army. *American Journal of Sociology, 112*(1), 1–45.

Viterna, J. S. (2013). *Women in war: The microprocesses of mobilization in El Salvador.* Oxford University Press.

Von Knop, K. (2007). The female jihad: Al Qaeda's women. *Studies in Conflict and Terrorism, 30*, 397–414.

Wang, P. (2011). Women in the LTTE: Birds of freedom or cogs in the wheel. *Journal of Politics and Law, 4*, 100–108.

Ward, O. (2010). Why Chechnya's Black Widows are driven to kill. *The Star.* https://www.thestar.com/news/insight/why-chechnyas-black-widows-are-driven-to-kill/article_9dc34aa2-5bf9-577c-b6dc-eec5e9a44d22.html

Weinberg, L., & Eubank, W. (2011). Women's involvement in terrorism. *Gender Issues, 28*, 22–49.

Weine, S. (2019). Rehabilitating the Islamic State's women and children returnees in Kazakhstan. Just Security. https://www.justsecurity.org/67694/rehabilitating-the-islamic-states-women-and-children-returnees-in-kazakhstan/

West, K. (2015) The female guerrilla fighters of the PKK. *Middle East Eye.* http://www.middleeasteye.net/in-depth/features/female-guerrilla-fighters-pkk-2044198184.

White, J. (2022). *Gender mainstreaming in counterterrorism policy: Building transformative strategies to counter violent extremism.* Routledge.

White, P. J. (2000). *Primitive rebels or revolutionary modernizers? The Kurdish national movement in Turkey.* Zed Books.

Williams, B. G. (2014). The brides of Allah: The terror threat of Black-Widow suicide bombers to the Winter Olympics. *Huffington Post.* https://www.huffpost.com/entry/the-brides-of-allah-the-t_b_4761027

Williams, S. (2016). The tough legacy of Ulrike Meinhof. *Medium.* https://medium.com/latterly/the-tough-legacy-of-ulrike-meinhof-af1387dace69

Winter, C., & Margolin, D. (2017). The mujahidat dilemma: Female combatants and the Islamic State. *CTC Sentinel, 10*(7), 25–30.

Wood, R. M. (2019). *Female fighters: Why rebel groups recruit women for war.* Columbia University Press.

Wood, R. M., & Thomas, J. L. (2017). Women on the frontline: Rebel group ideology and women's participation in violent rebellion. *Journal of Peace Research, 54*, 31–46.

Yousef, O. (2023). Moms for Liberty among conservative groups named "extremist" by civil rights watchdog. NPR. https://www.npr.org/2023/06/07/1180486760/splc-moms-for-liberty-extremist-group

Yuzik, Y. (2013). Russia's New Black Widows. *Foreign Policy.* https://foreignpolicy.com/2013/10/24/russias-new-black-widows/

Zimmer, B. (2014). The Deadly Web of "Black Widows." *The Wall Street Journal.* https://www.wsj.com/articles/the-deadly-web-of-8216black-widows8217-1390611562

Types of Terrorism

III

Types of Terrorism

CHAPTER 6

Ideological Terrorism

Far-Left versus Far-Right Political Extremism

Learning Objectives
1. To describe the origins of left- and right-wing political division.
2. To understand the contexts that gave rise to emergence of extremist ideologies across the world.
3. To examine the core far-left extremist ideologies.
4. To examine the core far-right extremist ideologies.
5. To analyze the history and the current state of ideological extremism in the United States.

6.1 INTRODUCTION

Ideologies have played a significant role in various types of terrorist movements across the world. Originally used by the French (as *idéologie*) during the French Revolution, the word **ideology** refers to a particular set of beliefs, ideas, and principles that explain how society should be organized (Cambridge University Press n.d.; Cranston 2024). Ideologies provide cultural, political, and economic models or goals to achieve their proposed social order (i.e., change the world). Several political ideologies emerged during the nineteenth and twentieth centuries—including socialism, communism, anarchism, fascism, and Nazism—when secular beliefs gained prominence over traditional religious beliefs. This chapter will explain the origins, history, characteristics, and significance of ideologies in terms of their influence on extremism and terrorism. As you read this chapter, keep in mind that holding extremist ideologies does not, on its own, make one a terrorist. As discussed in Chapter 1, terrorism occurs when individuals or groups use strategic violence against innocent civilians in a way that is designed to affect a larger audience and instill fear to achieve their objectives. In the case of ideological terrorism, those objectives are influenced by beliefs about how society should be organized.

6.2 ORIGINS OF THE LEFT AND RIGHT

In today's world, the terms "left" and "right" are used to refer to opposing ends of the **political spectrum** for liberals and conservatives, but these terms were originally coined during the French Revolution, and they were initially used as literal descriptions of the physical seating arrangements at the French National Assembly (Carlisle 2019). This split goes back to summer of 1789, when delegates from the aristocracy and revolutionaries met to decide the future of France. Soon after the storming of the Bastille in July 1789, anti-royalist revolutionaries, who were unhappy with the king and the economic situation in France, wanted to draft a new constitution to limit the royal authority's power over the public. One of the biggest debates was how much power and authority should be vested in the monarchy (King Louis XVI). Two main factions emerged at the National Assembly during these debates: (1) the commoners and revolutionaries, who wanted to limit the King's power to a symbolic one, abolish his absolute veto right, and establish democracy in France; and (2) the aristocracy and conservatives, who were loyal to the King and supported the continuation of the monarchy; they believed that the King, his dynasty, and the Church should rule France with unlimited authority (Andrews 2020). As the debates continued, those who wanted the change of rule, the progressives (commoners and the less powerful clergy) sat on the left side of the president of the National Assembly, whereas those who wanted to keep the existing power structure, the traditionalists or the nobility (those who were loyal to the king and the religious clerics), sat on the right side of the president.

Over time, this physical seating arrangement of the French politicians in the legislature began to be used to reference the opposing political ideologies—"the left" and "the right" as we know today. This terminology soon spread to other countries. Political parties from Bolshevik Russia to the United States began identifying themselves with these terms (Carlisle 2019). This characteristic political polarization continues to exist as a visible feature in contemporary politics.

6.2.1 Political Spectrum

Based on their emphasis on different policies and interests, the ideologies of the left and the right differ significantly from each other. For example, the left is characterized as pro-change, revolutionary, and the protector of the lower economic and social classes. It is usually known for working toward the goal of reducing unjustified inequalities that disadvantage certain segments of the population. Liberalism, socialism, communism, and anarchism are the leading ideological movements that emerged under leftward ideological thought.

In contrast, the right is characterized by its interest in dominant structures and the notions of tradition, hierarchy, and authority as well as free enterprise and private property. Unlike the left, the right view argues that social inequality in society is inevitable, a normal feature of life, and the government should not intervene. Conservatism, monarchism, Nazism, and fascism are the prominent ideologies that emerged as right-wing perspectives.

All of these ideologies are placed on an imaginary line called the political spectrum, which is used to describe political parties according to their ideology, views, and preferred policies. This line can be considered a scale with two opposite ends, one side representing the right, the other side representing the left. As can be seen in Figure 6.2, each of these ideologies has a different place on the political spectrum, depending on their basic principles and position on various social issues (e.g., how to best organize society and the economic system).

For example, scholars place anarchism on the furthest left side of the political spectrum because this particular ideology is considered to be the most extreme leftist thought, which favors the total destruction of the power elites. On the other hand, fascism is considered to be the most extreme right-wing ideology, and thus it is located at the furthest right of the political spectrum (Maddox & Lilie 1984).

FIGURE 6.1   The left vs. right divide in French Parliament. *Source:* BnF Gallica.

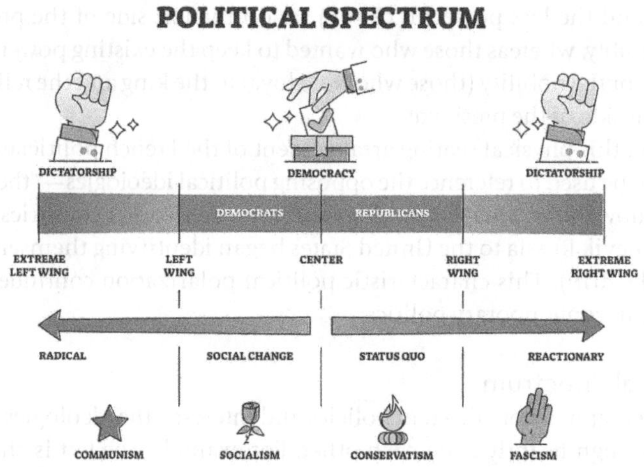

POLITICAL SPECTRUM

FIGURE 6.2 The left vs. right political spectrum. *Source:* VectorMine/
Shutterstock.

6.3 FAR-LEFT IDEOLOGIES

Extremist left-wing political thought (otherwise known as the **far-left** or radical left)
is often associated with extreme revolutionary views such as anarchism and communism, and is characterized by strong opposition to capitalism and globalization.
Advocates of leftward ideologies support progressive policies, such as greater social and
economic equality through the re-distribution of wealth acquired by the elites to the
disadvantaged segments of the society. It is crucial to understand the basic arguments
of extremist left thought because the history of the world is replete with examples of
violent terrorist attacks, forced indoctrinations, political repressions, mass killings,
and genocide committed by far-left militant organizations and governments that
sought to bring change to society through violence, instead of via traditional political
processes. This section will focus on the two main radical left ideologies: anarchism
and communism.

6.3.1 Anarchism

The word "anarchy" comes from the ancient Greek word "anarchos," which means
leaderless or without a ruler, or without authority (Cranston 2024). **Anarchism** is the
philosophical thought that favors anarchy. As mentioned previously, anarchism is
placed farthest to the left on the political spectrum. In the nineteenth century, French
political philosopher Pierre-Joseph Proudhon became known for advocating for
anarchism. In his seminal work *What is Property?* Proudhon argued that crime is
merely the product of private property and authority, and thus he speculated the
eventual dissolution of authority and establishment of a natural social order. Modern
anarchist thought was developed in France and then spread to the rest of the world
in the early twentieth century.

Anarchism favors establishing a noncoercive society without an official governing body. Opposition to the state, authority, and coercive forms of power are the central tenets of anarchism. According to this ideology, the existence of an authoritative governing body is unnecessary and harmful (Cranston 2024). Instead, anarchists believe in the unrestricted development of human society (completely free from domination) by abolishing human-made laws. Anarchists favor social equality and noncoercive consensus-building in decision-making.

Between the early twentieth century and end of World War II, in response to the race toward industrialization, anarchist movements developed in several different parts of the world, including countries like France, Russia, China, Japan, and Argentina. During this period anarchists carried out influential revolutions, such the Paris Commune, the Russian Civil War, and the Spanish Civil War. Anarchism played a significant role in workers' struggles for emancipation. For example, when heavily armed French radicals took control of Paris from the French government in 1871 (known as the Paris Commune), not only did they establish a secular system of social democracy by separating church and state affairs, but they also made significant improvements to workers' lives by reducing the mandatory working hours imposed by the elite, ending work in the evening, and banning child labor (Wheeldon 2021).

Revolutionary political violence known as propaganda of the deed—acts of violence directed at the ruling class to bring down the state and the authority—were adopted by anarchist groups during this period. Anarchists engaged in several violent attacks against the ruling class in attempts to inspire the population and catalyze major revolutions. Prominent people killed by anarchists during this era include US President William McKinley, President Sadi Carnot of France, and King Umberto I of Italy. These assassinations of government officials, heads of state, and wealthy business owners to change society through revolutionary means created an image of anarchists as violent, militant, and ruthless. Indeed, two years after the assassination of President McKinley by a second-generation Polish immigrant, the United States Congress, at the recommendation of President Theodore Roosevelt, enacted the Immigration Act of 1903 (also known as Anarchist Exclusion Act), which allowed law enforcement to deport suspected anarchist immigrants from the country (Fine 1955).

Historians generally agree that the anarchist movements lost their momentum by the end of World War II, mostly due to the rise of right-wing totalitarian regimes in Europe. For example, in Italy and Germany, the fascist governments headed by Mussolini and Hitler (described later in this chapter) completely destroyed the presence of anarchists in their countries. The Bolshevik revolution in Russia also led Russian anarchists to turn into supporters of communism. However, beginning in the 1960s, a new kind of anarchism emerged. During this era, anarchist ideas became influential among groups that were anti-Americanism, anti-globalization, anti-NATO, or anti-war, as well as other groups with agendas driven by environmental and economic injustices. These groups frequently engaged in riots and protests to spread their opinions. Most of these protests ended in violent encounters with police and significant property destruction.

One prominent example of these protests is the 1999 Seattle World Trade Organization protest, also known as the Battle of Seattle. It was organized by a coalition of anarchists who sought to bring attention to various issues—workers' rights, environmental issues, and the detrimental effects of global trade (Frantilla n.d.). This protest is considered the first internet-organized international mobilization by anarchists. It is estimated that more than 50,000 protesters gathered around the Paramount Convention Center in Seattle, Washington, where the WTO meeting was being held (Scruggs 2019). Protesters initially utilized peaceful means—such as chaining themselves to metal pipes, blocking the entrances to the convention center, and organizing street parties—to prevent the opening ceremony, which eventually led to the cancellation of workshops organized by the meeting committee. However, in reaction to the brutal response of the police—who used rubber bullets, pepper spray, detention, and tear gas—some protesters began to throw bottles and sticks at the police and destroy property, and they vandalized and looted major corporations such as Starbucks, Nike, and Nordstrom (Sawicki 2013). To anarchists and radicals, this mass protest and demonstration was a success as the WTO had to cancel the conference.

6.3.2 Is Anarchism Inherently Violent and Chaotic?

One major misconception about anarchism is that it is an inherently violent and chaotic ideology. In part, this misconception has resulted from media representations of anarchists in the West that have often been negative, depicting the members of these groups as violent and lawless (Wittel 2015). However, while anarchism favors "no rulers/no authority," it does not favor life "without rules," as is commonly assumed (Flood 2021). Anarchists simply reject domination and control by the state. They argue that the state creates unwanted dependency as the laws and regulations are often created by (or according to the desires of) the rich and powerful (Wittel 2015). Instead, anarchists aim for a society where nonhierarchical, voluntary, horizontal structures reject the capitalist economy and collectively learn to rule themselves via direct democracy (Flood 2021). They argue that each person should have a right to fully participate in any political decision made. As the anarchist philosophical thinker Peter Kropotkin stated in 1910, with anarchism "society is conceived without government—harmony in such a society being obtained, not by submission to law, or by obedience to any authority, but by free agreements concluded between the various groups, territorial and professional, freely constituted for the sake of production and consumption, as also for the satisfaction of the infinite variety of needs and aspirations of a civilized being" (Kropotkin 1995).

6.3.3 Communism

Communism is an ideology and form of government that aims to eliminate socioeconomic class struggles by creating a classless society in which all means of production and products (such as education, agriculture, and transportation) are communally owned by the people. The origins of this ideology go back to eighteenth-century France, to Joseph Victor d'Hupay, a philosopher who argued that people should live in communes in which all property and wealth are commonly owned (instead of individual ownership) and social ranks and classes are abolished (Deutsche Welle 2022). It is important to note that the Greek philosopher Plato also mentioned a communist society where ownership of all materials and goods are shared among the people; this was in his famous writing *Republic*, from around 375 BCE.

However, the contemporary version of communism was developed in 1848 by German philosopher Karl Marx (who spent most of his life in exile in England and

France) and German economist Friedrich Engels in their well-known book *The Communist Manifesto.* According to Marx, the rise of factories and the capability of mass production for profit during the Industrial Revolution, which had not been seen in any other period of human history, created a large working-class population that was exploited and oppressed by the rich. He argued that the Industrial Revolution allowed the rich to accrue massive wealth at the expense of a large, impoverished working class (Service 2010).

Marx blamed capitalism for society's problems (poverty, inequality, shortened lives of the working class), and his manifesto offered an alternative ideal for society—the replacement of capitalism with communism. As with anarchism, Marx and Engels highlighted the importance of the French Revolution for a future global scale proletarian (working-class) revolution. During the final stages of this transformation, they argued, class struggles would come to an end and society would live cohesively in social equilibrium, without the unnecessary influence of class and family structures and without the influences of religion and property (Pop-Eleches & Tucker 2020). As Marx stated in his 1875 writing *Critique of the Gotha Program*, "from each according to his ability, to each according to his needs." In other words, under the communist ideology, everyone in society would work to the best of their abilities and goods and services would be distributed freely according to each person's needs. In a classless society where everyone shares wealth according to their needs, people would not be motivated by greed—as in the free-market capitalist societies—as there would be no competition for greater status. In such a society, there would be no rich and poor or oppression of the working class due to economic equality and fairness—everything from mines to factories would be publicly owned and operated for the benefit of all. And the presence of a strong central government would provide citizens with all their basic needs: food, education, healthcare, and housing.

6.3.4 Soviet Union: The First Communist State

In 1917, the Bolsheviks—the extremist wing of the Russian Social Democratic Party—initially led by Vladimir Lenin and then Joseph Stalin, would make Russia the first nation in the world to put Marx and Engel's communism ideals into practice and create a communist government. Following Marx's guidelines, Stalin established a ruling class composed of the workers—the proletariat—who were supposed to rule the country temporarily during the transition from a capitalist economy into a communist one. Marx and Engels named this stage the "dictatorship of the proletariat," or rule by the working class. To liberate the working class, the state must first take control of all means of production. However, the owners of the means of production—the capitalist class or bourgeoisie—would not willingly give up their land and wealth. Therefore, the proletariat was tasked with suppressive coercion, including oppression, tyranny, and mass murder, against any kind of resistance (especially by the wealthy bourgeoise) to the success of the revolution. This mass social violence, argued Lenin, was necessary to exert absolute control over all aspects of Russian society and to ensure that people accepted this new system. According to well-regarded Russian historian Roy Medvedev, approximately 20 million Russians perished during this time—in labor camps, through forced collectivization and punitive famine policies (known as Holodomor), or they were executed for belonging to opposition parties

FIGURE 6.3 Vintage Soviet propaganda poster: Long Live the USSR! Blueprint for the Brotherhood of all Working Classes of all the World's Nationalities!, 1935. *Source:* Steve Knight from Halstead, United Kingdom, CC BY 2.0, via Wikimedia Commons.

or families of former nobility, merchants, and state officials. Millions of others were blacklisted, arrested, driven from their homes, and sent to labor camps (Keller 1989).

These numbers do not include the casualties that resulted during the Red Terror and the Great Purge. The Red Terror refers to the atrocities (political repression, mass killings, and executions) committed by the Bolsheviks during Lenin's term—specifically the fight between the Bolsheviks (known as the Reds) and the members of the military and supporters of the monarchy (known as the Whites). Even though the true extent of casualties during this era is impossible to determine, partly due to secrecy and censorship, it is estimated that approximately 200,000 Russians were executed by the Bolshevik Secret Police in an attempt to silence the regime's enemies, the dissidents (Blakemore 2020). The Red Terror lasted until 1921, when the Bolsheviks won the civil war. The brutal campaign to eliminate the dissenting members of the Communist Party, led by Joseph Stalin following Lenin's death in 1924, is referred to as the Great Purge or the Great Terror. It is estimated that more than 700,000 people, including 30,000 members of the Red Army—mostly Lenin supporters and Bolshevik generals and admirals who challenged Stalin—were executed between 1936 and 1938. As a result of the "dictatorship of the proletariat," Russia (the Soviet Union beginning in 1922) became one of the world's richest and most powerful states. It operated as the only revolutionary Marxist state on earth—a one-party state without the existence of any kind of dissent.

The Soviet Union initially became an ally of the United States, a liberal democracy, during World War II. However, in the 1950s, the US and Soviet Russia began a race to develop nuclear weapons, an era known as the **Cold War**. The two powers abstained from attacking each other because they both knew that a war involving nuclear weapons would annihilate them both, regardless of who attacked first. This would later be known as mutual assured destruction (Metcalfe 2022).

Even though the Soviet Union and the US did not engage in direct military conflict, they started a global scale proxy war (including the Korean and Vietnam Wars), each side economically and militarily supporting their allied regimes around the world. Both states organized coups, engaged in assassination attempts, and supported insurgencies in order to install their regimes in several different countries; their political influence also divided Europe in what was known as the Iron Curtain, with countries connected to the Soviet Union on the east side and capitalist NATO members on the West side (Hamilton 1990; Stuster 2013).

6.3.5 The October Crisis of 1962 (The Cuban Missile Crisis)

The 1962 Cuban Missile Crisis, also known as the October Crisis of 1962, was one of the most significant Cold War confrontations. It began when the Soviet Union installed more than 29 medium-range nuclear-armed missiles in Cuba, which could strike the US within a few minutes; this was ostensibly to protect the island nation from a potential US invasion. At the time, Cuba, a Caribbean island only 90 miles south of Florida, had been under Soviet military and economic control under its leftist revolutionary leader Fidel Castro. The US, unhappy with the existence of a Soviet-friendly regime so close to its borders, had already tried to overthrow the Castro government with the Bay of Pigs invasion in 1961. Financed and directed by the CIA, approximately 1,400 Cubans, trained by Americans, landed on an isolated spot on the island known as Bay of Pigs. After

FIGURE 6.4 "Everything for the Front," a USSR World War II propaganda poster. *Source:* El Lissitzky, Public domain, via Wikimedia Commons.

less than a half a day of fighting, Castro's army killed hundreds of CIA-trained exiles and captured more than 1,100 of them (Weldes 1999).

From a Soviet standpoint, the installation of ballistic missiles in Cuba was crucial: it would deter the US government from invading the Cuban territories again due to the threat of the missiles being launched at targets across the United States. It was also a retaliatory tactic, as the United States had installed several nuclear weapons targeting Soviet territories in Turkey and various Western European countries. However, believing that the presence of ballistic missiles so close to the US was unacceptable, the United States, under the leadership of President John F. Kennedy, responded with a naval blockade (or naval quarantine) around Cuba, blocking the Soviet Union from providing additional military equipment and missiles. Later, Kennedy explained the gravity of the situation to the US public in a television broadcast, declaring that the US was prepared to use military power to neutralize this dangerous Soviet threat (Blight et al. 1987).

Tension mounted over the following days: Soviet ships carrying nuclear weapons came very close to the US Navy, and an American reconnaissance jet was shot down while

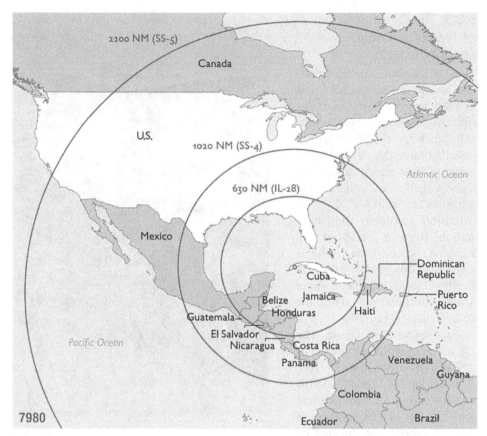

FIGURE 6.5 Map of Northern America showing the full range of the nuclear missiles (IL-28, SS-4, and SS-5) stationed on Cuba. *Source:* Defense Intelligence Agency, DID Graphics+1(202) 231-8601, Public domain, via Wikimedia Commons.

flying over Cuban territories. US invasion forces were deployed to Florida in response to these developments. However, on October 28, the crisis ended when the Soviet Union agreed to remove its ballistic installations from Cuba; in exchange, the United States had to remove their nuclear missile installations from Turkey and promise to not invade Cuba. The Kennedy administration accepted the Soviet Union's terms, and the crisis was concluded by late November 1962. The Cuban missile crisis is important because it is the closest that the world had ever come to a global scale nuclear war (Kennedy 2011).

6.3.6 Why Did an Ideology of Liberation Ultimately Fail and Lead to the Death of Millions?

Even though approximately one third of the world lived under communism during the twentieth century, contrary to Marx's vision, a global scale communist revolution, inspired and instigated by working-class people, has never materialized. Historically, the Soviet Union and China have been the most prominent communist superpowers (Pruitt 2019).

The Soviet Union collapsed in 1991, concluding the Cold War and reducing the prevalence and political influence of communism worldwide. As of 2024 there are five remaining communist-led states: China, North Korea, Cuba, Vietnam, and Laos. However, none of these countries were able to eliminate personal property ownership or create a classless society as Marx advocated in his manifesto. China, even though it officially identifies itself as a communist regime, has incorporated elements of capitalism (e.g., free market) into its economic system to survive the fate of the Soviet Union.

FIGURE 6.6 Chinese propaganda posters from Great Leap Forward (1958–1962). *Source:* Wang Liuying (王柳影), Xin Liliang (忻礼良), Meng Muyi (孟幕颐), Xu Jiping (徐寄萍), Zhang Biwu (张碧梧), Wu Shaoyun (吴少云), Jin Zhaofang (金肇芳), Yu Weibo (俞微波), Lu Zezhi (陆泽之), Public domain, via Wikimedia Commons.

Communist states engaged in mass murders on a scale that has not been seen with any other ideology. It is estimated that approximately 100 million people lost their lives under various communist regimes, including in Russia, China, North Korea, Cambodia, and Ethiopia. Most of these casualties occurred through mass famines and mass murders, which forced people to give up their private property and work according to the regimes' orders (Somin 2017). For example, between 1958 and 1962 under Mao Zedong's Great Leap Forward policy—in which people's homes, lands, livestock, and personal belongings were collectivized—more than 45 million Chinese people (mostly peasants) lost their lives (Dikötter 2018). This is the biggest mass murder in the history of the world. Under the Soviet **gulag system**, a prison system composed of hundreds of worksites, more than 18 million people were forced to work on the construction of canals, roads, and railroads, in mines, and on other industrial projects for 14 hours a day, under harsh conditions, and without adequate food. It is estimated that more than 1.5 million people lost their lives in gulags between 1919 and 1953 (Ivanova et al. 2015). Similarly, during the communist leader Pol Pot's reign of terror in Cambodia (1975–1979), more than one million Cambodians perished in Killing Fields, where people were shot or spaded and then buried collectively across 20,000 mass graves.

Researchers speculate that there are three main reasons for the failure of communism worldwide. First, the communist regimes did not reward individual effort, innovation, or contribution; without profit or competition, there was no incentive for people to work hard and be productive. Many people showed little effort and reserved their energy for the underground economy, where they could make a profit. Soviet workers developed a maxim that addressed the major flaw in their economic system: "We pretend to work and they pretend to pay us" (Tanas 2015). Second, unlike the democratically elected governments in capitalist societies, power in communist regimes has been controlled by a very small group of elites (e.g., the Bolsheviks in Russia), who often exploited the system and used it

FIGURE 6.7 Human skulls of victims of the Khmer Rouge stacked at the Killing Fields of Choeung Ek memorial in Phnom Penh, Cambodia. *Source:* Public domain, via Wikimedia Commons.

for their own benefit. Third, communist regimes were inherently violent, exerting full control over all aspects of life, including freedom of speech, religion, and economic activity. Even though Marx had promised a society in which the working class would enjoy prosperity and liberation, when put into practice, they encountered massive poverty and enslavement. Later, the communist regimes had to build walls to prevent their people fleeing into capitalist societies that offered them greater opportunities, such as in East Germany.

6.4 FAR-LEFT TERRORIST GROUPS

As noted, proponents of extreme ideologies become terrorists when they resort to violence to achieve their goals. Historically, far-left terrorist groups tend to be affiliated or aligned with communist organizations or parties, with many originating in university settings as offshoots of the student protest movements of the 1960s. As an example, we describe three historical cases of far-left terrorist groups: the Revolutionary Armed Forces of Colombia (FARC), the Japanese Red Army (JRA), and the Italian Red Brigades (BR). Each group employed violence in their attempts to create revolutionary change that would overthrow the existing government and address the needs of disadvantaged segments of the population—rural peasants (FARC), Palestinians (JRA), and the working class (BR).

6.4.1 Revolutionary Armed Forces of Colombia (FARC)

The **Revolutionary Armed Forces of Colombia (FARC**; Fuerzas Armadas Revolucionarias de Colombia in Spanish) was a Colombian Marxist-Leninist guerrilla group that emerged in 1964 following a decade-long civil war. During the period of 1948–1958 known as La Violencia, intense political violence erupted between Colombia's Conservative and Liberal political parties (Rabasa et al. 2006). The Conservatives, including large landowners, sought to reclaim ancestral lands from the Liberals, including reformist rural peasants, who fought to defend the countryside. Resulting in over 200,000 deaths, this civil war continued until the parties agreed to establish the National Front, an arrangement in which the parties would alternate holding the presidential office and have equal representation in other governmental positions (Oritz 2002).

Some liberal and communist guerilla groups, however, resisted this agreement and established their own communities in the countryside, termed "independent republics," in order to support the needs of the rural population. One such group, created by Pedro

Antonio Marín Marín (also known as Manuel Marulanda Vélez), developed into the FARC after it was attacked by the Colombian military in 1964. The group fought back and banded together with other reformist communities. Feeling neglected by the conservative government and with the goal of improving living conditions in the countryside, the FARC initially organized to defend their communities, but later aimed to overthrow the conservative Colombian government. In late 1960 the group expanded its role to provide educational and medical services, train guerrillas, and carry out attacks (Oritz 2002).

FARC military tactics included bombings, assassinations, hijackings, and kidnappings, as well as guerrilla attacks on Colombian political, military, and economic targets. Following a Maoist "people's war" doctrine, the FARC gradually extended its control over the countryside and then sought to isolate government forces in urban areas (Rabasa et al. 2006). The FARC funded itself through ransoms, which it gained by kidnapping politicians and elites, and drug trafficking. Researchers from Colombia's National Centre for Historical Memory recently estimated that more than 260,000 people died as a result of the FARC's guerilla violence—in addition to the 200,000 killed previously during La Violencia, prior to FARC's establishment (AP 2018).

Although the FARC engaged in peace talks with the government throughout the 1980s and 1990s—and together with the Colombian Communist Party established an official leftist political party, Patriotic Union (Unión Patriótica: UP), in 1985—violence continued as FARC members found the negotiations to be inadequate. It was not until 2016, after over five decades of guerrilla violence, that the FARC signed a peace deal with the Colombian government. FARC members gave up their arms in exchange for a number of concessions from the government, including programs to address poverty and inequality in rural areas that had been hitherto neglected (e.g., providing jobs, and building schools and roads) as well as opportunities for former FARC leaders to hold political offices and avoid incarceration (Suárez & Rueda 2021).

In 2021, the United States removed the FARC from its Foreign Terrorist Organizations list, after 24 years of this official recognition. In its place, however, the US added two FARC splinter groups—the Revolutionary Armed Forces of Colombia People's Army (FAR-EP) and Segunda Marquetalia—which are associated with FARC guerrilla leaders who rejected the peace deal (Blazakis 2022).

6.4.2 Japanese Red Army (JRA)

Founded by Fusako Shigenobu in 1971, the goal of the **Japanese Red Army (JRA)** was to achieve a worldwide Marxist-Leninist revolution and overthrow the Japanese government through terrorism. Shigenobu, a woman employed in a working-class office job with the Kikkoman soy sauce company, became involved in leftist political activism after starting night classes at Meiji University in the mid-1960s. At that time youth social movements, particularly on college campuses, were prominent. Notable protests erupted over the Vietnam War and the US-Japan Mutual Security Treaty, which allowed US military forces to remain in Japan to provide security following World War II. While participating in these movements, Shigenobu affiliated with the Japanese Red Army Faction (JRAF, a far-left militant group) and the Black Panthers, developing a robust commitment to anti-racism and anti-imperialism (Gerteis 2021). Her subsequent dedication to Palestinian nationalism and founding the JRA led to Shigenobu being recognized as the face of international terrorism in the 1970s, similar to Osama bin Laden's recognition in the 2000s (Box & McCormack 2004).

Convinced that violence was the only way to bring about revolution, in 1971 Shigenobu led a group of RAF members to Lebanon to commit themselves to international terrorism with the **Popular Front for Liberation of Palestine (PFLP)**. As a desk worker in the PFLP's Beirut office, Shigenobu translated propaganda to facilitate recruitment in Japan. Shigenobu's Japanese arm of the PFLP, the JRA, only recruited about 25 armed members but had hundreds of sympathizers in Japan. The JRA depended on the PFLP for financing, weapons, and training, and utilized tactics such as bombing, hijacking, and hostage-taking.

On May 30, 1972, the JRA, on behalf of the PFLP, committed an international terrorist attack in Israel, which Shigenobu is believed to have masterminded. Three JRA members arrived on a flight from Rome at the Lod Airport in Tel Aviv, retrieved assault rifles and hand grenades in the baggage claim area, and began firing at random. The attack killed 26 people and wounded 80 (Reich 2022).

Following the Lod Airport massacre, the JRA went on to commit numerous other attacks, either in support of Palestinian liberation or in efforts to free jailed JRA members. Attacks included the hijacking of Japan Airlines flight 747 to Libya and destruction of the plane (1973); hostage-taking at a Shell Oil refinery in Singapore (1974); hostage-taking at the French embassy in the Hague, Netherlands (1974); seizure of the consulate building at the US embassy in Kuala Lumpur, Malaysia, in demand of the release of seven JRA prisoners (1975); the hijacking of a Japan Airlines plane in Bombay, India (1977); and the bombing of a US military facility in Naples, Italy (1988) (US Department of State 1990).

In 2000, after living for 30 years as a fugitive in the Middle East, Shigenobu was arrested for her role in the 1974 siege of the French embassy in the Hauge, in which two French police officers were shot. Shigenobu declared the JRA disbanded in 2001, following her conviction. She was released from a Tokyo prison in May 2022, after serving a 20-year sentence (Kageyama 2022). While Shigenobu maintains her innocence, in a 2017 letter to a *Japan Times* reporter, she stated: "Our hopes were not fulfilled and it came to an ugly end" (McKirdy 2017). The Japanese Red Army was recognized on the US list of Foreign Terrorist Organizations from 1997 (the origin of the list) to 2001.

6.4.3 Red Brigades (BR)

Primarily active from 1970 to 1981, the **Italian Red Brigades** (BR; Brigate Rosse in Italian) was the largest and most enduring terrorist group in Italy's history, with thousands of active members during its peak. As the case with other far-left ideological terrorist groups, the Red Brigades emerged out of the university student and worker movements of the late 1960s. At the time, Italy had experienced rapid industrialization and a migration of people from the south to the urban areas of the north in search of employment. Poor living and working conditions and a perceived lack of support from union leaders and the Italian government led to widespread student and worker protests that escalated into violent clashes with the police. In an effort to extend the movement from the factories to broader society and coordinate the activities of the worker and student groups, ultra-leftist University of Trento student activists Renato Curcio, Mara Cagol, and Alberto Franceschini founded the Collettivo Politico Metropolitano in Milan. In 1970, this group developed into the Red Brigades (Sundquist 2010).

As a Marxist-Leninist organization, the goal of the Red Brigades was to establish a "dictator of the proletariat" through three phases:

1. "armed propaganda," in which the group sought to gain the support of factory workers and develop a class consciousness through intimidation and attacks on property (e.g., arson of factory managers' cars, raids of offices);
2. "attack the heart of the state," which involved an extension of violence to human political targets, including kidnapping and assassinations; and
3. "generalized civil war," with the unrealized goal of overthrowing the state.

The Red Brigades achieved its longevity in part due to its organizational structure and strict rules regarding clandestine operations (Jamieson 1990). The organization was hierarchical with three levels: columns, brigades, and cells. At least six columns were established in cities including Milan, Genoa, Turin, Rome, Naples, and the Veneto Region to organize efforts specific to the region. Each column consisted of several brigades with cells of up to 10 members under their command. As a clandestine operation, each brigade operated independently, and members were often unknown to each other (Irrera 2014; Sundquist 2010). This structure enabled the organization to operate for several years before the Italian law enforcement understood that they were dealing with a sophisticated terrorist group.

Altogether, data from the University of Maryland's Global Terrorism Database indicate that the Red Brigades was responsible for 220 attacks, which resulted in 223 deaths.

The 1974 kidnapping of Genoa Assistant State Attorney Mario Sossi represented the Red Brigades' shift to phase two of their revolutionary agenda: attacking the heart of the state. The BR released Sossi one month later in exchange for a court order for the release of eight incarcerated Red Brigade affiliates (the order was later blocked). Other notable attacks included the 1974 killing of two members of the right-wing Italian Socialist Movement party and the 1977 shooting of newspaper editor Carlo Casalegno. In 1978, the Red Brigades kidnapped Aldo Moro, president of the Christian Democratic party and a former prime minister, killing five of his bodyguards during the operation. Upon the refusal of the Italian government to release 13 imprisoned Red Brigade members, police found Moro's dead body in an abandoned car (Al-Khoury 2020).

The activities of the Red Brigades declined in the 1980s, as an increasing number of its members were arrested. In 1988, the group completed its final attack, the kidnapping of a chemical engineer in Venice (Al-Khoury 2020). A successor group, the Red Brigades Fighting Communist Party (BR-PCC), continued to commit attacks, reportedly under the guidance of incarcerated BR leaders. Although the Red Brigades as originally formed had ceased to exist as a unified organization in the 1980s, attacks of the BR-PCC and other nonaffiliated actors (under the name Red Brigades) continued until 2002 (Irrera 2014).

6.5 FAR-RIGHT IDEOLOGIES

Extremist **far-right** political ideology has been associated with or characterized by nationalistic, xenophobic, racist, chauvinist, homophobic, Islamophobic, anti-Semitic, authoritarian, and other reactionary views, and is frequently associated with fascism and Nazism (Jupskås & Segers 2020). Proponents of these ideologies often believe in the superiority of the White race over others and argue that White people should control society and subjugate or remove undesirable elements (i.e., other races). They often perceive minorities, immigrants, members of the LGBTQ+ community, people with disabilities, and different racial groups as threatening the survival of their nation, state, religion, and culture, and therefore favor harsh policies that will disadvantage these groups. Unlike advocates of left-wing ideologies, far-right groups believe in *inequality* among people. Some scholars define this ideology as "anti-democratic opposition towards equality" (Carter 2018), while others argue that attitudes toward equality are what distinguishes right-wing groups from left-wing groups (Jupskås 2020; Yturbe 1997).

It is important to understand the basic tenets of extreme right-wing politics, as proponents of this ideology have engaged in horrific anti-democratic and anti-egalitarian acts such as ethnic cleansing, forced assimilation, genocide, and violent attempts in order to achieve their goals. Most importantly, extremist right-wing political parties and groups have gained momentum in democracies across several parts of the world—from Europe to the US, from India to Brazil, and from Myanmar to Israel—and have engaged in violent, politically motivated atrocities, targeting immigrants, ethnic and religious minorities, and left-wing groups and politicians. Far-right groups thus pose a significant threat to stability and peace across the world. As a point of historical reference, this section will focus on the two main radical right-wing ideologies, fascism and Nazism.

6.5.1 Fascism

Fascism can be defined as a political ideology or regime headed by an autocratic leader in which the government controls all aspects of a society—including business, the economy, and labor—through the forceful suppression of opposition. In fascist systems, the state takes precedence over individual interests and emphasizes the use of extreme nationalism, militarism, and the rule of a powerful leader over the citizens, denigrating concepts such as individual rights, economic equality, liberal democracy, and political dissent. The term "fascism" comes from an emblem used in the ancient Roman Empire—the "fasces"—an ax that is tightly reinforced by several sticks, symbolizing the penal authority and unity around one leader in the Roman Empire (Broich 2021). Fascist governments came to power in several parts of Europe and across the world between 1919 and the end of World War II in 1945 (Waxman 2019).

Scholars describe fascism as an ultra-nationalist worldview that favors a forcibly monolithic and strongly controlled nation under a dictator. Different from the other extreme ideologies, fascists talk about the superiority of their race and the importance of racial hygiene—the separation of unfit groups and the establishment of racial purity (Broich 2021). Fascist rhetoric may emphasize how strong and successful their nation was in the past, and use violent, nationalist views as a means of rebirthing this mythic past. For fascism to be successful it requires not only the absence of opposition, but also active political engagement and society's support for the regime (Stanley 2020). Democracy is a threat to fascists, because it can result in socialism, which in turn threatens capitalism and the existence of strong nation-states. Some describe fascists as the armed hands of capitalist interests (Wolff 2020). Excluding certain groups of people from the society, rejecting individual rights and liberties, rejecting socialist economic principles, and dismantling democracy are some of the key principles of fascism that aim to expand a nation's influence and power.

Several countries were ruled by fascist leaders in the twentieth century, such as Italy under Benito Mussolini, Germany under Adolf Hitler, and Spain under Francisco Franco

(Weisberger 2021). The term "fascism" was first used (and coined) by Mussolini in 1919. Mussolini was a journalist and, oddly enough, a member of the left-wing Socialist Party in Italy before World War I. He was expelled from the Party because he harshly criticized the party administrator's stance on World War I that it was best for Italy to stay neutral. Contrary to this, Mussolini argued that it was crucial for Italy to join the war and fight with the Allies (the coalition of countries led by France, the United Kingdom, Russia, Italy, Japan, and the United States).

After dismissal from the Socialist party, Mussolini lost his job as the editor of *Avanti* (Forward), an anti-militarist, antinationalist, and anti-imperialist left-wing newspaper. However, obtaining significant financial aid from the French and British governments and wealthy Italian businessmen, Mussolini founded his own newspaper (*The People of Italy*), a pro-war

FIGURE 6.8   Benito Mussolini and Adolf Hitler stand together on a reviewing stand during Mussolini's official visit in Munich. *Source:* Muzej Revolucije Narodnosti Jugoslavije, Public domain, via Wikimedia Commons.

fascist newspaper that advocated for war and Italian nationalism to confront the country's current economic and political crisis.

Through this outlet, Mussolini gradually became the voice of the fascist movement in Italy and founded a new political party, the National Fascist Party (1922–1943), by gathering hundreds of discharged soldiers and veterans, renegade socialists, anti-Marxist revolutionaries, nationalists, and other discontented Italians. Mussolini named the nucleus of his political party *fasci di combattimento*, meaning "militant brotherhood" or "fighting bands bound together very tightly." His party's agenda was that democracy was a failed system responsible for the current failed economic and political system in the country, and the Italian population had to be gathered around a new system in which people were organized under the state power. Anything (or anyone) that would potentially obfuscate this new system must be violently quashed. Indeed, violence was the core of this new system (Griffin 2013).

Support for Mussolini grew quickly, and he was soon able to establish the paramilitary wing of the National Fascist Party—the "Blackshirt Militia" (Squadrists), an armed and uniformed fascist squad composed of former soldiers who would sweep the Italian countryside and terrorize the local population to intimidate the followers of left-wing groups and parties and increase support for Mussolini. Using this military

FIGURE 6.9   Italian fascist dictator Benito Mussolini in military uniform with microphone making a speech on raised podium waving to ecstatic crowds in Rome, Italy in the 1930s. *Source:* Fábio Reis Borges, CC0, via Wikimedia Commons.

group, Mussolini murdered the prominent members of the largest and most populous party in Italy, the Socialist Party; killed, exiled, or imprisoned thousands of dissidents; closed the activities of the opposition press and trade unions; and made opposition to his totalitarian power impossible (Wolff 2020). In 1922, he seized power in the country, garnering significant support from middle-class Italians.

The cost would be very high for Italy, however—soon the democratic system was abolished; opposition parties, free speech and press, and trade unions would be outlawed; and the whole population was put under the surveillance of spies and secret police. The interests of the powerful businessmen were prioritized over the interests of the lower- and middle-class Italians. Mussolini applied policies such as Industrial Motherhood—a eugenics ideal involving enforced fertility—in order to accelerate the production of more and "better" White Italian children, who would serve as soldiers in the Italian colonies in Africa (Garvin 2015). Under his leadership, women were regarded as baby factories and were given medals for giving birth to certain number of children.

Italy would live under this dictatorship for 20 years, engaging in violent authoritarianism in and outside of its territories—it killed thousands of Ethiopian people with gas bombs during their imperialist conquest to revive the ancient Italian Empire, established an alliance with Hitler, implemented anti-Semitic laws, and deported more than 20 percent of Italian Jews to Germany to be killed by the Nazis (Gornstein 2020).

6.5.2 Nazism (National Socialism)

Nazism (National Socialism), a form of fascism, is a political ideology that was embraced by many Germans between the years of 1933 and 1945. The word "Nazi" represents the shortened version of *Nationalsozialist Deutsche Arbeiterpartei* (NSDAP)—the National Socialist German Workers' Party, a far-right party which rose to power under Hitler's leadership in 1933. It was a dismissive term (along with the term "Sozi"), used by the political opponents of the party when NSDAP was not popular among the Germans during the 1920s. Before the establishment of NSDAP, Germans would use the term "Nazi" as a pejorative, referring to a clumsy person. Contrary to common knowledge, the word "Nazi" was never used by Hitler nor by the other members of the NSDAP. Instead, the terms "Nazi" and "Nazism" were created by the opposition (Kalu 2019).

Similar to fascism, national socialism is opposed to the concepts of democracy, liberalism, human rights, and the rule of law, favoring the establishment of a

FIGURE 6.10   The dead body of Benito Mussolini (second from left) next to his mistress Claretta Petacci and those of other executed fascists, on display in Milan on April 29, 1945, in Piazzale Loreto. Angry crowds strung up his corpse to the iron girders of a gas station, spat on it, and stoned it. *Source:* Vincenzo Carrese, Public domain, via Wikimedia Commons.

nationalist state whose population is strictly obedient to its leaders. Most importantly, Nazism believes in the concept of racial inequality (i.e., the racial superiority of Germans) and warns the public against the dangers of communism.

It is important to examine the economic and historical context in the aftermath of World War I in order to understand the rise of national socialism in Germany. In 1919, along with the rest of the Central Powers (Ottoman Empire, Austria-Hungary, and the Kingdom of Bulgaria) who lost the war against the Allied Powers, Germany was forced to sign a peace agreement—the Treaty of Versailles—in Paris. The provisions of this treaty caused humiliation, anger, frustration, hate, and mass demonstrations among Germans, as the German military was disbanded (except for a very small army composed of monarchist officers), large reparations were requested, and the country's territory was divided. The country was presented with an uncertain future as Germans faced poor economic conditions, high rates of unemployment, economic and political instability, and the absence of a military power (Wilde 2020). Further, Germans were forced to accept full responsibility for starting the war, and hence pay heavy reparations for years.

During such a distressed time, Adolf Hitler, via his National Socialist Party, promised the public a way out of Germany's current problems, capitalizing on people's anger and resentment toward the current regime, the Weimar Republic—the ruling democratic government that signed the peace treaty with the Allied Powers. Hitler, who was a great admirer of Mussolini, simply adopted the tactics and policies of the Italian Fascist Party into his National Socialist Party agenda in Germany (Gornstein 2020; Waxman 2019).

He argued that Germany, especially the German army members who were demilitarized by the peace treaty, had been "stabbed in the back" by the politicians who led the Weimar Republic. The dissatisfied, angry public believed in this middle-aged politician, who had recently completed a prison sentence for attempting to overthrow the Weimar

FIGURE 6.11 Adolf Hitler walking in an honorary formation during the launch ceremony of the aircraft carrier "Graf Zeppelin". *Source:* Bundesarchiv, Bild 183-2006-0810-500/CC-BY-SA 3.0, via Wikimedia Commons.

government. Hitler would use this jail time to write his well-known book *Mein Kampf* (My Struggle), which detailed his right-wing nationalist rebirth strategies, centered on anti-communism, anti-Semitism, re-armament, extreme nationalism, and expansion into non-German territories. These strategies would resonate with some of the former soldiers who were left unemployed after the peace treaty, and with the people affected by the Great Depression—the middle- and lower-class Germans. Due to fear of the spread of communism in Germany, the wealthy business class also supported Hitler and helped to finance his armed wing (SA, the paramilitary wing of the National Socialist Party) to dominate the violent street fights with the communists.

Even though he was gaining popularity among the Germans, Hitler was not elected to serve as the Chancellor of Germany. In 1933, President Paul von Hindenburg invited him to lead the coalition government because the only other alternative was the German Communist Party. The Conservatives, wealthy business class, and industrialists thought they could more easily control a right-wing party led by Hitler than the communists who had a broader support among the German public, and who were calling for a nationwide revolution similar to the one in Russia.

In 1933, shortly after Hitler was appointed as Chancellor, the national assembly building (Reichstag) was burned down in an arson attack by a young Dutch construction worker who was a sympathizer of communism. Exploiting the widespread fears of a potential communist uprising in German society, Hitler first declared an emergency rule, and a month later passed the Enabling Act, which allowed him to issue decrees directly, without the authorization of the National Assembly and the president of Germany (Lindseth 2003).

The decree curtailed individual freedoms and suspended all constitutional protections of the German public—freedom of speech, the right to assembly and privacy, access to free press—and the police were given the right to tap phones and intercept correspondence. The majority of the communist deputies at the national assembly were detained indefinitely, and more than 40,000 Germans were arrested and tortured by the SA and then sent to concentration camps. Using the Enabling Act, Hitler obtained his dictatorial powers and abolished all opposition parties, declared the National Socialist Party as the only legal party in Germany, and received the title of Fuhrer (the supreme leader): the chancellor and commander in chief of the army. He established his undisputed authority by subsuming the police, army, bureaucrats, and politicians to himself. Subordination to Hitler and membership to NSDAP became mandatory for all civil servants (Lewy 2009).

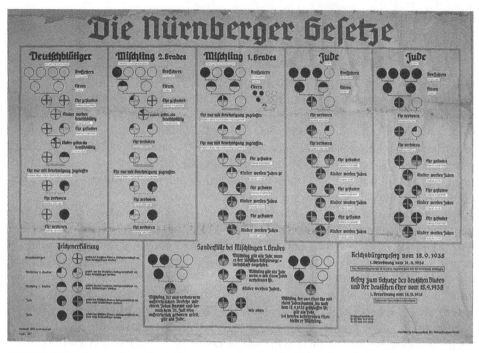

FIGURE 6.12   A chart from Nazi Germany explaining the Nuremberg Laws of 1935.
Source: DennisPeeters, Public domain, via Wikimedia Commons.

German citizens actively supported these extreme measures because there was finally order and a feeling of security in the country. The street fighting and killings had stopped. Many Germans hoped there was a new and bright future ahead for the country. However, Hitler was slowly mobilizing the crowds toward a German Volksgemeinschaft, a national and racial community under the New Order. Hitler's agenda resulted in the Holocaust, the genocide of approximately 11 million people in a state-sponsored effort to eliminate the perceived "undesirables," especially the Jewish population of Germany but also others including disabled people, Roma, and gay people (Kunkeler 2021; Laqueur 1965).

Putting his ideas on race into practice—that Germans, allegedly from the Aryan race, are the strongest and most valuable of all races—Hitler led a brutal campaign against Jews. NSDAP members believed that it was important to separate Jews from other Germans to protect and strengthen the purity of the German race. In 1935, they enacted the Nuremberg Laws, prohibiting Jews (along with Black people, Roma, and their descendants) from being full citizens of Germany and marrying or having sexual relationships with Germans.

The laws also required Jews to wear a yellow badge in public, and Jewish people were ostracized and excluded from the public life. As years passed, the NSDAP regime enacted additional laws making it impossible for Jews to remain in Germany. Jewish properties were confiscated by the state, synagogues were burned, businesses were attacked, and hundreds of thousands of Jews were arrested and sent to concentration camps. The *Vernichtung*—annihilation of Jews—would only come to a stop after the defeat of Germany in World War II in 1945. Germany was divided, the NSDAP and its ideology became illegal, and its members were convicted of crimes against humanity (Craig 1978). Unfortunately, remnants of this dangerous ideology are still present in today's politics, across several countries including the United States.

6.6 FAR-RIGHT TERRORIST GROUPS

Far-right extremist violence is often motivated by notions of racial, ethnic, or religious supremacy. A major issue in combatting far-right violence is the debate concerning its classification—is it terrorism, or is it a hate crime (Blazak 2011; Koehler 2016)? Whereas a hate crime is "a criminal act that is motivated by a bias toward the victim . . . or perceived group identity" (Blazak 2011, 245), terrorism takes this further in that it is strategic and intended to instill fear among a larger audience. These different definitions lead to variations in how these crimes are investigated and prosecuted.

In addition, a key characteristic of right-wing terrorism is that it often tends to be perpetuated by lone actors, rather than groups. While there are exceptions, the deadliest terrorist attacks motivated by a right-wing ideology in recent history were committed by individuals, acting alone, without clear connections to particular groups. For example, in 2011, Anders Behring Breivik killed eight people with a bomb attack in Oslo and then killed another 69 people in a mass shooting in Utøya, Norway. More recently, in the United States, Robert Gregory Bowers killed 11 people in a shooting at a synagogue in Pittsburgh, Pennsylvania, in 2019; White nationalist Patrick Wood Crusius killed 23 people in a shooting at a Walmart in El Paso, Texas, in 2019; and Payton Gendron, motivated by the far-right great replacement theory, killed 10 Black people in a shooting at a supermarket in Buffalo, New York, in 2022 (Koehler 2016; Sneed & Li 2022).

In addition to these **lone actor terrorists**, far-right extremist groups have engaged in violence and acts of terrorism to further their ideology. As examples, we review the cases of the National Socialist Underground (NSU), Combat 18, and the Proud Boys.

6.6.1 National Socialist Underground (NSU)

The **National Socialist Underground (NSU)** had engaged in far-right terrorist activities, including murder, bombings, and burglaries, dating back to 2000. The group was only discovered in 2011, though, after two of its members failed in an attempted bank robbery and took their own lives, and the third member set an apartment on fire and subsequently turned herself over to police. The NSU's three key members were born and raised in the German Democratic Republic (East Germany): two men, Uwe Mundlos and Uwe Böhnhardt, and one woman, Beate Zschäpe, along with over 100 **neo-Nazi** supporters. The trio met in the early 1990s as teenagers at a club for right-wing extremists in Jena, Germany. This was a time when, following the reunification of Germany in 1990, the neo-Nazi movement and far-right extremist violence directed toward immigrants in eastern Germany escalated (McGowan 2014).

The trio began their participation in extremist activities as the Comrade Group, joining anti-immigration and anti-globalization rallies organized by the National Democratic Party of Germany (NPD), Germany's extreme, right-wing neo-Nazi party, which involved attacking Vietnamese immigrants and defacing property with neo-Nazi graffiti. From there, they started creating and planting bombs—one at a football stadium, another at a town square—which led authorities to search their homes. After uncovering extremist far-right propaganda, explosives, and weapons, the police issued arrest warrants for

Mundlos, Böhnhardt, and Zschäpe. In response, the three went into hiding ("underground") and became the NSU.

Between January of 1998 and November of 2011, the NSU led a terror campaign throughout Germany in which they targeted migrants, particularly those of Turkish origin, whom they considered "enemies of the German nation" (von der Behrens 2018, 85). Between 2000 and 2007, the group murdered 10 individuals—eight men of Turkish or Kurdish origin, one Greek man (who, to them, appeared Turkish), and one German female police officer. Most were shot with the same weapon, a Česká 83 pistol with a silencer, in broad daylight. The NSU also committed three nail bomb attacks—explosives containing hundreds of 10 cm-length nails that were aimed at migrants—and a series of eight robberies of banks, post offices, and a supermarket, in which two people were injured (von der Behrens 2018).

In November 2011, police discovered the bodies of Mundlos and Böhnhardt in a van, their deaths determined to be suicide. Shortly thereafter, Zschäpe set fire to the apartment the three shared, presumably to destroy evidence. A few days later, she turned herself into police. In searching the remains of the apartment, investigators discovered a confessional video in which an animated Pink Panther character presented evidence of the NSU's murders. In July 2018, after a five-year trial in the Higher Regional Court in Munich, Zschäpe was sentenced to life in prison. Four supporters of the NSU were also tried for assisting the terrorist group with weapons and transportation and received sentences from 2.5 to 10 years. Despite a lengthy and heavily publicized trial, critics continue to raise questions about German authorities' handling of violent far-right extremism as well as the possibility that authorities protected the NSU (Hillebrand 2018).

These crimes were investigated by different agencies and were not connected to the NSU until 2011. The murders of the nine migrants were erroneously attributed to the Turkish mafia or the Kurdistan Worker's Party (PKK), despite a lack of evidence confirming a connection to these groups (von der Behrens 2018). That the NSU was able to evade German authorities for well over a decade led many to question the competence of the German police, accusing the authorities of institutional racism and being "blind in the right eye" when it comes to right-wing extremism (Koehler 2016; McGowan 2014). Following the NSU trial, a number of measures were taken to strengthen Germany's response to far-right extremism, such as consolidating databases and enhancing procedures for sharing information (Hillebrand 2018).

6.6.2 Combat 18

Named after Adolph Hitler (A and H being the first and eighth letters of the alphabet), **Combat 18** is a neo-Nazi terrorist group that originated in the United Kingdom in 1992 and spread throughout Europe, the United States, and Canada. Paul David "Charlie" Sargent started the group as an armed branch of the UK-based neo-Nazi music promotion and right-wing extremist political organization, Blood & Honour. However, Combat 18 has since distinguished itself from Blood & Honour with its violent terror campaign against immigrants, ethnic minorities, and leftists. With the motto "whatever it takes," Combat 18's stated goal is to create all-White nations. The group recruits members through neo-Nazi skinhead music festivals as well as the website Stormfront, and has associations to football hooliganism in Europe.

In addition to using violent intimidation and spreading xenophobic, threatening rhetoric through its magazines and distribution of neo-Nazi skinhead music, Combat

FIGURE 6.13 Combat 18 is a neo-Nazi, White supremacist organization that originated in the United Kingdom in the early 1990s. The name number 18 is the numerical representation of Adolf Hitler's initials, with A as the first letter of the alphabet, and H as the eighth. The group is known for its extreme far-right ideology, advocating for racial purity, anti-Semitism, and violence against minority groups. *Source:* Rijndaal, Public domain, via Wikimedia Commons.

18's members have been charged with arson and murder in numerous countries, including England, Germany, Denmark, the Czech Republic, and the United States. For example, in 1997, Danish authorities intercepted letter bombs that Combat 18 members had mailed from Sweden to targets in London (Boyes 1997). In 2010, three members of Combat 18 fired upon the Suleymaniye Mosque in Perth, Western Australia, causing $15,000 AUD in damages to the mosque (Global Terrorism Database 2024). Between 2010 and 2018, Greek authorities charged Combat 18 members with more than 30 bomb attacks targeting left-wing headquarters and Jewish memorials.

In 2019, Combat 18 escalated its threat to German security with the assassination of the pro-refugee politician Walter Lübcke, a member of the Christian Democratic Union of Germany. Following the act, hateful and celebratory responses to Lübeck's death proliferated online among far-right supporters. This incident, as well as a subsequent lone-actor attack on a synagogue and the aforementioned NSU terror spree, prompted the German government to ban Combat 18 and deploy over 200 police to search the homes of leading Combat 18 members across six German states in January 2020. In his speech regarding the ban, German Interior Minister Horst Seehofer stated: "Today's ban gives a clear signal: right extremism and anti-Semitism have no place in our society . . . the hideous murder of Walter Lübeck and the act of terror in Halle last year have shown us, brutally, that right-wing extremism and anti-Semitism are a significant danger to our free society" (BBC 2020).

Other nations have responded similarly to the threat of Combat 18. In the UK, Combat 18 members are not permitted to work for a number of British agencies including the prison service, armed forces, and police. In 2019, Canada added both Combat 18 and Blood & Honour to its list of terrorist organizations. This official designation as a terrorist organization enables Canada to more easily prosecute Combat 18 members and supporters of terrorist-related activities.

6.6.3 Proud Boys

The **Proud Boys** is an all-male far-right extremist group that espouses an Islamophobic, anti-Semitic, homophobic, transphobic, misogynistic, and xenophobic ideology. Although the group denies White supremacist motivations, Proud Boys members frequently join events sponsored by other groups that advocate **White supremacy**. According to Stanford University's Center for International Security and Cooperation, the Proud Boys is "semi-accelerationist in that it advocates violence in readiness for civil war in the United States. Most of the group's public activity involves protesting or attending political rallies and events, typically with the intent to provoke violence" (CISAC 2022). While it is considered a hate group in the US, Proud Boys is officially designated as a terrorist organization in both Canada and New Zealand. According to the University of Maryland's Profiles of Individual Radicalization in the United States (PRIUS) database, as of December 2021, 83 Proud Boys members have been charged with ideologically motivated crimes in the United States (Copland 2022; Public Safety Canada, n.d.).

The group was founded in 2016 by Gavin McInnes, the cofounder of *Vice* magazine. McInnes was born in England, raised in Canada, and immigrated to the United States when *Vice* moved its headquarters from Montreal to New York City. Through his writings that disparaged Muslims, feminists, transgender people, and non-Whites, and his talk show, aired by Compound Media, McInnes became known for his far-right political views and frustration with politically correct (PC) culture. In 2016, together with other anti-PC colleagues, he formed the Proud Boys. In McInnes's announcement regarding its formation, he declared the Proud Boys "Western chauvinists who refuse to apologize for creating the modern world" (McInnes 2016). Other stated goals of the group include promoting traditional gender roles, ending welfare, closing country borders, and opposing Islam and the "war on Whiteness."

An intense initiation process, akin to those in fraternal organizations, is required for men to become official Proud Boys members (McInnes 2016). Nonetheless, researchers estimate that Proud Boys membership grew to 6,000 official members throughout the United States and Canada by the end of 2017, and the group had over 40,000 followers on its social media accounts. Membership is more difficult to estimate today, as Meta

FIGURE 6.14 During the January 6 rally in Washington, DC, the Proud Boys, a far-right, self-described "Western chauvinist" organization, were among the various groups present. During the rally, some members of the Proud Boys were reported to have actively participated in storming the US Capitol building, leading to violence, vandalism, and the disruption of the certification process for the 2020 presidential election results. *Source:* Becker (1999); CC BY 2.0, via Wikimedia Commons.

(the social media company that owns Facebook, Instagram, and WhatsApp) closed the Proud Boys' accounts in 2018. However, Enrique Tarrio, the leader from 2018 to 2021, claims that the group gained 20,000 new members in 2020 alone (CISAC 2022).

Since its founding, the Proud Boys has demonstrated a proclivity for violence at protest events. For example, during a 2018 speech by McInnes in New York, 10 Proud Boys members were arrested for attempted assault, gang assault, and rioting in fights between Proud Boys and counterprotesters. In August of 2020, the Proud Boys were heavily involved in violent counterdemonstrations aimed at protests over the murder of African American man George Floyd by a White Minneapolis police officer. During this time, Proud Boys member Alan Swinney was sentenced to 10 years in prison for the unlawful use of a weapon to shoot at and threaten protesters (Levenson 2021). In December of 2020, Enrique Tarrio vandalized a Black Lives Matter banner during a protest in Washington, DC. When he was arrested for this act he was in possession of high-capacity firearm magazines, which are illegal to carry in the district (Moore 2021).

The Proud Boys were heavily involved in the January 6 insurrection at the US Capitol in 2021. Following the defeat of then-president Donald Trump, hundreds of his supporters marched toward the Capitol, pushed through barricades, and stormed the building, resulting in extensive violence, property destruction, and five deaths. Individuals with ties to several far-right groups, including the Oath Keepers and the Three Percenters, participated in the attack; however, of those charged with crimes during the incident, the largest number (54) were affiliated with the Proud Boys (Copland 2022). Moreover, on June 6, 2022, a federal grand jury charged five members of the Proud Boys, including its leader, Tarrio, with seditious conspiracy—conspiring to overthrow the government of the United States (DOJ 2022).

Following the Capitol breach and subsequent arrests, the Proud Boys dissolved its national leadership, and instead activity has been generated among local chapters. In particular, Proud Boys members have increasingly attended town council gatherings and school board meetings. They've sought to gain influence on issues such as LGBTQ+ rights, facial mask mandates, COVID-19 vaccination, and instruction on critical race theory and inclusive curricula in schools (Bellware 2022; Frenkel and Feuer 2021). Membership in the Proud Boys has grown since the Capitol riots; local chapter numbers increased from 43 in 2020 to 72 in 2021. Analysts note that their increase in activities at the local level has enabled the Proud Boys to gain influence more openly in mainstream politics (Brady 2022).

Given the current salience and threat to domestic security posed by extremist violence, we discuss the activities of ideological extremists in the United States from both the far left and far right in greater detail in the following section.

FIGURE 6.15   Proud Boys incited violence and destruction during the pro-Trump rally in Washington, DC, in 2020, to stop vote counting. *Source:* TapTheForwardAssist, CC BY-SA 4.0, via Wikimedia Commons.

6.7 IDEOLOGICAL EXTREMISM IN THE AMERICAN CONTEXT

The violent far-left and far-right ideologies (e.g., communism, national socialism) common in Europe during the twentieth and twenty-first centuries are also present in the United States. Communists, socialists, fascists, and national socialists (i.e., Nazis) have been active in the US during various time periods. As of 2024, far-left groups are marginal in most places, and they have gone through a significant process of de-radicalization. Extreme right-wing violence, however, has been on the rise (Flood 2021; Weisberger 2021). This section will briefly explain the history of far-left and far-right extremist groups in the United States.

6.7.1 The Far Left in the US: 1920s–1960s

Like their European counterparts, far-left groups in the US in early twentieth century organized around issues such as class struggles and minority rights, and then centered around the desire to correct a perceived injustice. Compared to right-wing groups, members of extreme left-wing groups typically have educational backgrounds, and their cadres are more likely to include minorities (Blumberg 1986). For example, the **Communist Party of the United States of America (CPUSA)**, one of the leading leftist organizations in the US

since its founding in New York City in 1919 until its disbanding in 1989, included a high number of Jewish members. Receiving funding from the Soviet Union, the CPUSA played significant roles in many aspects of social life in the US, from the workers' rights and job security to housing struggles and defending the rights of African Americans, women, LGBTQ+ individuals, and immigrants, among other oppressed groups. During this time, communists and sympathizers of communism were labeled "Reds" because of their perceived allegiance to the Soviet Union (which had a red flag).

Even though it was established as a legal party, the Communist Party was forced underground at the start of the Cold War between the Soviet Union and the United States. The party members were believed to have engaged in espionage and intelligence activities on American soil with the aim of

FIGURE 6.16 The Foley Square trial of American Communists, officially known as the "Smith Act trials," were a series of prosecutions that took place in the United States during the Cold War era. Ultimately, all 11 defendants were convicted and sentenced to prison terms. However, the convictions sparked controversy and debate over issues of free speech, political dissent, and the constitutionality of the Smith Act. Some viewed the trials as a violation of civil liberties, while others saw them as necessary measures to protect national security during the Cold War. *Source:* World Telegram & Sun photo by C.M. Stieglitz/Library of Congress.

shaping public opinion, and over the years, the US government took some harsh actions that had profound effects on American society. For example, during the First **Red Scare** (1917–1920), the government enacted many laws such as the Espionage Act of 1917 and the Sedition Act of 1918 to criminalize speech (printed or spoken) against the government, monitored radicals, and also threatened the public with deportation from the country if they supported communism. The police engaged in brutal raids against suspected leftist groups, which would later be known as Palmer Raids. Thousands of individuals were arrested (of whom many were not guilty of any crime but simply had a foreign accent) and many were put on a ship (the *USS Buford*) and deported to the Soviet Union (Cowley 2023). Because of the government repression, people became less likely to call themselves leftists during this era, as doing so would cause them to lose their job and face potential deportation.

The Second Red Scare occurred between 1940 and 1950. US law enforcement agencies were aware of some Soviet espionage activities with the aid of leftist American citizens on American soil. The leaders were suspicious that American communists were working as teachers, college professors, artists, journalists, and even Hollywood celebrities and using these positions to influence society with the ideology of communism. There were some actual cases of espionage, such as the theft of atomic secrets by Soviet American agents Julius and Ethel Rosenberg (who were sentenced to death and electrocuted in 1953), that contributed to this fear climate. However, many scholars agree that right-wing politicians were simply exploiting these isolated incidents to create an atmosphere of fear in the nation. For example, the right-wing Republican politician Joseph McCarthy publicly argued that communists had infiltrated federal agencies, such as the State Department, the White House, the Department of Treasury, and even the US Army (Storrs 2015).

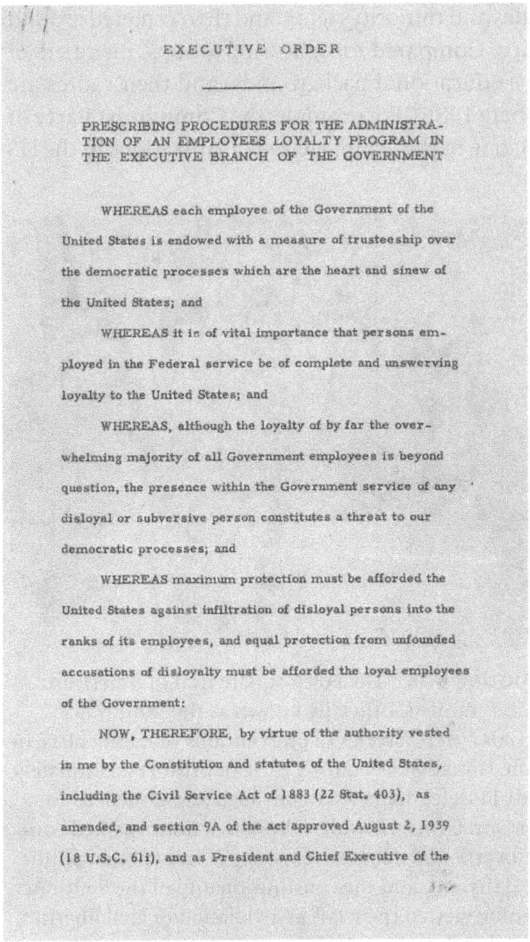
EXECUTIVE ORDER

PRESCRIBING PROCEDURES FOR THE ADMINISTRATION OF AN EMPLOYEES LOYALTY PROGRAM IN THE EXECUTIVE BRANCH OF THE GOVERNMENT

WHEREAS each employee of the Government of the United States is endowed with a measure of trusteeship over the democratic processes which are the heart and sinew of the United States; and

WHEREAS it is of vital importance that persons employed in the Federal service be of complete and unswerving loyalty to the United States; and

WHEREAS, although the loyalty of by far the overwhelming majority of all Government employees is beyond question, the presence within the Government service of any disloyal or subversive person constitutes a threat to our democratic processes; and

WHEREAS maximum protection must be afforded the United States against infiltration of disloyal persons into the ranks of its employees, and equal protection from unfounded accusations of disloyalty must be afforded the loyal employees of the Government:

NOW, THEREFORE, by virtue of the authority vested in me by the Constitution and statutes of the United States, including the Civil Service Act of 1883 (22 Stat. 403), as amended, and section 9A of the act approved August 2, 1939 (18 U.S.C. 61i), and as President and Chief Executive of the

FIGURE 6.17 The Executive Order 9835 (known as the Loyalty Order). *Source:* Harry S. Truman, public domain, via Wikimedia Commons.

Due to the anti-Soviet paranoia created by politicians, President Truman initiated the Second Red Scare by issuing the Loyalty Order, which required all federal employees to be tested to see whether they were loyal to the country (Fariello 2008). Thousands of people were questioned about their loyalty to the United States and a majority of them, including teachers, celebrities, intellectuals, and anyone who simply disagreed with the political views of McCarthy, were fired from their jobs. The suspected communists were alienated by their friends and family and had difficulty finding new employment (Storrs 2003). The public did not criticize the undemocratic tactics used to persecute suspected radicals even though a majority of the accused people had done nothing other than join a political party. At this time, the American public was convinced that communism was a threat to the future of the United States following international events such as the Soviet Union's successful test of a nuclear bomb and the communist takeover of China by Mao Zedong.

6.7.2 Far-Left Extremist Groups After the 1960s

Prominent examples of extreme left-wing groups in the United States in the latter half of the twentieth century are **Weather Underground** (a student-led group that emerged in opposition to US involvement in the Vietnam War and American imperialism); the **Symbionese Liberation Army** (a California-based group that aimed to create small homelands for minority groups and fought against racism, monogamy, and all institutions that sustained capitalism); the New World Liberation Front (another California-based militant group that engaged in tens of bombings); the Animal Liberation Front (a group that fights against the abuse and exploitation of animals); Earth Liberation Front (a group that engages in economic sabotage to stop the exploitation and destruction of the environment); and most recently Antifa, an anti-fascist and anti-racist movement that emerged after Donald Trump was elected to the US presidency.

The 1960s–1980s was the period in which far-left extremist groups were most militarily active. During this period groups such as Weather Underground, the Symbionese Liberation Army, and New World Liberation Front targeted political and economic conventions, engaged in riots, and conducted arson attacks, drive-by shootings, small-scale bombings of important government buildings, bank robberies, and even murdered law enforcement officers.

The far-left groups that emerged during the 1990s and 2000s—**Animal Liberation Front (ALF)** and **Earth Liberation Front (ELF)**—have targeted animal research facilities, biomedical industries that use live animals for scientific research, meat processing factories and fur producers, timber mills, and government

FIGURE 6.18   The Weather Underground members, along with Vietnam veterans march in anti US-Vietnam war protests (1976). *Source:* Public domain, via Wikimedia Commons.

facilities that house wild animals. Their violence has been primarily aimed at property destruction (via arson), rather than human targets. For example, in 1987, the ALF burned down an animal laboratory at the University of California with the stated motivation of retaliating "in the name of thousands of animals tortured each year in campus labs" (Brown 2019). The ALF and ELF have been heavily targeted by the federal law enforcement agencies, due to strong corporate lobbying activities of groups such as Americans for Medical Progress, the Foundation for Biomedical Research, and the National Board of Fur Farm Organizations.

6.7.3 The Far Left Today: Antifa

As mentioned, the frequency of left-wing terrorism significantly diminished by the end of the Cold War, and the far left has undergone a profound process of deradicalization in the United States. Most scholars agree that the threat of far-left terrorism is minimal. For example, a recent comprehensive analysis was conducted by the Center for Strategic and International Studies by collating cases from reputable terrorism datasets including START GTD, the RAND Database of Worldwide Terrorism Incidents, and the Anti-Defamation League's Hate, Extremism, Anti-Semitism and Terrorism Map. It found that between 1994 and 2020, far-left extremist groups were responsible for only one fatality (Jones & Doxsee 2020). Even so, the far left has undergone a resurgence beginning 2016 with the election of Donald Trump as the president of the United States (Bogel-Burroughs & Garcia 2020).

Even though they may have multiple ideologies, the far-left groups that emerged during this era have organized themselves around the issues of social justice and political correctness. They have orchestrated demonstrations—and sometimes violent retribution against symbols of the state—advocating for human rights, racial equality, immigrant rights, and personal liberties; protesting police brutality against minorities; and confronting fascism and other perceived injustices and restrictions imposed by the government.

The most prominent far-left extremist movement is the anti-fascist, anti-racist organization **Antifa**, which Donald Trump attempted to designate as a terrorist organization. Antifa is a loosely organized, secretive, and leaderless group whose members are organized into autonomous local cells without a chain of command. Rather than being a centralized unified organization, it is a group composed of several left-wing movements and activists that have come together to counter the threat posed by racist and fascist organizations on the far right, and has organized protests against groups that posit homophobic, xenophobic, authoritarian, racist, and fascist ideas.

Wearing black and with their faces covered, members of the group often engage in nonviolent peaceful demonstrations and

FIGURE 6.19 An Antifa protest against deportation. *Source:* Fibonacci Blue, CC BY 2.0, via Wikimedia Commons.

protests such as speeches, marches, community organizing, mutual aids for refugees and disaster survivors, and poster and flyer distributions, but they also believe in the use of violence against the racist and fascist groups because the agendas of such groups— according to Antifa—encourage violence against marginalized communities (Flood 2021). Antifa thus organizes activities that aim to prevent far-right groups from speaking in public, publish the identities of White supremacists online, and have used violence and property destruction to disrupt far-right gatherings.

The group gained nationwide media attention with the 2017 UC Berkeley protests when they attempted to stop the extreme right hate speech event organized by alt-right commentator Milo Yiannopoulos. Antifa protesters, some carrying signs reading

FIGURE 6.20 A protester standing under a sign reading "White Supremacy Is Terrorism" in a counterprotest in San Francisco. *Source:* Amaury Laporte, CC BY 2.0, via Wikimedia Commons.

"Stand Against Hate," threw rocks and commercial grade fireworks at the police, smashed the windows of the student union center where the speech was scheduled to take place, and pepper-sprayed and assaulted Trump supporters and event organizers. It is estimated that the protests caused more than $100,000 in damage (Park & Lah 2017).

The group has been harshly criticized not only by right-wing groups, but also by several other left-wing groups and prominent names on the left for their use of direct violence and physical confrontation with the police, which they argue is only counterproductive and feeds into the arguments presented by the alt-right groups that the far left, in general, is violent.

6.7.4 The Far Right in the US

Domestic right-wing extremism in the United States often centers around issues of nationalism, Christian religious radicalism, radical anti-government beliefs, and White supremacy, and has historically resulted in far more human casualties than any other type of domestic terrorist activity in the nation (Piazza 2017; Simi & Bubolz 2017). Similar to the far left, the American far right is not a monolithic organization; it encompasses an array of different movements with any variety of different causes.

A majority of the right-wing extremist groups glorify historical fascist agendas, the ones that were advanced by Mussolini and Hitler. As Madeleine Albright, former head of the US State Department, stated, "the core fascist ideologies espoused by Hitler and

Mussolini are still present in the United States and there are clear symptoms that they are on the rise" (Waxman 2019; Weisberger 2021).

Reports that utilize multiple sources of data confirm the threat of right-wing violence is greater than other types of extremism in the United States. For example, a report published by the International Centre for Counter Terrorism indicated that between 2001 and 2016 right-wing extremists were responsible for more fatalities within the US than were any other type of extremists (Liang & Cross 2020). According to the Anti-Defamation League, more than 75 percent of approximately 435 violent terrorist attacks in the US between 2010 and 2019 were committed by right-wing domestic extremists (Danvers 2021). The head of FBI's National Security Branch, Jill Sanborn, told lawmakers that the country needs a new unit to tackle the threat of right-wing extremism (Lucas 2022).

Most scholars agree that four main belief systems shaped far-right ideological motivations in the United States during the twentieth century: White superiority over other races, nativism, anti-communist hostility, and anti-Semitism. After the end of the Cold War, far-right groups began to organize so-called patriotic groups and then diverted their attention to the federal government, arguing that government was the source of all problems. However, more recently, far-right groups have begun to focus on several other issues, such as preventing gun control, abortion, and immigration, and typically espouse homophobic, Islamophobic, and xenophobic rhetoric. The following section will provide a brief overview of far-right violence in the United States.

6.7.5 White Supremacy, the Ku Klux Klan (KKK), and Neo-Nazis

White supremacy is probably the most well-known example of far-right ideological motivation in the US. Far-right violence in the nation began with traditional White supremacy: the opposition to racial equality. With the end of slavery after the Civil War, White conservative Southerners who maintained pro-slavery desires created the **Ku Klux Klan**—the oldest and most infamous American hate group—in Tennessee. The KKK led a violent campaign of terrorist violence in opposition to the progressive policies of the Reconstruction Era. As the group increased in number, it used violent intimidation tactics to prevent Black people (and White people who supported racial equality) from voting. KKK members also occupied important positions in the government in order to maintain White hegemonic control in the country.

FIGURE 6.21   The Ku Klux Klan was founded at the end of the US Civil War to repress the rights and freedoms of African Americans. *Source:* Library of Congress https://www.loc.gov/item/2016842489/.

For example, during the 1868 presidential election, thousands of Black people were killed by the KKK, and an additional several thousand were either lynched, raped, or tarred and feathered, along with other humiliating tactics employed by the organization's members (Cunningham 2013). Even though the initial agenda of the KKK was to target Black Americans, beginning in 1915 the group started to attack Catholics, immigrants (namely Jewish people who immigrated to the United States), and communist sympathizers. During this time, members of the KKK often made religious claims—that White people were God's chosen people, and non-Whites and Jews were subhuman with Satanic origins—as an argument in defense of their racist attacks (Gordon 2017).

The KKK's violent activities gained momentum once again during the 1960s, with the advent of the civil rights era. Several civil rights activists and Black civilians were killed in Klan bombings. Trying to escape this racial terror, approximately six million Black Americans left the Southern states in what would come to be known as the Great Migration (Tolnay 2003). Beginning in the 1970s—particularly after the end of the Vietnam War in 1975—KKK chapters began merging with neo-Nazi groups (e.g. the National Socialist Legion, Skinheads) to form an organized White power movement. Similar to White supremacists, neo-Nazis have mobilized around issues pertaining to race, anti-Semitism, and more recently in opposition to immigration, feminism, and LGBTQ+ rights (Kunkeler 2021).

6.7.6 The Alternative Right (Alt-Right)

The **alternative right**, commonly known as the alt-right, is a loosely connected network of far-right nationalist groups composed of mostly young White men, and is widely known for espousing anti-egalitarian, anti-Semitic, anti-Muslim, anti-immigrant, anti-women, and White supremacist ideas (Simi et al. 2016). The term was coined in 2008 by the head of the National Policy Institute, Richard Spencer. Different from the earlier versions of far-right extremist groups, the alt-right is known for their extensive use of social media, online platforms, and chat boards such as 4chan., Reddit, and X/Twitter. Social media, along with Donald Trump's presidential candidacy, were instrumental in engendering the sudden growth of the alt-right among American youth. The group members, despite knowing that Trump did not share their vision of a White ethno-state, applauded many of his policies—banning Muslim immigration to the US, curtailing immigration in general, and building a wall along the US-Mexico border. Trump's campaign slogans, such as "Make America Great Again," resonated with alt-right ideals and goals regarding the national rebirth of the country, and indeed similar slogans were used by Hitler and Mussolini (Gornstein 2020).

FIGURE 6.22 Proud Boys March for Trump, Washington, DC, December 2020. *Source:* Elvert Barnes, CC BY-SA 2.0, via Wikimedia Commons.

The alt-right embraces White ethnonationalism as their core value and maintains the notion that the White race and White identity is under attack, which they refer to as White genocide. They posit that social justice initiatives are hoaxes and the greatest threat to their liberty—attempts by so-called progressives to undermine Western civilization and the future of White generations. The alt-right emphasizes cultural and racial homogeneity and promotes the establishment of a White separatist ethno-state (Colley & Moore 2022). It asserts that conservative politicians who favor globalism, multiculturalism, and immigration are traitors. Other than the so-called traitor Republicans, the group has also organized propaganda campaigns against refugee settlements from Muslim countries, the Black Lives Matter movement, feminism, political correctness, multiculturalism, and immigration reforms.

Initially created as an online movement, the alt-right attempted to establish itself as a live, in-the-street movement by organizing the 2017 "Unite the Right" rally in Virginia, which ended in violent clashes with left-wing demonstrators. Far-right protesters engaged in violence, assaulting and firing guns at left-wing demonstrators. Thirty-five-year-old White supremacist James Alex Fields Jr. rammed his car into a crowd of counterprotesters, killing one and injuring 35 others. These violent acts were celebrated online by the members of the alt-right, while the group's extreme violence generated negative sentiment among the broader American public (Topinka 2022).

6.7.7 Far-Right Single-Issue Extremism

As with far-left groups, the far right also includes some smaller domestic terrorist movements that organize around narrow **single issues** such as abortion, immigration, religion, women, and gun control. The oldest of these groups, religious anti-abortion extremists (e.g., the Army of God), perceive abortion as the murder of innocent lives and justify the use of violence—including bombings, arson, vandalism, the destruction of medical facilities, stalking, intimidation, kidnapping, and the murder of doctors and nurses who provide abortion care—as a duty to protect the lives of fetuses (Spillar 2022).

Religious extremist groups are perhaps best known for targeting abortion clinics and doctors willing to perform abortions. For example, American Coalition of Life Activists, a Christian far-right extremist group, labels the clinical staff who conduct abortions as "war criminals" and regularly publishes a hit list, which includes the photos, names, home addresses, telephone numbers, and other personal information of doctors and nurses who provide abortion services. It is estimated that anti-abortion extremists have

FIGURE 6.23   Alt-right members preparing to enter Emancipation Park in Charlottesville, Virginia, holding Nazi, Confederate, and Gadsden "Don't Tread on Me" flags. *Source:* Anthony Crider, CC BY 2.0, via Wikimedia Commons.

carried out more than 7,200 acts of violence and killed 11 people—including doctors, clinic employees, security guards, and police officers—since abortion was legalized in the United States in the late 1970s with the *Roe v. Wade* Supreme Court ruling, which has since been overturned (Durkee 2022).

Involuntary celibates (incels) have been identified as the newest far-right domestic terrorism threat in the United States. Incels are an online, gender-based, ideology-driven, anti-feminist extremist group composed of men who engage in violent rhetoric and violence against women because of their inability to find sexual partners. The group is also racist, as they attack women who have sex with non-White men (Pitcavage 2019). Unfortunately, the incel ideology has been extremely lethal. Since 2014, dozens of women have lost their lives because of targeted violence by this group (Sganga 2022). Incels favor the use of violence and murder as a means of broader societal intimidation and subjugation of women. Similar to other alt-right groups, incels engage in recruitment and mobilization via online communication tools such as 4chan, Telegram, Reddit, PUAHate.com, and 8kun. Through male-dominated platforms, incels radicalize each other on different topics from male supremacy and the dehumanization of women to pro-rape discussions.

Incel violence often comes from lone actors rather than organized efforts. Due to the absence of a central command and control apparatus, it is extremely difficult for law enforcement agencies to track and prevent these atrocities. A prominent example of an incel attack occurred in 2014 at the University of California, Santa Barbara, when a twenty-year-old misogynist gunman killed six students via a shooting spree and stabbings and injured 14 others by vehicle ramming. Elliot Rodger, the shooter, posted a YouTube video in which he explained his motivation as punishing women for not sleeping with him. In his 107,000-word manifesto, he said, "I had no choice but to exact revenge on society that had denied me sex and love. I am the true victim in all of this. I am the good guy" (BBC 2018; Skolnik 2022).

6.8 POLITICAL SPECTRUM: A STRAIGHT LINE OR A HORSESHOE?

As explained in detail at the beginning of this chapter, the political spectrum is widely portrayed as an imaginary straight line, with extreme right and left ideologies placed at opposite ends and the middle of the line being the political center. The left wing is typically characterized by social equality, reform, rights, and progress, whereas the right wing is characterized by authority, tradition, nationalism, and hierarchy.

An alternative depiction developed by the French philosopher Jean-Pierre Faye, the **horseshoe theory**, argues that rather than being a simple straight line, the political spectrum is actually a horseshoe shape, with the middle-rounded part representing the political center and both ends of the horseshoe, bending toward each other, representing the extreme right and left. According to this theory, extreme right and extreme left are not opposite ideologies. Instead, they resemble one an other (Elhefnawy 2022).

The horseshoe theory argues that the ideologies on the far left (such as communism) and the far right (fascism) may look like opposites, but when one closely examines their polices and goals it is possible to see that they are making similar arguments, only in support of different groups—for example, they differ on who should have rights and

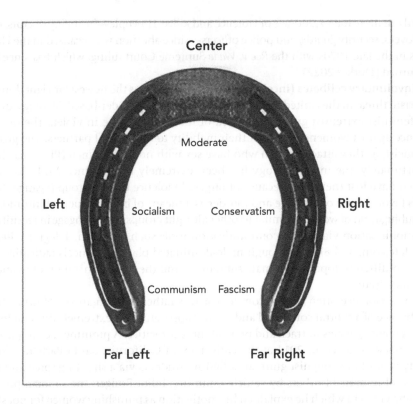

FIGURE 6.24 The horseshoe theory is a political concept that suggests that the far left and the far right, despite being at opposite ends of the political spectrum, can sometimes share more in common with each other than with moderate or centrist political positions. The theory proposes that both extremes exhibit authoritarian tendencies, intolerance of dissent, and a willingness to use violence to achieve their goals.

whose rights should be revoked. Both communism and fascism, even though located at the opposite ends of the political spectrum, favor a very strong, centralized state that controls all aspects of life for its population (Tangian 2020; Wright 2022).

Another example pertains to race. Far-right groups such as White supremacists are often concerned with White genocide, and blame Jews, Muslims, immigrants, and LGBTQ+ individuals for the ills of society. In their view, White dominance is threatened because of affirmative action and other multicultural movements that prioritize racial and ethnic minorities over White people. These groups justify discrimination against minorities. Certain far-left groups, in comparison, argue that White men are responsible for social inequalities—that it is harder for racial minorities to prosper because White people have oppressed them. Certain far-left groups argue that gun ownership should be limited because of the high number of casualties caused by mass shootings. Some far-right groups, in contrast, argue that abortion should be illegal, considering it murder of a fetus—no different than killing a person. Both sides favor taking rights away from individuals; they just differ on whose rights should be restricted.

6.9 CONCLUSION

Throughout history, extremist ideologies have been associated with terrorist movements across the world. Ideologies are critical for the organization of society, providing cultural, political, and economic models to achieve social order. But when taken to the extreme, certain ideologies can produce violent outcomes. Again, it is important to emphasize that extremism on its own is not terrorism. The majority of those who hold extremist views do not engage in violence. However, as illustrated by the historical review of ideological extremism provided in this chapter—as well as the case studies of contemporary extremist violence—extremist ideologies have led to horrific violence throughout history and remain significant threats today.

Key Lessons

Lesson 1

Ideologies have played a significant role in various types of terrorist movements across the world.

Lesson 2

Political ideologies are placed on an imaginary line called the political spectrum, with two opposite ends, one side representing the right and the other side representing the left.

Lesson 3

Far-left, extremist left-wing political thought has often been associated with extreme revolutionary views such as anarchism and communism and is often characterized by their strong opposition to capitalism and globalization.

Lesson 4

Marx and Engels argue that the rise of factories and capability of mass production for profit during the Industrial Revolution allowed the rich to accrue massive wealth at the expense of an impoverished large working class. They argued that under communism class struggles would end and people would live cohesively in social equilibrium.

Lesson 5

Communist states engaged in mass murders at a scale that has not been seen with any other form of ideology, including fascist right-wing authoritarians such as Hitler.

Lesson 6

Anarchism favors the establishment of a noncoercive society without an official governing body.

Lesson 7

While anarchism favors "no rulers/no authority," it does not favor life "without rules." Anarchists simply reject domination and control by the state. Instead, they aim for a society where voluntary and horizontal structures reject the capitalist economy and collectively learn to rule themselves via direct democracy.

Lesson 8

Far-right political ideology has been characterized by nationalistic, xenophobic, racist, chauvinist, homophobic, Islamophobic, anti-Semitic, authoritarian, and other reactionary views and is often associated with fascism and Nazism.

Lesson 9

Scholars describe fascism as an ultra-nationalist worldview that favors a forcibly monolithic and strongly controlled nation under a dictator. Fascists often focus on the superiority of their race and the importance of racial hygiene: the separation of unfit groups from their race in order to establish racial purity.

Lesson 10

Today, far-left groups are marginal in most places in the United States, and they have gone through a significant process of de-radicalization. Extreme right-wing violence, however, has been on the rise.

Lesson 11

The horseshoe theory argues that rather than being a simple straight line, the political spectrum is actually a horseshoe shape. According to this theory, extreme right and extreme left are not opposite ideologies. Instead, they highly resemble each other.

KEY WORDS

alternative right (alt-right)
anarchism
Animal Liberation Front (ALF)
anti-fascists (Antifa)
Cold War
Combat 18
communism
Communist Party of the United States
    of America (CPUSA)
Earth Liberation Front (ELF)
far left
far right
fascism
gulag system
horseshoe theory
ideology
involuntary celibates (incels)
Italian Red Brigades (BR)

Japanese Red Army (JRA)
Ku Klux Klan
lone actor terrorists
National Socialist Underground
    (NSU)
Nazism (National Socialism)
neo-Nazis
political spectrum
Popular Front for Liberation of Palestine
    (PFLP)
Proud Boys
Red Scare
Revolutionary Armed Forces of
    Colombia (FARC)
single-issue extremism
Symbionese Liberation Army
Weather Underground
White supremacy

RECOMMENDED SOURCES

Research Articles & Books

Ackerman, G. A., & Burnham, M. (2021). Towards a definition of terrorist ideology. *Terrorism and Political Violence*, *33*(6), 1160–1190.

Bjørgo, T., & Ravndal, J. A. (2022). *Extreme-right violence and terrorism: Concepts, patterns, and responses*. International Centre for Counter-Terrorism..

Carter, E. (2018). Right-wing extremism/radicalism: reconstructing the concept. *Journal of Political ideologies*, *23*(2), 157–182.

Doering, S., Davies, G., & Corrado, R. (2023). Reconceptualizing ideology and extremism: toward an empirically-based typology. *Studies in Conflict & Terrorism*, *46*(6), 1009–1033.

Haner, M., Sloan, M. M., Pickett, J. T., Cullen, F. T., & O'Neill, V. (2023). How politics constrain the public's understanding of terrorism. *Social Forces*, *102*(1), 157–179.

Hofmann, D. C. (2020). How "alone" are lone-actors? Exploring the ideological, signaling, and support networks of lone-actor terrorists. *Studies in Conflict & Terrorism*, *43*(7), 657–678.

Holt, T. J., Stonhouse, M., Freilich, J., & Chermak, S. M. (2021). Examining ideologically motivated cyberattacks performed by far-left groups. *Terrorism and political violence*, *33*(3), 527–548.

Jasko, K., LaFree, G., Piazza, J., & Becker, M. H. (2022). A comparison of political violence by left-wing, right-wing, and Islamist extremists in the United States and the world. *Proceedings of the National Academy of Sciences*, *119*(30), e2122593119.

McAlexander, R. J. (2020). How are immigration and terrorism related? An analysis of right-and left-wing terrorism in Western Europe, 1980–2004. *Journal of Global Security Studies*, *5*(1), 179–195.

Miller-Idriss, C. (2022). Hate in the homeland: The new global far right.

Piazza, J. A. (2017). The determinants of domestic right-wing terrorism in the USA: Economic grievance, societal change and political resentment. *Conflict management and peace science*, *34*(1), 52–80.

Silva, J. R., Duran, C., Freilich, J. D., & Chermak, S. M. (2020). Addressing the myths of terrorism in America. *International Criminal Justice Review, 30*(3), 302–324.

Simi, P., & Bubolz, B.F. (2017). Far right terrorism in the United States. In G. LaFree & J. D. Freilich (Eds) The handbook of the criminology of terrorism (pp. 295–309). Hoboken, USA: John Wiley & Sons, Inc

Tangian, A. (2020). Policy representation across the political spectrum. In *Analytical Theory of Democracy* (pp. 405–446). Springer, Cham.

News Articles & Government and Think Tank Reports

What is fascism?
    Author(s): John Broich
    Source: The Conversation

The escalating terrorism problem in the United States.
    Author(s): Seth G. Jones, Catrina Doxsee, & Nicholas Harrington
    Source: Center for Strategic and International Studies (CSIS)

What is right-wing extremism?
    Author(s): Anders Ravik Jupskås & Iris Beau Segers
    Source: Center for Research on Extremism (C-REX)

Surveying the landscape of the American far right.
    Author(s): Mark Pitcavage
    Source: Program on Extremism at The George Washington University

How Are Socialism and Communism Different?
    Author(s): Sarah Pruitt
    Source: HISTORY

Lessons from a century of communism.
    Author(s): Ilya Somin
    Source: The Washington Post

What to Know About the Origins of Fascism's Brutal Ideology?
    Author(s): Olivia B. Waxman
    Source: TIME

What is anarchism all about?
    Author(s): Andreas Wittel
    Source: The Conversation

What is the Threat to the United States Today?
    Source: New America

Socialism, anti-fascism and anti-abortion on Prevent list of terrorism warning signs
    Author(s): Vikram Dodd
    Source: The Guardian

Mental health and terrorism: more people flagged to authorities have 'mixed, unstable, unclear' views than Islamist ideologies
    Author(s): Barry Richards
    Source: The Conservative

Which Ideology Has Inspired The Most Murders In Terrorist Attacks On U.S. Soil?
    Author(s): Alex Nowrasteh
    Source: Forbes

Attacks by White Extremists Are Growing. So Are Their Connections.
    Author(s): Weiyi Cai & Simone Landon
    Source: The New York Times

Rise of the far right: a disturbing mix of hateful ideologies
    Author(s): Jamie Grierson
    Source: The Guardian

The misogynist incel movement is spreading. Should it be classified as a terror threat?
    Author(s): Lois Beckett
    Source: The Guardian

Documentaries, Videos, and Other Educational Media

Extremism in America
    Producers: Christopher Hastings & Scott Michels
    Source: PBS

Pathways to Violent Extremism
    Featuring: John Horgan
    Source: National Institute of Justice

American Insurrection
  Producers: A.C. Thompson, Karim Hajj, &
  Jacqueline Soohen
  Source: PBS
Turning Point: 9/11 and the War on Terror
  Producer(s)/Director(s): Brian
  Knappenberger
  Source: Netflix
An American Bombing: The Road to April
19th
  Producer(s)/Director(s): Marc Levin &
  Daphne Pinkerson
  Source: HBO

Michael Flynn's Holy War
  Producer(s)/Director(s): Paul Abowd &
  Jacqueline Soohen
  Source: PBS
White Noise
  Producer(s)/Director(s): Noah Baumbach
  Source: The Atlantic
America After 9/11
  Producer(s)/Director(s): Michael Kirk
  Source: PBS
United States of Conspiracy
  Producer(s)/Director(s): Michael Kirk
  Source: PBS

REFERENCES

Al-Khoury, D. (2020). Radicalisation: old and new a comparative analysis of the Red Brigades and the Islamic State. *Quality & Quantity, 54*(3), 867–885.

Andrews, N. J. (2020). The romantic socialist origins of humanitarianism. *Modern Intellectual History*, 17(3), 737–768.

AP (2018, August 2). Report puts Colombia conflict's death toll at 260,000-plus. https://apnews.com/article/687aabf1f89044ddb08d8cae7afd0f60.

BBC (2018). Elliot Rodger: How misogynist killer became "incel hero." https://www.bbc.com/news/world-us-canada-43892189

BBC (2020, January 23). Germany bans Combat 18 as police raid neo-Nazi group. BBC. https://www.bbc.com/news/world-europe-51219274

Bellware, K. (2022, June 13). Proud Boys disrupt drag queen reading event, prompting hate-crime probe. *Washington Post*. https://www.washingtonpost.com/nation/2022/06/13/proud-boy-drag-queen/

Blakemore, E. (2020). How the Red Terror set a macabre course for the Soviet Union. *National Geographic*. https://www.nationalgeographic.com/history/article/red-terror-set-macabre-course-soviet-union

Blazak, R. (2011). Isn't every crime a hate crime? The case for hate crime laws. *Sociology Compass*, 5(4), 244–255.

Blazakis, J. M. (2022, January 26). US has taken FARC off its terrorist list, giving insight into Biden's foreign policy. *The Conversation*.https://theconversation.com/us-has-taken-farc-off-its-terrorist-list-giving-insight-into-bidens-foreign-policy-174667.

Blight, J. G., Nye, J. S., & Welch, D. A. (1987). The Cuban missile crisis revisited. *Foreign Affairs*, 66(1), 170–188.

Blumberg, M. (1986). Comparative analysis of violent left- and right-wing extremist groups in the United States. Presentation. Annual Meeting of the American Society of Criminology.

Bogel-Burroughs, N. & Garcia, S. E. (2020). Who is Antifa, the movement Trump wants to declare a terror group? *New York Times*. https://www.nytimes.com/article/what-antifa-trump.html

Box, M., & McCormack, G. (2004). Terror in Japan: The Red Army (1969–2001) and Aum Supreme Truth (1987–2000). *Critical Asian Studies*, 36(1), 91–112.

Boyes, R. (1997). Letter bombs mark shift to terrorism by British neo-Nazis. *The Times*, 2.

Brady, E. (2022, March 9). Number of Proud Boys chapters almost doubled from 2020 to 2021: Report. *Newsweek*. https://www.newsweek.com/number-proud-boys-chapters-almost-doubled-2020-2021-report-1686510

Broich, J. (2021). What is fascism? The Conversation. https://theconversation.com/what-is-fascism-153947

Brown, A. (2019). The green scare: How a Movement That Never Killed Anyone Became the FBI's No. 1 Domestic Terrorism Threat. Intercept. https://theintercept.com/2019/03/23/ecoterrorism-fbi-animal-rights/

Cambridge University Press. (n.d.). Ideology. In *Cambridge Dictionary*. https://dictionary.cambridge.org/us/dictionary/english/ideology (accessed June 3, 2022).

Carlisle, M. (2019, September 12). What to know about the original of 'left' and 'right' in politics, from the French Revolution to the 2020 presidential race. Time. https://time.com/5673239/left-right-politics-orgins/

Carter, E. (2018). Right-wing extremism/radicalism: Reconstructing the concept. Journal of Political Ideologies, 23(2), 157–182.

CISAC (2022). Mapping militant organizations. Proud Boys. Stanford University. https://cisac.fsi.stanford.edu/mappingmilitants/profiles/proud-boys#text_block_32645

Colley, T., & Moore, M. (2022). The challenges of studying 4chan and the alt-right: "Come on in the water's fine." *new media & society*, 24(1), 5–30.

Copland, E. (2022, January 5). START releases data on Proud Boys ahead of Capitol Riot anniversary. *National Consortium for the Study of Terrorism and Responses to Terrorism.* https://www.start.umd.edu/news/start-releases-data-proud-boys-ahead-capitol-riot-anniversary

Cowley, M. K. (2023, July 31). Red scare. *Free Speech Center.* https://firstamendment.mtsu.edu/article/red-scare/

Craig, G. A. (1978). *Germany, 1866–1945.* Clarendon Press.

Cranston, M. (2024). Ideology. *Encyclopedia Britannica.* https://www.britannica.com/topic/ideology-society/the-sociology-of-knowledge

Cunningham, D. (2013). *Klansville, USA: The rise and fall of the civil rights-era Ku Klux Klan.* Oxford University Press.

Danvers, W. (2021). Right-wing extremism: An international threat. *Just Security.* https://www.justsecurity.org/74919/right-wing-extremism-an-international-threat/

Deutsche Welle (2022). Communism. https://www.dw.com/en/communism/t-39415002

Dikötter, F. (2018). *Mao's great famine: The history of China's most devastating catastrophe, 1958–62.* Bloomsbury.

DOJ (2022, June 6). Leader of Proud Boys and four other members indicated in federal court for seditious conspiracy and other offenses related to U.S. Capitol breach. US Department of Justice. https://www.justice.gov/opa/pr/leader-proud-boys-and-four-other-members-indicted-federal-court-seditious-conspiracy-and

Durkee, A. (2022). Attacks on abortion providers surged in 2021, report finds as Supreme Court overturns Roe v. Wade. *Forbes.* https://www.forbes.com/sites/alisondurkee/2022/06/24/attacks-on-abortion-providers-surged-in-2021-report-finds-ahead-of-roe-v-wade-ruling/?sh=37cf24e15419

Elhefnawy, N. (2022). What is fascism? The view from left, center and right: A note. https://papers.ssrn.com/sol3/papers.cfm?abstract_id=4056103

Fariello, G. (2008). *Red scare: Memories of the American inquisition.* Norton.

Fine, S. (1955). Anarchism and the assassination of McKinley. *American Historical Review,* 60(4), 777–799.

Flood, D. (2021). Anarchism in practice is often radically boring democracy. Sapiens. https://www.sapiens.org/culture/anarchism-democracy/

Frantilla, A. (n.d.). World Trade Organization protests in Seattle. Seattle City Archives. https://www.seattle.gov/cityarchives/exhibits-and-education/digital-document-libraries/world-trade-organization-protests-in-seattle

Frenkel, S. & Feuer, A. (2021, January 20). 'A total failure': The Proud Boys now Mock Trump. *The New York Times.* https://www.nytimes.com/2021/01/20/technology/proud-boys-trump.html?smid=fb-share&fbclid=IwAR3l99pdYtopyb_zhrDncSWjpgtqzNslGqPHR5aoBtDKkmPSWN1tYyG3iTo

Garvin, D. (2015). Taylorist breastfeeding in rationalist clinics: Constructing industrial motherhood in fascist Italy. *Critical Inquiry,* 41(3), 655–674.

Gerteis, C. (2021). *Mobilizing Japanese youth: The Cold War and the making of the sixties generation.* Cornell University Press.

Global Terrorism Database. (2024). Combat 18. University of Maryland National Consortium for the Study of Terrorism and Responses to Terrorism. https://www.start.umd.edu/gtd/search/IncidentSummary.aspx?gtdid=201002040023

Gordon, L. (2017). *The second coming of the KKK: The Ku Klux Klan of the 1920s and the American political tradition.* Liveright Publishing.

Gornstein, L (2020). What is fascism? And what does it mean in 2020 America? CBS News. https://www.cbsnews.com/news/what-is-fascism/

Griffin, R. (2013). The nature of fascism. Global Terrorism Database https://www.start.umd.edu/gtd/search/IncidentSummary.aspx?gtdid=201008250033

Hamilton, L. H. (1990). The USSR and Marxist revolutions in the third world. Cambridge University Press.

Hillebrand, C. (2018). Beate Zschäpe guilty: The five-year neo-Nazi trial that shook Germany. *The Conversation.* https://theconversation.com/beate-zschape-guilty-the-five-year-neo-nazi-trial-that-shook-germany-99816

Irrera, D. (2014). Learning from the past: Case of the Red Brigades in Italy. *Counter Terrorist Trends and Analyses, 6*(6), 16–20.

Ivanova, G. M., Raleigh, D. J., Mikhailovna, G., & Flath, C. A. (2015). *Labor camp socialism: The gulag in the Soviet totalitarian system.* Routledge.

Jamieson, A. (1990). Entry, discipline and exit in the Italian Red Brigades. *Terrorism and Political Violence, 2*(1), 1–20.

Jones, G. S., & Doxsee, C. (2020). The escalating terrorism problem in the United States. Center for Strategic & International Studies. https://www.csis.org/analysis/escalating-terrorism-problem-united-states

Jupskås, A. R. (2020). What is right-wing radicalism? Center for Research on Extremism. https://www.sv.uio.no/c-rex/english/groups/compendium/what-is-right-wing-radicalism.html

Jupskås, A. R., & Segers, I. B. (2020). What is right-wing extremism? Center for Research on Extremism. https://www.sv.uio.no/c-rex/english/groups/compendium/what-is-right-wing-extremism.html

Kageyama, Y. (2022, May 28). Japan terrorist group founder freed after serving time. AP News. https://apnews.com/article/middle-east-japan-kuala-lumpur-malaysia-48318a6c2ac37910272118d87d3e676d.

Kalu, M. C. (2019). Everyone knows the word "Nazi" but how did the term come into being? War History Online. https://www.warhistoryonline.com/instant-articles/the-origin-of-the-term-nazi.html?chrome=1&A1c=1

Keller, B. (1989). Major Soviet paper says 20 million died as victims of Stalin. *New York Times.* https://www.nytimes.com/1989/02/04/world/major-soviet-paper-says-20-million-died-as-victims-of-stalin.html

Kennedy, R. F. (2011). *Thirteen days: A memoir of the Cuban missile crisis.* Norton.

Koehler, D. (2016). Right-wing extremism and terrorism in Europe. *Prism, 6*(2), 84–105.

Kropotkin, P. (1995). 'Anarchism,' from the Encyclopedia Britannica. In M. S. Shatz (Ed.), *Kropotkin: "The Conquest of Bread" and other writings* (pp. 233–247). Cambridge University Press.

Kunkeler, N. (2021). What is Nazism? Center for Research on Extremism. https://www.sv.uio.no/c-rex/english/groups/compendium/what-is-nazism.html

Laqueur, W. (1965). The roots of Nazism. *The New York Review.* https://www.nybooks.com/articles/1965/01/14/the-roots-of-nazism/

Levenson, M. (2021, December 10). Self-proclaimed Proud Boys member gets 10 years for violence at Portland protests. *New York Times.* https://www.nytimes.com/2021/12/10/us/proud-boys-alan-swinney-sentenced.html

Lewy, G. (2009). *The Catholic Church and Nazi Germany.* Da Capo Press.

Liang, C. S., & Cross, M. J. (2020). White crusade: How to prevent right-wing extremists from exploiting the internet. Geneva Centre for Security Policy. https://dam.gcsp.ch/files/doc/white-crusade-how-to-prevent-right-wing-extremists-from-exploiting-the-internet

Lindseth, P. L. (2003). The paradox of parliamentary supremacy: Delegation, democracy, and dictatorship in Germany and France, 1920s–1950s. *Yale Law Journal, 113,* 1341–1349.

Lucas, R. (2022). The justice department will create domestic terrorism unit to counter rising threats. NPR. https://www.npr.org/2022/01/11/1072123333/justice-department-domestic-terrorism-unit

Maddox, W. S., & Lilie, S. A. (1984). *Beyond liberal and conservative: Reassessing the political spectrum*. Cato Institute.

Marx, K. (1875). Critique of the Gotha Programme. https://www.marxists.org/archive/marx/works/1875/gotha/ch01.htm

McGowan, L. (2014). Right-wing violence in Germany: Assessing the objectives, personalities and terror trail of the national socialist underground and the state's response to it. *German Politics, 23*(3), 196–212.

McInnes, G. (2016, September 15). Introducing: The Proud Boys. *Taki's Magazine*. https://www.takimag.com/article/introducing_the_proud_boys_gavin_mcinnes/

McKirdy, A. (2017, June 8). Imprisoned Japanese Red Army founder Shigenobu holds out hope for revolution. *The Japan Times*. https://www.japantimes.co.jp/news/2017/06/08/national/imprisoned-japanese-red-army-founder-shigenobu-holds-hope-revolution/#:~text=The%20imprisoned%20founder%20of%20the,to%20alter%20the%20pacifist%20Constitution

Metcalfe, T. (2022). What is mutual assured destruction? *Live Science*. https://www.livescience.com/mutual-assured-destruction

Moore, E. (2021, January 4). D.C. Police arrest leader of the Proud Boys ahead of far-right protests. NPR. https://www.npr.org/2021/01/04/953349879/d-c-police-prepare-for-far-right-protests-as-congress-counts-electoral-votes

Park, M. & Kyung, L (2017). Berkeley protests of Yiannopoulos caused $100,000 in damage. CNN. https://www.cnn.com/2017/02/01/us/milo-yiannopoulos-berkeley/index.html

Piazza, J. A. (2017). The determinants of domestic right-wing terrorism in the USA: Economic grievance, societal change and political resentment. *Conflict Management and Peace Science, 34*(1), 52–80.

Pitcavage, M. (2019). Surveying the landscape of the American far right. George Washington University Program on Extremism. https://extremism.gwu.edu/sites/g/files/zaxdzs2191/f/Surveying%20The%20Landscape%20of%20the%20American%20Far%20Right_0.pdf

Pop-Eleches, G., & Tucker, J. A. (2020). Communist legacies and left authoritarianism. *Comparative Political Studies, 53*(12), 1861–1889.

Pruitt, S. (2019). How are socialism and communism different? History. https://www.history.com/news/socialism-communism-differences

Public Safety Canada. n. d. https://www.publicsafety.gc.ca/cnt/ntnl-scrt/cntr-trrrsm/lstd-ntts/crrnt-lstd-ntts-en.aspx

Rabasa, A., Chalk, P., Cragin, K., Daly, S. A., Gregg, H. S., Krasik, T. W., O'Brien, K. A., & Rosenau, W. (2006). Beyond al-Qaeda: Part 2: The outer rings of the terrorist universe. Rand Corporation. https://apps.dtic.mil/sti/citations/ADA458206.

Reich, A. (2022, May 30). On this day: 50 years since JRA terrorists commit Lod Airport massacre. *Jerusalem Post*. https://www.jpost.com/israel-news/article-708078

Sawicki, K. S. (2013). Seattle WTO protests of 1999. https://www.britannica.com/event/Seattle-WTO-protests-of-1999

Scruggs, G. (2019). What the "Battle of Seattle" means 20 years later. Bloomberg. https://www.bloomberg.com/news/articles/2019-11-29/what-seattle-s-wto-protests-mean-20-years-later

Service, R. (2010). *Comrades! A history of world communism*. Harvard University Press.

Sganga, N. (2022). New secret service report details growing incel terrorism threat. CBS News. https://www.cbsnews.com/news/incel-threat-secret-service-report/

Simi, P., & Bubolz, B.F. (2017). Far right terrorism in the United States. In G. LaFree & J. D. Freilich (Eds.), *The handbook of the criminology of terrorism* (pp. 295–309). Wiley.

Simi, P., Windisch, S., & Sporer, K. (2016). Recruitment and radicalization among US far right terrorists. START. https://www.start.umd.edu/pubs/START_RecruitmentRadicalizationAmongUSFarRightTerrorists_Nov2016.pdf.

Skolnik, J. (2022). Secret Service report details growing threat of "incel" terrorism. *Salon*.

https://www.salon.com/2022/03/15/secret-report-details-growing-of-incel-terrorism/

Sneed, K., & Li, D. K. (2022, June 15). Hate crime charges filed against Buffalo shooting suspect who allegedly killed 10 at supermarket. ABC News. https://www.nbcnews.com/news/us-news/hate-crime-charges-filed-buffalo-shooter-killed-10-supermarket-rcna33709

Somin, I. (2017). Lessons from a century of communism. *Washington Post*. https://www.washingtonpost.com/news/volokh-conspiracy/wp/2017/11/07/lessons-from-a-century-of-communism/

Spillar, K. (2022). The anti-abortion movement has a long history of terrorism. A Roe repeal will make it worse. *Ms. Magazine*. https://ms-magazine.com/2022/05/06/anti-abortion-violence-terrorism-roe-v-wade/

Stanley, J. (2020). *How fascism works: The politics of us and them*. Random House.

Storrs, L. R. (2015). McCarthyism and the second red scare. *Oxford research encyclopedia of American history*. https://doi.org/10.1093/acrefore/9780199329175.013.6

Storrs, L. R. Y. (2003). Red scare politics and the suppression of popular front feminism: The loyalty investigation of Mary Dublin Keyserling. *Journal of American History, 90*(2), 491–524.

Stuster, J. D. (2013). Mapped: The 7 governments the U.S. has overthrown. *Foreign Policy*. https://foreignpolicy.com/2013/08/20/mapped-the-7-governments-the-u-s-has-overthrown/

Suárez, A. & Rueda, M. (2021, December 1). Explainer: What are Colombia's ex-FARC splinter groups? AP News. https://apnews.com/article/colombia-united-states-south-america-armed-forces-revolutionary-armed-forces-of-colombia-492c423824351ff8d-c1ed4bba761d200

Sundquist, V. H. (2010). Political terrorism: An historical case study of the Italian Red Brigades. *Journal of Strategic Security, 3*(3), 53–68.

Tanas, O. (2015). Putin revives Soviet deal of pretend-work-and-pay to hide crisis. Bloomberg. https://www.bloomberg.com/news/articles/2015-08-17/putin-revives-soviet-deal-of-pretend-work-and-pay-to-hide-crisis

Tangian, A. (2020). *Analytical theory of democracy: History, mathematics and applications*. Springer.

Tolnay, S. E. (2003). The African American "great migration" and beyond. *Annual Review of Sociology*, 209–232.

Topinka, R. (2022). The politics of anti-discourse: Copypasta, the alt-right, and the rhetoric of form. *Theory & Event, 25*(2), 392–418.

US Department of State. (1990). The Japanese red army. *Studies in Conflict and Terrorism, 13*(1), 73–78.

Von Der Behrens, A. (2018). Lessons from Germany's NSU case. *Race & Class, 59*(4), 84–91.

Waxman, O. (2019). What to know about the origins of fascism's brutal ideology. *Time*. https://time.com/5556242/what-is-fascism/

Weisberger, M. (2021). What is fascism? Live Science. https://www.livescience.com/57622-fascism.html

Weldes, J. (1999). *Constructing national interests: The United States and the Cuban missile crisis*. University of Minnesota Press.

Wheeldon, T. (2021). The Paris Commune, 150 years on—from the siege of the capital to "Bloody Week." France24. https://www.france24.com/en/france/20210318-from-the-siege-of-paris-to-the-bloody-week-the-commune-150-years-on

Wilde, R. (2020). How the Treaty of Versailles contributed to Hitler's rise. ThoughtCo. https://www.thoughtco.com/treaty-of-versailles-hitlers-rise-power-1221351

Wittel, A. (2015). What is anarchism all about? *The Conversation*. https://theconversation.com/what-is-anarchism-all-about-50373

Wolff, E. C. (2020). What is fascism? Center for Research on Extremism-University of Oslo. https://www.sv.uio.no/c-rex/english/groups/compendium/what-is-fascism.html

Wright, L. T. (2022). Horseshoe theory and why the radical left and right wing are the same. Soapboxie. https://soapboxie.com/us-politics/horseshoe-theory-political-left-and-right

Yturbe, C. (1997). On Norberto Bobbio's theory of democracy. *Political Theory, 25*(3), 377–400.

CHAPTER 7

Nationalistic Terrorism

*Ethnic Nationalism and Nonstate
Terrorist Violence*

Source: Everett Collection/Shutterstock.

Learning Objectives
1. To understand the concepts of nationalism, nationalistic terrorism, and ethno-nationalist terrorism.
2. To describe the emergence and history of nationalism.
3. To examine the different types of nationalism (ethnic vs. civic).
4. To understand the drivers of nationalist terrorist campaigns.
5. To analyze the emergence, development, and current status of some of the bloodiest nationalist terrorist organizations across the world.

7.1 INTRODUCTION

The emergence of nationalism is a prominent feature of modern history, and it is an idea that originated with two concepts: (1) **nation**, and (2) **state** (Mylonas & Tudor, 2021). In simple terms, a nation can be described as a group of people who are bound together based on some common defining features such as history, religion, language, culture, or ethnicity. A state is an association of people with its own sovereign political organization and independent government within a clearly defined territorial boundary, and which is often internationally recognized by other states. As the definition implies, states have formal institutions with the authority to enforce a system of rules over the people living in their territories. An important detail to note is that nations can be spread across multiple states (e.g., the Kurds in Iran, Iraq, and Syria) and states can encompass multiple nations (e.g., Spain, Turkey, and the United Kingdom). In other words, not every nation has a state as of 2024 (e.g., Basque people, Palestinians), and some states may contain multiple nations.

With this information in mind, nationalism can be described as the principle that the nation and the state should be congruent, or identical. Nationalism favors an individual's identification with their own nation—that loyalty and allegiance to the nation-state surpasses other individual and group interests (Kohn 1938; 2022). Nationalists also favor the superiority of their own nation over all others and advocate for the interests of their nation, especially with the aim of gaining political independence and popular sovereignty over their homeland (Mylonoas & Tudor, 2021). Nationalists aim to build, promote, and maintain a single national identity and unity based on some social characteristics such as ethnicity, culture, language, or religion (Calhoun 1997).

Nationalism was one of the salient causes of World War I, among several other conflicts and violent movements that threatened peace and security around the world during the twentieth and twenty-first centuries. It has been the driving force of many freedom, justice, and independence movements across the world, especially after the 1940s. States and ethnic groups embraced nationalism to legitimize violence against minorities and ruling elites (colonizers) to achieve their racial, ethnic, or religious goals (Breuilly 1993). This chapter will explain the origins, history, and significance of nationalism (particularly ethnic nationalism) in terms of its influence on extremism and terrorism.

7.2 A BRIEF HISTORY OF NATIONALISM

Contrary to the common assumption that nationalist ideologies date far back in history, nationalism is a modern movement. It was not until the end of the eighteenth century that the idea of nationalism became a widely recognized sentiment in world politics

(Mylonoas & Tudor, 2021). Historians often cite the French Revolution as the first expression of nationalist ideals. Before then, people lived under some type of territorial authorities, but their loyalty or political allegiance was not determined by their nation. Allegiances were determined by some other hierarchical affiliation such as religion, sect, dynasty, or feudal lord. Throughout most of the human history the idea of a nation-state was nonexistent, and civilizations were primarily formed around religions (e.g., the Holy Roman Empire) (Tagore 2017).

FIGURE 7.1 Symbol of French nationalism during revolution: Liberty Leading the People. *Source:* Eugène Delacroix, CC BY-SA 2.0, via Wikimedia Commons.

However, beginning with the French Revolution and the spread of popular sovereignty—the idea that people should be able to govern themselves—nationalism grew and spread from France across the rest of the world (Kohn 1939). With the overthrowing of the monarchy in France, revolutionaries drew up a new constitution that defined the rights of citizens and established new ruling principles for the leaders of their new sovereign state. France became a democratic sovereign state composed of free and self-governing citizens (Keitner 2012).

The revolutionaries also developed a new collective identity which emphasized citizens' loyalty to the state—regardless of their ethnicity or home country—to France as a nation. Education would only be provided in French (replacing all regional dialects), and the use of national symbols, flags, anthems, narratives, patriotic music, and other national identifiers quickly gained importance in the public sphere. The new three colored French flag was adopted to represent the progressive idea of the new French nation—living under liberty, equality, and fraternity (i.e., brotherhood), rather than the authoritarianism and inequality of the past. These efforts enabled France to be a sovereign state and intensified French people's loyalty to their nation, replacing former loyalties—to feudal authorities, the king, noblemen, and religious clerics, for instance.

Napoleon Bonaparte played an important role in the promotion and spread of French nationalism. He used the idea of the nation and nationalism as a powerful political force to justify his polices, such as military campaigns and invasions of other European countries that expanded the borders of France across Europe (Rowe 2013). He convinced the French public that these expansionist policies were predicated on the idea of spreading fraternity, liberty, and equality—the enlightened ideals of the French Revolution—to the people of European countries who were suffering under tyrannical monarchical rulers, and thus he rationalized his invasion of European countries as liberating people, bringing peace to their countries, and spreading the political achievements of the French Revolution. Citizens of several European countries, such as Germany and Italy, initially welcomed Napoleon's invasions of their territories in the hopes of gaining liberty and protection against their tyrannical rulers. Napoleon had provided these new territories with written rules and constitutions, such as the Napoleonic Code in France, that safeguarded the rights of the people. He was initially seen as liberator and modernizer by many Europeans, leading victorious campaigns against Austria, Holland, Belgium, Switzerland, Italy, Russia, Germany, Spain, and Portugal and annexing these European territories into France, which led the French armies to dominate Europe for almost 10 years during his reign.

However, as Napoleon became increasingly despotic and imperialistic, he unintentionally facilitated the birth of nationalism, patriotism, and liberty within the nations that were under his control (Kohn 1939). The oppression and conquest of European nations had ignited within them a counterreactionary spirit of nationalism. For example, historians widely accept that the unification of the German states into a liberated, democratic, and politically united Germany and the Italian states into a united Italy were because of growing anti-French sentiment in reaction to Napoleon's oppressive rule and to the spread of the core ideals of the French Revolution throughout Europe (Keitner 2012).

Napoleon's nationalist imperialism provoked harsh reactions in the occupied territories (e.g., Spain, Austria, Germany, Belgium, Poland, and Russia) and led these countries to unite against France. It also increased the spread and diffusion of nationalistic ideas (national autonomy, unity, and identity) among them. In other words, these countries discovered their own national consciousness and the importance of their own cultural unity through their hatred of the French invaders. The very nationalist ideals that brought Napoleon success in Europe had also defeated him by fostering national consciousness among his enemies (Alter 1994). For this reason, some historians call Napoleon the "national awakener" of the European people or the "father" of the rise of national movements in Europe. The British experience of nation-building was also shaped by Napoleon's aggressive expansionist policies in Europe. In a response to the increased threat of Napoleon's invasion of England, the concepts of "British Nation," "Great Britain," and "Britishness" were constructed to increase the loyalty and solidarity of Scottish and Welsh people to the English kingdom (Colley 1992).

For all of these reasons, the famous German historian Thomas Nipperdey explained: "Napoleon Bonaparte became the liberator and nation-builder for some; the oppressor, the despot, the 'Corsican usurper' and 'scourge of God' the 'son of hell' or 'sublime monster' for others—but the rather unexpected catalyst and trigger for a new epoch in European history for all" (Nipperdey & Daniel 1996).

7.2.1 Ethnic Nationalism versus Civic Nationalism

In his seminal work *Nationalism: A Study in Its Origins and Background*, the American philosopher, historian, and one of the first modern scholars of nationalism, Hans Kohn, describes two distinctive types of nationalism: civic and ethnic (Kohn & Calhoun 2017). According to Kohn, both types of nationalism were developed in the eighteenth and nineteenth centuries.

Civic nationalism is based on the idea that anyone (regardless of their ethnic origin) who shows loyalty to the institutions and civic values of a nation belongs to that nation. It is founded on the principle of human rights and personal freedom, and it has a unifying character, rather than a divisive one—it is based on the idea of unity in diversity (Tamir 2019). Civic nationalists welcome the diversity of sovereign people who adhere to the institutions, values, and political objectives of a democratic community. Nationality is not based on ethnic origin in civic nationalism; instead it is political, based on an individual's choice and it is absorbed into citizenship (Larin, 2020). An individual can choose to be a member of a nation based on the association of like-minded individuals under the civic model of nationhood.

The second type of nationalism, **ethnic nationalism** (also known as classical nationalism), which stems from the German Volksgemeinschaft (see Chapter 6), emphasizes the importance of ethnicity and cultural homogeneity in the formation of a nation (Breton 1988). A nation under this type is based on ethnicity and people who share a common descent, language, culture, religion, and history. Ethnic nationality cannot be acquired; it is an inherited privilege determined by pre-existing characteristics (Tamir 2019). Due to its aversion to diversity and highly restrictive nature, scholars describe this type of nationalism as primitive, tribal, conservative, exclusive, and divisive (Mylonas & Tudor, 2021; Larin, 2020).

Nations that have promoted ethnic nationalism have also engaged in harmful acts such as authoritarianism, colonization, military aggression, and intolerance toward other ethnic, religious, and cultural groups; in the case of Nazi Germany, these policies escalated as far as ethnic cleansing and genocide. As explained in Chapter 6, the German conception of ethnic nationalism under Adolf Hitler's NSDAP party led to a historical catastrophe in Europe. Hitler rallied the German people to believe in German racial superiority (i.e., Aryan supremacy) to rationalize his military offensives and horrific acts toward other nations and ethnic groups in Germany (Kohn & Calhoun 2017).

Noting these characteristics, scholars classify the two types of nationalism, civic and ethnic, as good and bad, respectively. For example, French sociologist Dominique Schnapper labels ethno-centric states as primitive, "failed states" and describes their condition as "social groupings that have not come yet to full political maturity, that do not

FIGURE 7.2 A Nazi propaganda calendar from 1938, showing the idealized concept of a healthy German family as the core of the Volksgemeinschaft, a pure "Aryan" family, with Nazi ideal racial types (a blond father, mother, and young child) and a flying eagle in the background. *Source:* Ludwig Hohlwein, Public domain, via Wikimedia Commons.

FIGURE 7.3 Nedeljko Cabrinovic (second from right, 1895–1916), the Serb nationalist who assassinated Archduke Franz Ferdinand (1863–1914) and Duchess Sophie Chotek (1868–1914). The bombing engendered World War I in 1914.

share a civic understanding of the nation." (Quoted in Brubaker, 1999).Civic nationalism, in comparison, is considered to be an indispensable characteristic of culturally developed, progressed nations and societies

As stated, ethnic nationalism (or ethnonationalism) was one of the main causes of World War I. The assassination of the Archduke of Austria, Franz Ferdinand, in 1914 was a nationalistic act by a Serbian nationalist. It played a significant role in the collapse of the major empires, such as the Austria-Hungarian and Ottoman Empires (Roshwald 2002). During the nineteenth century, the idea of ethnic nationalism penetrated certain nations in Europe and ignited the formation of several new nation-states—Austria, Hungary, Poland, Romania, Serbia, Greece, Montenegro, and Bulgaria (Denitch 1996). It sparked militarism and fascism among countries until the end of World War II. Not only have acts motivated by ethnic nationalism led to the deaths of millions of people but they have also led to some of the worst crimes that human beings have ever committed—such as Nazi Germany's policy of racial purity and the extermination of Jews and other groups (Rummel, 2022).

Ethnic nationalist political appeals were discredited and discouraged with the end of World War II. The term "nationalism" also took on increasingly negative connotations from that point on. Major international organizations such as NATO (1949) and the United Nations (1945) were established to increase military, economic, and political cooperation among the countries, which in turn led to a significant decrease in expressions of nationalism across Europe and the rest of the world.

However, after the 1950s, new forms of nationalism emerged across Europe, Asia, North America, South America, and Africa among certain state and nonstate actors, mainly for two goals: (1) to fight for their independence within a larger ruling power's territorial border, and (2) to end their colonial status. Several terrorist organizations with nationalist separatist goals emerged in Western developed societies, especially during the late 1960s. The most prominent examples of these groups are the Irish Republican Army (IRA) in the United Kingdom, Basque Homeland and Freedom (ETA) in Spain, National Liberation Front of Corsica (FLNC) in France, and **Liberation Front of Quebec (FLQ)** in Canada.

During the same time, national struggles for independence in colonized communities of Africa also accelerated—mainly driven by the desire for political independence from colonizers and occupying forces. The people of occupied or colonized territories employed their national identities (often described as "national awakening") in attempts to regain their national autonomy. Anti-colonial struggles were led by several groups such as the **Irgun Zvai Leumi** in Palestine, **Popular Liberation Movement of Angola**,

National Liberation Front in Algeria, and most prominently, the **African National Congress** in South Africa. These groups engaged in bloody attacks in urban areas against schools, clinics, railways, and ports to drive the colonial powers (e.g., British, French, and Portuguese) out of their territories and gain independence (Hoffman 1998).

In the 1970s and 1980s, other lethal terrorist organizations emerged, but this time in less economically and politically developed countries, such as the **Kurdistan Workers' Party (PKK)** in Turkey, the **Abu Sayyaf Group** in the Philippines, the **Liberation Tigers of Tamil Eelam (LTTE)** in

FIGURE 7.4 Nelson Mandela (1918–2013) was a South African anti-apartheid revolutionary, political leader, and philanthropist who played a pivotal role in ending apartheid and establishing a multiracial democracy in South Africa. *Source:* Keating, Maureen, photographer/LC-RC15-1994-655, no. 8 [P&P]/Roll Call portion of CQ Roll Call Photograph Collection (Library of Congress).

Sri Lanka, and the **National Organization of Cypriot Struggle (EOKA)** in Cyprus. In the 1990s, nationalistic terrorist violence emerged in the territories previously controlled by the Soviet Union, following the breakdown of the communist regime in the region including the **Kosovo Liberation Army (UCK)** in the Federal Republic of Yugoslavia, Chechen groups in Russia, and Serbian groups in Bosnia.

As of 2024, even though the number of nationalistic terrorist organizations has diminished, several groups with nationalistic inspirations still operate in different parts of the world. Examples of contemporary nationalist movements include the Tibetans and Uyghurs in China, Palestinians in Gaza and the West Bank, Chechens in Russia, and the Kurds in Iraq, Syria, Turkey, and Iran. These struggles led by oppressed national groups have often led to violent clashes and killings of non-nationals. Depending on who you ask, these groups can be described as heroic and patriotic, or cruel and terroristic.

7.2.2 Nationalistic (Ethnic Nationalist) Terrorism

Ethnic nationalist terrorism is the deliberate use of violence by a subnational group to achieve its agenda, often centered around the goal of separating its territory and society from the state in which it is located (Byman 1998; Reinares 2005). The short history of nationalism is abundant with examples of nonstate terrorist violence motivated by the idea of nationalism (Byman 1998), and several groups throughout the world have utilized nationalistic rhetoric as a means of mobilizing support for their causes. We will examine some examples later in this chapter. Ethnic nationalist terrorism has been regarded as the most prevalent type of terrorism in terms of number of attacks and casualties (Boylan 2016). Not only have ethnic nationalist terrorist groups been more destructive, but they have also proven themselves to be more resilient than terrorist groups motivated by other ideologies, whether they be religious, far right, or far left. Historically, nonstate actors from the Middle East to Europe and Africa have engaged in terroristic violence for nationalistic reasons for the sake of their ethnic identity groups, sometimes to gain an increased autonomy in the territories in which they live, and other times for separatist purposes—to secure an independent sovereign homeland for their group. In doing so, these groups often rallied their people (with whom they have ethnic, religious, and cultural ties) around the belief that their society is oppressed, treated unfairly, denied individual rights and basic freedoms, and persecuted by the more powerful ruling authority, whether it is an occupying, imperial, or dominating power (Crenshaw 1981).

Distinct from the other types of terrorism, ethnic terrorism is committed in the name of ethnic identity. Nationalism has become the justifying ideology and collective force to ignite nonstate terrorist violence among nation-based groups against rivals (those with different national identities, often in the majority) in their territories (Sullivan 2015). To achieve their goals (e.g., make the host states capitulate), ethnic nationalist terrorist groups often orchestrate attacks directed at symbols of the state (such as the police, military, and politicians), and also toward civilians and civilian infrastructure, especially if they view the civilians of the majority group as complicit in the discriminatory policies and practices imposed by the host state (Harff & Gurr 2018; Toft 2003). Civilians have also been targeted for the purposes of undermining the state's authority, to force the mediation process and to create a climate of fear among the rival hostile population in the hopes of driving them out of their ethnic geographical territories. For example, during the 1940s, members of the Jewish terrorist group Irgun Zvai Leumi (National Military Organization) deliberately killed hundreds of Arab noncombatant peasants in parts of Palestine to force them to evacuate the areas desired by the Jewish settlers (O'Ballance 1979). Labeled as a terrorist by the British colonial authorities in Palestine, the leader of Irgun, Menachem Begin, would later explain that "the massacre was not only justified, but there would not have been a State of Israel without these massacres" (O'Ballance 1979, 26).

7.2.3 Drivers of Nationalistic Terrorist Campaigns

There may be several disparate motivational causes for the emergence of ethnic nationalist terrorism. Some of the rationales that ethnic groups give for resorting to terroristic violence include:

- Political dissatisfaction or grievances with the ruling elite
- Political discrimination and exclusion by the ruling majority
- Bans on cultural elements (ethnic, linguistic, and religious practices) by the host state
- Failure of the ruling elite to offer inclusive political and economic rights and opportunities for the minority ethnic group
- Unavailability of political channels for the ethnic groups to voice their opinions and concerns
- Identity creation and keeping existing ethnic identities alive
- Retaliation and rebellion against repression of the ruling majority
- Oppressive and repressive policies applied by the host state (restrictions on free speech and public gathering, not providing due process in law enforcement, violating personal security and privacy, widespread arrests and imprisonments, increased monitoring of the ethnic community)

As explained earlier, the main characteristic of ethnic nationalist terrorism is that it involves engaging in acts of violence in the name of a particular ethnic identity (nation) within a geographically concentrated area (Davenport & Inman 2012). However, it is important to clarify two issues here. First, even though fighting on behalf of an ethnic identity is the unique motivational driver for ethnic nationalist terrorism, groups that initially launch campaigns of terrorism with ethno-nationalistic goals may also embrace some other religious or political ideological identities over time. Groups can evolve from one type of terrorism to another. For example, ETA (Basque Fatherland and Liberty) in Spain and the PKK (Kurdistan Workers' Party) in Turkey were initially established as secular nationalist terrorist groups, but over time they both embraced the Marxist-Leninist worldview and adjusted their military trainings and educational programs according to this far-left ideology (Crenshaw 2008; Sullivan 2015). Another example is the Lebanese religious group **Hezbollah**. Although Hezbollah started its activities as a religious group seeking to turn Lebanon into a Shia Islamic state, the group evolved to focus on improving the lives and rights of Shias in Lebanon, rather than solely focusing on its pan-Islamist ideology (Harb 2011).

Second, and more importantly, terrorism scholarship warns readers that the relationship between nationalism and terrorism is often more complex than the simple goal of pursuing an ethnic group's own collective interests and safeguarding an independent homeland or gaining increased autonomy within a specified territory. Terrorism is not simply the product of ardent nationalism. Even though the media and politicians often focus on terrorists' brutality, as British historian Eric John Ernest Hobsbawm describes, contemporary nonstate terrorist groups result as "symptoms, not significant historic agents" (Hobsbawm 2007, 136). We need to look behind the surface (or "search what lies beneath") to understand the complex contexts that gave rise to nationalistic terrorism—the factors that lead aggrieved minority communities to become susceptible to radicalization and engagement in terrorism. In doing so, attention should be given to the nonstate actor as well as the national and state context in which the terrorism occurs (English 2019; 2015). We will return to this point at the end of the chapter.

As mentioned previously, not every nation has a state, and most states contain multiple nations or ethnic identities. It is in these multiethnic societies, ruled under a host state, that ethnic terrorism occurs. As an illustration, the following section presents cases of nationalistic terrorist organizations across the world, including Spain, the United Kingdom, Israel, South Africa, Cyprus, and Turkey. In doing so, we examine the situations that have led to the formation of these ethnic nationalist terrorist organizations, the factors that have led the groups to adopt terrorist tactics and violence, and these groups' strategies and operations. However, the reader should be cautioned that terrorism itself, especially nationalist terrorism, is a contentious moral issue. Many difficult questions arise when examining the contexts in which ethnic nationalist terrorism arises. For example, what constitutes an illegitimate regime? Do state actions (or inactions) affect the rise of ethnic nationalist terrorism? What type of actions are acceptable to defeat an illegitimate ruling power to establish a sovereign homeland? Is it immoral to show solidarity toward oppressed national groups who engage in violent atrocities (i.e., mass murders, ethnic cleansing) in the name of nationalism? Is it okay for an ethnic group to win liberation through violence and terror? Does providing concessions to ethnic nationalist terrorist groups mean rewarding violence? Should we call nationalist groups "terrorists" or "freedom fighters"? (Goertzel 1988; Nathanson 2010; Steinhoff 2007). As explained in Chapter 1, one person's terrorist is another person's freedom fighter. For example, the ETA may be viewed as a terrorist organization by Spain, but they are considered freedom fighters for the Basque nation. The previous questions are important to keep in mind when reading the following case studies. The issue of ethnic nationalist terrorism must be understood within a specific political and social context. There is often a reason behind every attack, bombing, and assassination carried out by these groups (Horgan 2008; 2017).

FIGURE 7.5 Ireland, Northern Ireland, and the United Kingdom are three distinct entities with complex historical and political relationships. Map of the countries of the United Kingdom. *Source:* Dank, Jay, CC BY-SA 4.0, via Wikimedia Commons.

7.3 THE IRA AND THE UNITED KINGDOM

Established in 1917, the **Irish Republican Army (IRA)** is a nationalist republican paramilitary group seeking to end British rule in Northern Ireland and to reunify the Irish territories as a fully independent sovereign state (White 1989). The group has operated for almost a century under several iterations and names, but all for the same cause: an independent Ireland, free from British rule. Even though the IRA has never been listed as a terrorist organization by the United States, it has been acknowledged as one of the most dangerous terrorist organizations in the world by both British and Irish authorities.

With a degree of autonomy, Ireland had been ruled by the United Kingdom since the early twelfth century. However, in the twentieth century, nationalism began to gain widespread support among the Irish, as in the rest of the world. It was during this time that the first IRA (known as the Original IRA) was formed by the civilian Irish militia group. The group staged a failed rebellion against the

British in Dublin, in 1916, which was known as the Easter Uprising. Following this uprising, the majority of its members were imprisoned and sentenced to death. However, the remaining members started a campaign of guerilla warfare against the British (including ambushes, assassinations, bombings, raids, and sabotage) throughout the Irish War of Independence from 1919 to 1921 (Townshend 1979). Eventually, the IRA forced the British government to negotiate the future of Ireland. At the end of the war the parties signed the Anglo-Irish Treaty, which ended the three-year-long fighting between the two groups and divided Ireland into Southern Ireland and Northern Ireland. Northern Ireland, encompassing the predominantly Protestant Irish areas (often regarded as unionist or loyalist), chose to stay as a part of the United Kingdom. Irish Catholics, in contrast, gained the right to establish their Irish Free State across the area known as Southern Ireland (including 26 out of the 32 counties in Ireland), with its capital in Dublin, as a dominion of the British Empire, an autonomous community under British rule (Alonso 2007; Wilkinson 1974).

However, soon after the enactment of this treaty, the IRA split into two factions. The Pro-Treaty faction (called Regulars), featuring the majority of the IRA's membership, supported the peace treaty and a self-governing Ireland under British sovereignty. The Anti-Treaty faction (called Irregulars), on the other hand, featured a minority of IRA members; they opposed the treaty and waged a war to overthrow the new Irish state. Irregulars saw the treaty as a betrayal of Irish independence. A year-long civil war erupted, but this time between the two Irish groups: the pro-treaty Regulars and the anti-treaty Irregulars. Eventually, the Irregulars lost the Irish Civil War but continued their occasional attacks (including bombings, raids, and street battles) on both sides of the Irish border. During World War II, the Irregulars collaborated with Nazi Germany, seeking weapons for their fight, and proposed a joint invasion of Northern Ireland. The IRA assisted Germany with sabotage and espionage activities in Britain with the hope that the Nazis could help them reunite Ireland and drive the British forces out of Northern Ireland (English 2012). The group also signed a pact with Stalin's Soviet Union that required them to provide intelligence about British forces on the island in return for financial benefits.

Until the late 1960s, the IRA did not enjoy widespread support among the predominantly Catholic Republic of Ireland, nor the Protestant Northern Ireland. The group's activities were outlawed by both Irish governments, mainly because of its violence and pro-Soviet and pro-German agitation during World War II. Further, the IRA's shootings, bombings, and sabotage attacks in Northern Ireland between 1942 and 1944 had alienated the Irish society by associating the group with Nazis (Shanahan 2008).

However, the situation dramatically changed for the IRA during the early 1970s when the minority Catholic Irish population in Northern Ireland faced various types of discrimination (e.g., housing, job, employment, voting rights) by the ruling Protestant government and the loyalist society. Upon the partition of Ireland, Catholics in Northern Ireland had been reduced to second-class citizens. Protestants were given priority when it came to housing, jobs, and other economic opportunities due to their fierce loyalty to Britain. The Catholic minority was seriously disadvantaged in local government constituencies due to the political manipulation of electoral district boundaries that had created undue advantage for Protestants. Catholics were denied government jobs, including those in the police force and the army (Bosi 2012).

FIGURE 7.6 A group of children gathered at an Irish Republican Army (IRA) checkpoint on the Lecky Road, Derry. From August 1969 to July 1972 the Bogside and Creggan districts of Derry were no-go areas for the security forces. The areas were openly patrolled by members of both wings of the IRA. Some permanent checkpoints were built by the IRA within a few hundred meters of similar British Army posts. *Source:* Eamon Melaugh (cain.ulster.ac.uk/melaugh).

Due to this widespread discrimination, the Catholics formed the Northern Ireland Civil Rights Association to better protect their rights. Even though the group had mostly engaged in nonviolent street demonstrations to force the Northern Ireland government to end its discrimination against them, they became subjected to a violent crackdown by the Royal Ulster Constabulary (the Irish Protestant police force) and counterprotests by the Protestant loyalist society. The fights between the Catholics and the Protestant police force reached their height during the summer of 1969, which is known as the beginning of a 30 year-long conflict known as the Troubles. Britain deployed the British Army to help Northern Ireland suppress the demonstrations. Scores of Catholic civilians were shot by the police, Catholics' homes and business were burned down by arson attacks from angry Protestant mobs, and thousands of Catholics were forced to relocate from Belfast. The Loyalist paramilitaries' looting of Catholic businesses and homes was completely ignored by the police (Hewitt 1981; White 1989).

The IRA in Northern Ireland was caught unprepared. The group did not have enough weapons and thus failed to protect the Catholics from the brutal attack of the loyalists and the Royal Constables. Over the next few months, though, the IRA started a retaliatory bombing campaign against military, economic, and political targets within Northern Ireland and England. Its cadre increased in numbers as many young Catholic nationalists in Northern Ireland had been radicalized by the violence and decided to join the ranks of the IRA to better protect their people. They quickly organized hundreds of cells within Northern Ireland to defend the Catholic communities besieged by the Protestant police force and civilians and then launched a brutal guerilla campaign (bombing, assassinations, and ambushes) against the British Army. Business and commercial areas in Northern Ireland were also frequently targeted in the IRA's massive bombing campaign to deter further investment into the country and bring economic activity to a halt in Northern Ireland (Hewitt 1981).

However, this widespread use of indiscriminate violence by the IRA led to the emergence of yet another two factions within the group, toward the end of 1969: (1) the Dublin-based Official IRA (the Officials), and (2) the Belfast-based Provisional IRA (the Provos). The Officials were comprised of the majority of the IRA members who championed political negotiations and parliamentary participation (instead of terrorist violence) to achieve the goal of a united Irish Republic. The Officials embraced a Marxist-Leninist political revolutionary ideology, as the leadership of this faction believed that the problems in Northern Ireland were not only driven by religious and nationalistic divisions, but also by the exploitation and manipulation of working-class individuals. They also refused to supply the Catholics in Northern Ireland with weapons, arguing that armed struggle would alienate the working-class Protestant Irish from the unified Ireland ideal (Rekawek 2011; Shanahan 2008). The Provos included the minority IRA members who opposed a nonvio-

FIGURE 7.7 A mural in Derry depicting the Bloody Sunday, on which British soldiers opened fire on a civil rights demonstration in the city of Derry (also known as Londonderry), resulting in the deaths of 14 unarmed civilians and the injury of many others. This incident had significant political and social consequences and is one of the most contentious and tragic events in the history of the Troubles. *Source:* Keith Ruffles, CC BY 3.0, via Wikimedia Commons.

lent political peace process in Northern Ireland and believed in the use of guerilla warfare and terrorism to end what they viewed as the British occupation of the region (Bosi 2012; Horgan & Taylor 1997).

The Provisional IRA (Provos) engaged in a three-phase systematic terrorist campaign. This included:

1. Defending the Catholic minority from discrimination against the Protestant loyalist mobs and the Protestant majority police force in Northern Ireland
2. Indiscriminate retaliation against the Protestant communities and the Royal Constabulary in attempts to collapse the Northern Ireland government
3. Infliction of heavy casualties on British military targets in Northern Ireland and England through a continuous guerilla campaign to force the British to withdraw from Ireland.

With the disappearance of the Official IRA, the group soon became known as, simply, the IRA and enjoyed extensive funding from Irish Americans, which enabled them to obtain weapons and armory from international arms dealers. It is also believed that the IRA engaged in organized criminal activities, such as extortion, bank robbery, smuggling, and counterfeiting to generate revenue (Jackson 2005; Rekawek 2011).

The IRA's cadres continued to increase in numbers as the British Army and Royal Constabulary engaged in their own violent atrocities, including the introduction of a new law by the British government enabling the security forces to conduct arbitrary internment of Catholics suspected of having ties with the IRA and withholding trial. This governmental policy led to violence and political unrest among the Catholics. Sympathy and support for the IRA surged when 13 unarmed civilians were shot dead and more than 15 others seriously injured by British paratroopers during a peaceful anti-internment civil rights march in 1972. This incident would be noted in history as Bloody Sunday (or the Bogside Massacre) (Wilkinson 1997). The killings led to widespread anger among the crowd and the British Embassy in Dublin was burned to the ground by the demonstrators. As a result of Bloody Sunday, the British government suspended the Northern Ireland Parliament and began to impose direct rule in the region beginning in 1972 (Walsh 2000).

Even though there is not a consensus on the total number of IRA conflict-related deaths, it is estimated that from the late 1960s onward the Provisional IRA killed approximately 1,800 people (3,000, according to MI5), including 650 civilians, largely through bombing campaigns that targeted soldiers, civilians, politicians, army barracks, shopping centers, and royal parks (Lavery 2002). The Official IRA harshly criticized the Provisional IRA's violence because it was impeding their goal of uniting Southern Ireland with Northern Ireland by creating a sectarian conflict. Additionally, the Irish were garnering a negative perception worldwide. Numerous secret peace talks between the Provos and the British government failed, and the Provisional IRA carried out several high-profile attacks in England. The Birmingham pub bombings, which killed 21 civilians and injured a further 182, were attributed to the IRA, although the organization did not claim credit. There were the Hyde Park and Regent's Park bombings in 1982, which killed 11 soldiers and injured more than 50 civilians, as well as the assassination of Lord Mountbatten (the uncle of Prince Philip, the Queen's husband) and the assassination attempt on British Prime Minister Margaret Thatcher at Brighton's Grand Hotel. Naturally, the collateral damage inflicted on the civilians—such as in pubs, shopping centers, and subway stations—by the IRA was unwelcomed by the Irish Catholics. For example, after the Warrington area shopping center bombing in 1993 (in which two children lost their lives and many others were injured), thousands of Irish gathered in downtown Dublin to express disgust and shame over the IRA-inflicted civilian deaths. IRA bombings were condemned as "utterly inhuman and barbaric" (Moseley 1993). Despite all of this bloodshed and economic damage—the Baltic Exchange bombing in 1992, for example, is estimated to have caused 800 million pounds worth of damage and the Bishopsgate bombing in 1993 is estimated to have caused one billion pounds in damage—Britain still did not capitulate (Kowalski 2018; Rogers 2000).

Over the next two decades the political faction of the IRA, known as Sinn Fein (meaning "ourselves alone") began to play a more prominent role than the armed faction, the Provisional IRA, by starting a political settlement with Britain. Sinn Fein engaged in multiple ceasefires with loyalist paramilitary groups and officials of Northern Ireland. The first meeting to negotiate peace talks between Sinn Fein (since 1922) and the British government officials occurred in 1997, at which Sinn Fein agreed to decommission the Provisional IRA from all arms and agreed to uphold principles of nonviolence. In April 1998, after months of negotiations, the British and Irish governments signed the Good Friday Agreement (also known as the Belfast Agreement), which increased the rights of Catholics in Northern Ireland, by promising the establishment of a power-sharing government, a Protestant-Catholic coalition government (Richards 2001). Most importantly, the paramilitary groups on both sides agreed to disarm themselves and the IRA agreed that Northern Ireland would remain a part of the United Kingdom as long as the majority of the population wishes so. Further, the Protestant majority Royal Ulster Constabulary was disbanded and a majority of the British troops left the country upon the signing of the accord (Taylor 2014).

FIGURE 7.8   On January 5, 1969, the slogan "You are now entering Free Derry" was painted on a gable wall, marking the area's declaration of independence from British control. The Free Derry Corner, where the original slogan was painted, remains a significant landmark and symbol of the nationalist community's struggle during the Troubles. This historical site stands as a reminder of the conflict and the ongoing quest for civil rights and political change in Northern Ireland.

The complete disarmament and peace did not come quickly. The accord was seriously jeopardized as significant setbacks occurred due to the dissident republican nationalists' disagreement with the conditions of the Good Friday Agreement. For example, a splinter group called the Real IRA carried out the deadliest terrorist attack in Irish history, the Omagh car bombing, where approximately 30 people were killed and hundreds were injured, just three months after the peace agreement (Dingley 2001). However, in 2005, the IRA formally announced an end to its almost four decades-long military campaign and that going forward, it would work to achieve its aims solely through peaceful political and democratic means. Two months later, an international independent arm-decommissioning body verified that the IRA had decommissioned all of its arsenal. Today, small-scale IRA splinter groups, such as the Real IRA and Continuity IRA, continue practicing terrorism at a very low rate. Theirs is the same

FIGURE 7.9 The front cover of the Belfast agreement. The agreement ended the violent period known as Troubles and made substantive changes to Northern Ireland's peace, constitutional settlements and institutions. *Source:* Courtesy of Whytes.com.

century-old objective: a united Ireland, free from British influence (Ó Dochartaigh 2015; Tonge et al. 2011).

7.4 BASQUE FATHERLAND AND LIBERTY (ETA)

Euskadi Ta Askatasuna **(Basque Fatherland and Liberty)**, commonly known as ETA, was a nationalist and separatist organization that operated in a region known as Basque from 1959 to mid-2018, with the goal of creating an independent Basque state. Basques are a culturally and linguistically distinct Christian group that has lived in a region that falls under the jurisdiction of modern-day Spain and France (Sanchez-Cuenca 2007). The majority of the Basques (approximately two to three million, according to a 2001 census) live in Basque parts of Spain, whereas only a small fraction (approximately 150,000) live in the French side of the Basque region (Eustat 2021). Historically, the Basques have never had an independent state but enjoyed varying degrees of autonomy under different Spanish and French rulers over time (Sullivan 2015).

The group has been classified as a terrorist organization by Spain, France, the United Kingdom, Canada, the United States, and several other countries in Europe, and has engaged in some of history's bloodiest attacks, including bombings, sabotage, assassinations, and the kidnapping of prominent people, the ultimate goal being to establish a sovereign Basque state in northern Spain and southwestern France (Woodworth 2004). It should be noted, though, that many of the attacks (especially the bombings) carried out by ETA were preceded by a warning phone call to authorities, to allow civilians to evacuate the area before the explosions occurred. The group also targeted major tourist areas and shopping centers to sabotage Spain's revenue. One report estimates that ETA's attack on the tourism industry cost Spain more than 11 billion dollars between 1994 and 2003 (Council on Foreign Relations 2008). Many of ETA's victims were Spanish government officials, police and military officers, politicians, newspaper publishers, and judicial figures. The Spanish government estimates that through its almost six decades of existence, ETA carried out over 1,600 terrorist attacks and killed more than 800 people

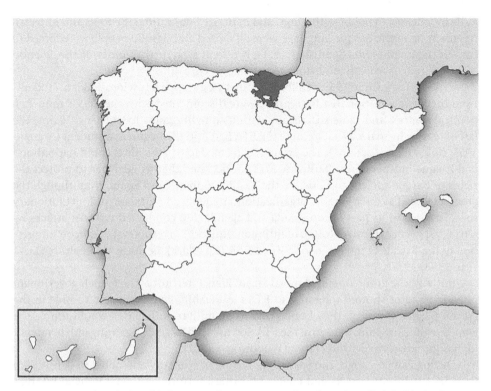

FIGURE 7.10 The relationship between the Basque people, who primarily inhabit the Basque Country (Euskal Herria), a region that spans parts of northern Spain and southwestern France, and the respective governments of Spain and France has been a complex and historically significant one. *Source:* Mutxamel, CC BY-SA 1.0, via Wikimedia Commons.

(approximately 400 of the victims were civilians) and left thousands more injured (Cosido 2002; Euronews 2021).

The origin of ETA goes back to the Basque Nationalist Party (PNV), a Christian conservative political party that operated in exile in Paris throughout the rule of fascist Spanish dictator, Francisco Franco. Eluding the fates of other dictators in Europe, Franco rose to power in 1939, after crushing the democratically elected socialist government in Spain during the Spanish Civil War. Unlike the previous Spanish government, which offered a large degree of autonomy to the Basque Country, which is linguistically and ethnically different from the majority of Spain, Franco actively attacked the Basques, overturning the privileges (e.g., self-determination) provided by former administrations (Sullivan 2015). He ordered the bombing of Basque areas during the Spanish Civil War to suppress Basque nationalist sentiments, an attack that destroyed the town of Guernica. This air raid would later be considered the first large-scale civilian bombing in human history.

Under Franco's repressive military dictatorship, the government's top priority was to achieve national unity in Spain. The ethnic minorities within Spain (the Basques and Catalans), and most prominently the Basque culture, tradition, and language, were all banned, and Basque intellectuals were imprisoned and tortured for their political views. The existing Basque literature was burned, and the language was prohibited from use on radio broadcasts, in public gatherings, and in future publications. Schools and universities teaching in the Basque language were all closed and Basque people were forced to convert their names into Spanish ones. Franco went even further, ordering the deletion of Basque language from tombstones (Sanchez-Cuenca 2007).

ETA was founded in 1959 in Bilbao, Spain, by a group of left-wing dissident students from the Basque Nationalist Party; they were discontented with the PNV's moderate political stances, and more specifically with its unwillingness to use arms against the fascist regime in Spain. What became the ETA had initially begun as a student forum in 1953, called Ekin ("Action"). The group was formed to discuss ideas about nationhood and Basque independence (Sullivan 2015). It declared that its goal was to protect the rights of Basque society and liberate the Basque country from Spain. Even though the group emerged as a nationalist organization, it embraced Marxism and revolutionary socialist ideas in its party propaganda and agenda and conducted terrorist attacks by setting off small explosives (often of little consequence) in response to Franco's suppression of the Basque language, national symbols (e.g., flags), heritage, and culture (Llera et al. 1993).

Initially, the group operated mostly from French territory. The French government often ignored or showed tolerance to ETA's leadership, enabling them to hide in the French Basque Country; they hoped that ETA's military offensives would topple the Franco regime in Spain. In return, the ETA downplayed its goal of gaining independence for Basque territories within France (Woodworth 2001).

During Franco's reign, the Spanish government violently attempted to defeat ETA; they made arbitrary arrests and enacted beatings, torture, and extra judicial killings. Almost all prominent figures of ETA were arrested by the early 1970s and condemned to death in military trials, known as Burgos trials, though some ETA members had their sentences downgraded to life in prison due to domestic and international pressures (Sullivan 2015).

The most notorious terrorist act carried out by ETA was the 1973 assassination of Admiral Luis Carrero Blanco, the prime minister of Spain, which occurred with the detonation of a massive bomb buried underground on a Madrid side street near a church. Blanco was Franco's chosen successor as the next president of Spain, someone who would continue the realization of his fascist vision (Agirre 1975). Many Spanish liberals praised the killing of Franco's successor, even though the attack was carried out by Basque separatists, arguing that in a way, the killing of Blanco facilitated Spain's smooth transition into democracy. Upon Franco's death of a heart attack in 1975, King Juan Carlos, in the absence of an obvious successor for Franco, had returned control of Spain to a democratically elected parliament (Mujal-Leon 2019).

Factionalism divided ETA several times throughout its six decades of history. First, during late 1960s, ETA was divided into two factions. ETA-V was comprised of separatist nationalists who pursued the goal of national autonomy and independence by removing the Spanish authorities from the Basque region. ETA-VI, in contrast, favored a Marxist-Leninist ideology and focused on the complete overthrow of the Spanish national government and the establishment of a communist regime throughout Spain. ETA-VI was more of an internationally oriented communist group than a separatist one (Llera et al. 1993; Sullivan 2015).

ETA-VI, unable to attract the population to its cause, dissolved within a short period of time. ETA-V, on the other hand, following the death of Franco in 1975, further divided into two factions. The ETA-Military group favored the use of violence and terrorism to protect the rights of the Basque people and achieve independence. The ETA-Political Military (ETA PM) advocated peaceful political negotiations alongside armed struggle. During the 1980s, the majority of the ETA-Political Military members abandoned violence and accepted the partial amnesty Spain's new democratic government had offered to incarcerated ETA members; they continued their activities under a new political party, Euskadi Ezkerra (Left of the Basque Country). ETA PM members who rejected the amnesty continued their activities by joining the ranks of ETA-Military. The ETA we know today originated from the ETA-Military (Hamilton 1999) and reclaimed the original group name, Euskadi Ta Askatasuna (Sanchez-Cuenca 2007).

Despite Spain's gradual transition to democracy in the late 1970s, ETA continued to terrorize Spain by refusing to recognize its constitutional democracy, even though the 1978 constitution had enshrined the recognition of the country's ethnic minorities. The group carried out its most violent attacks during this period, killing more than 200 individuals, mostly civilians, despite the central government in Madrid granting significant autonomy to the Basque region—including their own parliament, education, and health systems. On a massive scale, the group engaged in vandalism, arson, kidnappings, and shootings, robbed local banks and post offices, planted roadside bombs, and even extorted local Basque entrepreneurs, who were coerced into making financial contributions under the pretext of "revolutionary taxes" (Duerr 2017).

In 1983, the Spanish Interior Ministry established an illegal, clandestine group called the GAL (Antiterrorist Liberation Groups) that was tasked with killing members of ETA and civilians believed to have connections to ETA members. GAL often operated in the French Basque area and kidnapped, tortured, and murdered more than 26 Basque people between 1983 and 1987 (Woodworth 2001). It is believed that many of these killings targeted the Basque people in general and had nothing to do with actual ETA members.

During this time public attitudes toward ETA changed significantly not only among the Spanish people but also among the Basque population, as ETA continued its brutal attacks despite the

FIGURE 7.11 The 2006 Barajas bombing at Madrid's Barajas International Airport. A van loaded with explosives was detonated by the Basque separatist group ETA (Euskadi Ta Askatasuna) in the airport's parking lot. The Barajas bombing led to widespread condemnation both within Spain and internationally, and it intensified the calls for a resolution to the Basque conflict. Subsequently it contributed to increased pressure on ETA, which eventually declared a permanent ceasefire in 2011 and dissolved in 2018, bringing an end to its violent activities. *Source:* Enrique Dans, CC BY 2.0, via Wikimedia Commons.

democratic regime having made significant political concessions. In 1997, more than 500,000 Spanish and Basque people carried out the largest anti-ETA protest in Spanish history in response to the kidnapping and subsequent assassination of twenty-nine-year-old Miguel Angel Blanco, a politician from the ruling Popular Party in the Basque region. Blanco's murder marked a turning point for public opinion. Basque people, who once supported or refrained from voicing their opposition to ETA, now united with the rest of Spain to condemn the bloodshed and damage caused by ETA and reject the group's principles (Gil-Alana & Barros 2010). The slogan "Yes to Basques, no to ETA" was born during these protests. In the days following Blanco's murder more than six million people across Spain, including ETA's own supporters, orchestrated street demonstrations to demand an end to ETA violence (BBC 2017; Murua 2017). As well as pressure from the Basque people, the ETA's political wing encouraged a change in strategy, away from violence and toward peaceful means.

ETA attempted several unsuccessful peace negotiations with the Spanish authorities between 1989 and 2006. For example, the group declared a permanent ceasefire with the new socialist government in Spain in March of 2006. They pledged to cease all armed activities and follow a national process modeled after the Good Friday Agreement (the Belfast Agreement), which brought peace to Northern Ireland (Cox et al. 2006).

However, after less than eight months, in December 2006, some factions from ETA detonated a massive car bomb in a parking lot of the Madrid Barajas International Airport, which killed two civilians and ended the peace negotiations. Approximately four years later, in 2010, the group declared another ceasefire, but this time with a serious intent to cease all of its armed activities and bring a definitive end to its operations and the disbandment of the group. In 2011, with the presence of international negotiators including the former United Nations Secretary General Kofi Annan, the former prime minister of Norway, and the leader of Sinn Fein, Gerry Adams, the ETA announced its dissolution and ended an almost 60-year armed campaign for independence (Whitfield 2014). As a result of constructive negotiations with the Spanish and French authorities, the group surrendered its weapons and explosives in 2017. A year later, in 2018, ETA announced via video conference that it was formally dismantling its entire organizational structure, reading the following text:

> With this declaration, Euskadi ta Askatasuna, the Basque socialist revolutionary organization for national liberation, wishes to give news of its decision:
>
> ETA considers that the international conference that has recently taken place in the Basque country is an initiative of enormous significance. The agreed resolution includes all the elements for an integral solution of the conflict, and it has attained the support of a wide spectrum of the Basque society and the international community.
>
> A new political time is emerging in the Basque country. We have an historical opportunity to find a just and democratic solution for the centuries-old political conflict. Dialogue and agreement should outline the new cycle, over violence and repression. The recognition of the Basque country and the respect for the will of the people should prevail over imposition.
>
> This has not been an easy road. The cruelty of the fight has taken away the lives of many comrades. Many others are still suffering in prison and in exile. Our recognition and deepest tribute goes out to them.

From here on the road will not be easy either. Facing the imposition that still exists, every step, every achievement, will be the result of the effort and fight of Basque citizens. During these years the Basque country has accumulated the necessary experience and strength to address this path and it also has the determination for doing it. It is time to look at the future with hope. It is also time to act with responsibility and courage.

Therefore, ETA has decided the definitive cessation of its armed activity. ETA calls upon the Spanish and French governments to open a process of direct dialogue with the aim of addressing the resolution of the consequences of the conflict and to overcome the armed confrontation. Thorough this historical declaration, ETA shows its clear, solid and definitive commitment.

Lastly, ETA calls upon the Basque society to commit to this process until freedom and peace are achieved.

Long live the free Euskal Herria! Long live Basque socialism! No rest until independence and socialism!

Basque country, October 20, 2011

Euskadi ta Askatasuna

Today, the Basque people enjoy a high degree of autonomous government. Though not fully independent, they speak their own language, have their own police and schools (with teaching conducted in Basque) and courts, and have the right to collect taxes within their territories. Basques are more integrated in Spain than ever before (Shepard 2002).

As we have seen in this case study, terrorists do not operate in vacuum. They are not simply seeking violence. If the previous rulers in Spain had not suppressed the cultural, economic, social, and linguistic rights of the Basque people, if they had continued to offer them the autonomy that was granted for centuries before Franco, then Spain might have remained free of ethnic-nationalist terrorism (Peleg & Kempf 2006).

7.5 THE KURDISTAN WORKERS' PARTY (PKK)

The Kurdistan Workers' Party, commonly known as the PKK (the abbreviation for the Kurdish Partiya Karkeren Kurdistan), is a Kurdish militant organization established in 1974 in Turkey and considered to be one of the deadliest and longest-lasting terrorist organizations in the Middle East, having caused more than 40,000 casualties. As of 2024, Kurds are one of the world's largest ethnic communities that does not have a dedicated state (Ahmed & Gunter 2005; McKiernan 2006). Emerging in the mid-1970s in the shadow of groups such as the Palestine Liberation Organization, the PKK embraced a Marxist-Leninist ideology and trained its recruits in the teachings of the Mao Tse-tung and other revolutionary groups in Russia, China, and Vietnam (McDowall 2000). Its most influential leader was Abdullah Öcalan, popularly known as "Apo." Even though the group emerged as a nationalist separatist group with the goal of establishing an independent Kurdish state, it later embraced the goal of greater autonomy within Turkey. The PKK is listed as a terrorist organization by several countries and international organizations, including the European Union, the United States, Canada, and Australia.

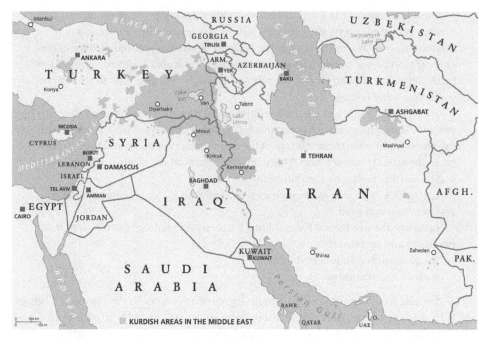

FIGURE 7.12 Kurds are an ethnic group with a distinct language and culture, and they primarily inhabit several regions in the Middle East. *Source:* Peter Hermes Furian/Shutterstock.

The PKK launched its first armed struggle in 1984, killing 18 police officers (White 2000). Since then its primary targets have been the police, military, and village guards. With a few exceptions, the group has continued to follow a policy of limited war—targeting only the members of Turkish security forces as a means of retaliation (Haner 2017).

Scholars widely agree that the PKK emerged in response to repressive measures imposed by the Turkish state aimed at accelerating the cultural assimilation of the Kurds. Such methods included village evacuations, a ban on the Kurdish language, extrajudicial murders, violence, and torture (Haner 2017). It is important to look at the historical incidents that led to the rise of this group.

Even though the origins of the Kurds are unknown, it is widely accepted that they are descended from the nomadic tribes of Medes, an Indo-European tribe. Historically, the Kurds lived in areas located between the Persian Gulf and the Caspian Sea, surrounded by four countries in present-day Middle East: Turkey, Iraq, Iran, and Syria (Romano 2006; White 2000). Historically, Kurds are known for their submission to central governments, whether it be Persia, the Ottoman Empire, or the Russian Empire—in other words, they have voluntarily assimilated into dominant cultures rather than pursuing their own interests (Romano 2006; van Bruinessen 1978).

However, beginning in the early twentieth century, a Kurdish nationalist identity arose, mostly in response to the assimilation policies of the new Turkish state. Unlike the ruling Ottoman Empire (which was based on civic nationalism), the new state was established on the idea of Turkishness and excluded the Kurdish minority from the public sphere. It was made very clear by the President of Turkey that "only the Turkish nation is entitled to claim ethnic and national rights in this country. No other element has any such right" (Romano 2006, 118). Various Turkish governments pursued forced assimilation by prohibiting Kurds to use the Kurdish language, banning Kurdish publications, replacing Kurdish place names (and other references to the Kurdish language) with Turkish ones, and closing all Kurdish-speaking schools and social and political organizations (Lewis 1968; McDowall 2000; McKiernan 2006). Due to the mandatory use of the Turkish language, thousands of Kurds had to drop out of school. Additionally, the first constitution of the republic, in 1924, had forbidden the use of Kurdish language in public places and a new law (law number 1505) had allowed the state officials to expropriate the Kurdish areas and then redistribute to Turkish-speaking population (White 2000). The implementation of these policies caused widespread resentment among the Kurdish population (Olson 1996). Essentially, Kurds were denied existence within the country (Romano 2006).

In response to these assimilation policies, between the 1920s and the late 1970s the Kurds reorganized around several clandestine groups and revolted against the Turkish Republic (e.g., the Sheikh Said rebellion, Mount Ararat rebellion, and Dersim rebellion), but their revolts were met with brutal repression campaigns. For example, after the Sheikh Said rebellion in 1925, Turkish authorities gave complete autonomy to the military and established a Tribunal of Independence under which judges were given the direct power to apply capital punishment (McDowall 2000, 195). As a result, hundreds of Kurdish villages were destroyed and thousands of innocent women, men, and children were killed (Romano 2006, 35). Further, Ankara passed the settlement law that amounted to a forced evacuation for residents of non–Turkish-speaking areas (McKiernan 2006, 93). The Kurdish population was dispersed to remote areas in an effort to extinguish their language and identity.

The Turkish government was similarly ruthless after the Dersim rebellion in 1937, eliciting collective suicides among the Kurdish population (Dersimi 1992). Forty thousand Kurds died during the military offensives (McDowall 2000, 93; White 2000, 83). As a result of the Kurds' defeat in this rebellion, Kurdish national ambition was silenced in Turkey until the 1970s (White 2000, 83).

During the late 1970s a new national awakening begun among the Kurds in Turkey, but this was due to the mandatory relocation of Kurdish children for educational purposes in majority Turkish places, the economic deprivation of Kurds from the mechanization of agriculture, and their resulting dislocation (to find better job opportunities in bigger Turkish cities). Due to migration (as well as forceful deportations) from the eastern to western parts of the country, the children of peasant Kurds began to acquire increased levels of education and obtain high-status occupations such as engineers, doctors, and journalists. Those young Kurds would later participate in social, political, and cultural lifestyles of the modern cities and gather to discuss the future of Kurdish identity (Romano 2006). University education had also exposed the poor Kurdish youth to the ideas of nationalism, socialism, and the struggle against the racist policies applied by the Turkish state. Soon, these Kurds had embraced leftist (Marxist) ideas and joined various leftist groups, even traveling to Lebanon to get training on leftist ideologies. Returning to Turkey, they organized mass protests in major cities in both the east and west, calling for increased rights for the repressed Kurds and also for the empowerment of democracy (McDowall 2000).

To erase this new emerging Kurdish national aspiration, Turkish bureaucrats once again engaged in a denial policy by arguing that there was no nation of Kurds, and the

FIGURE 7.13   PKK has a long history of including women in its ranks and promoting female participation within its cadres. This sets the PKK apart from many other armed groups in the Middle East and reflects the organization's commitment to gender equality and women's rights. *Source:* Kurdishstruggle, CC BY 2.0, via Wikimedia Commons.

Turks and the Kurds were brothers and compatriots (McDowall 2000). Further, the use of Kurdish language was again prohibited (law 2932), Kurds were warned that even Kurdish folk songs had to be sung only in Turkish to prevent separatist and national agendas, and Kurdish families were prohibited from giving their children Kurdish names (law 1587) (Haner 2017).

The PKK was established in 1974 as a Marxist-Leninist organization, the aim being to start a violent revolution against the Turks (O'Ballance 1996) in response to their racist, anti-Kurdish policies (Romano 2006, 125). Until the mid-1970s, the Kurds' approach was to seek wider participation in Turkish political, economic, and social life through democratic means. However, the closed nature of the Turkish political system prevented the Kurds from achieving their goals via peaceful means. With the establishment of the PKK, Kurds engaged in an armed struggle to protect their identity and achieve the goal of liberation (Bal and Laciner 2004). The PKK promised the Kurds a new Kurdish state in which they did not have to learn the Turkish culture and language, in which they could freely develop their own identity, culture, and language (Romano 2006).

The group soon became a viable threat to the state, as the PKK began assassinating the Kurdish leaders appointed by the Turkish government. Further, the PKK established its own state institutions in Kurdish majority areas, parallel to the institutions established by the Turkish state. Kurds, often not fluent in Turkish and unfamiliar with the mechanisms of Turkish courts, police, and other state institutions, preferred to visit the parallel institutions that served them in their own language (Romano 2006). Seeing this, many of the poor Kurdish youth joined the PKK (McDowall 2000). After starting with almost with no economic or social resources, the PKK developed into a mass organization with large support—an important challenge to the establishment of the Turkish state. The PKK's ranks further swelled because of the Turkish state's brutal attempts to eradicate them, in which they targeted people who simply sympathized with the PKK and subjected them to torture. Many of these repressed and tortured individuals went on to join the PKK (Romano 2006). Finally, some Kurdish women willingly joined the PKK to escape from the strict patriarchal control common in Middle Eastern societies. Kurdish women saw the PKK as an opportunity to escape their community; it is not surprising that almost one-third of the PKK's ranks is female (Romano 2006, 78).

In the 1990s, Turkish officials started to implement fundamental changes aimed at ending conflict with the Kurdish population. For example, President Özal enacted two laws allowing the use of the Kurdish language among the Kurdish people and the publication of Kurdish newspapers. He also freed many political prisoners by approving a limited amnesty (White 2000, 162). By the mid-2000s, the Turkish Republic officially recognized the existence of a Kurdish problem for the first time in its history after many years of repression, denial of identity, unaccounted murders, kidnapping, village evacuations, and forced migration (Akyol 2015; Dalay 2015; Ensaroglu 2013). The acting government of the time declared that they would facilitate reconciliation by implementing democratic measures, including the granting of equal citizenship status to the Kurds (Ensaroglu 2013). As of 2024, Kurds are able to gather freely and protest for their democratic rights without the intrusion of the Turkish law enforcement. As Middle Eastern scholar De Bellaigue stated: "After the speeches there will be a concert, with songs sung in Kurdish. And after that, everyone will go home. No arrests; no torture; no killings. Eastern Anatolia has changed for the better" (de Bellaigue 2010, 252).

In response to these democratic openings provided by the Turkish government, the incarcerated leader of the PKK, Apo, issued a historic letter in 2013 (Akyol 2015; Ensaroglu 2013):

> We have now reached a point where guns must go silent and ideas and politics must speak. We will unite in the face of those who try to split us. From now on, a new period begins when politics, not guns, will come to the fore. It is now time for armed elements to withdraw outside the country. (Öcalan 2013)

Despite these improvements, there has yet to be a permanent peace agreement between the PKK and Turkey (as there was between Spain and ETA, or the United Kingdom and the IRA). This is mostly because of the Turkish public's strong opposition to peace and Kurdish assimilation. Many Turks, especially those who lost loved ones during the conflict, do not welcome the government's conciliatory approach. Turkish nationalists view the peace process as a betrayal of the martyred security officials and murdered innocent individuals who lost their lives during this 40-year-long fight (Ensaroglu 2013; Marcus 2015). On several occasions, thousands of Turks have taken to the streets of major cities to demonstrate against the democratic opening for the Kurds (Ensaroglu 2013). Unfortunately, Turkish society still lacks a full understanding of the origin of the conflict between the Turks and Kurds. Being subjected to state propaganda for more than 30 years, the people in Turkey view the PKK as a violent terrorist organization (Romano 2006).

Even though the PKK is considered a terrorist organization, most intellectuals accept that its existence and activities mean that it is impossible for the Turkish government to ignore the Kurdish problem in Turkey (Romano 2006, 121). The PKK succeeded in bringing the Kurdish plight to the public agenda after the destruction of the Kurds in the 1930 uprising in Dersim. Using armed struggle, the PKK forcefully brought the Kurds' concerns to the center of public attention. In this way, the PKK was able to negate the long-established Kurdish psychology of impotence (i.e., feelings of hopelessness) (Romano 2006, 160).

7.6 IRGUN ZVAI LEUMI (IRGUN), THE NATIONAL MILITARY ORGANIZATION

Irgun Zvai Leumi (Irgun) was a Jewish right-wing nationalist paramilitary organization that operated in Palestine when it was under British mandate between 1931 and 1948. Members of Irgun separated from an older well-known Jewish paramilitary organization

ארגון צבאי לאומי

IRGUN ZWAÏ LÉUMI BE-EREZ JISRAËL
ORGANISATION MILITAIRE NATIONALE JUIVE D'EREZ JISRAËL
JEWISH NATIONAL MILITARY ORGANISATION OF EREZ JISRAËL
An Irgun poster for distribution in Central Europe.

FIGURE 7.14 1931 Irgun propaganda poster distributed in Europe to prompt mass Jewish immigration to Palestine. *Source:* Irgun, Public domain, via Wikimedia Commons.

known as Haganah (Defense), which operated under the Jewish Agency (Fromkin 1975). Irgun is known to model itself after the nationalist Irish Republican Army. Group members firmly believed that the permanent solution to Jewish nationalist interests could be solved only through the creation of a Jewish sovereign state within the historical boundaries of Palestine, and the use of brutal violence, including terrorism, was justified to achieve this goal (Lavi 2005). Irgun engaged in a bloody terrorist campaign against the British, Arabs, and even some Jews who denounced the group's activities (Morris 2009).

In 1940, some Irgun members left the group and established a new faction, Lehi—an even more extremist faction that engaged in bank robberies, assassinations, and murder against the British security forces and the Arab civilians. Irgun has been described as a terrorist organization by the Jewish Agency, Britain, the United States, the United Nations, and some other countries and international organizations (Heller 2012). In an open letter published by the *New York Times* in 1948, Albert Einstein, along with several other prominent Jews, condemned Irgun (and its predecessor Herut) as a "terrorist, right-wing, chauvinist organization in Palestine"—the Jewish version of "Nazi and Fascist Parties" (Massad 2006):

> To the Editors of the *New York Times*:
>
> Among the most disturbing political phenomena of our times is the emergence in the newly created state of Israel of the "Freedom Party," a political party closely akin in its organization, methods, political philosophy and social appeal to the Nazi and Fascist parties. It was formed out of the membership and following of the former Irgun Zvai Leumi, a terrorist, right-wing, chauvinist organization in Palestine.
>
> Before irreparable damage is done by way of financial contributions, public manifestations in Begin's behalf, and the creation in Palestine of the impression that a

large segment of America supports Fascist elements in Israel, the American public must be informed as to the record and objectives of Begin and his movement.

Attack on Arab Village

A shocking example was their behavior in the Arab village of Deir Yassin. This village, off the main roads and surrounded by Jewish lands, had taken no part in the war, and had even fought off Arab bands who wanted to use the village as their base. On April 9, terrorist bands attacked this peaceful village, which was not a military objective in the fighting, killed most of its inhabitants 240 men, women, and children and kept a few of them alive to parade as captives through the streets of Jerusalem. Most of the Jewish community was horrified at the deed, and the Jewish Agency sent a telegram of apology to King Abdullah of Trans-Jordan. But the terrorists, far from being ashamed of their act, were proud of this massacre, publicized it widely, and invited all the foreign correspondents present in the country to view the heaped corpses and the general havoc at Deir Yassin.

The Deir Yassin incident exemplifies the character and actions of the Freedom Party.

Within the Jewish community they have preached an admixture of ultra-nationalism, religious mysticism, and racial superiority.

During the last years of sporadic anti-British violence, the IZL and Stern groups inaugurated a reign of terror in the Palestine Jewish community. Teachers were beaten up for speaking against them, adults were shot for not letting their children join them. By gangster methods, beatings, window-smashing, and widespread robberies, the terrorists intimidated the population and exacted a heavy tribute.

The people of the Freedom Party have had no part in the constructive achievements in Palestine. They have reclaimed no land, built no settlements, and only detracted from the Jewish defense activity. Their much-publicized immigration endeavors were minute, and devoted mainly to bringing in Fascist compatriots.

New York, December 2, 1948

Irgun is one of the rare examples of a paramilitary group that transitioned from being a terrorist group to a political party. The group did not initially enjoy widespread support from the Jewish community in Palestine and was strongly opposed by the largest Jewish paramilitary group of its time, the Haganah (which would form the official Israeli army in 1948). During its height, Irgun was estimated to have about 4,000 active members. Even though it was established in 1931, Irgun's terrorist violence started in 1937 when it began to violently challenge the British authority in Palestine and inflamed animosity between the Arabs and Jews (Atkins 2004).

7.6.1 How Did Irgun Emerge?

After the end of the First World War, Palestine, which had been a part of the Ottoman Empire for centuries, was invaded by the British forces. Arabs, which comprised the majority of the population in Palestine, had helped the British to defeat the Turkish Otto-

FIGURE 7.15 In 1947, Jewish refugees arrived in Palestine with a banner proclaiming: "The Germans destroyed our families and homes—don't you destroy our hopes." Jewish immigration from Germany did increase significantly in the years leading up to World War II as a response to growing persecution and anti-Semitic policies enacted by the Nazi regime. While 1935 marked a crucial year with the passage of the Nuremberg Laws, which stripped Jews of their German citizenship and instituted a range of discriminatory measures, the mass exodus of Jews from Germany began earlier and continued throughout the 1930s. *Source:* Public domain, via Wikimedia Commons.

man forces during World War I in return for establishing their independent Arab state in the region. However, the British rejected this pledge of independence after their victory in the war against the Turks.

Jews in the region had also started to have issues with the British and the establishment of the British Mandate in Palestine. Beginning 1931, Irgun and other Jewish organizations came into serious conflict with the British over various issues. The British limited the number of Jewish immigrants from Europe into Palestine, prevented the acquisition of arms by Jews in Palestine, and were ineffective at protecting Jewish settlers from Arab nationalists. Most importantly, British and Jewish citizens disagreed on the political future of the Palestine (Clancy-Smith et al. 2001).

Britain's unsympathetic approach toward Zionism, or Jewish nationalism—such as not allowing mass Jewish immigration into Palestine to establish their own state, along with their failure to keep their promises to the Arabs—quickly exacerbated the relationship among Britain and the Arab and Jewish communities.

Arabs, discontent with the political situation, started to attack growing Jewish settlements in their territories, fearing that Jews would outnumber them in the near future. Jews, in return, blamed the British forces for failing to protect their isolated settlements and argued for the need to establish their own self-defense security forces. Even though this request was rejected by the British officials on the grounds that such a military force would further incite the already aggrieved Arabs (by Jewish Zionist activities), Jews formed the Haganah, an underground paramilitary force to be used solely for the self-defense of Jews in Palestine (Harms & Ferry 2005).

Arabs were not only disgruntled by the unkept promises of having their independent state, but they now began to fear that they would be a minority in their homeland, as the British had started to allow mass Jewish immigration into Palestine per Article 2 of the League of Nations (United Nations) Covenant: "Britain should place the country under such political, administrative, and economic conditions as will secure the establishment of the Jewish national home." Anti-Jewish riots and street demonstrations erupted in several cities as Jewish immigration increased in scale in the mid-1930s, especially after Adolf Hitler was appointed as the Chancellor of Germany. Approximately 30,000 Jews entered Palestine in 1933 alone, fleeing persecution in Germany (Clancy-Smith et al. 2001). The significant increase in the number of Jews immigrating into Palestine increased the intensity of unrest among the Arabs. To end the European Jewish immigration into Palestine, Arabs started the Great Arab Revolt in 1936, leading a guerrilla war by attacking government targets in city centers (e.g., telephone and rail lines, oil pipelines, police and military personnel and posts), ambushing main roads, and attacking the Jewish settlements in the countryside, destroying their livestock and agricultural fields (Amar-Dahl 2016; Hughes 2015).

Thanks to Haganah's placement of its fighters in defensive positions across the country, the Jewish casualties were not very high. However, this large-scale Arab violence in response to Jewish settlement across Palestine led to major criticisms among national-

FIGURE 7.16   A female officer of the Haganah gives a demonstration in the handling of a Sten gun during the War of Independence. Haganah was the main paramilitary organization of the Jewish community in Palestine. Women played significant roles in Haganah, from armed struggle to safeguarding property, securing of local communities, and escorting convoys. *Source:* Haganah Museum, Public domain, via Wikimedia Commons.

ist members of the Haganah-Bet (a splinter ultra-nationalist military) against Haganah's policy of using violence only for "self-defense." According to this policy, Haganah forces were not allowed to engage in any kind of retaliatory act against the Palestinians; they could only engage in self-defense of Jewish communities in Palestine, regardless of the scale of violence they faced (Pappe 2022). Opposing this policy, approximately 2,000 Haganah-Bet members gathered and established a new Jewish paramilitary organization in 1937, the Irgun Zvai Leumi. The group, different from other Jewish underground organizations, encouraged the use of indiscriminate violence and terror to gain the respect of the British and Arabs in the region (Bauer 1966; Charters 2007).

Beginning 1937, after Britain's failed attempt to divide Palestine into two separate states comprised of Arabs and Jews, Irgun initiated its first attacks against the Arabs, killing dozens and injuring more. "Black Sunday," for instance, saw Irgun execute four simultaneous terrorist attacks, killing several civilians across Jerusalem. In the following years, Irgun started systematic bombing attacks in crowded public places where Arabs lived, such as the 1938 grocery store bombing in Haifa, which killed more than 50 Arab civilians and injured several others (Black 2017; Cipriani 2017).

However, contrary to Irgun's expectations that their campaign of attacks would scare the Arabs and deter them from engaging in further violence, these actions only escalated the intercommunal violence in Palestine, inciting Arab counterattacks. As argued by Haganah and the Jewish Agency, Irgun's brutal violence strategy endangered, rather than protected, the future of the Jewish community in Palestine. Jews in Palestine denounced Irgun for violating the principle of using force only for self-defense, for undermining the security of Jews, and distrusting the political struggle in Palestine. The group was also asked by the Jewish Agency to stop all paramilitary activities which could potentially lead to a civil war between the Arabs and Jews.

In 1939, with the approaching danger of a second world war in Europe, the British government wanted to bring an absolute end to the intercommunal violence in Palestine. The government arranged a conference in London between the Arab and Jewish community leaders to consider potential options for the future of Palestine. The conference failed, as the Arab and Jewish parties refused to sit at the same negotiation table and opposed the compromise solutions proposed by Britain (Sheffer 1973). Instead, the British government published the MacDonald White Paper, imposing its own solution for the future of Palestine. The paper's central tenets were as follows:

1. Jewish immigration into Palestine to be strictly limited to a certain number
2. Restrictions to be imposed on further Jewish land purchase
3. A two-to-one ratio of Arabs to Jews to be maintained in Palestine
4. Discontinuation and decommissioning of paramilitary groups such as Haganah
5. Independent status to be granted to Palestine within 10 years (Cohen 1973)

FIGURE 7.17 Aftermath of 1946 Irgun Bombing of King David Hotel. The attack targeted the King David Hotel, which served as the headquarters of the British Mandatory authorities and housed offices of the Secretariat of the Government of Palestine and the British military command. The Irgun members disguised themselves as Arab workers and planted explosives in the basement of the hotel. The bombing killed 91 people, including British, Arab, and Jewish civilians, as well as soldiers and government officials. It caused extensive damage to the hotel and nearby buildings. *Source:* Gordon Trevor Moore, CC BY-SA 4.0, via Wikimedia Commons.

Both sides strongly opposed Britain's plan. Soon after the British solution was announced, Jewish groups started a campaign of violence against the British rule in Palestine: government offices were ransacked, the Immigration Department was burned down, tax offices were bombed, bridges connecting Palestine to its neighboring countries were blown up, the central post office in Jerusalem and several telephone booths over the country were bombed, and the Land Registry Office was destroyed. Countless police officers were killed in isolated attacks. Countless others were kidnapped as hostages. Irgun offensives also targeted the British Air Force bases across Palestine, killing paratroopers and destroying several fighter planes. They also targeted high level British officials.

For example, Lord Moyne, British Prime Minister of State in the Middle East, was assassinated by Lehi members (a splinter faction of Irgun) in 1944 in Cairo (Cohen 1979). During this time Arab villages, markets, coffee shops, public transportation facilities, and other crowded places continued to be the target of Irgun violence. Irgun officials often defended their use of violence against civilian Arabs as a response to immigration quotas placed on Jewish refugees in Palestine during the zenith of Hitler's anti-Semitic policies in Germany.

The situation worsened in 1946, when Irgun blew up the British Embassy in Rome (which they viewed as the center of British efforts to monitor and stop Jewish immigration into Palestine) and the British headquarters of the Government Secretariat and Army Command in the southern wing of King David Hotel in Jerusalem (Charters 2007; Hoffman 2020). More than 90 civilians and soldiers, including Arab and British soldiers, lost their lives and hundreds of others were seriously injured. Attacks and acts of sabotage continued to increase during the following months, which led to the killing of more British soldiers (Quillen 2002). Across the country, civilian social and economic life came to a halt. The implementation of martial law, which sought to end the Jewish terrorist activities, meant the army assumed the distribution of groceries. Even though Irgun (and its faction Lehi) had not enjoyed widespread support from Palestinian Jews and had been condemned by the Jewish Agency and Haganah several times, collective punishment due to repressive countermeasures and the inconvenience

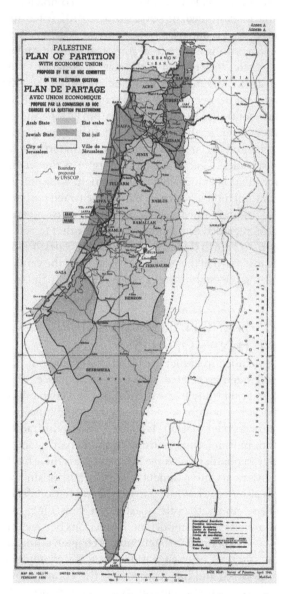

FIGURE 7.18 1947 United Nations partition plan for Palestine at the end of the British Mandate. The plan aimed to partition Palestine into separate Jewish and Arab states, with Jerusalem under international administration. *Source:* Zero0000A/RES/181(II), Public domain, via Wikimedia Commons.

resulting from the implementation of the martial law began to alienate the Jews and elicit sympathy and support for the terrorists (Segev 2000).

In the face of escalating terrorist violence and following a recommendation by the United Nations in 1947, Britain announced the cessation of all military and civilian activities in Palestine and decided to completely withdrawal from the region. Mutual attacks continued, however (Miller 2010). For example, Irgun carried out the Deir Yassin massacre (as noted in the letter to the *New York Times*) in an Arab village located in Jerusalem, killing hundreds of unarmed civilian Arabs (Morris 2005).

After the creation of the state of Israel in 1948, Irgun disbanded its organizational structure and many of its members joined the official Israel Defense Forces (IDF). The tensions between the IDF and Irgun continued for a while, however, as some Irgun members continued to smuggle arms from Europe and engage in military confrontations with the official Israeli Army. In late 1948, the newly established Israeli government outlawed Irgun and declared both Irgun and Lehi terrorist organizations. David Ben-Gurion, the first leader of Israel, denounced Irgun as the "enemy of the Jewish people." Some Irgun members later formed an extreme right-wing political party named Herut (Freedom) and continued their activities within the Israeli parliament (Pedahzur 2012).

Irgun is a historically notable terrorist organization: its activities and tactics have been regarded as a model by several other terrorist groups across the world, from Vietnam to French Canada. Ironically, the Palestinian Liberation Organization, which will be discussed in the next chapter, adopted the very same tactics and tools utilized by Irgun during the establishment of Israel to free their land from illegal Jewish settlements.

7.7 NATIONALISM IN AMERICA: CONFLATING PATRIOTISM WITH NATIONALISM

As detailed in earlier case studies, throughout history, ethnic nationalist motivations have been associated with extreme violence. In contrast, civic nationalism, which is based on loyalty to the institutions and civic values of a nation, is considered a positive feature of modern societies. Similarly, the concept of **patriotism**, or the affective attachment to one's nation, is viewed as an admirable characteristic. These two concepts, nationalism (ethnic nationalism) and patriotism, however, are often used interchangeably in popular discourse. In recent years there has been a rise of nationalist and far-right movements, often under the guise of patriotism, throughout Europe and North America (Koehler 2016). While patriotism and nationalism both involve some form of pride in one's country, the often-destructive consequences of ethnic nationalism necessitate an awareness of the important distinctions between these two concepts (Viroli 1995).

As explained throughout this chapter, ethnic nationalism is an ideology that favors the interests of one's nation (over, for example, foreigners, immigrants, and ethnic minorities) and has accrued negative connotations. Ethnic nationalism, in particular, espouses national superiority and dominance over other countries and highlights the importance of unity based on shared culture, ethnicity, religion, or language (i.e., cultural background). It is militant, aggressive, morally dangerous, and has a divisive character that is rooted in rivalry or resentment. It can lead to intolerance, isolation, and an irrational hatred or fear of people from other cultures. English critic George Orwell refers to nationalism as "the worst enemy of peace" (Orwell 2018). Due to its characteristics, nationalism is often described as the evil twin of patriotism.

Patriotism, on the other hand, has a history of more than 2,000 years and it is simply the love of one's country. It has a benign, positive connotation. It often involves the common elements of civic nationalism, such as positive attitudes, sentiments, pride, attachment, and devotion toward one's own country and its institutions (Hanson & O'Dwyer 2019). Unlike ethnic nationalism, patriotism focuses on the importance of shared values regardless of individuals' ethnicity, language, beliefs, and opinions. Patriotism respects and appreciates cultural differences and values. It is not a political virtue as nationalism, but an attachment to one's nation based on affection and peace. Patriotism and ethnic nationalism are distinct and correspond to differing social and political attitudes. For example, in an analysis of six data sets of representative surveys conducted both in the United States and internationally, researchers consistently found that people who express high levels of nationalism, including feelings of national superiority and competition with other countries, report hostility toward immigrants, whereas those who express high degrees of patriotism, measured as admiration for one's country, show no greater prejudice than the average citizen (de Figueiredo & Elkins 2003).

In recent years, in the United States as throughout the rest of the world, individuals and groups claiming to be patriots have contributed to an increase in social problems—hate crimes, political polarization, and civic unrest—driven by ethnic nationalism. Some scholars argue that at no time in history since World War I have nationalist sentiments been this strong. For example, in 2020, in opposition to the absence of restrictive immigration policies in the union, globalization, and joblessness, nationalism was the driving force for Britain to withdraw from the European Union (popularly known as Brexit).

Similarly, in the United States, Donald Trump led a campaign with nationalistic appeals that conflated national pride and patriotism with ethnic nationalism, using slogans such as "Make America Great Again" and "America First" and blaming outsiders (e.g., immigrants stealing American jobs, Muslims hating the US, and Mexicans bringing crime into the country) for the country's social ills and economic concerns (Longley 2019). Research suggests that this rhetoric appealed to a large proportion of Americans who endorse views consistent with "restrictive" expressions of nationalism, which set racial and ethnic (White) and religious (Christian) boundaries on who can be considered an American (Devos & Banaji 2005). Americans who advance restrictive definitions of being "truly American" tend to be White, male, and reside outside of urban areas, and these demographic characteristics are consistent with those of Donald Trump's support base (Bonikowski & DiMaggio 2016). To the extent that such exclusive notions of national identity continue to generate support among the American population, it is important to keep in mind the violent history associated with ethnic nationalism. We consider the connection between nationalism and violence further in the following section.

7.7.1 Is Nationalism Inherently Violent?

The world has witnessed various episodes of guerilla warfare and terrorist conflicts by nonstate actors over the last several decades in which nationalism was the primary motivating factor. According to a study executed by a well-known political scientist, during the nineteenth century more than a quarter of all wars were initiated because of nationalism, and today nationalism is the leading cause of violence for almost all wars, including ethnic cleansing and genocide campaigns, violent insurgencies, and terrorism (Wimmer 2012).

History has shown that when nationalists (especially state actors) achieve power, they openly advocate for the use of violence and either turn their societies into totalitarian governments or start civil wars by persecuting civilians and ethnic minorities. For example, the belief in Aryan (German) superiority in Nazi Germany led to global disorder, World War II, and the Holocaust. The idea of nationalism more recently caused the former state of Yugoslavia to dissolve and ultimately be replaced by seven independent states in 1991. Nationalism caused more than 100,000 casualties in ethnically divided Bosnia and also led to the genocide of more than 8,000 Muslims by Serbian nationalists in the town of Srebrenica. Hundreds of thousands of Tutsi people have been killed in Rwanda by Hutus, and thousands of Muslims in Myanmar have been killed through ethnic cleansing campaigns solely motivated by nationalistic reasons. In 2018, the United Nations Secretary General announced that the rise of nationalism around the globe had made it hard and impossible for the UN to do its job (United Nations 2018).

Despite this history, whether nationalism directly causes violence is a subject of debate among several scholars. For example, in his book *Nationalism and War*, Hutchinson (2017) argues that even though many modern wars have a nationalistic character, this does not necessarily mean that the ideology of nationalism was their cause. Nationalism often serves as a mediating factor in the eruption of violence. For example, the presence of significant societal and demographic changes, revolutionary upheavals (e.g., collapse of a state), military failures (humiliation in a war), unexpected transformations in geopolitical environments that threaten the status of a group, the lack of political power, and competing claims on territorial borders can all lead to nationalistic radicalization and, in turn, collective violence (Hutchinson 2017).

It is important to follow historical trajectories and developments to understand that the link between nationalism and violence is not direct, but instead is dependent on contextual factors. For example, some scholars argue that the idea of nationalism has limited motivational effect in environments with abundant economic resources and effective, nondiscriminatory formal political institutions and channels. However, it can lead to brutal violence among groups in an environment with ineffective and discriminatory political institutions (e.g., state coercion, nonresponsive governments), and with limited economic resources (Lange 2013). In such an environment, nationalism may lead a group to seek to eliminate the others in an attempt to increase their community's share of resources. Likewise, nationalism can cause individuals to become frustrated and angry with the problems facing their national community (especially economic problems) and can lead to the scapegoating of minorities as the source of the grievance.

Similarly, Irish political scientist Sinisa Malešević (2013) defends the position that nationalism is not inherently violent, but rather nationalist ideologies can be radicalized into organized violent action by additional factors. Malešević argues that it is not the ideology of nationalism but the increased capacities of state and nonstate actors of the late nineteenth and early twentieth centuries that were vital in the proliferation of revolutions, insurgencies, terrorism, genocide, and other intercommunal violence. These capacities include new industrial and technological developments in the area of warfare—such as the invention of fighter planes, automatic guns, and powerful explosives such as dynamite—along with the mass production of weaponry, canned food, advancements in telecommunications and mass transportation, and the establishment of modern military units.

7.8 CONCLUSION

Nationalism is considered a modern movement. Ethnic nationalism—the use of ethnicity and cultural homogeneity in the formation of a nation—has been linked to authoritarianism, colonization, military aggression, and intolerance toward other ethnic, religious, and cultural groups. In terms of the numbers of attacks and casualties, ethnic nationalist terrorism has been the most prevalent type of terrorism throughout history. Although the number and impact of ethnic nationalist terrorist organizations has declined over time, there has been a resurgence of nationalist sentiment in recent years and the dangers of ethnic nationalism must be kept in mind. However, it is important to emphasize a major point in our examination of terrorist violence. It is not the ideology on its own that produces violence. In order to understand any type of terrorism, it is critical to comprehend the context in which it arises. Each of the case studies presented in this chapter detailed a complex set of social, political, and economic factors at play in the emergence of ethnic nationalist terrorism.

Key Lessons

Lesson 1

Contrary to common knowledge that nationalist ideologies date far back in history, nationalism is a modern movement. French Revolution is known to be the first expression of nationalist ideals in the world. Throughout most of the human history, the idea of a nation-state was nonexistent, and civilizations were primarily formed around religions.

Lesson 2

Not every nation has a state as of 2024 (e.g., Basque people, Palestinians), and some states may contain multiple nations.

Lesson 3

Nationalism favors an individual's identification with their own nation and the premise that loyalty and allegiance to the nation-state surpasses all other individual and group interests.

Lesson 4

Civic nationalism is based on the idea that anyone (regardless of their ethnic origin) who shows loyalty to the institutions and civic values of a nation belongs to that nation. It is founded on the principle of human rights and personal freedom, and it has a unifying character, rather than a divisive one.

Lesson 5

Ethnic nationalism emphasizes the importance of ethnicity and cultural homogeneity in the formation of a nation. It cannot be acquired; it is determined by birth.

Lesson 6

Nations that have promoted ethnic nationalism have engaged in harmful acts, including authoritarianism, colonization, military aggression, and intolerance toward other ethnic, religious, and cultural groups.

Lesson 7

Ethnic nationalist terrorism has been regarded as the most prevalent type of terrorism in terms of number of attacks and casualties.

Lesson 8

Even though fighting on behalf of an ethnic identity is the unique motivational driver for ethnic nationalist terrorism, groups that initially launch campaigns of terrorism with ethno-nationalistic goals may also embrace some other religious or political ideological identities over time. Groups can evolve from one type of terrorism to another.

Lesson 9

The relationship between nationalism and terrorism is often more complex than the simple goal of pursuing an ethnic group's own collective interests and safeguarding an independent homeland or gaining increased autonomy within a specified territory. Terrorism is not simply the product of ardent nationalism.

Lesson 10

While patriotism and nationalism are often used interchangeably in the modern day, there are important distinctions between these two concepts.

Lesson 11

Whether nationalism directly causes violence is a subject of debate among several scholars.

KEY WORDS

Abu Sayyaf Group
African National Congress
Basque Fatherland and Liberty (ETA)
civic nationalism
ethnic nationalism
Hezbollah
Irgun Zvai Leumi
Irish Republican Army (IRA)
Kosovo Liberation Army (UCK)
Kurdistan Workers' Party (PKK)

Liberation Front of Quebec (FLQ)
Liberation Tigers of Tamil Eelam (LTTE)
nation
National Liberation Front
National Organization of Cypriot Struggle (EOKA)
patriotism
Popular Liberation Movement of Angola
state

RECOMMENDED SOURCES

Research Articles & Books

Boylan, B. M. (2016). What drives ethnic terrorist campaigns? A view at the group level of analysis. *Conflict Management and Peace Science, 33*(3), 250–272.

Brubaker, R. (1999). The Manichean myth: Rethinking the distinction between 'civic' and 'ethnic' nationalism. *Nation and national identity: The European experience in perspective*, 55–71.

Brubaker, R., & Laitin, D. D. (1998). Ethnic and nationalist violence. *Annual Review of sociology, 24*(1), 423–452.

Byman, D. (1998). The logic of ethnic terrorism. *Studies in Conflict & Terrorism, 21*(2), 149–169.

Choi, S. W. (2022). Leader nationalism, ethnic identity, and terrorist violence. *British Journal of Political Science, 52*(3), 1151–1167.

Crenshaw, M. (1981). The causes of terrorism. *Comparative politics, 13*(4), 379–399.

English, R. (2019). Nationalism and terrorism. In E. Chenoweth, R. English, S. Kalyvas, and A. Gofas (Eds.), *The Oxford handbook of terrorism* (pp. 268–282). Oxford University Press.

Hanson, K., & O'Dwyer, E. (2019). Patriotism and nationalism, left and right: AQ-methodology study of American national identity. *Political Psychology, 40*(4), 777–795.

Lange, M. (2013). When does nationalism turn violent? *Nationalism and War*, 124.

Malešević, S. (2013). Is nationalism intrinsically violent? *Nationalism and Ethnic Politics, 19*(1), 12–37.

Tagore, R. (2017). *Nationalism*. Penguin UK.

Toft, M. D. (2010). The geography of ethnic violence. In The Geography of Ethnic Violence. Princeton University Press.

Wilkinson, P. (2000). Nationalism and its consequences: A review. *Terrorism and Political Violence*, *12*(2), 123–130.

Viroli, M. (1995). For love of country: An essay on patriotism and nationalism. Clarendon Press.

News Articles & Government and Think Tank Reports

The disruptive power of ethnic nationalism
   Author(s): Shlomo Ben-Ami
   Source: Australian Strategic Policy Institute (ASPI)
What's Behind a Rise in Ethnic Nationalism? Maybe the Economy
   Author(s): Robert J. Shiller
   Source: The New York Times
The Rise of Ethnonationalism and the Future of Liberal Democracy
   Author(s): Jocelyne Cesari, Jack A. Goldstone, Pankaj Mishra, & Stewart M. Patrick
   Source: Council on Foreign Relations
Biden calls white supremacy greatest terrorism threat as 2024 race heats up
   Author(s): Toluse Olorunnipa
   Source: The Washington Post
How 'great replacement' theory led to the Buffalo mass shooting
   Author(s): Michael Feola
   Source: The Washington Post

Documentaries, Videos, and Other Educational Media

Organized White Nationalism and Terrorism | Preserving Democracy
   Producer(s)/Director(s): Dana Roberson
   Source: PBS Learning Media
Prof. Richard English - Nationalism, Terrorism and Religion
   Featuring: Richard English
   Source: The University of Edinburgh YouTube channel
The Rise of Ethnic Nationalism
   Featuring: Shlomo Ben-Ami
   Source: UCLA Younes & Soraya Nazarian Center for Israel Studies
Charlottesville: Race and Terror
   Producer(s)/Director(s): VICE News Tonight
   Source: VICE News YouTube Channel
How America can respond to white nationalist violence
   Featuring: Eric Ward & Jelani Cobb
   Source: PBS News YouTube Channel

REFERENCES

Agirre, J. (1975). *Operation Ogro: The execution of Admiral Luis Carrero Blanco*. Quadrangle.

Ahmed, M. M., & Gunter, M. M. (Eds.). (2005). *The Kurdish question and the 2003 Iraqi War*. Mazda Publishers.

Akyol, M. (2015). Who killed Turkey-PKK peace process? Al-Monitor. http://www.al-monitor.com/pulse/originals/2015/08/turkey-syria-iraq-pkk-peace-process-who-killed-kurds.html

Alonso, R. (2007). *The IRA and armed struggle*. Routledge.

Alter, P. (1994). Nationalism. Hodder Education Publishers.

Amar-Dahl, T. (2016). *Zionist Israel and the Question of Palestine: Jewish Statehood and the History of the Middle East Conflict*. De Gruyter Oldenbourg.

Atkins, S. E. (2004). *Encyclopedia of modern worldwide extremists and extremist groups*. Greenwood Publishing Group.

Bal, İ., & Laçiner, S. (2004). *Avrasya Stratejik Araştırmalar Merkezi: Ethnic terrorism in Turkey and the case of the PKK: Roots, structure, survival and ideology*. Frank Cass.

Bauer, Y. (1966). From cooperation to resistance: The Haganah 1938–1946. *Middle Eastern Studies*, *2*(3), 182–210.

BBC (2017). What is ETA? https://www.bbc.com/news/world-europe-11183574

Black, I. (2017). *Enemies and neighbors: Arabs and Jews in Palestine and Israel, 1917–2017.* Atlantic Monthly Press.

Bonikowski, B., & DiMaggio, P. (2016). Varieties of American popular nationalism. *American Sociological Review, 81*(5), 949–980.

Bosi, L. (2012). Explaining pathways to armed activism in the Provisional Irish Republican Army, 1969–1972. *Social Science History, 36*(3), 347–390.

Boylan, B. M. (2016). What drives ethnic terrorist campaigns? A view at the group level of analysis. *Conflict Management and Peace Science, 33*(3), 250–272.

Breton, R. (1988). From ethnic to civic nationalism: English Canada and Quebec. *Ethnic and Racial Studies, 11*(1), 85–102.

Breuilly, J. (1993). *Nationalism and the state.* Manchester University Press.

Brubaker, R. (1999). The Manichean myth: Rethinking the distinction between "civic" and "ethnic" nationalism. In H. Kriesi, K. Armingeon, H. Siegrist, & A. Wimmer (Eds.), *Nation and national identity: The European experience in perspective* (pp. 55–71).

Byman, D. (1998). The logic of ethnic terrorism. *Studies in Conflict & Terrorism, 21*(2), 149–169.

Calhoun, C. J. (1997). *Nationalism.* University of Minnesota Press.

Charters, D. (2007). Jewish terrorism and the Modern Middle East. *Journal of Conflict Studies, 27*(2), 80–89.

Cipriani, R. (2017). For a historical-sociological approach to the City of Haifa. *Journal of Mediterranean Knowledge, 2*(2), 187–205.

Clancy-Smith, J. A., Gershoni, I., & Tucker, J. E. (2001). *The war for Palestine: Rewriting the history of 1948.* Cambridge University Press.

Cohen, M. J. (1973). Appeasement in the Middle East: The British white paper on Palestine. *The Historical Journal, 16*(3), 571–596.

Cohen, M. J. (1979). The Moyne assassination, November, 1944: A political analysis. *Middle Eastern Studies, 15*(3), 358–373.

Colley, L. (1992). *Britons: Forging the nation 1707–1837.* Yale University Press.

Cosido, I. (2002). Spanish policy against terrorism: The Guardia Civil and ETA. Grupo de Estudios Estrategicos. http://www.gees.org/articulos/spanish-policy-against-terrorism-the-guardia-civil-and-eta

Council on Foreign Relations (2008). Basque Fatherland and Liberty (ETA) (Spain, separatists, Euskadi ta Askatasuna). https://www.cfr.org/backgrounder/basque-fatherland-and-liberty-eta-spain-separatists-euskadi-ta-askatasuna

Cox, M., Guelke, A., & Stephen, F. (Eds.). (2006). *A farewell to arms? Beyond the Good Friday Agreement.* Manchester University Press.

Crenshaw, M. (1981). The causes of terrorism. *Comparative Politics, 13*(4), 379–399.

Crenshaw, M. (2008). The debate over "new" vs. "old" terrorism. In I. A. Karawan, W. McCormack, & S. E. Reynolds (Eds.), *Values and violence: Intangible aspects of terrorism* (pp. 117–136). Springer.

Dalay, G. (2015). Is Turkey's Kurdish peace process on the brink? Al Jazeera. http://studies.aljazeera.net/en/reports/2015/09/20159813236393942.html

Davenport, C., & Inman, M. (2012). The state of state repression research since the 1990s. *Terrorism and Political Violence, 24*(4), 619–634.

De Bellaigue, C. (2010). *Rebel land: Unraveling the riddle of history in a Turkish town.* Penguin.

de Figueiredo Jr., R. J., & Elkins, Z. (2003). Are patriots bigots? An inquiry into the vices of in-group pride. *American Journal of Political Science, 47*(1), 171–188.

Denitch, B. D. (1996). *Ethnic nationalism: The tragic death of Yugoslavia.* University of Minnesota Press.

Dersimi, N. M. (1992). *Hatıratım.* Ankara, TR: Öz-GeYayınları.

Devos, T., & Banaji, M. R. (2005). American=white? *Journal of Personality and Social Psychology, 88*(3), 447–466.

Dingley, J. (2001). The bombing of Omagh, 15 August 1998: The bombers, their tactics, strategy, and purpose behind the incident. *Studies in Conflict and Terrorism, 24*(6), 451–465.

Duerr, G. (2017). Independence through terrorism? The linkages between secessionism and terrorism in the Basque Country. In S. N. Romaniuk, F. Grice, D. Irrera, & S. Webb (Eds.), *The Palgrave handbook of global counterterrorism policy* (pp. 459–477). Palgrave Macmillan.

English, R. (2012). *Armed struggle: The history of the IRA*. Pan Books.

English, R. (Ed.) (2015). *Illusions of terrorism and Counter-terrorism*. Oxford University Press.

English, R. (2019). Nationalism and terrorism. In E. Chenoweth, R. English, S. Kalyvas, & A. Gofas (Eds.), *The Oxford handbook of terrorism* (pp. 268–282). Oxford University Press.

Ensaroglu, Y. (2013). Turkey's Kurdish question and the peace process. *Insight Turkey*, 15(2), 7–17.

Euronews (2021). ETA ten years on: The key moments that led to the end of the Spanish terror group. https://www.euronews.com/2021/10/20/eta-ten-years-on-the-key-moments-that-led-to-the-end-of-the-spanish-terror-group

Eustat (2021). Population and housing census 2021. Press Release. Euskal Estatistika Erakundea. https://en.eustat.eus/elem/ele0019100/not0019114_i.pdf

Fromkin, D. (1975). The strategy of terrorism. *Foreign Affairs*, 53(4), 683–698.

Gil-Alana, L. A., & Barros, C. P. (2010). A note on the effectiveness of national anti-terrorist policies: Evidence from ETA. *Conflict Management and Peace Science*, 27(1), 28–46.

Goertzel, T. (1988). The ethics of terrorism and revolution. *Studies in Conflict & Terrorism*, 11(1), 1–12.

Hamilton, C. (1999). *The gender politics of ETA and radical Basque nationalism 1959–1982*. Dissertation, Royal Holloway, University of London.

Haner, M. (2017). *The freedom fighter: A terrorist's own story*. Routledge.

Hanson, K., & O'Dwyer, E. (2019). Patriotism and nationalism, left and right: AQ-methodology study of American national identity. *Political Psychology*, 40(4), 777–795.

Harb, Z. (2011). *Channels of resistance in Lebanon: Liberation propaganda, Hezbollah and the media*. Bloomsbury Publishing.

Harff, B., & Gurr, T. R. (2018). *Ethnic conflict in world politics*. Routledge.

Harms, G., & Ferry, T. M. (2005). *The Palestine-Israel conflict: A basic introduction*. Pluto.

Heller, J. (2012). *The Stern Gang: Ideology, politics and terror, 1940–1949*. Routledge.

Hewitt, C. (1981). Catholic grievances, Catholic nationalism and violence in Northern Ireland during the civil rights period: A reconsideration. *British Journal of Sociology*, 32(3), 362–380.

Hobsbawm, E. J. (2007). *Globalization, democracy, and terrorism*. Little, Brown.

Hoffman, B. (1998). *Inside terrorism*. Victor Gollancz.

Hoffman, B. (2020). The bombing of The King David Hotel, July 1946. *Small Wars & Insurgencies*, 31(3), 594–611.

Horgan, J. (2008). From profiles to pathways and roots to routes: Perspectives from psychology on radicalization into terrorism. *ANNALS of the American Academy of Political and Social Science*, 618(1), 80–94.

Horgan, J. G. (2017). Psychology of terrorism: Introduction to the special issue. *American Psychologist*, 72(3), 199.

Horgan, J., & Taylor, M. (1997). The provisional Irish Republican army: Command and functional structure. *Terrorism and Political Violence*, 9(3), 1–32.

Hughes, M. (2015). Terror in Galilee: British-Jewish collaboration and the special night squads in Palestine during the Arab Revolt, 1938–39. *Journal of Imperial and Commonwealth History*, 43(4), 590–610.

Hutchinson, J. (2017). *Nationalism and war*. Oxford University Press.

Jackson, B. A. (2005). Provisional Irish Republican Army. *Aptitude for Destruction*, 2, 93–140.

Keitner, C. I. (2012). *The paradoxes of nationalism: The French Revolution and its meaning for contemporary nation building*. SUNY Press.

Koehler, D. (2016). *Right-wing terrorism in the 21st century: The 'National Socialist Underground' and the history of terror from the far-right in Germany*. Routledge.

Kohn, H. (1938). I. Nationalism. In F. P. Davidson & G. S. Viereck (Eds.), *Before America decides* (pp. 13–26). Harvard University Press.

Kohn, H. (1939). The nature of nationalism. *American Political Science Review*, 33(6), 1001–1021.

Kohn, H. (2022). *A History of Nationalism in the East*. Routledge.

Kohn, H., & Calhoun, C. (2017). *The idea of nationalism: A study in its origins and background*. Routledge.

Kowalski, R. C. (2018). The role of sectarianism in the Provisional IRA campaign, 1969–1997. *Terrorism and Political Violence, 30*(4), 658–683.

Lange, M. (2013). When does nationalism turn violent? In J. A. Hall and S. Malešević *Nationalism and War* (pp. 124–144). Cambridge University Press.

Larin, S. J. (2020). Is it really about values? Civic nationalism and migrant integration. *Journal of Ethnic and Migration Studies, 46*(1), 127–141.

Lavery, B. (2002). I.R.A. apologizes for civilian deaths in its 30-year campaign. *New York Times*. https://www.nytimes.com/2002/07/17/world/ira-apologizes-for-civilian-deaths-in-its-30-year-campaign.html

Lavi, S. (2005). The use of force beyond the liberal imagination: Terror and empire in Palestine, 1947. *Theoretical Inquiries in Law, 7*(1), 199–228.

Lewis. B. (1968). The *emergence of modern Turkey*. Oxford University Press.

Llera, F. J., Mata, J. M., & Irvin, C. L. (1993). ETA: From secret army to social movement: The post-Franco schism of the Basque nationalist movement. *Terrorism and Political Violence, 5*(3), 106–134.

Longley, K. (2019). Why Donald Trump is just following in Ronald Reagan's footsteps on race. The Washington Post. https://www.washingtonpost.com/outlook/2019/08/04/why-donald-trump-is-just-following-ronald-reagans-footsteps-race/

Malešević, S. (2013). Is nationalism intrinsically violent? *Nationalism and Ethnic Politics, 19*(1), 12–37.

Marcus, A. (2015). Turkey's Kurdish guerrillas are ready for war. *Foreign Policy*. http://foreignpolicy.com/2015/08/31/turkeys-kurdish-guerillas-are-ready-for-war/

Massad, J. (2006). The persistence of the Palestinian question: Essays on Zionism and the Palestinians. Routledge.

McDowall, D. (2000). *A modern history of the Kurds*. I.B. Tauris.

McKiernan, K. (2006). *The Kurds: A people in search of their homeland*. Macmillan.

Miller, R. (Ed.). (2010). Britain, Palestine and empire: The mandate years. Ashgate.

Morris, B. (2005). The historiography of Deir Yassin. *Journal of Israeli History, 24*(1), 79–107.

Morris, B. (2009). *One state, two states*. Yale University Press.

Moseley, R. (1993). A sense of shame in Ireland. *Chicago Tribune*. https://www.chicagotribune.com/news/ct-xpm-1993-03-27-9303270091-story.html

Mujal-Leon, E. M. (2019). Spain: The PCE and the post–Franco era. In D. Albright (Ed.), *Communism and political systems in Western Europe* (pp. 139–174). Routledge.

Murua, I. (2017). No more bullets for ETA: The loss of internal support as a key factor in the end of the Basque group's campaign. *Critical Studies on Terrorism, 10*(1), 93–114.

Mylonas, H., & Tudor, M. (2021). Nationalism: What we know and what we still need to know. *Annual Review of Political Science, 24*(1), 109–132.

Nathanson, S. (2010). *Terrorism and the ethics of war*. Cambridge University Press.

Nipperdey, T., & Daniel, N. (1996). *Germany from Napoleon to Bismarck, 1800–1866*. Princeton University Press.

O'Ballance, E. (1979). *Language of violence: The blood politics of terrorism*. Presidio Press.

O'Ballance, E. (1996). *The Kurdish struggle, 1920–94*. Macmillan.

Öcalan, A. (2013). Liberating life: Women's *revolution. Cologne, Germany*: International Initiative Edition and Mesopotamian Publishers, Neuss.

Ó Dochartaigh, N. (2015). The longest negotiation: British policy, IRA strategy and the making of the Northern Ireland peace settlement. *Political Studies, 63*(1), 202–220.

Olson, R. W. (Ed.). (1996). *The Kurdish nationalist movement in the 1990s: Its impact on Turkey and the Middle East*. University Press of Kentucky.

Orwell, G. (2018). *Notes on nationalism*. Penguin.

Pappe, I. (2022). *A history of modern Palestine*. Cambridge University Press.

Pedahzur, A. (2012). *The triumph of Israel's radical right*. Oxford University Press.

Peleg, S., & Kempf, W. (2006). Experiencing terrorism in Spain: The case of ETA. In S. Peleg & W. Kempf (Eds.) *Fighting terrorism in the liberal state* (pp. 40–47). IOS Press.

Quillen, C. (2002). A historical analysis of mass casualty bombers. *Studies in Conflict and Terrorism, 25*(5), 279–292.

Rekawek, K. (2011). *Irish republican terrorism and politics: A comparative study of the Official and the Provisional IRA*. Routledge.

Reinares, F. (2005). *Root causes of terrorism*. Routledge.

Richards, A. (2001). Terrorist groups and political fronts: The IRA, Sinn Fein, the peace process and democracy. *Terrorism and Political Violence, 13*(4), 72–89.

Rogers, P. (2000). Political violence and economic targeting aspects of provisional IRA strategy, 1992–97. *Civil Wars, 3*(4), 1–28.

Romano, D. (2006). *The Kurdish nationalist movement: Opportunity, mobilization and identity*. Cambridge University Press.

Roshwald, A. (2002). *Ethnic nationalism and the fall of empires: Central Europe, the Middle East and Russia, 1914–23*. Routledge.

Rowe, M. (2013). The French Revolution, Napoleon, and nationalism in Europe. In J. Breuilly (Ed.), *The Oxford handbook of the history of nationalism* (pp. 127–148). Oxford University Press.

Rummel, R. J. (2022). *Democide: Nazi genocide and mass murder*. Routledge.

Sanchez-Cuenca, I. (2007). The dynamics of nationalist terrorism: ETA and the IRA. *Terrorism and Political Violence, 19*(3), 289–306.

Segev, T. (2000). *One Palestine, complete: Jews and Arabs under the British mandate*. Macmillan.

Shanahan, T. (2008). *Provisional Irish Republican Army and the morality of terrorism*. Edinburgh University Press.

Sheffer, G. (1973). Intentions and results of British policy in Palestine: Passfield's white paper. *Middle Eastern Studies, 9*(1), 43–60.

Shepard, W. S. (2002). The ETA: Spain fights Europe's last active terrorist group. *Mediterranean Quarterly, 13*(1), 54–68.

Steinhoff, U. (2007). *On the ethics of war and terrorism*. Oxford University Press.

Sullivan, J. L. (2015). *ETA and Basque nationalism (RLE: terrorism & insurgency): The fight for Euskadi 1890–1986*. Routledge.

Tagore, R. (2017). *Nationalism*. Penguin.

Tamir, Y. (2019). Not so civic: Is there a difference between ethnic and civic nationalism? *Annual Review of Political Science, 22*, 419–434.

Taylor, P. (2014). *The Provos: The IRA and Sinn Fein*. A&C Black.

Toft, M. D. (2003). *The geography of ethnic violence*. Princeton University Press.

Tonge, J., Shirlow, P., & McAuley, J. (2011). So why did the guns fall silent? How interplay, not stalemate, explains the Northern Ireland peace process. *Irish Political Studies, 26*(1), 1–18.

Townshend, C. (1979). The Irish Republican Army and the development of guerrilla warfare, 1916–1921. *English Historical Review, 94*(371), 318–345.

United Nations (2018). Rising Nationalism Threatens Multilateralism's 70-Year 'Proven Track Record' of Saving Lives, Preventing Wars, Secretary-General Tells Security Council. UN Meetings Coverage and Press Releases. https://press.un.org/en/2018/sc13570.doc.htm

Van Bruinessen, M. (1978). *Agha, shaikh and state: On the social and political organization of Kurdistan*. University of Utrecht.

Viroli, M. (1995). *For love of country: An essay on patriotism and nationalism*. Clarendon Press.

Walsh, D. (2000). *Bloody Sunday and the rule of law in Northern Ireland*. Springer.

White, P. J. (2000). *Primitive rebels or revolutionary modernizers: The Kurdish Nationalist movement in Turkey*. Zed Books.

White, R. W. (1989). From peaceful protest to guerrilla war: Micromobilization of the Provisional Irish Republican Army. *American Journal of Sociology, 94*(6), 1277–1302.

Whitfield, T. (2014). *Endgame for ETA: Elusive peace in the Basque Country*. Oxford University Press.

Wilkinson, P. (1974). *Political terrorism*. Macmillan.

Wilkinson, P. (1997). Reflections on Bloody Sunday. *Terrorism and Political Violence, 9*(2), 132–134.

Wimmer, A. (2012). *Waves of war: Nationalism, state formation, and ethnic exclusion in the modern world*. Cambridge University Press.

Woodworth, P. (2001). *Dirty war, clean hands: ETA, the GAL and Spanish democracy*. Cork University Press.

Woodworth, P. (2004). The war against terrorism: The Spanish experience from ETA to al-Qaeda. *International Journal of Iberian Studies, 17*(3), 169–182.

CHAPTER 8

Religious Terrorism

Terrorist Violence Motivated by Religious Imperatives

Learning Objectives

1. To understand the nature, history, and role of religions pertaining to their influence on terrorism and political violence.
2. Identify the distinctive characteristics of religious terrorism that separate it from nationalistic and ideological terrorism.
3. To discuss whether religions should be seen as a cause of terroristic violence.
4. To explore whether particular religions are more prone to violence than others.
5. To explain the different motivational aspects (drivers) for religiously inspired terrorism.
6. To explain the historical examples of violence carried out in the name of Abrahamic religions, giving special attention to their cultural, historical, and geographical contexts.

8.1 INTRODUCTION

Violence in the name of religion is deeply embedded within the history of faiths, with early examples dating back to Jewish Zealots between 66–73 BC in Roman-occupied Israel (Hoffman 1998). During the past few decades, religious terrorism has become an important national security issue for many governments around the world. Often, in the contemporary West, terrorism is widely perceived as an act of violence committed by religious fanatics (Lewis & Dawson 2018).

Even though there is no scholarly consensus on what elements constitute a religion, the term "religion" often denotes a set of social practices (e.g., morals, ethics, rules, sacred texts, holy places) and common beliefs regarding the origin, nature, and purpose of life and the universe, and fate after death. Religions often have sacred texts and scriptures that provide the basis for religious beliefs, and their worshippers participate in devotional and ritual activities and observances such as prayers, religious services, and holidays.

Religion, as a concept, has played a significant role in human affairs and world history for centuries. Historically, religion,

FIGURE 8.1 Islam (622 CE; symbol on right), Christianity (0 CE; symbol on left), and Judaism (1300 BCE; bottom center symbol) represent the three Abrahamic religions because they all trace their spiritual lineage back to the biblical figure Abraham. These three religions share historical and theological connections through their common Abrahamic heritage, but they also have distinct beliefs, practices, and traditions. *Source:* ApChrKey, CC BY-SA 4.0, via Wikimedia Commons.

rather than ethnicity, served as a primary social (group) identity (Esposito 2003). Not only have religions served as a binding force in societies by bringing individuals together and generating close-knit communities, but they have also provided a sense of purpose to their followers through symbolic, material, and social resources (Gregg 2018). Groups have also used religious identities to mobilize their followers to challenge existing social and political orders (Wessinger 2009).

8.2 RELIGIOUS TERRORISM

Given this information, **religious terrorism** can be broadly described as a strategy in which violence, influenced by interpretations of religious texts, beliefs, or clerical authorities, is used to achieve political or divine goals. Some scholars consider it as a form of political violence, more specifically violence perpetrated in the name of religion by religiously motivated individuals (Gunning & Jackson 2011). Different from the other types of terrorism covered in the previous chapters, in this type of terrorism, religion itself is used as the motivation, justification, and organization for the acts of terrorism (Juergensmeyer 2005). Perpetrators of religious terrorism often see their use of violence as a sacramental act or religious duty in the name of God (Hoffman 1998) and believe they will receive spiritual rewards, such as God's blessings, religious merits, and heavenly luxuries, for their violence (Juergensmeyer 2007). They see themselves as soldiers and representatives of God on Earth, fighting on behalf of divine justice.

Religion can also provide moral justification for violence by demonizing enemies and showing the struggle as a sacred fight between satanic powers and God's soldiers. As a result, religious terrorists can kill with moral impunity; they believe they will receive heavenly rewards for their violence. It is this aspect of religious terrorism that makes it far more destructive and lethal than ideological or nationalistic terrorism.

Academic researchers have identified three distinctive characteristics of religiously motivated terrorist organizations. These are:

1. Having transcendent goals (as opposed to having clearly defined pragmatic goals that are political and economic in nature), such as establishing a religious state, returning to an idealized period of history, or destroying civilization to hasten the return of the Messiah (Laqueur 1999; Cook 2003; Cronin 2003; Gunning & Jackson 2011; Juergensmeyer 2005).
2. Seeing violence as a sacramental/divine duty committed in the name of God (Juergensmeyer 2005; Ranstorp 1996).
3. Being unamenable to negotiation and indiscriminate in the use of violence, as they do not care about the earthly constituency and focus instead on heavenly rewards (Juergensmeyer 2005).

Historically, there have been many instances in which religion, including the three Abrahamic traditions—Judaism, Christianity, and Islam—and others such as Hinduism, Buddhism, and Odinism was used as the key factor in motivating and sustaining non-state terrorist violence. Until the beginning of nineteenth century, in which ideologies such as nationalism and anarchism emerged, religious beliefs and motivations were the sole drivers of terrorism (Rapoport 2002). Many of the brutal terrorist attacks that occurred in the late twentieth and early twenty-first centuries were carried out in the name of religion (Juergensmeyer 2021).

As political scientist David Rapoport explains in his seminal work "The Four Waves of Modern Terrorism" (2002), even though the issue of religious terrorism was overshadowed by ideological and ethnic nationalist motivated terrorism during the early twentieth century, beginning in the late 1970s, modern religious terrorist groups began to resurge and dominate world affairs. Religion, once again, became the major driving force behind international terrorism between the 1990s and 2000s. Some scholars argue that religious terrorism is the "new terrorism of the right" (Laqueur 1999), as religious imperatives have increasingly motivated terrorist acts through far-right extremist nationalist identity in Western Europe and North America during the past decade (Henne 2019). Even though there are clear-cut boundaries between left-wing and religiously inspired terrorism, nowadays, religiously motivated terrorist and hate groups often contain elements of right-wing terrorism—racism, fascism, and nationalism (Gregg 2014).

It is important to note that despite the fact that Islam and its followers have been commonly associated with religious terrorism during the past few decades (Haner et al. 2020), violence in the name of religion has been practiced by groups claiming all religious faiths. This chapter will provide examples of historical and contemporary religiously motivated terrorist groups of different religious faiths and discuss whether religion should be seen as a cause of terroristic violence. It will also cover the goals and targets of religious terrorism, and current trends in religiously inspired terrorism and hate crimes in the United States and abroad. It will also consider whether certain religions are more prone to violence than others.

As explained earlier in this textbook, the study of terrorism in general, and terrorism's association with religion more specifically, is a contentious topic. Religion is a broad, multifaceted, and complex cultural phenomenon that includes texts, rituals, spiritual leaders and followers, and social and political factors. Findings from decades of academic research indicate that many people have biased understandings of terrorism and hold prejudiced connotations of specific religions with regard to their association with violent extremism. Due to the sensitivities associated with this issue, readers should approach the topics discussed in this chapter from an informed perspective, paying special attention to the cultural, historical, and geographical contexts of specific incidents. It is important to consider all of the factors that are used to justify and promote violence in the name of faith to correctly understand the sources of religiously motivated terrorism.

8.2.1 Religion's Role in Motivating Terrorism

As many of the terrorist acts that occurred during the last few decades were committed in the name of religious convictions, a number of scholars from the fields of political science, sociology, criminology, and religious studies have proposed different theoretical perspectives to explain the complicated role of religion in terrorism. Some posit that religions propagate myths that are extremely dangerous and can lead to violence. From this perspective, a society would do well to eradicate all religious beliefs (Avalos 2005; Harris 2008; Henne 2019). In contrast, and more commonly, others argue that religion is irrelevant to the motivations for terrorism (secondary in importance to other factors, such as nationalism) and that it would be dangerously reductive to blame terroristic violence on religion. These scholars point to the fact that especially in the modern world, politics have become more and more entwined with religion (Lewis & Dawson 2018).

For example, even though groups like the Irish Republican Army and Jewish Irgun Zvai Lemu had strong religious identities, academic research indicates that their grievances were experienced by large numbers of people and were not religious in nature. Nationalism and political issues (along with economic and social tensions) played a more dominant role in their recruits' radicalization into terrorism and their subsequent violent acts (Hoffman 1998; Juergensmeyer 2007). In these cases, religious beliefs were infused into nationalist struggles. Political, ethnic, and other motivations, which are often conflated with religious traditions and ideas, led to violence (Armstrong 2014). When one looks at the long history of terrorism, even though religious motivations have had profound effects on violence, there have often been other factors, intertwined with religious influences, that generate nonstate terrorism. These include foreign military presence and invasions, globalization, political repression, legitimacy of state power, political leadership, religious repression and discrimination, economic inequality, territorial occupation, oppression by the competing political actor, shared grievances, and social upheavals.

Additionally, scholars argue that far from being the cause of terroristic violence, religion itself is a restraining force upon terrorism because religions are peaceful in nature and religious identities are a source of love, affection, and compassion (Cavanaugh 2009; Masaeli & Sneller 2017). For example, the mainstream teachings of the major world religions, Islam, Judaism, and Christianity, are all nonviolent. Many of the texts, figures, and symbolic stories contained in the Bible are also found in the Torah and Qur'an. Most people regard their religion as peaceful and refuse to believe that their own beliefs can lead to violence. As political scientist Mark Juergensmeyer (2007) explains, most Muslims refuse to believe that the perpetrators of the 9/11 attacks represent the true believers of Islam. Instead, it is the particular interpretation of sacred texts by certain groups within certain local contexts that can contribute to different understandings of what the religion is about and may lead to violence under the guise of religious beliefs. Additionally, leaders may use religion to frame their political goals in sacred terms in efforts to rally their masses to their cause (Bloom 2004; Pape 2003). In other words, religion is often used as a medium—grievances such as alienation and marginalization are depicted in religious terms and expressed through religious ideologies. Even though some acts of terroristic violence may include religious elements in their motives, these acts do not represent the normative traditions of religion (Pape 2006).

Religious conflicts are seldom about religion itself. According to this group of scholars, religion does not directly lead to the outbreak of violence; however, it has the potential to intensify violence when religious ideas and identities are embraced in a conflict situation (Stern 2003; Toft 2007). Religious motivations can serve as a strong promoter of terrorism when they are blended with social, economic, and political factors in shaping people's thoughts and actions (Gregg 2018). For example, in her book *Thieves of State: Why Corruption Threatens Global Security*, researcher Sarah Chayes argues that even though there is no single explanatory power behind extremism, violent religious radicalization into terrorism is often found within corrupt political systems in which powerful leaders co-opt public institutions and engage in systematic abuses against their citizens. According to Chayes, in the absence of independent legal systems and established political institutions, people turn to religious extremism to protect themselves from unscrupulous leaders (Chayes 2015). In support of this argument, she points out that many ex-Taliban detainees in US-controlled prisons cited corruption (not religious ideals or goals) as their reason for joining the ranks of the Taliban (Chayes 2015).

Similarly, Marc Sageman, a former senior CIA officer and a leading terrorism expert at the Foreign Policy Research Institute, challenges the argument that religion is a root cause leading individuals into violent extremism. In his book *Understanding Terror Networks*, Sageman (2004) claims that even al-Qaeda's emergence into the world scene as a bloody terrorist organization was simply a strategic response to geopolitical factors, such as the Soviet and American occupation of Muslim territories across the Middle East and Asia. Further supporting this argument, University of Chicago political scientist Robert Pape, analyzing more than 450 demographic profiles of suicide terrorists worldwide from 1980 to 2001 in his seminal work *Dying to Win*, came to the conclusion that religious fanaticism (more specifically Islamic fundamentalism) has nothing to do with individuals' motivation to engage in terrorism. Pape discovered that people engage in **suicide terrorism** to end foreign military occupations or coerce modern liberal democracies to make territorial concessions from the region that terrorists view as their homeland. It is not religious fervor but the presence of religiously different foreign combat forces in a valued territory that leads individuals to use suicide terrorism as a strategic tactical tool (Pape 2006). Pape argues that in the absence of sophisticated military capacities, people turn to the easiest form of military engagement—using their bodies as bombs—as a social survival tactic to oust the foreign powers from their own territories.

Groups use this tactic because they are aware that resorting to suicide terrorism has worked several times in the past, forcing Americans, Israelis, French, Russians, and others to leave the occupied territories (Lebanon, Gaza Strip, West Bank, and Chechnya respectively) and give concessions to locals. For example, Hezbollah emerged and began to use suicide attacks only after Israel invaded Lebanon in 1982 with tens of thousands of troops. The group stopped its suicide attacks after the American, French, and Israeli forces withdrew their military forces from Lebanon following the 1983 Marine barracks suicide attacks, which killed more than 200 US soldiers and approximately 60 French military personnel. Even though suicide terrorism is often infused by religious motivations, these acts are in fact driven by rational calculations and nationalist sentiments.

As British political scientist Richard English stated, "It would be an error to say if only you could just detach religion and get rid of it, the terrorist threat would somehow evaporate" (English 2020). In other words, eradicating all forms of religious beliefs would not remove the issues of terrorism from our world. Further supporting this argument, Juergensmeyer (2021) argued that for the most part of human history, religion was simply a part of the societal culture of a group or a region. When the society engaged in violent atrocities, its religious identity and ideology, by association, was also considered to be violent. As explained in detail in previous chapters, followers of secular ideologies such as Stalin's Soviet Union and Jacobins' France during the French Revolution also engaged in extreme cruelties and murders, slaughtering millions of innocent men and women to further their agendas. In neither of these cases was religion the cause of violence or terror. It would be erroneous to assume that religious identities are the unique instigators of terrorism.

Motivational Aspects of Religious Terrorism

Given the consensus that religious terrorism is not caused by religion itself, what leads groups to commit acts of terrorism in the name of religion? Researchers have identified four broad categories of motivation:

1. to initiate the apocalypse that will destroy the world
2. for fundamentalist aspirations (to create a religious country, government, or religious and racial purification of a region)
3. to defend a predominantly religious region from secularization attempts
4. to campaign for justice (Gregg 2014; Hoffman 1995; Juergensmeyer 2021; Ranstorp 1996).

First, **apocalyptic terrorism**, in which followers are motivated by some transcendent aims, is considered the most dangerous form of terrorism. This is because groups motivated to end the world carry out indiscriminate attacks against society with no consideration for their potential political, moral, or pragmatic outcomes (Juergensmeyer 2021). Unlike ideologically motivated and nationalist terrorist groups, which constantly seek popular support for their actions, apocalyptic terrorist groups do not consider the outcomes of their actions because they believe in "ending the world and the return of the Messiah," as described in all Abrahamic religions. To cleanse the world from what they perceive as a global level of corruption, infidelity, sin, and depravity, apocalyptic terrorists believe that the initiation of a global level catastrophe is a necessary divine mission that would annihilate society and allow the Messiah's return to start a new peaceful world (Saiya 2020). Due to its inherent objectives and history of unrestrained use of violence, apocalyptic terrorism is considered irrational, ruthless, and closed to negotiation.

Second, **fundamentalist aspirations** can provide a powerful force in the radicalization of individuals into religiously motivated terrorist organizations. **Fundamentalism** can simply be described as a strict adherence to a belief system and reactions to changes that threaten this belief system (Emerson & Hartman 2006). Even though fundamentalism itself is not necessarily violent, the term has gained negative connotations and is often used to describe radical and violent religious movements.

In the casual pathway to religious terrorism via fundamentalism, religious authorities and figures play a key role in shaping their followers' actions and beliefs regarding violence and terrorism (Reeve 1999). Some groups have acted with the desire to establish a governmental authority run by religious clerics within a state's border or across a region, encompassing several states. These groups often argue that their religion had been corrupted by new interpretations and outside influences, and the only way to revive the old golden age (i.e., when the religion was practiced perfectly) is to purge these new understandings and the people who follow them. If the "corrupt" society does not cooperate, they see violence as a necessary means. Fundamentalist terrorists work toward the goal of enforcing their religious beliefs on a collective system or society. While doing this, they do not seek to win the support of sympathizers from the opposing society; instead, they subject the opposing society to a process of dehumanization and demonization. As a result, punishing and destroying the opposing side with extreme violence is viewed as a part of a non-negotiable war carried out in the name of God.

Even though the fundamentalist motivations for violence are often associated with Islamist groups (e.g., ISIS), the same motivations have been practiced by groups from other religions and by some cults. As will be explained in detail throughout this chapter, groups that operate with the motivation of establishing a religious government often engage in serious human rights violations toward religious minorities (which often leads to refugee crises) as they force people to conform to their understanding of the religion (Almond et al. 2011).

Relatedly, some fundamentalist groups engage in religious terrorism with the motivation to cleanse their societies from other religious influences in order to create a religiously pure state. For them, the world is divided into "right" and "wrong," and there is only one true religion. There is no space for other religions in their societies. They aim to impose their religious views on other segments of society and resort to violence if their goal of creating a religiously purified state is blocked by other groups (Roszak 1995).

Third, extreme **secularization** attempts by states can also lead to violence in the name of religion. The competition between religion and secularism—the principle of separation of state from the religious institutions—emerged in late seventeenth- and eighteenth-century Europe. The result, in most cases, was the restriction of religion to churches and the use of nonreligious thought as the central force in society for establishing social and political order. However, the relegation of the church and religious values to the margins of the society was not welcomed by some segments within the major religions. Several groups across the world (e.g., Christian militia groups in the United States, al-Qaeda in the Middle East) have seen secularization as the destruction of religious faith and thus engaged in violence, arguing that religious values are at stake and that with God on their side, they are defending these values (Juergensmeyer 2021). The groups in this category see their fights as a battle between good (themselves/believers) and evil (Satan/infidels/nonbelievers). For this reason, groups fighting secularization often select names to reflect that they are the representatives of their faith, such as Hezbollah (Party of God), **Aum Shinrikyo** (The Supreme Truth), and Jund al-Haqq (Soldiers of Truth) (Ranstorp 1996).

Fourth, campaigns for justice can also motivate the formation of religiously inspired terrorist organizations. Societies, when threatened by powerful outsiders, may adhere to religious ideologies and rally their people by framing issues as existential threats to their community and sacred values (Hall 2013; Perliger & Pedahzur 2016). Traumatic events such as military invasions, brutal repressions by foreign powers, persecution, limited access to economic resources, social inequality, and living under colonialism can all serve as catalysts for seeking justice. By framing these hardships as a threat to their communities, religious leaders can initiate violent campaigns for addressing injustices by using their emotional connection with the society. These leaders use religion as a powerful moral tool, often citing religious scriptures, narratives, and beliefs to motivate their followers to take action for justice and social or political change. While earthly goals, such as the liberation of an occupied territory, are perceived as a top priority for a religiously motivated group's agenda, these groups often do not depict themselves as fighting for material gains. They see themselves as fighting a battle against the enemies of God; they see violence as prescribed and sanctified by God (Burstein 2018). Religious groups under this category have engaged in terroristic violence and retaliatory attacks in an attempt to force the foreign powers to withdraw from their territories. By participating in these groups, members are given an opportunity to exact vengeance against the sources of their grievances.

8.3 EXTREMISM IN JUDAISM

One of the first examples of the use of terrorism as a tactic is often attributed to a first-century Jewish political and religious group, commonly known as the **Jewish Zealots**. The term "zealot" (*Kanna'im* in Jewish) describes a person who is passionately devoted to a cause and is fanatical in pursuit of their religious ideals and generally refuses to compromise. Zealots strongly opposed the paganistic and polytheistic Roman rule in Palestine and were concerned about the religious and national future of Jewish people under this cosmopolitan culture. For the Zealots, it was unacceptable to be ruled by the Roman appointed leaders; the Jewish God of Israel was the only true ruler. The Zealots targeted not only the Romans but also Jews who were friendly with the Romans because for them, cooperation with Rome was equal to recognizing Caesar as lord, in place of God.

8.3.1 The Early Period: The Sicarii

Sicarii (from the Greek word sikarioi, meaning "Dagger Men"), a subgroup of Zealots, are known as the most extremist Jews, having engaged in assassinations and terrorist acts against the ruling Romans and their Jewish sympathizers. It is argued that the bloodthirsty reign of the Roman Empire and the appointment of Herod the Great as King of Judaea gave impetus for the emergence of the Sicarii. Further, the introduction of the Roman and Greek institutions, such as the gymnasium and the arena, and the idolatry use of images and trophies provoked the Jews, as these new places were found to be antagonistic to the spirit of Judaism. In their opposition to the Roman Empire, the Zealots, who emerged as a resistance group, were mainly inspired by religious motives. The group viewed itself as defenders of the Mosaic law and the Jewish nation.

Soon after Herod died, the Sicarii started an aggressive revolt against the rule of the Roman empire and its taxation (which they perceived as Roman enslavement) from 66 to 70 BCE, known as First Jewish-Roman War. They traveled in crowded public places, such as markets and theaters, and assassinated Roman soldiers and Jews who cooperated with the Romans. They used daggers called sicar (easily concealable short knifes) hidden beneath their cloaks, and then blended into the crowd to prevent detection. The Sicarii were also known to destroy storehouses of grains and wood to force the inhabitants of Jerusalem to fight against the Roman occupation, out of desperation.

FIGURE 8.2 The term "Sicarii" comes from the Latin word "sicarius," meaning "dagger-men" or "assassins." The Sicarii were known for their use of concealed daggers, which they used for assassinations and acts of insurgency against Roman authority and their collaborators. The daggers used by the Sicarii were typically small, easily concealable, and designed for close-quarters combat. They were often carried by individuals within their robes or clothing, allowing them to strike unexpectedly. These weapons were instrumental in the Sicarii's guerrilla tactics and targeted killings. *Source:* FotoGuy 49057, CC BY 2.0, via Wikimedia Commons.

The Sicarii, believing that their martyrdom would be rewarded by God, attacked and looted Jewish villages, destroyed property, slaughtered the highest priest (along with other priests) in the Temple Mount, led the destruction of the Jewish Temple and city of Jerusalem, and engaged in horrific acts, such as cutting off the hands of Roman prisoners. Further, the Sicarii were known to raid and massacre Jewish men, women, and children whom they considered as apostate and collaborators with the Romans. Due to their reign of terror, in the New Testament the Zealots are refereed as *lestes*, meaning bandits, robbers, and plunderers (Denova 2021).

The Zealots' revolt was unsuccessful, and Jerusalem again fell under the rule of the Romans. In the following years, Romans went after the remaining members of the Sicarii. A majority of the Sicarii had fled Jerusalem and settled in a fortress called Masada, after slaughtering the Roman troops stationed there. After three months of siege the Romans were able to breach the walls of Masada, but they had discovered that the Sicarii (approximately 1,000 men, women, and children) had committed mass suicide, rather than surrender to the Romans.

8.3.2 The Modern Period

Jewish terrorism during the modern period can be grouped into two main categories: (1) the anti-colonial wave (Zionist terrorism), and (2) the religious wave. During the anti-colonial wave, various Jewish groups (e.g., Irgun, Lehi, Haganah) committed acts of terrorism initially against the British mandate and then toward the Arab population in Palestine as a part of their national liberation struggle (i.e., to remove the British from Palestine) and goal of penetrating the Jewish communities in Muslim areas of Europe in their quest for a Jewish state. A majority of the violence that occurred during this time (1930s–1970s) was executed by secular Jewish Zionist groups. Scholars often categorize this period as Jewish political terrorism (Liebman 1983; Sprinzak 1987). During the religious wave (from the 1970s to date), most of the violence was directed at Palestinian Arabs by groups such as Gush Emunim (The Block of the Faithful), the Jewish Underground, and followers of the Kahane legacy with profoundly religious rhetoric, motivation, and objectives (Pedahzur & Perliger 2009). Some scholars also categorize this period as Jewish religious-nationalist terrorism, since most of the violence that occurred during this era included ethno-nationalist, political, and other factors along with a heavy focus on religious scriptures, rites, and motivations (Aran & Hassner 2013).

8.3.3 Gush Emunim (The Block of the Faithful)

Gush Emunim was an ultra-religious (and also nationalist) fundamentalist Zionist Jewish group, established by the followers of Rabbi Abraham Isaac Kook, the first chief Rabbi of Palestine, and organized around messianic ideas and the goal of creating Jewish settlements across Palestine. The group was established in 1974 to protest the American plan to return the territories captured by Jews back to the Arabs (withdrawal from Sinai and the Golan Heights), as demanded by a peace initiative (Newman 2013). Due to the nature of its mission, "the Land of Israel, for the people of Israel, according to the Torah of Israel," some scholars describe this group as the "Extreme Religious New Zionism" (Avruch 1979; Weissbrod 1982).

Acting according to religious scriptures, members of the group strongly believed that it was God's imperative for the Jews to have a sovereign state across the Land of Israel, as

FIGURE 8.3 The IDF evacuating illegal settlers sent to Judea and Samaria by the Gush Emunim movement. The Gush Emunim movement is a right-wing Israeli movement advocating for Jewish settlement in the West Bank and Gaza Strip, territories captured by Israel during the Six-Day War in 1967. Over the years Gush Emunim has been instrumental in establishing and expanding many Israeli settlements in these areas, often leading to tensions with Palestinians and the international community. *Source:* Asher Koralik/Dan Hadani collection/National Library of Israel/The Pritzker Family National Photography Collection, CC BY 4.0, via Wikimedia Commons.

defined in the Bible. Rabbi Kook, and later his son Rabbi Kook Junior, convinced their followers that the establishment of a Jewish state in Israel would lead to redemption and the start of the Messianic Era. The group had a divine imperative: to forcefully settle in the Land of Israel to fulfill their perceived God given right and bring the Messiah (Sprinzak 1987). They believed that this was an important sacred mission for all Jews that required devotion to the point of martyrdom, and thus no opposition should be tolerated. In a public announcement delivered in 1979, Rabbi Kook Junior stated: "We are commanded by the Bible, not by the government. The Bible overrides the government, it is eternal and this government is temporary and invalid" (Weissbrod 1982, 269).

Even though many secular and Orthodox Jews, and the former secular Israeli government led by the Labor Party, opposed the ideals of this movement, the group's message resonated among a large majority of the Jewish community (MacGilivray 2016). The new right-wing Likud party government boosted Gush Emunim members' efforts to start new settlements beyond the Israeli borders by actively supporting their efforts, providing military assistance and economic funds required for the new settlements (Weissbrod 1982). Many Jews volunteered to become settlers and joined the ranks of Gush Emunim by starting small communities near large Arab populations. They established illegal outposts in Palestinian territories as part of the strategy of settling Israelis in these areas. However, the groups started to disappear from the scene toward the mid-1980s, especially after Israeli police arrested many key members of Gush Emunim who were planning a major attack against the Arab population in the country and to destroy holy Muslim landmarks (e.g., Al-Aqsa Mosque and the Dome of the Rock) in 1984 (Sprinzak 1987).

8.3.4 The Followers of Kahane's Legacy (Kahanism) and the Jewish Defense League

Kahanism is another example of an ultra-religious, right-wing Jewish ideology based on the views of Rabbi Meir David Kahane, an American-born extremist Orthodox rabbi. Using the post-Holocaust slogan "Never Again," Rabbi Kahane formed the militant **Jewish Defense League (JDL)** in New York City in 1968, with the aim of uniting and protecting the Jewry in the United States. He argued that Jewish Americans were at the risk of another Holocaust, this time at the hands of African Americans and Hispanics. From late 1960s to mid-1970s, the JDL trained and armed its recruits and ran thuggish style patrols throughout the city under the guise of protecting vulnerable Jews from anti-Semitic acts. The group became known worldwide for starting a ruthless bombing campaign against Soviet targets in New York City to pressure the Soviet Union to allow the migration of Jews into other countries. The JDL attacked homes, torched cars, and bombed Soviet-owned buildings, such as the New York office of the Soviet Airline, Aeroflot, and the Soviet Cultural Building. The group also targeted high-profile Palestinians, Arabs, and Arab sympathizers in the United States. In 1971, after the JDL was designated as a terrorist group in the United States by the FBI and faced severe criminal persecution, Kahane and his family immigrated to Israel to avoid incarceration (Sprinzak 1991).

In Israel, Kahane formed a religious political party named "Kach" (Thus!), which had an apocalyptic agenda: expulsion of the Arab population from Israel and from the occupied Palestinian territories to hasten the imminent arrival of the Messiah. After three losses in general elections, Kahane entered the Israeli Parliament (Knesset) in 1984. There he delivered speeches throughout Israel, calling for the dissolution of Israel's democratic parliament and the establishment of a Jewish Theocracy ruled by strict interpretations of the Torah, Tanakh, and Talmud. He further argued that ethnic cleansing of Christian and Muslim Arabs in Israel was not only a necessity, but also an act of duty to God (Freidman 1986). Kahanists openly argued for a wide scale war in the Middle East—Jewish armies marching through neighboring countries, destroying churches and mosques, and forcing Christian and Muslims to abandon their beliefs or be killed (Magnusson 2021).

During his political career Kahane proposed several controversial bills, such as stripping non-Jews of their Israeli citizenship, subjecting non-Jews in Israel to extra taxes, and making sexual intercourse and marriage between Jews and Arabs illegal and punishable by law. Kahan strictly believed that Jews were God's chosen people and that they should not mix with non-Jews in any way (Ghanem & Khatib 2017). He delivered speeches stating, "The Arab is a cancer in our midst. And you don't co-exist with cancer. A cancer you either cut out and throw out or you die. Is better to have a Jewish state that is hated by the whole world than an Auschwitz loved by it" (Hasan 2021).

In 1985, the followers of Kahane murdered American Palestinian activist Alex Odeh via bombing in Los Angeles, because he had called for a two-state solution in Palestine. In 1986, Kahane introduced a draft law for demolishing the Al-Aqsa Mosque in Jerusalem. Once his attempts failed at the Knesset, he incited his followers to attack the al-Aqsa

FIGURE 8.4 Leader of the Kach right-wing movement Meir Kahane speaking before his followers in Tel Aviv. *Source:* Dan Hadani collection/National Library of Israel/The Pritzker Family National Photography Collection, CC BY 4.0, via Wikimedia Commons.

FIGURE 8.5 Clashes following the Ibrahim Mosque massacre. In 1994, a tragic event unfolded when Baruch Goldstein, a Jewish radical extremist, carried out a heinous massacre at the Ibrahim Mosque in Hebron. His brutal attack on praying Muslims resulted in the deaths of 29 Palestinians and left another 150 wounded. Goldstein, a resident of the Jewish enclave of Hebron known as Kiryat Arba, was associated with the racist and extreme right-wing Kach Party. Armed with a Galil rifle, he opened fire into the crowd, unleashing more than 100 bullets over several minutes. *Source:* Gideon Markowiz/Photographer: Israel Press and Photo Agency (I.P.P.A.)/Dan Hadani collection, National Library of Israel/CC BY 4.0, via Wikimedia Commons.

Mosque with the goal of rebuilding a Jewish Temple in its place. He encouraged his activists to assault and harass Palestinians. Due to his ultra-racist electoral rhetoric and overt extremism, in 1988, Kahane was banned from politics in Israel and his party, the Kach Movement, was barred from the 1988 Israeli parliament elections. Kahane was assassinated by an Egyptian American in 1990 while speaking to a crowd of Orthodox Jews during a Zionist conference at a New York City hotel (Friedman 1990; Pedahzur & Perliger 2009). However, his followers continued to carry out Kahane's violent and brutal legacy.

In 1994, soon after the Oslo Peace Accords were signed by Palestinian and Israeli officials in Washington, DC, Baruch Goldstein, a US-born Israeli military officer who adopted Kahanist ideology, committed the largest mass murder in Israeli history. Goldstein fired more than 100 rounds of bullets on Muslim worshippers at the Ibrahim Mosque in Hebron, in the West Bank, killing 29 and wounding more than 150, before he was beaten to death by the survivors (Ashrawi 2014). Some scholars argue that this incident was a major antecedent to the unending cycle of violence between the Arabs and Jews, as Palestinian groups started suicide bombing campaigns in retaliation against Kahane followers' brutal attacks on their communities. In 1994, following the Ibrahim Mosque attack, the Israeli government declared Kach (and also its offshoot, Kahane Chair) a terrorist organization (Pedahzur & Perliger 2009).

A year later, in 1995, Yigal Amir, a follower of Kahanist ideology and admirer of Goldstein, assassinated the liberal Israeli Prime Minister, Yitzhak Rabin, to stop the peace process with the Palestinians. Today, scholars argue that Kahane's legacy of religious fascism and racism are still alive and have been embraced by new radical movements (e.g., Kahane Was Right Movement) (Pedahzur 2012; Pedahzur & Perliger 2009). Kahanists have risen to powerful political positions and continue to promote Kahane's original extremist rhetoric, such as denying housing to Arabs and even condoning the murder of Arab children on the grounds that they may pose a threat to Jews in the future. The leading expert on Jewish right-wing and religious terrorism, Professor Ehud Sprinzak, explains, "Not a single Israeli I know has made a greater contribution to the brutalization of the nation and its public spirit than did Kahane" (Sprinzak 1990).

8.4 EXTREMISM IN CHRISTIANITY

Christian terrorists justify their atrocities through interpretations of the Bible and Christian scriptures, doctrines, and rituals, which are often different from those of conventional Christian traditions and beliefs. Notably, nonviolence, peace, and unconditional love are central to the teachings and basic tenets of religion of Christianity. Jesus himself was known to exemplify the virtue of nonviolence. According to the Bible, not only did he forbid revenge (e.g., an eye for an eye) but he also asked his followers to love their enemies. For example, Jesus commanded his followers to stop defending him as he was

FIGURE 8.6 Peter the Hermit, a charismatic preacher and religious figure, played a significant role in inciting the First Crusade. He fervently preached across Europe, rallying Christians to take up arms and reclaim the Holy Land from Muslim control. *Source:* Unknown author, public domain, via Wikimedia Commons.

arrested and tortured by the Romans, telling them "for all who draw the sword will die by the sword" (Matthew 26:52). Scholars often describe the religion of Christianity as "a faith rooted in absolute nonviolence" (Saiya 2022, 84).

However, the basic tenets of Christianity—peace and pacifism—were challenged with the start of the Holy Wars (i.e., the crusades) in the twelfth century, under the guise of spreading the Christian faith. During this era, violence in the name of God began to be viewed as a noble and sacred duty for devoted Christians. Religious authorities approved the conquering, persecution, and extermination of non-Christian societies. During the crusades that took place between the eleventh and thirteenth centuries, armies gathered by the Catholic Church committed violent atrocities in their attempt to liberate the Holy Land from those they perceived as infidels. This included massacring thousands of Jews, Muslims, and Heterodox Christians, setting fire to the Great Synagogue in Jerusalem, and partially destroying the al-Aqsa Mosque. Pope Urban II defended these killings, proclaiming that "God wills it" (Saiya 2022, 92). Similarly, during the Inquisition efforts that took place in Spain for more than 400 years starting in the late 1400s, tens of thousands of Jews and Muslims were brutally killed, and hundreds of thousands of them were forcefully exiled to other parts of the world. The Catholic monarchs justified these killings as a divine order from God to create a uniformly Christian Spain. Terrorism in the name of Christianity continued during the age of colonialism. Religious authorities provided spiritual approval for Protestant Christians' genocidal violence against the native inhabitants of the new territories across the world, from America to Africa and Asia.

Starting from the first acknowledged incident of Christian terrorism, the Gunpowder Plot, the following section will discuss how a religion based on the notion of complete nonviolence has been used by groups and individuals to incite terrorism and political violence. As is the case with the other major world religions, the religion of Christianity

FIGURE 8.7 Inquisition in Spain. Thousands of Jews and Muslims were burned at stakes during the inquisition headed by the Roman Catholic Church. *Source:* Wood engraving by H.D. Linton after Bocourt after T. Robert-Fleury. Wellcome Collection, public domain. Wellcome Collection. https://wellcomecollection.org/works/mjwa6gf4

contains movements, and individuals within them, that have engaged in violence, terrorizing racial and religious minorities and committing mass murders, kidnappings, and beheadings (Eichenwald 2015; Saiya 2022). Although the mainstream media does not provide it much coverage relative to Islamist-related terrorism (e.g., ISIS), violent Christian terrorism is a reality in several different parts of the world today, including the United States (Christian Identity movement), Africa (Lord's Resistance Army in Uganda), India (National Liberation Front of Tipura), Brazil (Soldiers of Jesus), and China (Eastern Lightning).

8.4.1 The Gunpowder Plot (Jesuit Treason)

The **Gunpowder Plot**, one of the first known examples of Christian terrorism, was a failed assassination attempt of King James of England in the sixteenth century. Organized by Roman Catholics in an attempt to end the English Protestant government and replace it with Catholic leadership, the group planned to blow up the English House of Lords (Parliament) with barrels of gunpowder during the re-opening of the Parliament in 1605. The plan was to kill the king, queen, and the current members of parliament to create an opportunity for a quick and easy takeover of the country by the English Catholics (Haynes 1994).

However, the massacre was prevented and the plot was revealed by an anonymous letter sent to Lord Monteagle, brother-in-law of one of the conspirators, warning him not to attend the November 5 gathering. Thanks to this warning, the plotter (Guy Fawkes) was arrested just before detonating the bomb with a fuse and box of matches. Thirty-six barrels of gunpowder (approximately 1.5 tons) were found hidden under the coal and wood in the basement of the Parliament building, more than enough to raze it. In the following weeks, the government captured and arrested all of the plotters and then executed them. Later, the Protestant government used the revelation of this ruthless plot to further persecute the Catholics in England. New anti-Catholic legislation was introduced, eliminating Catholics' rights to vote and run in elections and the recusancy law, which required all Catholics to attend the Anglican Church services, was enforced.

8.4.2 Lord's Resistance Army (LRA)

Headquartered in Uganda, the **Lord's Resistance Army (LRA)** is a terrorist organization established in the late 1980s with the goal of creating a new government based on Christianity's Ten Commandments. Initially started as a conflict between the Acholi people of

Northern Uganda (resisting colonialism) and the tribes of Southern Uganda (British supporters), the group embraced a religious outlook in 1986 with the establishment of the Holy Spirit Movement, led by Alice Lakwena. Lakwena preached that she was guided by God and that the Acholi people could overthrow the government of Uganda if they followed her messages from God. The Holy Spirit Movement was defeated by Ugandan troops in 1987. However, a Catholic altar boy, Joseph Kony, a distant relative of Lakwena, established the Lord's Resistance Army in 1988 (initially named the United Holy Salvation Army), a violent terrorist group, with the remnants of the Holy Spirit Movement.

Similar to Alice Lakwena, Kony preached that he was receiving messages directly from God and that God had tasked him to prepare an army to overthrow the current government and establish a Christian theocracy with the Ten Commandments as its constitution. The LRA heavily recruited child soldiers and carried out a violent indiscriminate terrorist campaign that included murder, torture, rape, and massacring of entire villages, completely disrupting life and spreading fear and insecurity in Uganda for almost two decades. Most of the violence at the hands of the LRA has been directed at Acholi communities, as Jospeh Kony failed to draw support among his own people for his mission. Kony is known to force LRA members to kill, mutilate, and rape Acholi people to discourage them from cooperating with the official government forces. The group also has a reputation for abducting thousands of children (estimated to be between 60,000 and 100,000) and women to use them as child soldiers and sex slaves (Cascais 2022). In 2005, the International Criminal Court in The Hague, Netherlands, issued arrest warrants against Joseph Kony and indicted him and his top commander team with 33 crimes, including sexual enslavement, rape, murder, forced enlisting of child soldiers, and intentionally directing attacks against civilians.

Even though the group leadership and many of its supporters were expelled from Uganda by the end of 2006—and is now spread out across remote border areas of South Sudan, Democratic Republic of Congo, and Central African Republic—the LRA still terrorizes local populations by attacking villages and forcefully recruiting child soldiers. Today the group acts similar to a criminal gang and finances its terroristic missions by slaughtering elephants (for the ivory trade), and through gold and diamond mining in Central Africa.

8.4.3 Soldiers of Jesus: The Neo Pentecostalist Evangelical Christian Violence

Soldiers of Jesus (Bonde de Jesus) is a violent neo-Pentecostalist terrorist organization in Brazil. Pentecostalism is a decentralized Protestant evangelical movement seeking to return Christianity to its original pure form as it was practiced in the Apostolic Age of the Early Church. The term "Pentecostal" comes from an incident described in the Bible—the Pentecost, the descent of the Holy Spirit upon the Apostles and followers of Jesus in Jerusalem. Pentecostals argue that all Christians should seek a postconversion experience that they describe as baptism with the Holy Spirit—repenting for their sins and accepting Jesus as their Lord and Savior to live a spirit filled life. They argue that once baptized, individuals may be given spiritual gifts by the Holy Spirit to perform miracles such as healing the sick, speaking in unknown tongues, and raising people from death. Several Pentecostal spiritual leaders have claimed to receive direct revelations from God. Loud praying via songs, intense

FIGURE 8.8 Invading five favelas, the Soldiers of Jesus created the Israel Complex, leading a holy war against their rivals. *Source:* chensiyuan, CC BY-SA 4.0, via Wikimedia Commons.

emotional experiences, divine healing by exorcism, and mass baptisms are common elements of evangelical worship services at Pentecostal churches (DW 2022). Pentecostals also have a strict behavior manual for individuals, especially for women, which forbids women from wearing pants, stipulates allowable lengths of skirts, and prohibits them from wearing make-up and going to the beach. Finally, monetary donations are an important part of Pentecostalism. Members are required to give their money in order to establish a close alliance with God.

Neo-Pentecostalism is currently the fastest growing denomination of the Protestant religion in Brazil. Experts argue that Pentecostalism has such a growing influence on all aspects of the society that Brazil, the world's largest Roman Catholic country, is expected to be completely evangelical by 2030 (DW 2022). A majority of members come from impoverished backgrounds with limited education. Beginning in the 1990s, Pentecostals entered Brazilian politics by offering church-endorsed candidates for various offices, most of the time their own bishops and pastors. Neo-Pentecostals view political participation as a religious duty, a spiritual war in which Pentecostals are fighting against demonic forces within the government. This Christian group has become a very powerful political force, proposing significant changes to Brazil's existing laws on sexuality and gender diversity (anti-LGBTQ+), family life (anti-abortion), and freedom of speech and worship. Evangelical churches within the Pentecostal movement operate drug-trafficking factions and paramilitaries that carry out attacks against the members of Catholic community in Brazil (Phillips, 2024).

Recently, the movement, with the help of narco-criminal groups (as a result of neo-Pentecostal missionary efforts on incarcerated gang members and drug lords) and paramilitary forces, invaded and seized control of five neighborhoods on the outskirts of Rio de Janeiro. There they established an independent zone, which they call Complexo do Israel (Israel Complex). Calling their armed forces "the Army of the Living God," the group established checkpoints around the Israel Complex to prevent the entry of Brazilian police and military, raised Israeli flags to the highest spots around the neighborhood (in reference to Pentecostal belief that the return of Jews back to Israel is a necessary step toward the return of Christ), and exercised control over approximately 130,000 residents. Casting themselves as defenders of Christ in a holy war, the group sells drugs and regulates social life in the complex by using violence to convert Catholics and people from other religions into Pentecostalism (Dalby 2020). Christian symbols are incorporated into their weapons, uniforms, and even on cocaine packages in the form of Israeli flag (the Star of David).

The group has waged a holy war against so-called evil, including Catholicism, Afro-Brazilian religions, and other minority religions viewed as Satan's work, and destroyed several Afro-Brazilian temples and Catholic institutions (Hinz et al. 2021). Afro-Brazilian celebrations have been outlawed in the complex and members of other religious groups have been subjected to murder campaigns and torture at the hands of Soldiers of Jesus (Phillips 2022). With no support or protection from the Brazilian government, several nonevangelical places of worship have been closed due to the threats and intimidation from Soldiers of Jesus. For example, in 2020, an Afro-Brazilian temple that was preparing to celebrate its 50th year in the area was burned to the ground and all of its sacred items were stolen by the Soldiers of Jesus. An article in the *Washington Post* indicates that Soldiers of Jesus engage in stoning children, murdering priests, raiding the houses of Catholics and Afro-Brazilians at night to forcefully convert people into their sect, and ransacking the property of anyone whose faith does not align with their own. They often force priests and religious figures to incinerate their churches and religious places by pointing a gun at their heads. They rationalize their violence by shouting, "All evil has to be undone in the name of Jesus!" (McCoy 2019).

8.4.4 The National Liberation Front of Tripura (NLFT)

The **National Liberation Front of Tripura (NLFT)** is a Baptist Christian terrorist organization operating in the Tripura region of India (Northeast India). Tripura is a region equal to the size of Northern Ireland. According to its 2022 census it has a population of over four million people, of which more than three million are Bengali Hindus. NLFT has been engaging in brutal violence following a militant Christian discourse since the late 1980s, with the ultimate goal of separating Tripura from India and establishing a Christian theocratic government in their territories. The NLFT is known to have zero tolerance for the other religions in India, which include Hindus, Sikhs, Muslims, Buddhists, Catholics, and Protestants. It calls its armed wing the "National Holy Army," and finances its armed activities through supplies of weapons and money provided by the Baptist Church of Tripura.

NLFT members are most known for their forced conversion of Bengali Hindu people (mostly villagers) to Christianity. Scholars note that this group engages in cruel methods including rape, torture, and killing as a means of intimidation to force Hindus and other religious minorities convert to their extreme form of Christianity. They have openly threatened to kill Hindus, the religious majority in India, and prevent them from celebrating their annual religious festivals. The NLFT desecrated Hindu religious institutions by painting their walls with Christian

FIGURE 8.9 The National Liberation Front of Tripura (NLFT) is a terrorist organization based in the northeastern Indian state of Tripura. Established with the aim of seceding from India and establishing an independent Tripuri state, the NLFT has been involved in various acts of terrorism, including bombings, assassinations, and extortion. *Source:* Germenfer, CC0 1.0 Universal Public Domain Dedication, Via Wikimedia.

symbols (crosses) using blood and they have kidnapped and executed several prominent Hindu religious leaders who resisted attempts to force their conversion to Christianity (Adam et al. 2007).

8.4.5 Eastern Lightning: The Church of the Almighty God

Eastern Lightning (Dongfang Shandian), also known as the Church of Almighty God, is a highly secretive, organized, and violent Christian terrorist organization founded in the Henan Province of China in 1990. At the time of writing, the group is estimated to be active in at least 20 provinces across China and have about three to four million members. Acting with an apocalyptic (doomsday) focus, the followers of the group believe that the world is coming to an end, and they have a religious duty to kill as many "demons" as possible. The group is led by a former physics teacher, Zhao Weishan, who calls himself the "Highest Priest," claiming to receive direct revelations from God to prepare people for the apocalypse.

The group believes that God showed himself in three different eras throughout world history, first as "Jehovah," then as "Jesus Christ," and now as "Lightning (Almighty God)"—a thirty-year-old nondescript Chinese female Messiah who currently lives in the Henan Province of China. According to the group, the world is now in its final stage, which they describe as "the Age of Kingdom." They claim that the authority of the Bible is over and all believers should follow the female Messiah and dispose of their Bibles (as they are outdated). The followers are taught that all existing Christian denominations and sects have lost the true meaning of the Holy Spirit and that mankind can be saved from their sins and made fully clean only through the teachings of the female Messiah. They also call their followers to engage in an apocalyptic struggle against the ruling Communist Party in China, which they refer to as the "great red dragon" (Hume 2015). Eastern Lightning appeals to many in China who are dissatisfied with the ruling government.

Eastern Lightning has carried out deadly attacks against thousands of nonbeliever individuals in China, including prominent church leaders. They have engaged in financial inducement, beatings, poisoning, kidnappings, bribing, intense brainwashing, and blackmailing with sexual entrapments to recruit new members. They use poison for most of their killings, as it is harder to trace and thus many murders are ruled as natural causes (Shea 2013). The group reaches out to church leaders and offers them large sums of money and other financial benefits to lead their congregation into their church. If they are unsuccessful, they try to lure the pastors into fornication with attractive women and then secretly take photographs and videos to blackmail them into accepting the teachings of Eastern Lightning. If they can't lure the pastors into sexual temptation, they kidnap them and then take their photographs with nude girls after drugging them, using the compromising photographs as a threat if they still resist the group's conversion efforts (Shea, 2013).

Eastern Lightning's primary recruits come from the poor, middle-aged Christian homemakers, and members of underground house churches (illegal religious meeting groups in China). The followers of the Eastern Lightning travel door to door and ask people, especially housewives whose husbands are migrant workers and spend most of the year in cities working at factories, to join their group and leave their children, husbands, and property behind or they will be punished by God with a fatal disease or another form of deadly judgment. Once they join the group, members live in communes and follow the group's way of life with total devotion, which requires them to donate all of their savings to the group's purpose. Reports indicate that the group blinds, impairs, or removes the tongues and ears of individuals who refuse to accept the teachings of the Church of Almighty God or try to leave the group (Hong, 2017). For example, in 2014, a woman who refused to listen to the preaching of Eastern Lightening members while eating at a McDonald's was brutally beaten to death inside the restaurant, in front of a large crowd. The killers, who were all caught and later executed by the Chinese government, stated without remorse that the victim was a demon and had an evil spirit (Hume 2015).

Reports from the region also indicate that thousands of women and members of house churches vanished in the last decade, and no one knows whether they were converted into Eastern Lightning or killed. As Dennis Balcombe, an American pastor who preaches in China, explains, "[Eastern Lightning] are extremely violent and use sex to try to convert people. I have heard stories of people being burned, beaten, and told to kill their children" (Shea 2013).

8.4.6 Christian Extremism and Terrorism in the United States

Extremist Christian groups have also shown their capacity for violence, fanaticism, and terrorism in the United States. For the purposes of this section, violence committed in the name of Christianity in the United States has been grouped in to two main categories: (1) anti-abortion violence, and (2) anti-minority violence.

The Army of God (AOG)

The **Army of God (AOG)** is a Christian fundamentalist terrorist organization that has been active in the United States since the 1980s. The group is composed of a wide network of Christians who openly promote massive property damage (through bombings and arson) and brutal killings of abortion providers, medical staff who assist with abortion procedures, and, more recently, killings of LGBTQ+ individuals. Viewing God as the general of their so-called army, the group cites verses from the Bible in defense of their killings. The group leadership developed and posted online a guide on how to make bombs and carry out arson and acid attacks against abortion clinics (Mason 2002).

The group, which views itself as "pro-life," encourages its followers to stop abortion at all costs through the murder of physicians, clinic workers, and other staff. The AOG initially began by vandalizing and invading facilities, harassing doctors and nurses, and blocking women's access to abortion clinics. It carried out its first deadly attack in 1993, when navy veteran Michael Griffin shot and killed David Gunn, an abortion provider in Pensacola, Florida. Since then, the AOG has been distributing "Wanted" posters in print and online that advertise the names, photographs, home addresses, and phone numbers of abortion providers in the United States and encourage their murder by AOG followers. Gunn was murdered as a result of such a poster distributed at a Pro-Life rally in Alabama. A leading follower of the Army of God defended the murderer of Gunn, stating, "He didn't shoot Mother Teresa, he shot a mass murderer such as Saddam Hussien [sic] or Hitler. I don't even think it is accurately termed 'murder.' God is the only one who knows whether Gunn would ever have repented or if he would have killed another 5,000 babies and probably three or four women who probably weren't Christians either" (Bader & Baird-Windle 2015).

FIGURE 8.10   A "Wanted" poster distributed by Army of God reads "Tiller the Killer, Dr. Death . . . Wanted by God". *Source:* https://feminist.org/wp-content/uploads/2020/06/exhibit-d.jpg.

FIGURE 8.11   Rev. Donald Spitz is a controversial figure known for his extreme anti-abortion views and activism. He has been involved with various anti-abortion organizations and has gained attention for his provocative and confrontational tactics in promoting his beliefs. *Source:* RevSpitz, CC BY-SA 3.0, via Wikimedia Commons.

The group's radical Pentecostal leader Rev. Donald Spitz is also known to publish anti-Black racist writings to incite violence among his followers. For example, in 2002, Spitz posted sensationalist, fabricated stories on the group's official website, such as "White woman carjacked, raped, and executed by African-Americans," "NAACP calls for the murder of police officers," and "[African Americans say] let's rape these white girls, kill them and throw them off the bridge" (SPLC 2022).

Recently, Spitz made highly critical statements about the US government, accusing its leaders of failing to uphold Christian values. For example, after Eric Rudolph—the 1996 Olympic Park bomber who was also involved in a series of bombing attacks against abortion clinics, gay bars, police officers, and doctors—was captured by the police in 2003, Spitz delivered a speech saying, "this is an example of our government taking the side of the abortionists to persecute the Christians." He called Eric Rudolph and other followers of the AOG "martyrs" and described their actions as "justifiable murders," and has provided financial help for indicted members of the AOG over the last two decades (Whyte 2018). Spitz said that the biggest problem that these "martyrs" are facing "is not regret, nor any kind of Christian remorse for breaking the commandment that thou shalt not kill—it's their close proximity to homosexual sex in prison" (Whyte 2018).

In 2022, several Army of God members reunited publicly at the

ReAwaken America gathering in New York, spearheaded by retired Army general and former advisor to Donald Trump, Michael Flynn. Similar to the Army of God, ReAwaken America uses religious rhetoric ("They hate you because they hate Jesus") to encourage its followers to join in spiritual warfare to restore the nation's Christian roots. The group practices mass baptism where thousands of members, one by one, enter a large metal tub filled with water, escorted by a pastor, to "put on the whole armor of God." ReAwaken America incites violence by spreading misinformation, making

FIGURE 8.12 Protests by Army of God members during abortion doctor George Tiller's funeral services at College Hill United Methodist Church. *Source:* Allen Graham, PDImages/Shutterstock.

claims such as "immigrants are taking your place," "vaccines are creating a genocide," "homosexuals are sinful people who don't honor God," and "Democrats are baby-butchering mongrels," and arguing that Christians need to act to save the country from these demonic forces (Smith & Lardner 2022).

Christian Identity

Christian identity (also known as Identity Christians) is a religious, anti-Semitic, and racist extremist Protestant group that operates across hundreds of small churches in every region of the United States and in some other English-speaking countries including Canada, England, Ireland, Australia, and South Africa. Even though the membership of Christian Identity has declined in the past decade, the group's ideology has been instrumental in radicalizing existing neofascist extremist groups.

Origins of Christian Identity go back to nineteenth-century England, to the Protestant members of the Church of England and an idea known as Anglo-Israelism (also known as British-Israelism), which argues that Anglo-Saxons and Germans are the true descendants of the biblical Lost Tribes of Israel. The modern doctrine of Christian Identity, however, developed from the so-called two-seed line theory. According to this theory, there are two lines of descendants from Eve. The first one consists of the offspring of Eve and Adam, the sons Abel and Seth. The second one comes from Eve's affair with the Serpent (Satan) in the gardens of Eden, and thus their son, Cain.

Christian Identity followers argue that the Jews came from Cain. In other words, they are Satan's descendants. Arguing that Jews are children of Satan, adherents of this movement believe that European descended White people are the true Israelites, God's servants and chosen people, favored by God with promises made in the Bible. Christian Identity followers cite verses from the Bible (e.g., John 8:44, "You [Jews] belong to your father, the devil, and you want to carry out your father's desires") as a justification of their hatred of Jewish people. Due to this belief, adherents of Christian Identity have a hostile attitude toward American evangelical Protestants and other Christian fundamentals because they reject the belief that the return of Jewish people to Israel is essential for the fulfillment of the end-time prophecy (the second coming of the Messiah) (SPLC 2022). They also view other races as subhuman, arguing that God created non-Whites out of mud without souls, before he created Adam and Eve (ADL 2017). They argue that the true Israelites (White European people) are rightfully entitled to the divine promises mentioned in the Bible. Finally, Identity Christians believe in millenarism, that the world is in its final stages and Jesus Christ will return after a period of tribulation in which the White race will battle the Jews. Unlike evangelicals in the US, Identity Christians view the apocalypse as a racial holy war and themselves as God's soldiers (ADL 2017).

Since they view themselves as the true Israelites, Identity Christians read the Hebrew Bible, celebrate Jewish holidays, and follow strict Jewish religious rules (e.g., dietary restrictions such as not eating pork). The Southern Poverty Law Center describes Christian Identity as the most radical Christian group in the country due to its extreme governmental ideologies. Followers of Christian Identity reject the authority and legitimacy of the US government and law enforcement agencies, as the adherents of the group believe that the country is run by Jews. These ideas led group members to isolate themselves from mainstream society and live in smaller groups with likeminded individuals in obscure communes, such as Elohim City in Oklahoma (ADL 2017). Today, a majority of the Christian Identity members live in areas of the country that have few Jewish and non-White people, such as the Ozarks, northern New England, and the Midwest, and withdraw themselves from mainstream society.

A notable example of such a communal group is the Covenant, the Sword, and the Arm of the Lord (CSA). Until a 1985 siege by the FBI, CSA members lived on a farm in Arkansas and prepared their recruits for the imminent doomsday. They believed that the United States was a Zionist-occupied government, and in 1983 they published a manifesto openly calling for a war against the government for "the Advancement of Christ's Kingdom." Since their emergence in the United States during the 1970s the CSA has influenced several anti-government movements in the nation and as well as dozens of White nationalist terrorist attacks, including hate crimes, synagogue bombings, mass shootings, and murders.

FIGURE 8.13 The 1995 bombing of the Alfred P. Murrah Federal Building is noted as the nation's deadliest domestic terrorist attack, which inspired a generation of hate-filled extremists. *Source:* NASA employee, public domain, via Wikimedia Commons.

The Identity Christians are well-known for their connection to Timothy McVeigh, who carried out the April 1995 truck bombing attack against the Alfred P. Murrah Federal Building in Oklahoma City, killing 168 (including 19 children who were staying at the daycare facility in the building) and injuring approximately 900 individuals. The attackers used a rental truck containing a homemade bomb composed of agricultural fertilizer and fuel oil to destroy the federal building.

For several years the incident was known as the nation's worst single act of domestic terrorism in terms of the number of casualties (only superseded by the September 11 attacks). The US media initially depicted this bloody attack as an Islamist terrorist attack and created widespread anti-Muslim outrage throughout the nation for more than two days. However, the arrest of two military veterans of the Persian Gulf War, Timothy McVeigh and Terry Nichols, presented the American public with a difficult realization that the perpetrators were Christian Identity followers who perceived the destruction as a justifiable attack against the US government and death of innocent individuals as a collateral damage.

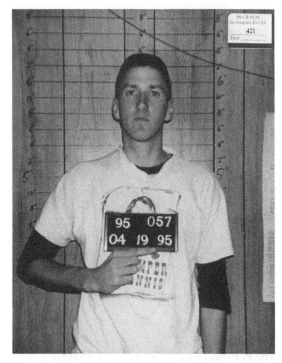

FIGURE 8.14　Mugshot of Timothy McVeigh, one of the two conspirators of the Oklahoma City Bombing of 1995. *Source:* United States Federal Government, public domain, via Wikimedia Commons.

Even though McVeigh has never publicly acknowledged his connections to Christian Identity, law enforcement officials linked him to the group based on three discoveries: McVeigh's explicit praise of *The Turner Diaries*, a book commonly read and distributed by Christian Identity followers; McVeigh's former connections to the Christian Identity compound in Elohim City, Oklahoma (Wexler 2015); and the importance of the attack date, April 19, which is shared with the anniversaries of two notable federal government acts against the Christian Identity group. On April 19, 1993, the FBI raided and burned down the heavily armed religious Branch-Davidian Compound at Waco, Texas, and Christian Identity follower Richard Snell was executed on April 19, 1995. McVeigh later claimed during the trials that he had carried out this massacre to avenge the killings of more than 70 Christian Identity members by the FBI at the Waco siege. To further justify his killings, he also cited additional government acts abroad and within the US, including the death of Iraqi civilians in the Gulf War and the 1992 killing of Randy Weaver's wife and son by federal agents during the Ruby Ridge standoff. Weaver was a religious White supremacist who was modifying assault weapons for White nationalist groups (Wexler 2015). In a letter that he sent to one of his friends while waiting for his execution, McVeigh wrote:

> Borrowing a page from US foreign policy, I decided to send a message to a government that was becoming increasingly hostile, by bombing a government building and the government employees within that building who represent that government.

FIGURE 8.15 The 51-day standoff between the FBI and the cult members ended in a fire and deaths of 80 members of the Branch Davidian compound in Waco, Texas, in 1993. *Source:* United States Government, public domain, via Wikimedia Commons.

Bombing the Murrah federal building was morally and strategically equivalent to the US hitting a government building in Serbia, Iraq, or other nations . . . culminating in the Waco incident, federal actions grew increasingly militaristic and violent, to the point where at Waco, our government—like the Chinese—was deploying tanks against its own citizens . . . It was in this climate then, that I reached the decision to go on the offensive—to put a check on government abuse of power where others have failed in stopping the federal juggernaut run amok. (McVeigh 2001)

The Phineas Priesthood (Phineas Priests)

The **Phineas Priesthood** is an American domestic terrorist organization in which adherents follow a religious ideology based on a story found in the Old Testament, "the Phineas action." According to the story, a Midianite prophet, known as Balaam, encouraged women to seduce the men of Israel by tempting them to commit adultery and forget the commandments of God. Under the influence of these beautiful women, several Jews were plunged into sexual immorality and began to believe in a Midianite pagan god, participating in ritualistic sexual practices. These sinful acts were thought to have invoked God's wrath and as a punishment, God inflicted a deadly plague upon the Jewish people. God told Moses (in Numbers 25: 4–5) that the only way to save his tribe from this plague was to kill all of the men who participated in this sinful behavior. While Moses was conveying God's command to his followers in an assembly, an Israeli man named Zimri openly defied these orders by taking a Midianite princess into his tent to have sexual encounter with her. Phineas (who would later be the first highest priest of Israel), in accordance with God's command, grabbed a spear and killed this interfaith couple in their tent. Due to Phineas's righteous act (Numbers 25:11-13), God ended the plague against the Israelites and rewarded Phineas and his family with a covenant of peace and a permanent priesthood.

Several individuals in the United States, following an idea that originated in a 1990 book *Vigilantes of Christendom: The Story of the Phineas Priesthood* by White supremacist author Richard Kelly Hoskins, interpret Phineas's brutal actions as God's order to kill interracial couples. Hoskins describes this Biblical event in his book as God's calling of his devoted believers to murder "race-mixers" and their friends. Hoskins describes several characters in his book who have, throughout the centuries, committed violent atrocities in order to defend God's law: the purity of races. The followers of this ideology believe in a religious justification for their violent behavior—that they will be rewarded by God if they murder interracial couples. Similar to Christian identity adherents, Hoskins describes the Jews of today as the descendants of Eve and Satan and claims that White people are the real descendants of the biblical Jews. Some argue that Phineas Priesthood is a form of Christian Identity movement. In his book Hoskins also describes his mission of opposing homosexuality and abortion, along with outlawing racial "interbreeding" and encouraging people to seek revenge for crimes committed against the White race by following the Biblical example of Phineas (Rosin 1999).

The Phineas Priesthood is not an actual organization or group, as there is no leader, governing body, or membership process. Despite that, adherents have engaged in several violent acts including bank robberies, abortion clinic bombings, newspaper publisher bombings, attacks on Jewish facilities, and plans to blow up FBI buildings across the country. Most recently, in 2014, a Texas man named Larry McQuilliams, who described himself as "the highest priest in the fight against anti-God people," shot more than 100 rounds of bullets into buildings in downtown Austin (a federal courthouse and police station) and also tried to burn down the Mexican consulate. After the incident police discovered the book *Vigilantes of Christendom* in McQuilliams's car, along with a list of 34 other targets marked on a map that he had planned to attack (Holpuch 2014).

The Concerned Christians

Founded by Monte Kim Miller in 1985 in Denver, Colorado, **Concerned Christians** is a doomsday cult and a terrorist organization that has planned to carry out violent terrorist activities to hasten the second coming of the Messiah (Center for Israel Education 1999). Miller, who worked as a marketing executive at Proctor & Gamble, considered himself the end-time prophet of God and urged his followers to take Christianity back to its apocalyptic roots and declare all existing Christian churches and denominations corrupt. Through his radio programs and biweekly newspaper, Miller repeatedly attacked the Orthodox Catholic Church and the World-Faith movement, as well as evangelical Christian doctrines (Leppäkari 2014). The group is also known for their mission to forcefully convert all Jews to Christianity and expel Muslims from Israel (Center for Israel Education 1999; Henderson 2015). He claimed that he was the modern-day incarnation of Christ and that he channels messages from God regarding current issues. Miller is also known to have collected large sums of donations from his followers, considered spiritual extortion (Kenworthy 1999; Rosin 1998). According to witness testimonies, he would demand donations. His followers explained that "refusal to pay would result in not only the family, but also the attendees of their Bible study, going to hell" (Barker 2021). Further, in 1996, Miller instructed his followers to prepare to die for God: "Jesus Christ died on the cross and we have a duty to die. The Lord's judgment has been with the Earth for 2,000 years and now judgment is ready to begin" (Rosin 1998).

According to Miller, the United States is led by Satan, the apocalypse will be soon, and his followers are the only true Christians in the world. In 1998, Miller prophesized two future incidents to his followers through his radio program, *Our Foundation*. First, he was one of the two witnesses of Revelation 11, and he would be violently killed in the streets of Jerusalem toward the end of 1999 but would be resurrected three days later (Rosin 1998). Second, a big earthquake would wipe Denver off the map on October 10, 1998, and the occurrence of this destruction would be a "Gathering message" from God for the true believers. Shortly after this announcement, 72 members of the Concerned

Christians abandoned their homes and belongings and disappeared from their jobs, family members, and friends. American officials, unaware of the group members' whereabouts, warned Israel and Mexico that the group members may travel there to escape the prophesized destruction of Denver and fulfill Miller's violent apocalyptic prophesy (Kenworthy 1999).

On January 3, 1999, Israeli authorities arrested 14 members of the group (including children) in Jerusalem on charges that group was planning to carry out a bloody confrontation with law enforcement officers to instigate the second coming of Christ. After the official interrogation, Israeli authorities declared that the Concerned Christians were about to start a gunfight with Israeli police in the Old City, where they believe the tomb of Jesus lies. They also planned to destroy Islamic and Jewish Holy sites such as the Al-Aqsa Mosque and Temple Mount, which they believed must be destroyed to start the return of Jesus Christ (Center for Israel Education 1999). All of the group members were deported from Israel to United States on January 5, 1999. Back home, the group members stayed at a downtown hotel in Denver and refused to talk to anyone, including the police; they severed their ties with their family members and prepared themselves for the final days of the world. The members denied all the allegations made against them by the Israeli officials (Leppäkari 2014).

8.5 EXTREMISM IN ISLAM

Of the Abrahamic religions, Islam is most often conflated with terrorism, even though its central message is similar to those of Judaism and Christianity—peace. Western politicians and the media are often quick to sensationalize acts of terrorism that claim to be committed in the name of Islam; however, they often fail to label the same acts as terrorism when committed by Christians (Johnson 2017). As we present the topic of Islamist terrorism, it is important to keep in mind that terrorism is not in the province of any specific religion and individuals have carried out violent atrocities in the name of all religions.

This section will discuss the causes and consequences of violent atrocities that were committed in the name of Islam. We will look in detail at Salafism, a key movement that emerged in the nineteenth century that influences the radical Islamist terrorism witnessed in the twenty-first century. We will first provide an overview of the main sects within the religion of Islam to provide context for the emergence of Salafism.

Soon after the death of the Islamic Prophet Muhammed in 632 CE, Muslims split into two sects, the Sunnis and the Shias (or Shiites), over a dispute about who should lead the Muslim community. A smaller group of Muslims argued that the political and religious succession for the guidance of the Muslim community should stay with the prophet Muhammed's descendants. They argued that the son-in-law and cousin of prophet Muhammad, a young apostle, Ali ibn Abi Talib, should be the new leader. The majority of Muslims, on the other hand, based on the prophet Muhammed's teachings and lifestyle, argued that the legitimate religious authority had to be elected by the Muslim community, rather than following a succession of bloodline in prophet's family. They offered a candidate, Abu Bakr, who had demonstrated leadership qualities and was one of the older apostles in the Prophet Muhammed's close circle. Over time, supporters of Ali came to be known as Shia (or Shiite) and those who supported Abu Bakr became known as Sunnis. Historians often compare this split in Islam to the Great Schisms of

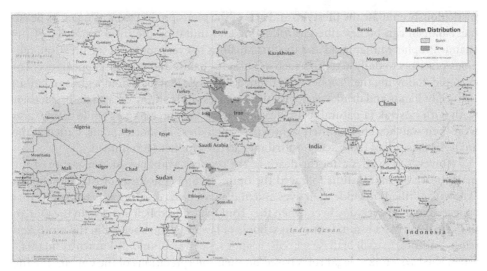

FIGURE 8.16   The global distribution of Sunni and Shia Muslims. *Source:* United States Central Intelligence Agency (1995). Muslim distribution: Islamic countries. Map Library of Congress.

1054, when Christians were divided into two, as Orthodox Christians considered Jesus Christ to be the head of the church, whereas Catholics accepted the Pope as the absolute authority over the Church (BBC 2013).

Even though this divide started purely out of a political dispute over leadership succession, over time, as these two groups showed hostilities and continued to separate from each other into distinct communities, they developed major theological differences. Today, Sunnism and Shiism are still the two main sects of the Islamic tradition. According to a 2015 report by Pew Research Center, there are more than 1.8 billion Muslims in the world, and the overwhelming majority of Muslims practice the Sunni strand (Pew Research Center 2017).

8.5.1 Salafism (Salafi Movement)

Salafism is a contemporary Sunni Islamist school of thought that emerged during the late nineteenth and early twentieth centuries. The word *"salaf"* comes from the Arabic saying *"al-salaf al-salih,"* meaning "the pious predecessors," which is often used to describe the first three generations of Muslims. According to Islamic resources, Prophet Muhammed said, "the best people are those living in my generation (Prophet Muhammad and his companions who directly learned from the Prophet), then the ones who come after them (the followers), then those who followed them [followers of the followers]." Collectively, these three generations are known as Salaf in the Islamic world. Based on this text, some Islamic scholars argue that the first three generations of Muslims were the best ones the religion has ever seen. They called these generations the "pious predecessors," who are believed to live and exemplify the purest, pristine, and most correct version of Islam.

Originating from this saying, the followers of the modern-day Salafi movement argue that to recreate the most authentic form of Islam, they must follow and meticulously emulate the lifestyles and acts of the pious predecessors as much as possible. Salafism can be described as following and imitating the lived examples of the Islamic Prophet Muhammad and the first Muslims in every sphere of the life, from religious practices to daily activities such as culinary habits and outward appearance. For example, following the Prophet Muhammed's lifestyle, Salafists hold a glass or cup in their right hands and drink water with three pauses while sitting on a chair, brush their teeth with miswak (a natural teeth cleaning twig), use three fingers while eating, and wear their watches only on their right wrists; men dress in shorter pants, cuffed at the ankle, because all of these acts are attributed to the Prophet Muhammed.

However, centuries after the death of the prophet Muhammed, a majority of the mainstream Sunni Muslims followed the opinions and consensus of Islamic scholars (known as ijtihad) to guide their lives and find answers to contemporary questions that appeared in their everyday lives, when they couldn't find explicit answers in the Qur'an or in tradition. As a result, four main schools of law in Islam emerged in the ninth and tenth centuries. In each of these schools, Islamic scholars, commonly known as "ulama," established systemized legal rules based on their interpretations of the Qur'an, the life and practices of Prophet Muhammed, and the first Muslims to cover all possible social, economic, political, and legal situations. For centuries, these laws regulated the social and religious lives of Muslims, from marriage and divorce, to trade, punishments, conduct of war, inheritance, and administration of the state (Meleagrou-Hitchens 2018).

However, unlike the majority of Sunni Muslims, Salafists questioned and rejected the consensus provided by the Islamic scholars over the centuries simply because they appeared later than the pious predecessors. Salafists view these opinions as heretic and hold the perspective that mainstream Islam has been corrupted by these new interpretations and practices. Instead, being inspired by the teachings of the fourteenth-century scholar Ibn Taymiyya (1263–1328), Salafists rely on literal interpretations of only two original sources (regardless of time and context) to guide their lives and purify their religion: (1) the Qur'an, and (2) the sayings and traditions of the Prophet Muhammed. While mainstream Sunni Muslims accept the guidance of Islamic scholars, according to Salafists, any information that is not directly found in scriptural evidence, such as the interpretations of Islamic scholars, is invalid (Wagemakers 2016).

It should be noted that Salafism emerged largely in response to European colonialism and the occupation of Muslim lands in the Middle East and North Africa during the late nineteenth century. The group holds hostility toward Western imperialism and culture. The followers of the Salafist movement believe that by following the lifestyles of Salaf and the writings of the Scriptures in their own lives, they can recreate the golden ages of Islam by stripping it from all the heretics, including the four schools of law which emerged in the late ninth century.

8.5.2 Is Salafism Linked Extremist and Terrorist Activity?

During the last 50 to 60 years, Salafism inspired several groups across the Middle East and North Africa. However, Salafists are not a homogenous group, and they constitute a minority among the general Muslim population. Experts estimate that less than 1 percent of all Muslims in the world follow Salafist ideology (Parvez 2017b). Salafists encompass a large variety of beliefs that range from the goal of purifying Islam to the strict application of the Sharia law (religious rules derived from the Qur'an and the deeds and sayings of the Prophet Muhammed) and encouraging a fight against non-Muslims who are seen as occupying Muslim lands. For this reason, Western scholars often categorize Salafists into three distinct groups:

1. quietist: a group that focuses on religious education and missionary activities, staying away from worldly politics;
2. political Salafists: a group that favors activism and political participation;
3. jihadists: a very small group within the Salafists that uses military action when deemed necessary to oppose apostate rulers of Muslim countries and invading forces.

Some jihadist Salafists argue that the problems with Muslim society today are the result of the Western secularization attempts and thus Muslim societies have to be ruled by the laws set by God (Allah) in the Qur'an in order to flourish again. If the ruling government does not follow the Scripture or does not accept the sovereignty of God, they recommend that their followers excommunicate the officials and build forces to fight against secular Muslim rulers. Salafists in this group also believe that leaders of Muslim states deserve to be killed for their application of man-made laws, instead of using the laws of Sharia (Wagemakers 2016).

Even though it constitutes a very small group among Muslims, Salafism has become a topic of increased interest among scholars and researchers from varied fields during the last two decades. This is because extreme jihadist groups such as ISIS and al-Qaeda have claimed to be ideologically inspired by certain components of this movement. An increased number of state leaders, politicians, and journalists in the United States and across the West have equated the Salafist tradition to an ideology that favors or justifies terrorism and political violence, citing the Salafist tradition's conservative aspects, such as Sharia law, and specifically views that challenge the many liberal values of the West, such as gender equity (Fahmi 2020).

On the other hand, scholars have warned political officials and the media that it is dangerous to equate people's religious faith and practices to terrorism, as the majority of Salafists refute the teachings of Salafist Jihadists and perceive groups such as ISIS and al-Qaeda as deviant outliers (Meleagrou-Hitchens 2018). Further, such an approach not only offends Salafists worldwide, but it also fuels hatred and fear toward Muslims everywhere by casting suspicion on all Muslims, as we have witnessed from bloody mosque shootings across the US, Canada, and Australia. Most importantly, viewing Salafism as a breeding source of terrorism leads us to a serious misunderstanding of the factors and drivers that lead individuals into extremist groups (Coolsaet 2016; Haner et al. 2020; Parvez 2017a). To more effectively fight against the drivers of violent extremism, we have to scrutinize the context—the certain environments and historical moments that gave rise to radical interpretation of Islam.

8.5.3 Al-Qaeda

Al-Qaeda (also known as The Base) is a Salafist Jihadi terrorist organization founded by Osama bin Laden in the late 1980s. The Soviet invasion of Afghanistan in the late 1970s and the subsequent support provided to the Afghan **Mujahideen** by the United States played an important role in the emergence of al-Qaeda. Toward the end of 1979, approximately 30,000 Soviet troops entered Afghanistan to defend the Afghan communist government—the pro-Soviet regime which had come to power by toppling the demo-cratically elected government in 1978—against the anti-communist Muslim fighters. With the economic and military support of the Soviet Union, the Afghan communist regime carried out a purge of the anti-communist population, commonly known as Mujahideen (meaning those who engage in jihad).

In response to this, the United States, as the adversary of the Soviet Union during the Cold War, provided economic, military, and training support to the Mujahideen, which helped the rebellion grow across the countryside of Afghanistan. In this context, the US government (via the CIA Operation Cyclone) funded the production of millions of textbooks and news articles (for Afghan school-aged children and Muslims across the world) that glorified jihad and martyrdom as a religious obligation against the enemies of Islam. In response to this, thousands of young Muslim volunteers (mostly Arabs) trav-eled to Afghanistan to fight against the Moscow-backed communist regime in Kabul. Over time, the Afghan Mujahideen, along with the foreign fighters who joined them, became successful in neutralizing the Soviet military control in the country. In 1988, after 10 years of bloodshed, the Soviet Union signed an accord with the United States and Afghanistan agreeing to fully withdraw its troops from the invaded territories (Davis 2002; Hansen 2007).

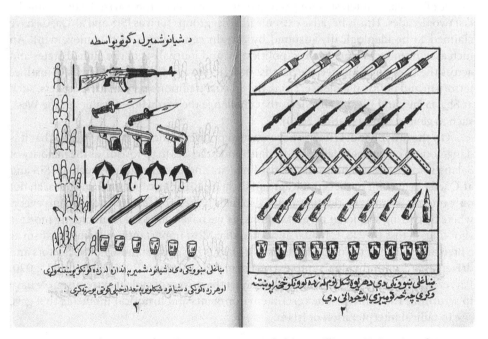

FIGURE 8.17 In the 1980s, the US government awarded $60 million to University of Ne-braska at Omaha to produce children's books for Afghan kids, urging them to take up arms against Russians. These books glorified jihad by repeatedly saying "Jihad is the kind of war that Muslims fight in the name of God to free Muslims and Muslim lands from enemies of Islam. If infidels invade, jihad is the obligation of every Muslim". *Source:* Pashto and Math, Grade 1, Ar-chives and Special Collections, Dr. C. C. and Mabel L. Criss Library, University of Nebraska at Omaha.

The war ended, but there were two major consequences for the stability of the region and the world. Thousands of young Muslims had traveled to conflict zones to liberate Afghanistan from the Soviet communist regime, as several of them developed extremist views; as well-trained fighters with years of experience fighting Russian soldiers, they returned to their home countries after the withdrawal of the Soviet Union from Afghanistan. Two important individuals emerged from this war: (1) a well-educated young Saudi billionaire who was born into one of the country's wealthiest families, Osama bin Laden, who would later establish al-Qaeda, and (2) Abu Musab al-Zarqawi, a Jordanian national and former street thug, who would later create ISIS. Both bin Laden and Zarqawi had left their lives to fight as Mujahideen against the Soviet occupation.

Bin Laden was the leader of the logistical network, al-Qaeda, an unofficial agency that was helping Muslim volunteers (from other Muslim countries in the Middle East, the Balkans, and parts of Africa) travel to Afghanistan to support Afghan Muslims' fight against the Soviet Union. Through the same organization, he was also known to provide logistical and humanitarian aid to Afghan Mujahideen, using the wealth he acquired from his family. Reports indicate that during his 10-year stay in Afghanistan, beginning in 1979, not only did he take part in front-line battles, but he also used his father's construction company equipment to help the Mujahideen build shelters, tunnels, hospitals, and roads over the rugged terrain of Afghanistan. The organization stopped its activities in 1988, after the defeat of the Soviets, and bin Laden returned to Saudi Arabia.

Back in Saudi Arabia, bin Laden became very discontent with the ruling Saudi family who welcomed more than 500,000 American troops into the country during the Gulf War in 1990, to carry out attacks against another Muslim country, Iraq. American forces had destroyed much of the Iraqi Army and annihilated critical infrastructure—sewage, water, electricity, communication, and oil—crippling the lives of millions of Iraqis. Arguing that the US military presence in Saudi Arabia was no different than the Soviet occupation of Afghanistan, bin Laden left the country and resettled in Sudan. From there, he moved back to Afghanistan and reestablished al-Qaeda headquarters there in the mid-1990s. There he started oppositional activities, heavily criticizing Saudi Arabia and other Muslim countries as well as Western powers that had large military presences in Muslim lands.

Al-Qaeda issued statements during this era indicating that its primary goal was to drive out American military forces from Muslim lands—Saudi Arabia, Yemen, and Somalia. As American journalist Peter Bergen, who met with bin Laden in 1997 in Afghanistan, explained, bin Laden "could have chosen a different path at several points in his life, but the introduction of American troops into Saudi Arabia turned his sort of latent anti-Americanism into a passionate hatred of the United States" (Davies 2021). During this interview, bin Laden told Bergen that "the United States government is unjust, criminal, and tyrannical. The US today has set a double standard, calling whoever goes against its injustice, a terrorist. It wants to occupy our countries, steal our resources, impose agents on us to rule us, and then wants us to agree to all this. If we refuse to do so, it says we are terrorists" (CNN 2021).

In 1995, and then in 1996, bin Laden issued two letters, one addressed to the King of Saudi Arabia, titled "Open Letter to King Fahd," and a second one to American military command in Saudi Arabia, "Declaration of War against the Americans Who Occupy the

Land of the Two Holy Mosques." Despite being issued on different dates, both letters conveyed similar messages, such as asking the Saudi family to stop squandering its oil money and share it with the people, and warning Americans of the upcoming danger of guerilla war if they did not leave the holy Islamic sites in Saudi Arabia. Beginning in 1995, al-Qaeda-inspired Arabs began to carry out deadly terrorist attacks against American targets in Saudi Arabia. First, a truck bombing close to a US military base in the capitol of Saudi Arabia, Riyadh, killed seven individuals, including five American soldiers. A year later, in 1996, a Saudi Shiite group carried out another massive truck bombing at the US military housing complex Khobar Towers, Saudi Arabia, killing 19 US soldiers and wounding more than 400. It is still unknown by the intelligence community whether bin Laden or al-Qaeda were directly involved in these two attacks.

By circulating information about injustices occurring in the Islamic world at the hands of Western powers, bin Laden managed to turn al-Qaeda into a global network. For example, in a magazine published in 1996 (Washington Post 1998), he cited examples of massacres carried out by Western forces in an effort to increase support for al-Qaeda. These included:

1. The 1996 Qana massacre in Lebanon during which 106 civilian Lebanese were deliberately killed (according to a United Nations investigation) inside a UN shelter by artillery bombing from the Israeli Defense Forces (Center for Israel Education 2022).
2. The death of approximately 500,000 Iraqi children (according to a UNICEF report) as a consequence of United States-imposed sanctions (embargo on food, medicine, and appropriation of the oil revenue) on Iraq (Geneva International Centre for Justice 2022; Sponeck 2006).
3. The intentional withholding of arms and weapons from the Muslims of Bosnia while they were subjected to ethnic cleansing, mass rape, and massacre at the hands of Christian Serbs who were obtaining heavy artillery and weapons from Israel (Brown 2016; Daalder 1998).

FIGURE 8.18   A Soviet helicopter downed by Afghan Mujahideen. *Source:* Peretz Partensky/Langton Labs.

Between 1996 and 1998, bin Laden participated in several interviews with journalists from Western media outlets including the *Washington Post*, *Time* magazine, British documentary makers, and the American television channel ABC. In each of these interviews, he asked for US troops to leave Saudi Arabia and the holy Islamic sites. In August 1998, two months after he was officially acknowledged as the leader of "a terrorist organization called al-Qaeda," al-Qaeda carried out simultaneous bombing attacks against US embassies in

Kenya and Tanzania. Using trucks loaded with thousands of pounds of TNT, these attacks killed 12 Americans and more than 200 locals. In an interview with John Miller of ABC, bin Laden denied al-Qaeda's involvement in the bombings of the US embassies in Africa. In 1999, bin Laden was charged for conspiring to kill American nationals abroad by the US Attorney's Office and for the first time, he appeared on the FBI's Ten Most Wanted Fugitives list (PBS 2022).

FIGURE 8.19 The *USS Cole* was towed away from the port city of Aden, Yemen, into open sea after the attack. *Source:* DoD photo by Sgt. Don L. Maes, US Marine Corps, public domain, via Wikimedia Commons.

Two horrific attacks occurred in the upcoming year. First, in 2000, a suicide attack was orchestrated by al-Qaeda in Yemen against a destroyer ship of the United States Navy, the *USS Cole*, while it was docked in Aden Harbor for a fuel stop. Two al-Qaeda-affiliated suicide bombers with a small fishing boat loaded with C4 explosives hit the vessel from the port side, causing a massive explosion that killed 17 US sailors. And then came the terrorism of September 11, 2001, when 19 Saudi Arabs affiliated with al-Qaeda hijacked four American commercial airplanes and crashed them into three different locations—the World Trade Center towers in New York, the Pentagon in Virginia, and a rural field in Pennsylvania.

A month later, the US government responded with Operation Enduring Freedom, invading Afghanistan, destroying the al-Qaeda bases in the country, and killing thousands of suspected al-Qaeda militants. Bin Laden evaded the security forces for a decade, until May 2011, when he was killed by US Navy Seals in a fortified compound located in Abbottabad, Pakistan.

Whether or not bin Laden accepted his involvement in the 9/11 attacks is a topic of controversy. According to a statement distributed from his hideout via fax on September 16, 2001, bin Laden denied his involvement in the planning and implementation of this devastating attack, saying: "The U.S. is pointing the finger at me but I categorically state that I have not done this" (The Globe & Mail 2011). However, in a 2003 audio message that was distributed by Al Jazeera and alleged to be from bin Laden, he acknowledged al-Qaeda's involvement in the attacks, calling American governmental officials criminals and rationalizing the attacks as avenging the oppression of Muslims (Cochran 2001).

8.5.4 Islamic State (IS)

The **Islamic State (IS)**, also known as the Islamic State of Iraq and Syria (ISIS), its Arabic acronym, DAESH, or the Islamic State of Iraq and the Levant (ISIL), is a Sunni Salafist terrorist organization. It was founded by another Mujahideen supporter, Abu Musab al-Zarqawi, in 1999, and is widely known for its brutal public executions. As with al-Qaeda,

FIGURE 8.20   US Army paratroopers prepare to board C-17 Globemaster III's in support of Operation Iraqi Freedom on March 23, 2003. *Source:* Tech. Sgt. Stephen Faulisi, US Air Force, public domain, via Wikimedia Commons.

to understand the rise of ISIS it is important to look at the historical incidents associated with the emergence of this organization in Middle East.

8.5.5 Occupation of Iraq (The Second Persian Gulf War, 2003–2011)

In March 2003, approximately three years after the 9/11 attacks, coalition forces led by the United States (including troops from Great Britain) invaded Iraq. According to US officials, the primary justifications for this invasion were (1) to destroy the weapons of mass destruction (WMD) allegedly possessed by the Iraqi army (an American accusation which was later proved to be erroneous); (2) to end Saddam Hussein's alleged support for al-Qaeda terrorism (although a US bipartisan committee concluded in 2004 that there was no evidence indicating a collaborative relationship between al-Qaeda and Saddam's Iraq); and (3) to free the Iraqi people from Saddam Hussein's dictatorship.

The coalition air forces defeated Saddam Hussein's secular Sunni Iraqi Army via airstrikes aimed at government and military installations across the country in less than a month and started their ground invasion of Iraq beginning in mid-April 2003. Most of the Iraqi forces simply did not resist the advancing coalition forces. Toward the end of May, the country largely fell under the control of the United States. The Coalition Provisional Authority was established and control was given to an American diplomat Paul Bremer, as Iraq's chief executive authority. Bremer was given the power to rule the country by authoritative decree and was subject to the authority of the United States Secretary of Defense, Donald Rumsfeld.

De-Ba'athification of the Iraqi Society
Over his short career of slightly more than a year in Iraq, Bremer issued several decrees. First, Bremer issued the Order (Decree) 1: De-Ba'athification of Iraqi Society on May 16, 2003. Order 1 removed Sunnis (Ba'ath Party members) from all governmental and civil positions (in educational institutions and hospitals) and permanently banned them from seeking employment in the public sector. This purge of Baathists left thousands of educated Iraqis (e.g., doctors, teachers, politicians, civil servants) unemployed and highly discontent with the American-led coalition forces.

Dissolution of the Iraqi Army
Within a week, Bremer signed Order (Decree) 2: Dissolution of Entities—the disbandment of Iraqi Army personnel, security officers, and the Iraqi intelligence infrastructure. Overnight, hundreds of thousands of well-trained Iraqi men became unemployed. Extremely angry with this decision, they roamed the streets of Baghdad, criticizing and threatening the coalition government and asking them to reverse their decision. These

former soldiers (approximately 400,000) would come to form the backbone of the Iraqi insurgency against the American occupation, which would last for years and claim the lives of thousands. In a 2012 *Newsweek* article, Colin Powell, the secretary of state for the Bush administration, wrote about this decision:

> When we went in, we had a plan, which the president approved. We would not break up and disband the Iraqi Army. We would use the reconstituted Army with purged leadership to help us secure and maintain order throughout the country . . . The plan the president had approved was not implemented. Instead, Secretary Donald Rumsfeld and Ambassador Paul Bremer, our man in charge in Iraq, disbanded the Army and fired Baath Party members down to teachers. We eliminated the very officials and institutions we should have been building on, and left thousands of the most highly skilled people in the country jobless and angry—PRIME RECRUITS FOR INSURGENCY. (Powell 2012)

In subsequent years, many of these experienced foot soldiers and senior commanders of Saddam Hussein's secular army would serve in the top military and administrative cadres of ISIS.

In the following days Bremer established the Iraqi Interim Governing Council, of which all members were directly selected by the US government from among the Iraqis who supported the American invasion of Iraq. Bremer would later ask this interim Iraqi government to approve the implementation of the highly controversial first Iraqi Constitution. The constitution, drafted by the Coalition Provisional Authority, included clauses such as the privatization of the Iraqi oil resources and banning political parties opposed to US occupation from playing an active role in the future of Iraq. Before he left Iraq, Bremer issued Order (decree) 17, which provided total immunity from the Iraqi legal process to the American government and all non-Iraqi military and civilian personnel associated with the Coalition Provisional Government.

Even though the failed leader Saddam Hussein was caught hiding in a hole close to his childhood home in the city of Tikrit, and his sons were both killed by US troops in 2003, the situation further deteriorated over the following years. First, the United Nations Chief Weapons Inspector, David Kay, testified before the US Senate in 2004 (also later confirmed by a US Presidential Commission on Iraq in 2015) that there was not a single trace of weapons of mass destruction present in Iraq. This finding contradicted the Bush administration's claims that Saddam had a huge stockpile of chemical, biological, and nuclear weapons ready to be used against the West. Kay told US Senate members: "We were all wrong, and that is most disturbing" (CNN 2004).

The Blackwater Security Consulting USA

Being exempt from any kind of legal prosecution by the Iraqi criminal justice system, heavily armed operatives of the US-contracted security firm Blackwater USA engaged in serious human rights violations against Iraqi civilians. Knowing that they were not bound by the US Code of Military Justice and that they could act with absolute impunity in Iraq, Blackwater engaged in mass atrocities. These ranged from torture to mass murder of Sunni Iraqis, which naturally provoked anger among the locals. Most of the killings committed by Blackwater personnel were described as "trigger-happy slaughter" instead of a legitimate fight with insurgents (Flynn & Sahib 2006).

Torture and Prisoner Abuse at Abu Ghraib Prison Complex

In February 2004, *The New Yorker* published the summary of an official report (which wasn't meant to be shared with the American public) detailing the devastating acts carried out inside the American-run Abu Ghraib prison. Based on evidence and witness reports, the author of the report, Major General Taguba, described the systematic and illegal abuses by American soldiers and the intelligence community as "sadistic, blatant, and wanton criminal." He further reported:

> Breaking chemical lights and pouring the phosphoric liquid on detainees; pouring cold water on naked detainees; beating detainees with a broom handle and a chair; threatening male detainees with rape; allowing a military police guard to stitch the wound of a detainee who was injured after being slammed against the wall in his cell; sodomizing a detainee with a chemical light and perhaps a broom stick, and using military working dogs to frighten and intimidate detainees with threats of attack, and in one instance actually biting a detainee.

The official report did not include photographic evidence because of their "extremely sensitive and disturbing nature." However, the television channel CBS brought public attention to leaked photographs of the horrific abuse of the civilian Sunni Iraqi men, women, and teenagers at the hands of American soldiers, after being arrested at random security sweeps and at military checkpoints. These photographs provided further evidence that the prisoners were subjected to torture, assault, indecent acts, dehumanization, and maltreatment. They showed prison cells splattered with blood, battered faces of dead prisoners, naked prisoners forced to assume humiliating poses as American soldiers taunted them, naked Iraqi prisoners piled on top of each other in the shape of a pyramid, and other vulgar and humiliating acts (Hersh 2004; NPR 2016). Eric Fair, an American interrogator who worked at Abu Ghraib and Fallujah, later stated that what they were doing could not be explained as "enhanced interrogation techniques," as the US government called them. According to him, "it was torture." "We hurt people, and not just physically . . . We destroyed them emotionally" (NPR 2016).

FIGURE 8.21 An Abu Ghraib naked prisoner is covered in mud and what appears to be feces. A baton-wielding prison guard appears to be ordering a detainee to walk a straight line with his ankles handcuffed. *Source:* US Government copyright, public domain, via Wikimedia Commons.

Establishment of al-Qaeda in Iraq

Public outrage over these human rights violations by Blackwater contractors and American soldiers broke out in Iraq and in several other places throughout the world, including the United States, as the photographic evidence aired on television news and social media outlets. Playing on Iraqis' feelings of anger and hatred toward Americans, Abu Musab Al-Zarqawi founded al-Qaeda in Iraq (AQI) in 2004. Under the banner of AQI, Sunnis were transformed into an organized force and began to engage in retaliatory attacks.

Highly enraged and provoked by the killings that occurred at the hands of Blackwater Security Consulting, AQI-inspired Sunnis ambushed and killed four Blackwater employees in the city of Falluja in 2004. The bodies of the US contractors were then brutally mutilated and burned, and their blackened corpses were hung from a nearby bridge. The full video of the atrocity was shared with the rest of the world (Flynn & Sahib 2006; Gettleman 2004). Similarly, soon after the media's release of evidence of torture against the Iraqi prisoners, AQI kidnapped American businessman Nicholas Berg in Iraq and beheaded him while videotaping the incident. AQI claimed this was a retaliatory action against the humiliations of Iraqi prisoners at Abu Ghraib prison.

Purge of Iraqi Sunnis

In November 2004, after the killing of Nicholas Berg, US troops, with the support of the newly established Iraqi army, composed of strictly Shias, carried out a large military assault on Fallujah, the stronghold Sunni Iraqis. According to the Pentagon, 1,200 insurgents were killed during this operation in which US Marines conducted house-to-house searches to rid the region of Sunni extremists. However, the Red Cross indicated that more than 800 of those killings were of Iraqi civilians. Soon after this large-scale operation, in 2005 Iraq's control was given to the Iranian-backed Shia government. Shiites controlled much of the parliament and Nouri Al-Maliki, a senior Iraqi politician who had strong ties to Iran, became the first prime minister of the country in 2006. During the same year, the US killed al-Qaeda leader Zarqawi in an airstrike.

Although US officials thought that the establishment of democracy in the country (e.g., the newly elected government), coupled with the killing of Sunni extremist Zarqawi, would bring an end to the insurgency in Iraq, peace was not achieved. Beginning in 2006, a brutal sectarian conflict devastated the country. The Sunni population was systematically excluded from the mainstream economic and political life in Iraq and subjected to assassination, widespread torture, and incarceration for years without trial. A wave of looting and reprisal began against the former regime's supporters, the Sunnis, which was largely ignored by the new ruling Shia government of Iraq. This eventually led to enormous chaos with brutal killings. Even the nonviolent protests carried out by Sunnis were harshly policed and thousands of Sunnis were jailed by American soldiers in a camp called Bucca. There, they were held in the same cells with mostly non-Iraqis, hardened al-Qaeda operatives.

Notably, this mixing of hundreds of thousands of Sunni civilian Iraqis who were detained at military checkpoints and house searches with seasoned violent radicals in the American-run Camp Bucca prison complex led to the socialization and then radicalization of these noncombatant civilians (McCoy 2014). It is estimated that at least nine top commanders of ISIS had been incarcerated in Camp Bucca. The deceased leader of the group, a former academic and the self-proclaimed caliph, Abu Bakr al-Baghdadi, had become radicalized at Camp Bucca, according to Iraqi terrorism expert Hisham al-Hashimi: "At Camp Bucca, Baghdadi absorbed the jihadist ideology and established himself among the big names. He met . . . the officers in Saddam's army [at Camp Bucca], and despite their Ba'ath origins they impressed him with their military knowledge. He also influenced them with his religious background—mainly his expertise in Quranic studies" (Hashem 2015).

Jeremi Suri, American historian and distinguished professor at the University of Texas at Austin, explained, "Their time in prison deepened their extremism and gave them opportunities to broaden their following. . . . The prisons became virtual terrorist universities: The hardened radicals were the professors, the other detainees were the students, and the prison authorities played the role of absent custodian" (Thompson & Suri 2014). Similarly, prion commander James Skylar Gerrod would also say via his Twitter account that "Many of us at Camp Bucca were concerned that instead of just holding detainees, we had created a pressure cooker for extremism" (McLaughlin 2014).

WikiLeaks: The Iraq War Logs

In November 2008, Barack Obama, who campaigned to withdraw all American forces from Iraq, was elected as the new president of the United States. In 2009, keeping his pre-election promise, Obama ordered the gradual withdrawal of US troops from Iraq, beginning with the immediate retreat of US combat forces from major Iraqi cities, including Bagdad and Mosul. In December 2011, after approximately nine years of fighting, the US formally completed its military withdrawal from Iraq, marking the end of the US-Iraq war. The war is estimated to have cost trillions of dollars and killed more than 4,500 American soldiers and more than 100,000 Iraqis (according to US officials), including both civilians and fighters by 2006 (Council on Foreign Relations 2022).

In 2010, approximately 400,000 classified US documents from the Iraq war were published online by the whistle-blowing organization **WikiLeaks**. These documents indicated a completely different picture of human costs to the Iraqis themselves than the one reported in the American political discourse and news media. Julian Assange, the owner of the website, argued that he made the **Iraq War Logs** public to expose the truth about the conflict (BBC 2010). The documents revealed that Iraqi civilian casualties were much higher than reported to the world, that private military contractors such as the Blackwater Security Consulting employees were unnecessarily torturing and killing members of the Iraqi public, and that US forces were ignoring the wide-scale torture and purge of Sunnis by the Shias.

The documents, named "U.S. Army Sigacts (Significant Actions)," described in detail how Sunni Iraqi detainees were subjected to torture by tools such as electric drills, electrocution, or cutting the detainees' fingers and burning them with acid, with the knowledge of US military officials. They also included information on how large numbers of civilian Iraqis were killed by US forces at checkpoints or during routine operations and how these killings were hidden from the public. Further, these classified documents revealed how Iran's Islamic Revolution Guards were training and providing arms to the new Shia Iraqi Army to help their efforts of purging the Sunni population (BBC 2010). Later empirical studies conducted by scholars revealed that in contrast to the statistics provided by the US military in public statements, more than 650,000 Iraqis (civilians and military) were killed during the war and approximately 600,000 children were living on the streets of Iraq as orphans (Cole 2011; Tirman 2022).

8.5.6 The Arab Spring

In late 2010, a wave of pro-democracy uprisings spread across the Middle East and North Africa, beginning first in Tunisia (Jasmine Revolution) and then Egypt (January 25 Revolution), wherein people revolted against authoritarianism, poverty, and corruption. Inspired by the successful overthrowing of governments in Tunisia and Egypt, people of authoritarian regimes in other Arab countries also engaged in large-scale protests and armed revolts to topple their governments (and to dismiss unpopular officials) in order to establish modern democratic governments: in chronological order, Yemen, Bahrain, Libya, and finally Syria. It became known as the **Arab Spring**.

Different from the other Arab countries that were also swept by large-scale public uprisings, in Libya, NATO forces led by French, British, and American military launched an airstrike campaign against the ruling government led by Muammar al-Qaddafi. The effort was intended to help the rebels' efforts to topple him (Al-Jazeera 2020). In Syria, the situation was similar. The dictator Bashar al-Assad had violently cracked down the protesters who were calling for his resignation from the presidential authority of Syria, turning the revolt into a protracted civil war which was spread through the country. Assad, worried about a potential foreign intervention against Syria to remove him from power, as it had just happened in Libya to Qaddafi, made a tactical move to allow the rise of extremist groups in Syria. In mid-2011, Assad released thousands of incarcerated hard-line extremists and jihadists from Syrian prisons with official amnesties and intentionally allowed them to join and mix with the rebels, tolerating the rise of extremism, which made it ethically difficult for Western countries led by the United States to back them against the secular rule of Assad (Laub 2021). Assad hoped that with this move the West would join behind him to take down the hardline jihadists, instead of attacking him as they did to Qaddafi in Libya (Lewitt 2021).

8.5.7 Emergence of ISIS

Back in Iraq, Abu Bakr al-Baghdadi, the new leader of al-Qaeda in Iraq (AQI), sent a unit of his fighters to Syria to support the rebels and recently released extremists against the Assad regime. With these fighters Syrian rebels captured major cities in Syria such as Raqqa, along with military assets and weaponry. In the meantime, al-Baghdadi also carried out a series of bombing attacks under the name "Breaking the Walls" against the Shia-controlled prisons in Iraq; this was in order to save incarcerated Sunnis from torture and oppression. These attacks eventually freed hundreds of incarcerated Sunnis and grew al-Baghdadi's army even stronger. Finally, in April 2013, al-Baghdadi traveled to Syria and announced to the world that he was taking control of the AQI allied groups in Syria and merging them with his group in Iraq, under the name Islamic State in Iraq and Syria (ISI). In less than a year, ISIS carried out several deadly attacks against Iraqi security forces and by mid-2014 had taken control of major cities in Iraq such as Fallujah, Raqqa, Mosul, Tikrit, and Ramadi.

FIGURE 8.22 A group of Islamic State fighters in Sinai, Egypt. The Islamic State (IS), also known as ISIS or ISIL, emerged as a significant threat in the early 2010s, primarily in Iraq and Syria. IS used sophisticated propaganda tactics and social media to recruit fighters and supporters from various parts of the world, including Europe, Africa, and Asia. *Source:* Zezoyo, CC BY-SA 4.0 DEED, via Wikimedia.

Many Sunnis welcomed the arrival of ISIS into Iraq, as they viewed them as their protectors against the oppressive Iranian and American backed Shia regime in Iraq. ISIS, growing by the thousands, destroyed the newly established Iraqi Army and gained access to advanced heavy weaponry given to the Iraqis by the Americans. In a short period, a large part of Syria and almost half of Iraq fell under the control of ISIS.

Over time ISIS built an army; seized control of dams, major oil and gas fields in Iraq and Syria; and called for fighters, doctors, nurses, engineers, teachers, and other civilians from all over the world to immigrate to territories controlled by the group. Due to its military achievements, ISIS recruited more than 40,000 foreign fighters from about 120 countries. Soon it operated like a state, building roads, schools, hospitals, and infrastructure that were essential for the everyday life of its citizens. ISIS provided cozy lifestyles, job opportunities, and monthly payments for individuals who travel to Syria and Iraq to join its ranks. Statements obtained from incarcerated ISIS fighters indicate that recruits were not only presented with the comfort of living in houses and apartments, but also were provided with opportunities to further their education and occupational experiences. ISIS won over the Sunnis, who had been violently purged since the 2003 invasion of Iraq, providing the safety and security that they were denied for almost a decade by the Shia-controlled Iraqi government.

ISIS also provided the opportunity for Sunnis to exact vengeance on the enemy forces. Sunnis all around the world, watching highly graphic content on social media, joined the ISIS ranks and engaged in violence (e.g., beheadings and mass murders of Western journalists, tourists, and aid workers on camera) as an act of revenge for years of suffering.

On August 19, 2014, ISIS beheaded American journalist James Foley as a response to then-President Obama's announcement of the authorization of the first American airstrike against ISIS forces in Iraq. In less than a month, ISIS beheaded another American Israeli journalist, Steven Sotloff, as a response to the Obama-ordered targeted airstrikes and military intervention in Iraq (Carter & Fantz 2014). In response to continued airstrikes, ISIS carried out brutal international terror attacks in 29 countries including France, England, Turkey, and Belgium, killing at least 2,000 people.

Scholars argue that the United States' invasion of Iraq contributed to the emergence of ISIS (BBC 2004). Former President Obama has acknowledged that "ISIL is a direct outgrowth of al-Qaeda in Iraq, that grew out of our invasion, which is an example of unintended consequences" (Haaretz 2015). Supporting this argument, recent academic research based on interviews with ISIS prisoners in Iraq and elsewhere indicates that recruits were drawn not by religion but by anger and a desire of revenge over how they and their families had suffered under US occupation. These resentments, combined with the consequences of the policies implemented in Iraq—leaving over half a million Iraqi military personnel unemployed and detaining civilians together with extremists at Camp Bucca—further created a context ripe for radicalization.

8.6 CONCLUSION

This chapter reviewed multiple cases of religious terrorism from each of the three major Abrahamic religions—Judaism, Christianity, and Islam. What should be clear to the reader is that terrorism is not in the provenance of any one specific religion. While the exact role of religion in terrorism is contested among scholars, most agree that religion is not a direct cause of terrorism. Religiously motivated groups have developed transcendental goals based on their extremist interpretations of the faith, and have resorted to violence to achieve those goals. What is dangerous about religious terrorism is that these individuals view their violence as a duty or mission in the name of God, and therefore are not concerned with its consequences; they believe they will be divinely rewarded for their acts. As the case studies illustrate, it is important to understand the cultural, historical, and geographical contexts that give rise to acts of terrorism in order to correctly understand the sources of religiously motivated terrorism. Religious beliefs can serve as a strong motivator of terrorism when they blend with social, economic, and political factors to shape people's thoughts and actions.

Key Lessons

Lesson 1

Religion, as a concept, has played a significant role and powerful influence in human affairs and world history throughout the centuries, as religious identities have often served as a strong group identifier—informing a group's understanding of us versus them.

Lesson 2

Interpretations of religion can provide moral justification for violence by demonizing the enemies and showing the struggle as a sacred fight between satanic powers and God's soldiers.

Lesson 3

Religious terrorists can kill with moral impunity, as they believe in receiving heavenly rewards for their brutal acts. It is this aspect of religious terrorism that makes it far more destructive and lethal than secular and leftist ideologies.

Lesson 4

Today, religiously motivated terrorist and hate groups often contain the elements of right-wing terrorism—racism, fascism, and nationalism.

Lesson 5

Despite the fact that Islam and its followers have been commonly associated with the issue of religious terrorism (especially by right-wing politicians and media outlets), violence in the name of a religion has been practiced by all religions and faiths.

Lesson 6

It is important to understand the cultural, historical, and geographical contexts of specific incidents that gave rise to acts of terrorism in order to correctly understand the sources of religiously motivated terrorism.

Lesson 7

Religious beliefs can serve as strong motivators of terrorism when they are blended with social, economic, and political factors in shaping people's thoughts and actions.

KEY WORDS

al-Qaeda
apocalyptic terrorism
Arab Spring
Army of God (AOG)
Aum Shinrikyo
Christian identity
Concerned Christians
Eastern Lightning

fundamentalism
Gunpowder Plot
Gush Emunim
Iraq War Logs
Islamic State (IS/ISIL/ISIS)
Jewish Defense League (JDL)
Jewish Zealots
Kahanism

Lord's Resistance Army (LRA)
Mujahideen
National Liberation Front of Tripura
  (NLFT)
Phineas Priesthood
religious terrorism

Salafism
secularization
Sicarii
suicide terrorism
Soldiers of Jesus
WikiLeaks

RECOMMENDED SOURCES

Research Articles & Books

Almond, G. A., Appleby, R. S., & Sivan, E. (2011). *Strong religion: The rise of fundamentalisms around the world.* University of Chicago Press.

Aran, G., & Hassner, R. E. (2013). Religious violence in Judaism: Past and present. *Terrorism and Political Violence, 25*(3), 355–405.

Armstrong, K. (2014). *Fields of blood: Religion and the history of violence.* Anchor.

Burstein, A. (2018). Armies of God, armies of men: A global comparison of secular and religious terror organizations. *Terrorism and Political Violence, 30*(1), 1–21.

Cavanaugh, W. T. (2009). *The myth of religious violence: Secular ideology and the roots of modern conflict.* Oxford University Press.

Cronin, A. K. (2002). Behind the curve: Globalization and international terrorism. *International security, 27*(3), 30–58.

Emerson, M. O., & Hartman, D. (2006). The rise of religious fundamentalism. *Annual review of Sociology,* 127–144.

Esposito, J. L. (2003). *Unholy war: Terror in the name of Islam.* Oxford University Press, USA.

Gregg, H. S. (2014). Defining and distinguishing secular and religious terrorism. *Perspectives on Terrorism, 8*(2), 36–51.

Henne, P. (2019). Terrorism and religion: An overview. *Oxford Research Encyclopedia of Politics.*

Hoffman, B. (1995). "Holy terror": The implications of terrorism motivated by a religious imperative. *Studies in Conflict & Terrorism, 18*(4), 271–284.

Johnson, D. (2017). Hate in God's name. Southern poverty and Law center. Retrieved from https://www.splcenter.org/20170925/hate-god%E2%80%99s-name

Juergensmeyer, M. (2005). Terror in the mind of God: The global rise of religious violence. *Police Practice and Research, 6*(2), 201–208.

Juergensmeyer, M. (2021), Religious Terrorism at the Turn of the Twenty-First Century. In *The Oxford Handbook of the History of Terrorism.*

Lewis, J. R., & Dawson, L. L. (2018). Introduction: Religion and Terrorism. *Numen, 65*(2–3), 117–124.

Pedahzur, A., & Perliger, A. (2009). *Jewish terrorism in Israel.* Columbia University Press.

Ranstorp, M. (1996). Terrorism in the Name of Religion. *Journal of international affairs,* 41–62.

Rapoport, D. C. (1983). Fear and trembling: Terrorism in three religious traditions. *American Political Science Review, 78*(3), 658–677.

Stern, J. (2003). Terror in the Name of God. New York: Ecco.

News Articles & Government and Think Tank Reports

Religious conservatism doesn't make a terrorist. But crime and exclusion can.
  Author(s): Z. Fareen Parvez
  Source: The Guardian

Who exactly are 'radical' Muslims?
  Author(s): Z. Fareen Parvez
  Source: The Conversation

Colin Powell on the Bush Administration's Iraq War Mistakes.
  Author(s): Colin Powell and Jake Chessum
  Source: Newsweek
You Shouldn't Blame Islam for Terrorism. Religion Isn't a Crucial Factor in Attacks.
  Author(s): Mehdi Hasan
  Source: The Intercept
The myth of religious violence
  Author(s): Karen Armstrong
  Source: The Guardian
Terror: Can We Blame Religion?
  Author(s): Donald Winchester
  Source: Vision.org
Secrets of the extreme religious right: Inside the frightening world of Christian Reconstructionism.
  Author(s): Paul Rosenberg
  Source: Salon
Holy Hate: The Far Right's Radicalization of Religion
  Author(s): Daryl Johnson
  Source: Southern Poverty & Law Center (SPLC)
Yes, let's have a frank and open discussion about the causes of extremism and terrorism
  Author(s): Adrian Cherney
  Source: The Conversation
The Cult Who Kidnaps Christians and Is at War with the Chinese Government.
  Author(s): Matt Shea
  Source: VICE
Christian Identity.
  Author(s): Southern Poverty & Law Center
  Source: Southern Poverty & Law Center webpage

What ISIS Really Wants
  Author(s): Graeme Wood
  Source: The Atlantic
How Disbanding the Iraqi Army Fueled ISIS.
  Author(s): Mark Thompson
  Source: TIME
Terrorism, war and the problem of "religious violence"
  Author(s): Tony Coady
  Source: ABC News
Religious extremism main cause of terrorism, according to report
  Author(s): George Arnett
  Source: The Guardian
Examining Religion and Violence
  Author(s): Damien Cave
  Source: The New York Time
It's not the religion that creates terrorists, it's the politics
  Author(s): Giles Fraser
  Source: The Guardian
Doesn't religion cause most of the conflict in the world?
  Author(s): Rachel Woodlock, Antony Loewenstein, Jane Caro, & Simon Smart
  Source: The Guardian
6 facts about religious hostilities in the Middle East and North Africa
  Author(s): Katayoun Kishi & Angelina E. Theodorou
  Source: Pew Research Center
How strong is the link between faith and terrorism?
  Author(s): Reza Aslan
  Source: CNN

Documentaries, Videos, and Other Educational Media

Terror in the Name of God
  Featuring: Jessica Stern
  Source: C-Span
Terrorism and Religion
  Featuring: John Esposito
  Source: C-Span
How religious are so-called 'Islamic terrorists'?
  Featuring: Mehdi Hasan
  Source: Al Jazeera English YouTube channel

Blowback: How ISIS Was Created by the U.S. Invasion of Iraq
  Featuring: Mehdi Hasan
  Source: The Intercept
Unholy War: Terror In the Name of Islam
  Featuring: John Esposito
  Source: GBH Forum Network YouTube Channel
God & Country
  Producer(s)/Director(s): Dan Partland

How Religion Started the Bloodiest Wars In
Human History | Holy Wars | Chronicle
  Producer(s)/Director(s): Chronicle
  Source: Chronicle-Medieval History
  Documentaries YouTube channel
How a new Christian right is changing US politics
  Featuring: Barbara Plett Usher
  Source: BBC News YouTube Channel

Does ISIS Have Any Religious Legitimacy
  Featuring: Graeme Wood & Mehdi Hasan
  Source: MSNBC YouTube Channel
Former Undercover CIA Officer Talks War and
Peace
  Featuring: Amaryllis Fox
  Source: AJ+ YouTube channel

REFERENCES

Adam, J., De Cordier, B., Titeca, K., & Vlassen-root, K. (2007). In the name of the father? Christian militantism in Tripura, Northern Uganda, and Ambon. *Studies in Conflict & Terrorism*, 30(11), 963–983.

ADL (2017). Christian identity. ADL. https://www.adl.org/resources/backgrounders/christian-identity

Al-Jazeera (2020). What is the Arab Spring, and how did it start? https://www.aljazeera.com/news/2020/12/17/what-is-the-arab-spring-and-how-did-it-start

Almond, G. A., Appleby, R. S., & Sivan, E. (2011). *Strong religion: The rise of fundamentalisms around the world*. University of Chicago Press.

Aran, G., & Hassner, R. E. (2013). Religious violence in Judaism: Past and present. *Terrorism and Political Violence*, 25(3), 355–405.

Armstrong, K. (2014). *Fields of blood: Religion and the history of violence*. Anchor.

Ashrawi, H. (2014). Kahane's legacy. *The Hill*. https://thehill.com/blogs/congress-blog/foreign-policy/199475-kahanes-legacy/

Avalos, H. (2005). *Fighting words: The origins of religious violence*. Prometheus Books.

Avruch, K. A. (1979). Traditionalizing Israeli nationalism: The development of Gush Emunim. *Political Psychology*, 1(1), 47–57.

Bader, E. J., & Baird-Windle, P. (2015). *Targets of hatred: Anti-abortion terrorism*. St. Martin's Press.

Barker, J. (2021). Concerned Christians. Watchman Fellowship. https://www.watchman.org/profiles/pdf/concernedchristiansprofile.pdf

BBC (2004). Iraq war illegal, says Annan. BBC. http://news.bbc.co.uk/2/hi/middle_east/3661134.stm

BBC (2010). Wikileaks: Iraq war logs 'reveal truth about conflict'. BBC. https://www.bbc.com/news/world-middle-east-11612731

BBC (2013). Sunnis and Shia in the Middle East. BBC News. https://www.bbc.com/news/world-middle-east-25434060

Bloom, M. M. (2004). Palestinian suicide bombing: Public support, market share, and outbidding. *Political Science Quarterly*, 119(1), 61–88.

Brown, J. (2016). Supreme Court rules against exposing Israel's role in Bosnian genocide. *+972 Magazine*. https://www.972mag.com/israels-involvement-in-bosnian-genocide-to-remain-under-wraps/

Burstein, A. (2018). Armies of God, armies of men: A global comparison of secular and religious terror organizations. *Terrorism and Political Violence*, 30(1), 1–21.

Carter, C. J., & Fantz, A. (2014). ISIS video shows beheading of American journalist Steven Sotloff. CNN. https://www.cnn.com/2014/09/02/world/meast/isis-american-journalist-sotloff/index.html

Cascais, A. (2022). The last throes of Uganda's Lord's Resistance Army. *DW*. https://www.dw.com/en/uganda-lord-resistance-army-final-days/a-60535944

Cavanaugh, W. T. (2009). *The myth of religious violence: Secular ideology and the roots of modern conflict*. Oxford University Press.

Center for Israel Education (1999). Christian extremists denied entry to Israel. CIE. https://israeled.org/christian-extremists-denied-entry-to-israel/

Center for Israel Education (2022). 106 Lebanese civilians killed at Qana. https://israeled.org/106-lebanese-civilians-killed-at-qana/

Chayes, S. (2015). *Thieves of state: Why corruption threatens global security.* Norton.

CNN (2004). Transcript: David Kay at Senate hearing. CNN. https://transcripts.cnn.com/show/se/date/2004-01-28/segment/02

CNN (2021). Osama bin Laden: Fast facts. https://edition.cnn.com/2013/08/30/world/osama-bin-laden-fast-facts/index.html

Cochran, J. (2001). Entire Osama bin Laden statement broadcast. ABC News. https://abcnews.go.com/International/story?id=80278&page=1

Cole, J. (2011). Post-American Iraq by the numbers. Informed Comment. https://www.juancole.com/2011/12/post-american-iraq-by-the-numbers.html

Cook, D. (2003). The recovery of radical Islam in the wake of the defeat of the Taliban. *Terrorism and Political Violence, 15*(1), 31–56.

Coolsaet, R. (2016). Facing the fourth foreign fighters wave: What drives Europeans to Syria, and to IS? Insights from the Belgian case. Egmont Institute. https://www.jstor.org/stable/resrep06677.1

Council on Foreign Relations (2022). 2003–2011, the Iraq War. Council on Foreign Relations. https://www.cfr.org/timeline/iraq-war

Cronin, A. K. (2003). Behind the curve: Globalization and international terrorism. *International Security, 27*(3), 30–58.

Daalder, I. (1998). Decision to intervene: How the war in Bosnia ended. Brookings Institute. https://www.brookings.edu/articles/decision-to-intervene-how-the-war-in-bosnia-ended/

Dalby, C. (2020). Brazil's evangelical gangs waging war on Afro-Brazilian religions. Insight Crime. https://insightcrime.org/news/analysis/brazil-evangelical-christian-gangs/

Davies, D. (2021). Osama bin Laden biography goes inside Al-Qaida leader's final hideout. NPR. https://www.npr.org/2021/08/04/1024238643/osama-bin-laden-biography-peter-bergen

Davis, C. (2002). "A" is for Allah, "J" is for jihad. *World Policy Journal.* https://www.jstor.org/stable/40209794?seq=1

Denova, R. I. (2021). *The origins of Christianity and the New Testament.* Wiley.

DW (2022). How Pentecostal churches are changing Brazil. DW. https://www.dw.com/en/how-pentecostal-churches-are-changing-brazil/a-63283164

Eichenwald, K. (2015). How uninformed U.S. politicians help ISIS. *Newsweek.* https://www.newsweek.com/2015/08/21/why-not-war-radical-islamist-terrorists-361360.html

Emerson, M. O., & Hartman, D. (2006). The rise of religious fundamentalism. *Annual Review of Sociology,* 127–144.

English, R. (2020). 10-Minute Talks: Religion and the history of terrorism. *The British Academy.* https://www.thebritishacademy.ac.uk/podcasts/10-minute-talks-religion-and-the-history-of-terrorism/

Esposito, J. L. (2003). *Unholy war: Terror in the name of Islam.* Oxford University Press.

Fahmi, G. (2020). Why reforming Islam to fight violent extremism is a bad idea. Chatham House. https://www.chathamhouse.org/2020/11/why-reforming-islam-fight-violent-extremism-bad-idea

Friedman, R. I. (1990). *The false prophet: Rabbi Meir Kahane; from FBI informant to Knesset member.* Hill.

Flynn, S., & Sahib, K. (2006). The day the war turned. GQ. https://www.gq.com/story/fallujah-private-contractors-lawsuit

Geneva International Centre for Justice (2022). Razing the truth about sanctions against Iraq. https://www.gicj.org/positions-opinons/gicj-positions-and-opinions/1188-razing-the-truth-about-sanctions-against-iraq

Gettleman, J. (2004). Enraged mob in Falluja kills 4 American contractors. *New York Times.* https://www.nytimes.com/2004/03/31/international/worldspecial/enraged-mob-in-falluja-kills-4-american.html

Ghanem, A. A., & Khatib, I. (2017). The nationalisation of the Israeli ethnocratic regime and the Palestinian minority's shrinking citizenship. *Citizenship Studies, 21*(8), 889–902.

Globe & Mail (2011). Osama bin Laden in photos. https://www.theglobeandmail.com/news/world/osama-bin-laden-in-photos/article634570/

Gregg, H. S. (2014). Defining and distinguishing secular and religious terrorism. *Perspectives on Terrorism, 8*(2), 36–51.

Gregg, H. S. (2018). Religious resources and terrorism. *Numen, 65*(2–3), 185–206.

Gunning, J., & Jackson, R. (2011). What's so "religious" about "religious terrorism"? *Critical Studies on Terrorism, 4*(3), 369–388.

Haaretz (2015). WATCH: Obama, "ISIL is a direct outgrowth of Al-Qaida in Iraq which grew out of our invasion. Haaretz. https://www.haaretz.com/israel-news/2015-03-17/ty-article/obama-isis-grew-out-of-our-invasion/0000017f-e3ee-d38f-a57f-e7fe19fa0000

Hall, J. R. (2013). Religion and violence from a sociological perspective. In M. Juergensmeyer, M. Kitts, & M. Jerryson (Eds.), *The Oxford handbook of religion and violence* (pp. 363–374). Oxford University Press.

Haner, M., Wichern, A., & Fleenor, M. (2020). The Turkish foreign fighters and the dynamics behind their flow into Syria and Iraq. *Terrorism and Political Violence, 32*(6), 1329–1347.

Hansen, M. (2007). Soviet-era textbooks still controversial. *Lincoln Journal Star.* https://journalstar.com/special-section/news/soviet-era-textbooks-still-controversial/article_4968e56a-c346-5a18-9798-2b78c5544b58.html

Harris, S. (2008). *Letter to a Christian nation.* Vintage.

Hasan, S. (2021). The making of the Jewish extremist Meir Kahane. TRT World. https://www.trtworld.com/magazine/the-making-of-the-jewish-extremist-meir-kahane-46868

Hashem, A. (2015). The many names of Abu Bakr al-Baghdadi. Al-Monitor. https://www.al-monitor.com/originals/2015/03/isis-baghdadi-islamic-state-caliph-many-names-al-qaeda.html

Haynes, A. (1994). *Gunpowder Plot: Faith in rebellion.* Sutton Publications.

Henderson, A. (2015). 6 modern-day Christian terrorist groups our media conveniently ignores. Salon. https://www.salon.com/2015/04/07/6_modern_day_christian_terrorist_groups_our_media_conveniently_ignores_partner/

Henne, P. (2019). Terrorism and religion: An overview. *Oxford research encyclopedia of politics.* https://doi.org/10.1093/acrefore/9780190228637.013.693

Hersh, S. M. (2004). Torture at Abu Ghraib. *The New Yorker.* https://www.newyorker.com/magazine/2004/05/10/torture-at-abu-ghraib

Hinz, K., Borges, D., Coutinho, A., & Andriez, T. A. (2021). The rise of Brazil's neo-Pentecostal narco-militia. Open Democracy. https://www.opendemocracy.net/en/democraciaabierta/rise-narco-militia-pentecostal-brazil-en/

Hoffman, B. (1995). "Holy terror": The implications of terrorism motivated by a religious imperative. *Studies in Conflict & Terrorism, 18*(4), 271–284.

Hoffman, B. (1998). Old madness new methods. *Rand Review, 22*(2), 1998–1999.

Holpuch, A. (2014). Texas man in Austin rampage was "homegrown, American extremist." *The Guardian.* https://www.theguardian.com/us-news/2014/dec/02/texas-austin-rampage-homegrown-american-extremist

Hong, B. (2017). Is This The Scariest Doomsday Sect in China? The Daily Beast. https://www.thedailybeast.com/is-this-the-scariest-doomsday-sect-in-china

Hume, T. (2015). "Eastern Lightning": The banned religious group that has China worried. CNN. https://www.cnn.com/2014/06/06/world/asia/china-eastern-lightning-killing/index.html

Johnson, D. (2017). Hate in God's name. Southern Poverty Law Center. https://www.splcenter.org/20170925/hate-god%E2%80%99s-name

Juergensmeyer, M. (2005). Terror in the mind of God: The global rise of religious violence. *Police Practice and Research, 6*(2), 201–208.

Juergensmeyer, M. (2007). Does religion cause terrorism? In J. R. Lewis (Ed.), *The Cambridge companion to religion and terrorism* (p. 11–22). Cambridge University Press.

Juergensmeyer, M. (2021). Religious terrorism at the turn of the twenty-first century. In C. Dietze & C. Verhoeven (Eds.), *The Oxford handbook of the history of terrorism* (pp. 591–605). Oxford University Press.

Kenworthy, T. (1999). Relatives left in dark about kin who joined Christian cult leader. *Washington Post.* https://www.washingtonpost.com/archive/politics/1999/01/08/relatives-left-in-dark-about-kin-who-joined-christian-cult-leader/bf430d35-d98d-4f46-92e1-bf9a03d89492/

Laqueur, W. (1999). *The new terrorism: Fanaticism and the arms of mass destruction.* Oxford University Press.

Laub, Z. (2021). Syria's civil war: The descent into horror. Council on Foreign Relations. https://www.cfr.org/article/syrias-civil-war

Leppäkari, M. (2014). Apocalyptic management by Monte Kim Miller. *Journal of Religion and Violence, 2*(1), 122–133.

Lewis, J. R., & Dawson, L. L. (2018). Introduction: Religion and terrorism. *Numen, 65*(2–3), 117–124.

Lewitt, M. (2021). The Assad regime's business model for supporting the Islamic State. Washington Institute for Near East Policy. https://www.washingtoninstitute.org/policy-analysis/assad-regimes-business-model-supporting-islamic-state

Liebman, C. S. (1983). Extremism as a religious norm. *Journal for the Scientific Study of Religion, 22*(1), 75–86.

MacGilivray, I (2016). The impact of Gush Emunim on the social and political fabric of Israeli society. E-International Relations. https://www.e-ir.info/2016/07/21/the-impact-of-gush-emunim-on-the-social-and-political-fabric-of-israeli-society/

Magnusson, E. (2021). "Frightening proportions": On Meir Kahane's assimilation doctrine. *Nordisk Judaistik/Scandinavian Jewish Studies, 32*(2), 36–53.

Masaeli, M., & Sneller, R. (Eds.). (2017). *The root causes of terrorism: A religious studies perspective.* Cambridge Scholars Publishing.

Mason, C. (2002). Killing for life: The apocalyptic narrative of pro-life politics. Cornell University Press.

McCoy, T. (2014). How the Islamic State evolved in an American prison. *Washington Post.* https://www.washingtonpost.com/news/morning-mix/wp/2014/11/04/how-an-american-prison-helped-ignite-the-islamic-state/

McCoy, T. (2019). "Soldiers of Jesus": Armed neo-Pentecostals torment Brazil's religious minorities. *Washington Post.* https://www.washingtonpost.com/world/the_americas/soldiers-of-jesus-armed-neo-pentecostals-torment-brazils-religious-minorities/2019/12/08/fd74de6e-fff0-11e9-8501-2a7123a38c58_story.html

McLaughlin, J. (11 July 2014). Was Iraq's top terrorist radicalized at a US-run prison? *Mother Jones.* https://www.motherjones.com/politics/2014/07/was-camp-bucca-pressure-cooker-extremism/

McVeigh, T. (2001). The McVeigh letters: Why I bombed Oklahoma. *The Guardian.* https://www.theguardian.com/world/2001/may/06/mcveigh.usa

Meleagrou-Hitchens, A. (2018). Salafism in America: History, evolution, radicalization. George Washington University Program on Extremism. https://extremism.gwu.edu/sites/g/files/zaxdzs2191/f/Salafism%20in%20America.pdf

Newman, D. (2013). Gush Emunim and the settler movement. In J. Peters & D. Newman (Ed.), *Routledge handbook on the Israeli-Palestinian conflict* (pp. 274–284). Routledge.

NPR (2016). "It was torture": An Abu Ghraib interrogator acknowledges "horrible mistakes." NPR. https://www.npr.org/sections/parallels/2016/04/04/472964974/it-was-torture-an-abu-ghraib-interrogator-acknowledges-horrible-mistakes

Pape, R. A. (2003). The strategic logic of suicide terrorism. *American Political Science Review, 97*(3), 343–361.

Pape, R. (2006). *Dying to win: The strategic logic of suicide terrorism.* Random House.

Parvez, Z. F. (2017a). Religious conservatism doesn't make a terrorist. But crime and exclusion can. *The Guardian.* https://www.theguardian.com/commentisfree/2017/jun/06/religious-conservatism-terrorist-crime-exclusion-theresa-may

Parvez, Z. F. (2017b). Who exactly are "radical" Muslims? *The Conversation.* https://theconversation.com/who-exactly-are-radical-muslims-73098

PBS (2022). Osama bin Laden v. The U.S.: Edicts and statements. https://www.pbs.org/wgbh/pages/frontline/shows/binladen/who/edicts.html

Pedahzur, A. (2012). *The triumph of Israel's radical right.* Oxford University Press.

Pedahzur, A., & Perliger, A. (2009). *Jewish terrorism in Israel.* Columbia University Press.

Perliger, A., & Pedahzur, A. (2016). Counter cultures, group dynamics and religious terrorism. *Political Studies, 64*(2), 297–314.

Pew Research Center (2017). The changing global religious landscape. https://www.pewresearch.org/religion/2017/04/05/the-changing-global-religious-landscape/#global-population-projections-2015-to-2060

Phillips, T. (2022). Christ and cocaine: Rio's gangs of God blend faith and violence. *The*

Guardian. https://www.theguardian.com/world/2022/jan/23/christ-and-cocaine-rios-gangs-of-god-blend-faith-and-violence

Phillips, T. (2024). Rio's 'narco-pentecostal' gangs accused of ordering Catholic churches to close. The Guardian. https://www.theguardian.com/world/article/2024/jul/10/brazil-gang-boss-drug-trafficking-closing-churches

Powell, C. (2012). Colin Powell on the Bush administration's Iraq War mistakes. *Newsweek*. https://www.newsweek.com/colin-powell-bush-administrations-iraq-war-mistakes-65023

Ranstorp, M. (1996). Terrorism in the name of religion. *Journal of International Affairs, 50*(1), 41–63.

Rapoport, D. C. (2002). The four waves of rebel terror and September. *Anthropoetics, 8*(1), 1–11.

Reeve, S. (1999). *The new jackals: Ramzi Yousef, Osama bin Laden, and future of terrorism.* Northeastern University Press.

Rosin, H. (1998). Cult leader and followers vanish, leaving worried relatives. *Washington Post.* https://www.washingtonpost.com/archive/politics/1998/10/17/cult-leader-and-followers-vanish-leaving-worried-relatives/9999f38f-36a5-44c1-995e-7661a40f7806/

Rosin, H. (1999). L.A. shooting may have been initiation rite. *Washington Post.* https://www.washingtonpost.com/wp-srv/national/longterm/hatecrimes/stories/beliefs081299.htm

Roszak, T. (1995). *The making of a counter culture: Reflections on the technocratic society and its youthful opposition.* University of California Press.

Sageman, M. (2004). Understanding terror networks. University of Pennsylvania Press.

Saiya, N. (2020). Confronting apocalyptic terrorism: Lessons from France and Japan. *Studies in Conflict & Terrorism, 43*(9), 775–795.

Saiya, N. (2022). *The global politics of Jesus: A Christian case for church-state separation.* Oxford University Press.

Shea, M. (2013). The cult who kidnaps Christians and is at war with the Chinese government. *Vice.* https://www.vice.com/en/article/7be5ya/the-chinese-cult-who-kidnap-christians-and-paint-snakes

Smith, M. R., & Lardner, R. (2022). Michael Flynn is recruiting an "Army of God" in growing Christian nationalist movement.

PBS. https://www.pbs.org/newshour/politics/michael-flynn-is-recruiting-an-army-of-god-in-growing-christian-nationalist-movement

SPLC (2022). Christian Identity. Southern Poverty Law Center. https://www.splcenter.org/fighting-hate/extremist-files/ideology/christian-identity

Sponeck, H. C. V. (2006). *A different kind of war: The UN sanctions regime in Iraq.* Berghahn Books.

Sprinzak, E. (1987). Fundamentalism, terrorism, and democracy: The case of the Gush Emunim underground. Woodrow Wilson Center Occasional Paper no. 4. Smithsonian Institution.

Sprinzak, E. (1990). Kahane: The Nightmare That Liberal Ideologues Could Not Imagine: Israel: The slain rabbi believed he represented mainstream Judaism and was on his way to power. In fact, he helped brutalize a nation. *Los Angeles Times.* https://www.latimes.com/archives/la-xpm-1990-11-11-op-5885-story.html

Sprinzak, E. (1991). Violence and catastrophe in the theology of Rabbi Meir Kahane: The ideologization of mimetic desire. *Terrorism and Political Violence, 3*(3), 48–70.

Stern, J. (2003). *Terror in the name of God.* Ecco.

Thompson, A., & Suri, J. (1 October, 2014). How America helped ISIS. *The New York Times.* https://www.nytimes.com/2014/10/02/opinion/how-america-helped-isis.html

Thompson, M. (2015). How disbanding the Iraqi Army fueled ISIS. *Time.* https://time.com/3900753/isis-iraq-syria-army-united-states-military/

Tirman, J. (2022). Iraq: The human cost. MIT Center for International Studies. http://i.a.cnn.net/cnn/2006/images/10/11/human.cost.of.war.pdf

Toft, M. D. (2007). Getting religion? The puzzling case of Islam and civil war. *International Security, 31*(4), 97–131.

Wagemakers, J. (2016). Salafism. Oxford Research Encyclopedias. https://oxfordre.com/religion/display/10.1093/acrefore/9780199340378.001.0001/acrefore-9780199340378-e-255

Washington Post (1998). Calls to action. https://www.washingtonpost.com/wp-srv/inatl/longterm/eafricabombing/stories/action082398.htm

Weissbrod, L. (1982). Gush Emunim ideology—from religious doctrine to political action. *Middle Eastern Studies*, *18*(3), 265–275.

Wessinger, C. (2009). Deaths in the fire at the Branch Davidians' Mount Carmel: Who bears responsibility? *Nova Religio*, *13*(2), 25–60.

Whyte, L. (2018). Has Trump's White House 'resurrected' Army of God anti-abortion extremists? *The Open Democracy.* https://www.opendemocracy.net/en/5050/army-of-god-anti-abortion-terrorists-emboldened-under-trump/

Wexler, S. (2015). *America's secret jihad: The hidden history of religious terrorism in the United States.* Catapult.

The Operations of Terrorist Organizations

Targets and Tactics

When, Where, and How Terrorists Kill

Source: Journalist 1st Class Preston Keres, Public domain, via Wikimedia Commons.

Learning Objectives

1. To classify terrorist targets into different categories based on their tangible and intangible qualities.
2. To learn the nature and history of targets and tactics that have been widely used by terrorist organizations across the world.
3. To analyze and compare patterns in terrorists' targeting and tactics, both in the United States and worldwide.
4. To explore the key factors that influence the terrorists' target selection process.
5. To explain why and when terrorists target undefended civilians.

9.1 INTRODUCTION

In September 1972, eight members of the Palestinian group **Black September** infiltrated the Olympic village in Munich, West Germany, and killed two Israeli athletes and held nine other members of the Olympic team hostage (Doubek 2022).

On April 19, 1995, a US Army veteran destroyed a federal office building in Oklahoma City with a massive truck bomb, killing more than 160 people, including 19 children (Cooper 2020).

FIGURE 9.1 The Munich Massacre refers to a tragic event that occurred during the 1972 Summer Olympics in Munich, West Germany. A Palestinian terrorist group known as Black September took 11 members of the Israeli Olympic team hostage. The terrorists demanded the release of Palestinian prisoners held in Israeli jails and sought to draw international attention to the Palestinian cause. The situation escalated into a violent confrontation at the Fürstenfeldbruck airbase, where the terrorists and hostages were taken. During a botched rescue attempt by German authorities, all 11 Israeli hostages were killed, along with one German police officer and five of the eight terrorists. *Source:* Spielvogel, CC BY-SA 4.0, via Wikimedia Commons.

On September 11, 2001, al-Qaeda operatives hijacked four commercial airplanes, crashing two of them into the twin towers of the World Trade Center in New York, one into the Pentagon in Washington, DC, and another into an agricultural field in Pennsylvania. Overall, more than 3,000 people were killed and massive property destruction caused (Haner et al. 2021).

On January 7, 2015, two men armed with Kalashnikov type assault rifles stormed the offices of the French satirical magazine, Charlie Hebdo, in Paris France, and systematically killed 17 individuals, including editorial staff and cartoonists (BBC 2015).

In June 2015, a White supremacist entered a predominantly Black church in Charleston, South Carolina and fired 74 rounds, killing nine worshippers, saying, "I have to do it. You rape our women and you're taking over our country. And you have to go" (Foster & Sanchez 2015).

In July 2019, a left-wing Antifa extremist attempted to blow up the US Immigration and Customs Enforcement (ICE) detention center in Tacoma, Washington using a 500-gallon propane tank, before he was shot dead by the police (Allam 2020).

And in May 2020, an extreme right-wing US Air Force Staff Sergeant killed two and injured three other law enforcement personnel in Oakland, California during a peaceful Black Lives Matter protest, in an attempt to ignite a nationwide civil war (Derysh 2020).

There are countless examples of terrorist groups causing widespread death and destruction, using a range of tactics and methods, while in pursuit of their goals, whether it is a regime or policy change, territorial concession, social control, or simply the maintenance of the status quo (Wither & Mullins 2016).

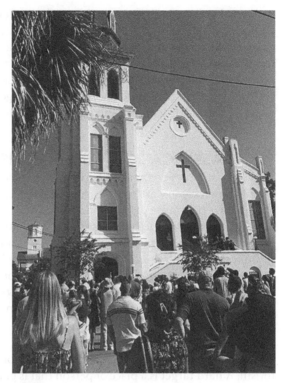

FIGURE 9.2 Crowds gather in front of the Emanuel African Methodist Episcopal Church in Charleston, South Carolina, following Dylann Roof's racially motivated attack on June 17, 2015. Roof later confessed to the shooting, stating his intention to incite a race war. *Source:* Kellyjeanne9, CC BY-SA 4.0, via Wikimedia Commons.

Even though terrorist groups show wide variation in their target selections and come from a wide range of ideological backgrounds with different goals, motives, and histories, one striking commonality among them is that terrorists' choice of targets is rarely random. Target selection is almost always the result of a carefully planned, deliberate, and (to them) rational decision-making process (Abrahms & Mroszczyk 2021; Ahmed 2018; Asal et al. 2009; Drake 1998a; Silke 2010). Contrary to frequent media depictions and claims of politicians, terrorists are not mindless and indiscriminate bloodthirsty individuals (Polo 2020). Most terrorists weigh the costs and benefits of their attacks and operate within a delineated framework. Several factors influence terrorists' selection of targets and victims, such as the group's ideology, its military capabilities, its access to weapons, its strategic objectives, and the security environment in which it operates. Social factors such as public opinion, international pressure, political cost, and the potential newsworthiness of an attack also shape terrorists' targeting decisions.

This chapter will cover three interrelated topics. We will first discuss the diverse types of tactics and targets of terrorist organizations, with a specific focus on who terrorists target and how these targets differ depending on the ideology of the groups involved. Second, we will identify the many different attack methods used by terrorist groups. Third, we will examine the factors that determine terrorists' target selection, and more specifically why the victims of terrorism are targeted and how the targeting decisions of terrorist groups vary. Consistent with the existing literature, our focus will be on explaining how ideological beliefs correspond to differences in terrorist targeting strategies and the circumstances under which undefended civilians are more likely to be targeted in terror attacks.

9.2 CLASSIFICATION OF TERRORIST TARGET TYPES

A "target" can be defined as a person, object, or a place selected as the recipient of an attack. It could be a religious institution, school, government building, security official, or some other kind of prominent person (Jones et al. 2020). Targets of terrorist violence are diverse, and it is a frivolous task to categorize them into mutually exclusive groups. There are many categories of terrorist targets beside the commonly known "soft" and "hard" targets (Schmid 2020). A review of the existing literature indicates six areas of target selection considerations, based on factors such as (1) the protection level of a target ("hard" vs. "soft"), (2) the target's official status (military vs. civilian), (3) extent of planning required, (4) intended audience of the attack, (5) target victim type, and (6) purpose of the attack.

9.2.1 Hard Targets versus Soft Targets

The protection level of a target is the most common factor used to classify targets of terrorism. A **hard target** is a place or person that is guarded and protected from threats by strong physical security measures (e.g., guards, checkpoints, physical deterrents such as walls, CCTV cameras, and metal detectors). It is often risky for terrorists to carry out attacks against hard targets because of the increased likelihood of being captured or killed. Public access to hard targets is often prevented and limited to specific individuals, as hard targets are usually staffed by security personnel. Another important characteristic of hard targets is that the staff who work at these places are aware of the risk of becoming a target of terrorist activity at any time. They go through regular security training about these risks and are required to be observant of such risks (Asal et al. 2009). Due to these reasons, hard targets are considered unattractive to terrorists. Examples of hard targets include military bases, airports, government buildings, international summits, airlines, prisons, heads of states, ambassadors, politicians, diplomatic missions, power stations, and nuclear plants.

A **soft target**, on the other hand, is a location, place, or a person that is vulnerable to attacks due to a lack of security measures and protections in place. Unlike hard targets, soft targets are often welcoming environments. They attract large civilian populations who have no reason to believe that they will be a target of a terrorist attack and thus take few precautions, and are also easily accessible to the public with no or limited security. Due to their open and accessible nature, soft targets are attractive to terrorists. Further, an attack on a soft target that includes a large civilian population can have a long lasting detrimental psychological effect on the general population. Examples of soft targets include shopping centers, libraries, hotels, night clubs, hospitals, transportation systems, movie theaters, restaurants, places of worship, pedestrian zones in urban centers, and other recreational public venues that are frequented by large numbers of civilians.

It is important to note that some soft targets can later transition into hard targets due to past tragic events. For example, international sporting events such as the Olympics have been targeted by groups from various ideologies including Christian and Islamist fundamentalists, as well as nationalist and separatist groups. Due to these attacks, nations that are selected to host Olympic events are now required to take stringent security measures for the safety of the athletes and spectators. Airports are another notable example of a soft target that has transitioned into a hard target. Shortly after the 9/11 attacks, countries around the world implemented strict security measures (e.g., full body scanners, metal detectors, limitations on what can be passed through security checkpoints) to prevent such a tragic event from occurring again. Several other critical infrastructures (e.g., power grids, telecommunication centers, water treatment plants) that would have been historically considered soft targets have transitioned into hard targets as a potential attack toward these installations would cause extensive damage to the normal functioning of societies and the well-being of communities.

FIGURE 9.3 Hotel Europa, often referred to as "the Hardboard Hotel," was a hub for international press and journalists who were covering the conflicts between the IRA and the loyalists (Morrison 2020). The hotel also served as a meeting point for politicians, high-ranking British soldiers, and paramilitaries during the Troubles. Between 1970 and 1994 it was damaged by explosions 33 times, earning the dubious distinction of being "the most bombed hotel in the history of the world." Experts suggest that the IRA targeted the hotel repeatedly because it was a landmark building that guaranteed maximum media coverage after each attack (Meredith 2017). *Source:* Murat Haner.

9.2.2 Military versus Civilian Targets

Another commonly used classification of terrorist targets is based on the official status of the places and persons under attack: military versus **civilian targets**. **Military targets** include individuals who have an official status with the security forces of the government (e.g., police, military, and others) and facilities and installations that are owned by the security forces (e.g., military barracks, police stations). Military targets often consist of combatants with the power to use lethal force and thus they are also considered hard targets.

Civilian targets, in contrast, consist of places and individuals that are not members of security forces, such as private citizens and civilian businesses. Compared to military targets, civilian targets have limited or no security and thus they are more easily accessible than military targets. Examples include infrastructure such as shops, restaurants, schools, hospitals, shopping malls, and places of worship, and individuals such as students, shoppers, tourists, and religious figures. Even though attacks against undefended civilians are newsworthy and relatively easy to carry out, such attacks typically have counterproductive national and international consequences for the reputation of the terrorist groups. Groups that target civilians are often labeled as violent and immoral and run the risk of losing support from their popular base (Polo 2020).

9.2.3 Preplanned Targets versus Targets of Opportunity

Most terrorist operations involve careful and extensive planning and prior coordination concerning the selection of targets, surveillance, the date and time of the attack, the weapons to be used, the attack type, intelligence gathering, and the training necessary to carry out the attacks. Even though the degree of planning varies, attacks toward targets that involve complex operations are defined as **preplanned targets**. Examples of preplanned targets include 9/11, the 1995 Tokyo subway sarin gas attack by Aum Shinrikyo cult members, al-Qaeda's 1998 bombing of US Embassies in Kenya and Tanzania, and the 2011 Norway attacks by far-right extremist Anders Behring Breivik.

It is important to note that preplanned attacks can be aimed at specific individuals (such as presidents) or specific locations that include unknown individuals (Drake 1998a). For example, during the 2004 Madrid train bombings, the terrorists carried out a series of coordinated attacks (using 10 bombs hidden in backpacks and small bags) against the commuter train system of Madrid, killing approximately 200 civilians and injuring more than 1,800 (CNN 2023). Even though the terrorists devised an elaborate plan to kill civilians by targeting the train system, they did not intend to kill those specific individuals; rather, they targeted passengers in general.

Targets of opportunity, on the other hand, refer to the vulnerable enemy targets (e.g., police, military) that appear in an unexpected time and place when an attack has not been preplanned or arranged. Terrorists may take advantage of the opportunity, especially if they see this unexpected opportunity as a legitimate target—a person they believe deserves to be killed or a thing that they believe must be annihilated.

9.2.4 Physical Targets (Targets of Violence) versus Psychological Targets (Targets of Attention)

Decades of research indicates that most terrorist attacks are executed to send a message to the perceived enemies, rather than solely to kill them. It can be argued that each attack has two aspects: (1) the killing of an enemy target, and (2) sending a message to the adversary government and society (Schmid 1988). Scholars identify two targets of violence associated with each attack: (1) the **physical target (target of violence)**, and (2) the **psychological target (target of attention)**. Physical targets are the actual targets that terrorists aim to kill or destroy. Psychological targets, on the other hand, are the primary audiences that the terrorists aim to influence by their attacks (Wither & Mullins 2016). Government officials, policymakers, members of the adversary group or society, and potential supporters of terrorist groups can all be classified as psychological targets.

Members of major religious groups have targeted the Olympic games because such attacks often bring widespread news coverage, which makes it easier for the group to air their cause to their audience as well as the international community. Terrorists are not targeting these games because they dislike sports or have issues with specific athletes. By carrying out these highly sensational and attention-generating attacks, they send a message either to the host government or to the governments of the athletes (Silke 2010). Even though they may kill an athlete during such an attack, the governments are the real primary target (i.e., psychological target) of their acts.

9.2.5 Classification by Target Victim Type and Attack Location
Another commonly used classification is the type of victims involved and the attack locations. The Global Terrorism Database classifies terrorist target types into the following 22 categories by their victims' characteristics and the place of the attacks:

1. business
2. government
3. police
4. military
5. abortion-related
6. airports and aircraft
7. foreign government entities (e.g., embassies, consulates, diplomatic staff)
8. educational institution
9. food or water supply
10. journalists and media
11. maritime (includes ports and maritime facilities)
12. nongovernmental organization
13. private citizens and property
14. religious figures/institutions
15. telecommunication
16. terrorists/nonstate militias
17. tourists
18. transportation (other than aviation)
19. unknown
20. utilities
21. violent political parties
22. other

The Global Terrorism Index (GTI) reports that are annually produced by the Institute for Economics & Peace (IEP), which provide a comprehensive summary of key global trends in terrorism over the past decade, employ a similar target classification. The GTI reports classify targets into six categories as:

1. military, police
2. citizens
3. public figures, institutions
4. businesses
5. critical infrastructure
6. other

9.2.6 Classification by Purpose of Attack

Based on the terrorists' reason for an attack, targets have been classified into the following four categories (Drake 1998a):

1. symbolic
2. functional
3. logistical
4. expressive/emotional

FIGURE 9.4 On August 27, 1979, Lord Louis Mountbatten, a prominent member of the British royal family, was assassinated in a terrorist attack by the Irish Republican Army (IRA). Lord Mountbatten was on a family vacation in Mullaghmore, Ireland, when a bomb planted on his boat by the IRA exploded, killing him, his fourteen-year-old grandson Nicholas Knatchbull, and others. The assassination of Lord Mountbatten marked a high-profile and symbolic target for the IRA, as Lord Mountbatten was a decorated war hero and uncle to Prince Philip, the husband of Queen Elizabeth II. *Source:* Allan Warren, CC BY-SA 3.0, via Wikimedia Commons.

It is important to note that these categories are not mutually exclusive; a target that is attacked for its symbolic value may also have functional and logistical value for a terrorist group.

Symbolic Targets

A **symbolic target** follows from the goal of inflicting heavy psychological damage on the enemy. Terrorists may attack certain prominent individuals or places to force their perceived enemies to make a specific policy change or simply draw attention to their cause. For example, on August 27, 1979, an Irish Republican and member of the Provisional Irish Republican Army (PIRA) assassinated a British Royal family member, Lord Louis Mountbatten, while he was lobster fishing with his friends and family members; they used a radio-controlled bomb placed under his yacht. The IRA later announced that the goal of this assassination was to bring global attention to the conflict in Ireland and inflict terror on British officials to drive them out of Northern Ireland (Clancy 2023). According to Irish nationalists, Mountbatten was a legitimate target because he was representing the British royal family.

Functional Targets

A **functional target** is one in which the destruction of the place or murder of a person is deemed imperative to the continued operation and cause of the terrorist group. In other words, these targets pose an existential threat to the terrorists. For example, in 1992, the IRA destroyed a forensic lab in Northern Ireland with a 3,000-pound homemade explosive because of the lab's crucial role in analyzing evidence concerning terrorism-related charges against Irish Republicans (Kearney 2017). By completely gutting the lab and eliminating the forensic evidence (e.g., exhibits and case files) to be used in court, the IRA disrupted the prosecution of the cases, hence slowing down the functioning of the judicial system in the country for a long period.

Logistical Targets

Terrorist groups need financial resources to fund their daily necessities (food, transportation, housing, communication, weapons) as much as their ongoing military operations. Terrorist groups utilize various methods to obtain money and materials, such as fundraising from their support base, illicit drug or sex trading, and targeting logistical resources. A **logistical target** is one that is attacked by terrorists to provide them with resources. For example, both the ETA in Spain and the PKK in Turkey are known to force their wealthy supporters to contribute financially to their cause under the guise of a "revolutionary tax." These groups contact the rich business owners in their regions and ask them to pay an annual tax and threaten to disrupt their economic and business activities if they decline to do so.

Expressive Targets

Terrorists are human beings. Even though most terrorist organizations have some ethical guidelines and rules that lay out the conditions of engagement with enemy targets, terrorists may sometimes act emotionally in response to a specific situation or stimulus. In other words, as with all the other military units, terrorists are not immune to violations of their rules. Simply having rules of conduct does not guarantee that all members of a terrorist group will follow the code all of the time, especially since the actual combat environment is physically and emotionally turbulent. In this context, the persons and places that are targeted by terrorists due to emotion-based motivations and desires are classified as **expressive targets**. A major example of an expressive target is when terrorist actions are motivated by a desire for vengeance. For example, even though the PKK has very strict rules not to kill individuals who are not in combat, a retired Turkish military member, who was known to be one of the most notorious torturers of Kurdish inmates, was assassinated by a PKK member while he was riding a public bus in Istanbul (Haner 2017).

9.3 TERRORIST TACTICS AND ATTACK TYPES

Terrorists have the potential to use a variety of **tactics**, ranging from conventional operations such as shooting, assassination, and **bombing** to very complex and unconventional operations such as hijacking, kidnapping, and bioterrorism, often determined by two key elements: the ultimate goals and objectives in carrying out an attack, and the group's organizational capabilities and available resources. If the goal of a group is to force a government to negotiate (e.g., for the release of prisoners, or to extort money), then they are most likely to use tactics that are not initially deadly, such as hijacking a plane or kidnapping prominent individuals. These kinds of operations often require extensive planning, logistics, and intelligence gathering. Alternatively, if a terrorist group simply wants to inflict pain on their perceived adversaries, then they often use less risky tactics such as bombings, assassinations, and armed assaults.

The groups' organizational capabilities also play an important role in determining the type of tactics used in terrorist operations. Most terrorist groups are able to construct bombs with rudimentary skills that can be learned online. However, not all groups have the competence or monetary resources needed to construct advanced level explosive devices, such as vehicle borne explosives, which require multiple level triggering methods. Even though there have been some instances in the past, not all terrorist groups have the capability to acquire radioactive material for use in constructing a dirty bomb.

Depending on their capacity and motives, terrorists have a wide range of tactics at their disposal. Even though the academic literature identifies several types of terrorist tactics and operations, the focus here will be on the eight major types of tactics that are frequently employed by terrorist organizations:

1. armed assault
2. assassination
3. bombing
4. hijacking
5. raiding
6. sieging and hostage-taking
7. sabotage (facility/infrastructure attack)
8. suicide attacks

Before explaining these tactics, it is important to note that when groups carry out attacks they may use more than one tactic simultaneously, such as hijacking and mass casualty or destruction, as was the case with the 9/11 attacks. Also, using these techniques, terrorists may carry out two different types of attacks: (1) **discriminate attacks**, in which groups only attack enemy combatants, such as legitimate military targets such as military officials, installations, and police officers, or (2) **indiscriminate attacks**, where the groups strike randomly, failing to distinguish between combatants and protected individuals and objects such as civilians and civilian infrastructure.

Even though chemical, biological, radioactive, and nuclear weapons—or **weapons of mass destruction (WMD)**—can have a significant psychologically and physically destructive effect on the critical structures of society and human lives, this section will focus on the most commonly used type of terrorists tactics, because to date only one terrorist organization has been able to use them (recall the cult of Aum Shinrikyo that carried out the 1995 Tokyo subway sarin gas attack that killed more than 50 commuters). Realistically, the risk of terrorist groups accessing and using such weapons is extremely low (though not impossible). It should be noted, however, that despite the low level of risk associated with accessing such weapons, governments and international organizations around the world stay alert (mostly due to the availability of such weapons in nations like North Korea) and take precautionary steps to make sure that terrorists do not have access to the materials, expertise, and other enabling capabilities to develop and use WMDs (United Nations 2023).

9.3.1 Armed Assault

The Global Terrorism Database describes **armed assault** as terrorist actions with the primary motivation of killing or physically harming an adversary, using lethal weapons such as firearms, sharp instruments, and incendiary devices (such as hand grenades). Assault is often an effective terrorist tactic because of its random nature. Not only do these types of tactics create a general sense of vulnerability among the general public, but they also demonstrate the inability of governments to protect their own citizens, and thus disrupt the daily activities of individuals. They are also highly mediatic events, often resulting in cover-

FIGURE 9.5   Paris rally in support of the victims of the Charlie Hebdo shootings on January 7, 2015, in Paris, France. The shootings targeted the offices of Charlie Hebdo, a satirical French magazine known for its provocative cartoons and commentary on various topics, including religion and politics. Two heavily armed shooters, Saïd and Chérif Kouachi, stormed the magazine's headquarters during an editorial meeting. They opened fire, killing 12 people and injuring several others. The attack was motivated by the belief that Charlie Hebdo had insulted Islam through its cartoons, particularly those featuring the Prophet Muhammad. *Source:* sébastien amiet;l, CC BY 2.0, via Wikimedia Commons.

age and publicity at the global level. The Charlie Hebdo shootings in Paris, for example, in which two aggrieved brothers shot and killed 12 employees of the satirical French magazine, received broad international coverage from Europe to the United States (Kreuz 2020).

9.3.2 Assassination

Assassination can simply be defined as the murder of an important public figure, such as a head of state, government leader, political party leader, celebrity, prominent member of a social or political movement, or other senior leader, such as a high-ranking military official. Assassinations have been widely used throughout history in all parts of the world to draw attention to terrorists' causes, to exact revenge against a perceived oppressor, or simply to undermine the authority of a ruling government.

The assassination of important figures can make a terrorist group seem militarily powerful. Such operations achieve two goals: spread fear among the enemy, and bring publicity to the group. As described in detail in the Global Terrorism Database, the killing of a random soldier or a police officer is simply an armed assault; however, if the individual is specifically selected to be killed (e.g., killing a prominent soldier), the act is considered an assassination.

Assassinations are devastating not only because of their sudden and secret nature, but also due to the intense emotional effect that they have on the society. The assassination of Archduke Franz Ferdinand of Austria-Hungary by a Serbian terrorist (a member of the Black Hand) in 1914 led to the start of the First World War, which cost the lives of more than 40 million military and civilian individuals. Another example comes from the United States. Four individuals who served as president have been assassinated (Lincoln, Garfield, McKinley, and Kennedy), and dozens of others were unsuccessfully targeted by assassins. After each attempt there was serious political turmoil in the nation that attracted widespread national and international media coverage, unintentionally advertising the power of terrorist groups to annihilate even the well-protected, highest-level elected officials in the world.

9.3.3 Bombings and Mass Casualty Attacks

Historically, terrorist organizations have commonly used various types of explosives (in terms of lethality and complexity) as weapons. Today, improvised explosive devices (IEDs) or bombs remain an appealing tool for groups that are seeking to cause mass casualties, destroy large infrastructures, and create widespread panic and an atmosphere of fear. Unfortunately, instructions for bomb manufacturing are readily available online, and the materials necessary to construct a bomb can easily be found in any hardware or auto supply store. Terrorist groups are now able to improvise bombs, creating them in several different shapes and forms so that they are disguisable, increasing their portability and thwarting the preventative efforts of law enforcement. By improvising, groups are able to target critical locations in the hearts of cities and other crowded public locations, disguising their explosives as a box, luggage, or pressure cooker, or by delivering them as a package in the mail, concealing them in containers such as recycling and trash bins at city centers, or transporting them with vehicles.

FIGURE 9.6 The US Navy aircraft carrier *USS Bunker Hill* afire after being hit by two "Kamikaze" suicide planes off Okinawa, May 11, 1945. The kamikaze attacks during World War II represent one of the most well-known and systematic uses of aircraft as suicide weapons in military history. *Source:* Naval History & Heritage Command, Public domain, via Wikimedia Commons.

Using vehicle-borne IEDs, terrorists are able to create extremely powerful bombs, increasing the capacity and damage radius of the explosives. A compact car can carry up to a 500 pounds of explosives whereas a delivery truck can carry up to 10,000 pounds of the same material (DHS 2023). The concealed portability of large amounts of explosives enables terrorist groups to carry out mass casualty attacks on target populations (e.g., embassies, religious complexes, government buildings, shopping districts, city streets with thousands of people nearby), as well as cripple everyday life by destroying critical services such as electricity, water, communication, and transportation for days or even weeks. All of this damage can be inflicted

FIGURE 9.7   The attacks of September 11, 2001, were tragic and unprecedented. The hijackers deliberately crashed two planes, American Airlines Flight 11 and United Airlines Flight 175, into the North and South Towers of the World Trade Center in New York City, causing both towers to collapse within hours. A third plane, American Airlines Flight 77, was flown into the Pentagon in Arlington, Virginia. *Source:* rds323, Public domain, via Wikimedia Commons.

on the perceived enemy with minimal risk of being caught, through the use of remote-controlled detonators, timers, or simply by parking and leaving an explosive loaded vehicle close to a target location, as per the Oklahoma City bombing.

With the 9/11 attacks on the World Trade Center and the Pentagon, the world was introduced to a new type of highly destructive weapon: commercial planes loaded with jet fuel. Historically, planes have been used to transport and drop explosives on enemy targets, such as the atomic bombs dropped on Hiroshima and Nagasaki during World War II. Aside from that, the Japanese army employed kamikaze missions, a type of suicide bombing mission designed to destroy enemy targets by intentionally crashing fighter planes into American navy assets, causing large-scale destruction and military casualties (Hone 2020). However, 9/11 marked the first time a terrorist group used the actual planes as bombs. Hijackers crashed two Boeing 767 airplanes, one owned by American Airlines and one by United Airlines, each carrying thousands of gallons of highly flammable jet fuel, into the two towers of the World Trade Center. The impact started an intense fire, which is believed to have caused the melting of the steel beams and the collapse of the towers (Sonenshine 2021).

9.3.4 Hijacking

Hijacking is another type of terrorist tactic in which terrorists forcefully seize control of an aircraft, land vehicle, or ship while it is in transit. During these operations, terrorists hold the passengers or the commodity hostage as a bargaining tool against a government or organization and ask for their demands to be met or that the operator of the vehicle change the route to a new destination. Hostages can be killed or the cargo can be damaged if the adversary does not comply with the demands (e.g., ransom payments, safe passage to another country, or freeing of prisoners). Hijackings are different from hostage-taking incidents in the sense that the target in the former category is a vehicle, regardless of whether there is a passenger in it.

While 9/11 can be considered the most infamous and tragic hijacking incident, there have been hundreds of other hijackings dating back to the 1910s, the earliest days of aviation (Macola 2021). In 1948, six pro-communist Greeks who needed to travel to Yugoslavia to avoid prosecution hijacked a commercial plane that was traveling from Athens to Thessaloniki and forcefully changed the route to then Skopje, Yugoslavia (Kokkinidis 2022). In 1976, Air France flight 139, which was en route from Tel Aviv to Paris, was hijacked by members of the Popular Front for the Liberation of Palestine (PFLP) and the German left-wing group, the Red Army Faction. The hijackers demanded five million dollars as a ransom payment and the release of Palestinian individuals form Israeli prisons in exchange for the safe release of the 240 passengers on board (Simon 2019).

9.3.5 Raiding

Raids, also known as surprise attacks, are one of the most frequently used fighting tactics in terrorism. They are often executed with a large number of fighters equipped with heavy weapons and conducted for a short period of time, often during an overnight mission. The goal is not to capture and seize a building, land, or individuals, but to surprise and demoralize the adversary with heavy casualties and destruction of their equipment, position, and installations at an unexpected time. Raids can also be conducted to collect information, to disrupt the plans of the enemy, or to free prisoners kept by the adversary. It is crucial for the terrorists who carry out raid missions to retreat to their safe havens (defense positions) before the adversary responds in a coordinated way (via air or land forces) with more advanced weapons (Haner 2017). Raid missions always end with withdrawal.

9.3.6 Siege and Hostage-Taking

A **siege** is the military takeover of a place, such as a school, bank, theater, or shopping mall by terrorist groups in which hostages are seized as a bargaining tool and typically released once the terrorists' demands are met. In 2004, 32 armed separatist Chechens wearing bomb belts violently took over a school in Beslan, North Ossetia, and held more than 1,000 people as captives in the school's gymnasium. Barricading the entrances with explosives, the group asked the Russian government to pull its troops out of Chechnya. The attack resulted in the death of more than 300 people, mostly children, after the Russian forces stormed the building to kill the attackers (BBC 2017).

Hostage-taking incidents are desirable tools for groups who are seeking to advertise their cause around the world and influence public opinion. As mentioned in the previous chapters, the live broadcasted beheadings of British, Japanese, and American Islamic State captives in Syria garnered international media attention and created tremendous pressure on the respective governments to meet the demands of the IS. Such attacks often create a dilemma for governments as the solution to end these types of crises often leaves some discontent. If the governments agree to negotiate and execute the demands of violent groups (e.g., pay the ransom or release prisoners), then they are accused of appeasing

FIGURE 9.8 The Beslan school siege was a horrific hostage crisis that occurred in the Russian town of Beslan, North Ossetia, in September 2004. The siege began on the morning of September 1 when a group of heavily armed terrorists, mostly belonging to Chechen and Ingush extremist groups, took more than 1,100 people hostages, the majority of whom were children. Approximately 334 people lost their lives during the Beslan school siege, including hostages, terrorists, and Russian security forces. *Source:* Leon, CC BY-SA 3.0, via Wikimedia Commons.

terrorists. The alternative option, however—engaging in a military style rescue mission—is risky because such operations often end up with fatal consequences, as we saw in the Beslan school example.

Groups also engage in hostage-taking missions for financial reasons. US Treasury officials have publicly warned the international community that hostage-taking for ransoming is the second greatest financial resource (falling right behind direct state sponsorship) for terrorist organizations worldwide. Corroborating this, statistics from the same agency indicate that between 2008 and 2023, at least $165 million dollars have been paid as ransom to various terrorist organizations worldwide (Ferran & Keneally 2023).

9.3.7 Sabotage (Facility or Infrastructure Attack)

Sabotage is the deliberate destruction of nonhuman targets, such as places, property, or equipment (bridges, roads, factories, dams, pipelines, train tracks, warehouses, hotels, machinery) that are owned by the adversary. Distinct from the other tactics, sabotage is often aimed at *things*, not humans, even though people may get hurt during such operations (e.g., an arson attack toward an enemy building may inadvertently kill individuals residing in that building). A notable example of a sabotage is the bombing attacks conducted against the Nord Stream pipelines, which carry natural gas from Russia to Germany, by Pro-Ukrainian paramilitaries. The lines became inoperable after the attack, causing financial loss (estimated to be $500 million) to Russian state-owned gas company, Gazprom (Entous et al. 2023). Vladimir Putin called the sabotage against the pipelines an "act of international terrorism" (Reuters 2022).

Sabotage of civil and military infrastructure through ransomware—a type of malware attack launched by hackers to encrypt and exfiltrate data on electronic systems until a ransom is paid for their release—is also a growing concern today. These attacks have become a critical threat to the national security and economic stability of many countries around the world (Craig 2021). In 2017, the US shipment company Federal Express was attacked by WannaCry 2.0 global ransomware, which caused the company to lose more than $300 million in ransom payments and system downtimes (Cook 2021). The Wanna-Cry outbreak, which was suspected to be sponsored by a terrorist organization supported by the North Korean government, caused even more damage in other countries. In the United Kingdom alone, the malware shut down computer systems in more than 80 National Health Service organizations, blocked access to patient records, and forced hospitals to postpone surgeries and cancel patient appointments (Collier 2017).

9.3.8 Suicide Attacks

Suicide attacks (also known as suicide bombings) help groups cause devastating physical and psychological casualties for the adversary, and due to the media attention they receive, advertise their goals and missions to a broader audience. In this type of attack, terrorists use their own bodies as the explosive delivery and guidance system (Aman 2007). The only downside as far as the terrorist group is concerned is the certain death of the attackers. Compared to other tactics, suicide attacks are highly effective and precise in the annihilation of the targets, as the bomber can disguise themselves within a crowd and detonate highly explosive materials mixed with shrapnel in close proximity to their victims, leading to highly graphic casualties. In suicide operations, the perpetrator does not need to make an escape plan.

Statistics indicate that a single terrorist attack of suicide bombing, on average, kills more people than any other form of terrorism (Hafez 2007; Horowitz 2015). This is normal

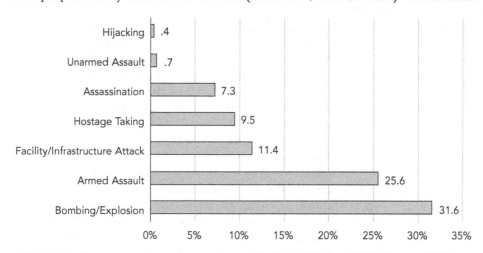

FIGURE 9.9 Terrorist tactics used across the world, 2019–2020 (n=16,975). *Source:* START (National Consortium for the Study of Terrorism and Responses to Terrorism) (2022). Global Terrorism Database 1970–2020 [data file].

and expected, as the ability to conceal explosive materials and also the ability to control the timing of an explosion gives an advantage to terrorists who are seeking the maximum level of casualties on the adversary and also makes it harder for law enforcement agencies to guard the public against such threats (Almogy et al. 2004). Due to these tactical advantages, some scholars call suicide bombers "smart bombs": a bomb that can pinpoint its target, travel into restricted zones, revise and update the plans as necessary, and choose the timing of detonation. Suicide bombing operations are cost effective for terrorist groups because terrorists can inflict large destruction and many deaths on the adversary while suffering only a single casualty (the bomber) (United States Institute of Peace 2023).

As described in Chapter 2, suicide attacks are effective psychological tools for terrorists to inflict fear on society, along with the casualties and injuries that they cause. The unexpectedness of the attacks and the large number of deaths that result from them have the power to influence the everyday social activities of people. As these attacks increase in frequency, the public feels unsafe and may limit social activities (Hutchinson 2007). A notable suicide bombing took place on May 22, 2017, after US singer Ariana Grande's concert at Manchester Arena, in England. With 22 children and adults killed and over 200 injured, the incident was marked as Britain's deadliest terror attack in over a decade (Radde 2023).

9.4 TRENDS IN TERRORIST TACTICS AND TARGET TYPES

Terrorist groups can employ several different types of tactics depending on their goals, ability, and the availability of resources. An analysis of the trends shows important regional differences in the tactics used by groups across the world. According to data obtained from Global Terrorism Database, there were approximately 17,000 terrorist attacks in the world between 2019 and 2020, and bombings or explosions (32 percent) were the most commonly used tactic worldwide.

However, during the same time period, sabotage (facility or infrastructure attack) was the most common terrorist tactic employed by the terrorists in the United States (49 percent of attacks). Bombing, on the other hand, accounted for less than 5 percent of all incidents that occurred at this time in the United States. Analyses of these trends are important because they help law enforcement agencies craft effective counterterrorism measures and prevention efforts to better confront the threat of terrorism. Looking at

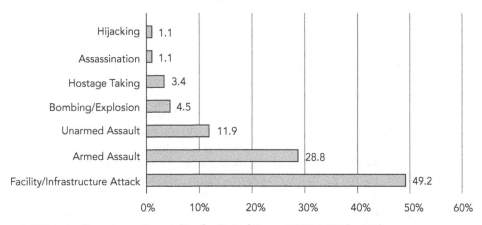

FIGURE 9.10 Terrorist tactics used in the United States, 2019–2020 (n=175).

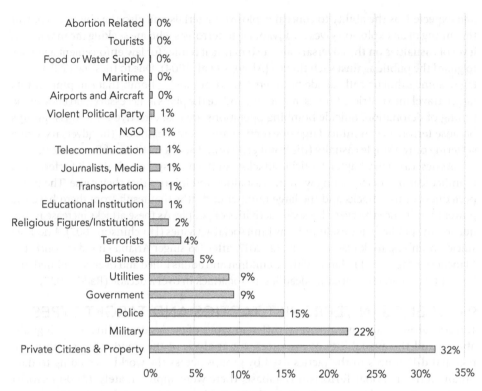

FIGURE 9.11   Terrorist target types across the world, 2019–2020.

these visualizations, it is easy to see that terrorists often favor conventional tactics, such as shootings (armed assault), bombings, and facility attacks. Even though some have been used in a few instances in the history of terrorism, unconventional tactics such as nuclear, chemical, and bioterrorism are not widely used by terrorist groups. The RAND Terrorism Chronology Database, which includes cases of terrorism globally, indicates that since 1968, less than 1 percent of all terrorist attacks or plots (52 out of 8000 recorded incidents) showed some kind of evidence that terrorists attempted to use chemical, biological, or nuclear weapons (Schmid 2020).

As with tactics of terrorism, it is extremely important to analyze trends in terrorist targets. Identifying likely terrorist targets may help intelligence and law enforcement agencies devise plans to increase security measures for potential target locations. An analysis of these trends indicates clear regional differences in target selection. According to the Global Terrorism Database, between 2019 and 2020 most terrorist attacks in the world targeted private citizens and property (32 percent) (often due to their race, ethnicity, or religion), followed by military (22 percent) and police (15 percent) individuals and installations.

However, when we examine the trends in the United States, a different reality emerges. The statistics indicate that during the same period, terrorists and extremists in the United States primarily attacked religious figures and institutions (31 percent of attacks) (particularly mosques, synagogues, and Black churches), followed by private citizens and property (29 percent), and the police (15 percent). Unlike the global pattern, attacks against military installations and officials were not a common terrorist target

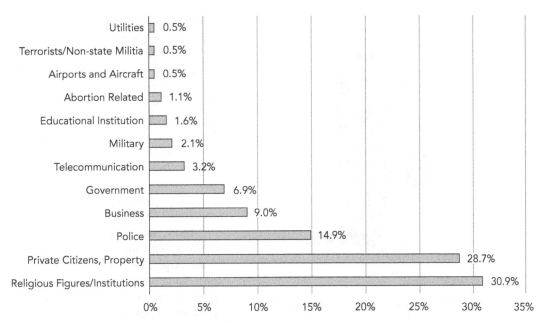

FIGURE 9.12 Terrorist target types across the United States, 2019–2020.

choice in the US. Abortion clinics (including women's health clinics and medical staff) and telecommunication infrastructure are frequent targets of terrorism in the US, whereas both categories do not constitute notable terrorist targets across the rest of the world.

9.5 KEY FACTORS THAT INFLUENCE TERRORISTS' SELECTION OF TARGETS

As we learned in previous sections, terrorists' choice of targets is almost endless and varies significantly. However, the existing academic literature indicates that the majority of attacks carried out by terrorist groups are discriminate in nature, and terrorists' selection of specific targets during these attacks is a function of several factors (Ahmed 2018; Asal et al. 2009; Drake 1998a; Hoffman 1993; Abrahms & Mroszczyk 2021; Schmid 2020; Silke 2010; Wright 2013) including, but not limited to:

1. ideology
2. strategic and tactical objectives of the group
3. internal factors
4. external factors

9.5.1 The Ideology of a Group

Ideology is considered one the central factor in terrorists' selection of targets (Asal et al. 2009; Drake 1998b). As covered in Chapter 6, ideology can be defined as a particular set of beliefs, ideas, and principles that explain how society should be organized (Cranston 2024). As leading expert in terrorist target selection Charles J. M. Drake (1998b) states, even though terrorists aim to attract media attention and humiliate their enemies with their violent attacks, ideology is the key factor in the targeting process for terrorists

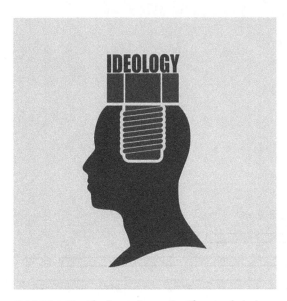

FIGURE 9.13   Ideology plays a significant role in influencing the formation, objectives, and actions of terrorist groups, ranging from recruitment to defining targets and justification for violence. It's important to note that terrorist groups can have a wide range of ideologies, including religious, political, nationalist, ethnic, and ideological motivations. Understanding and addressing the ideological motivations of terrorist groups is a crucial aspect of counterterrorism efforts. *Source:* GrAl/Shutterstock.

because it sets out the initial ethical framework and boundaries within which terrorists operate. Supporting this argument, a research report prepared by the Pearson Institute also indicates that ideological motivations are the most consistent predictor of terrorists' target selection, even when other strategic conditions (e.g., anticipated military and judicial government response) are controlled (Wright 2013).

More specifically, ideology dictates legitimate and illegitimate targets and influences the professional conduct of a group's fighters. The actions of terrorists typically adhere to some code of ethical conduct that guides the use of violence, including the circumstances under which violence can be used, the types of violence that can be legitimately employed, and who can be targeted. Terrorist groups vary in the ideologies they adopt, their commitment to their ideology, and in their use of violence. However, ideologies constrain goals and strategies that groups pursue and hence play an important role in providing the rationale for their actions and in identifying the boundaries for the use of violence against targets (Sanín & Wood 2014).

As we learned in Chapter 6, far-right groups in the United States (namely White supremacists), in line with their ideology, often target civilians—racial and religious minorities, and immigrants—using murder and assault. These targets and tactics are in line with said groups' White supremacist ideology; they believe they should control and dominate society. Proponents of this ideology also posit the so-called White genocide theory (or the Great Replacement), which argues that White people are endangered within the United States because political and economic elites are trying to further a multiethnic, multicultural, and multireligious order (i.e., European and American descendant White people in the nation are being deliberately replaced by non-White immigrants). Far-right groups often see immigrants, minorities, and progressive movements, as well as White people who support diversity, as legitimate targets. As observed by Heidi Beirich, the director of the Intelligence Project at the Southern Poverty Law Center, some White supremacists in the United States openly favor genocide and ethnic cleansing of non-Whites and religious minorities to further their agendas (Sanchez 2017). Theories such as the Great Replacement have been a major driving ideological

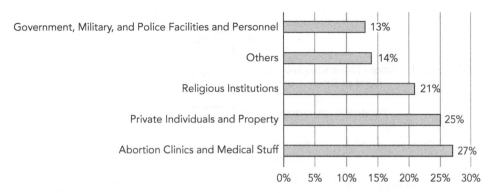

FIGURE 9.14 Right-wing terrorist and extremist targets in the United States, 1994–2020 (n=411).

force, defining the perceived enemies of far-right groups in the US as immigrants, Muslims, Hispanics, Asians, and Black people (Ware 2022).

The CSIS data also indicated that the targets of far-right groups have changed over time, mostly due to the recent upsurge in extreme White supremacist online activity, along with the election of Donald J. Trump as president in 2016. When researchers analyze the same dataset for the years between 2015 and 2020, the results indicate a different reality. During 2015 through 2020, right-wing extremist groups and individuals across the nation targeted private individuals, namely immigrants, Black people, Hispanics, and Muslims, the most (42 percent), followed by religious institutions (32 percent), and then government, police, and military installations (8 percent).

In contrast, contemporary far-left groups have often organized themselves around issues of animal rights, protection of forest lands, and most recently social justice and political correctness (e.g., human rights and personal liberties, police killings of minorities, confronting fascism). In line with their ideologies, these groups orchestrate demonstrations and have carried out arson and vandalism attacks against property such as animal research facilities, biomedical industries that use live animals for scientific research, meat processing factories and fur producers, timber mills, and government facilities that house wild animals to cause financial loss as a repercussion for the maltreatment of the earth and animals. Unlike the far-right groups that attack individuals via homicide and assault, far-left groups are often associated with low levels of lethal violence. Their use of violence is primarily aimed at property destruction (via arson and vandalism), as the killing of humans would conflict with their ideology. Both the Animal Liberation Front (ALF) and the Earth Liberation Front (ELF) officially declared on several occasions that their attacks will never target humans or animals because doing so would violate their ideology of saving animals (US House of Representatives 2002).

The selection of targets is quite different when we examine the CSIS data for far-left extremist groups in the United States. Between 1994 and 2020, far-left groups across the nation committed more than 210 violent attacks, primarily directed toward businesses (52 percent) (e.g., meat, poultry, oil, lumber, fur industries); followed by government, police, and military installations and personnel (17 percent); then private individuals and property, mostly due to their role in right-wing politics and environmental issues (17 percent); and higher educational institutions such as universities and pharmaceutical laboratories that conduct experimental research on animals (7 percent) (Jones et al. 2020).

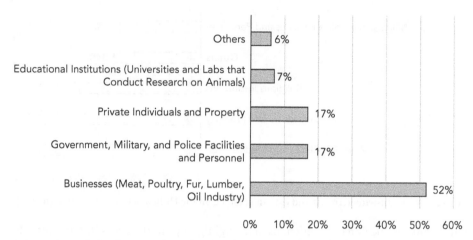

FIGURE 9.15 Left-wing terrorist and extremist targets in the United States, 1994–2020 (n=219).

As seen in these examples, ideology has a direct impact on target selection. Terrorists operating in the same areas of the world (e.g., the United States) can significantly differ in their selection of targets due to their divergent sets of beliefs. Not only does a group's ideology define how it views the immediate environment, but it also helps to identify potential enemies and targets that can be attacked to achieve its goals. By categorizing individuals as legitimate and illegitimate targets based on the role they play and carrying out violent attacks within the borders of these constraints, terrorists save themselves from feelings of guilt. They feel justified in attacking their targets because in their eyes, the victims deserve the punishment. The psychological process of dehumanization helps terrorists transform their targets into objects and representatives of the source of the problem. Through dehumanization, terrorists come to view the members of the enemy group as subhuman, perpetrators of injustice and suffering who are responsible for their government's atrocities.

Ideologies help terrorist groups displace the blame for the consequences of their actions for the adversary. During the Battle of Algiers, for example, the National Liberation Front of Algeria (FLN) targeted French civilians, settlers (known as Pied-Noirs), and tourists in Algeria. The FLN viewed them as symbols of French colonialism in their country and displaced the culpability for their deaths on the French government and military for not leaving Algeria (Sajed 2023).

Some scholars criticize the influence of ideologies on target selection, citing examples of groups that share similar ideological orientations but have strikingly different targeting strategies (Abrahms & Mroszczyk 2021). Even though both al-Qaeda and ISIS are believed to share the same worldviews (i.e., Islamism), al-Qaeda have openly criticized and condemned ISIS several times for its indiscriminate suicide bombings, hostage executions, and targeting of Shia Muslims in Iraq and Syria (Dearden 2017). After the Islamic State brutally killed more than 300 civilians, including 30 children in a 2017 mosque attack in Sinai, Egypt, al-Qaeda and other extremist groups pledged to take revenge against ISIS (Lister 2017).

What scholars often forget to consider here is that even though these two groups may share the same ideology, the contextual factors that gave rise to al-Qaeda and ISIS were different. As described in the previous chapters, al-Qaeda was particularly dissatisfied with the American military presence in Saudi Arabia and the existing local dictators throughout the Middle East, who were being backed by powerful Western countries (Ware 2022). Al-Qaeda carried out attacks in the United States and across different countries in Europe to force them to withdraw from the Middle East. ISIS, however, emerged as a consequence of the US military invasion of Iraq. The group carried out indiscriminate civilian attacks in Iraq and Syria because they viewed Shia Muslims, Kurds, and other ethnic and religious minorities as collaborators in the US invasion. Other factors, such as the new Shia regime's violent suppression of the Sunni population after the invasion, also contributed to ISIS's horrific methods of killing of civilians and hostages.

9.5.2 Strategic and Tactical Objectives of the Group

Even though ideology is recognized as the leading motivational element for terrorists' target selection, it is not the only factor. Along with ideology, it is the group's strategic objectives that are salient in target selection. Leading scholars in the field of terrorism claim that ideology by itself is not enough to explain the target selection preferences of terrorist groups (Crenshaw 1981; 1987; Dugan et al. 2005; Pape 2003; Perry & Hasisi 2015; Abrahms et al. 2017). Instead, they argue that terrorists carry out attacks against various targets in such a way to put pressure on their perceived psychological target and then produce the desired outcome. The process of target selection is based on a rational choice model.

American political scientist Robert Pape of the University of Chicago criticizes the conflation of ideology, particularly the religious ideologies, with terrorists' choice of targets. He argues that terrorists are rational actors, as are the rest of people in society, and thus their behavior seeks to maximize their interests. They use terrorist tactics to coerce governments into making concessions (e.g., withdraw from their territories, acknowledge their cultural, social, and economic rights). More specifically, Pape (2003; 2005) discovered that individuals use suicide terrorism to attack their enemies not because of their religious ideology, but because historical examples show that this tactic actually works both militarily and politically. As discussed in the previous chapters, in 1984, US President Ronald Reagan ordered the complete withdrawal of American military forces from Lebanon following the October 1983 Beirut suicide truck bombings of US Marine Corps barracks, which claimed the lives of more than 300 American and French soldiers. The group that carried out the attack later publicly announced that the aim was to force the occupying forces out of Lebanon by frightening them into compliance and threatening that more incidents with similar consequences would occur if they did not comply with the group's demands (Glass 2018). In the end, the terrorists achieved their goal as US politicians and the American public were convinced that a full withdrawal from Lebanon was necessary to prevent further casualties.

Even though the United States had invested in building large military installations (with hundreds of fighter jets and heavy weaponry) in Saudi Arabia for decades, two years after the 9/11 attacks, Secretary of Defense Donald Rumsfeld announced that US troops would be withdrawing from the country. It became clear that a large presence of

(a)   (b)

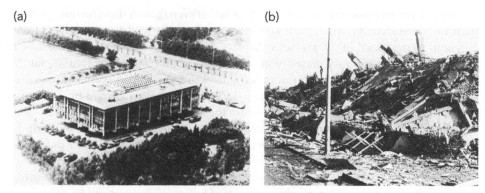

FIGURE 9.16 The 1983 Beirut barracks bombings were two suicide truck bombings that occurred on October 23, 1983, in Beirut, Lebanon. The attacks targeted the barracks of the United
States Marine Corps and the French Paratroopers. The attacks were devastating, resulting in a high
number of casualties. The attack was part of a broader campaign against Western military presence
in Lebanon. In the aftermath of the bombings, the US and French forces eventually withdrew
from Lebanon. *Source:* Photo (a) from the Long Commission Report, Public Domain, via Wikimedia;
Photo (b) from by SSgt Robert E. Kline, public domain, via Wikimedia Commons.

American troops in Saudi Arabia was a grave risk to the lives of Americans serving in the
region. As mentioned in the previous chapters, bin Laden and many Muslims were out-
raged by the presence of such a large non-Muslim military force in the territories that
housed the holiest sites in Islam (Mecca and Medina) and viewed them as occupying
forces. In 2003, US officials transferred control of the Prince Sultan Air Base to Saudi
officials and relocated to Al Udeid Air Base in Qatar (van Natta Jr. 2003).

Understanding the strategic logic that drives terrorist violence is important for
designing effective counterterrorism measures. Compared to their adversaries (e.g.,
states, governments), terrorists are comparatively weak in terms of the quantity and quality of their fighters and weaponry capabilities. It is too risky for them to counter their
adversaries directly in a military style full-scale war. However, terrorists devise strategies
to achieve their goals, in consideration of this power imbalance. A review of literature
reveals six primary categories of strategic objectives that terrorist groups may pursue to
achieve their goals (Crenshaw 1981; Drake 1998a):

1. threat elimination
2. compliance
3. disorientation
4. attrition
5. provocation
6. advertisement

The strategic objective of **threat elimination** consists of attacks that are targeted
toward enemy individuals and installations that pose a threat to the well-being and
interests of a terrorist group and its members. Targeted killings of enemy soldiers, police
officers, collaborators, informers, or the destruction of military installations, barracks,
and border control towers that restrict the activities of a group are all examples of threat
elimination. Eradicating these threats helps terrorist groups achieve their respective goals

and missions more easily. For example, during the Troubles, the dissident Irish republican group Ulster Volunteer Force (UVF) often targeted enemy equipment and personnel that threatened their activities. In December 1969, the group detonated a car bomb right in front of a central detective bureau in Dublin, Ireland, targeting both the officers and the nearby telephone exchange headquarters.

Compliance, on the other hand, refers to the targeting of places and individuals that are important to the adversary government (i.e., the psychological target) to frighten them into fulfilling the demands of the group or facing more severe consequences. This strategic objective requires terrorists to establish control of the enemy, either by inflicting extensive damage or holding someone important in captivity. In March 1978, the Italian far-left group the Red Brigades kidnapped the prime minister of Italy, Aldo Moro, and held him under detention while negotiating their demands with the Italian authorities. The group asked the

FIGURE 9.17 Aldo Moro, an Italian politician and leader of the Christian Democracy (DC) party, was abducted by members of the Red Brigades in 1978. The Red Brigades demanded the release of several imprisoned members in exchange for Moro's release. They also called for a political trial against the Italian government. Despite efforts by various intermediaries, including the Pope, to negotiate Moro's release, the Italian government did not meet the Red Brigades' demands. On May 9, 1978, Aldo Moro's body was found in the trunk of a car in the center of Rome. He had been shot multiple times. *Source:* Public domain, via Wikimedia Commons.

Italian government to free some left-wing incarcerated terrorists in exchange for Moro. When their demands were not met, they executed the prime minister and left his body in the trunk of a car parked in a historic district of Rome (Moss 1981).

The strategic objectives of **disorientation** (creating confusion) and **attrition** (reducing an enemy's strength) involve seemingly random and indiscriminate attacks to disrupt and paralyze everyday social, economic, and political activities of the adversary society. Unlike the strategic objective of compliance, attacks that involve disorientation and attrition do not ask the adversary to comply with a specific request. The goal is to create chaos—a constant feeling of fear, anxiety, and worry among the members of the adversary society—and make the public lose their faith in their government's capacity to protect them. Through such strategies, groups try to convince the enemy that they are strong and able to inflict serious casualties when they wish to do so. A prime example is Zionist terrorist group Irgun's bombing campaigns against the British government forces

FIGURE 9.18 The Jewish terrorist group Irgun carried out the bombing of the King David Hotel, which served as the headquarters for the British Mandatory authorities in Jerusalem. The group viewed British authorities as an obstacle to Jewish immigration and the establishment of a Jewish state in Palestine. *Source:* Lakeview Images/Alamy Stock Photo.

in Palestine in order to establish a Jewish state. In July 1946, Irgun members detonated a massive explosive at the King David Hotel, the administrative headquarters of the British rule in Palestine, killing almost 100 individuals (UK Parliament 2006). The attack, along with several other bombing campaigns, was designed to undermine the British public's support for its presence in Palestine and eventually force the British military forces out of the country. The British public and political leadership became convinced that maintaining control over Palestine was not worth the cost in economic losses and casualties. The same bombing tactics were used by the IRA in Northern Ireland and England to inflict psychological damage (fear and worry) on the British public so that they would pressure their governments to withdraw from Irish territories.

The strategic objective of **provocation** is a prime example of how terrorists are highly rational when they carry out their attacks. Provocation can simply be defined as the use

FIGURE 9.19 This photograph was taken at "barrier 15" in lower Waterloo Street in Derry, Ireland, before the anti-internment parade on Bloody Sunday reached the area. At this barrier, the photographer was threatened by the soldier on the left of the picture. The soldier had threatened to shoot if the photographer did not stop taking photographs. At this point a friend of the photographer, Barney McGuigan, pulled him away and said, "You're going to get yourself into trouble." Barney McGuigan was shot dead approximately 30 minutes later. *Source:* Eamon Melaugh (cain.ulster.ac.uk/melaugh).

of terrorist tactics by groups in order to encourage governments to take extremely harsh repressive measures against the terrorist group and its supporters and sympathizers (Blankenship 2018). In some cases, terrorists may carry out violent atrocities to elicit brutal retaliation and restrictions of civil liberties, which may unintentionally radicalize civilians into supporting the terrorists and their cause. In this respect, provocation achieves two goals: it makes the repressive government and its agents unpopular among the public, and it increases the popularity of terrorist groups by presenting them as defenders of the repressed (Kydd & Walter 2006). In Turkey, between the 1970s and 1990s, the Turkish government engaged in extensive human rights violations among the Kurdish civilian population in the southeastern parts of the country. As a response to the PKK's terrorism campaign, they implemented countless states of emergencies and put the military and other security officials in charge of the administration of the region. Living under these undemocratic and repressive measures, along with the civilian collateral damage caused by the Turkish security forces, many Kurds became convinced that supporting the PKK was the only way to protect their interests in the region (Haner 2017). Similar incidents (e.g., disproportionate use of force, curtailment of civil rights, internment without trials, extrajudicial killings) also led to the radicalization of Irish people into cadres of the IRA. For example, the 1972 Bloody Sunday massacre in which 26 unarmed Irish civilian Catholics were shot (13 died) by British paratroopers during a peaceful civil rights march led to heavy condemnation of the British presence in Ireland and boosted support for the PIRA; many Irish people who had not yet been radicalized flocked to the PIRA in order to get revenge on the British.

The strategic objective of **advertisement** encourages terrorists to carry out attacks against targets that would guarantee maximum media attention. Potential press coverage of an attack is extremely important for terrorist groups for several reasons. First, terrorist groups need to gain publicity to make their audience aware of their existence and to advertise their cause to potential future recruits. They need widespread media attention, which can be achieved through violent and destructive actions. Following the widespread American television coverage of the infamous Trans World Airlines Flight 847 (flying from Cairo to San Diego) hijacking in 1985, British Prime Minister Margaret Thatcher told news agencies and members of the American Bar Association that nations "must try to find ways to starve the terrorists and the hijacker of the oxygen of publicity on which they depend" (Apple Jr. 1985).

Carrying out deadly attacks against the members of the adversary society and its security officials can boost the morale of a group, and that of the society it represents. This is particularly true if they are experiencing cruelty and abuse from the security forces. Third, terrorist acts almost always serve as a communication strategy to a more powerful adversary (Pape 2005; Weimann 1987). Research analyzing the emergence of terrorist movements often indicates that groups turn to terrorism when they are prevented

FIGURE 9.20 TWA Flight 847 Captain John Testrake with hijacker in Beirut. The hijacking of Trans World Airlines Flight 847 was a high-profile act of terrorism that occurred in 1985. The hijacking received extensive media coverage, particularly on television. The incident occurred in 1985 when television news was a major source of information for the public, and it quickly became a major news story both in the United States and internationally. Television networks provided live coverage of key developments in the hijacking, including the release of hostages and the demands of the hijackers. This live reporting added to the drama and sense of urgency surrounding the situation. *Source:* FAA, public domain, via Wikimedia Commons.

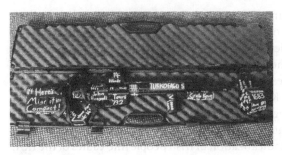

FIGURE 9.21 Gun used in Christchurch attack, marked with text referencing extreme right-wing ideology and previous terrorist attacks. On March 15, 2019, a White supremacist shooter attacked two mosques in Christchurch, New Zealand, during Friday prayers. The attacker live-streamed the first mosque shooting on Facebook using a helmet-mounted camera. Tech companies and social media platforms faced criticism for their role in allowing the video to spread rapidly. It brought attention to the rise of far-right extremism and the use of social media for the dissemination of extremist content. It also led to discussions about the role of technology companies in preventing the spread of violent and harmful content online. *Source:* Brenton Tarrant, public domain, via Wikimedia Commons.

from voicing their grievances through legitimate political and democratic outlets (Haner 2017; Hoffman 2006; Richardson 2007). When their voices are unheard or ignored, groups may amplify their grievances through violent acts. Through use of violence, terrorists convey a powerful message—that they are able to inflict pain and suffering if concessions are not made.

Aircraft hijackings, bombings of concert arenas, sporting events, and shopping centers, and kidnappings of prominent politicians and business tycoons are salient examples of attacks that terrorists carry out in order to gain attention. The kidnapping and subsequent killing of Israeli athletes during the 1972 Munich Olympics—the first time a terrorist incident reached a global audience of more than 900 million people during a live broadcast—is considered the most notable example of a terrorist attack for advertisement. With this attack, the Black September group brought the largely ignored and prolonged Palestinian-Israeli conflict into the international agenda. Only one month after the attacks, the United Nations gave the Palestinian Liberation Organization observer status in its international assembly (Doubek 2022).

The Christchurch mosque shootings in New Zealand, in 2019, is also evidence of terrorists' desire for publicity. The suspect, Brenton Tarrant, live-streamed via Facebook his massacre of more than 50 individuals during Friday prayer. Tarrant even posted on the online message board 8chan: "Well lads, it's time to stop shitposting and time to make a real-life effort post. I will carry out and [sic] attack against the invaders, and will even live stream the attack via Facebook." His live broadcast of the murder of Muslim worshippers was watched by more than 4,000 individuals on Facebook before the company removed it from the site. Not only did the attack send shockwaves around the world, but it also led to a widespread increase in White supremacist acts of violence (Clun & Noyes 2019; Tsikas 2020).

9.5.3 Internal Factors

In addition to ideology and strategic objectives, terrorists' decision-making processes are also affected by internal factors such as the capability of a group and its material and human resources. These internal factors are often thought of as constraints placed upon groups because the absence of these resources limits the attacking and targeting capabilities and target preferences of terrorist groups.

Scholars often classify the internal factors into two categories—tangible and intangible (Drake 1998a). Examples of tangible internal factors include physical means such as the availability of weapons, ammunition, financial resources, communication resources, and vehicles, the availability of instructors, and the number of recruits. Without these means, terrorists cannot undertake effective attacks against their perceived enemies. The operation of a terrorist organization is similar to the operation of a businesses in everyday society. They both need financial resources to fund their ongoing daily operations (e.g., food, housing, and other needs that are essential to the healthy functioning of a group). Without sufficient financial resources, terrorists cannot obtain powerful and sophisticated weapons and ammunition, including the material required for explosives. The absence of quality weaponry and ammunition places restrictions on the kind of targets that terrorists can successfully attack. For example, it would be pointless to try to destroy an armored enemy vehicle (e.g., tank) with standard rifles.

Intangible means, on the other hand, include factors and qualities that enable groups to use their tangible means and resources in the most effective ways possible. Examples include the availability of experienced leadership, the quality of training available to recruits, the discipline established within a group, the capability of combatants, and other technical skills. For example, a growing number of scholars today argue that the targeting of civilians is often not a strategy adopted by the leadership of terrorist groups, but the rogue behavior of individuals who act against the wishes of the leadership. Terrorist groups tend to prohibit their fighters from targeting noncombatants and condemn and repudiate such acts, even apologizing to the adversary society (Abrahms & Potter 2015; Abrahms & Mroszczyk 2021). Human factors (e.g., relations within the group, psychological state of fighters, personal agendas, individual differences in moral judgments) in target selection cannot be ignored.

9.5.4 External Factors

Terrorists' decision-making is also influenced by external factors—factors that are considered to be outside of the control of a group. External factors can be both **restrictive** and **encouraging** in nature. Restrictive external factors prevent or deter groups from carrying out missions that they would normally undertake. As mentioned before, terrorists are rational actors. They are aware that there are limits when it comes to their targeting choices. These limits can be imposed by their supporters, the media, international actors, or simply by the security environment in which they operate (Silke 2010). The risk of getting caught or killed may deter terrorists from targeting a security official who is well protected. Potential negative (national and global) publicity may put pressure on terrorist groups to avoid targeting certain places and individuals (or even refraining from using certain tactics). Terrorists frequently seek to ensure their targeting choices are not unpopular among their supporters and the international community. They aim to maximize their attacks on targets that are unpopular among the aggrieved community, and may try to minimize the loss of life against certain targets. For example, killing a publicly liked person (e.g., an artist, TV star, politician, or religious figure) or civilians (especially children and women) may cause a group to be rejected by their supporters, with sympathizers cutting financial help, denying group members the use of their resources and facilities, and informing law enforcement of the group's activities.

Even though the emotional toll of many civilian deaths is more influential than the killing of military and other security officials, in terms of imposing fear and the communication of group's causes, terrorists' killing of undefended civilians makes it easier for authorities to label a group as a terrorist organization in the global arena. To win a broader base of popular support internationally and to differentiate themselves from oppressive governments, terrorists restrain their targeting choices to specific individuals and places. Rather than civilians, terrorists may target symbols of the state (police, military, judicial officers, power lines, oil lines, transportation infrastructure) to convey a message that they are discriminate in their use of violence.

A prominent example of this is the abduction and murder of Prime Minister Aldo Moro in 1978 by the Red Brigades. This act produced a significant backlash, even among the left-wing trade unions in Italy. Soon after this incident, the Red Brigades' decision to kill popular labor movement figure Guido Rossa, an Italian trade unionist and factory worker, further isolated and eroded their popular support. More than 250,000 factory workers attended Guido's funeral, heavily condemning the Red Brigades' actions. It is argued that the Red Brigades' unpopular assassinations and violence against these figures produced such a large anti-communist blowback across Italy that it blocked Italian Communists' road to power in government (Broder 2018).

Corroborating this example, research analyzing different groups across the world indicates that the indiscriminate use of violence against civilians and popular targets (compared to violence against military and government officials) produces counterproductive results for terrorist groups. These include eroding peaceful resolution prospects with the adversary government, alienating actual or potential supporters of the group, exposing the group to direct government retaliation, and eventual demise of the group (Abrahms 2013; Abrahms & Gottfried 2016; English 2016; Kydd & Walter 2002; Stanton 2016).

External factors can also serve as **encouraging factors** for terrorists to carry out violent attacks against certain targets. For example, the motivation to gain approval from their constituencies, out-group antagonism (e.g., existence of strong religious, ethnic, or social divide), the desire to punish informers, and an adversary governments' repressive strategies may incentivize terrorist groups to carry out attacks against civilians (Asal et al. 2019; Polo 2020). This is especially true when governments carry out indiscriminate attacks against a group's support base, under the guise of preventing terrorism. Such attacks mitigate terrorists' constraints against targeting civilians. Indiscriminate government repressions of the general population can provide an incentive and justification for terrorist groups to carry out direct retaliatory attacks against out-group civilians without the risk of losing their popular support and legitimacy. Such retaliatory attacks against the civilians of out-groups can actually boost the morale of sympathizers and supporters and encourage (i.e., radicalize) the previously uncommitted, moderate population to join terrorist organizations (Kalyvas 2004; Wood 2003).

9.6 CONCLUSION

Throughout history, terrorists have attacked multiple types of targets using a variety of tactics. Classifying them is a challenging task. Researchers have identified six key characteristics of targets that shape their selection including (1) their level of protection,

(2) whether they are military or civilian, (3) the amount of planning necessary, (4) the intended audience of the attack, (5) the type of victims targeted, and (6) the purpose of the attack. Data show that certain tactics tend to be more popular (e.g., bombing, armed assault, hostage-taking) or less popular (e.g., chemical, biological, radioactive, and nuclear weapons) among terrorists, depending on two key factors: the terrorists' goal in carrying out an attack, and the group's organizational capabilities and available resources.

A key theme in this chapter is that terrorists' attack decisions are rarely indiscriminate. Instead they are largely rational—targets and tactics are carefully chosen to maximize the group's interests. While a group's ideology is recognized as the main determinant in target selection—setting the ethical boundaries within which the group operates—terrorists must also take additional factors into consideration. These include the strategic and tactical objectives of the group, internal factors (the abilities and resources of the group) and external factors (the security environment, social and political developments, public opinion). Altogether, terrorists' target and tactic selections are calculated.

For several reasons—negative media attention, alienation of sympathizers, repercussions from the international community—targeting undefended civilians is typically avoided. However, research indicates that under certain circumstances, terrorists have made rational choices (from their perspective) to attack noncombatants without causing backlash among their supporters—when doing so targets out-group civilians in response to indiscriminate repression. As noted throughout this chapter, it is important to continue to examine historical cases and current trends in terrorists' target and tactic selection (over time and regionally), to strategically inform counterterrorism measures and policy.

Key Lessons

Lesson 1

Even though terrorist groups come from a wide range of ideological backgrounds with different goals, motives, and histories, one striking commonality among them is that terrorists' choice of targets is rarely random. Target selection is almost always premeditated, and it is the result of a carefully planned deliberate, logical, and rational decision-making process.

Lesson 2

Terrorists' potential to use a variety of tactics is often determined by two important elements: (1) their ultimate goal and objectives by carrying out an attack, and (2) the group's organizational capabilities and available resources.

Lesson 3

Analyses of trends in terrorists' use of tactics and selection of targets are important because they help law enforcement agencies craft effective counterterrorism measures

and prevention efforts to better tackle the threat of terrorism.

Lesson 4

The existing academic literature indicates that a majority of the attacks carried out by terrorist groups are discriminate in nature, and terrorists' selection and choice of specific targets during these attacks is a function of several factors.

Lesson 5

Even though terrorists aim to attract media attention and humiliate their enemies with their violent attacks, ideology is the key factor in the targeting process for terrorists because it sets out the initial ethical framework and boundaries within which terrorists operate.

Lesson 6

Using their ideologies as a moral guide, terrorists identify their enemies and differentiate between legitimate targets and forbidden targets, and can perpetrate violent attacks against certain targets without the sense of guilt or shame.

Lesson 7

When one examines the terrorism statistics for any time period and region of the world, it is clear that terrorists' tactics and targets often correspond with their specific ideologies.

Lesson 8

Terrorists strategically select and attack their targets in such a way that the adversary is forced into meeting their demands. Terrorists' target selection process is rational.

Lesson 9

Terrorists restrict their targeting choices to prevent the risk of alienating their supporters and sympathizers. They need to make sure that their targeting choices are not unpopular among their supporters and the international community.

Lesson 10

The motivation to gain approval from their constituencies, out-group antagonism, a desire to punish informers, and adversary governments' repressive strategies may incentivize terrorist groups to carry out attacks against undefended civilians.

KEY WORDS

advertisement
armed assault
assassination
attrition
Black September
bombing
civilian targets
compliance
discriminate attacks
disorientation
expressive targets
functional targets
hard targets
hijacking
hostage-taking
indiscriminate attacks
logistical targets

military targets
preplanned targets
provocation
raids
sabotage
siege
soft targets
suicide attack
symbolic targets
tactic
targets of attention (psychological targets)
targets of opportunity
targets of violence (physical targets)
threat elimination
weapons of mass destruction (WMD)

RECOMMENDED SOURCES

Research Articles & Books

Abrahms, M., & Gottfried, M. S. (2016). Does terrorism pay? An empirical analysis. *Terrorism and Political Violence, 28*(1), 72–89.

Abrahms, M., Ward, M., & Kennedy, R. (2018). Explaining civilian attacks: Terrorist networks, principal-agent problems and target selection. *Perspectives on Terrorism, 12*(1), 23–45.

Ahmed, R. (2018). Terrorist ideologies and target selection. *Journal of Applied Security Research, 13*(3), 376–390.

Blankenship, B. (2018). When do states take the bait? State capacity and the provocation logic of terrorism. *Journal of Conflict Resolution, 62*(2), 381–409.

Drake, C. (1998). Terrorists' target selection. Springer.

Drake, C. J. (1998). The role of ideology in terrorists' target selection. Terrorism and Political Violence, *10*(2), 53–85.

Hemmingby, C., & Bjørgo, T. (2018). Terrorist Target Selection: The Case of Anders Behring Breivik. *Perspectives on terrorism*, *12*(6), 164–176.

Hoffman, B. (1993). Terrorist targeting: Tactics, trends, and potentialities. *Terrorism and Political Violence*, *5*(2), 12–29.

Horowitz, M. C. (2015). The rise and spread of suicide bombing. *Annual Review of Political Science*, *18*, 69–84.

Moghadam, A. (2003). Palestinian suicide terrorism in the second intifada: Motivations and organizational aspects. *Studies in Conflict and Terrorism*, *26*(2), 65–92.

Pape, R. (2006). *Dying to win: The strategic logic of suicide terrorism*. Random House Trade Paperbacks.

Polo, S. M. (2020). The quality of terrorist violence: Explaining the logic of terrorist target choice. *Journal of Peace Research*, *57*(2), 235–250

Richardson, L. (2007). *What terrorists want: Understanding the enemy, containing the threat*. New York: Random House.

Schmid, A. P. (2020). *Layers of Preventive Measures for Soft Target Protection against Terrorist Attacks*. International Centre for Counter-Terrorism (ICCT).

News Articles & Government and Think Tank Reports

Thatcher urges the press to help 'starve' terrorists.
   Author(s): R. W. Apple Jr.
   Source: The New York Times
50 years ago, the Munich Olympics massacre changed how we think about terrorism.
   Author(s): James Doubek
   Source: NPR
The Tactics and Targets of Domestic Terrorists.
   Author(s): Seth G. Jones, Catrina Doxsee, & Nicholas Harrington
   Source: Center for Strategic and International Studies
IRA Belvoir Park science labs bomb targeted NI justice.
   Author(s): Vincent Kearney
   Source: BBC
How Far-Right Terrorists Choose Their Enemies.
   Author(s): Jacob Ware & Clin P. Clarke
   Source: Foreign Policy (FP)
Terrorism, ideology, and target selection.
   Author(s): Austin L. Wright
   Source: The Pearson Institute
Terrorism as a Strategy of Retribution
   Author(s): Graig R. Klein
   Source: The International Centre for Counter-Terrorism (ICCT)

Documentaries, Videos, and Other Educational Media

Munich 72 and Beyond Producer(s)/Director(s): Global Sports Development and Sidewinder Films
   Source: YouTube
9/11: As Events Unfold
   Producer(s)/Director(s): Transportation Security Administration
   Source: YouTube
First Woman to Hijack a Plane: Leila Khaled
   Producer(s)/Director(s): Real Stories
   Source: Real Stories YouTube channel
9/11, 2001 as it happened Producer(s)/Director(s): The Sydney Morning Herald and The Age
   Source: The Sydney Morning Herald and The Age YouTube Channel
Bishopsgate bombing
   Producer(s)/Director(s): BBC
   Source: BBC London YouTube channel
Europe's most bombed hotel: The Europa Hotel in Belfast
   Producer(s)/Director(s): Abdallah Elbinni
   Source: Al Jazeera English YouTube Channel
Turning Point: 9/11 and the War on Terror
   Producer(s)/Director(s): Brian Knappenberger
   Source: Netflix
Italy The Moro Kidnapping
   Producer(s)/Director(s): Associated Press
   Source: AP Archive YouTube Channel

REFERENCES

Abrahms, M. (2013). The credibility paradox: Violence as a double-edged sword in international politics. *International Studies Quarterly, 57,* 660–671.

Abrahms, M., Beauchamp, N., & Mroszczyk, J. (2017). What terrorist leaders want: A content analysis of terrorist propaganda videos. *Studies in Conflict & Terrorism, 40*(11), 899–916.

Abrahms, M., & Gottfried, M. S. (2016). Does terrorism pay? An empirical analysis. *Terrorism and Political Violence, 28*(1), 72–89.

Abrahms, M., & Mroszczyk, J. (2021). Terrorist target selection. In M. Haner & M. Sloan (Eds.), *Theories of terrorism* (pp. 151–171). Routledge.

Abrahms, M., & Potter, P. B. K. (2015). Explaining terrorism: Leadership deficits and militant group tactics. *International Organization, 69,* 311–342.

Ahmed, R. (2018). Terrorist ideologies and target selection. *Journal of Applied Security Research, 13*(3), 376–390.

Allam, H. (2020). "I am Antifa": One activist's violent death became a symbol for the right and left. NPR. https://www.npr.org/2020/07/23/893533916/i-am-antifa-one-activist-s-violent-death-became-a-symbol-for-the-right-and-left

Almogy, G., Belzberg, H., Mintz, Y., Pikarsky, A. K., Zamir, G., & Rivkind, A. I. (2004). Suicide bombing attacks: Update and modifications to the protocol. *Annals of Surgery, 239*(3), 295.

Aman, M. (2007). *Preventing terrorist suicide attacks.* Jones & Bartlett Learning.

Apple Jr., R. W. (1985). Thatcher urges the press to help "starve" terrorists. *New York Times.* https://www.nytimes.com/1985/07/16/world/thatcher-urges-the-press-to-help-starve-terrorists.html

Asal, V. H., Rethemeyer, R. K., Anderson, I., Stein, A., Rizzo, J., & Rozea, M. (2009). The softest of targets: A study on terrorist target selection. *Journal of Applied Security Research, 4*(3), 258–278.

Asal, V., Phillips, B. J., Rethemeyer, R. K., Simonelli, C., & Young, J. K. (2019). Carrots, sticks, and insurgent targeting of civilians. *Journal of Conflict Resolution, 63*(7), 1710–1735.

BBC (2015). Charlie Hebdo attack: Three days of terror. BBC. https://www.bbc.com/news/world-europe-30708237

BBC (2017). Beslan school siege: Russia "failed" in 2004 massacre. BBC. https://www.bbc.com/news/world-europe-39586814

Blankenship, B. (2018). When do states take the bait? State capacity and the provocation logic of terrorism. *Journal of Conflict Resolution, 62*(2), 381–409.

Broder, D. (2018). Historically compromised. *Jacobin.* https://jacobin.com/2018/05/red-brigades-aldo-moro-pci-historic-compromise

Clancy, P. (2023). Lord Louis Mountbatten's assassination by the IRA. British Heritage. https://britishheritage.com/history/lord-mountbatten-death#:~:text=Mountbatten%20and%20three%20members%20of%20his%20holiday%20party%20died%20while,the%20vessel%20the%20night%20before.

Clun, R. & Noyes, J. (2019). Christchurch shooting live: Ardern confirms NZ to toughen gun laws. *Sydney Morning Herald.* https://www.smh.com.au/world/oceania/christchurch-shooting-live-questions-over-alt-right-hate-monitoring-following-shooting-20190317-p514zk.html

CNN (2023). Spain train bombings fast facts. https://www.cnn.com/2013/11/04/world/europe/spain-train-bombings-fast-facts/index.html

Collier, R (2017). NHS ransomware attack spreads worldwide. *Canadian Medical Association Journal,* 189 (22) E786–E787.

Cook, S. (2021). 2021 Ransomware statistics and facts. Comparitech. https://www.comparitech.com/antivirus/ransomware-statistics/

Cooper, K-L. (2020). Oklahoma City bombing: The day domestic terror shook America. BBC. https://www.bbc.com/news/world-us-canada-51735115

Craig, T. (2021). HVAC industry needs to prevent ransomware from entering systems. *The News.* https://www.achrnews.com/articles/145402-hvac-industry-needs-to-prevent-ransomware-from-entering-systems

Cranston, M. (2024). Ideology. *Encyclopedia Britannica.* https://www.britannica.com/topic/ideology-society/the-sociology-of-knowledge

Crenshaw, M. (1981). The causes of terrorism. *Comparative Politics, 13*(4), 379–399.

Crenshaw, M. (1987). Theories of terrorism: Instrumental and organizational approaches. *Journal of Strategic Studies, 10*(4), 13–31.

Dearden, L. (2017). Al-Qaeda leader denounces Isis "madness and lies" as two terrorist groups compete for dominance. *The Independent.* https://www.independent.co.uk/news/world/middle-east/al-qaeda-leader-ayman-al-zawahiri-isis-madness-lies-extremism-islamic-state-terrorist-groups-compete-middle-east-islamic-jhadis-a7526271.html

Derysh, I. (2020). Far-right "Boogaloo boy" killed officer after using Black Lives Matter protest as cover: Prosecutors. *Salon.* https://www.salon.com/2020/06/17/far-right-boogaloo-boy-killed-officer-after-using-black-lives-matter-protest-as-cover-prosecutors/

DHS (2023). Communicating in crisis: A fact sheet from the National Academies and the Department of Homeland Security. https://www.dhs.gov/xlibrary/assets/prep_ied_fact_sheet.pdf

Doubek, J. (2022). 50 years ago, the Munich Olympics massacre changed how we think about terrorism. NPR. https://www.npr.org/2022/09/04/1116641214/munich-olympics-massacre-hostage-terrorism-israel-germany

Drake, C. (1998a). Terrorists' target selection. Springer.

Drake, C. J. (1998b). The role of ideology in terrorists' target selection. *Terrorism and Political Violence, 10*(2), 53–85.

Dugan, L., LaFree, G., & Piquero, A. R. (2005). Testing a rational choice model of airline hijackings. *Criminology, 43*(4), 1031–1065.

English, R. (2016). *Does terrorism work? A history.* Oxford University Press.

Entous, A., Barnes, J. E., & Goldman, A. (2023). Intelligence suggests pro-Ukrainian group sabotaged pipelines, U.S. officials say. *New York Times.* https://www.nytimes.com/2023/03/07/us/politics/nord-stream-pipeline-sabotage-ukraine.html

Ferran, L., & Keneally, M. (2023). Inside terrorist hostage negotiations: The price of freedom. ABC News. https://abcnews.go.com/Blotter/fullpage/inside-terrorist-hostage-negotiations-price-freedom-25114240

Foster, P., & Sanchez, R. (2015). "You rape our women and are taking over our country," Charleston church gunman told black victims. *The Telegraph.* https://www.telegraph.co.uk/news/worldnews/northamerica/usa/11684957/You-rape-our-women-and-are-taking-over-our-country-Charleston-church-gunman-told-black-victims.html

Glass, A. (2018, October 23). Reagan condemns Beirut bombing, Oct. 23, 1983. *Politico.* https://www.politico.com/story/2018/10/23/reagan-condemns-beirut-bombing-oct-23-1983-921655

Hafez, M. M. (2007). *Suicide bombers in Iraq: The strategy and ideology of martyrdom.* US Institute of Peace Press.

Haner, M. (2017). *The freedom fighter: A terrorist's own story.* Routledge.

Haner, M., Sloan, M. M., Cullen, F. T., Graham, A., Lero Jonson, C., Kulig, T. C., & Aydın, Ö. (2021). Making America safe again: Public support for policies to reduce terrorism. *Deviant Behavior, 42*(10), 1209–1227.

Hoffman, B. (1993). Terrorist targeting: Tactics, trends, and potentialities. *Terrorism and Political Violence, 5*(2), 12–29.

Hoffman, B. (2006). *Inside terrorism.* Columbia University Press.

Hone, T. (2020). Countering the Kamikaze. United States Naval Institute. https://www.usni.org/magazines/naval-history-magazine/2020/october/countering-kamikaze#:~:text=During%20the%20first%20four%20months,of%20more%20than%2034%20percent.

Horowitz, M. C. (2015). The rise and spread of suicide bombing. *Annual Review of Political Science, 18*, 69–84.

Hutchinson, W. (2007). The systemic roots of suicide bombing. *Systems Research and Behavioral Science: The Official Journal of the International Federation for Systems Research, 24*(2), 191–200.

Jones, S. G., Doxsee, C., & Harrington, N. (2020). The tactics and targets of domestic terrorists. Center for Strategic & International Studies. https://www.csis.org/analysis/tactics-and-targets-domestic-terrorists

Kalyvas, S. N. (2004). The paradox of terrorism in civil war. *Journal of Ethics, 8*, 97–138.

Kearney, V. (2017). IRA Belvoir Park science labs bomb targeted NI justice. BBC. https://www.bbc.com/news/uk-northern-ireland-41306262

Kokkinidis, T. (2022). Flashback to first aircraft hijacking in Greece. Greek Reporter. https://greekreporter.com/2022/09/12/flashback-to-first-plane-hijacking-in-greece/

Kreuz, R. J. (2020). Charlie Hebdo shootings served as an extreme example of the history of attacks on satirists. *The Conversation.* https://theconversation.com/charlie-hebdo-shootings-served-as-an-extreme-example-of-the-history-of-attacks-on-satirists-145527

Kydd, A. H., & Walter, B. F. (2002). Sabotaging the peace: The politics of extremist violence. *International Organization, 56,* 263–296.

Kydd, A. H., & Walter, B. F. (2006). The strategies of terrorism. *International security, 31*(1), 49–80.

Lister, T. (2017). Why the massacre of Muslims in Sinai was too extreme for al Qaeda. CNN. https://www.cnn.com/2017/11/27/middleeast/egypt-sinai-attack-isis-al-qaeda/index.html

Macola, I. G. (2021). The world's most infamous aeroplane hijackings. Airport Technology. https://www.airport-technology.com/features/world-most-infamous-aeroplane-hijackings/

Meredith, F. (2017, January 6). Life goes on at the most bombed hotel in the world. *Irish Times.* https://www.irishtimes.com/life-and-style/people/life-goes-on-at-the-most-bombed-hotel-in-the-world-1.2901861

Morrison, K. (2020, November 11). Belfast's great survivor: The Europa Hotel. *Al Jazeera.* https://www.aljazeera.com/features/2020/11/11/belfasts-great-survivor-the-hotel-europa

Moss, D. (1981). The kidnapping and murder of Aldo Moro. *European Journal of Sociology, 22*(2), 265–295.

Pape, R. (2005). *Dying to win: The strategic logic of suicide terrorism.* Random House.

Pape, R. A. (2003). The strategic logic of suicide terrorism. *American Political Science Review, 97*(3), 343–361.

Perry, S., & Hasisi, B. (2015). Rational choice rewards and the jihadist suicide bomber. *Terrorism and Political Violence, 27*(1), 53–80.

Polo, S. M. (2020). The quality of terrorist violence: Explaining the logic of terrorist target choice. *Journal of Peace Research, 57*(2), 235–250.

Radde, K. (2023). British intelligence missed a chance to stop the 2017 Ariana Grande concert attack. NPR. https://www.npr.org/2023/03/02/1160746721/ariana-grande-concert-attack-manchester-arena-mi5-report

Reuters (2022). Putin calls "sabotage" against Nord Stream an "act of international terrorism" —Kremlin. Reuters. https://www.reuters.com/world/putin-calls-sabotage-against-nord-stream-an-act-international-terrorism-kremlin-2022-09-29/

Richardson, L. (2007). *What terrorists want: Understanding the enemy, containing the threat.* Random House.

Sajed, A. (2023). Between Algeria and the world: Anticolonial connectivity, aporias of national liberation and postcolonial blues. *Postcolonial Studies, 26*(1), 13–31.

Sanchez, R. (2017). Who are White nationalists and what do they want? CNN. https://www.cnn.com/2017/08/13/us/white-nationalism-explainer-trnd/index.html

Sanín, F. G., & Wood, E. J. (2014). Ideology in Civil War: Instrumental adoption and beyond. *Journal of Peace Research, 51,* 213–226.

Schmid, A. (1988). Goals and objectives of international terrorism. In Slater, R. O. & Stohl, M. (Eds.) *Current perspectives on international terrorism* (pp. 47–87). Palgrave Macmillan.

Schmid, A. P. (2020). *Layers of preventive measures for soft target protection against terrorist attacks.* International Centre for Counter-Terrorism.

Silke, A. (2010). Understanding terrorist target selection. In A. Richards, P. Fusey, & A. Silke (Eds.), *Terrorism and the Olympics: Major event security and lessons for the future* (pp. 49–71). Routledge.

Simon, S. (2019). Opinion: Remembering Pilot Michel Bacos, hero of the 1976 Entebbe hijacking. NPR. https://www.npr.org/2019/03/30/708229313/opinion-remembering-pilot-michel-bacos-hero-of-the-1976-entebbe-hijacking

Sonenshine, T. D. (2021). What to tell your kids about 9/11. *The Hill.* https://thehill.com/opinion/education/571682-what-to-tell-your-kids-about-9-11/

Stanton, J. A. (2016). *Violence and restraint in civil war: Civilian targeting in the shadow of international law.* Cambridge University Press.

Tsikas, M. (2020). Life in prison looms for Australia's Christchurch gunman, now NZ's first convicted terrorist. *The Conversation.* https://theconversation.com/life-in-prison-looms-for-australias-christchurch-gunman-now-nzs-first-convicted-terrorist-134780

UK Parliament (2006). Sixtieth anniversary of bombing of King David hotel. https://edm.parliament.uk/early-day-motion/31213/sixtieth-anniversary-of-bombing-of-king-david-hotel

United Nations (2023). Chemical biological, radiological and nuclear terrorism. United Nations Office of Counter-Terrorism. https://www.un.org/counterterrorism/cct/chemical-biological-radiological-and-nuclear-terrorism

United States Institute of Peace (2023). Suicide bombers in Iraq: Questions and answers. USIP.https://www.usip.org/publications/suicide-bombers-iraq-questions-and-answers

US House of Representatives (2002). Oversight hearing before the subcommittee on forests and forest health. Committee on Resources. https://www.govinfo.gov/content/pkg/CHRG-107hhrg77615/html/CHRG-107hhrg77615.htm

Van Natta Jr., D. (2003). The struggle for Iraq: Last American combat troops quit Saudi Arabia. *New York Times.* https://www.nytimes.com/2003/09/22/world/the-struggle-for-iraq-last-american-combat-troops-quit-saudi-arabia.html

Ware, J. (2022). How far-right terrorists choose their enemies. *Foreign Policy.* https://foreignpolicy.com/2022/02/09/far-right-terrorism-extremism-target-selection-jihad-enemy/

Weimann, G. (1987). Media events: The case of international terrorism. *Journal of Broadcasting & Electronic Media, 31,* 21–39.

Wither, J. K., & Mullins, S. (Eds.). (2016). *Combating transnational terrorism.* Procon.

Wood, E. J. (2003). *Insurgent collective action and civil war in El Salvador.* Cambridge University Press.

Wright, A. L. (2013). Terrorism, ideology, and target selection. The Pearson Institute. https://thepearsoninstitute.org/sites/default/files/2017-02/9.%20Wright_Terrorism,%20ideology.pdf

CHAPTER 10

Terrorism and the Media

Communication Strategies
and Their Consequences

AllSides Media Bias Chart™

Ratings based on online, U.S. political content only – not TV, print, or radio.
Ratings do not reflect accuracy or credibility; they reflect perspective only.

L   **L**   **C**   **R**   **R**

LEFT	LEAN LEFT	CENTER	LEAN RIGHT	RIGHT
AlterNet	abc NEWS			The American Conservative
The Atlantic	AP			THE AMERICAN SPECTATOR
DEMOCRACY NOW!	AXIOS	BBC NEWS	THE DISPATCH	BREITBART
DAILY BEAST	Bloomberg	The CHRISTIAN SCIENCE MONITOR	THE EPOCH TIMES	Blaze media
HUFFPOST	CBS NEWS	Forbes	FOX BUSINESS	CBN
The Intercept_	CNN	MarketWatch	NATIONAL REVIEW (news)	DAILY CALLER
JACOBIN	The Guardian	NEWSNATION	NEW YORK POST (news)	Daily Mail
Mother Jones	INSIDER	Newsweek	reason	DAILY WIRE
MSNBC	NBC NEWS	REUTERS	THE WALL STREET JOURNAL (opinion)	The Post Millennial.
THE NEW YORKER	The New York Times (news)	RealClear Politics	Examiner	FOX NEWS
The New York Times (opinion)	npr	THE HILL	The Washington Times	the FEDERALIST
The Nation.	POLITICO	THE WALL STREET JOURNAL (news)		IJR INDEPENDENT JOURNAL REVIEW
SLATE	PROPUBLICA			NATIONAL REVIEW (opinion)
Vox	TIME			NEW YORK POST (opinion)
	The Washington Post			NEWSMAX
	USA TODAY			WASHINGTON FREE BEACON
	yahoo! news			OAN

AllSides Media Bias Ratings™ are based on multi-partisan, scientific analysis.

Visit AllSides.com for balanced news and over 2,400 rated sources.

AllSides does not own the rights to third party logos.

Version 9.2

© AllSides 2024

Source: Reprinted with permission of AllSides Media Bias Chart™.

Learning Objectives
1. To explain terrorists' use of and dependence on the media.
2. To examine the media's role in the social construction of terrorism.
3. To identify the parties in competition to frame events and issues in the media.
4. To consider the impact of terrorism media frames on public perceptions of terrorism and counterterrorism measures.
5. To explain the impacts of disinformation and media bias.

10.1 INTRODUCTION

In Chapter 1, we defined terrorism as the use of violence against noncombatants to intimidate or coerce people in the pursuit of political or social objectives. To accomplish its goals, terrorism is aimed at affecting a large audience (beyond the immediate victims). By definition, terrorism relies on **publicity**. If news of an attack does not reach an audience, it will not succeed in furthering the terrorists' cause. As the change sought by terrorists typically requires the attention of parties beyond those directly affected by an attack, terrorists rely on the media—print, television, and the internet and social media—to communicate. In addition to publicizing their cause, the media are also used to facilitate critical functions of terrorist groups such as recruiting, generating resources (i.e., money), and impression management—controlling their image to appeal to their support base or potential supporters. In pursuit of the strategic objective of advertisement, discussed in Chapter 9, terrorists carefully select their tactics and targets in order to maximize their desired media attention.

The ways in which the media respond to attacks, in turn, contributes to the social construction of terrorism and terrorists among the public. The knowledge that most people have about terrorism comes from the media. People's understanding of what constitutes an act of terrorism, where, how, and why terrorism occurs, and who terrorists are, is largely based on the news they consume; the images and videos they view. As discussed in Chapter 2, the media strongly influences public opinion, and media reports may contribute to increased fear, stereotyping, and prejudice. A number of factors have been shown to influence how different

FIGURE 10.1 The media play a significant role in shaping public perception, and it can both amplify and mitigate the impact of terrorism. Responsible and ethical media coverage is essential to strike a balance between informing the public and preventing the amplification of terrorism's harmful effects. *Source:* JoeBakal/Shutterstock.

incidents are portrayed to the public, including standards and **journalism ethics**, potential impacts on ratings and profits of the media companies, and the interests of the government, political elites, and security forces, as well as public opinion itself. Because public understandings of terrorism influence support for political officials, counterterrorism policy, criminal sanctions, social relations within society, and personal well-being, it is critical to examine the elements that influence media consumption and the media's reporting of terrorism. This chapter will discuss the role of the media in terrorism, starting with the various ways in which terrorists use the media and then covering the competing interests that influence how news about terrorism is presented to the public.

10.2 TERRORISM AS ADVERTISEMENT

On April 15, 2013, brothers Tamerlan and Dzhokhar Tsarnaev used a toy car's remote control to detonate two homemade bombs consisting of pressure cookers, nails, and BB pellets near the finish line of the Boston Marathon. The explosions killed two spectators and injured 264 others. The subsequent four-day manhunt and shootout resulted in the deaths of two police officers and suspect Temerlan Tsarnaev. On the evening of April 19, Dzohkhar Tsarnaev was found hiding in a dry-docked boat in Watertown, Massachusetts (START 2024; Ray 2023). Through bloodstained writings on the boat in which he hid, Tsarnaev revealed Islamic extremist motivations for the attack (Katersky & McPhee 2015).

The target selected for the attack—the Boston Marathon—is an annual sporting event that draws athletes from across the world to its 26.2-mile running course, plus half a million spectators, and hundreds of thousands of television viewers worldwide (Ray 2023). The event already attracts tremendous media attention, but the bomb attack—and the multiday pursuit of the suspects that followed—engendered a significant global audience. US news networks experienced sizable spikes in ratings during this time, with CNN ratings up 194 percent, Fox News up 48 percent, and MSNBC up 37 percent (Collins 2013). The attack also generated an unprecedented number or reports from "citizen journalists," as spectators took to social media, and Twitter in particular, to communicate their experiences, and post images, descriptions, and news tips (Minkoff 2018; Olsen 2018; Reider 2013). During the time of the attack and search there were 27.8 million tweets from the public, making the terrorist attack the most discussed event on Twitter in 2013. This Twitter response also had a knock-on effect on the reporting of official news outlets (e.g., mistakenly reporting an arrest), as journalists utilized social media sources to expedite the publication of their stories (Minkoff 2018; Rieder 2013).

Apparently, according to handwritten notes that Dzhokhar Tsarnaev provided to the FBI during his hospitalization, the brothers, both American citizens, were self-radicalized and acted independently. They selected their tactic and constructed the bombs before determining their target. Although they were initially planning a 4th of July attack, the date of the Boston Marathon happened to fall just as they were completing the bombs (earlier than anticipated), and they seized the opportunity (Winter 2018). Public health researchers have found that repeated exposure to news coverage of the bombings corresponded to elevated stress among Americans, even if they resided outside of the region directly affected by the attack (Holman et al. 2014).

As with numerous other terrorist attacks noted in this text, the Tsarnaev brothers strategically selected a target that enabled them to cause massive destruction and command the attention of a broad audience. While they may not have anticipated the **citizen reporting** on Twitter, the marathon is a major event with an international audience that receives widespread media coverage.

Research has shown that certain features of attacks tend to draw media attention. An analysis of attacks that occurred between 1980 and 2001 (before 9/11) revealed that most incidents worldwide during that time received little news coverage. However, some attacks were sensationalized in the news, and those attacks were the ones that were associated with casualties, linked to **domestic terrorist** groups, and targeted airlines or used hijacking as a tactic (Chermak & Gruenewald 2006). Following 9/11, which reshaped Americans' perception of terrorism and terrorists (see Chapter 2), the key feature that influenced the amount of coverage that a terrorist attack received was whether the perpetrator was Muslim (Kearns et al. 2019). Analyses of newspaper

NON-MUSLIM PERPETRATOR = 15 HEADLINES

MUSLIM PERPETRATOR = 105 HEADLINES

FIGURE 10.2 The portrayal of Muslims in the media as terrorists is a problematic and unfair stereotype that has been a subject of significant concern and criticism. It's important to recognize that such portrayals are inaccurate and harmful, as they contribute to negative stereotypes, discrimination, and bias against Muslims. *Source:* Illustration by Mona Chalabi.

coverage of all attacks that occurred in the United States between 2006 and 2015 revealed that terrorist attacks with Muslim perpetrators received 357 percent more news coverage than other attacks. The Boston Marathon bombing alone received 13 percent of terrorism news coverage during this time period (2006–2015). Attacks received more media attention when the perpetrator was arrested, the attack targeted law enforcement or the government, and the attack resulted in fatalities (Kearns et al. 2019).

10.3 TERRORISTS' DIRECT USE OF MEDIA IN ACTS OF VIOLENCE

In Chapter 4 we discussed how the worldwide expansion of the internet provided terrorists with new tools for recruitment and radicalization. The Islamic State of Iraq and Syria (ISIL/ISIS), in particular, has developed a reputation for its media savvy. In addition to using online media for recruitment and fundraising, ISIS has become known for its video-recorded executions. In August of 2014, ISIS released a video-recorded execution of American journalist James Foley via the Al-Hayat Media Center (ISIS's media

FIGURE 10.3 The ISIS execution of James Foley was a tragic and widely publicized event that occurred in 2014. This horrific act was condemned worldwide and had several significant consequences. The video's dissemination through social media highlighted the use of online platforms by terrorist groups to spread propaganda and recruit individuals.

wing) account on the social media platform Diaspora. The video showed a masked ISIS insurgent holding a knife to Foley's head, followed by the image of his beheaded body. The last scene in the video showed the insurgent with a second American hostage and communicated a threat to execute him if the United States did not cease military operations in Iraq. Less than a month later, ISIS released a beheading video featuring the second hostage, American journalist Steven Sotloff. Three additional beheading videos of British and American aid workers followed (Carter 2014; Friis 2015). Since 2014, ISIS has released over 2,000 videoed executions (Ramussen 2018).

Despite social media companies' efforts to censor the videos, they spread widely across the internet and screen-captured images from them appeared in major print media outlets. The executions were noted as a turning point in terrorist violence—the Secretary of Defense at the time, Chuck Hagel, described the acts as "beyond anything we have ever seen," and President Barack Obama asserted that ISIS was "unique" in its brutality (Friis 2015, 736). These images contributed to the reframing of ISIS from a "regional" and "humanitarian" problem to a national security threat, with politicians using them to justify military action and policy, and gain public support for their agendas (Friis 2015).

Importantly, however, this type of violence was not new—terrorist groups have used **beheadings** as a murder method for centuries—nor was the visual recording of these gruesome acts, as the tactic is believed to have emerged in the 1990s during the First Chechen War. What was new was the **digital technology** that enabled the rapid proliferation of **visual media**. The internet has enabled terrorist groups such as ISIS to distribute images of its violence to people who would not otherwise witness such events, directly communicating with international audiences and encouraging the perception that its own violence is more exceptional than other violence that is not broadcasted (Friis 2015).

As touched on during Chapter 9's discussion of the Christchurch mosque shootings, terrorists—often far-right extremists, as in the Christchurch case—have also **livestreamed** their attacks on social media, resulting in direct, unfiltered publicity. For example, Payton Gendron, the White supremacist who carried out the 2022 mass shooting at a supermarket in a predominantly Black neighborhood of Buffalo, New York, livestreamed the attack on a platform called Twitch. Prior to the attack, Gendron used the Discord app to notify users of his livestreaming plan. Although Twitch removed the video within two minutes of the start of the attack, and only 22 people viewed the stream in real time, the footage received enough airtime and viewership to be downloaded and shared widely. In his manifesto, Gendron explicitly indicated that the livestream of the Christchurch mosque shootings along with another livestream of a 2019 synagogue attack in Halle, Germany, contributed to his radicalization (Perrigo 2022).

It is clear from these examples that the internet has become an important tool for terrorists, facilitating their sustenance and publicizing their mandate. Many social media platforms have responded by removing harmful content and malicious accounts, and using machine learning techniques to moderate posts. However, this censorship raises concerns about freedom of speech. Mainstream news networks contend with similar conflicts. Journalists often take great risks in their coverage of terrorism—traveling to conflict zones, interviewing key informants, and covering gruesome tragedies, while following a code of professional ethics. According to the Society of Professional Journalists, journalists' ethical guidelines include the following principles: (1) seek truth and report it, (2) minimize harm (balance the public's need for information against potential harm or discomfort), (3) act independently, and (4) be accountable and transparent (Abubakar 2020; SPJ 2023). When reporting about terrorism, the principle of minimizing harm can be particularly challenging, as journalists carefully negotiate between educating the public and providing a propaganda outlet for terrorists, while considering issues of national security (Abubakar 2020; Nacos et al. 2011). It should also be noted that much of the "news" circulating today (e.g., via social media) is not written by journalists who are committed to these ethical principles. Some of it is not even written by humans but rather generated by artificial intelligence tools that produce realistic-looking fake news reports, generated and spread to affect public opinion on political and social issues (Swenson 2023). It is critical to examine news sources and their credibility. The remainder of the chapter will consider the tensions and the complex processes at play in the media's coverage of terrorism.

10.4 THE MEDIA'S PORTRAYAL OF TERRORIST AND TERRORIST ATTACKS

As mentioned at the start of the chapter, the media plays a critical role in constructing the public's understanding of terrorism and terrorists. The public forms a conception of terrorism based on information communicated through media. It is important to consider the different factors that shape the media's portrayal of terrorism. Although the **free press**—the right of news organizations to report without government intervention (censorship)—is fundamental to a well-functioning democracy, the relationship between the government and media outlets is often more complicated than the principle implies.

Reporters Without Borders, an International nonprofit organization dedicated to protecting freedom of information, publishes an annual World Press Freedom Index. This measure ranks the extent to which the press is free from government influence in each nation based on two factors: (1) the number of abuses documented against the media and journalists related to their work, and (2) survey responses from media specialists including journalists, researchers, academics, and human rights activists within each nation (RSF.org). Freedom of press is measured as a scale, rather than a dichotomy (e.g., free/not free) because, even in nations with a free press, various factors influence reporting, including the interests of governments and political elites, depending on the current social and political climate. Looking to the results of the 2024 index, North Korea, Afghanistan, Syria, and China ranked among the lowest—nations with the least freedom of information. On the other end of the scale—with the greatest freedom of press—are Norway, Denmark, Sweden, the Netherlands, and then Finland, all considered "good" according to the index's classification. Out of 180 nations the United States ranked 55th, down from

45th last year, with the report noting that "major structural barriers to press freedom persist in this country, once considered a model for freedom of expression." Russia ranked 162nd, having dropped in rank from the previous year due to the adoption of laws, following the invasion of Ukraine, that created punishment (up to 15 years in prison) for the spread of false information about the Russian military (Duggal & Ali 2023). Ukraine itself, meanwhile, placed 61st. Figure 10.4 shows the global freedom of press rankings.

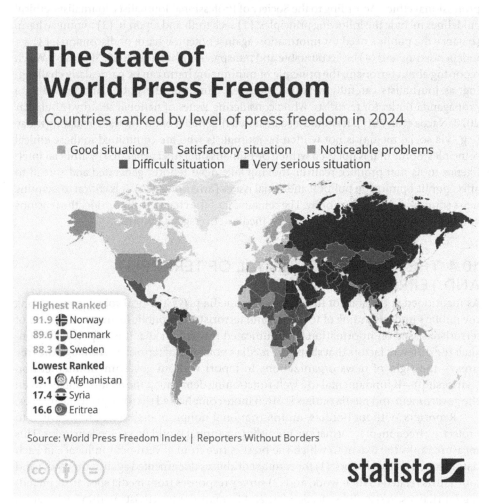

The State of World Press Freedom

Countries ranked by level of press freedom in 2024

- Good situation
- Satisfactory situation
- Noticeable problems
- Difficult situation
- Very serious situation

Highest Ranked
91.9 Norway
89.6 Denmark
88.3 Sweden

Lowest Ranked
19.1 Afghanistan
17.4 Syria
16.6 Eritrea

Source: World Press Freedom Index | Reporters Without Borders

statista

FIGURE 10.4   Freedom of the press is a critical component of democratic societies, allowing for the free flow of information, transparency, and accountability. However, in the context of terrorism, there are several considerations. Governments may impose censorship or content restrictions on media outlets, preventing them from publishing or broadcasting certain information related to terrorism. Some governments may resort to intimidation, harassment, or threats against journalists who investigate or report on terrorism-related issues. A free press plays a crucial role in holding governments accountable, investigating wrongdoing, and providing the public with diverse perspectives and information.

10.4.1 Media Framing

Although there are a variety of news sources today, that present diverse perspectives, including those on **social media**, the news content published through mainstream media sources is filtered and crafted to present a story to the public. Certain topics are selected as newsworthy by journalists and editors, and selected details are conveyed in the news stories. Through a process called **framing**, the media define the issue, diagnose its causes, make a moral assessment, and suggest remedies (Entman 1993). As demonstrated by the Freedom of Press Index, the extent to which media frames are free from the influence of governments and other stakeholders varies.

Robert Entman, American journalist and Professor of Media and Public Affairs, defines framing as "selecting and highlighting some facets of events or issues, and making connections among them so as to promote a particular interpretation, evaluation, and/or solution" (2004, 95).

Further, Entman (2004, 45) notes that "ideally, a free press balances official views with a more impartial perspective that allows the public to deliberate independently on the government's decisions. But in practice, the relationship between governing elites and news organizations is less distant and more cooperative than the ideal envisions, especially in foreign affairs."

Entman (2004) developed the **cascading network activation** model, depicted in Figure 10.5, to illustrate the multiple points of influence in reporting related to US foreign policy. While an explanation of the full model is beyond the scope of this text, the image is instructive for our purposes. For issues relating to foreign policy (and national security), such as terrorism, the news begins at the top of the model, with the administration's first public statements about the event. These statements go through other political elites (reporters' contacts) to journalists. Journalists consult their networks (e.g., politicians, topic experts, witnesses) and their editors to determine the relevant perspectives on the issue, noting divergence or consensus in ideas and assess the interpretations of their competitors (other news outlets). That research then goes into the construction of the frames that they ultimately present to the public. At each step in the process, groups compete to have their perspective represented in the news stories.

As with a cascading waterfall, each level in the model makes its own contribution to the flow of information, and as shown by the feedback loops, different levels in turn influence each other. Importantly, the media takes public opinion into consideration in the construction of news frames; however, Entman points out that public opinion, which is largely determined by opinion polling, is shaped by news frames. The polling topics and questions, including their wording and response options, are based on the frames provided by the media. Data on public opinion is confined within those frames. Entman (2004) further argues that the parties represented in the model have motivations that come into play in creating frames—the government wants support for its national security strategy, politicians want to be re-elected, journalists want to advance their careers, media companies want profits, and so on. All parties represented in the model act with varying degrees of uncertainty and competence. Given the speed at which news is provided to audiences, public officials and the media rarely have the opportunity to consider all relevant facts and opinions before responding.

10.4.2 Framing Competition: Beyond Political Elites

Political elites often have tremendous weight in the production of news frames. However, they are not (and should not be) the only source of information on political and social issues. In reporting on a story, journalists consult their professional networks, often including topic experts such as correspondents, pundits, academics, and representatives from civil service organizations. These experts are frequently quoted in news stories and often appear on televised news programs to provide context and expert analysis. Other experts and spokespersons have their own perspectives that they wish to have included in the framing of events. The background and potential agenda of those granted the authority to contribute their insights on topics should be carefully considered in assessing their contribution to knowledge on the topic.

An extensive examination of expert evaluation that entered the framing of terrorism following the attacks of 9/11 was provided by sociologist Christopher Bail. Bail (2015) identified 120 civil society organizations with interests in the status of Muslims in the United States and conducted an analysis of more than 300,000 documents from these organizations (including press releases, research reports, and tax documents) and

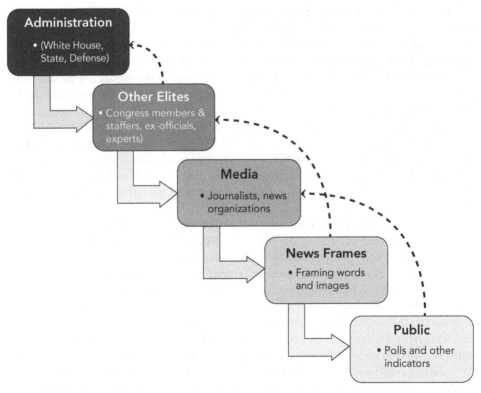

FIGURE 10.5 Cascading Network Activation refers to the process by which information, ideas, or narratives spread through interconnected networks or systems. It emphasizes how the media's role in agenda-setting and framing can trigger a cascade effect, influencing how information and narratives spread and ultimately shape public perception and societal priorities.

measured how frequently information from each organization was utilized by the mainstream news media. Most of these organizations, including groups such as the Islamic Society of North America (ISNA), the Arab American Institute (AAI), and the Council on American Islamic Relations (CAIR), engage in efforts to condemn terrorism and provide accurate portrayals of Muslims to the public. Other "fringe" organizations, including the Middle East Media Research Institute (MEMRI), the Middle East Forum (MEF), and the Investigative Project on Terrorism (IPT), have acted to promote an anti-Muslim agenda and their opinions and interpretations of events have received considerable attention in the mainstream media.

These **anti-Muslim organizations** appear to be objective sources for information about Middle Eastern and Muslim culture. MEMRI explains their mission as "exploring the Middle East and South Asia through their media, MEMRI bridges the language gap between the West and the Middle East and South Asia, providing timely translations of Arabic, Farsi, Urdu-Pashtu, Dari, Turkish, Russian, and Chinese media, as well as original analysis of political, ideological, intellectual, social, cultural, and religious trends" (memri.org/about). Information provided by this organization has been regularly cited by media outlets including Fox News, the *New York Times*, *Washington Post*, and the *Boston Globe*. Bail notes, however, that in 2004 "University of Michigan historian Juan Cole denounced MEMRI for 'cleverly cherry-pick[ing] the vast Arabic press . . . for the most extreme and objectionable articles.' Cole claimed to have 'looked at the newspapers [in the Muslim world] that ran both tolerant and extremist opinion pieces on the same day, and checked MEMRI, to find that only the extremist one showed up" (Bail 2015, 82). Other accusations include providing incorrect translations of Middle Eastern Media to suggest the promotion of violence among Muslims. Similarly, the MEF is a conservative American think tank that publishes the journal *Middle East Quarterly*, which is frequently criticized for its anti-Muslim publications. And the IEP has been accused of providing inaccurate translations of Islamic terminology, in ways that depict Muslims as intolerant and aggressive, as well as spreading claims that American Muslim organizations were launching a "stealth jihad" to establish an Islamic empire in the West (Bail 2015, 94).

Bail's analysis reveals that these anti-Muslim organizations influenced mainstream media (and continue to do so) through the use of emotional and sensationalized reports and commentary that attracted the attention of the media and the public. In doing so, they generated substantial contributions from donors that enabled them to continue to push their agendas of shaping the media portrayal of Islam to the public. Another tactic used by these organizations is the use of Muslim-looking spokespersons who, by their names and appearances, were able to gain authority on the topic of the Muslim faith and culture, while communicating information harmful to Muslims (Bail 2015).

Other so-called experts have had significant impacts on the media's construction of terrorism and related concerns—so much so that in recognizing this bias, on May 26, 2004, the editors of the *New York Times* issued an apology for insufficient scrutiny in their reporting of issues related to the Iraq War. Regarding its review of articles published prior to the war and during its early stages, the editors wrote:

> We have found a number of instances of coverage that was not as rigorous as it should have been. In some cases, information that was controversial then, and seems questionable now, was insufficiently qualified or allowed to stand unchallenged.

Looking back, we wish we had been more aggressive in re-examining the claims as new evidence emerged—or failed to emerge.

They depended at least in part on information from a circle of Iraqi informants, defectors and exiles bent on "regime change" in Iraq, people whose credibility has come under increasing public debate in recent weeks.

Complicating matters for journalists, the accounts of these exiles were often eagerly confirmed by United States officials convinced of the need to intervene in Iraq. Administration officials now acknowledge that they sometimes fell for misinformation from these exile sources. So did many news organizations—in particular, this one.

From the Editors, "The Times and Iraq," *New York Times*, May 26, 2004

In the case of terrorism, and of the attacks of 9/11 in particular, biased information entered mainstream media and contributed to the social construction of terrorism. These frames of terrorism and of Muslims as terrorists dominated the media, receiving reinforcement and sustenance from multiple sources (as shown in the cascade model). Many scholars point to the terrorist attacks of 9/11 as an event that produced news frames across media outlets in the United States that were highly consistent with the government's preferred frames (Altheide 2017; Nacos et al. 2011). The attacks have been described as a "black swan" event—an occurrence that to most Americans was so unexpected and had unimaginable consequences that time is demarcated in terms of "before" and "after" (Dugan & Fisher 2023). Americans experienced a drastic change to their perceived vulnerability to terrorism.

During this time within the United States, there was a notable absence of frames that competed with those presented by President George W. Bush. Starting with his initial televised speeches to the public, the former president told a story in which "good Americans" were victims of the unjustified actions of "evil terrorists." He also framed the situation as controllable, offering and gaining support for a military response, a **Global War on Terror**, and security policies that limited citizens' civil liberties (Loseke 2009; 2013).

The attacks of 9/11 and the Western media's response to them, have played the most critical role in constructing Americans' (and citizens of other Western nations') understanding of terrorism. We

FIGURE 10.6 On May 26, 2004, the editors of the *New York Times* published an editorial titled "From the Editors: The Times and Iraq," in which they apologized to their readers for their misleading coverage of the Iraq War. The letter said: "Over the last year this newspaper has shone the bright light of hindsight on decisions that led the United States into Iraq. We have examined the failings of American and allied intelligence, especially on the issue of Iraq's weapons and possible Iraqi connections to international terrorists. We have studied the allegations of official gullibility and hype. It is past time we turned the same light on ourselves". *Source:* Haxorjoe, CC BY-SA 3.0, via Wikimedia Commons.

next discuss the multiple ways in which, following the initial framing of 9/11, bias is evidenced in the media and has contributed to stereotyping and prejudice among the public, as well as national security concerns.

10.4.3 Biased Media Frames and Their Consequences

Prior to 9/11, several scholars had already identified a "culture of fear" among Americans, in which phenomena deemed fearful captures the attention of the public and motivates support for proclaimed remedies. In turn, politicians use these fears to achieve their goals (Best 2018; Furedi 2018; Glassner 1999; Nacos et al. 2011). A particular concern about Muslims as dangerous outsiders was already present in American society as well. Muslims and Arabs have historically been vilified as threats to national security in both entertainment and news media (Akram et al. 2009; Shaheen 2014; Tehranian 2008). Regarding the culture of fear and perceptions of terrorism, sociologist David Altheide (2017, 133) argued that "tying terrorism coverage to an expansive discourse of fear has contributed to the emergence of the politics of fear, or decision makers' promotion and use of audience beliefs and assumptions about danger, risk, and fear in order to achieve certain goals." (In an analysis of President Bush's first four televised speeches after the 9/11 attacks, Loseke (2009, 508–509) highlights the language used to frame terrorism as something that Americans must fear:

> [Bush] explicitly directs his audience to evaluate the events of September 11 as a "threat to our way of life" (September 20), a "deadly new threat . . . a threat to our freedoms" (November 8). According to the president, Americans must now live in "the face of continuing threat" and under the "dark threat of violence" (September 20). The magnitude of these threats is enormous because "thousands of these terrorists in more than 60 countries" (September 20) "have threatened other acts of terror" (November 8).
>
> Hence, while the "Story of September 11" might have constructed the events of that day as a one time occurrence, as something that would never happen again, these events rather become symbolic, they serve as a warning of what Americans should expect in the future. This most certainly encourages the anticipation of threat.

Given the existing culture of fear and concerns about Muslims, the Bush administration's framing of terrorism easily resonated with the American public and enabled the advancement of policies, through three presidential administrations, that limited American citizens' civil liberties (such as the Patriot Act) and harmed Muslims (such as the National Security Entry-Exit Registration System (NSEERS).

This framing was supported in the mainstream news media, often with the input of political elites and civil society organizations as noted previously. Stories explained terrorism as foreign, with Muslims and Middle Easterners as dangerous enemies of a morally superior United States. For example, the language used in news reports during the Global War on Terror communicated good versus evil. US military personnel were often called "soldiers," while Iraqi fighters were called "gunmen" or "guerillas." Deaths at the hands of Iraqis were referred to as "gruesome," while deaths caused by US military personnel were portrayed as simply unavoidable (Altheide 2022). The language used to communicate news matters constructs the interpretation and evaluation of the issue. Different words can be used to describe similar actors and actions, and this difference sends clear messages to the public.

FIGURE 10.7 In 2017, the "I Am a Muslim Too" event was organized to show support for American Muslims and to reject increasing discrimination, Islamophobia, hate crimes, and anti-Muslim policies targeting the Muslim community in the United States. The event attracted a diverse group of participants, including people from different faiths, backgrounds, and political affiliations. Public figures, activists, and community leaders also joined to express their solidarity. The event aimed to emphasize unity, inclusivity, and support for religious freedom and diversity in the United States. *Source:* REUTERS/Carlo Allegri.

In addition to constructing evaluations of actors as good or evil, media frames also demonstrate the construction of terrorism as foreign and Muslim (and not domestic or non-Muslim/ Christian). Through an examination of media coverage of 11 terrorist incidents that occurred in the United States between 2011 and 2016 (from the *New York Times, Washington Post, USA Today,* CNN, MSNBC, and Fox News), Powell (2018) found that attacks with a perpetrator who had international or Islamic connections were quickly labeled as "terrorism" in the media. In articles about attacks with foreign or Islamic associations, a great deal of attention was given to the perpetrator's foreign ties, religious background, and foreign sources of their radicalization. For example, although both Tsarnaev brothers were US citizens at the time they committed the Boston Marathon bombing, extensive media attention was focused on the possibility that Tamerlan was radicalized abroad. Moreover, before any suspects in the bombing were even identified, the media theorized about Islamic ties (Powell 2018). The Global Terrorism Database includes the following incident:

> A suicide bomber detonated an explosives-laden RV in front of an AT&T Inc. building in downtown Nashville, Tennessee, United States. The assailant was killed, three people were injured, and several buildings were damaged in the blast. No group claimed responsibility for the incident; however, authorities attributed the attack to Anthony Warner, an unaffiliated individual, who issued a warning minutes prior to the attack. Sources noted that Warner held anti-government views and believed in several conspiracy theories, but it is uncertain if these inspired the attack. According to a neighbor, Warner stated "Nashville and the world is never going to forget me" a week prior to the attack.

Despite the fact that this incident meets the definition of terrorism (used in this text and by the GDT), it was not described as such in the media. Rather than "suicide terrorism" or even a "bombing" or "attack," it was largely referred to as a "mysterious motor home blast" (Barr 2021; Hassan 2020). Anthony Quinn Warner, the bomber, was not a Muslim (no religion was identified), he was White and described as "paranoid" and a "loner." Similar patterns have been demonstrated in multiple research studies—attacks with foreign and Muslim perpetrators receive substantially more media coverage than those with other perpetrators, and attacks in which the perpetrator is foreign or Muslim are much more likely to be labeled as terrorism in the first place (Kearns et al. 2019; Mitnik et al. 2020; Morin 2016; Powell 2018).

Another pattern identified in the media's framing of terrorism concerns the motivations for attacks. In the cases of Muslim perpetrators and those with foreign ties, emphasis in news coverage is placed on religious background, international connections, and possible ties to (or inspiration from) Islamist terrorist organizations. In comparison, when the perpetrator is a non-Muslim American, the attack is often framed as the result of mental illness (as in the case of Warner) (Betus et al. 2021). In doing so, the media excuses the behavior of the American (non-Muslim) terrorist as mental illness, while suggesting that the actions of the Muslim terrorist are part of a much larger threat. Mental illness, in this context, is a personal problem, and after the perpetrator is captured or

FIGURE 10.8 The Nashville Christmas bombing, also known as the Nashville bombing, occurred on the morning of December 25, 2020, in downtown Nashville, Tennessee, near the AT&T transmission building. Anthony Quinn Warner was identified as the perpetrator of the bombing, which involved detonating a recreational vehicle (RV) filled with explosives in downtown Nashville. *Source:* FBI database.

killed, they no longer pose a threat to society. The larger threat of Islamic extremism, especially with foreign connections, however, remains even after the perpetrators are killed or apprehended, because it is thought to be a part of an ongoing agenda of international terrorism (Powell 2018). The attitudes of the American public reflect this logic. Americans are more likely to view an attack as an act of terrorism if it was carried out by a Muslim (Huff & Kertzer 2018).

As discussed in Chapter 2, since 9/11, Muslims in the United States have suffered the consequences of the media's framing of terrorism. They have been subjected to increased discriminatory counterterrorism measures including profiling, unfettered surveillance, eavesdropping, unlawful searches, and immigration restrictions, and have experienced increases in hate-based crimes including outright murder (Dugan & Fisher 2023). Empirical studies have shown that general media coverage that portrays Muslims as terrorists or extremists directly creates fear and worry about terrorism among the public and generates out-group prejudices (e.g., Kishi 2017; Nellis & Savage 2012; Powell 2018).

FIGURE 10.9 The US Capitol attacks that occurred on January 6, 2021, were widely described by public officials, experts, and organizations as acts of domestic terrorism. *Source:* Tyler Merbler from USA, CC BY 2.0, via Wikimedia Commons.

10.5 THE JANUARY 6 US CAPITOL ATTACK: TERRORISM OR NOT?

Social psychological research has long demonstrated that people are motivated to maintain a positive evaluation of others like themselves (i.e., in-group members) and devalue outsiders (i.e., out-group members). **Social identity theory** pioneer Henri Tajfel (1978) argues that individuals form group-level identities based on their social category memberships (e.g., nationality, race, ethnicity, religion). In doing so, we differentiate ourselves from others based on those social categories. To enhance the status and evaluation of our own group, we tend to think favorably of our own group members (i.e., "us") and distance ourselves from the out-group (i.e., "not us"). For the largely Christian or otherwise non-Muslim American population, the idea of a Muslim (out-group) enemy was consistent with these distinctions, and large numbers of the non-Muslim American population already endorsed this view.

As suggested by trends in the labeling of attacks committed by non-Muslim Americans as crime but not terrorism, designating an in-group member as the enemy creates more conflict. This can be seen with the case of the January 6, 2021 attacks on the US Capitol. As the US Congress was about to certify the presidential election results, with Joe Biden as the winner, Donald Trump supporters stormed the Capitol building, seeking to disrupt the affirmation. This attack resulted in severe consequences for the nation including seven fatalities; assault-related injuries to 140 police officers; over $30 million in damages to the Capitol; arrests of 725 individuals; psychological trauma endured by congresspersons, security personnel, employees, and members of the public; and a crisis for American democracy (Agiesta 2022; Chapell 2021; US DOJ 2022). Some of the crimes committed by individuals involved in the Capitol attack meet the following federal definition of **domestic terrorism**, which was included as an amendment to US federal statute 18 (Crimes) US Code 2331, with the 2001 passing of the Patriot Act:

"domestic terrorism" means activities that—
  (A) involve acts dangerous to human life that are a violation of the criminal laws of the United States or of any State;
  (B) appear to be intended—
    (i) to intimidate or coerce a civilian population;
    (ii) to influence the policy of a government by intimidation or coercion; or
    (iii) to affect the conduct of a government by mass destruction, assassination, or kidnapping; and
  (C) occur primarily within the territorial jurisdiction of the United States

Many political elites and security experts have labeled the attack as domestic terrorism, including the United States House Select Committee to Investigate the January 6 attack and US FBI Director Christopher Wray (AP 2021), among others. Yet there is considerable disagreement in the media about whether or not the acts are indeed terrorism. Some express concern about far-right extremism and endorse the terrorism label for the events of January 6, while others have discounted the threat, labeling it instead as legitimate political discourse (Dugan & Fisher 2023; Haner at al. 2023). Even those who have similar political views have drawn media attention for their disagreement. For instance, the *New York Times* reported a heated conflict between former Fox News host Tucker Carlson and US Senator Ted Cruz, both Republicans, in which Carlson accused Cruz of purposefully lying when he labeled the Capitol attack terrorism. Cruz subsequently apologized for his use of the terrorism label (Savage 2022).

Public opinion on the events of January 6, 2021, also reflects this disparity. A national survey conducted on the same day of the attacks reported that of 1,397 registered voters who had heard about the event, 93 percent of Democrats viewed "the storming of the Capitol building as a threat to democracy," while only 27 percent of Republicans viewed this event as such a threat (Sanders et al. 2021). A nationally representative survey conducted in 2022 found that respondents who supported former President Donald Trump were more likely than others to reference the January 6 events using positive terms including "peaceful," "a good thing," and "mostly good citizens" (Piazza & Van Doren 2022).

Scholars have suggested that these conflicting views are due, in part, to the dominance of the media's framing of terrorism following the 9/11 attacks and supported by existing perceptions of Muslims as an out-group. The characteristics of the participants in the January 6 Capitol attack—mostly White and Christian—were inconsistent with that frame. Criminologists Laura Dugan and Daren Fisher (2023) argue that the decades-long focus on the 9/11 terrorism frame contributed to a lack of attention to the growing, and now more deadly threat of far-right extremism in the United States; since 9/11, far-right extremists have attacked 331 percent more frequently than Islamic extremists, and have killed 75 percent more people in the United States.

10.6 DISINFORMATION AND TERRORISM

During his presidency, Donald Trump frequently called journalists and mainstream news outlets "fake news." While media bias and false or misleading news stories were not new during Trump's term in office, the spread of fake news about a number of issues (e.g., the COVID-19 virus, conspiracy theories) was proliferating online, and **disinformation** about voter fraud played a key role in the January 6 Capitol attack (Bond & Allyn 2021). Spreading false information itself is not an act of terrorism; however, research has shown that it contributes to violent extremism (Piazza 2021).

False information can take different forms. **Misinformation** is information that is false or misleading but is spread without an intent to deceive. Think of people reposting news stories they believe to be true, unknowingly sharing false information with others. In contrast, **disinformation** is content that is false and deliberately intended to harm someone or something, and malinformation is content that is based in reality (has

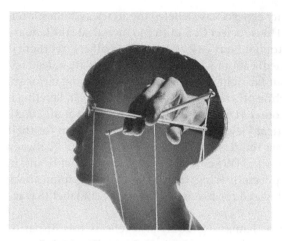

FIGURE 10.10 The spread of misinformation through social media has become a growing concern in recent years. Social media platforms enable information to spread rapidly, often reaching a large audience within seconds. *Source:* SvetaZi/Shutterstock.

some truth to it) but is deliberately spread to cause harm (Carmi et al. 2020). Social media has enabled disinformation and malinformation to spread exponentially. So-called bots (software applications that run automatically) amplify news stories, meaning that disinformation can gain prominence on user's news feeds, giving the appearance of major news. These disinformation campaigns often originate from foreign state-linked groups seeking to gain political influence (Hunt 2021; Johnson 2018; Rhodes 2022; Seldin 2021). Through a recent 150-nation analysis of the connection between disinformation and domestic terrorism, political scientist James Piazza (2021) found that disinformation increased political polarization, which in turn led to terrorism. These false narratives target political and social issues in a way that increases political division and opposition, out-group intolerance, distrust in governmental authorities, and dissatisfaction with major social institutions, which can then lead to acts of violence (DHS 2023; Hawdon et al. 2019). These false narratives impact individuals and groups because they resonate with existing ideologies and appeal to emotion (Johnson 2018; Vosoughi et al. 2018; Walter et al. 2022).

A notable, direct example of the impact of disinformation on violence is the "Pizzagate" incident in the United States. During the 2016 presidential election cycle, a disinformation-based conspiracy theory spread on social media claiming that presidential candidate Hilary Clinton was at the center of a human trafficking and child sex ring operating out of pizza restaurants in Washington, DC. Protests in front of pizza establishments and threats of violence erupted over these rumors. Then, on December 4, 2016, with the intent of rescuing abused children, Edgar Welch drove from North Carolina to Washington, DC, entered the Comet Ping Pong pizza restaurant armed with an AR-15 assault rifle, a revolver, and a pocketknife. He searched the restaurant, found no evidence of wrongdoing, and fired his gun two or three times. Analyses of the disinformation that circulated regarding this conspiracy theory revealed that many of the social media posts originated from the Czech Republic, Cyprus, and Vietnam, and were often produced by bots (Fisher et al. 2016).

Similar violent incidents have occurred around the world, ignited by disinformation spread through social media. In 2019, a hundred-person mob burned two men alive in Puebla, Mexico, after disinformation about "child kidnappers" spread on the instant messaging application WhatsApp. Likewise, lynch mobs in India have killed dozens of people due to child kidnapping disinformation spread on WhatsApp (Funke & Benkelman 2019).

As with the case of social media posts that display acts of terrorism, major social media platforms have attempted to control the spread of disinformation by suspending accounts, removing or flagging dangerous posts, or by providing counternarratives and education. However, social media companies have had limited success in combating disinformation and, again, must negotiate the line between the freedom of speech and protecting the public. Nonprofit organizations such as the Poynter Institute and AllSides are also working to fight disinformation. Through its initiative MediaWise, the Poynter Institute provides media literacy training, free of charge, to the public through its initiative MediaWise and provides a news fact-checking resource online through its initiative PolitiFact (see www.poynter.org/). Working to educate the public about biased news, AllSides offers competing perspectives on news stories, identifying whether they are written from a right, left, or center political viewpoint. Regarding media bias, AllSides' website states: "Everyone is biased—and that's okay. There's no such thing as unbiased news. But hidden media bias misleads, manipulates and divides us. So everyone should learn how to spot media bias" (see www.allsides.com). AllSides also provides a ranking of the political leaning or bias of hundreds of news sources, so that readers can be aware of the perspectives that are represented in their news stories. Efforts such as these can help the public navigate the vast array of news sources available today.

10.7 CONCLUSION

Many terrorism experts and public officials recognize that terrorism and the media have a symbiotic relationship. Terrorists depend on the media to accomplish their goals of affecting large audiences and gaining publicity. Likewise, in reporting about terrorism, the media capture their own audiences and their profits depend on these shocking, emotion-laden events. Technology enables news reports, images, and videos of terrorist attacks to spread rapidly across the world, but the media must carefully balance their mission of educating the public about current events with the terrorists' agendas of spreading propaganda for their cause.

In addition to providing coverage in ways that minimize the benefits to terrorists, journalists also must negotiate multiple parties and information sources, all seeking to have their perspectives represented in news coverage. Biased information is frequently presented in news media, whether it is from governments trying to gain support for their national security policies, political elites seeking public approval, organizations pushing a particular agenda, or media companies wanting to maximize profits in an increasingly competitive market. Since most people do not have direct experience with terrorism, the ways in which it is framed by the media play a critical role in the social construction of terrorism and terrorists for the public. As evidenced by the post-9/11 terrorism frame (foreign, Muslim), this social construction can have severe consequences on public understanding, the well-being of those affected, and national security.

Key Lessons

Lesson 1

By definition, terrorism relies on publicity. If news of an attack does not reach an audience, it will not succeed in furthering the terrorists' cause.

Lesson 2

Terrorists strategically select targets that enable them to cause massive destruction and command the attention of a broad audience.

Lesson 3

The internet has enabled terrorist groups to distribute images of its violence to people who would not otherwise witness such events, directly communicating with international audiences.

Lesson 4

Journalists follow professional codes of ethics; however, not all news is produced by journalists who are bound by such guidelines.

Lesson 5

The free press is the right of news organizations to report without government intervention. The extent to which presses are free varies by nation.

Lesson 6

Through a process called framing, the media define the issue, diagnose its causes, make a moral assessment, and suggest remedies.

Lesson 7

Multiple parties, including the government, political elites, security forces, civil society organizations, topic experts, media companies, and others compete to have their preferred frames of terrorism represented in the media.

Lesson 8

The background and potential agenda of those granted the authority to contribute their insights on topics should be carefully considered in assessing their contribution to knowledge on the topic.

Lesson 9

Following the attacks of 9/11 biased information entered mainstream media and substantially contributed to the social construction of terrorism among Americans.

Lesson 10

The 9/11 media frame that portrays Muslims as terrorists or extremists creates fear and worry about terrorism among the public and generates out-group prejudices.

Lesson 11

Social identity theory argues that individuals form group-level identities based on their social category memberships (e.g., nationality, race and ethnicity, religion).

Lesson 12

There is considerable disagreement in the media about whether or not the January 6 attack on the US Capitol included acts of terrorism. Scholars have suggested that these conflicting views are due, in part, to the dominance of the media's framing of terrorism following the 9/11 attacks and supported by existing perceptions of Muslims as an out-group.

Lesson 13

Disinformation, content that is false and deliberately intended to harm someone or something, increases political polarization, which can lead to terrorism.

KEY WORDS

anti-Muslim organizations
beheadings
cascading network activation
citizen reporting
digital technology

disinformation
domestic terrorism
framing
free press
Global War on Terror

journalism ethics
livestreamed attacks
misinformation
political elites

publicity
social identity theory
social media
visual media

RECOMMENDED SOURCES

Research Articles & Books

Abubakar, A. T. (2020). News values and the ethical dilemmas of covering violent extremism. *Journalism & Mass Communication Quarterly, 97*(1), 278–298.

Altheide, D. L. (2007). The mass media and terrorism. *Discourse & Communication, 1*(3), 287–308.

Bail, C. A. (2015). *Terrified: How anti-Muslim fringe organizations became mainstream.* Princeton University Press.

Betus, A. E., Kearns, E. M., & Lemieux, A. F. (2021). How perpetrator identity (sometimes) influences media framing attacks as "terrorism" or "mental illness". *Communication Research, 48*(8), 1133–1156.

Chermak, S. M., & Gruenewald, J. (2006). The media's coverage of domestic terrorism. *Justice Quarterly, 23*(4), 428–461.

Dugan, L., & Fisher, D. 2023. Far-right and jihadi terrorism within the United States: From September 11th to January 6th. *Annual Review of Criminology, 6*, 131–153.

Glassner, B. (1999). *The culture of fear: Why Americans are afraid of the wrong things.* New York: Basic Books.

Huff, C., & Kertzer, J. D. (2018). How the public defines terrorism. *American Journal of Political Science, 62*(1), 55–71.

Kearns, E. M., Betus, A. E., & Lemieux, A. F. (2019). Why do some terrorist attacks receive more media attention than others? *Justice Quarterly, 36*(6), 985–1022.

Loseke, D. R. (2009). Examining emotion as discourse: Emotion codes and presidential speeches justifying war. *The Sociological Quarterly, 50*(3), 497–524.

Mitnik, Z. S., Freilich, J. D., & Chermak, S. M. (2020). Post-9/11 coverage of terrorism in the New York Times. *Justice Quarterly, 37*(1), 161–185.

Powell, K. A. (2018). Framing Islam/creating fear: An analysis of US media coverage of terrorism from 2011–2016. *Religions, 9*(9), 257.

News Articles & Government and Think Tank Reports

Pizzagate: From rumor, to hashtag, to gunfire in D.C.
   Author(s): Marc Fisher, John Woodrow Cox, & Peter Hermann
   Source: The Washington Post

More misinformation-related attacks.
   Author(s): David Shedden
   Source: Poynter Institute for Media Studies

Assaults against Muslims in U.S. surpass 2001 level.
   Author(s): Katayoun Kishi
   Source: Pew Research Center

Social media companies vowed to stop videos of terror attacks. Buffalo showed they have more work to do.
   Author(s): Billy Perrigo
   Source: TIME

On Boston bombing, media are wrong—again.
   Author(s): Rem Rieder
   Source: The USA Today

From the editors; The Times and Iraq.
   Source: The New York Times

Documentaries, Videos, and Other Educational Media

Terrorism and the Media
  Producer(s)/Director(s): CBC News
  Source: CBC News: The National YouTube
  channel
The Media's Role in Covering Terrorism
  Featuring: Josh Gerstein, P.J. Crowley,
  Christopher Dickey, Ira Rosen, Producer,
  Kristen Saloomey, Eric Schmitt
  Source: The Aspen Institute YouTube channel
Social Media and Combating Terrorism
  Featuring: Ron Johnson, Peter Bergen,
  Hany Farid, Frances Townsend
  Source: C-Span
Max Abrahms discusses the role of social
media in terrorism

Featuring: Max Abrahms
Source: CGTN America
Terrorism and the United States: An Ironic
Perspective
  Featuring: Ron Hirschbein
  Source: California State University Chico
  Media
Terrorism Lawsuits Against Social Media
Companies
  Featuring: Jeff Breinholt, Will Mackie,
  Annie E. Kouba, Katie A. Paul
  Source: Program on Extremism at George
  Washington University YouTube Channel

REFERENCES

Abubakar, A. T. (2020). News values and the ethical dilemmas of covering violent extremism. *Journalism & Mass Communication Quarterly, 97*(1), 278–298.

Agiesta, J. (2022, July 26). CNN poll. January 6 hearings haven't changed opinions much, but most agree Trump acted unethically. CNN. https://www.cnn.com/2022/07/26/politics/cnn-poll-january-6-trump/index.html

Akram, S. M., Johnson, K. R., & Martinez, S. (2009). The demonization of persons of Arab and Muslim ancestry in historical perspective. In Martínez, S. (Ed.), *International migration and human rights* (pp. 98–114). University of California Press.

Altheide, D. L. (2017). *Terrorism and the politics of fear.* Rowman & Littlefield.

Altheide, D. L. (2022). Media logic, terrorism, and the politics of fear. In N. Ribeiro & C. Schwarzenegger (Eds.), *Media and the dissemination of fear: Global transformations in media and communication research* (pp. 275–299). Palgrave Macmillan.

Bail, C. A. (2015). *Terrified: How anti-Muslim fringe organizations became mainstream.* Princeton University Press.

Barr, L. (2021, March 15). FBI report finds Nashville bomber wanted to kill himself, not motivated by terrorism: Authorities said he was driven by "eccentric conspiracy

theories." ABC News. https://abcnews.go.com/Politics/fbi-report-finds-nashville-bomber-wanted-kill-motivated/story?id=76471078

Best, J. (2018). *American nightmares: Social problems in an anxious world.* University of California Press.

Betus, A. E., Kearns, E. M., & Lemieux, A. F. (2021). How perpetrator identity (sometimes) influences media framing attacks as "terrorism" or "mental illness." *Communication Research, 48*(8), 1133–1156.

Bond, S., & Allyn, B. (2021, October 22). How the "stop the steal" movement outwitted Facebook ahead of the Jan. 6 insurrection. National Public Radio. https://www.npr.org/2021/10/22/1048543513/facebook-groups-jan-6-insurrection

Carmi, E., Yates, S. J., Lockley, E., & Pawluczuk, A. (2020). Data citizenship: Rethinking data literacy in the age of disinformation, misinformation, and malinformation. *Internet Policy Review, 9*(2), 1–22.

Carter, C. J. (2014, August 20). Video shows ISIS beheading U.S. journalist James Foley. CNN. https://www.cnn.com/2014/08/19/world/meast/isis-james-foley/index.html

Chapell, B. (2021, February 24). Architect of the Capitol outlines $30 million in damages from pro-Trump riot. NPR. https://www.npr

.org/sections/insurrection-at-the-capitol/ 2021/02/24/970977612/architect-of-the-capitol-outlines-30-million-in-damages-from-pro-trump-riot

Chermak, S. M., & Gruenewald, J. (2006). The media's coverage of domestic terrorism. *Justice Quarterly*, 23(4), 428–461.

Collins, S. (2013, April 19). CNN sees huge ratings spike with Boston bombing, manhunt coverage. *Los Angeles Times*. https://www .latimes.com/entertainment/tv/la-xpm-2013-apr-19-la-et-st-cnn-sees-huge-ratings-spike-with-boston-bombing-manhunt-coverage-20130419-story.html

Dugan, L., & Fisher, D. 2023. Far-right and jihadi terrorism within the United States: From September 11th to January 6th. *Annual Review of Criminology*, 6, 131–153.

Duggal, H., & Ali, M. (2023, May 3). Map: What is the state of press freedom today? Al Jazeera. https://www.aljazeera.com/news/ 2023/5/3/map-what-is-the-state-of-press-freedom-in-the-world-today

Entman, R. M. (1993). Framing: Towards a clarification of a fractured paradigm. *Journal of Communication*, 43(4), 51–58.

Entman, R. M. (2004). *Projections of power: Framing news, public opinion, and U.S. foreign policy.* University of Chicago Press.

Fisher, M., Cox, J. W., & Hermann, P. (2016, December 6). Pizzagate: From rumor, to hashtag, to gunfire in D.C. *Washington Post*. https://www.washingtonpost.com/local/ pizzagate-from-rumor-to-hashtag-to-gunfire-in-dc/2016/12/06/4c7def50-bbd4-11e6-94ac-3d324840106c_story.html

Friis, S. M. (2015). "Beyond anything we have ever seen": Beheading videos and the visibility of violence in the war against ISIS. *International Affairs*, 91(4), 725–746.

Funke, D., & Benkelman, S. (2019, April 4). More misinformation-related attacks. *Poynter*. https://www.poynter.org/fact-checking/2019/ misinformation-is-inciting-violence-around-the-world-and-tech-platforms-dont-have-a-plan-to-stop-it/Institute.

Furedi, F. 2018. *How fear works: The culture of fear in the 21st century.* Bloomsbury.

Glassner, B. (1999). *The culture of rear: Why Americans are afraid of the wrong things.* Basic Books.

Haner, M., Sloan, M. M., Pickett, J. T., Cullen, F. T., & O'Neill, V. (2023). How politics constrain the public's understanding of terrorism. *Social Forces.* https://doi.org/10.1093/sf/soac132

Hassan, M. (2020, December 30). Mehdi Hasan on the privileges afforded to the Nashville bomber. MSNBC. https://www .msnbc.com/all-in/watch/mehdi-hasan-on-the-privileges-afforded-to-the-nashville-bomber-98627141613 2020

Hawdon, J., Bernatzky, C., & Costello, M. (2019). Cyber-routines, political attitudes, and exposure to violence-advocating online extremism. *Social Forces*, 98(1), 329–354.

Holman, E. A., Garfin, D. R., & Silver, R. C. (2014). Media's role in broadcasting acute stress following the Boston Marathon bombings. *Proceedings of the National Academy of Sciences*, 111(1), 93–98.

Huff, C., & Kertzer, J. D. (2018). How the public defines terrorism. *American Journal of Political Science*, 62(1), 55–71.

Hunt, J. S. (2021). Countering cyber-enabled disinformation: Implications for national security. *Australian Journal of Defence and Strategic Studies*, 3(1), 83–88.

Johnson, J. (2018). The self-radicalization of white men: "Fake news" and the affective networking of paranoia. *Communication Culture & Critique*, 11(1), 100–115.

Katersky, A., & McPhee, M. (2015, March 10). What Boston Marathon bombing suspect Dzhokhar Tsarnaev wrote in blood-stained boat. ABC News. https://abcnews.go.com/US/ boston-marathon-bombing-suspect-dzhokhar-tsarnaev-wrote-blood/story?id=29534415

Kearns, E. M., Betus, A. E., & Lemieux, A. F. (2019). Why do some terrorist attacks receive more media attention than others? *Justice Quarterly*, 36(6), 985–1022.

Kishi, K. (2017). Assaults against Muslims in U.S. surpass 2001 level. Pew Research Center. https://www.pewresearch.org/short-reads/2017/11/15/assaults-against-muslims-in-u-s-surpass-2001-level/.

Loseke, D. R. (2009). Examining emotion as discourse: Emotion codes and presidential speeches justifying war. *Sociological Quarterly*, 50(3), 497–524.

Loseke, D. R. (2013). Keynote address: Empirically exploring narrative productions of meaning in public life. *Qualitative Sociology Review, 9*(3), 12–30.

Minkoff, R. (2018). Accuracy and ethics in reporting the Boston bombing. Loyola University Center for Digital Ethics & Policy. https://www.luc.edu/digitalethics/researchinitiatives/essays/archive/2018/accuracyandethicsinreportingthebostonbombing/

Mitnik, Z. S., Freilich, J. D., & Chermak, S. M. (2020). Post-9/11 coverage of terrorism in the New York Times. *Justice Quarterly, 37*(1), 161–185.

Morin, A. (2016). Framing terror: The strategies newspapers use to frame an act as terror or crime. *Journalism & Mass Communication Quarterly, 93*(4), 986–1005.

Nacos, B. L., Bloch-Elkon, Y., & Shapiro, R. Y. (2011). *Selling fear: Counterterrorism, the media, and public opinion.* University of Chicago Press.

Nellis, A. M., & Savage, J. (2012). Does watching then affect fear of terrorism? The importance of media exposure on terrorism fear. *Crime & Delinquency, 58*(5): 748–768.

New York Times. (2004, May 26). From the editors: The Times and Iraq. *New York Times.* https://www.nytimes.com/2004/05/26/world/from-the-editors-the-times-and-iraq.html

Olsen, E. (2018, April 15). How the Boston Marathon bombings changed Twitter, media and how we process tragedy. NPR. https://www.npr.org/2023/04/15/1170082886/marathon-bombings-twitter-media-boston-strong

PBS (2021, March 2). Watch: FBI chief Chris Wray calls Jan. 6 "domestic terrorism," defends intel. PBS News. https://www.pbs.org/newshour/politics/watch-live-fbi-chief-chris-wray-to-face-questions-about-extremism-capitol-riot

Perrigo, B. (2022, May 17). Social media companies vowed to stop videos of terror attacks. Buffalo showed they have more work to do. *Time.* https://time.com/6177640/buffalo-shooting-twitch-social-media/

Piazza, J. A. (2021). Fake news: The effects of social media disinformation on domestic terrorism. *Dynamics of Asymmetric Conflict,* 1–23.

Piazza, J., & Van Doren, N. (2022). It's about hate: Approval of Donald Trump, racism, xenophobia and support for political violence. *American Politics Research, 51*(3), https://doi.org/10.1177/1532673X221131561.

Powell, K. A. (2018). Framing Islam/creating fear: An analysis of US media coverage of terrorism from 2011–2016. *Religions, 9*(9), 257.

Ramussen, D. M. (2018, September 12). Islamic State propaganda is more than just pure evil. University of Copenhagen. https://uniavisen.dk/en/islamic-state-propaganda-is-more-than-just-pure-evil/

Ray, M. (2023). Boston Marathon bombing of 2013. Britannica. https://www.britannica.com/event/Boston-Marathon-bombing-of-2013

Rhodes, S. C. (2022). Filter bubbles, echo chambers, and fake news: How social media conditions individuals to be less critical of political misinformation. *Political Communication, 39*(1), 1–22.

Rieder, R. (2013, April 19). On Boston bombing, media are wrong—again. *USA Today.* https://www.usatoday.com/story/money/columnist/rieder/2013/04/18/media-boston-fiasco/2093493/

Sanders, L., Smith, M., & Ballard, J. (2021, January 7). Most voters say the events at the U.S. Capitol are a threat to democracy. YouGov America. https://today.yougov.com/topics/politics/articles-reports/2021/01/06/US-capitol-trump-poll

Savage, C. (2022, January 7). Was the Jan. 6 attack on the Capitol an act of "terrorism"? *New York Times.* https://www.nytimes.com/2022/01/07/us/politics/jan-6-terrorism-explainer.html

Seldin, J. (2021, January 27). US security officials warn of "heightened" domestic threat. Voice of America News. https://www.voanews.com/usa/us-security-officials-warn-heightened-domesticthreat

Shaheen, J. (2014). *Reel bad Arabs: How Hollywood vilifies a people.* Olive Branch Press.

Society of Professional Journalists. (2023). SPJ code of ethics. https://www.spj.org/ethicscode.asp

START (2024). Global Terrorism Database. University of Maryland, National Consortium for the Study of Terrorism and Responses to Terrorism. https://www.start.umd.edu/gtd/

Swenson, A. (2023, May 14). AI-generated disinformation poses threat of misleading voters in 2024 election. PBS News Hour. https://www.pbs.org/newshour/politics/ai-generated-disinformation-poses-threat-of-misleading-voters-in-2024-election

Tajfel, H. E. (1978). *Differentiation between social groups: Studies in the social psychology of Intergroup relations.* Academic Press.

Tehranian, J. (2008). *Whitewashed: America's invisible Middle Eastern minority.* NYU Press.

US Department of Justice (2022). One year since the Jan. 6 attack on the Capitol. https://www.justice.gov/usao-dc/one-year-jan-6-attack-capitol

Vosoughi, S., Roy, D., & Aral, S. (2018). The spread of true and false news online. *Science, 359*(6380), 1146–1151.

Walter, D., Ophir, Y., Lokmanoglu, A. D., & Pruden, M. L. (2022). Vaccine discourse in white nationalist online communication: A mixed-methods computational approach. *Social Science & Medicine, 298,* 114859.

Winter, T. (2018, October 23). Boston Marathon bomber told FBI agents he and his brother acted alone, court documents say. NBC News. https://www.nbcnews.com/news/crime-courts/boston-marathon-bomber-told-fbi-agents-he-his-brother-acted-n923556

CHAPTER 11

Financing Terrorism

How Terrorists Raise, Store, and Transfer Funds

Source: Shutterstock/David Orcea.

Learning Objectives
1. To explain why financing is an important aspect of daily life for terrorist groups.
2. To define various means and methods terrorists use to finance their organizational and operational needs.
3. To compare and contrast the legal and illicit ways in which terrorists finance their operations.
4. To explore the key methods terrorists use to store and transfer their funds.
5. To explain the major national and international measures designed to counter the financing of terrorism and their impact on society.

11.1 INTRODUCTION

Terrorism financing includes the processes of (1) raising, (2) storing, and (3) transferring funds acquired through various means to enable terrorist organizations to achieve two important goals: (1) plan and execute terrorist acts, and (2) maintain the daily functioning of their organizations (Clarke 2015; United Nations 2023a). Regardless of their ideological orientation or philosophy, terrorist organizations require significant resources to fund their operations and organizational activities. Terrorism or violent conflicts often cannot occur unless the aggrieved groups have access to significant funding. Access to money (as well as the ability to move it around the world) is a key enabler of terrorism and violent extremism (Vision of Humanity 2023). A growing body of scholars argues that depriving terrorists from financial resources is one of the most important steps in countering terrorist threats and curtailing extremist activities.

Unlike individual states and international organizations, in which ruling authorities and officials have the advantage of taxing their citizens to finance their military expenditures, terrorists must rely on other sources of income, including criminal (e.g., human trafficking, drugs trade, fraud, counterfeiting, robbery, smuggling, and extortion) and legitimate (e.g., running front businesses and charitable organizations) activities, to generate funds and support their agendas.

This chapter will discuss why terrorists need funds and the role of financing in the operations of terrorist organizations, provide an overview of the different means that terrorists use to fund their activities, and examine the efforts undertaken by governments and international organizations to thwart the financing of terrorism. The chapter will conclude with a discussion of the ethical considerations surrounding measures aimed at combating terrorism financing.

11.2 WHY DO TERRORISTS NEED FUNDS?

In a sense, terrorists and terrorist groups operate just like legitimate organizations, businesses, and other official governing bodies. All of them need money as a source of security and a means of achieving their respective goals. Indeed, all individuals need resources to meet their basic needs such as food, shelter, and clothing. States and other official governing bodies need money to provide basic services that are essential to the healthy functioning of a society such as healthcare, the construction of critical infrastructure (e.g., roads, bridges, libraries, power plants, hospitals), security and rule of law (via the criminal justice system, police, courts, corrections), coverage for public employee salaries, and other services such as defense, transportation, public works (e.g., sewers, snow removal, signage), and disaster management. Terrorist organizations are not exempt from this crucial need—terrorist groups need a constant supply of money for their sustenance, the achievement of their objectives, and the continuation of their activities (Shapiro & Siegel, 2007). They cannot survive for long without sufficient and stable financial resources.

Terrorists' funding needs can be broadly grouped into two general categories: (1) money needed to maintain the daily functioning and reputation of an organization, and (2) financial resources needed for carrying out terrorist acts.

11.2.1 Money Needed for Planning and Execution of Attacks

Whether perpetrated by an individual (i.e., lone wolf) or a group, the planning and execution of every terrorist attack requires financial resources. Varying costs may be associated with terrorist attacks including those related to the planning and preparation of operations, training of recruits, reconnaissance of targets, purchase of instruments (weapons, explosives, and other munitions), travel and lodging required for a specific act, and retaining operatives (Attah 2019; Barrett 2011). A lack of sufficient funding can be a limiting factor in carrying out an attack. Investigations led by the FBI revealed that Ramzi Yousef, the mastermind of the 1993 World Trade Center bombing (using a rented van filled with 1,200 pounds of explosives), originally planned to destroy one tower with the blast and let the debris of the falling tower knock down the second tower in order to kill tens of thousands of people with the destruction and resultant cyanide gas (Mylroie 1995; Raphaeli 2003). The attack did not go as planned, however, because Yousef and his coconspirators lacked the funding to obtain material that would be powerful enough to destroy the entire tower. The terrorists were so financially desperate that they returned to the rental car center to reclaim the deposit fee for the van they used to bomb the tower (2002).

Even though terrorist attacks cannot be achieved without adequate financing, it is important to note that compared to the funds required for the sustenance of terrorist organizations (explained in the next section), the actual cost of a terrorist attack can be relatively inexpensive (Allam &

FIGURE 11.1 The availability of 3D printing technology makes it possible for individuals to create firearms at home, bypassing traditional regulations and background checks. This raises legal and regulatory concerns regarding firearm control and public safety. The ease of access to 3D printed gun designs can potentially enable individuals with malicious intent, such as terrorists, to produce untraceable firearms. This poses challenges for law enforcement agencies in tracking and preventing illegal firearm activities. *Source:* Sujan/Shutterstock.

TABLE 11.1　Examples of the Direct Cost of Terrorist Attacks

Attack	Year	Estimated Cost
London Transport System Attacks	2005	£8,000
Madrid Train Bombings	2004	$10,000
Istanbul Truck Bombings	2003	$40,000
Jakarta JW Marriott Hotel Bombing	2003	$30,000
Bali Bombings	2002	$50,000
USS Cole Attack	2000	$10,000
East Africa US Embassy Bombings	1998	$50,000

Source: Adapted from FATF (2008).

Gadzinowski 2009; Crimm 2004). A 2012 report by the US Department of Defense indicated that a remote-controlled bomb costs about $400, and a suicide vest can be built for about $1,200 dollars (Temple-Raston 2014). In many cases terrorists self-finance their acts by using cheap, readily available materials such as propane tanks, alarm clocks, suitcases, batteries, and plastic bottles filled with gas. Of growing concern today is the ability to construct guns using 3D printers. In 2019, a far-right extremist in Germany killed two people using a 3D printed weapon, which he created at his home following a blueprint he had downloaded from the internet. During the same year, British police arrested another right-wing extremist who was preparing for a massacre—a 3D printer, several firearm blueprints, and a manifesto were found in his home. Terrorists now have the ability to produce not only handguns, but also fully automatic weapons, such as AR-15 and AK47 rifles, using 3D printers a fraction of their retail cost (Abbasi 2021).

　　A 2008 report published by international money laundering and terrorist financing watchdog, Financial Action Task Force revealed that in general, terrorists do not need much funding to carry out devastating attacks (see Table 11.1). The report highlighted that the London public transportation system attacks (that killed 52 and injured more than 700) cost the terrorists just around 8,000 GBP. The resultant cost of the attacks to society, in comparison, including material damage to infrastructure and associated decreases in retail sales, tourism, restaurants, and other businesses due to the fear caused by the attacks is estimated to be more than $1.4 billion USD (Jordan 2005). Carrying out terrorist acts can be quite inexpensive, compared to the tremendous consequences they can create.

11.2.2　Money Needed to Maintain the Daily Functioning (Day-to-Day Expenses) and Reputation of an Organization

In addition to the operational costs needed to carry out attacks, terrorist groups need funding to sustain the daily functioning of their organizations. Significant sources of funding are often required (and must be sustained) to support the complex organizational infrastructure of groups. Andrew Silke, a prominent criminologist and terrorism scholar, argues that even though it is certainly possible to start an insurgency with limited funds, it is difficult to maintain a long-term, successful campaign without the availability of significant financial resources. More specifically, he argues that "a lack of money will not stop a terrorist campaign from starting, but it will seriously inhibit the growth and longevity of that campaign and will also inhibit the intensity, sophistication, and overall impact" (Silke 2000, 123).

These organizational costs, which help to sustain critical group functions, can generally be grouped into four main categories:

- basic needs
- production and dissemination of recruitment materials
- provision of services (including social services)
- support for the families of killed or captured insurgents

First, terrorist organizations need money to run their camps and operate their training facilities. In doing so, they need to provide their members with basic necessities such as food, shelter, clothing, electricity, and water. These necessities all require funding, and most of them are essential for the survival of group members.

Second, in order to attract the attention of their support base and recruit new members, terrorist groups need to develop and disseminate recruitment materials such as letters, emails, radio advertisements, magazines, books, newspapers, and pamphlets. Regardless of whether this goal is achieved through printed materials, verbally (i.e., word of mouth), or via online media campaigns, terrorists need money to recruit new members, communicate their goals, and spread their ideology.

FIGURE 11.2 *Dabiq* was an English-language online magazine published by ISIS (Islamic State of Iraq and Syria) as part of its propaganda efforts. ISIS used the magazine to promote its extremist ideology, recruit followers, and communicate its messages to a global audience. *Source: Dabiq* magazine.

Third, terrorist groups may need funding to procure various services such as training and education for recruits, rent of safe houses and sleeper cells, travel, communication needs, healthcare, building, bribing officials, forging passports, seeking the expertise of specialists (e.g., engineers, IT specialists, accountants), and paying salaries to their members and mercenaries. These groups may also need funding for supporting social, political, and economic activities within their support base. Terrorist groups across the world have political establishments or fronts that operate within the existing legal sphere of the respective adversary societies (Gross 2010), which help them to legitimize and popularize their cause and ideology. Even though these political extensions often publicly distinguish themselves from their military wings, they rely on financial support from the main entity to fund activities such as distributing campaign materials, organizing political rallies and meetings, working to register voters from their support base, and delivering campaign speeches. Terrorist groups often need funding to provide humanitarian and social services to their support base, such as healthcare, education, and security which helps them soften their reputation. Groups such as Hamas, Hezbollah, the PKK, and the IRA have all reportedly provided education, schooling, hospitals, and court services to their support bases (Johnson & Jensen 2010; 2005).

Fourth, groups need funding to support the family members of insurgents who were imprisoned or killed in action (FATF 2008).

FIGURE 11.3 Sinn Féin has historically had strong links to the IRA. While the two organizations were separate entities, many of their members and leaders were associated with both. Sinn Féin was often seen as the political voice of the republican movement, advocating for the same objectives as the IRA but through peaceful means. *Source:* Rathfelder, CC BY-SA 4.0, via Wikimedia Commons.

For terrorist groups, publicity and legitimacy are extremely important elements. One way to establish these is to give confidence to their fighters that in case something happens to them, the group would take care of their loved ones. Providing these kinds of benefits not only promotes the popularity and legitimacy of terrorist organizations but also increases the willingness of individuals to join their cadres. Groups such as the PKK, IRA, Hezbollah, and several others are all known to provide regular pensions to the widows and orphans of their deceased fighters (Johnson & Jensen 2010).

11.3 SOURCES OF TERRORIST FINANCING

Terrorist organizations have engaged in a wide range of activities to accomplish their fundraising goals. As depicted in Table 11.2, terrorists generate funds from multiple channels including **foreign state support**; **legitimate sources** such as donations, **charities**, legal businesses, and **front companies**; **diaspora funding**, cultural and social events, and real estate investments; and illegitimate activities such as **theft**, **fraud**, **smuggling**, **burglary**, kidnapping, **tax fraud**, **protection rackets**, **drug trafficking**, human smuggling, **extortion**, and **money laundering** (Allam & Gadzinowski 2009; Morais 2002). The methods used by terrorist groups to raise funds often depend on several factors, such as the ideology and the geographic location in which the groups operate, and the opportunity structures that are available for fundraising.

This section will explore the various means and tools of terrorist financing, starting with a brief discussion of how some nations and regional and global powers have provided financial support to terrorist and insurgent groups throughout the world.

TABLE 11.2   The Many Different Means of Terrorist Financing

(1) State Sponsorship	(2) Legitimate Resources	(3) Illegitimate Resources
• Passive support (e.g., providing safe haven to terrorist groups, allowing them to engage in fundraising activities) • Active support (e.g., provision of direct financial and military support)	• Donations from sympathizers • Front businesses • Diaspora funding • Real estate investments • Abuse of charities and other nonprofit organizations • Membership fees • Sales of publications • Fundraising campaigns • Self-financing	• Fraud • Kidnapping for extortion • Counterfeiting • Human smuggling • Drug trade and trafficking • Tax fraud • Robbery • Smuggling • Revolutionary taxes • *Illicit trade* of commodities (e.g., oil, diamonds, gold)

We will also explain how regional factors and opportunity structures directly influence the financing options for terrorist groups.

11.3.1 State Sponsorship for Terrorist and Insurgent Groups

Financial support provided by states and nations (i.e., state sponsorship) has been an important source of revenue for terrorist groups across the world, especially during the Cold War era. State sponsorship of terrorism remains a concern, however. In 2009, international efforts to disrupt terrorism financing captured more than $280 million in state support to terrorist organizations (Levi 2010).

Nation-states may sponsor groups for various reasons such as to disrupt the internal security of rival states (e.g., as in the Cold War era), to protect their social, political, military, and economic interests, to increase their regional and global reach and influence, to gain support of friendly ethnic and religious groups, to ignite regime changes in line with their foreign policy objectives, and to destabilize their perceived enemies or competitors (Davis 2021).

State sponsorship of terrorism can be grouped into two main categories: (1) passive, and (2) active support. **Passive support** includes activities such as allowing the terrorist groups to use their territories as a safe haven (i.e., sanctuary) or give them a free hand to engage in recruitment and fundraising activities within their borders. Syria and Iraq are known to provide safe haven for Kurdistan Workers' Party (PKK) members, a group designated as a terrorist organization by NATO, the US, and Turkey. Throughout Ireland's struggle for independence from Britain, the United States provided sanctuary and support to the members of Irish militant groups. As another example, during the Cold War period the United States government provided direct financial and military support to Afghan guerilla fighters to fight against the Soviet-friendly communist regime in Afghanistan and permitted Islamist extremists such as Abdallah bin Azzam and Osama bin Laden to travel to the United States. Azzam is known to have visited several US states including New York, Texas, California, and Indiana, and launched an official recruitment bureau (the Service Bureau) to convince Muslims to travel to Afghanistan to fight against the Russians and to donate money to their jihadi activities. His magazine, *Al-Jihad*, which was launched to raise awareness of the Afghan cause, was distributed all over the United States, selling thousands of copies each month (Hegghammer 2020).

Active support, in contrast, includes activities such as providing direct financial and military support, including the provision of intelligence, tactical training, and war equipment to enhance a group's military capabilities. As explained in Chapter 6, especially during the Cold War era, even though the United States and the Soviet Union did not engage in direct attacks against each other, both countries provided political, financial, and military help to insurgent groups across the world fueling lengthy and brutal fights (also known as proxy wars) in places like Angola, Afghanistan, Nicaragua, and Cuba (Davis 2021).

FIGURE 11.4 C 130 transport aircraft of the civil company Southern Air Transport. The SAT is an airline of the CIA founded in 1947 to support US covert activities, and has operated in Southeast Asia, El Salvador, Nicaragua, Angola. *Source:* G B_NZ, CC BY-SA 2.0, via Wikimedia Commons.

After the communist revolution succeeded in Cuba, the United States attempted to assassinate Fidel Castro multiple times and provided military and financial support to insurgents to carry out the Bay of Pigs invasion, to end Castro's regime. During Ronald Reagan's presidency, the US government covertly backed the contras in Nicaragua by providing them with funding and training to topple the communist Sandinista government. This financial support and training stopped only when it was discovered that the Reagan administration was benefitting from the profits of arms sales to Iran (known as Iran-Contra Affair).

Other examples of active state sponsorship of terrorism include cases such as Iran's military and financial support for Hamas and Hezbollah in Israel, Syria's opening of its borders to PKK members and providing them with military training camps and financial resources to fight against Turkey, and India's supply of weapons and ammunitions to Tamil Tigers (LTTE) insurgents in their fights against the Sri Lankan government. During Muammar al-Qaddafi's rule, Libya provided financial support and offered sanctuary to several terrorist groups across the world including the Provisional Irish Republican Army, Kurdistan Workers' Party, and the Palestinian Liberation Organization (Clarke 2015; Johnson & Jensen 2010).

It can be argued that active state sponsorship of terrorism in regional and global conflicts has diminished significantly. Scholars often cite two main reasons for this. First, with the end of the Cold War, groups which had ideological allegiance to the US or the Soviet Union lost their military and economic subsidies and with the decline of state sponsorship, they began to rely increasingly on criminal and other activities to fund their operations and sustain their organizations (Morais 2002). Second, terrorist groups experienced a significant decline in funding from nation-state sponsors due to measures that were developed to fight against terrorism financing. Especially after 9/11, sponsoring a terrorist organization became costly for states. Facing increased international scrutiny and devastating consequences such as economic and political sanctions and isolation in the international arena, several states (e.g., Sudan, Yemen, and Libya) stopped their support for terrorism. As the state sponsorship of terrorism declined, groups turned to other funding possibilities.

Currently, the US Department of State designates four countries as state sponsors of terrorism due to their repeated provision of support for acts of international terrorism: (1) Cuba, (2) North Korea (Democratic People's Republic of Korea), (3) Iran, and (4) Syria (US Department of State 2023b). This list is updated regularly, with new countries added and other countries removed from the list as conditions change. A country could be removed if they renounce terrorism, if there is a fundamental shift in the leadership and policies of the government accused, or if strategic circumstances in the US require them to do so. Even though Iraq was designated as a state sponsor of terrorism in 1979, it was removed from the list three years later, in 1982 with the beginning of the Iraq-Iran War, so that the United States could provide military and financial support to Iraq. However, Iraq was listed again as a state sponsor of terrorism in 1990 and removed from the list in 2004, following the US invasion of the country. Other countries such as Libya, South Yemen, and Sudan were formerly listed as state sponsors of terrorism, and they have been de-listed at different times due to changing conditions in their territories.

An important critique of such lists is that the inclusion and exclusion of countries is often politically driven. Michael Oppenheimer, professor in the Princeton School of Public and International Affairs, stated in an interview that "countries that wind up on that list are countries we don't like. Other countries and outside powers support terrorism, and objectively speaking are terrorists, and the ones we don't like are on the list, and the ones we're allied with are not on the list. It's all about double standards" (McCluskey 2014).

11.3.2 Legitimate Sources

Terrorists are often thought to obtain their funds through illicit activities. In reality, terrorists do not solely rely on illegal sources to fund their activities. Research indicates that the financing of terrorism largely relies on money obtained from legitimate sources such as storefront businesses (e.g., bars, drinking clubs), donations from charitable organizations and other nonprofits, sales of publications, and solicitations, among other legal outlets (Gardella 2003; Maximilian & Teichmann 2018).

For terrorists, seeking funding from legitimate sources is often necessary and a result of a rational decision-making process (Clarke 2015). As it will be explained in detail in the final section of this chapter, measures developed to identify and prevent terrorism financing largely focus on criminal activities (e.g., money laundering) and suspicious transactions made through official financial systems. When terrorists generate funds through legitimate channels, they lower the risk of detection. Using these businesses, terrorists can finance their activities over a long period of time, without raising suspicion (Davis 2021). Further, legitimate businesses can enable terrorists to hide the origins of funds acquired through illegitimate activities (e.g., drug trafficking). Terrorists may run businesses to use them as fronts for money laundering (Dalyan 2008).

This is such a serious issue that scholars and government officials agree that one of the biggest barriers in combatting the financing of terrorism emanates from the fact that funding for terrorist acts is often generated from legal sources which makes detection and investigations difficult, if not impossible (Allam & Gadzinowski 2009; Brooks et al. 2005). Commingling the funds acquired through illegitimate resources with legitimate ones makes their origins untraceable (Raphaeli 2003), and it is difficult for law enforcement officials to prove the illegal origin of funds when they come from legitimate sources. Knowing these loopholes, terrorists can move large sums of money through the financial system without triggering a legal response. This section will explore the three main types of terrorist financing methods in the legitimate arena:

1. Donations and fundraising campaigns
2. Front businesses
3. Self-financing

Donations and Fundraising Campaigns

Donations made by individuals to charities, religious institutions, and other nonprofit organizations (e.g., hospitals, orphanages, educational institutes, political movements) and funds acquired through various types of fundraising campaigns and cultural activities (e.g., festivals, magazine subscriptions, and sales of merchandise) constitute an important source of legitimate income for terrorist groups across the world (Morais 2002). The financing of terrorism through charitable donations and fundraising activities is a long-known historical technique, with the first examples dating back to Provisional Irish Republican Army and Palestinian Liberation Organization.

As explained in the previous chapters, terrorist groups cannot survive without an active support base—a group of likeminded individuals (based on determinants such as religion, geography, culture, ethnicity, ideology) who often share the group's grievances and believe in similar causes. Using these support bases, terrorist organizations recruit fighters into their cadres. However, not all members of a support base are suited for armed conflict or are willing to become official group members. Instead, they may be more interested in supporting the goals and ideals of the group through other means, such as by organizing fundraising activities or providing money through donations (Brooks et al. 2005).

Groups may use charitable organizations and nonprofits, established in broad range of categories (e.g., religious, educational, health, and food aid programs) to solicit funding from their support networks and wealthy individuals and channel it to high-risk areas under the cover of charity work (Davis 2021). These activities may be organized either in their home region or abroad, in locations where the aggrieved group has diaspora communities—groups of like-minded individuals who leave their homelands and settle in other countries for various reasons. The Provisional Irish Republican Army (PIRA) and the Kurdistan Workers' Party (PKK) are prime examples of groups that have relied heavily on diaspora support to fund their activities. The PIRA, through the Irish diaspora in the United States and the PKK, through the Kurdish diaspora located across several countries in Europe and Australia, obtained significant financial support from their identity-based networks.

French officials estimated that in 2016, the PKK raised nearly $6 million dollars from its front organizations and charities in France to cover its ongoing military and political activities in Turkey and the Middle East (Davis 2018; TE-SAT 2018). Beginning in the late 1960s, the PIRA solicited several million dollars of funding from the Irish diaspora in the United States, through a charity called Irish Northern Aid (NORAID) (Hanley 2004). NORAID's fundraising events, which were held at several locations

TABLE 11.3 Crowdfunding

Online Platform	Amount Raised
GiveSendGo	$5,400,887.03
GoFundMe	$579,657.25
OurFreedomFunding	$64,148.00
FundRazr	$57,635.00
GoFundMe	$50,385.85
RootBocks	$37,581.12
DonorBox	$28,667.25
Fundly	$20,015.00
GoGetFunding	$7,096.00
Total	**$6,246,072.50**

across the US from New York to Philadelphia, Boston, and San Francisco, not only provided the Provisional IRA with financial means, but also helped the group sustain a publicity campaign across the country (Collins 2022).

Terrorists exploit commonly used financial systems and also seek new methods to fund their operations, as they need to be one step ahead of officials to sustain their activities. In particular, terrorists have embraced online banking and other modern financial technologies that many people rely on for their daily activities, largely due to their convenience and the ability for donors and recipients of funds to remain anonymous. **Crowdfunding** (e.g., funding a cause or a project by soliciting relatively small amounts of money from a large number of people via the internet) (SEC 2022) through various online platforms such as Facebook, Telegram, Twitter, PayPal, and GoFundMe has become a popular fundraising tool for terrorist organizations (see Table 11.3). The use of online crowdfunding platforms by extremists to raise funds for their ideologically driven activities is a concerning and evolving issue. According to a 2023 Anti-Defamation League report far-right extremists generated more than six million dollars from 324 campaigns between 2016 and 2022 (ADL 2023).

The combined use of social media outlets and new financial technologies (e.g., cryptocurrencies) not only allows terrorist groups to easily reach out to their support base and obtain funding from all over the world in real time, but also provides anonymity for donors, protecting them from potential legal repercussion. According to a testimony submitted to the US House of Representatives in 2021, between 2005 and 2015 almost all of the far-right extremist groups in the United States tracked by the Global Project Against Hate and Extremism (GPAHE) had a PayPal button on their website to solicit online donations from their followers (House of Representatives 2021). Foreign terrorist groups such as ISIS, al-Qaeda, and others have also learned to leverage new technologies, soliciting cryptocurrency donations from around the world using online platforms (Savage 2020). In 2019, the al-Qassam Brigades in Palestine solicited donations on Twitter with the assurance to their followers that Bitcoin donations were anonymous and untraceable. The group also provided video instructions on their official webpage to demonstrate how to make anonymous donations using unique Bitcoin addresses generated for each donor (Faridvar 2020; Phillips 2020). When government efforts focused on preventing donations made by PayPal or Bitcoin, terrorist organizations advised their followers to use more secure and anonymous cryptocurrencies, such as Monero—a cryptocurrency that obscures transaction amounts, balances, transaction histories, and addresses.

Front Businesses

Besides soliciting funds using organizations with charitable and nonprofit statuses, terrorist organizations have also resorted to front businesses in different fields to mobilize funds and resources for their campaigns (Morais 2002). A large number of terrorist groups across the world, from al-Qaeda to the ETA, PKK, LTTE, PIRA, and the Loyalists, are known to operate ordinary businesses such as pubs, taxicab services, construction companies, fish farms, delivery services, restaurants, auto shops, and guesthouses, under which legitimate and illicit funds are mixed. This enables the groups to conceal and launder the proceeds of funds obtained from their legal and illegal activities (Clarke 2015). **Front companies** not only allow terrorists to raise funding to sustain their activities, but also enable them to launder the funds obtained through illegal activities. ISIS invested in several front businesses in Iraq and Syria, including car dealerships, restaurants, factories (e.g., tile, cement, and chemical products), and even private hospitals, to hide the origins of money looted from bank vaults or earned through extortion activities and oil and minerals sales in the black market. Using these businesses, ISIS not only generated significant income, but it was also able to move its money acquired through criminal enterprises into the legitimate economy (Warrick, 2018).

Al-Qaeda's deceased leader bin Laden owned a large transnational network of commercial ventures and front companies (aside from his father's multibillion dollar construction firm) such as a European fertilizer wholesaler (Wadi al-Aqiq), a Sudanese road Construction firm (Al-Hiraj), banks, export-import ventures, and LLCs (holding companies) in Luxembourg, Switzerland, and Amsterdam that he allegedly used to fund cells of operatives to carry out attacks against American interests (Mintz 1998).

As another example, the Liberation Tigers of Tamil Elam (LTTE), a militant terrorist group operating in Sri Lanka since the late 1970s, is known to operate a wide range of businesses, including video stores, gas stations, restaurants, grocery stores, travel agencies, and telecommunication retailers in Europe and North America. The group has also accrued revenue from newspaper sales and by operating TV channels (e.g., Tharisanam TV, National TV of Tamil Eelam), which have had tens of thousands of subscribers from Europe, the Middle East, and North Africa (Davis 2021).

Both the Provisional IRA and Loyalist terrorist groups in Ireland ran legitimate business enterprises, such as drinking clubs and pubs as one of the main sources of cash income for their activities. Using false accounting practices (e.g., underinvoicing and overinvoicing traded goods), or selling beverages stolen from delivery trucks in their clubs, the loyalists were able to transfer large amounts

FIGURE 11.5 US Army personnel stand guard duty near a burning oil well in the Rumaylah Oil Fields in Southern Iraq. At the height of its power, the Islamic State of Iraq and Syria (ISIS) obtained significant revenue from oil sales. ISIS controlled and exploited oil fields in Iraq and Syria, using them as a major source of funding for its operations. The revenue generated allowed ISIS to finance its operations, including the recruitment of fighters, the purchase of weapons and equipment, the establishment of governance structures, and the funding of terrorist attacks both within its territory and abroad. *Source:* Arlo K. Abrahamson, public domain, via Wikimedia Commons.

of money into their paramilitary activities without alerting officials (Clarke 2015; Gardella 2003; Silke 2000). The ETA in Spain and the PKK in Turkey are also known to engage in front businesses, such as operating restaurants, bars, parlors, and shops where proceeds of sales are donated to groups' prospective activities (FATF 2008).

Self-Financing

Terrorists also **self-finance**—raise or provide money on their own—to carry out their attacks (Barrett 2011; Pieth 2002). As mentioned previously, carrying out an attack can be relatively inexpensive. Studies indicate that in recent years almost all right-wing, anti-Islamic, homophobic, anti-feminist, and incel (involuntary celibate) motivated attacks in the US and across the world were carried out by individuals who used their own funding resources (Smith et al. 2010). The Norwegian terrorist Anders Behring Breivik, who killed 77 people in 2011 with a 2,100-pound bomb attack at the Norwegian Government Quarter in Oslo and later with a mass shooting at a children's summer camp, raised money on his own to finance his attacks (Taylor 2019). In his 1,500-page manifesto, Breivik noted that he worked for nine years to generate the funding required to carry out the attacks (and publicize his manifesto), which he estimated to be around $316,000. This included $33,000 for armor and weapons, up to $110,000 for explosives, $22,000 for logistics, transport, and lodging, and $152,000 for the creation of the compendium (i.e., printing and distributing his anti-Islamic, anti-feminist, and militant manifesto titled, *2083: A European Declaration of Independence*). During his trial, it was discovered that Breivik used money from several resources, including funds from his own start-up companies (through

FIGURE 11.6 Anders Behring Breivik carried out a bombing in Oslo's government district and later conducted a mass shooting at a Workers' Youth League (AUF) camp on the island of Utøya. These attacks resulted in the deaths of 77 people, making it one of the deadliest terrorist incidents in Norway's history. Breivik claimed that he self-financed his attacks. He mentioned in his manifesto, titled "2083: A European Declaration of Independence," that he had acquired funds through various means, including the sale of property and investments. He also claimed to have used his own savings to purchase materials and firearms for the attacks. *Source:* Johannesen, Nærings- og handel departementet, https://www.flickr.com/photos/nhd-info, CC BY 2.0, via Wikimedia Commons.

which he made about $150,000–$200,000), investments in the stock market, personal savings, and borrowing money through nine different credit card providers (which gave him access to an additional $30,000), to prepare, finance, and execute these bloody attacks on his own (Ravndal 2012; Taylor 2011).

The White supremacist and neo-Nazi terrorist Brenton Tarrant, who carried out the 2019 mass shootings at two mosques (which claimed the lives of 51 individuals) in New Zealand, relied on his own funds (Dearden 2020). In his 74-page manifesto, Tarrant claimed that he invested in a cryptocurrency called BitConnect (Bambrough 2019) to purchase high-powered firearms with military specification sighting and telescoping systems, 7,000 rounds of ammunition, military style ballistic armor, and tactical vests, as well as cover the costs of reconnaissance activities including travel to mosque sites and the purchase of a drone to study the entry and exit doors of the mosques (Reuters 2020).

11.3.3 Illegitimate Sources

Even though classic money laundering operations are often highlighted by the media when it comes to **illegitimate sources** of terrorist financing, in reality, terrorist groups draw on a wide range of criminal activities in order to fund their organizations. These range from low-level acts such as robbery, fraud, kidnapping, counterfeiting, and credit card fraud, to high-level organized crime including drugs, arms, and human trafficking, smuggling, sales of valuable minerals and oil in the black market, and taxation through coercion and intimidation (Gardella 2003; Johnson & Jensen 2010). These activities often involve violence or the threat of violence and may conflict with groups' ideologies. Nevertheless, terrorist organizations often depend on illegal activities for their sustenance.

The six main types of illegitimate funding sources used by terrorist organizations include:

1. Fraud
2. Kidnapping for extortion or ransom
3. Counterfeiting
4. Human smuggling and drug trafficking
5. Illicit trade of commodities (e.g., oil, diamonds, gold)
6. Other means (e.g., revolutionary taxes, robbery, smuggling, protection rackets, prostitution rackets, illegal gambling)

Fraud

Fraud, the intentional use of deception for material or monetary gain, is a frequently used fundraising tactic for terrorist groups. The LTEE, IRA, Hezbollah, al-Qaeda, and ISIS are known to generate money through several types of fraudulent activities, such as income tax fraud, unemployment benefits fraud, food stamp fraud, credit card fraud, identity theft, student loan fraud, and welfare fraud. Terrorists increasingly rely on fraud, because it often involves low-risk activities with less severe repercussions if caught compared to other types of crimes. According to a 2022 National Terrorist Financing Risk Assessment Report compiled by the US Department of Treasury, domestic violent extremist groups (DVEs) in the United States heavily engage in minor crimes, such as food stamp and credit card fraud, to generate revenue to fund their illicit activities (NTFRA 2022).

Similar tactics have been used by other groups across the world. Both the IRA and members of the Loyalist paramilitaries in Northern Ireland have falsified government welfare applications to claim unemployment benefits (commonly known as dole payments) and engaged in tax fraud to fund their activities (Davis 2021; Silke 2000). Al-Qaeda is known to generate revenue from passport forgery schemes. A former member of the group, Shadi Abdullah, who was arrested in Germany in 2003 provided the police with detailed information about how al-Qaeda raised hundreds of thousands of dollars by selling fake passports and through fraudulent fundraising activities to buy hand grenades and pistols to carry out their planned attacks in Europe (Horowitz 2003; Isikoff 2003).

Before its demise by Sri Lankan forces in May 2009, members of the Liberation Tigers of Tamil Eelam (LTTE) also engaged in several types of fraudulent activities across the world. In Switzerland, the group used fake paycheck slips, false identities, doctored credit reports, and other documents to obtain tens of thousands of credit cards and loans from Swiss banks, which were later used to purchase firearms. In England, LTTE members who worked at gas stations cloned thousands of credit cards from British customers and installed credit card cloning devices in ATMs to steal financial information and withdraw money from customer accounts (SATP 2023). Experts estimate that more than 60 million pounds were stolen from customers at over 200 gas stations across the UK (Townsend 2007). In 2007, the group carried out Norway's largest credit card scam, gaining more than five million Norwegian crowns through stolen and fake credit cards (Kumar 2008).

Kidnapping for Extortion or Ransom

As explained in Chapter 9, **kidnapping** for ransom is a popular fundraising tool for terrorist groups. David S. Cohen, the undersecretary for terrorism and financial intelligence at the US Treasury Department, stated in 2012 that "kidnapping for ransom has become today's most significant source of terrorist financing" (Callimachi 2014). Compared to other criminal methods (e.g., bank robbery, counterfeiting, and fraud), kidnapping for ransom and extortion is not only a relatively easy method to obtain funding, but it is also a lucrative business. Groups may target local prominent individuals (e.g., politicians, businessmen) or foreigners (e.g., tourists from wealthy countries) to obtain ransom payments from their families, governments, or insurance companies.

The Italian Red Brigades, the ETA (Basque Homeland and Liberty), ERP (People's Revolutionary Army), IRA, al-Qaeda, PKK, ISIS, and several others have all used kidnapping for ransom to raise funds. The Argentinian far-left Marxist-Leninist group, People's Revolutionary Army (ERP), carried out more than 180 kidnappings of prominent individuals, obtaining approximately $76 million in revenue (Lewis 2002). In 1973, the group kidnapped Exxon executive Victor Samuelson, the manager of an oil refinery in Argentina, and received $14.2 million ($10 million in cash and $4.2 million in food, medicine, and construction materials) in ransom payments (Kandell 1974). In 1981, the IRA kidnapped the owner of a chain grocery store, Ben Dunne and demanded 500,000 British Pounds from his family (Little 2019). In 1993, Basque Homeland and Liberty (ETA) members in Spain kidnapped Spanish businessmen Julio Iglesias Zamora while he was on his way home from work and held him captive for 117 days, until his family agreed to pay $2.3 million as ransom (Reuters 1993).

Most recently, the Abu Sayyaf Group (ASG), an Islamist terrorist organization that seeks to establish an independent state in southern Philippines, has become known for its kidnappings of Western foreign nationals for ransom payments. In 2000, the group kidnapped three French journalists (members of the France 2 TV Channel) and received $5.5 million in ransom payments in return for their release (CPJ, 2000). It is estimated that the ASG generated more than $35 million from kidnapping activities between 1992 and 2008 (UNODC 2023). Al-Qaeda (in the Middle East and Africa) has kidnapped foreigners, politicians, civil servants, and civilians for ransom. According to

FIGURE 11.7 Abu Sayyaf is a militant group based in the southern Philippines that kidnapped two German nationals, Stefan Viktor Okonek and Henrike Dielen, from their yacht off the coast of Sabah, Malaysia, in 2014. They were released after several months, reportedly after a ransom was paid.

a *New York Times* report, between 2008 and 2014, al-Qaeda and its affiliates (e.g., al-Qaeda in the Islamic Maghreb, in Northern Africa, in the Arabian Peninsula, in Yemen, al-Shabaab, Boko Haram) received approximately $125 million in ransom payments from European governments. Kidnapping has become such a profitable business for the group that experts now believe that al-Qaeda finances most of its operational and organizational activities from the ransoms paid by Europeans to free their prisoners (Callimachi 2014). A book published by an al-Qaeda operative in 2014 devoted a chapter to kidnapping and offered its recruits several tips on how to carry out successful kidnapping operations (e.g., defining the purpose of kidnapping and providing strategies for protecting themselves) (New York Times 2014).

Counterfeiting

Counterfeiting, the fraudulent imitation of a trusted brand or product to seek profit by taking advantage of its reputation, is another illegal venue for terrorist fundraising (IACC 2023). Terrorist groups may engage both in the production and trade of counterfeited goods. Compared to other illicit methods of fundraising such as drug trade, human smuggling, kidnapping, and bank robberies, the act of counterfeiting is a lucrative business because it is a low-risk activity (in terms of getting caught or potential casualties) with high profit margins. It also tends to carry less moral guilt for group members, as it does not typically generate condemnation and revulsion from the support base (Silke 2000). Further, groups can obtain large profits from the sales of counterfeited goods, without involvement in the actual production of the fabricated goods.

Terrorist groups counterfeit a wide range of commodities, imitating consumer products such as designer clothing, shoes, handbags, watches, electronics, software, video games, pharmaceuticals, artwork, toys, baby formula, perfume, currency, books, and the piracy of music, and movies (often pornographic ones).

Research indicates that several terrorist groups have turned to counterfeiting because other illegal activities became difficult due to tighter governmental security approaches. Beginning in the 1970s, the IRA in Northern Ireland used bank robberies to supplement its traditional revenue generating strategies (e.g., newspaper sales). Throughout the late 1970s, the group robbed banks almost every other day. However, the government began to require banks to take strong security measures such as installing metal doors, surveillance cameras, and time locks on safes and doors (Faoleán 2023). In response, the IRA shifted to counterfeiting consumer products and bank notes, along with kidnaping prominent businesspeople. In 1983, the Irish police discovered hundreds of thousands of pounds of forged £10 notes during raids of suspected IRA members' premises. In 2009, a prominent leader of the Provisional IRA, Sean Garland, was indicted in the United States on charges that he conspired with North Korea to print and circulate hundreds of millions of fake $100 bills in the United Kingdom and other parts of the world (McDonald 2011).

Along with counterfeiting bank notes, the Provisional IRA and the Loyalists in Northern Ireland both engaged in counterfeiting consumer goods such as jeans, music CDs, and Hollywood movies. Counterfeiting big brand clothing became such a major revenue generator for the IRA that the group later bought factories in Turkey and Eastern European countries to produce these goods (Silke 2000). During the 1990s, the PIRA also set up chemical laboratories in Miami, Florida to produce counterfeit Ivomec, an anti-parasite veterinary drug, and sold their ineffective drug with high quality Ivomec labels printed in a farm in Northern Ireland (Cannon 2015). Until the scheme was discovered, it is estimated that at least 700 thousand large livestock were treated with this fake medicine in the US and across the world. Sales profits were transferred back to several bank accounts in Ireland (Safemedicines 2023).

Groups like al-Qaeda, ETA, PKK, FARC, Hezbollah, and several others are also known to raise substantial amounts of funds through counterfeiting merchandise. Investigations led by the FBI revealed that the perpetrators of the 1993 World Trade Center bombing financed their attack through funds collected from the sales of fake reproductions of major brand clothes in a Broadway store in New York City (UNIFAB 2016). In 2003, the former secretary general of Interpol, Ronald K. Noble, testified before the US Congress that beginning early 2000s, both al-Qaeda and Hezbollah started counterfeiting consumer goods such as Adidas and Nike shoes, electronic devices (e.g., Sony stereo equipment), Calvin Klein jeans, cigarettes, and computer software to further their gains from illicit activities (Johnston 2003).

Human Smuggling and Drug Trafficking

Raising funds through smuggling and trafficking can occur in two ways: (1) groups can directly engage in these criminal activities, or (2) they can generate revenue from taxing the groups that engage in smuggling and trafficking within their geographical area of influence (Berry et al. 2002).

Human smuggling (also known as migrant smuggling) involves the provision of services such as transportation across international borders or the procurement of fraudulent documents (e.g., passports, travel documents) (ICE 2023) for individuals who want to gain illegal access into a foreign country. Every year, millions of people around the world seek services from migrant smugglers in order to escape regional conflicts, poverty, government persecution, or simply to seek better living conditions elsewhere. According to the Financial Action Task Force (FATF), the proceeds earned from smuggling operations are estimated to be more than $10 billion annually (FATF 2022).

Terrorist groups may facilitate the smuggling of migrants, especially if they have territorial control over the areas through which the smuggling routes cross. In Africa, migrant smugglers pay a "safe passage toll" to various terrorist groups in exchange for using their area of control to transport migrants. Due to the decades-long political turmoil, poverty, and armed conflict in Syria, Iraq, and Afghanistan, millions of people pay terrorist and organized criminal groups to migrate to Turkey and Europe. The PKK is known to smuggle people from Turkey, Northern Iraq, Syria, and other places into Greece and Italy to generate funds for their operations (Sheinis 2012). Hezbollah and FARC have been reported to transport migrants from the Middle East and South America into the United States through cooperation with Mexican drug cartels, using their southern narcotics routes (Carter 2009).

Along with smuggling individuals, terrorist groups also derive funds from the global drug trade, ranging from receiving protection money from drug dealers to full scale involvement in the actual production and distribution of illegal drugs across the world. According to a 2003 US Senate hearing, approximately 40 percent of the US State Department's current list of designated foreign terrorist organizations are connected to the global drug trade and illegal narcotics production (US Senate 2003). FARC in Columbia first started generating revenue from the drug business by taxing the coca production (a tropical shrub from which cocaine is produced) by farmers in rural areas under its control. For years, the group destroyed crops of coca leaves produced by farmers who declined to pay the "protection fee" and taxed other narcotic traffickers involved in the manufacture and distribution of cocaine in the areas they controlled.

Beginning in the 1990s, FARC became directly involved in the production and distribution of cocaine in jungle laboratories (Otis 2018; Reuters 2017). Local farmers were forced to sell their crops only to FARC operated laboratories and hundreds of farmers who sold their crops to non–FARC buyers were brutally murdered. Soon FARC became the largest cocaine dealer in the world. In 2006, the United States government indicted the entire top leadership cadre of FARC on the grounds of importing

FIGURE 11.8 Human smuggling, often associated with terrorist groups and drug cartels, is a grave and complex issue that poses significant security and humanitarian challenges around the world. These groups engage in human smuggling for various reasons, including financial gain, recruitment, and facilitating the movement of individuals across borders. Both terrorist organizations and drug cartels charge fees to individuals seeking to be smuggled across borders, making it a profitable source of income. *Source:* Jasonctillmann, CC BY-SA 3.0, via Wikimedia Commons.

FIGURE 11.9   The Colombian government has undertaken various military and law enforcement operations over the years to destroy jungle laboratories associated with the Revolutionary Armed Forces of Colombia (FARC). FARC, a left-wing guerrilla group, has been involved in the production and trafficking of illegal drugs, particularly cocaine, as a means to finance its insurgency and fund its activities. *Source:* DEA Employee, public domain, via Wikimedia Commons.

more than $25 billion in cocaine into the United States and other countries and controlling more than 50 percent of the world's cocaine trade (Frieden 2006).

Groups such as the ETA, al-Qaeda, and the PKK have also used the drug-trafficking business to generate revenues. In 2002, investigations led by Spanish authorities revealed that the Basque separatist group ETA has had a "drugs for weapons" deal with various mafia groups in Italy, under which the ETA delivered drugs (mostly cocaine) to the mafia and, in return, received high-tech weaponry, such as missiles and launchers (Arostegui 2002). The PKK is also reported to have a significant stake in the international drug trade, controlling almost 70 percent of the drug market in Europe, according to an Interpol report. In 2008, the US Treasury Department designated the PKK as a significant foreign narcotics trafficker. The group buys unprocessed morphine (i.e., extracts from the seeds of the opium poppy) from countries such as Iran, Afghanistan, and Pakistan and then creates heroin in its laboratories established in its regions of influence. Along with production, the group also levies taxes on other international drug traffickers, which use the group's territories to transport their narcotic products into European countries (Levitt 2009).

It is important to note that despite these official reports, groups like the PKK and PIRA are known to publicly condemn the use and smuggling of drugs for profit. This is mostly because despite the large profit margins, drug smuggling does not morally align with the groups' ideologies. The PKK, for example, has never officially acknowledged or approved of generating revenue from drug dealing. On the contrary, the group carried out ruthless assassinations against individuals who produced or distributed drugs in its area of influence (Haner 2017; Silke 2000).

Illicit Trade of Commodities (e.g., Oil, Diamonds, Gold)

The financing of terrorism also largely depends on available local resources (Barrett 2009). The prime example of this is the case of ISIS, which had access to lands seized in Iraq and Syria between 2013 and 2017. Unlike any other terrorist group in history, ISIS generated significant revenue from a variety of sources including oil and gas sales, which built the group's reputation as the wealthiest terrorist group in the world. After taking over oil installations in Syria and Iraq, the group made approximately $3 million per day from illegal oil production and smuggling, according to the US intelligence officials (Al-Khatteeb & Gordts 2014).

ISIS also generated significant funding from antiquities looted from museums or unearthed by illegal excavations at archaeological sites located in Syria and Iraq. According to UNESCO, an international watchdog, antiquity plundering provided the group between hundreds of millions of dollars to $7 billion dollars in black market revenue (NBC News 2014). Antiquity plundering had become such a lucrative business for ISIS that it launched an official looting program (e.g., pillaging of cultural heritage

FIGURE 11.10 The damage of artifacts due to the illicit trade at Palmyra, Syria. ISIS has been reported to finance activities through the illicit trade of antiquities. The group has controlled territories in Iraq and Syria that are rich in archaeological sites and artifacts, and it has taken advantage of these resources to generate revenue through the looting and trafficking of valuable antiquities, including sculptures, artifacts, coins, and manuscripts, and smuggling and sales of stolen antiquities through the international black market to collectors, buyers, and art dealers worldwide. *Source:* UNESCO, CC BY-SA 3.0 IGO, via Wikimedia Commons.

sites), by issuing excavation permits to private individuals, helping them move the discovered artifacts into international markets, and imposing a 20 percent tax on sold items (Rose-Greenland 2016). Once ISIS discovered that it was a profitable business, it hired its own archeologists and bought excavation equipment to take over the trade itself. The group plundered antiques at such an industrial scale that thousands of stolen artifacts can be easily found from antique dealers in London, Geneva, Basel, Zurich, and many other European cities, according to a 2015 Guardian report (Shabi 2015).

Groups such as Hezbollah and Hamas have also raised money through the illicit trade of commodities. In 2023, a Hezbollah member in the United Kingdom was sanctioned for allegedly funding the group through the smuggling of diamonds mined in conflict zones in West Africa (Associated Press News 2023). US Department of Justice prosecutors revealed that Hezbollah made more than $440 million from importing and exporting diamonds, precious gems, artwork, and other goods (i24 News 2023). The illicit tobacco trade has also served as a significant source of income for the group. In 2013, 15 individuals of Palestinian origin were arrested in New York on charges of running a multimillion-dollar cigarette smuggling industry from which the profits were diverted into Hamas and other militant Islamist groups. The prosecutors estimated that the group made at least $55 million in sales of untaxed cigarettes which were sold in New York grocery stores (Hosenball 2013).

Groups such as al-Shabaab, Boko Haram, and the Lord's rhinos Army in Africa have engaged in the hunting and poaching of elephants and rhinoceroses to generate revenue, mostly due to the high profit margins, large consumer demands (especially from

Asian countries), and little risk of detection involved in decimating these animals. According to a 2015 testimony submitted to the US House of Representatives, the annual illegal wildlife trade is estimated to generate around $10–$20 billion-dollars, with the black-market price of elephant ivory ranging between $1,000 and $1,800 per pound and a rhino horn selling around $30,000 per pound (US House of Representatives 2015).

Other Activities

In addition to the aforementioned illegal activities, terrorist groups use other methods such as robbery, extortion, **revolutionary taxes**, retail and auto theft, siphoning government and international aids (e.g., al-Qaeda's stealing of reconstruction aid that was given to Iraq) (Barrett 2009), taxing local economic activities, charging toll fees on roads under their control, collecting protection fees from large local and international companies operating in their regions, issuing high-interest loans, engaging in maritime piracy, and operating illegal gambling and prostitution rackets.

The type of illegal economic activities a group utilizes is mostly determined by the opportunity structures and resources available to them in their area of influence and operation. In 1984, LTTE in Sri Lanka established a naval wing called the "Sea Tigers" to engage in maritime piracy, because the territory controlled by the group was surrounded by the Indian Ocean. The Sea Tigers had ships, large vessels, submarines, speed boats, and attack vessels that were not only used to attack Sri Lankan Navy, but also to smuggle weapons into their territories and attack merchant and fishing ships sailing in Indian Ocean (Møller 2009). Unlike the Somali pirates who attack ships to take crew members hostage to obtain ransom, LTTE Sea Tigers attacked Indian, Australian, Malaysian, Jordanian, Philippine, Chinese, and Sri Lankan ships to obtain material goods for their operational and organizational activities (Bowley 2022). In 1997, the Sea Tigers captured a Greek registered freighter loaded with more than 32,000 mortar bombs donated by the United States to the Sri Lankan armed forces and transported the arms into its off-coast jungle bases, to use against the Sri Lankan security forces. Through this naval force, LTTE also generated significant financial resources by carrying legitimate goods (such as timber, rice, cement, and fertilizer) and illegitimate cargo (weapons and ammunition for other paying terrorist groups) around the world (Garofano & Dew 2013).

FIGURE 11.11 The ivory and horn trade has been a source of revenue for various armed groups and terrorist organizations in Africa, particularly in regions where poaching of elephants and rhinos are prevalent. These groups exploit the illegal ivory and horn trade to fund their activities, purchase weapons, and sustain their operations. Poachers often tranquilize rhinos and remove their horns while they are still alive, causing tremendous pain and suffering.
Source: William Folwds, CC BY-SA 4.0, via Wikimedia Commons.

Another example of how existing opportunity structures shape the type of financial activities available to terrorist groups is the application of protection fees in war-ridden regions. In 2014, after seizing control of the vast majority of territories in Iraq and Syria, ISIS required the large international companies that were present in the region to pay protection fees in return for continuing their businesses without interruption. The French Lafarge SA cement company was one of them. In 2022, the US Department of Justice issued a $778 million fine to the company for providing material support to ISIS. Company officials pleaded guilty to the charges that between 2012 and 2014, Lafarge SA paid more than $10 million dollars to the Islamic State as a protection fee to ensure the continued operation of their plant in Syria (Javers & Mangan 2022).

11.4 CHANNELS OF TERRORIST FINANCING: HOW TERRORISTS MANAGE AND TRANSFER THEIR FUNDS

In addition to acquiring funds, managing (e.g., use and obscure) and transferring financial resources is an important consideration for terrorist groups. Security is of utmost concern, as most financial transactions occur through outside institutions, involving people who do not have ties with the terrorist groups. These transactions, which often move funds across different jurisdictions (sometimes across different countries and even continents), are vital for a group's activities. However, these transactions increase the risk of detection by law enforcement agencies.

Despite the risk, terrorist groups continually seek new methods and exploit loopholes in existing laws and regulations as well as emerging technologies to move funds across borders, circumvent legal sanctions, and hide their funds from the scrutiny of authorities. A review of the literature reveals that terrorists not only use unregulated channels, but also take advantage of official financial systems (e.g., banks), new payment methods such as cryptocurrency, and the cross-border transportation of currency, gold, and other valuables through couriers to manage and channel funds. This section will explore the two main methods terrorists use to move and manage their funds: (1) informal value transfer systems, and (2) official financial systems.

11.4.1 Informal Value Transfer Systems (IVTS)

The US Department of the Treasury Financial Crimes Enforcement Network (FinCEN) defines **informal value transfer systems (IVTS)** as "any system, mechanism, or network of people that receives money for the purpose of making the funds or an equivalent value payable to a third party in another geographical location, whether or not in the same form" (FinCEN Advisory 2003, 1). IVTS, also known as alternative remittance systems, pose a significant challenge to law enforcement and intelligence officials, as the majority of these transactions take place outside of conventional banking systems through unofficial business entities, and thus are not regulated by the measures that restrict terrorist financing through formal financial institutions (Hett 2008). Even though it is difficult to estimate the exact size of remittances, according to an IMF report, in 2011, annual IVTS transfers totaled approximately $1 trillion (Ratha 2023).

First used in the Indian subcontinent to settle trades among the remote villages and communities, the origins of IVTS go back several thousand years. Today, IVTS

TABLE 11.4 Steps Involved in a Traditional IVTS Transfer

Step 1	Sender gives currency to an IVTS operator in a country (e.g., the United States) and provides the operator information on destination city or country and a passcode.
Step 2	The IVTS operator in the US notifies their counterpart in destination country (e.g., Pakistan) by phone or email, regarding the money paid to recipient and the passcode.
Step 3	Sender calls the recipient and provides them with the password.
Step 4	Recipient goes to the IVTS operator at their city, gives them the code, and picks up the funds (minus the commission).
Step 5	No money is actually transferred between the countries. However, the transaction amounts among the IVTS operators are settled later through bank transfers, by sending cash with couriers, or traded with goods such as diamonds, gold, and gems.

Source: Adapted from FinCEN (2003).

are used in several parts of the world (especially in countries where formal banking networks are poorly established), and depending on the ethnic groups using them, they are called by different names such as "hawala" (transfer) in Arab and Muslim world; "hundi" (bill of exchange) in India; and "fei chien" (flying money) in China (McCulloch & Pickering 2005).

IVTS are based on a system of high-level trust (e.g., honor, family connections, and regional relationships) and cooperation, rather than profit, and they are widely used by immigrants and expatriates to send money back to family members in their home countries. Individuals prefer IVTS over official financial systems for four reasons. First, IVTS are the best option if bank transfers are not possible in the country of destination due to lack of reliable financial systems (e.g., banking infrastructure). Currently the only way to send money to remote war-ridden locations of Iraq and Syria and remote locations in India, South Asia, and Africa is through the hawala system, due to the lack of easily accessible formal financial institutions in these territories. Second, transfers through IVTS are much cheaper compared to official channels in which both the senders and recipients are charged tax, service, and foreign exchange fees (Morais 2002). IVTS transfers can also be sent from convenient locations, such as markets, small shops, and gas stations.

Third, regulated money transfers are often slower and may take several days due to compliance procedures. At the least, the sender

FIGURE 11.12 Somalian dealer waiting for customers at a money market in Hargeisa, Somaliland. Money markets in Somalia and Afghanistan could involve currency exchange, trade, and financial transactions conducted in an open-air or market-style setting.
Source: WorldRemit Comms, CC BY-SA 2.0, via Wikimedia Commons.

has to open an account with a bank to send money overseas. In contrast, an IVTS transfers funds almost instantly with minimal fees charged to the sender and with no paperwork involved (Passas 2003). Fourth and finally, transfers through IVTS are not subject to currency reporting requirements set by international regulators. These systems operate covertly (with no publicly available transaction records, such as sender's and recipient's names, addresses, or the destination country) and do not involve the physical movement of the money (Morais 2002). As a result of these secrecy and anonymity features, IVTS transfers pose a significant investigative and supervisory challenge to financial regulators and law enforcement authorities.

Alternative remittance systems are widely used for legitimate reasons (e.g., by immigrants or overseas workers in Europe and North America to send money back to their families) and serve as an important tool for underdeveloped and rural communities across the world because of their aforementioned advantages. However, due to these very same advantages, especially the fact that they leave no paper trail, these systems are also attractive to terrorists (CTITF 2009). Several terrorist plots in the US and across the world occurred through IVTS financing, to circumvent institutionalized banking systems as a method of avoiding detection. Post-9/11 investigations suggested that Taliban and al-Qaeda networks used IVTS (along with formal banking and Western Union transfers) to channel funds to finance their attacks in the United States (Cook & Smith 2011). In 2010, a Pakistani individual was arrested for sending $7,000 to another suspect via the hawala system, to carry out a car bombing attack at Times Square in New York City (Weizer 2010).

The hawala system has also been used in Europe to finance terrorist operations across the world. The perpetrators of the 9/11 attacks in the United States and the murderers of *Wall Street Journal* reporter Daniel Pearl in 2002 obtained financial means for their attacks through hawala transfers sent from IVTS centers located in Europe (Irujo 2015). Similarly, a large-scale intelligence operation carried out by Spanish officials in 2015 revealed a network of approximately 300 IVTS centers located inside regular businesses such as phone call centers, butcher shops, and neighborhood grocery stores, which were being used by al-Qaeda and ISIS to transfer funds between Europe and conflict regions (Moore 2015).

11.4.2 Official Financial Systems

Terrorists also take advantage of the financial systems that exist in the legal arena to clandestinely move their funds and prevent law enforcement officials from confiscating them. To do so, they often misuse the recent technological developments and innovations in payment systems that allow transactions through new channels and structures, with no or limited regulation. Examples include the use of digital currencies (e.g., cryptocurrencies), **online payment and processing systems** (e.g., PayPal), prepaid debit and credit cards, traveler's check and money orders, and smurfing transactions (making multiple cash deposits each below $10,000 to prevent triggering federal reporting requirements) through banks. More traditional methods, such as the off-shore financial centers (e.g., land-locked territories or tropical islands that offer financial services to nonresidents to generate revenue) also help terrorists hide and move their funds across jurisdictions— mostly due to the fact that financial transactions in these jurisdictions are not subject to robust regulations (IMF 2000). The following section will discuss the use of three major official methods used by terrorists to move funds across borders to circumvent reporting and detection systems: (1) prepaid debit and credit cards, (2) digital currencies, and (3) online payment and processing systems.

Prepaid Debit and Credit Cards

New and innovative payment products and services that have been developed for ease of use and customer convenience, such as payment network branded (e.g., Visa, Master-card, Discover) prepaid or loadable debit and credit cards (also known as open-loop cards), which are available for purchase at retail markets, have created challenges for law enforcement officials due to their growing use in terrorist financing (Johnson & Jensen 2010). According to a 2020 report, the global prepaid card market is estimated to generate approximately $4 trillion in revenue for financial institutions (Furber 2020).

Issued by major banks beginning in the early 2000s, prepaid cards allow bearers to pay for goods and services at any merchant and enable them to withdraw cash from global ATM networks. Unlike traditional debit or credit cards, the beneficiary does not need to provide any personal information to banks for an evaluation of their credit background or need to open a payment account with a financial institution to obtain these cards. Once obtained, these cards can be used to move funds around the world, make purchases, and withdraw cash when needed, or be passed to others, in a completely anonymous manner, with no required customer identification or verification measures required (FATF 2013).

Due to their highly secure and anonymous nature, prepaid cards are a preferred method of payment by terrorists. The perpetrators of 2015 Paris terror attacks, in which more than 130 people lost their lives and hundreds of others were critically injured, used prepaid debit cards to pay for their accommodations and purchase weapons in order to conceal their identities from officials (Seibt 2015). During the 2016 Jakarta bombing attacks at a major shopping and business district close to the presidential palace and US Embassy in Indonesia, the attackers used prepaid credit cards to transfer funds for their operation (BBC 2016).

Due to the same reasons, prepaid cards have also been a preferred method of cross border money transfer for terrorists. In 2019, police investigations during the trial of Joaquin Guzman (El Chapo), the leader of the major Mexican drug cartel Sinaloa, revealed that the cartel had been using prepaid debit cards to move its drug proceeds from the United States to South America. After the cards arrived in countries like Colombia and Ecuador, the cartel hired individuals from the public to withdraw the money from ATMs (Wolf 2019).

Digital Currencies

Also known as **cryptocurrencies**, digital currencies are a decentralized and encrypted alternative method of payment based on cryptography (sophisticated coding) to secure transactions. Unlike national currencies, there is no central regulating authority that maintains the value of a cryptocurrency. Instead, transactions are verified and recorded on a blockchain, a record in which all transactions are updated and held by currency holders (Dion-Schwarz et al. 2019).

Digital currencies are created through a process called "mining," which involves the use of high computer power and electricity to solve complex mathematical puzzles to generate coins. Instead of mining, one can simply purchase a cryptocurrency and then keep it in their "cryptographic wallets" (Ashford & Curry 2023). There are currently more than 22 thousand cryptocurrencies, with a total market capitalization of $1.1 trillion (Hicks & Adams 2023). Some of the major cryptocurrencies are Bitcoin, Ethereum, and Litecoin.

Due to features such as decentralization and anonymous trading, cryptocurrencies have enabled terrorists and other malicious actors to expand and disguise their funding methods (e.g., solicit donations, purchase weapons, and move their funds globally). Several digital currencies (e.g., Monero, MasterCoin, BlackCoin) are now designed to be completely anonymous and secure, allowing high-volume international transfers without the risk of detection. These systems can be accessed online from anywhere in the world. Transactions that occur through digital currency platforms are not subject to strict regulatory regimes implemented at financial institutions, that are designed to counter terrorist funding (e.g., know your customer rules, maintaining customer identifications, mandatory reporting of certain transactions, filing suspicious activities report). Using these currencies, individuals can easily hide the identity of the sender and the recipient, and the amount of money sent. Digital currency wallets can be obtained within minutes, with no personal identity verification procedures required, further complicating the law enforcement efforts to identify and disrupt potentially threatening terrorist activity.

For all of these features, most prominently for the ability to execute untraceable fund transfers, along with lax or inconsistent international regulatory oversight, digital currencies have attracted the attention of terrorist groups and lone-wolf actors (FATF 2015; Hett 2008). In 2014, ISIS released an online article titled "Bitcoin wa Sadaqat al-Jihad" (Bitcoin and Charity of Jihad) on an internet blog, detailing strategic reasons why Bitcoins should be used (e.g., being anonymous, untraceable, not being subject to legislation, and having a global distribution) instead of traditional fiat currencies (government issued moneys) to donate funds to the group (Bob 2018).

A 2021 report published by the Southern Poverty Law Center (SPLC) revealed the American

FIGURE 11.13 Cryptocurrencies provide a level of anonymity that can make it challenging to track financial transactions, and they have been used by extremist individuals and groups to fund their activities or spread their ideologies. Andrew Anglin, the founder of The Daily Stormer website, which advocates for the purity of the White race, publishes hate-filled, conspiratorial screeds against Black people, Jews, and women and has helped inspire at least three racially motivated murders, received at least 112 Bitcoins from a worldwide network of supporters between 2017 and 2021 (Kinetz & Hinnant 2021a). *Source:* Jorge Franganillo, CC BY 2.0, via Wikimedia Commons.

right-wing extremist groups' heavy reliance on the use of cryptocurrency as a means of breaking themselves free from the "Jewish controlled banking empire" (Hayden & Squire 2021). In 2017, for example, Andrew Anglin received about 15 Bitcoins as financial support for his planning and promotion of the hateful and deadly "Unite the Right" rally in Charlottesville, Virginia (Kinetz & Hinnant 2021b).

Online Payment and Processing Systems

Starting in the late 1990s, nonbank financial institutions began offering internet-based payment and processing systems to facilitate transactions among customers and merchants and to ease personal transfers among individuals. These services (e.g., PayPal, E-money, Zelle, e-gold, Stormpay) vary significantly in their scope and functionality and provide convenient features such as online access to prefunded accounts, ease of use for internet purchases, instant transfer of funds between accounts, and global reach to make and receive donations. Unfortunately, these very features which are designed to increase customer convenience also make them vulnerable to misuse by terrorist and criminal groups (Laksmi 2017). Many of these services can be set up using only a valid email address, with no other personal information required (Hett 2008).

PayPal, the online payment and processing system serves more than 200 million global users in 200 countries or regions, supporting 25 currencies. The company processes approximately 41 million transactions every day and provides an extremely easy way (compared to using banks) to instantly send and receive money abroad (Rozsa 2023). Due to these features, the system is also open to abuse by terrorists. In 2018, FBI investigations revealed that ISIS was using PayPal to transfer funds to its operatives across the world by depicting these transactions as compensation for equipment and goods purchased online. In one incident, an individual from Maryland was pretending to sell computer equipment online on eBay and in exchange was receiving funds from ISIS through PayPal ($8,700) to purchase weapons and ammunitions to be used in terrorist attacks inside the United States (DOJ 2018; Pascu 2017). A recent research study conducted by the International Centre for Counter-Terrorism (ICCT) discovered that between 2012 and 2020, terrorists used PayPal as a payment method in more than 18 percent of a total of 319 purchases of goods and services (e.g., travel tickets, firearms, bomb-making materials) for their attacks in the US (Whittaker 2022).

11.5 COUNTERING THE FINANCING OF TERRORISM

Combatting terrorism financing is a multijurisdictional, highly complex, and difficult endeavor requiring a degree of cooperation and reciprocity from national and international actors. Today, most countries, as well as international organizations (e.g., UN, FATF) have implemented some kind of measures to counter the global financing of terrorism. These measures significantly proliferated after the 9/11 attacks but have raised some concern as they created a major shift in the balance of power between states and individuals in liberal democracies (McCulloch & Carlton 2006). This section will provide a brief overview of the four major international and national efforts designed before and after the 9/11 attacks to "starve the terrorists of funding" (Morais 2002).

11.5.1 The International Convention for the Suppression of Financing of Terrorism

Designed to cut off funding for terrorist organizations, the International Convention for the Suppression of Financing of Terrorism was adopted by the General Assembly of the United Nations in December 1999. Even though the Convention abstained from providing a formal definition of terrorism (due to the reasons highlighted in Chapter 1), it required member states:

I. To pass domestic legislation to criminalize the collection and donation of funds for terrorist activities,
II. To facilitate international cooperation in police and judicial investigations regarding issues related to terrorist financing,
III. To identify, freeze, and seize any funds used or allocated for the purposes of carrying out terrorist acts (United Nations 2009).

With the ratification of the Convention, for the first time in the history of the UN, member states were required to take solid action against the financial aspect of terrorism with binding legal obligations, such as prosecution and extradition (US Congress 2000). As of 2023, more than 130 member-countries signed the Convention (United Nations 2023b).

11.5.2 Executive Order 13224: Blocking Property and Prohibiting Transactions with Persons Who Commit, Threaten to Commit, or Support Terrorism

On September 23, 2001, soon after the 9/11 attacks, then-President George W. Bush signed the Executive Order 13224, authorizing the US Department of State (in consultation with the Treasury and Justice Departments) to designate and freeze the assets of foreign individuals and entities that have either committed, or have the potential to commit, terrorist acts (Crimm 2004). The act also allowed the Department of Treasury to seize the assets of individuals, front organizations, subsidiaries and others that provide support (financial or material), services, or assistance to designated terrorist organizations (US Department of State 2023a). The Order was developed to freeze and seize terrorist funds, deny their access to international financial systems, and prevent their ability to raise funding in the future.

11.5.3 United Nations Security Council Resolution 1373

Initiated only five days after the issuance of Executive Order 13224, United Nations Security Council (UNSC) unanimously adopted Resolution 1373, requiring all member states to implement more effective counterterrorism measures. This resolution was basically the worldwide application of the US sanctions brought by Executive Order 13224 (McCulloch & Pickering 2005). Member states were required to designate persons or entities who commit, attempts to commit, or facilitate support for the commission of terrorist acts, freeze the funds and assets of listed individuals and organizations, prohibit aid provision to terrorists, and criminalize financial dealings with individuals designated as terrorists (Barrett 2009). The United Nations established the Counter-Terrorism Committee (CTC) to facilitate the implementation of these new obligations by the member states (Rosand 2003).

11.5.4 The Financial Action Task Force (FATF) Eight Special Recommendations

The Financial Action Task Force (FATF) is an international group currently composed of 36-member states (excluding Russia, whose membership was suspended in February 2023). The group was established in 1989 by the G7 countries to combat the issue of global money laundering by rouge states and criminal organizations. In October 2001, following the 9/11 attacks, FATF adopted "Eight Special Recommendations" to detect, prevent, and suppress the financing of terrorism and terrorist acts, to add to its existing 40 recommendations on money laundering (FATF 2023b). These recommendations, commonly viewed as the gold standard for combating the financing of terrorism, require countries to:

I.   Take immediate steps to ratify and implement the two United Nations instruments tackling the financing of terrorism: (1) the 1999 UN International Convention for the Suppression of the Financing of Terrorism, and (2) United Nations Security Council Resolution 1373.

II. Criminalize the financing of terrorism.

III. Implement measures to freeze, seize, and confiscate the funds, properties, and other valuable assets of those who financed, or who are planning to finance terrorism and terrorist acts.

IV. Require financial institutions to report suspicious activities and transactions that may be linked to terrorism financing to intelligence units and law enforcement agencies.

V.   Abstain from being a safe haven for individuals charged with financing of terrorism and when asked, cooperate with other countries to help facilitate investigations (e.g., legal assistance, extradition requests, information exchange) regarding the financing of terrorism in their jurisdictions.

VI. Take measures to license and register all institutions (including alternative remittance systems) that provide money and other valuable transfer services and make sure that these institutions follow the FATF recommendations.

VII. Require financial institutions to keep records of detailed information (e.g., name, address, account number) on money transfers, identify and verify customers' identity (with passport, identity cards, driving licenses), abstain from keeping anonymous accounts, and monitor suspicious activity transfers that do not contain complete originator information and keep customers' personal information and transaction records for at least five years in case an investigative request is made from a competent authority.

VIII. Ensure that terrorist organizations do not pose as legitimate nonprofit entities, exploit legitimate nonprofit organizations for their fundraising activities, or divert funds intended for legitimate purposes into their terrorist activities.

On a regular basis, FATF issues publicly available, online lists of countries and jurisdictions that have not adopted its recommendations regarding the financing of terrorism. These countries are categorized into two groups. The first includes blacklist countries (also known as high-risk jurisdictions) which have serious deficiencies in the area of money laundering and terrorist financing. As of 2023, only three countries—North

Korea, Iran, and Myanmar—are included on the blacklist. The second group, grey list countries (also known as jurisdictions under increased monitoring), includes jurisdictions that are currently working with FATF to address their regulatory deficiencies in the area of terrorist financing and money laundering (FATF 2023a). Noncompliance with FATF recommendations can be quite costly for member states. Between 2013 and 2016, the task force issued more than $10 billion in fines to international financial institutions for failing to follow its recommendations (Vision of Humanity 2023).

11.6 CONCERNS WITH THE INITIATIVES THAT TARGET THE FINANCING OF TERRORISM

Measures aimed at combatting the financing of terrorism have been subjected to heavy criticism for their practical, social, and political implications on individuals' civil rights and on the rule of law and democracy. These legislations gave such broadly defined, arbitrary, and far-reaching powers to governments (with no culpability) that scholars argued they would not have been ratified by democratic countries if the attacks of 9/11 hadn't occurred. These concerns are discussed in the sections below.

11.6.1 Demise of Alternative Remittance Systems and Associated Effects

The post-9/11 regulations severely curtailed the activities of the informal value transfer (alternative remittance) systems (e.g., hawala) across the world. Even though IVTS are largely used for legitimate reasons by immigrants (e.g., to send money back to their families and friends) and serve as an important tool for poor and impoverished communities where the banking system is not developed, they have become the major target of law enforcement and intelligence officials during the post–9/11 era (McCulloch et al. 2004).

As a result, hundreds of thousands of law-abiding individuals, mostly immigrants and expatriates, have been left with no readily available tools to send money back to their home countries. After the ratification of the post-9/11 measures, the offices of Al-Barakaat hawala in the United States, the largest informal value transfer system in Somalia, were raided and its assets were frozen—on the accusations that the Al-Barakaat Network was serving as major financial conduit for terrorist funds and it was providing material and logistical support to al-Qaeda (Department of Treasury 2004). When asked, US officials were unable to provide solid evidence showing such a connection between Al-Barakaat and the terrorist groups. However, the application of these sanctions led to a financial crisis in Somalia as foreign remittances through the hawala system were responsible for much of the income and international financial aid coming to this country (McCulloch & Pickering 2005; Schmemann 2002).

11.6.2 Lack of Due Process and Absence of Clear Criteria for Designations

The post-9/11 legislations provided government officials with extreme powers such as the ability to unilaterally designate a person or an entity as terrorist and freeze and confiscate their assets with no burden of proof or court process. In the post–9/11 era, individuals without evidence of criminal wrongdoing or a hearing could be targeted and designated as terrorists. Further, these regulations allowed officials to use the "guilt by association" norm; that is, to extend these sanctions to others, who somehow (even quite remotely) are associated with a designated terrorist (e.g., family member, relative, friend, coworker) (Cole 2003).

Neither the UN resolutions nor the US Executive Order provided a clear set of criteria or procedures for listing or de-listing groups and individuals, or a legal channel for the accused to challenge their designation (Zagaris 2002). Both regulations provided overarching discretionary powers to authorities even in situations where an actual crime has not yet occurred. These regulations authorized officials to bring criminal action against persons who, according to their judgment, *may* use their funds to carry out terrorist activities in the future. Scholars argue that these measures impinge too much upon civil liberties and democratic rights, as they do not focus on actual crimes, but on "crimes that may occur" in the future (Allam & Gadzinowski 2009; McCulloch & Carlton 2006).

There have been several examples of wrongful implementation of these measures that resulted in serious economic and legal consequences for individuals with no established links to terrorism. In 2002, an Australian businessman whose company coincidentally shared the same name with an organization blacklisted by the UN was subjected to the freezing and confiscation of his assets for approximately a month with no explanation or warning (McCulloch et al. 2004). His assets were unfrozen only after the media brought the incident to public attention as unlawful. During the same year, even though the US government provided no evidence of terrorist activity, it asked the Swedish authorities to freeze the assets of three Somali-born Swedish citizens after they were placed on the UN designated list of terrorists at the request of the United States. The decision was harshly criticized by Swedish authorities and society, as the Swedish government and courts had no authority or means to appeal this decision occurring in their jurisdictions against their own citizens (Schmemann 2002).

In 2009, in an attempt to provide more fair and clear procedures to monitor designations, the UN Security Council established a system for individuals and business entities who opposed their designations as financers of terrorism. The system allowed the appointment of an independent ombudsperson to examine complaints regarding wrongful designations and provide explanations to the complainant about why they were named on such lists. Nevertheless, critics argued that this new step was still short of democratic expectations as the ombudsperson had no authority to lift sanctions, remove individuals from the terrorist list, or even make specific recommendations to the sanctions committee regarding the listings (Wornship 2009).

11.6.3 Encompassing Activities That Do Not Involve Terrorism

Measures designed to combat terrorism financing have also been criticized because they can criminalize activities that don't involve terrorism, such as donating money to charities, humanitarian organizations, social justice movements, and international solidarity groups. Even though most charities operate in the legitimate financial arena and carry out important social and humanitarian functions, the post-9/11 measures depicted charities and other NGOs as potential fronts for terrorist financing and for transfer of illicit funds (Dalyan 2008).

Being aware of this potential exposure to criminal liability with heavy repercussions, individuals, especially Muslims in the Western world, have abstained from donating to NGOs and charities out of fear that they may later become subject to prosecution. Muslim leaders around the world have indicated that these vague measures led to a substantial decline in global philanthropy. This in turn impaired the ability of Islamic charities and welfare programs to serve marginalized communities in impoverished and war-torn regions of the world (Crimm 2004).

A 2015 news report revealed that not only individuals but also banks and other financial institutions have withdrawn themselves from operating in conflict-ridden regions to lower their risk of being targeted by post-9/11 anti-terrorism financing legislation. Several reports highlighted how US- and UK-based international humanitarian programs have had difficulty with banks and other financial institutions in sending financial help to conflict zones, such as Syria, Yemen, Sudan, Somalia, Pakistan, and Afghanistan. In 2014, the international women's rights group Madre (which operates in more than 40 countries) had trouble transferring funds to Iraq for its gender-based violence prevention program, because Western Union refused to handle these transfers without providing any explanation to the NGO. Prevention of international aid delivery is concerning and expected to have a much larger negative impact in the future. As acknowledged by Mercy Corps, an international humanitarian group working in dangerous areas of the world: "If these measures are preventing or deterring the responsible delivery of humanitarian aid into conflict zones, we will see civilian casualties greater than those from any military campaign" (Dawson 2015).

11.6.4 The Practical Utility of Preventing Financial Transactions
Scholars commonly argue that these legislative measures may not be effective in preventing the financing of terrorism, as terrorist groups have a diverse portfolio of methods to move their funds. If one option is not viable anymore these groups simply turn to other methods, or develop others, to raise and transfer their funds. It is not realistic to control or get rid of all available methods as a whole, because they are being used by millions of other law-abiding citizens every day.

11.7 CONCLUSION
Just like individuals and organizations in society, terrorists need funding in order to operate. While terrorist attacks themselves can be relatively inexpensive, terrorist groups often need to secure and maintain substantial amounts of money to support their existence and advance toward their goals. Throughout history, terrorists have used a number of methods to generate funding, from both legal and illegal sources. Often, the means by which terrorist groups accumulate funding conflict with their moral or ideological views (e.g., drug trafficking) but are undertaken nonetheless out of necessity. Methods of terrorism funding are also heavily influenced by the resources and opportunities available to them in their areas of operation and influence.

In addition to generating money, terrorists also need to secure and transfer it. To do so, terrorist groups often employ the same technologies and payment options that ordinary people use every day. This creates practical and ethical challenges, as nations engage in complex international efforts to combat the financing of terrorism.

Key Lessons

Lesson 1

Terrorism or violent conflicts often cannot occur unless these aggrieved groups have access to significant financial resources.

Lesson 2

How terrorists manage (e.g., use and obscure) and transfer their financial resources is an important issue that has implications for the security and sustainability of their operations.

Lesson 3

Compared to the funds required for the maintenance of organizational infrastructures, the actual cost of devastating terrorist acts can be quite inexpensive.

Lesson 4

The methods used by terrorist groups to raise funding often depend on several factors, such as the ideology and the geographic location that the groups operate within and the opportunity structures that are available for fundraising.

Lesson 5

The financing of terrorism largely relies on money obtained from legitimate resources such as storefront businesses (e.g., bars, drinking clubs), donations from charitable organizations and other nonprofits, sales of publications, solicitations, and from many other legitimate outlets.

Lesson 6

Terrorist groups also draw on a wide range of criminal activities to fund their organizations, which may range from low-level acts such as robbery, fraud, kidnapping, and counterfeiting to high-level organized transnational acts such as narcotics, arms, and human smuggling, sales of valuable minerals and oil in the black market, and taxation through coercion and intimidation.

Lesson 7

One of the biggest barriers in combatting terrorism financing emanates from the fact that funding for terrorist acts is often generated from legal sources which makes detection and investigations difficult, if not impossible.

Lesson 8

The combined use of social media outlets and the new financial technologies such as cryptocurrencies not only allows terrorist groups to easily reach out to their support base and obtain funding from all over the world in real time, but also provides anonymity for donors, protecting them from potential legal repercussion.

Lesson 9

Combatting the financing of terrorism is a multijurisdictional, highly complex, and difficult endeavor requiring a degree of cooperation and reciprocity from national and international actors.

Lesson 10

Measures aimed at combatting the financing of terrorism have been subjected to heavy criticism by many, for their practical, social, and political impacts on individuals' civil rights and the rule of law and democracy.

KEY WORDS

active support
burglary
charities
counterfeiting
crowdfunding
cryptocurrencies
diaspora funding
drug trafficking
extortion
foreign state support
fraud
front companies

human smuggling
illegitimate sources
illicit trade
informal value transfer systems (IVTS)
kidnapping
legitimate sources
money laundering
online payment and processing systems
passive support
protection rackets
revolutionary taxes
self-financing

smuggling
tax fraud

terrorism financing
theft

RECOMMENDED SOURCES

Research Articles & Books

Barrett, R. (2011). Preventing the financing of terrorism. *Case W. Res. J. Int'l L.*, *44*, 719.

Brooks, R. C., Riley Jr, R. A., & Thomas, J. (2005). Detecting and preventing the financing of terrorist activities: A role for government accountants. *The Journal of Government Financial Management*, *54*(1), 12.

Clarke, C. P. (2015). Terrorism, Inc.: The Financing of Terrorism, Insurgency, and Irregular Warfare: The Financing of Terrorism, Insurgency, and Irregular Warfare. ABC-CLIO.

Davis, J. (2021). Illicit money: Financing terrorism in the twenty-First century. Lynne Rienner Publishers.

Johnson, J. M., & Jensen, C. (2010). The financing of terrorism. *Journal of the Institute of Justice and International Studies*, *10*, 103.

Laksmi, S. W. (2017). Terrorism Financing and the Risk of Internet-Based Payment Services in Indonesia. *Counter Terrorist Trends and Analyses*, *9*(2), 21–25.

McCulloch, J., & Pickering, S. (2005). Suppressing the financing of terrorism: Proliferating state crime, eroding censure and extending neo-colonialism. *British Journal of Criminology*, *45*(4), 470–486.

Raphaeli, N. (2003). Financing of terrorism: Sources, methods, and channels. *Terrorism and Political Violence*, *15*(4), 59–82.

Silke, A. (2000). Drink, drugs, and rock'n'roll: Financing loyalist terrorism in Northern Ireland—Part two. *Studies in Conflict & Terrorism*, *23*(2), 107–127.

News Articles & Government and Think Tank Reports

What's behind far-right trend of using 3D tech to make guns?
Author(s): Hyder Abbasi
Source: Al Jazeera

How ISIS uses oil to fund terror.
Author(s): Luay Al-Khatteeb & Eline Gordts
Source: Brookings Institution

ETA has drugs-for-weapons deal with mafia.
Author(s): Martin Arostegui
Source: United Press International (UPI)

ISIS, other jihadists increase Bitcoin use after fall of Caliphate.
Author(s): Yonah Jeremy Bob
Source: The Jerusalem Post

Paying ransoms, Europe bankrolls Qaeda terror.
Author(s): Rukmini Callimachi
Source: The New York Times

Tackling the financing of terrorism.
Author(s): The United Nations Counter-Terrorism Implementation Task Force
Source: UNRCCA

Christchurch shooter donated thousands to far-right groups and websites before attack, report shows.
Author(s): Lizzie Dearden
Source: The Independent

Terrorists use of cryptocurrencies: technical and organizational barriers and future threats.
Author(s): Cynthia Dion-Schwarz, David Manheim, & Patrick B. Johnston
Source: RAND

Terrorist Financing.
Author(s): Financial Action Task Force
Source: FATF

Terrorism and digital financing: how technology is changing the threat.
Author(s): House Committee on Homeland Security
Source: US Congress

French company fined $777 million and pleads guilty to paying ISIS as terror group killed Westerners.
Author(s): Eamon Javers & Dan Mangan
Source: CNBC

'White Dissidents' Raise Millions in Cryptocurrency.
  Author(s): Erika Kinetz & Lori Hinnant
  Source: The PBS
Hawala: the ancient banking practice used to finance terror groups.
  Author(s): Jack Moore
  Source: Newsweek

How much does a terrorist attack cost? A lot less than you'd think.
  Author(s): Dina Temple-Raston
  Source: NPR

Documentaries, Videos, and Other Educational Media

Anti-Money Laundering / Counter-Financing of Terrorism
  Featuring: Yulia Minaeva
  Source: United Nations Office on Drugs and Crimes
Counter-Terrorism Financing and the Evolution and Adaptation of Terrorist Tactics
  Featuring: Jessica Davis
  Source: Social Sciences and Humanities Research Council of Canada (SSHRC) YouTube Channel
Reporting suspected money laundering and terrorist financing
  Source: Finansinspektionen, YouTube Channel
Crowdfunding for terrorism financing
Producer(s)/Director(s): The Financial Action Task Force (FATF) OECD
  Source: The Financial Action Task Force, YouTube Channel
Crime & Crypto: How cryptocurrencies enable money laundering & terror funding
  Featuring: Renato Mariotti
  Source: France 24
Anti-Money-Laundering, Counterterrorism Financing and Financial Crime

Featuring: Hue Dang
  Source: Amherst College YouTube Channel
Crypto's role in terrorist financing | Tech It Out
  Featuring: Ankit Tuteja
  Source: The World is One News (WION)
The role of cryptocurrency in financing terrorism
  Featuring: Ali Rogin & Ari Redbord
  Source: PBS
FATF Webinar Money Laundering and Terrorist Financing through the Arts and Antiquities Market
  Featuring: Tom Bergin, Viktor Ivanov, Paul Dergarabedian, Donna Yates, & Rena Neville
  Source: The Financial Action Task Force (FATF) YouTube Channel
Combating terrorism financing: What more can be done?
  Featuring: Demir Murat Seyrek, Ilkka Salmi, Rebecca Schönenbach, Stephen Reimer
  Source: European Policy Centre, YouTube Channel

REFERENCES

Abbasi, H. (2021). What's behind far-right trend of using 3D tech to make guns? Al-Jazeera. https://www.aljazeera.com/news/2021/7/31/what-behind-far-right-trend-using-3d-tech-make-guns

ADL. (2023). ADL crowdfunding report: How bigots and extremists collect and use millions in online donations. *ADL*. https://www.adl.org/resources/report/adl-crowdfunding-report-how-bigots-and-extremists-collect-and-use-millions-online

Al-Khatteeb, L. & Gordts, E. (2014). How ISIS uses oil to fund terror. Brookings. https://www.brookings.edu/articles/how-isis-uses-oil-to-fund-terror/

Allam, M., & Gadzinowski, D. (2009). Combating the financing of terrorism: EU policies, polity and politics. *EIPAScope, 2009*(2), 37–43.

Arostegui, M. (2002). ETA has drugs-for-weapons deal with mafia. UPI. https://www.upi.com/Defense-News/2002/10/03/ETA-has-drugs-for-weapons-deal-with-Mafia/80091033676439/

Ashford, K. & Curry, B. (2023). What is cryptocurrency? *Forbes*. https://www.forbes.com/advisor/investing/cryptocurrency/what-is-cryptocurrency/

Associated Press News (2023). UK, US sanction art dealer with suspected ties to Hezbollah. https://apnews.com/article/hezbollah-sanctions-terrorist-art-diamonds-fa25987e33c91dac573e014c12b24847

Attah, C. E. (2019). Financing terrorism in Nigeria. *Africa Development/Afrique et Développement*, 44(2), 5–26.

Bambrough, B. (2019). New Zealand mosque shooter's mention of bitconnect could setback Bitcoin acceptance. *Forbes*. https://www.forbes.com/sites/billybambrough/2019/03/22/new-zealand-mosque-shooters-mention-of-bitconnect-could-setback-bitcoin-acceptance/?sh=2fe1fb72352f

Barrett, R. (2009). Time to reexamine regulation designed to counter the financing of terrorism. *Case Western Reserve Journal of International Law*, 41, 7–18.

Barrett, R. (2011). Preventing the financing of terrorism. *Case Western Reserve Journal of International Law*, 44, 719–736.

BBC (2016). Jakarta attacks: Bombs and gunfire rock Indonesian capital. BBC. https://www.bbc.com/news/world-asia-35309195

Berry, L., Curtis, G. E., Hudson, R. A., & Kollars, N. A. (2002, May). A global overview of narcotics-funded terrorist and other extremist groups. Federal Research Division, Library of Congress.

Bob, Y. J. (2018). ISIS, other jihadists increase Bitcoin use after fall of Caliphate. *Jerusalem Post*. https://www.jpost.com/middle-east/isis-threat/isis-other-jihadists-increase-bitcoin-use-after-fall-of-caliphate-540079

Bowley, R. (2022). *Preventing the maritime facilitation of terrorism: Maritime terrorism risk and international law*. Taylor & Francis.

Brooks, R. C., Riley Jr, R. A., & Thomas, J. (2005). Detecting and preventing the financing of terrorist activities: A role for government accountants. *Journal of Government Financial Management*, 54(1), 12–18.

Callimachi, R. (2014). Paying ransoms, Europe bankrolls Qaeda terror. *New York Times*. https://www.nytimes.com/2014/07/30/world/africa/ransoming-citizens-europe-becomes-al-qaedas-patron.html

Cannon, D. T. (2015). War through pharmaceuticals: How terrorist organizations are turning to counterfeit medicine to fund their illicit activity. *Case Western Reserve Journal of International Law*, 47, 343–376.

Carter, S. A. (2009). Hezbollah uses Mexican drug routes into US. *Washington Times*. https://www.washingtontimes.com/news/2009/mar/27/hezbollah-uses-mexican-drug-routes-into-us/

Clarke, C. P. (2015). Terrorism, Inc.: The financing of terrorism, insurgency, and irregular warfare: The financing of terrorism, insurgency, and irregular warfare. ABC-CLIO.

Cole, D. (2003). *Enemy aliens: Double standards and constitutional freedoms in the war on terror*. The New Press.

Collins, R. (2022). New book examines Irish-American aid during the Troubles. *Irish Central*. https://www.irishcentral.com/news/thenorth/noraid-northern-ireland-troubles-robert-collins

Cook, M. D., & Smith, T. (2011). The Battle for money transfers: The allure of PayPal and Western union over familial remittance networks. *Journal of Information Warfare*, 10(1), 19–36.

CPJ (2000). As hostage crisis drags on, release of three French journalists delayed. Committee to Protect Journalists. https://cpj.org/2000/08/as-hostage-crisis-drags-on-release-of-three-french/

Crimm, N. J. (2004). High alert: The government's war on the financing of terrorism and its implications for donors, domestic charitable organizations, and global philanthropy. *William & Mary Law Review*, 45, 1341–1451.

CTITF (2009). Tackling the financing of terrorism. United Nations Counter-Terrorism Implementation Task Force. https://unrcca.unmissions.org/sites/default/files/ctitf_financing_eng_final.pdf

Dalyan, S. (2008). Combating the financing of terrorism: Rethinking strategies for success. *Defence Against Terrorism Review*, 1(1), 137–153.

Davis, J. (2018). PKK financing in Europe. Insight Intelligence. https://newsletter.insightthreatintel.com/p/pkk-financing-in-europe

Davis, J. (2021). Illicit money: Financing terrorism in the twenty-first century. Lynne Rienner Publishers.

Dawson, S. (2015). Anti-terrorist finance rules exact toll on aid to conflict zones. Reuters. https://www.reuters.com/article/us-aid-counterterrorism/anti-terrorist-finance-rules-exact-toll-on-aid-to-conflict-zones-idUSKBN0OR22E20150611

Dearden, L. (2020). Christchurch shooter donated thousands to far-right groups and websites before attack, report shows. *The Independent*. https://www.independent.co.uk/news/world/australasia/brenton-tarrant-christchurch-donations-generation-identity-b1768056.html

Dion-Schwarz, C., Manheim, D., & Johnston, P. B. (2019). Terrorists use of cryptocurrencies: Technical and organizational barriers and future threats. RAND Corporation. https://www.rand.org/pubs/research_reports/RR3026.html

Faoleán, G. Ó. (2023). Armed robberies, kidnappings and counterfeit cash: The many ways the IRA sought to finance itself during the Troubles. *Irish Times*. https://www.irishtimes.com/culture/books/2023/03/11/the-many-ways-the-ira-sought-to-finance-itself-during-the-troubles/

Faridvar, M. (2020). US announces disruption of 3 terror groups' cyber financing campaigns. Voice of America. https://www.voanews.com/a/usa_us-announces-disruption-3-terror-groups-cyber-financing-campaigns/6194388.html

FATF (2008). Terrorist financing. Financial Action Task Force. https://www.fatf-gafi.org/content/dam/fatf-gafi/reports/FATF%20Terrorist%20Financing%20Typologies%20Report.pdf

FATF (2013). Guidance for a risk-based approach to prepaid cards, mobile payments, and internet-based payment services. Financial Action Task Force. https://www.fatf-gafi.org/en/publications/Fatfrecommendations/Rba-npps-2013.html

FATF (2015). Emerging terrorist financing risks. Financial Action Task Force. https://www.fatf-gafi.org/en/publications/Methodsandtrends/Emerging-terrorist-financing-risks.html

FATF (2022). Money laundering and terrorist financing risks arising from migrant smuggling. Financial Action Task Force Report. https://www.fatf-gafi.org/en/publications/Methodsandtrends/Migrant-smuggling.html

FATF (2023a). Black and grey lists. https://www.fatf-gafi.org/en/countries/black-and-grey-lists.html

FATF (2023b). International standards on combating money laundering and the financing of terrorism & proliferation: The FATF Recommendations. https://www.fatf-gafi.org/content/dam/fatf-gafi/recommendations/FATF%20Recommendations%202012.pdf.coredownload.inline.pdf

FinCEN Advisory (2003). Informal value transfer systems. US Department of the Treasury. https://www.fincen.gov/sites/default/files/advisory/advis33.pdf

Frieden, T. (2006). U.S. indicts 50 Colombians it calls "narcoterrorists." CNN. https://www.independent.co.uk/news/world/americas/75m-bounty-on-colombian-rebels-in-us-war-on-drugs-471215.html

Furber, S. (2020). Prepaid cards' dark underbelly hides potential financial sector pain. S&P Global Market Intelligence. https://www.spglobal.com/marketintelligence/en/news-insights/latest-news-headlines/prepaid-cards-dark-underbelly-hides-potential-financial-sector-pain-58131927

Gardella, A. (2003). The fight against the financing of terrorism between judicial and regulatory cooperation. *Studies in International Financial Economic & Technology Law, 6,* 109–148.

Garofano, J., & Dew, A. J. (Eds.). (2013). *Deep currents and rising tides: The Indian Ocean and international security*. Georgetown University Press.

Glass, C. (2018). The unjust prosecution of the holy land foundation five. *The Intercept*. https://theintercept.com/2018/08/05/holy-land-foundation-trial-palestine-israel/

Gross, J. (2010). Talking with terrorists: Terrorist groups and the challenge of legitimization.

Journal of Public & International Affairs, 21, 93–114.

Haner, M. (2017). *The freedom fighter: A terrorist's own story.* Routledge.

Hanley, B. (2004). The politics of Noraid. *Irish Political Studies, 19*(1), 1–17.

Hayden, M. E., & Squire, M. (2021). How cryptocurrency revolutionized the white supremacist movement. Southern Poverty Law Center. https://www.splcenter.org/hatewatch/2021/12/09/how-cryptocurrency-revolutionized-white-supremacist-movement

Hegghammer, T. (2020). Why jihadists loved America in the 1980s. *The Atlantic.* https://www.theatlantic.com/politics/archive/2020/03/jihad-abdallah-azzam-america-osama-bin-laden/607498/

Hett, W. (2008). Digital currencies and the financing of terrorism. *Richmond Journal of Law and Technology. 15*(2), 1–43.

Hicks, C., & Adams, M. (2023). Different types of cryptocurrencies. *Forbes.* https://www.forbes.com/advisor/investing/cryptocurrency/different-types-of-cryptocurrencies/#:~:text=How%20Many%20Cryptocurrencies%20Are%20There,market%20capitalization%20of%20%241.1%20trillion

Horowitz, J. (2003). Briefly noted. *New York Times.* https://www.nytimes.com/2003/06/25/international/briefly-noted.html

Hosenball, M. (2013). New York says breaks cigarette-smuggling ring linked to militants. Reuters. https://www.reuters.com/article/us-crime-cigarettes-mideast/new-york-says-breaks-cigarette-smuggling-ring-linked-to-militants-idUSBRE94F1C320130516

i24 News (2023, April 19). US charges alleged Hezbollah financier with smuggling diamonds, art. *i24 News.* https://www.i24news.tv/en/news/international/1681915209-u-s-charges-alleged-hezbollah-financier-with-smuggling-diamonds-art

IACC (2023). What is counterfeiting/intellectual property (IP) theft? International Anti-counterfeiting Coalition. https://www.iacc.org/resources/about/what-is-counterfeiting

ICE (2023). Human trafficking vs. human smuggling. US Immigration and Customs Enforcement. https://www.ice.gov/sites/default/files/documents/Report/2017/CSReport-13-1.pdf

IMF (2000). Offshore financial centers: IMF background paper. International Monetary Fund. https://www.imf.org/external/np/mae/oshore/2000/eng/back.htm

Irujo, J. M. (2015). Network of 250 Spanish butchers and phone shops funding jihadists in Syria. *El Pais.* https://english.elpais.com/elpais/2015/02/02/inenglish/1422892172_955064.html

Isikoff, M. (2003). Distorted intelligence? Global Policy Forum. https://archive.globalpolicy.org/component/content/article/168-general/37692.html

Javers, E., & Mangan, D. (2022). French company fined $777 million and pleads guilty to paying ISIS as terror group killed Westerners. CNBC. https://www.cnbc.com/2022/10/18/lafarge-cement-to-plead-guilty-pay-more-than-700-million-on-charges-of-bribing-isis-as-terror-group-killed-westerners.html

Johnson, J. M., & Jensen, C. (2010). The financing of terrorism. *Journal of the Institute of Justice and International Studies, 10,* 103–116.

Johnston, D. (2003). Fake goods support terrorism, Interpol official is to testify. *New York Times.* https://www.nytimes.com/2003/07/16/us/threats-responses-money-trail-fake-goods-support-terrorism-interpol-official.html

Jordan, M. (2005). London calculates the cost of attacks. *Washington Post.* https://www.washingtonpost.com/archive/politics/2005/08/16/london-calculates-the-cost-of-attacks/9ac57b91-2cf5-414a-b3f6-cafe7137648e/

Kandell, J. (1974). Exxon subsidiary pays $14.2-million Argentine ransom. *New York Times.* https://www.nytimes.com/1974/03/14/archives/exxon-subsidiary-pays-142-million-argentine-ransom-special-to-the.html

Kinetz, E., & Hinnant, L. (2021a). Far-right cryptocurrency follows ideology across borders. Associated Press. https://apnews.com/article/cryptocurrency-coronavirus-pandemic-technology-business-europe-f7f754fc2c68b0eb0d712239323f26c3

Kinetz, E., & Hinnant, L. (2021b). "White dissidents" raise millions in cryptocurrency.

PBS. https://www.pbs.org/wgbh/frontline/article/far-right-extremists-raise-millions-cryptocurrency-bitcoin/

Kumar, S. A. (2008). Targeting LTTE's global network. International Institute for Counter-Terrorism (ICT). https://ict.org.il/targeting-lttes-global-network/

Laksmi, S. W. (2017). Terrorism financing and the risk of internet-based payment services in Indonesia. *Counter Terrorist Trends and Analyses, 9*(2), 21–25.

Levi, M. (2010). Combating the financing of terrorism: A history and assessment of the control of "threat finance." *British Journal of Criminology, 50*(4), 650–669.

Levitt, M. (2009). Contending with the PKK's narco-terrorism. Washington Institute for Near East Policy. https://www.washingtoninstitute.org/policy-analysis/contending-pkks-narco-terrorism

Levitt, M. A. (2002). The political economy of Middle East terrorism. *Middle East Review of International Affairs, 6*(4), 49–65.

Lewis, P. H. (2002). Guerrillas and generals: The "dirty war" in Argentina. Greenwood Publishing Group.

Little, I. (2019). Businessmen have often fallen foul of kidnap gangs on both sides of Irish border. *Belfast Telegraph.* https://www.belfasttelegraph.co.uk/opinion/news-analysis/ivan-little-businessmen-have-often-fallen-foul-of-kidnap-gangs-on-both-sides-of-irish-border/38512318.html

McCluskey, M. (2014). The United States' "outdated" terror list. Al Jazeera. https://www.aljazeera.com/features/2014/1/26/the-united-states-outdated-terror-list

McCulloch, J., & Carlton, B. (2006). Preempting justice: Suppression of financing of terrorism and the "war on terror." *Current Issues in Criminal Justice, 17*(3), 397–412.

McCulloch, J., & Pickering, S. (2005). Suppressing the financing of terrorism: Proliferating state crime, eroding censure and extending neo-colonialism. *British Journal of Criminology, 45*(4), 470–486.

McCulloch, J., Pickering, S., McQueen, R., Tham, J. C., & Wright-Neville, D. (2004). Suppressing the financing of terrorism. *Current Issues in Criminal Justice, 16*(1), 71–78.

McDonald, H. (2011). IRA veteran Sean Garland escapes extradition to US. *The Guardian.* https://www.theguardian.com/world/2011/dec/21/sean-garland-escapes-extradition-us

Mintz, J. (1998). Bin Laden's finances are moving target. *Washington Post.* https://www.washingtonpost.com/wp-srv/inatl/longterm/eafricabombing/stories/bin-laden082898.htm

Møller, B. (2009). Piracy, maritime terrorism and naval strategy (No. 2009: 02). DIIS Report. https://www.files.ethz.ch/isn/96541/2009-02_%20Piracy_maritime_terrorism_and_naval_strategy.pdf

Moore, J. (2015). Hawala: The ancient banking practice used to finance terror groups. *Newsweek.* https://www.newsweek.com/underground-european-hawala-network-financing-middle-eastern-terror-groups-307984

Morais, H. V. (2002). The war against money laundering, terrorism, and the financing of terrorism. *Lawasia Journal 2002*, 1–30.

Mylroie, L. (1995). The World Trade Center bomb: Who is Ramzi Yousef? And why it matters. *The National Interest, 42*, 3–15.

NBC News (2014). How terrorists tap a black market fueled by stolen antiquities. https://www.nbcnews.com/storyline/iraq-turmoil/how-terrorists-tap-black-market-fueled-stolen-antiquities-n137016?cid=eml_onsite#%247%20billion

New York Times (2014). Al Qaeda guide to kidnapping. *New York Times.* https://www.nytimes.com/interactive/2014/07/30/world/africa/31kidnap-docviewer3.html

NTFRA (2022). National terrorist financing risk assessment. US Department of Treasury. https://home.treasury.gov/system/files/136/2022-National-Terrorist-Financing-Risk-Assessment.pdf

Otis, J. (2018). Colombia is growing record amounts of coca, the key ingredient in cocaine. NPR. https://www.npr.org/2018/10/22/658547337/colombia-is-growing-record-amounts-of-coca-the-key-ingredient-in-cocaine

Pascu, L. (2017). ISIS used PayPal, eBay to get money into the US for terror attacks, FBI says. *Bitdefender.* https://www.bitdefender

.com/blog/hotforsecurity/isis-used-paypal-ebay-to-get-money-into-the-us-for-terror-attacks-fbi-says/

Passas, N. (2003). Informal value transfer systems, terrorism and money laundering. Report to the National Institute of Justice. Northeastern University.

Phillips, K. (2020). Feds seize millions of dollars in cryptocurrency raised by major terrorist groups, DOJ says. *USA Today.* https://www.usatoday.com/story/news/politics/2020/08/13/doj-cryptocurrency-seized-terrorist-financing-investigation/3363048001/

Pieth, M. (2002). Financing of terrorism: Following the money. *European Journal of Law Reform 4*(2), 365–376.

Raphaeli, N. (2003). Financing of terrorism: Sources, methods, and channels. *Terrorism and Political Violence, 15*(4), 59–82.

Ratha, D. (2023). Remittances: Funds for the folks back home. International Monetary Fund. https://www.imf.org/en/Publications/fandd/issues/Series/Back-to-Basics/Remittances

Ravndal, J. A. (2012). A post-trial profile of Anders Behring Breivik. *CTC Sentinel.* https://ctc.westpoint.edu/a-post-trial-profile-of-anders-behring-breivik/

Reuters (1993). Basque group frees captive. *New York Times.* https://www.nytimes.com/1993/10/30/world/basque-group-frees-captive.html

Reuters (2017). Colombia and FARC rebels to wage joint fight against coca cultivation. Reuters. https://www.reuters.com/article/uk-colombia-peace-idUKKBN15B29A

Reuters (2020). Factbox: New Zealand court hears how shooter planned deadly attacks. https://www.reuters.com/article/uk-newzealand-shooting-tarrant-planning-idAFKBN25K0GH

Rosand, E. (2003). Security council resolution 1373, the counter-terrorism committee, and the fight against terrorism. *American Journal of International Law, 97*(2), 333–341.

Rose-Greenland, F. (2016). How much money has ISIS made selling antiquities? More than enough to fund its attacks. *Washington Post.* https://www.washingtonpost.com/posteverything/wp/2016/06/03/how-much-money-has-isis-made-selling-antiquities-more-than-enough-to-fund-its-attacks/

Rozsa, A. (2023). What is PayPal and how does it work? *Wise.* https://wise.com/us/blog/what-is-paypal-and-how-does-it-work

Safemedicines (2023). Counterfeit drugs and terrorism: How can counterfeit drugs be useful to terrorists? The Partnership for Safemedicines. https://www.safemedicines.org/counterfeit-drugs-and-terrorism

SATP (2023). Incidents involving the LTTE outside Sri Lanka. South Asia Terrorism Portal. https://www.satp.org/satporgtp/countries/srilanka/database/outsidemajorincidents.htm

Savage, C. (2020). U.S. seizes Bitcoin said to be used to finance terrorist groups. *New York Times.* https://www.nytimes.com/2020/08/13/us/politics/bitcoin-terrorism.html

Schmemann, S. (2002). A nation challenged: Sanctions and fallout; Swedes take up the cause of 3 on U.S. terror list. *New York Times.* https://www.nytimes.com/2002/01/26/world/nation-challenged-sanctions-fallout-swedes-take-up-cause-3-us-terror-list.html

SEC (2022). Updated investor bulletin: Regulation crowdfunding for investors. US Securities and Exchange Commission. https://www.sec.gov/oiea/investor-alerts-bulletins/ib-crowdfunding

Seibt, S. (2015). Paris attacks: An unprecedented investigation. France 24. https://graphics.france24.com/paris-attacks-investigation-terrorism-belgium-bataclan-suspects/

Shabi, R. (2015). Looted in Syria—and sold in London: The British antiques shops dealing in artefacts smuggled by Isis. *The Guardian.* https://www.theguardian.com/world/2015/jul/03/antiquities-looted-by-isis-end-up-in-london-shops

Shapiro, J. N., & Siegel, D. A. (2007). Underfunding in terrorist organizations. *International Studies Quarterly, 51*(2), 405–429.

Sheinis, D. (2012). The links between human trafficking, organized crime, and terrorism. *American Intelligence Journal, 30*(1), 68–77.

Silke, A. (2000). Drink, drugs, and rock 'n' roll: Financing loyalist terrorism in Northern Ireland—Part two. *Studies in Conflict & Terrorism, 23*(2), 107–127.

Taylor, A. (2019). New Zealand suspect allegedly claimed "brief contact" with Norwegian mass murderer Anders Breivik. *Washington Post*. https://www.washingtonpost.com/world/2019/03/15/new-zealand-suspect-allegedly-claimed-brief-contact-with-norwegian-mass-murderer-anders-breivik/

Taylor, M. (2011). Norway gunman claims he had nine-year plan to finance attacks. *The Guardian*. https://www.theguardian.com/world/2011/jul/25/norway-gunman-attack-funding-claim

Teichmann, F. M. J. (2018). Financing terrorism through hawala banking in Switzerland. *Journal of Financial Crime 25*, 287–293

Temple-Raston, D. (2014). How much does a terrorist attack cost? A lot less than you'd think. NPR. https://www.npr.org/sections/parallels/2014/06/25/325240653/how-much-does-a-terrorist-attack-cost-a-lot-less-than-you-think

TE-SAT (2018). European Union terrorism situation and trend report. EUROPOL. https://www.europol.europa.eu/cms/sites/default/files/documents/tesat_2018_1.pdf

Townsend, M. (2007). Petrol station scam funds Tamil Tigers. *The Guardian*. https://www.theguardian.com/money/2007/apr/22/crime.scamsandfraud

UNIFAB (2016). Counterfeiting and terrorism. *UNIFAB*. https://www.unifab.com/wp-content/uploads/2016/06/Rapport-A-Terrorisme-2015_GB_22.pdf

United Nations (2009). International convention for the suppression of the financing of terrorism. UN Special Treaty Event. https://www.unodc.org/documents/treaties/Special/1999%20International%20Convention%20for%20the%20Suppression%20of%20the%20Financing%20of%20Terrorism.pdf

United Nations (2023a). Combating terrorist financing. UN Office on Drugs and Crime. https://www.unodc.org/unodc/en/terrorism/expertise/combating-terrorist-financing.html

United Nations (2023b). International convention for the suppression of the financing of terrorism. Treaty Collection. https://treaties.un.org/Pages/ViewDetails.aspx?src=IND&mtdsg_no=XVIII-11&chapter=18

UNODC (2023). Kidnapping for ransom and terrorism. United Nations Office on Drugs and Crime. https://www.unodc.org/e4j/en/organized-crime/module-16/key-issues/kidnapping-for-ransom-and-terrorism.html

US Congress (2000). International Convention for the Suppression of the Financing of Terrorism adopted by the United Nations General Assembly on December 9, 1999, and signed on behalf of the United States of America on January 10, 2000. https://www.congress.gov/treaty-document/106th-congress/49/document-text#:~:text=The%20Convention%20was%20adopted%20by,in%20the%20financing%20of%20terrorism.

US Department of Justice (2018). Maryland man sentenced to 20 years in prison for providing material support to ISIS and terrorism financing. US Department of Justice. https://www.justice.gov/opa/pr/maryland-man-sentenced-20-years-prison-providing-material-support-isis-and-terrorism#:~:text=Mohamed%20Elshinawy%2C%2032%2C%20of%20Edgewood,and%20attempting%20to%20provide%20material

US Department of State (2023a). Executive order 13224. https://www.state.gov/executive-order-13224/

US Department of State (2023b). State sponsors of terrorism. https://www.state.gov/state-sponsors-of-terrorism/

US Department of Treasury (2004). Testimony of R. Richard Newcomb, Director Office of Foreign Assets Control. US Department of the Treasury Before the House Financial Services Subcommittee on Oversight and Investigations. https://home.treasury.gov/news/press-releases/js1729

US House of Representatives (2015). Poaching and terrorism: A national security challenge. US House of Representatives Subcommittee on Terrorism, Nonproliferation, and Trade. https://www.govinfo.gov/content/pkg/CHRG-114hhrg94308/html/CHRG-114hhrg94308.htm

US House of Representatives (2021). Terrorism and digital financing: How technology is changing the threat. US House of Representatives Committee on Homeland Security.

https://www.congress.gov/event/117th-congress/house-event/LC67196/text?s=1&r=94

US Senate (2003). Narco-terrorism: International drug trafficking and terrorism—a dangerous mix. US Senate Hearing before the Committee on the Judiciary. https://www.govinfo.gov/content/pkg/CHRG-108shrg90052/html/CHRG-108shrg90052.htm

Vision of Humanity (2023). Preventing terrorist financing: Are regulations enough? https://www.visionofhumanity.org/combating-the-financing-terrorism/

Warrick, J. (2018). Retreating ISIS army smuggled a fortune in cash and gold out of Iraq and Syria. *Washington Post*. https://www.washingtonpost.com/world/national-security/retreating-isis-army-smuggled-a-fortune-in-cash-and-gold-out-of-iraq-and-syria/2018/12/21/95087ffc-054b-11e9-9122-82e98f91ee6f_story.html

Weizer, B. (2010). Charges of getting cash to failed times sq. bomber. *New York Times*.

https://www.nytimes.com/2010/09/16/nyregion/16shahzad.html?_r=2&

Whittaker, J. (2022). How do terrorists use financial technologies? ICCT. https://www.icct.nl/publication/how-do-terrorists-use-financial-technologies

Wolf, B. (2019). "El Chapo" renews U.S. law enforcement concerns about money laundering via prepaid cards. Reuters. https://www.reuters.com/article/bc-finreg-money-laundering/el-chapo-renews-u-s-law-enforcement-concerns-about-money-laundering-via-prepaid-cards-idUSKCN1QN218

Wornship, P. (2009). U.N. council streamlines terror sanctions delisting. Reuters. https://www.reuters.com/article/us-un-sanctions-idUSTRE5BG57120091217

Zagaris, B. (2002). The merging of the counter-terrorism and anti-money laundering regimes. *Law and Policy in International Business*, 34, 45–107.

Combating Terrorism and Political Violence

CHAPTER 12

Countering Terrorism

Considerations for Shaping Effective Security Strategies

Learning Objectives

1. To investigate the major challenges associated with counterterrorism efforts.
2. To examine role of deterrence-based logic in counterterrorism in terms of policy formation and public support.
3. To delineate the variety of counterterrorism options as well as their advantages and disadvantages.
4. To consider the importance of empirical evaluations of counterterrorism programs.
5. To assess the recommendations of counterterrorism experts and the United Nations in developing comprehensive counterterrorism policies.

12.1   INTRODUCTION

Previous chapters have discussed the complexity of terrorism, from variations in the radicalization process to diverse terrorist motives and the social and political contexts in which they develop. Governments and scholars struggle to agree upon a clear definition of terrorism itself. For these reasons, among others, combatting terrorism is a multifaceted undertaking.

Understandably the public is concerned about terrorism, particularly following a major attack in their nation, and generally wants the government to take measures to fight it. Despite the fact that terrorist attacks are a relatively rare occurrence in nonconflict areas, such as the United States, Americans consider fighting terrorism to be a top national security concern (Crenshaw & LaFree 2017). As recently as February 2023, a Pew Research Center poll found that 60 percent of Americans said that defending against terrorism should be a top priority for the president and Congress to address that year (Pew 2023). Similarly, a nationwide survey of American adults conducted in 2019 revealed that while about 26 percent of participants felt that the government is doing all it can to stop terrorist attacks, 60 percent said that the government could do more, and just 14 percent said that the government has done too much.

In terms of counterterrorism strategies, a majority of respondents agreed or strongly agreed with the following statements:

1. Strict border control policies are necessary to protect us from threats such as Islamic extremism and terrorism.
2. As a means of preventing terrorist attacks in the US, certain groups, including those who are US citizens, should undergo special, more intensive security checks before boarding airplanes in the US.
3. I am willing to accept further security screening and longer lines at the airport if it decreases the likelihood of a terrorist attack.
4. As a means of preventing terrorist attacks in the US, every person going into an office building or public place should be required to go through a metal detector.
5. As a means of preventing terrorist attacks in the US, mass transit systems like subways, buses, and trains should be required to institute security systems similar to what is found in airports (Haner et al. 2018).

TABLE 12.1   Agreement with Counterterrorism Measures: Percentages from a Nationwide Survey of American Adults

	General Agreement	Strongly Agree	Agree	Disagree	Strongly Disagree
Strict border control policies are necessary to protect us from threats such as Islamic extremism and terrorism.	60.6	29.7	30.5	22.8	17.0
As a means of preventing terrorist attacks in the US, certain groups, including those who are US citizens, should undergo special, more intensive security checks before boarding airplanes in the US.	57.0	19.6	37.4	24.6	18.3
I am willing to accept further security screening and longer lines at the airport if it decreases the likelihood of a terrorist attack.	72.2	27.1	45.1	16.7	11.1
As a means of preventing terrorist attacks in the US, every person going into an office building or public place should be required to go through a metal detector.	60.6	21.7	38.9	29.0	10.4
As a means of preventing terrorist attacks in the US, mass transit systems like subways, buses, and trains should be required to institute security systems similar to what is found in airports.	67.2	19.2	43.5	25.4	11.9

Source: Haner et al. (2018).

As the endorsement of these counterterrorism measures suggest, Americans show a tendency to be concerned about Islamist terrorism in particular, and threats from outside of the United States, and express a willingness to be inconvenienced if it means protecting the nation from terrorists. As discussed in Chapter 10, many scholars and government officials point to the terrorist attacks of 9/11 as responsible for this tendency. The 9/11 attacks have been described as a "black swan" event that was unimaginable and fundamentally changed perceptions of vulnerability to terrorism (Dugan & Fisher 2023). Following these unprecedented attacks, governments worldwide intensified their focus on counterterrorism (Crenshaw & LaFree 2017). New federal units and task forces were created, and numerous security measures were implemented in response to the attacks, and in many cases a concerned public supported these efforts.

This chapter will cover approaches to anti-terrorism and counterterrorism, along with their successes and challenges. Whereas **anti-terrorism** refers to measures that aim to prevent terrorist attacks from happening in the first place (e.g., security screening, efforts to

FIGURE 12.1 The terrorist attacks of September 11, 2001, had a profound and lasting impact on various aspects of society, including the perception of Muslims and Islam. These attacks played a significant role in fueling anti-Muslim rhetoric and sentiments in the United States and in some other parts of the world. Since the perpetrators were associated with al-Qaeda, a radical Islamist group, there was a tendency to associate Islam and Muslims with terrorism. *Source:* Anti-Fascistische Fotografie Actie (AFFA), public domain, via Wikimedia Commons.

prevent radicalization), **counter-terrorism** refers to responses to existing terrorist threats or attacks (e.g., implementing laws and freezing assets, military responses). In practice, these terms are often used interchangeably, with counterterrorism being the most commonly used term to describe efforts to address terrorism. Counterterrorism encompasses a range of interventions including, but not limited to (Lum et al. 2006):

- airport screening
- anti-terrorism home products
- arrest
- assassination
- bilateral agreements
- blast-resistant luggage
- buildings security
- closed-circuit television (CCTV)
- community and NGO efforts
- diplomatic efforts
- educational programs
- emergency preparedness
- foreign aid
- fortification of embassies
- gas masks distribution
- harsher punishment
- hostage negotiation
- imprisonment
- investigation strategies
- legislation (e.g., USA PATRIOT Act)

- medical antidotes
- media efforts/spinning
- metal detectors
- military interventions
- multilateral agreements
- psychological counseling
- punishment and sentencing
- religious interventions

- seal/tamper-proof devices
- situational crime prevention
- UN conventions
- UN resolutions
- vaccinations
- war
- weapons detection devices

Counterterrorism interventions may be employed at home or abroad, and their use depends on several factors including definitions and understandings of terrorism and terrorists, experiences with terrorism and attacks, perceived vulnerability, available resources, politics, and public opinion. We consider these factors and current research on counterterrorism in the sections that follow.

12.2 DETERRING TERRORISM: THE WAR ON TERROR

We begin our discussion of counterterrorism with the concept of deterrence. **Deterrence theory** is one of the oldest and most widely used criminological theories for explaining why people commit crimes and offering solutions to crime. Developed by Italian philosopher Cesare Beccaria in 1764, the theory posits that crime may be deterred with punishments that are certain, swift, and severe. This theory assumes that people are rational actors that weigh the potential costs and benefits of their actions. When perceived costs of engaging in criminal behavior outweigh the anticipated benefits, rational actors will refrain from committing the crime.

Deterrence may be specific or general. **Specific deterrence** refers to the prediction that individuals who do engage in crime will be deterred from committing future crimes due to the punishment that they experienced. **General deterrence** occurs when the general public is deterred from engaging in crime because they are aware of the punishments faced by those who do. Applied to the case of terrorism,

FIGURE 12.2 Cesare Beccaria, an Italian philosopher and criminologist, is renowned for his groundbreaking work in the field of criminal justice, particularly his essay titled "On Crimes and Punishments" (*Dei delitti e delle pene* in Italian). Published in 1764, Beccaria's essay laid the foundation for modern criminal law and significantly influenced the development of justice systems worldwide. Beccaria proposed that the primary purpose of punishment should be to deter individuals from committing crimes. He believed that punishments should be swift, certain, and severe enough to dissuade potential offenders. Beccaria's ideas laid the groundwork for the modern concept of deterrence in criminal justice. *Source:* Sailko, CC BY 3.0, via Wikimedia Commons.

it follows that terrorists may refrain from attacks if their perceived costs, relative to potential rewards, are substantial. Deterrence can take the form of punishment, including military occupation, increased policing, and drone strikes, that would decrease the appeal of terrorism to actors. It can also include measures that seek to deny terrorists anticipated benefits of an attack, including increased security measures (e.g., airport screening, protection of critical infrastructure) that signal to terrorists that an attempted attack would be futile (Moore & Jackson 2021). In practice, deterrence theory reasoning encourages an aggressive and commanding response to terrorism.

The **Global War on Terror** initiated by the United States following the terrorist attacks of 9/11 is an example of policy following the principles of deterrence. As noted, the attacks were so unprecedented that they fundamentally changed how people viewed their own vulnerability to terrorism. Populations worldwide called for swift, certain, and severe measures to be taken. Since 9/11, the counterterrorism strategies of numerous countries worldwide have followed deterrence-based logic. Based on the heightened perceived vulnerability to international terrorism that resulted from the attacks, the security focus was on potential threats from abroad. The United States and many other countries initially responded by doing everything they could to prevent another 9/11-type attack (Crenshaw & LaFree 2017). The US responded quickly and authoritatively with military responses in Afghanistan and Iraq, enhanced security and intelligence operations, coordinated global counterterrorism programs with international partners, and by establishing the **Department of Homeland Security (DHS)**.

Less than two weeks following the 9/11 attacks, Governor Tom Ridge of Pennsylvania was appointed as the first Director of the Office of Homeland Security. In November of 2022 the US Congress passed the Homeland Security Act, which founded the DHS as a stand-alone executive department that combined (in full or in part) 22 different federal departments and agencies, in an attempt to unify national security efforts (DHS 2023b). These departments are listed in Table 12.2. The six stated missions of the DHS are to:

- counter terrorism and homeland security threats
- secure US borders and approaches

FIGURE 12.3 The US response to the terrorist attacks of September 11, 2001, was swift and multifaceted. It included immediate military actions in Afghanistan and Iraq, the implementation of enhanced security and intelligence operations, the launch of global counterterrorism programs, the formation of the Department of Homeland Security (DHS) and the Transportation Security Administration (TSA), an increased focus on border security, and efforts to raise public awareness and preparedness regarding future potential terrorist attacks. *Source:* Photo by Chief Photographer's Mate Eric J. Tilford, public domain, via Wikimedia Commons.

TABLE 12.2 Department of Homeland Security Operational and Support Components

Component	Purpose
U. S. Citizen and Immigration Services (USCIS)	USCIS is the federal agency that oversees lawful immigration to the United States.
United States Coast Guard (USCG)	USCG is the only military organization within DHS and protects the maritime economy and the environment, defends our maritime borders, and saves those at risk.
United States Customs and Border Protection (CBP)	CBP's priority mission is to keep terrorists and their weapons out of the US. CBP also secures and facilitates trade and travel while enforcing regulations, including immigration and drug laws.
Cybersecurity and Infrastructure Security Agency (CISA)	CISA leads the national effort to understand, manage, and reduce risk to our cyber and physical infrastructure.
Federal Emergency Management Agency (FEMA)	FEMA supports our citizens and first responders to build, sustain, and improve our capability to prepare for, protect against, respond to, recover from, and mitigate all hazards.
Federal Law Enforcement Training Center (FLETC)	FLETC provides career-long training to law enforcement professionals to help them fulfill their responsibilities safely and proficiently.
United States Immigration and Customs Enforcement (ICE)	ICE promotes homeland security and public safety through the criminal and civil enforcement of federal laws governing border control, customs, trade, and immigration.
United States Secret Service (USSS)	USSS safeguards the nation's financial infrastructure and payment systems to preserve the integrity of the economy, and protects national leaders, visiting heads of state and government, designated sites, and National Special Security Events.
Transportation Security Administration (TSA)	TSA protects the nation's transportation systems to ensure freedom of movement for people and commerce.
Management Directorate	The Management Directorate is responsible for budget, appropriations, expenditure of funds, accounting and finance; procurement; human resources and personnel; information technology systems; facilities, property, equipment, and other material resources; providing biometric identification services; and identification and tracking of performance measurements relating to the responsibilities of the Department.
Science and Technology Directorate (S&T)	S&T is the primary research and development arm of the Department. It provides federal, state and local officials with the technology and capabilities to protect the homeland.
Countering Weapons of Mass Destruction Office (CWMD)	CWMD works to prevent attacks against the United States using a weapon of mass destruction (WMD) through timely, responsive support to operational partners.
Office of Intelligence and Analysis	The Office of Intelligence and Analysis helps the Homeland Security Enterprise with the timely intelligence and information it needs to keep the homeland safe, secure, and resilient.
Office of Homeland Security Situational Awareness (OSA)	OSA provides operations coordination, information sharing, situational awareness, common operating picture, and executes the Secretary's responsibilities across the homeland security enterprise.
Ombudsman Offices	An ombudsman analyzes, reports on, and raises complaints, concerns, and recommendations to the appropriate agency for resolution. This work is done with a commitment to neutrality, independence, and confidentiality. The ombudsman offices are separate and distinct from the agencies they oversee.

Source: Department of Homeland Security (2023b).

- secure cyberspace and critical infrastructure
- preserve and uphold the nation's prosperity and economic security
- strengthen preparedness and resilience
- champion the DHS workforce and strengthen the department

On October 26, 2001, President George W. Bush signed into law the **USA PATRIOT Act** (Uniting and Strengthening America by Providing Appropriate Tools Required to Intercept and Obstruct Terrorism). The PATRIOT Act relaxed existing privacy laws to increase the intelligence gathering capabilities of the government and facilitate information sharing between law enforcement and intelligence personnel that may detect and disrupt terrorist plots (DOJ 2023). The act permitted the monitoring of electronic communications and telephone records, and expanded access to personal records and the ability to engage in other surveillance techniques, without requiring probable cause (evidence to suggest that a crime was or will be committed). Amidst criticisms that the act violated the fourth amendment of the US Constitution (requiring a warrant and probable cause for searches) in collecting information from Americans who were not under criminal investigation (discussed in Chapter 13), the act was renewed in 2006 (the USA PATRIOT Act Improvement and Reauthorization Act of 2005), 2009, and 2011, with added civil liberties safeguards. In 2015, President Obama signed into law the USA FREEDOM Act (Uniting and Strengthening America by Fulfilling Rights and Ensuring Effective Discipline Over Monitoring), which replaced the PATRIOT Act. The FREEDOM Act extended many of the provisions of the PATRIOT Act while incorporating additional civil liberties protections including prohibiting the bulk collection of telephone metadata (in which the government obtains call data from all customers of a major service provider) and enabling technology companies to inform customers of records requests.

Together, these counterterrorism efforts illustrate deterrence theory logic, having been swift (initiated almost immediately following the attacks of 9/11), certain (increasing the likelihood of being caught and punished via the mobilization of military forces and extensive surveillance techniques), and severe (with consequences of war, death, and life imprisonment). At the time, the American public desired an authoritative response to the horrific and unprecedented attacks.

The application of deterrence theory-based logic to the issue of terrorism has been subject to multiple critiques. Importantly, while deterrence theory has been widely used to understand criminal behavior, terrorists differ from "typical" criminals. Terrorist attacks are designed to achieve political or social objectives and communicate to a larger audience. While research indicates that terrorists are rational decision-makers (in terms of their targets and tactics), terrorists' motivations vary widely and they may receive benefits from their actions, despite the consequences (e.g., communication of their goals, popular support). Terrorists' risk to benefit calculation may be difficult to comprehend and requires an understanding of what it is that terrorist groups value (Crenshaw & LaFree 2017). In addition, terrorists are rarely unitary actors. Terrorist groups are often led by a small number of top-ranking members, and group dynamics can affect decision-making processes. Terrorists' preferences have also been shown to change over time. It is challenging to craft a coherent approach to combat all terrorism (Moore & Jackson 2021). As criminologists Daren Fisher and Laura Dugan argue, the deterrence approach of the United States based on the perception that terrorists are foreign (international) and Muslim has had a number of consequences for Americans, including discrimination and increased hate crimes against American citizens and the diversion of attention away from the treat of domestic terrorism (Dugan & Fisher 2023).

Recognizing that a multifaceted approach is necessary to combat terrorism, the United States and other nations also employ a number of other counterterrorism methods. Many of these strategies can be broadly categorized as terrorism prevention programs. We describe different counterterrorism interventions in the following section.

12.2.1 Situational Crime Prevention

As with deterrence, **situational crime prevention (SCP)** originated in the field of criminal

FIGURE 12.4 President George W. Bush signs the USA PATRIOT Act, anti-terrorism legislation, October 26, 2001, in the East Room of the White House. The USA PATRIOT Act was a significant and controversial response to the 9/11 terrorist attacks, aimed at enhancing the government's surveillance and law enforcement powers to combat terrorism. The act significantly expanded the government's authority to combat terrorism but also generated debates about the balance between security and civil liberties. *Source:* Records of the White House Photo Office (George W. Bush Administration), 1/20/2001–1/20/2009, public domain, via Wikimedia Commons.

justice and has more recently been applied to terrorism. The approach recognizes that criminals take advantage of opportunities in given situations to commit crime. To reduce crime, the SCP approach changes the environment to increase the effort needed and risks associated with committing crime. Rather than focusing on the criminal's motives and root causes of crime, SCP addresses the opportunities to commit crime. An SCP approach to terrorism posits that four pillars create the opportunity structure of terrorism: (1) targets, (2) weapons, (3) tools, and (4) facilitating conditions (Clarke & Newman 2006). Criminologists Ronald Clarke and Graeme Newman developed a series of acronyms to aid in the identification of factors that facilitate or impede the planning and execution of a terrorist attack.

The acronym EVIL DONE indicates the most vulnerable targets are those that are exposed, vital, iconic, legitimate, destructible, occupied, near, and easy. The idea is that terrorists target sites or persons that are visible, important, feasibly destroyable and within reach. The acronym MURDEROUS refers to terrorists' selection of weapons and suggests that terrorists prefer those that are multipurpose (can be used in a variety of situations), undetectable (can be easily hidden), removable (easily carried), destructive, enjoyable (fun to use), reliable, obtainable, uncomplicated (are easy to use), and safe (minimize danger to the terrorist user). While no acronym was developed for the third pillar, tools, this pillar encompasses the resources terrorists use to carry out an attack including money, identification, transportation, and SCP interventions seek to deny terrorists access to these tools. ESEER is used to indicate the conditions that facilitate attacks.

Attacks are more likely when conditions are easy (e.g., a government is corrupt already), safe (e.g., a state has lenient identification requirements), excusable (e.g., government overreactions can advantage terrorists), enticing (e.g., the terrorists have community support), and rewarding (e.g., there is potential for financial or religious rewards). In each case, terrorists take advantage of targets, weapons, tools, and conditions that will increase the success of an attack. SCP recognizes this tendency and uses this theoretical framework to protect desirable targets—called **target hardening**—and limit access to weapons and opportunities favorable to attacks. The approach does not aim to eliminate terrorists, but instead seeks to prevent terrorist attacks by eliminating terrorists' opportunities for acts of violence (Clarke & Newman 2006; Freilich et al. 2019; LaFree & Freilich 2019).

The installation of enhanced security screening devices at airports is a popular example of the SCP approach. Terrorists cannot commit skyjackings if they are unable to get weapons onto the planes. However, while the SCP approach has been successful in addressing crime in general, additional research is needed on its applicability to the case of terrorism.

12.2.2 Terrorism Prevention and Deradicalization Programs

Whereas many deterrence-focused approaches to counterterrorism rely on **hard power**, or the use of coercion to achieve a desired outcome (e.g., military responses, economic sanctions), other terrorism prevention strategies utilize **soft power**, obtaining the desired outcomes through persuasion (e.g., countering radical ideologies, strengthening community relationships, and civic engagement). Much of the research on soft power terrorism prevention strategies comes from the field of public health. Following a medical model, prevention strategies can be categorized into three levels based on the delivery of the intervention and the target population. At the broadest level is **universal prevention**, which targets the entire population in an effort to strengthen public resilience. Next is **selective prevention**, which focuses on a subpopulation thought to be vulnerable or particularly at risk (e.g., of radicalization). Finally, **indicated prevention** involves screening processes for people who are already showing signs of the problem (e.g., extremist behaviors) (Schmid 2020a).

FIGURE 12.5 Airport security enhancements are a clear illustration of how the SCP approach seeks to prevent terrorists from gaining access to weapons or dangerous materials on airplanes. Enhanced security screening devices at airports include metal detectors, X-ray scanners for carry-on baggage, body scanners, explosive trace detection systems, and other advanced technologies. These devices are designed to detect prohibited items, including weapons and explosives, that passengers may attempt to bring onto aircraft. *Source:* Kitt Hodsden http://ki.tt, public domain, via Wikimedia Commons.

Terrorism prevention efforts are often described as **countering violent extremism (CVE)** programs, particularly those that aim for selective prevention and indicated prevention. Recognizing that extremism is not itself terrorism but often precipitates terrorism, CVE programs seek to prevent individuals from radicalizing to commit acts of violence. With the goals of eliminating the threat of terrorism, discouraging radicalization and the mobilization of terrorist groups and thwarting attacks, these strategies can be classified by their objectives and the point at which they are designed to intervene. As identified by the National Consortium for the Study of Terrorism and Responses to Terrorism (START), CVE programs include:

1. **Prevention programs**, or programs that "seek to prevent the radicalization process from taking hold in the first place and generally target a segment of society rather than a specific individual" (Vidino & Brandon 2012, 9);
2. **Disengagement programs**, which attempt to convince an individual to abandon involvement in a terrorist group; and
3. **Deradicalization programs**, which attempt to alter the extremist beliefs that an individual holds.

Prevention programs target individuals who may be at risk of radicalization to terrorism. In the United Kingdom, the Muslim Council of Wales delivered a CVE program called Prevent. The program targeted Imams and mosque committee members, Muslim women, and young Muslims and included meetings with local police and officials, radio discussions, training sessions on citizenship, civic engagement and British Muslim identity, and monthly sporting events. The goals of the program were to challenge extremist ideologies and support mainstream voices, disrupt individuals who promote violence, support individuals vulnerable to recruitment by terrorist groups, and address grievances (Sheikh et al. 2012).

In contrast, disengagement and deradicalization programs work with individuals who are already expressing radical beliefs or are involved in terrorist activity. Recall from Chapter 4 that deradicalization involves changing attitudes or ideologies that support terrorism and disengagement occurs when one refrains from engaging in terrorist actions. These programs are designed to change extremist attitudes and modify violent behavior with the goal of getting individuals to give up terrorism. A number of countries have such programs for persons who have been arrested or imprisoned for terrorism including Austria, Belgium, Germany, Great

FIGURE 12.6   The White House Summit on Countering Violent Extremism (CVE) was a high-profile event convened by the US government to address the challenges posed by violent extremism and radicalization, both domestically and internationally. The summit took place in February 2015 and aimed to bring together various stakeholders, including government officials, community leaders, civil society organizations, and experts to develop strategies and partnerships for countering extremism.

Britain, Indonesia, Iraq, Morocco, the Netherlands, Pakistan, Saudi Arabia, Singapore, Sri Lanka, Turkey, and Yemen (LaFree & Frelilich 2019: 393). In Sri Lanka, a program for detained former members of the Liberation Tigers of Tamil Eelam (LTTE) includes seven different programs: educational, vocational, psychological, spiritual, recreational, cultural and family, and community (Webber et al. 2018, 6). The program's goals include psychologically empowering the detainees and equipping them with the skills necessary to reintegrate into mainstream society.

Although the prevention of future acts of terrorism is an ultimate goal, CVE programs have been critiqued for a number of reasons. With the goals of selective prevention and indicated prevention, many programs, including those in Australia, Europe, Africa, and North America, have focused their efforts on Muslim communities. Following the post-9/11 perception that Muslims are at risk for radicalization, these programs seek to strengthen and build resilience in Muslim communities. However, an unintended consequence of these programs is that Muslim communities often feel stigmatized by the increased attention placed on them. Reports also indicate that some CVE programs have been used as an opportunity to gather intelligence and surveil Muslim neighborhoods (Mastroe & Szmania 2016). Further, due in part to issues cited in this text that complicate understandings of terrorism—variability in definitions of terrorism, terrorists' motivations, and pathways to radicalization—there is extremely limited evidence demonstrating their effectiveness. It is challenging to create a deradicalization program if the process of radicalization itself is not fully understood. There have been very few systematic research studies of CVE programs and counterterrorism initiatives in general, a topic that we discuss going forward (Crenshaw & LaFree 2017; Mastroe & Szmania 2016; Schmid 2020a).

12.2.3 The Effectiveness of Counterterrorism Initiatives
In their article "Counter-Terrorism Studies: A Glimpse at the Current State of Research (2020/2021)," distinguished fellow at the International Centre for Counter-Terrorism Alex Schmid and his colleagues note, "while much ink has been spilled on defining terrorism and on developing theories about terrorism, the same is not true for counterterrorism. Counterterrorism, as a reactive phenomenon, it would seem, is not in need of much explanation. As a consequence, counterterrorism is, in the words of Daniel Byman, professor in Georgetown University's School of Foreign Service, 'under-theorized and under-researched'" (Schmid et al. 2021, 155). A major reason for the lack of research on counterterrorism programs is that governments are (understandably) secretive about their strategies (Crenshaw & LaFree 2017). There is little available data on counterterrorism programs, and very few counterterrorism interventions have been studied by academic researchers.

The most comprehensive study of counterterrorism programs was conducted through the Campbell Collaboration, a nonprofit organization that encourages evidence-based policy formation by synthesizing data from academic research, by criminologist Cynthia Lum and colleagues. The researchers completed an extensive examination of published **program evaluations**—systematic studies that examine the effectiveness of programs. A key finding from the study was that there is an overall lack of evaluations of counterterrorism interventions. After an exhaustive search of all research that made reference to an evaluation of a program designed to prevent, detect, manage, and respond to terrorism events and an examination of over 20,000 reports, the researchers found only seven studies that were conducted with a "moderately rigorous" research design, which could be considered valid counterterrorism program evaluations (Lum et al. 2006).

Within the counterterrorism evaluation research that Lum and colleagues identified, five specific counterterrorism interventions were examined: metal detectors and security screening, military retaliations, United Nations resolutions against terrorism, fortifying embassies and protecting diplomats, and increasing the severity of punishment for acts of terrorism. Their findings regarding the effectiveness of these measures were

FIGURE 12.7 In 2018, Los Angeles Mayor Eric Garcetti declined a $425,000 federal grant for Countering Violent Extremism (CVE) programs due to significant opposition from civil rights organizations. Opposition to such programs is often rooted in concerns about potential discrimination and stigmatization, particularly when there are perceptions that CVE efforts disproportionately target and vilify specific communities, such as Muslims. *Source:* Neon Tommy, CC BY-SA 2.0, via Wikimedia Commons.

mixed. Overall, placing metal detectors at airports was found to reduce hijacking events; however, the research identified a **substitution effect** in which airplane hijacking was replaced with other types of terrorism (e.g., bombing, armed attacks, and hostage-taking). There is evidence to suggest that enhanced security focused on one type of terrorism may lead terrorists to seek other tactics and targets.

The military interventions examined were the United States' 1986 attack on Libya after it bombed the LaBelle Discotheque in West Berlin and military strikes by Israel on Palestine Liberation Organization (PLO) targets. In these cases, the researchers found that the military interventions actually led to short-term increases in terrorist attacks in the United States, the United Kingdom, and Israel, and found no long-term effects (i.e., no reduction in terrorism). The study found no evidence of effectiveness for fortifying embassies and protecting diplomats (i.e., target hardening) or increasing the severity of punishment for terrorist acts. The only UN resolution that was associated with reductions in terrorism was against skyjackings. Altogether, this extensive search for rigorous empirical evaluations of counterterrorism interventions uncovered little (if any) evidence of their effectiveness and identified some harmful consequences.

The major concern with the absence of research on counterterrorism is that policymakers lack evidence that the counterterrorism efforts they put in place are effective, particularly relative to the costs of their implementation. Military intervention carries the often-extensive costs of human life, social disruption, destruction, and the potential alienation or even radicalization of local populations. Enhanced security and intelligence gathering capabilities can infringe upon civil liberties, and as noted previously, CVE programs have resulted in increased prejudice and discrimination of targeted groups. We consider these issues in greater detail in Chapter 13.

Naturally, all counterterrorism efforts have financial costs. A 2018 report by the nonprofit, nonpartisan think tank, the Stimson Center, estimated that the United States spent a total of $2.8 trillion on counterterrorism-related initiatives between 2002 and 2017, including government-wide homeland security efforts, international programs, and military efforts (i.e., wars in Afghanistan, Iraq, and Syria). $979 billion (35 percent) of this total went to homeland security spending, supporting efforts related to border and transportation security, defending against catastrophic threats, domestic counterterrorism, emergency preparedness and response, intelligence and warning, and protecting critical infrastructure and key assets. Emergency and overseas contingency operations spending at the Department of Defense accounted for $1.7 trillion (60 percent), war-related spending by the Department of State and the US Agency for International Development (USAID) was $138 billion (5 percent), and spending on other types of counterterrorism-related foreign aid accounted for $11 billion (>.5 percent). Given the tremendous costs of counterterrorism in the United States alone, determining whether these efforts actually prevent or stop terrorism is critical.

12.2.4 Failed and Foiled Plots in the US

An additional data source on counterterrorism efforts comes from research conducted through the National Consortium for the Study of Terrorism and Responses to Terrorism (START) at the University of Maryland. START researchers collected data on 121 jihadist-linked plots to use violence against the United States between January 1993 and February 2016. While the data are limited in that they only cover jihadist-linked terrorism attempts, they provide valuable information about terrorists' intentions and the ways in which their plans were disrupted.

The researchers coded whether each plot was completed, successful, failed, or foiled, according to the following definitions:

- **Completed:** plots in which the actions intended by the perpetrator were carried out to their final stage of implementation, whether or not they had their intended physical impact.
- **Successful:** plots that achieved the kinetic action that was planned, regardless of the outcome in number of deaths, the response to the attack or the long-term consequences.
- **Failed:** plots that were unsuccessful because of something the would-be perpetrators did, a factor internal to the plot—either they made a mechanical mistake or they had a change of intention.
- **Foiled:** plots that were unsuccessful because of some kind of intervention, whether from members of the public, friends or family, or by government authorities; in the United States this is usually FBI or local or state law enforcement, sometimes with the assistance of the intelligence agencies of foreign governments (Crenshaw et al. 2017, 1).

Overall, the researchers found that most perpetrators (75 percent) were American citizens (young men), and about 25 percent of the plots had some link to a known terrorist organization. About one fifth of the plots targeted Washington, DC, or the surrounding area while more than one quarter of the plots targeted New York. Regarding motive, many of the individuals involved in the plots reported "opposition to the American use of military force against Muslims in civil conflicts abroad" (Crenshaw et al. 2017, 3).

Of the 121 plots during this time period, only 15 were successfully completed. An additional 10 plots were partially completed. Eighty-two percent of the jihadist-linked plots in the US were completely or partially foiled, primarily due to government surveillance or police informants and undercover FBI agents who gain insight during the early stages of the plot, a controversial technique considered in Chapter 13. Despite government interventions, 13 plots were foiled due to community tip-offs and in three cases, family members informed authorities. The distribution of types of sources responsible for the foiling of the plots is depicted in Figure 12.8.

While surveillance and **government informants** have played a role in foiling terrorist plots, these findings also highlight the importance of tips from members of the public. Researchers found that bystanders have prevented approximately 10 percent of the more than 5,000 attempted terrorist attacks against transportation systems worldwide since 1970 (Jenkins & Butterworth 2018). As a notable example in the US, in May 2010, two vendors in New York City's Times Square reported an oddly parked car to police, which was found to be loaded with explosives (Friedell 2018). Recognizing the value of information provided by the public, many countries have curated terrorism prevention programs that encourage the public to look out for possible terrorism-related behaviors. Originally implemented by British authorities in response to the Irish Republican Army's bombing attacks against the public transportation systems in England and Northern Ireland (Friedell 2018; Jenkins & Butterworth 2018; Pearce et al. 2020), these programs ask people to call a tip line with information if they observe something suspicious.

The US Department of Homeland Security (DHS) has been implementing the "If You See Something, Say Something" campaign since 2010. The program is advertised

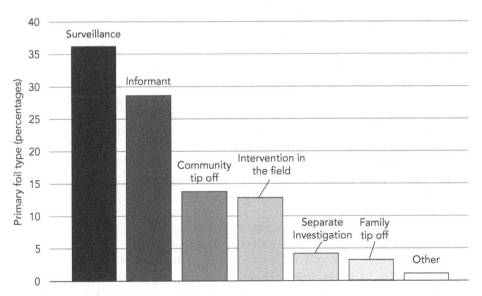

FIGURE 12.8   Primary foil types. *Source:* Crenshaw et al. (2017).

widely at airports and schools, on venue tickets, and public transportation to remind the public to report anything they have seen or heard that could suggest a terrorist threat (DHS 2023a). Noting that "suspicious" behavior can mean different things to different people, the campaign has an educational component to help the public understand what should be considered suspicious. Via presentations, pamphlets, and infographics, it instructs the public, "Whether you are on your way to work, shopping at a store, or traveling on vacation, remember: We all play a role in keeping our communities safe. Remember to stay alert and say something when you see something suspicious."

The following activities should only be reported if they are conducted in a manner that would arouse suspicion of terrorism.

- **Expressed or implied threat:** Communicating a spoken or written threat to commit a crime that could harm or kill people or damage a facility, infrastructure, or secured site.
- **Observation and surveillance:** A prolonged or unusual interest in facilities, buildings, or infrastructure beyond casual or professional interest.
- **Photography:** Taking pictures or videos of persons, facilities, buildings, or infrastructure in a covert manner, such as photos or video of security related equipment or personnel, infrequently used access points, or structure of a building.
- **Theft, loss, and diversion:** Stealing or diverting items—such as equipment, uniforms, or badges—that belong to a facility or secured site.
- **Testing or probing of security:** Challenging or testing a facility's security or IT systems to assess the strength or weakness of the target.
- **Aviation activity:** Operating or interfering with the operation of an aircraft that poses a threat of harm to people and property.
- **Breach or attempted intrusion:** Unauthorized people trying to enter a restricted area or impersonating authorized personnel.
- **Misrepresentation:** Presenting false information or misusing documents to conceal possible illegal activity.
- **Eliciting information:** Questioning personnel beyond mere curiosity about an event, facility, or operations.
- **Acquisition of expertise:** Gaining skills or knowledge on a specific topic, such as facility security, military tactics, or flying an aircraft.
- **Cyberattack:** Disrupting or compromising an organization's information technology systems.
- **Recruiting and financing:** Funding suspicious or criminal activity or recruiting people to participate in criminal or terrorist activity.
- **Sabotage, tampering, and vandalism:** Damaging or destroying part of a facility, infrastructure, or secured site.
- **Materials acquisition and storage:** Acquisition and storage of unusual materials such as cell phones, radio controllers, or toxic materials.
- **Weapons collection and storage:** Collection or discovery of unusual amounts of weapons including explosives, chemicals, or other destructive materials.
- **Sector-specific incident:** Actions that raise concern to specific sectors (e.g., a power plant) with regard to their personnel, facilities, systems, or functions.

Because **public reporting programs** rely on laypersons' understandings and interpretations of suspicious behavior possibility related to terrorism, education about what should and should not be reported is critical. Research has demonstrated that the general public may show biases against certain groups (e.g., Muslims, immigrants) in their judgments of whether an activity is suspicious or not, particularly if they already hold stereotyped perceptions of those groups (Carson & Politte 2021; Haner et al. 2022). As with other counterterrorism strategies, public reporting programs concern individuals who may have behaved suspiciously but have not yet committed a crime. These initiatives also raise concerns about infringing upon civil liberties (Williams et al. 2019)

12.3 THE UNITED NATIONS (UN) PLAN OF ACTION AND RECOMMENDATIONS FROM EXPERTS

It should be clear from the discussion in this chapter that while countries worldwide have expanded their counterterrorism efforts, substantial research is needed to understand the effectiveness of counterterrorism interventions as well as their potential consequences. Scholars observe that states cannot take a "one size fits all" approach to counterterrorism. As with the case of understanding radicalization into terrorism and terrorists' motives, it is essential to consider the context in which terrorism occurs in order to develop a plan to counter it (Crenshaw & LaFree 2017).

Highlighting the need to address the social and political contexts that give rise to terrorism, in addition to other counterterrorism interventions, the United Nations developed a Plan of Action to Prevent Violent Extremism, which was adopted by the UN General Assembly in 2016. The plan "calls for a comprehensive approach encompassing not only essential security-based counterterrorism measures but also systematic preventive steps to address the underlying conditions that drive individuals to radicalize and join violent extremist groups" (UN 2024). Developed through interagency collaboration and "high-level meetings of the UN General Assembly and Security Council, interactive briefings to Member States and outcomes of international and regional meetings," the Plan provides more than 70 recommendations to member states and the UN System. It recommends that each Member State develop its own national plan of action with an emphasis on the following seven priority areas, cited from the UN media brief, available on the UN's official website.

1. **Dialogue and conflict prevention**: In the framework of the broader prevention efforts of the Secretary-General, the recommendations include the need to engage opposing parties and regional actors earlier, and to forge international consensus and engage religious leaders.
2. **Strengthening good governance, human rights, and the rule of law**: In order to strengthen trust between government institutions and communities to prevent marginalization and exclusion, the recommendations include providing access to justice and strengthening fair, effective, accountable, and inclusive institutions; reforming national legal frameworks and penitentiary systems; and fostering basic service provision in a nondiscriminatory manner.
3. **Engaging communities**: For genuine community engagement, the recommendations include developing participatory strategies with civil society and local

FIGURE 12.9 The "See Something, Say Something" campaign is a public awareness initiative that has been recognized and promoted by the US Department of Homeland Security (DHS). The campaign encourages individuals to be vigilant and report any suspicious activity or behavior that they may observe to authorities. It is designed to engage the public in the effort to enhance security and prevent potential threats. The key message of the campaign is that everyone has a role to play in maintaining the safety and security of their communities. *Source:* Department of Homeland Security, public domain, via Wikimedia.

communities, adopting community-oriented policing models, and developing local and family-based mentorship programs.

4. **Empowering youth**: Harnessing the idealism, creativity and energy of young people and others who feel disenfranchised, the recommendations include supporting and enhancing young people's participation in PVE activities and integrating them into decision-making processes at local and national levels.

5. **Gender equality and empowering women**: Fostering women as a critical force for sustainable peace, the recommendations include investing in research on women's roles in violent extremism and ensuring that a portion of funds dedicated to addressing violent extremism are committed to support greater gender equality.

6. **Education, skill development, and employment facilitation**: To foster respect for human diversity and prepare young people to enter the workplace, the recommendations include investing in programs that promote global citizenship and provide comprehensive primary through tertiary education, including technical and vocational education.

7. **Strategic communications, the internet, and social media**: To communicate a vision that offers tangible change to the disillusioned and disenfranchised, recommendations include developing and implementing national communication strategies, and empowering victims to turn their suffering into a constructive force.

The plan is a call for a unified response in combatting terrorism. In his promotion of the plan, then-UN Secretary General Ban Ki-moon wrote:

> Many years of experience have proven that short-sighted policies, failed leadership, heavy-handed approaches, a single-minded focus only on security measures and an utter disregard for human rights have often made things worse. Let us never forget: Terrorist groups are not just seeking to unleash violent action, but to provoke a harsh reaction. We need cool heads and common sense. We must never be ruled by fear— or provoked by those who strive to exploit it (Ki-moon 2016).

Critics of the plan note that it is a recommendation and requires no formal commitment from UN member states. While many member states have attempted to develop national plans according to the UN guidance, other states have been hesitant to do so (Schmid 2020b). Nevertheless, in his edited *Handbook of Terrorism Prevention and Preparedness* (2020), Alex Schmid notes that the UN Plan is largely consistent with recommendations by top terrorism experts. While arguing that if all member states were to implement the recommendations of the Plan, it would significantly reduce violent extremism and terrorism, Schmid contends that "the most important thing to remember when it comes to terrorist strategy from nonstate actors is that the success of terrorists largely depends on the indirect effects caused by the reactions of governments, media, society and other parties to terrorist provocations and acts of revenge" (Schmid 2020b, 1122). Schmid follows with four key lessons learned about counterterrorism:

1. One important cause of nonstate terrorism is a desire to exact revenge for some perceived or real injustice that has not been adequately addressed by the existing political system. It is a greatly underestimated cause of terrorism.

If government actions are within the rule of law, respecting basic human rights and supported by the majority of citizens, there will be fewer people driven to terrorist acts by feelings of revenge. In other words, many acts of retaliatory terrorism by nonstate actors will be prevented. by avoiding acts of revenge (as opposed to rule of law-based law enforcement).

2. Another way of reducing nonstate terrorism relates to those acts of terrorism which are acts of *provocation*. Many terrorists want to produce an overreaction with their atrocities, expecting that the government will target and repress the terrorists' professed constituency as a whole, which is likely to drive new recruits into the arms of the terrorist organization. Governments should avoid falling into the trap of doing what terrorists expect. By not falling into the provocation trap, governments can prevent some further acts of terrorism.

3. A third way to prevent terrorism is to limit the possibilities for terrorists to obtaining free publicity with their public outrages. If half or more of the terrorist struggle is in the media, prevention should shift more strongly *to targeting the communication channels* and the mass and social media terrorists seeks to instrumentalize to reach various audiences. Without publicity for their cause, terrorists cannot hope to get very far. However, to reduce the amount of publicity for acts of terrorism, governments have to work closely with editors of mass media and operators of social media and mobilize public support for applying selective news blackouts. This, too, will prevent some acts of terrorism.

4. A fourth way of reducing terrorism is based on the fact that *terrorism is intimately linked to armed conflict*. Becoming a party to an armed conflict abroad might not always be avoidable for governments but should only be done as a last resort in cases of humanitarian emergencies and then only with a strong mandate from the United Nations. Resistance against foreign interventions allows local terrorists to gain support and leads to radicalization among sectors of the public abroad. Terrorism is intimately linked to conflict not only abroad but also on the domestic front. Preventing polarization in society, protecting minorities against hate crimes while engaging in strengthening social cohesion and resilience and engaging in conflict resolution goes a long way in preventing terrorism at home. (Schmid 2020b)

12.4 CONCLUSION

Following the terrorist attacks of 9/11, several countries worldwide bolstered their counterterrorism efforts following a deterrence-based approach. For many, this unprecedented attack called for a drastic and authoritative response. However, deterrence theory-based logic does not apply neatly to the case of terrorism. Terrorists differ from other criminals in that their motives, values, and the potential rewards they seek may be difficult to comprehend and predict. Drastic measures and harsh policies often have unintended consequences, such as infringement on human rights, increased prejudice and discrimination, alienation of communities, and even increased radicalization into terrorism.

Additional counterterrorism measures include those based on the principles of situational crime prevention and countering violent extremism. These approaches have their consequences, however, and there is an overall lack of evidence regarding the

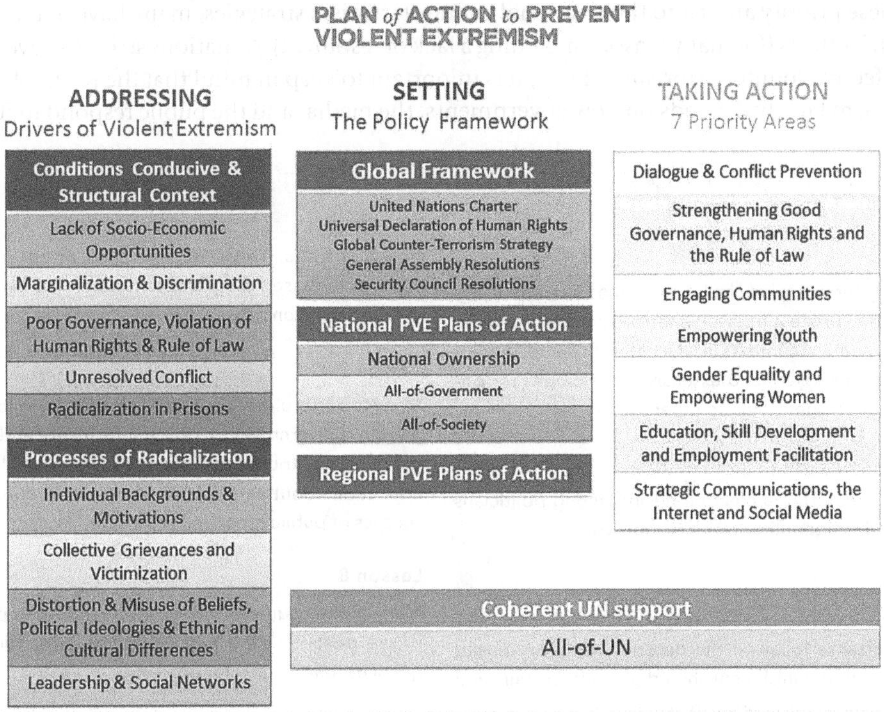

PLAN *of* **ACTION** *to* **PREVENT VIOLENT EXTREMISM**

ADDRESSING	SETTING	TAKING ACTION
Drivers of Violent Extremism	The Policy Framework	7 Priority Areas

Conditions Conducive & Structural Context
Lack of Socio-Economic Opportunities
Marginalization & Discrimination
Poor Governance, Violation of Human Rights & Rule of Law
Unresolved Conflict
Radicalization in Prisons

Processes of Radicalization
Individual Backgrounds & Motivations
Collective Grievances and Victimization
Distortion & Misuse of Beliefs, Political Ideologies & Ethnic and Cultural Differences
Leadership & Social Networks

Global Framework
United Nations Charter Universal Declaration of Human Rights Global Counter-Terrorism Strategy General Assembly Resolutions Security Council Resolutions

National PVE Plans of Action
National Ownership
All-of-Government
All-of-Society

Regional PVE Plans of Action

Dialogue & Conflict Prevention
Strengthening Good Governance, Human Rights and the Rule of Law
Engaging Communities
Empowering Youth
Gender Equality and Empowering Women
Education, Skill Development and Employment Facilitation
Strategic Communications, the Internet and Social Media

Coherent UN support
All-of-UN

FIGURE 12.10   The UN's efforts to prevent violent extremism are guided by a comprehensive framework that emphasizes addressing the underlying factors that contribute to radicalization and extremism. The Plan of Action to Prevent Violent Extremism was formally adopted in December 2015, and it outlines a multifaceted approach to preventing violent extremism at the global, national, and community levels. The plan emphasizes a preventive approach, focusing on addressing the root causes of violent extremism rather than solely responding to its manifestations. It highlights the importance of addressing factors such as social exclusion, marginalization, and grievances that can lead individuals toward extremism. *Source:* UN SG's Plan of Action to Prevent Violent Extremism, Secretary-General's Report, www.un.org/sites/www.un.org.counterterrorism/files/plan_action.pdf.

effectiveness of counterterrorism initiatives. Given the great potential consequences associated with counterterrorism interventions, as well as their financial costs, future empirical research on these efforts is imperative.

Recognizing that a unified and comprehensive approach to counterterrorism that not only includes security-based measures but also strives to address the underlying conditions that give rise to terrorism is needed, the United Nations developed a Plan of Action to Prevent Violent Extremism. The plan, which includes seven priority areas— dialogue and conflict prevention; strengthening good governance, human rights, and the rule of law; engaging communities; empowering youth; gender equality and empowering women; education, skill development, and employment facilitation; and strategic communications, the internet, and social media—is consistent with key recommendations of terrorism experts. While some UN member states have made strides to incorporate these priority areas into their national counterterrorism strategies, many have not made such efforts (for many reasons including a lack of resources). As nations strive to develop effective counterterrorism policies, it is important to keep in mind that the result of terrorism largely depends on how governments, the media, and the public respond to it.

Key Lessons

Lesson 1

Countering terrorism is a challenge due to variations in the radicalization process to diverse terrorist motives and the social and political contexts in which they develop, numerous tactics employed, and extensive possibilities for potential attack targets, among other factors.

Lesson 2

Major terrorist attacks create a desire among politicians and the public for authoritative responses.

Lesson 3

Much of the counterterrorism response following the 9/11 terrorist attacks followed the deterrence theory-based reasoning—that punishment should be swift, certain, and severe to deter future terrorism.

Lesson 4

The US response to the 9/11 attacks included military intervention, increased surveillance, enhanced security measures, and community-based programs, as well as the creation of the Department of Homeland Security.

Lesson 5

Situational crime prevention attempts to change the situational environment to limit the opportunities for terrorist attacks.

Lesson 6

Countering violent extremism programs seek to eliminate the threat of terrorism, discourage radicalization, and thwart attacks. The CVE approach often implements community-based programs to targeted audiences at risk for radicalization.

Lesson 7

Many terrorist plots fail or are foiled before reaching completion. Government or police informants and tips from the public contribute to the foiling of terrorist plots. Public education about actual terrorist threats is critical for the success of public reporting programs.

Lesson 8

Many of the counterterrorism interventions implemented in the post–9/11 era had negative unintended consequences, particularly for Muslims.

Lesson 9

The United Nations developed a Plan of Action to Prevent Violent Extremism, which encourages countries to develop a comprehensive approach to counterterrorism that not only includes security-based measures but also strives to address the underlying conditions that give rise to terrorism.

Lesson 10

In developing counterterrorism policy, it is important to recognize that the success of terrorists often depends on the responses of governments, the media, and the public generated by an attack.

KEY WORDS

anti-terrorism
countering violent extremism (CVE)
counterterrorism
Department of Homeland Security (DHS)
deradicalization programs

deterrence theory
disengagement programs
failed plot
foiled plot
general deterrence
government informants

Global War on Terror
hard power
indicated prevention
prevention programs
program evaluations
public reporting programs
selective prevention
situational crime prevention (SCP)

soft power
specific deterrence
substitution effect
surveillance
target hardening
universal prevention
USA PATRIOT Act

RECOMMENDED SOURCES

Research Articles & Books

Brooks, R. C., Riley Jr, R. A., & Thomas, J. (2005). Detecting and preventing the financing of terrorist activities: A role for government accountants. *The Journal of Government Financial Management, 54*(1), 12.

Carson, J. V., & Politte, H. (2021). Implicit bias within public reporting: A virtual reality experiment examining "suspicious" activity. Crime & Delinquency, 67(12), 2135–2162.

Freilich, J. D., Gruenewald, J., & Mandala, M. (2019). Situational crime prevention and terrorism: An assessment of 10 years of research. *Criminal Justice Policy Review, 30*(9), 1283–1311.

Haner, M., Sloan, M. M., Pickett, J. T., & Cullen, F. T. (2022). When do Americans "See Something, Say Something"? Experimental evidence on the willingness to report terrorist activity. *Justice Quarterly, 39*(5), 1079–1103.

LaFree, G., & Freilich, J. D. (2019). Government policies for counteracting violent extremism. *Annual Review of Criminology, 2,* 383–404.

Lum, C., Kennedy, L. W., & Sherley, A. (2006). Are counter-terrorism strategies effective? The results of the Campbell systematic review on counter-terrorism evaluation research. *Journal of Experimental Criminology, 2,* 489–516.

Moore, B., & Jackson, B. A. (2021). Terrorism and deterrence. In M. Haner & M. M. Sloan (Eds.), *Theories of terrorism: Contemporary perspectives* (pp. 262–283). Routledge.

Schmid, A. P. (2020a). Terrorism prevention: Conceptual issues (definitions, typologies, and theories). In A. P. Schimd (Ed)., *Handbook pf terrorism prevention and preparedness* (pp. 13–48). International Centre for Counter-terrorism.

Schmid, A. P., Forest, J. J., & Lowe, T. (2021). Counter-terrorism studies: A glimpse at the current state of research (2020/2021). *Perspectives on Terrorism, 15*(4), 155–183.

News Articles & Government and Think Tank Reports

Countering terrorism
  Source: North Atlantic Treaty Organization (NATO)
Countering Terrorism
  Source: United Nations
How to stop terrorism: EU measures explained
  Source: European Parliament
Five Things About Community-Based Terrorism Prevention Programs

Author(s):
  Source: National Institute of Justice (NIJ)
'Force alone is not the answer,' says UN counter-terrorism chief
  Source: United Nations
How Terrorism Ends
  Author(s): John B. Alterman
  Source: United States Institute of Peace

Why Protecting Education Would Prevent Terrorism
    Author(s): Moza Bint Nasser
    Source: TIME
What's In A Name? How to Fight Terrorism
    Author(s): Michael Howard
    Source: Foreign Affairs

Prevent: We prevent vulnerable people from being drawn into extremism
    Source: UK Counter Terrorism Policing
End the 'War on Terror'
    Author(s): Kenneth Roth
    Source: Human Rights Watch

Documentaries, Videos, and Other Educational Media

Terrorism and Counterterrorism
    Featuring: Martha Crenshaw
    Source: Stanford Program on International and Cross-Cultural Education (SPICE)
U.S. War Against Terrorism
    Featuring: President George Bush
    Source: C-Span
War on terrorism: Is the military the best way to fight extremism
    Featuring: Phil Gurski
    Source: Global News YouTube Channel
What Is Counterterrorism?
    Featuring: Irfan Saeed
    Source: National Museum of American Diplomacy
Countering Violent Extremism
    Featuring: Todd C. Helmus & Miriam Matthews
    Source: RAND
Counter-Terrorism Tactics Since 9/11
    Featuring: Terry Schappert
    Source: HISTORY YouTube channel
White House Summit on Combating Terrorism, International and Law Enforcement Leaders
    Source: C-Span

Rights & Freedoms While Countering Terrorism: UN Special Rapporteur's Briefing
    Featuring: Fionnuala D. Ní Aoláin
    Source: United Nations YouTube Channel
Richard English on the Effectiveness of Counter-Terrorism
    Featuring: Richard English
    Source: Oxford Academic YouTube Channel
The UK's international counter-terrorism policy
    Source: UK Parliament
Audrey Kurth Cronin: Counterterrorism Won't Work Against ISIS
    Featuring: Audrey Kurth Cronin
    Source: Carnegie Council for Ethics in International Affairs YouTube Channel
How Terrorism Ends: Understanding the Decline and Demise of Terrorist Campaigns
    Featuring: Audrey Kurth Cronin
    Source: George Mason University Television (gmu-tv) YouTube Channel

REFERENCES

Beccaria C. (1764). *On crimes and punishments and other writings.* University of Toronto Press
Carson, J. V., & Politte, H. (2021). Implicit bias within public reporting: A virtual reality experiment examining "suspicious" activity. *Crime & Delinquency, 67*(12), 2135–2162.
Clarke, R. V. G., & Newman, G. R. (2006). *Outsmarting the terrorists.* ABC-CLIO.
Crenshaw, M., Dahl, E., & Wilson, M. (2017). Jihadist plots in the United States. START. https://www.start.umd.edu/publication/jihadist-plots-united-states-interim-findings-infographic
Crenshaw, M. & LaFree, G. (2017). *Countering terrorism.* The Brookings Institution.
Department of Homeland Security. (2023a). If you see something, say something. https://www.dhs.gov/see-something-say-something
Department of Homeland Security (2023b). Operational and support components. https://www.dhs.gov/operational-and-support-components

Department of Justice (2023). Report to congress on implementation of 1001 of the USA PATRIOT Act. https://oig.justice.gov/sites/default/files/reports/23-115.pdf

Dugan, L., & Fisher, D. (2023). Far-right and Jihadi terrorism within the United States: From September 11th to January 6th. *Annual Review of Criminology, 6*, 131–153.

Freilich, J. D., Gruenewald, J., & Mandala, M. (2019). Situational crime prevention and terrorism: An assessment of 10 years of research. *Criminal Justice Policy Review, 30*(9), 1283–1311.

Friedell, D. (2018, December 30). 'See something, say something' seems to work. WTOP News. https://wtop.com/dc-transit/2018/12/see-something-say-something-seems-to-work/

Haner, M., Sloan, M. M., Cullen, F. T., Kulig, T. C., and Jonson, C. L. (2018). Fear of terrorism Survey. YouGov America.

Haner, M., Sloan, M. M., Pickett, J. T., & Cullen, F. T. (2022). When do Americans "see something, say something"? Experimental evidence on the willingness to report terrorist activity. *Justice Quarterly, 39*(5), 1079–1103.

Jenkins, B. M., & Butterworth, B. R. (2018). Does "see something, say something" work? Mineta Transportation Institute Publications. https://scholarworks.sjsu.edu/cgi/viewcontent.cgi?article=1253&context=mti_publication

Ki-Moon, B. (2016). UN Secretary-General's remarks at general assembly presentation of the plan of action to prevent violent extremism. United Nations. https://www.un.org/sg/en/content/sg/statement/2016-01-15/un-secretary-generals-remarks-general-assembly-presentation-of-the-plan-of-action-prevent-violent-extremism-delivered

LaFree, G., & Freilich, J. D. (2019). Government policies for counteracting violent extremism. *Annual Review of Criminology, 2*, 383–404.

Lum, C., Kennedy, L. W., & Sherley, A. (2006). Are counter-terrorism strategies effective? The results of the Campbell systematic review on counter-terrorism evaluation research. *Journal of Experimental Criminology, 2*, 489–516.

Mastroe, C., & Szmania, S. (2016). Surveying CVE metrics in prevention, disengagement and deradicalization programs: Report to the Office of University Programs, Science and Technology Directorate, U.S. Department of Homeland Security. National Consortium for the Study of Terrorism and Responses to Terrorism. https://www.start.umd.edu/pubs/START_SurveyingCVEMetrics_March2016.pdf

Moore, B., & Jackson, B. A. (2021). Terrorism and deterrence. In M. Haner & M. M. Sloan (Eds.), *Theories of terrorism: Contemporary perspectives* (pp. 262–283). Routledge.

Pearce, J. M., Parker, D., Lindekilde, L., Bouhana, N., & Rogers, M. B. (2020). Encouraging public reporting of suspicious behaviour on rail networks. *Policing and Society, 30*(7), 835–853.

Pew Research Center (2023). Strengthening the economy is Americans' top policy priority; dealing with COVID-19 is among the lowest. https://www.pewresearch.org/politics/2023/02/06/economy-remains-the-publics-top-policy-priority-covid-19-concerns-decline-again/pp_2023-02-06_political-priorities_00-01/

Schmid, A. P. (2020a). Conclusions: Terrorism prevention—The UN Plan of Action (2015) and beyond. In A. P. Schimd (Ed)., *Handbook of terrorism prevention and preparedness* (pp. 1103–1155). International Centre for Counter-terrorism.

Schmid, A. P. (2020b). Terrorism prevention: Conceptual issues (definitions, typologies, and theories). In A. P. Schimd (Ed)., *Handbook of terrorism prevention and preparedness* (pp. 13–48). International Centre for Counter-terrorism.

Schmid, A. P., Forest, J. J., & Lowe, T. (2021). Counter-terrorism studies: A glimpse at the current state of research (2020/2021). *Perspectives on Terrorism, 15*(4), 155–183.

Sheikh, S., Sarwar, S., & King, E. (2012). Evaluation of the Muslim Council of Wales' prevent work. Office for Public Management. https://www.gov.wales/sites/default/files/statistics-and-research/2019-08/120719muslimcouncilen.pdf

Stimson Center (2018). Stimson study group on counterterrorism spending: Protecting American while promoting efficiencies and accountability. https://www.stimson.org/

wp-content/files/file-attachments/CT_
Spending_Report_0.pdf

United Nations (2024). Plan of action to prevent violent extremism. https://www.un.org/
sites/www.un.org.counterterrorism/files/
plan_action.pdf

Vidino, L., & Brandon, J. (2012). Countering
radicalization in Europe. *London, International
Centre for the Study of Radicalisation and
Political Violence.* file:///C:/Users/melissasloan/
Downloads/3%20ICSR-Report-Countering-
Radicalization-in-Europe.pdf

Webber, D., Chernikova, M., Kruglanski, A. W.,
Gelfand, M. J., Hettiarachchi, M., Gu-nara-
nta, R., Lafreniere, M., & Belanger, J. J.
(2018). Deradicalizing detained terrorists.
Political Psychology, 39(3), 539–556.

Williams, M. J., Bélanger, J. J., Horgan, J., &
Evans, W. P. (2019). Experimental effects of
a call-center disclaimer regarding confiden-
tiality on callers' willingness to make disclosures related to terrorism. *Terrorism and
Political Violence*, 31(6), 1327–1341.

CHAPTER 13

Ethical Issues in Countering Terrorism

Emerging Technologies and Questionable Practices

Learning Objectives

1. To discuss the methods and practices employed by intelligence and security services in developed countries in the post–9/11 era in efforts to counter terrorism.
2. To consider contemporary technologies utilized in counterterrorism efforts, including the deployment of drones, cyberhacking, and activities falling within the realm of bulk data collection.
3. To examine contentious counterterrorism practices, such as the utilization of enhanced interrogation techniques, sting operations, entrapment operations, and extrajudicial killings.
4. To examine the complexity of ethical issues raised within the domain of counterterrorism.
5. To assess the potential repercussions and unintended consequences of counterterrorism practices adopted in the post–9/11 era.

13.1 INTRODUCTION

Ethics refer to rules of conduct or moral principles arising from a society's culture, customary standards, laws, and religious teachings that help individuals determine what is morally right and wrong or what kind of behavior is acceptable and what is not under specific conditions (Singer 2023). Like the case with most professionals, including those in medicine, law, science, academia, and journalism, counterterrorism officials are also bound by codes of professional conduct and moral principles that governs the use of violence during their operations. These include distinctions between legitimate and forbidden targets, rules of engagement, proportionality and de-escalation during attacks, and the treatment of enemy captives and detainees. The actions of military forces are restricted by the just cause and the just conduct principles (e.g., resulting from the Geneva Convention). Soldiers must follow certain rules of conduct to guide their use of violence, including under what circumstances violence can be used, what types of violence can be legitimately employed, and how enemy captives should be treated (Crawford 2003; Gordon 2006).

FIGURE 13.1 Ethics is a branch of philosophy that deals with the study of what is morally right and wrong. It explores questions about how humans should behave and make decisions in various aspects of life. *Source:* Jorgen Mcleman/Shutterstock.

However, as with any code of conduct, there have been occasional deviations and lapses in adherence. Particularly after the terrorist attacks of 9/11, a number of US counterterrorism practices that breached ethical standards were revealed. These include the establishment of **black sites** (extrajudicial domains that are not regulated by law), the use of enhanced interrogation techniques to obtain information from terrorist suspects, and the preventive detention of individuals without trials.

During the same period, it became evident that a variety of controversial practices made possible by technological advance-

FIGURE 13.2 The use of drones, specifically armed drones, by the United States for targeted killings and airstrikes in various parts of the world has been a subject of significant debate and controversy. *Source:* MOHAMMED HUWAIS/Stringer/Getty images.

ments were being employed in counterterrorism efforts, such as (1) the use of unmanned systems for targeted killing, and (2) the surveillance of the society under a practice called "bulk/mass data collection." These developments underscored the challenges of striking a balance between national security imperatives and the protection of fundamental human rights and personal privacy.

Commencing with the US invasion of Afghanistan, media reports and nongovernmental human rights organizations began shedding light on incidents of civilian casualties in the Middle East and Northern Africa resulting from automated weapons systems, notably drone attacks. For instance, in December 2013, a drone strike conducted by the US military in Yemen targeted suspected al-Qaeda operatives but tragically claimed the lives of 12 civilians and injured more than 15 individuals who were later revealed to be participants in a wedding procession (Human Rights Watch 2014a). Collateral damage from drone attacks reached such high levels during the post–9/11 era that scholars now argue that in conflict zones (e.g., Yemen, Afghanistan, Syria, Iraq), the probability of getting killed in a counterterrorism operation is greater than being a victim of an actual terrorist attack (Kurtulus 2012). Despite arguments justifying their use from a utilitarian ethics perspective, preemptive drone strikes raise significant concerns as they infringe upon human rights, including the right to a fair trial and due process for individuals (Harris & Monaghan 2018). These ethical dilemmas underscore the need for a reevaluation of the use of such technology in counterterrorism efforts.

In June 2013, Edward Snowden, an American citizen who had been working as an intelligence subcontractor for the **National Security Agency (NSA)**, made headlines by leaking thousands of classified documents. These documents exposed the "secret, massive, and indiscriminate" scope of technological surveillance activities carried out by American and British intelligence services worldwide (Bowcott 2014). Snowden's revelations ignited a global debate on the balance between national security and individual privacy rights, leading to calls for increased transparency and oversight in intelligence gathering and data collection practices (Szoldra 2016).

In the context outlined, the final chapter of this book considers the ethical dilemmas surrounding various counterterrorism practices. Initially, we will explore modern technologies employed in counterterrorism efforts, including the use of drones for **targeted killings**, computer hacking to access encrypted data, and activities falling under bulk data collection. Then our focus will shift toward historically long-standing and controversial counterterrorism practices. These encompass a range of activities, such as the use of enhanced interrogation techniques, sting and entrapment operations, extrajudicial killings, and the indefinite detention of individuals without trials.

It is important to note that while the examples of controversial counterterrorism practices presented later in this chapter occurred during the United States' efforts to combat terrorism in the post–9/11 era, this does not mean that the US is unique in its use of unethical practices. These instances of ethical breaches and human rights violations came to light due to the efforts of concerned American security personnel, journalists, politicians, and government officials. These issues generated extensive investigations and media coverage due to the high value placed on human rights in the United States as well as the demand for accountability. In response, the US government has sought to address these concerns. These instances illustrate both the potential danger of counterterrorism efforts and the importance of learning from mistakes in the creation of effective and ethical policies.

13.2 EMERGING TECHNOLOGIES AND THEIR USE IN COUNTERTERRORISM OPERATIONS

The emerging technologies that are used for counterterrorism purposes can be broadly classified into two major groups:

1. Use of unmanned aerial vehicles for targeted killing (UAV technologies and drones)
2. Mass data collection

Undoubtedly, innovative tools like drones, autonomous weapons, and bulk data collection and surveillance technologies are reshaping the landscape of modern counterterrorism warfare. While proponents of these emerging military and intelligence technologies often highlight potential benefits, such as reduced collateral damage, early detection of potential terrorist activities, and more effective terrorism prevention, they also raise significant ethical and human rights concerns. The upcoming section will consider what these technologies entail, how the United States and the United Kingdom utilize them, and what the long-term and unforeseen implications of their use might be.

13.2.1 Unmanned Aerial Vehicles (UAVs and Drones)

Unmanned aerial vehicles (UAVs), commonly referred to as **drones,** are remotely operated computer-based aerial systems frequently employed to carry out lethal counterterrorism operations and long-range surveillance on enemy targets. The use of drones, initiated under the George W. Bush administration to counter threats from al-Qaeda, has become a prominent choice of weapon for both the US military and the CIA. Drones offer a more covert and lethal means of combat compared to conventional warfare methods.

Advocates of these technologies also contend that drones entail lower human and financial costs compared to traditional armed conflicts.

Between 2004 and 2020, the United States conducted thousands of drone strikes across various regions of the world, including targets in countries like Afghanistan, Iraq, Libya, Somalia, Syria, and Yemen (FCNL 2021).

Experts argue that the scale of US drone warfare may be even larger in scope and geographical coverage, as the CIA has been known to use drone strikes outside of known war zones and their program remains largely secret to the public. Estimating the total

FIGURE 13.3 An MQ-9 Reaper unmanned aerial vehicle flies a combat mission over southern Afghanistan. The US government justifies drone strikes, particularly those involving targeted killings, through a combination of legal, strategic, and policy arguments. These justifications have evolved over time and continue to be a subject of debate and scrutiny. *Source:* US Air Force Photo/Lt. Col. Leslie Pratt, public domain, via Wikimedia Commons.

financial cost of US drone programs is difficult due to the use of these programs by different agencies within the US government (Acosta 2015). However, it is public information that the Department of Defense requested approximately $9 billion for the maintenance and continuous operation of the Pentagon's unmanned aerial vehicle (UAV) systems and associated technologies in the FY 2019 budget (Gettinger 2018). This substantial budget allocation highlights the significant financial investment in UAV technologies for military and counterterrorism purposes, underscoring the growing role of drones in contemporary defense strategies.

Who Do Drones Target?

Drones have been deployed for various purposes through foreign bases located overseas, targeting three distinct groups.

First, in the aftermath of the 9/11 attacks, drones were initially used to target members of various terrorist groups operating in regions officially declared as war zones. Examples include operations against ISIS in Iraq and Syria, as well as targeting al-Qaeda and Taliban operatives in Afghanistan.

Second, the US government has also employed the practice of "targeted killing," which involves the deliberate and premeditated use of drone attacks overseas to eliminate individuals designated as high-value targets. These individuals are placed on "kill lists," which are databases of terror suspects approved for either capture or killing. These lists are maintained by the Pentagon, CIA, and the US Department of Justice (Gerstein 2018). Within intelligence and military circles, this process of identifying, locating, and eliminating such targets is often referred to as "find, fix, finish" (FFF). The use of drones for targeted killings, in particular, has been a subject of intense debate and controversy (Zenko 2011).

Reenactment based on original radio traffic transcript of drone crew

Sensor: And, oh… and there it goes!

FIGURE 13.4   The concept of drone killings based on "suspicious patterns" (e.g., a convoy of vehicles traveling at night) is controversial and raises significant ethical, legal, and human rights concerns. Signature strikes involve the use of armed drones to target individuals or groups based on behavioral patterns, rather than specific intelligence indicating their direct involvement in terrorist or militant activities. This is a reconstruction of a tragic incident from 2010 involving a drone strike targeting a convoy of vehicles in Afghanistan. The strike was carried out by a Predator drone crew operating from Nevada. Regrettably, it resulted in the loss of 23 civilian lives, including members of several families. The screenshot comes from the *National Bird* documentary. *Source: National Bird* documentary film.

According to a 2010 report by the *Guardian* based on leaked Afghanistan war logs, the number of individuals placed on the Pentagon's kill list had exceeded 2,000 by the year 2009 (Davies 2010). These revelations highlight the extent and complexity of the US government's use of targeted killings as a counterterrorism strategy and the associated ethical and legal considerations.

Third, drones are also utilized to conduct "signature strikes," a highly controversial assassination tactic that was developed during Barack Obama's presidency. Signature strikes authorize the Pentagon and CIA to carry out drone strikes against individuals without knowing their identities, because their behavioral patterns may indicate involvement in terrorist activities (Currier 2015; Ackerman 2016). These suspicious behavioral signatures can encompass a wide range of activities, including carrying weapons, traveling in convoys of vehicles, participating in large gatherings, or using communication devices (Wolfendale 2021). The practice of signature strikes has sparked debates due to the inherent risks of misidentification and the potential for civilian casualties associated with such operations.

The use of drones in remote locations for remote killings has been criticized by many on several grounds (Currier 2015; Wolfendale 2021). These critiques can be grouped into three general categories: (1) effectiveness of drone targeting and the scope of civilian casualties, (2) the violation of human and due process rights, and (3) the fear among populations living under the drone threat.

Effectiveness of Drone Targeting and the Scope of Civilian Casualties

One of the primary issues with drone programs is the level of secrecy and the limited congressional oversight under which they operate. This secrecy makes it challenging to fully assess their effectiveness, considering factors such as the frequency of missed targets, the reasons for such failures, and the exact number of casualties caused by drone strikes. Researchers and the media often have to rely on data provided by local media outlets, nongovernmental organizations, and independent monitoring groups in conflict zones. Anonymous leaks from members of the intelligence community in the US and conflict zones also contribute to our understanding of these operations (Edney-Browne 2019).

Analyses of available data by human rights groups, even when based on partial estimates, raise doubts about the precision and accuracy of drone strikes (Bergen 2012). Data compiled by Reprieve, a human rights organization based in the US and UK, revealed that US efforts to kill 41 men on a kill list resulted in the deaths of approximately 1,100 civilians. Similarly, leaked reports to the media exposed that during the five-month

FIGURE 13.5   On August 29, 2021, the US military carried out a drone strike in Kabul in response to an imminent threat of a terrorist attack at the Kabul airport following the Taliban takeover of Afghanistan. The drone strike resulted in the tragic deaths of 10 Afghan civilians, including seven children. One of the victims was an aid worker for an international humanitarian organization. *Source:* Marcus Yam/ Getty images.

period of Operation Haymaker in Afghanistan, nearly 90 percent of those killed in airstrikes were not individuals on the kill lists but civilians (Ackerman 2014). In contrast to being a surgical operation, as described in 2011 by CIA official John Brennan (who later became the director of the CIA in 2013), the country specific reports highlight the fact that many drone strikes are unsuccessful and human tolls can be extremely heavy.

According to whistleblower accounts, obtaining accurate positive identifications and locations of suspects and poststrike assessments in remote regions is difficult due to the limited technology, military presence, and the extent of surveillance available. Targets are often located through metadata captured from electronic communications, commonly known as **signals intelligence (SIGINT)**. However, these systems often provide faulty intelligence in unconventional battlefields (e.g., places such as Yemen and Somalia), because most of this intelligence comes from foreign governments, which may have their own agendas (Currier 2015; Walker 2015). This is the primary reason why civilians are killed in drone operations. In 2012, the Obama administration authorized a US drone strike in Yemen that killed 12 civilians, including three children and a pregnant woman, but no alleged militants on the US military kill list (Open Society Justice Initiative 2015). In 2011, the deputy governor of Yemen's central Mareb province was killed in a US drone attack because Yemeni officials failed to disclose to the CIA that he was present at a gathering with suspected al-Qaeda members. US officials later acknowledged that they had been misled by Yemeni officials who had different interests than those of US security (Entous & Barnes 2011). These incidents underscore the complexity of conducting drone operations in regions with limited resources and unreliable intelligence, which can result in tragic consequences.

The Violation of Human and Due Process Rights

The reliance on drones for targeted killings has also led to criticism concerning the diminished emphasis on capturing, rather than killing, terrorists. This shift is driven by the belief that drones are a more efficient and less risky method for dealing with potential threats (Bender 2015). Critics argue that this approach deprives governments of valuable opportunities to gather intelligence, understand terrorist groups, and potentially bring individuals to justice through legal means. Overreliance on drone strikes for dealing with threats may limit the intelligence and strategic advantages gained through capture and interrogation.

Further, critics argue that drone operations are contrary to the US constitution and international laws because individuals, including the American citizens, may be killed without a chance to defend themselves in a court of law. In 2018, a federal judge accepted a lawsuit brought by an American journalist against the US government for his alleged inclusion on a kill list of approved drone strike targets. The judge ruled that American citizens have the right to due process before being placed on such lists, thus placing US citizens on kill lists without giving them notice, is a violation of their constitutional rights (Gerstein 2018).

The Constant Fear of Living Under the Drone Threat

Existing research suggests damaging and counterproductive effects of US drone strikes in conflict regions such as Pakistan, Yemen, and Somalia. A 2012 report jointly prepared by the International Human Rights and Conflict Resolution Clinic at Stanford University and the Global Justice Clinic at New York University revealed how civilian populations have been traumatized from the CIA's secretive drone missions in remote locations of Pakistan, where they strike homes, vehicles, and public areas without warning. Upon interviewing more than 130 locals, the researchers concluded that civilians, including women and children, were forced to live under the constant fear of an attack and the risk of getting killed at any time. These circumstances left them vulnerable to symptoms including anxiety, psychological trauma, insomnia, loss of appetite, extreme stress, and outbursts of anger and irritability (International Human Rights and Conflict Resolution at Stanford Law School & Global Justice Clinic at NYU School of Law 2012).

Similar conclusions were reached in a 2019 study conducted in Afghanistan. The lived experiences of people indicated how drone attacks and surveillance led to the avoidance of social, religious, and cultural activities and traditions within rural villages and towns, such as not attending weddings, religious festivals, funerals, and local political meetings, discontinuing family visits, and abstaining from activities that involve nighttime travel, out of fear that drone surveillance may mistakenly spot them as a potential target. One interviewee described life under drones: "Our life is like being in a prison. But the prison is big. You cannot meet at night, go for dinners, you cannot travel easily and without fear—you cannot continue to perform your culture and your celebrations. What kind of life is this?" (Edney-Browne 2019).

Further findings from academic research reveal that rescuers and medical professionals have also been targeted with secondary drone strikes, leading community members and health professionals to avoid helping victims in the aftermath of each attack. As one source reported: "Secondary strikes have discouraged average civilians from coming to one another's rescue, and even inhibited the provision of emergency medical assistance from humanitarian workers." (Woods 2012). Interviews with eyewitnesses indicated that drone strikes have changed the dynamics of social life, including cultural and social practices in these regions. Several parents removed their children from school because armed drones were hovering above their communities, including schools, 24 hours a day. People do not gather anymore in crowds out of fear that they may get targeted by drone operators (Woods 2012).

Findings also reveal that the drone programs may contribute to radicalization into terrorism. Critics argue that the great number of civilian casualties caused by drone strikes can fuel individuals' resentment and anger, pushing them toward participation in terrorism or supporting violent attacks against US interests in the region. This view is supported by a 2012 Pew Research Center Global Attitudes Survey, which found that almost 75 percent of Pakistanis viewed the United States as an enemy and held unfavorable attitudes toward Americans (Pew 2012).

A growing amount of evidence suggests that extremist groups use US drone strikes and associated collateral damage as a propaganda tool to fuel hatred and anti-American sentiment, bolstering ordinary individuals' participation in terrorism to exact revenge. When civilians, including loved ones, are killed in drone strikes, it can generate fear, deep-seated grudges, and hatred among affected populations. These negative emotions can in turn lead to radicalization and an increased willingness to engage in acts of terrorism as a means of revenge or retaliation against the United States. A 2004 Pentagon commission report reached similar conclusions. The report concluded that "Muslims do not hate our freedoms, but rather hate our policies" (Bandow 2010). Scholars cite this as the "blowback effect"—the unintended consequences of harsh counterterrorism interventions (Greenwald 2009).

A 2012 *New York Times* article declared that "drones have replaced Guantanamo as the recruiting tool of choice for militants" (Becker & Shane 2012). An *Independent* article published in 2010 stated, "the drones have killed some jihadis. But the evidence suggests they create far more jihadis than they kill" (Hari 2010). A senior advisor to the US Department of State in 2012 described this countereffective side of drones: "Every one of these dead non-combatants represents an alienated family, a new desire for revenge, and more recruits for a militant movement that has grown exponentially even as drone strikes have increased" (Shah 2016). Evidence suggests that even though they may provide an illusion of victory, drones do not win the hearts and minds of local populations, which is an essential element in the war against terrorism. Faisal Shahzad, a Pakistani born naturalized American citizen who planned to detonate a car bomb in New York's Times Square in 2010, had justified his plot by telling the judge that "When the drones hit, they don't see children, they don't see anybody. They kill everybody . . . I am part of the answer to the US terrorizing the Muslim nations and the Muslim people" (Greenwald 2012).

13.2.2 Mass Data Collection

Edward Snowden's leak of classified information in 2013 had a profound impact on the world by exposing the extensive and secretive surveillance activities conducted by US and UK intelligence agencies. The disclosures shed light on the scope and scale of data collection, encompassing not only the communications of ordinary individuals but also the private communications of world leaders and allies. While this chapter cannot cover the full detail of the revelations, notable **surveillance** practices revealed in Snowden's leak include:

- Eavesdropping on phone calls of world leaders (including the allies such as Germany, France, Canada, Israel, and the Republic of Korea).
- Forcing US phone companies (e.g., AT&T, Verizon) to surrender metadata such as phone numbers, locations, the time and duration of calls on an ongoing daily basis for calls made from the United States to other countries.
- Making financial deals with commercial encryption software companies (to which people rely on to protect the privacy of their personal data) to create backdoor (also known as trapdoors) accesses for NSA.
- Warrantless surveillance of domestic population, including journalists, activists, and human rights groups who do not have any kind of connection with terrorism.
- Tapping into fiber-optic cables laid beneath the Atlantic Ocean by establishing partnership with the major telecommunications corporations (known as corporate partner access) that carry a significant portion of global communication every day.
- Electronic eavesdropping on internal computer systems of European Union and United Nations offices located in the US and across the Europe.
- Collecting more than 200 million text messages per day across the globe to extract location information, contact networks, and business and credit card details of mobile phone users.
- Hacking into the internal computer network of the largest SIM card manufacturer in the world, Gemalto (Netherlands), which has more than 450 wireless network customers across the world, including AT&T, T-Mobile, Verizon, and Sprint; in order to obtain encryption keys (which protect the privacy of cellphone communications) and thus monitor mobile communications without a warrant or approval from the telecommunication companies or foreign governments (Ball 2013; Ball et al. 2013; BBC 2014; Scahill & Steele 2014; Webster 2014; West 2013).

The documents downloaded by Snowden from National Security Agency (NSA) and CIA computers revealed how these agencies compiled files on billions of people and institutions such as universities, hospitals, and private companies around the world. Americans, whose private communications were supposedly protected by the US Constitution, were not exempt from this mass surveillance program. The revelations indicated that regardless of one's citizenship status, the NSA and its counterpart in the UK, the **Government Communications Headquarters (GCHQ)**, intercepted all outgoing and incoming data through the major global undersea communication cables. Snowden's disclosures also highlighted the agencies' capabilities to remotely access and activate computer and phone cameras, enabling them to capture images and videos of individuals without their knowledge or consent. This raised significant privacy and security concerns, as it demonstrated the potential for invasive surveillance.

Edward Snowden's decision to disclose classified information to journalists was driven by his ethical concerns about the activities he was involved in while working at the NSA. He claimed that he initially attempted to address his concerns internally by raising them to his supervisors, but when his complaints were not adequately addressed, he felt compelled to take further action. In 2012, Snowden anonymously contacted journalists from *The Guardian*, a British newspaper, to share a sample of classified NSA documents. He wanted to provide evidence of the extent of the surveillance programs and convince them to meet with him in person. In May 2013, Snowden took a medical leave from his job under the pretext of seeking treatment for epilepsy. He then traveled to Hong Kong, where he met with journalists from *The Guardian*, including Glenn Greenwald and Laura Poitras, and shared thousands of secret documents

FIGURE 13.6   The National Security Agency (NSA) headquarters is located at Fort Meade in Maryland, United States. Fort Meade is a military installation that serves as the headquarters for various US intelligence and security agencies, in addition to the NSA. *Source:* National Security Agency, Public domain, via Wikimedia Commons.

detailing NSA surveillance programs. This disclosure of classified information to the media set in motion a series of events that would lead to widespread public awareness of government surveillance programs and ignite a global debate on issues of privacy, security, and government transparency.

In the immediate aftermath of the revelations, Director of National Intelligence James Clapper publicly denied that the NSA collected data on Americans. During a congressional hearing in March 2013, Clapper was asked directly whether the NSA collected any type of data on millions of Americans, to which he replied, "No." This statement later led to accusations that he had misled Congress. As more details from Snowden's leaks became public, it became increasingly clear that the NSA was engaged in widespread surveillance, including the bulk collection of phone records and internet communications. The US government eventually acknowledged the existence of these surveillance programs, such as PRISM (described in the next section) and the bulk metadata collection program (Greenwald & MacAskill 2013).

Opponents of digital mass surveillance argued that these powers given to law enforcement and government agencies were too broad, making it easy for these agencies to spy on people without accountability. The NSA was not able to produce significant evidence that its **mass data collection** program had indeed stopped any large-scale terrorist attacks against the United States (Elliott & Meyer 2013; McLaughlin 2015). A 2013 White House review panel concluded: "there has been no instance in which the NSA could say with confidence that the outcome [of a terror investigation] would have been any different" without the program (Isikoff 2013).

Snowden, who is currently an asylee in Russia, has been charged by the US Department of Justice for violating the 1917 Espionage Act and for theft of government property.

FIGURE 13.7 During his presidency, Barack Obama argued that certain mass surveillance programs and practices were necessary for national security and counterterrorism efforts. However, Obama's position evolved over time, and he also took steps to reform and limit some of these surveillance practices. *Source:* Debra Sweet, CC BY 2.0, via Wikimedia Commons.

Today, he is a controversial figure. For some, he is a champion of civil liberties and privacy rights; they argue that his actions exposed government overreach and surveillance programs that were conducted without adequate oversight. Supporters believe that his disclosures spurred important debates on surveillance and privacy, leading to policy changes and legal reforms. However, others view Edward Snowden as a traitor who violated his oath of secrecy and put national security at risk. They argue that his leaks compromised intelligence operations and revealed sensitive information to adversaries (Blankenship 2023).

Reports indicate that the NSA relied on two main laws to justify its surveillance programs:

1. Section 215 of the 2001 PATRIOT Act: to collect metadata (not the actual communication content but transactional data such as phone numbers, and duration, times, and geo-locations of calls) from American phone users on an ongoing basis (Debelak 2013).
2. FISA Amendment Act (FAA): to justify its electronic surveillance (the actual contents, videos, photo, contents of emails and text messages) for mass data collection (Macaskill & Dance 2013).

The following section will briefly examine two of the methods that NSA used for bulk data collection.

PRISM Program

The **PRISM Program**, perhaps the most controversial of the leaked programs, is a top-secret multiagency program that began in 2007. The program gave the NSA and the UK's GCHQ direct access to the servers of nine major internet companies including Google, Apple, Facebook, Microsoft, Yahoo, YouTube, Skype, AOL, and PalTalk. Even though the existing laws already allowed intelligence officials to request user communication details from internet companies, PRISM went further to provide direct access to these electronic communications without the need for individual court orders or a formal request to the communications company. This access allowed government officials to collect electronic communication materials such as the content of emails, video and voice chats, search history, photos, stored data, file transfers, online social networking details, logins, and location information of users designated as foreign targets. Communications of American

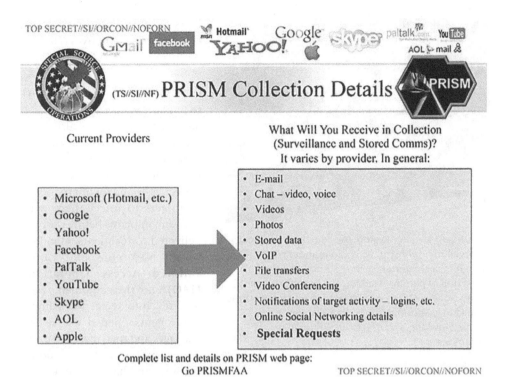

FIGURE 13.8 The leaked NSA slide on PRISM. PRISM refers to a controversial surveillance program conducted by the US National Security Agency (NSA), as revealed in documents leaked by Edward Snowden in 2013. PRISM was designed to collect and analyze electronic communications data, including emails, chat messages, and more, from major technology companies and online service providers. *Source:* NSA-PRISM-Slides, Internet Archive.

citizens may also be stored in the process (Gellman & Poitras 2013). The revelations indicated that the NSA ran these surveillance programs through partnerships with these major US telecom and internet companies and compensated them regularly. However, the companies in question claimed that the government was not able to log directly into their users' data (Webster 2014). Created with the Protect America Act of 2007, as a part of the US governments' post-9/11 electronic surveillance efforts, PRISM has been considered the biggest single contributor to intelligence reports prepared by the NSA (Dance 2013).

In the wake of the revelations, Americans raised concerns that the NSA's programs violated the fourth amendment of the US Constitution, which prohibits unreasonable searches and seizures. "Restore the Fourth" rallies emerged across more than 100 cities to condemn the US government's warrantless mass surveillance of domestic and foreign communications (Sottek & Kopfstein 2013). In 2014, more than 4,500 webpages across the world organized "The Day We Fight Back" protest, which called on people around the world to protest telecommunication surveillance, by displaying a banner advertisement on their homepages that read: "Dear Internet, we are sick of complaining about the NSA. We want new laws that curtail online surveillance. Today, we fight back," and providing

FIGURE 13.9 The "Restore the Fourth" movement emerged in response to revelations about government surveillance programs, such as PRISM and the bulk collection of phone metadata. The movement continues to be active today and engages in advocacy efforts related to government surveillance and privacy.
Source: Slowking, GFDL 1.2, via Wikimedia Commons.

links by which visitors may contact their representatives (Hattem 2014).

Intercepting Computer Shipments to Implant Malware

Snowden's revelations also indicated the presence of routing centers controlled by the NSA to intercept computer shipment deliveries bound for international customers to infect them with malware implants before they are delivered to recipients. Handled by an NSA elite unit called **Tailored Access Operations (TAO)**, once these shipments were diverted into secret workshops, TAO agents opened the sealed packages and then installed backdoor surveillance tools including malware and hardware to enable the NSA to penetrate targeted computers and retrieve data remotely. The agents then repackaged them with original factory seals and shipped them to their destination (Appelbaum et al. 2014). The Snowden files indicated that the NSA had implanted approximately 100,000 electronic devices across the world, which enabled the agency to gain access to entire networks in which these devices were used. The malware utilized included:

- CAPTIVATEDAUDIENCE (enables agents to take over targeted computer's microphone to record conversations happening nearby)
- GUMFISH (takes over the webcam and snaps photographs)
- FOGGYBOTTOM (records logs of internet browsing histories, steals login credentials used to access various websites)
- SALVAGERABBIT (steals data from removable flash drives that are connected to infected computers)

According to the files, this technology was not only being used on terrorist and extremist suspects, but also against systems administrators who work for foreign phone and internet service providers to gain covert access to communications processed by these companies (Der Spiegel 2013). The documents note that Britain's GCHQ hacked (with an operation code named Operation Socialist) a Belgian telecommunication company, Belgacom in 2010, whose major customers included the members of the European Commission, the European Council, and the European Parliament, through implanted devices to secretly monitor the electronic communications used in this network (Gallagher & Greenwald 2014).

13.3 QUESTIONABLE COUNTERTERRORISM PRACTICES

Aside from the more recent counterterrorism practices facilitated by technological developments, a number of other discoveries shocked the American public, the media, and members of the US government (Marks 2005). These developments can be broadly grouped under two categories:

1. The CIA's detention and interrogation programs, including:

   - The creation of extrajudicial domains that are not regulated by law
   - Preventive detention (indefinite detention without trial) of suspects
   - The use of torture and enhanced interrogation techniques

2. The use of anonymous **undercover informants** and entrapment operations against the domestic population.

13.3.1 CIA's Detention and Interrogation Programs

On December 9, 2014, the US Senate Intelligence Committee released a 528-page partially redacted executive summary on the CIA's detention and **interrogation programs**, disclosing the agency's extensive and systematic use of torture during the post–9/11 era. The summary, which was originally part of a 6,700-page classified report, was the result of an investigation of more than six million pages of CIA documents (including operational cables, intelligence reports, internal memos and emails, briefing materials, interview transcripts, contracts, and other records) over the course of more than five years. The investigation, which started in March 2009 as a bipartisan endeavor, arrived at 20 main conclusions, including:

1. The use of the enhanced interrogation techniques

FIGURE 13.10 The Senate Intelligence Committee Report on Torture, also known as the **Senate Torture Report**, is an extensive document that was released in December 2014. It is the result of a multiyear investigation by the United States Senate Select Committee on Intelligence into the use of enhanced interrogation techniques (often referred to as torture) by the **Central Intelligence Agency (CIA)** in the post–9/11 era.

was not an effective means of acquiring intelligence or gaining cooperation from detainees

2. The CIA's justification for the use of its enhanced interrogation techniques rested on inaccurate claims of their effectiveness

3. The interrogations of CIA detainees were brutal and far worse than the agency presented to policymakers and others

4. The CIA has actively avoided or impeded congressional oversight of the program (Kaplan 2014).

The US Senate Intelligence Committee initiated the review study after federal prosecutors disclosed that in November 2005, the CIA had destroyed 92 tapes containing harsh interrogations of al-Qaeda suspects during the years after the September 11 attacks. The revelation came as a part of a Freedom of Information Act lawsuit that was brought by the American Civil Liberties Union (ACLU), asking the US government to release the records of the treatment of prisoners who were under American custody in foreign facilities. Until then, most of the American public and members of the US government were unaware of the violent details of the techniques that were used to torture detainees held under suspicion of connection to al-Qaeda. The CIA claimed that they had destroyed the tapes because they had no intelligence value and they wanted to protect the identities of the undercover agents; however, the Senate Intelligence Committee voted 14–1 to investigate the issue further (Mazzetti 2009). The report revealed that between late 2001 and early 2009, CIA officials, aided by two outside contractor psychologists, had started a program of indefinite secret detention and the use of brutal interrogation techniques in violation of US law and international treaty obligations.

The discovery of a draft letter written by senior CIA lawyers and addressed to the US Attorney General indicated that CIA officials knew that the tactics (which were rebranded at the time as "enhanced interrogation techniques") were illegal, violating the US Torture Statute. The letter revealed that the CIA had asked the Justice Department for immunity from its illegal activities—a protection from the prosecution of CIA agents for the act of torture. However, when the Justice Department declined to issue immunity, the agency procured another method to cover its actions—the torture memos.

Torture Memos
Officially known as the Memorandum Regarding Military Interrogation of Alien Unlawful Combatants Held Outside the United States, the **torture memos** are a set of legal memorandums, exchanged between the Department of Justice, White House, CIA, and the Department of Defense regarding the protection of US officials from being charged with war crimes for the torture and coercion of detainees (Lewis 2002). Beginning on January 9, 2002, with a memo written by then-Deputy Assistant Attorney General John C. Yoo, currently a law professor at University of California, some of these memorandums provided legal arguments that neither the 1949 Geneva Conventions nor the 1996 War Crimes Act (18 U.S.C.) applied to al-Qaeda and Taliban detainees that were captured during the war in Afghanistan. Yoo argued in his first memo that nonstate actors (e.g., al-Qaeda and Taliban) could not be considered a part of international agreements governing wars, because the existing treaties only covered acts occurring in civil wars and traditional wars between nations. Therefore, unlawful combatants such as

al-Qaeda fighters were not legally entitled to the protections covered by the agreements (US Department of Justice 2002).

Supporting this argument, White House Counsel Alberto Gonzales issued another memo on January 25 to then-President Bush that the Department of Justice's determination was correct, and that President Bush should declare that both Taliban and al-Qaeda were outside of the protections safeguarded by Article 4 of the Geneva Convention because they were "unlawful combatants." Gonzales argued that declining "prisoner of war" status to al-Qaeda and Taliban members would protect US officials and members of the military from the War Crimes Act, in which punishment for some violations (Section 2441, inhumane treatment) could amount to the death penalty. Similar to the arguments made by the Department of Justice Official Yoo, Gonzales argued that the world was facing a new type of warfare which required a new approach toward the captured terrorists (Gonzales 2002).

Both Secretary of State Colin Powell and the State Department's legal adviser William Taft IV issued two separate memorandums (on January 26 and February 2) which argued that even though denying prisoner of war status to al-Qaeda and the Taliban would prevent the risk of domestic prosecution against US officials and provide flexibility to the American military in their treatment of detainees, such an approach would also carry several negative consequences. It could increase risk to the lives of US troops if they become captured, generate negative international reactions, and undermine public support for US military actions among European allies (Powell 2002). In light of the information provided by different agencies, President Bush issued a directive on February 7, 2002, ordering the Department of Defense and the members of the US Armed Forces to treat the captured members of al-Qaeda and Taliban humanely, regardless of the fact that they are not legally entitled to such treatment or protected by the Geneva Conventions (Bush 2002).

The Bybee Memos

Despite the president's directive, subsequent memos issued on later dates by the Office of Legal Counsel of the Department of Justice provided guidance on the use of torture practices against so-called high-value detainees (i.e., Taliban and al-Qaeda). First, on August 1, 2002, then-Assistant Attorney General Jay Bybee provided a legal basis and rationale for the use of enhanced interrogation techniques to extract information from detainees. The Department of Justice argued that an act can be cruel, inhumane, and degrading but not produce enough pain and suffering (physical or mental) to be considered torture as defined by the Section 2340A of Title 18 (the US torture code) and Article 4 of the Geneva Convention. More specifically, Bybee stated that for an act to constitute torture, "it must inflict pain that is difficult to endure"—it must be so intense that as a result the victim should suffer a serious injury such as "death, organ failure, permanent damage resulting in a loss of significant body function, or lasting psychological harm" (Bybee 2002a, 1, 12, 46).

The Department of Justice authorized US military personnel to use sensory deprivation techniques to interrogate detainees because even though "many of these techniques may amount to cruel, inhuman, or degrading treatment, they do not produce pain or suffering of the necessary intensity to meet the definition of torture" (Bybee 2002a, 2).

Further, the memo stated that officials who engage in torture cannot be held criminally liable if (1) defendants simply indicate that "they had acted in good faith that their conduct would not amount to the acts prohibited by the statue," and (2) the torture occurred as a result of necessity or self-defense (Bybee 2002a, 8, 46).

In a separate memo submitted by Bybee to the Acting General Counsel of the Central Intelligence Agency on August 1, 2002, the US Department of Justice provided the opinion that the agency's application of 10 interrogation techniques with high-level al-Qaeda members to encourage them to disclose information about future terrorist attacks would not violate the existing torture conventions and laws. The counsel indicated that the CIA had a "good faith belief that no prolonged mental harm would result using these methods in the interrogation of the subject, due to the presence of personnel with medical and psychological training who have the authority to stop the interrogation in case of an emergency (or if the techniques are used improperly) (Bybee 2002b, 16, 18). These techniques included:

- attention grasp
- walling
- facial hold
- facial slap (insult slap)
- cramped confinement
- wall standing
- stress positions
- sleep deprivation
- placing subject in a cramped confinement box with an insect
- waterboarding

The Bradbury Memos

On May 10 and 30 of 2005, the CIA sought further approval from the legal counsel of the Department of Justice for the use of harsher techniques in the interrogation of high value al-Qaeda detainees, arguing that the use of enhanced interrogation techniques are necessary to prevent future acts of terrorism (Bradbury 2005a, 2005b). These techniques, some of which are listed previously, comprise three categories (Bradbury 2005, 12, 13):

1. **Conditioning techniques**: techniques that demonstrate to the detainee that he has no control over basic human needs such as **dietary manipulation** (presenting detainees with bland, unappetizing diet), nudity (to cause psychological discomfort), and sleep deprivation (forcing the detainee undergoing this technique to wear a diaper).
2. **Corrective techniques**: techniques that involve some degree of physical interaction with the detainee to correct or startle him such as a facial slap, abdominal slap (striking the abdomen of the detainees with the back of open hand), facial hold, and attention grasp.
3. **Coercive techniques**: techniques that are used by the agency to put the detainee into more physical and psychological stress such as walling (slamming against a wall), water dousing (subjecting detainees to cold water), stress positions (techniques used to create muscle fatigue and humiliate and insult detainees), cramped confinement, and **waterboarding**.

Then-Assistant Attorney General Steven Bradbury concluded that none of these techniques would violate US torture law if they are applied in the presence of medical and psychological personnel, and these personnel are allowed to stop their use in the case of an emergency (Bradbury 2005a).

In another memo issued on May 30, 2005, Bradbury (2005b) argued that these techniques do not violate the obligations set forth by Article 16 of the United Nations Convention Against Torture and Other Cruel, Inhuman, or Degrading Treatment or Punishment due to jurisdictional issues. Bradbury argued that CIA interrogations do not take place in territories that are under United States' jurisdiction, which makes Article 16 of UN convention inapplicable and invalid, because the language used in this article has a limited predefined geographical scope defined as "territory under its jurisdiction" (Bradbury 2005b, 18). The Office of Legal Counsel concluded that the CIA's interrogation programs could not be subject to judicial inquiry.

Although not reported in the legal opinions, the Senate report revealed that the CIA was also using techniques such as "mock burials," "anal feeding," "rectal rehydration" without documented medical necessity, and "exposure to bright light and extreme temperatures." The report also revealed that detainees were sometimes threatened with a buzzing power drill, sexually threatened with a broomstick, or threatened with harm to their families, including threats to sexually abuse the mother of one detainee and to harm his children (Prokop 2014). Detainees were kept in completely dark cells, isolated, and shackled to walls, with constant loud music and provided with a bucket for human waste. They were subject to "rough takedowns" "in which approximately five CIA officers would scream at a detainee, drag him outside of his cell, cut his clothes off, and secure him with Mylar tape. The detainee would then be hooded and dragged up and down a long corridor while being slapped and punched" (Senate Select Committee on Intelligence 2014, 4). A clandestine officer described these harsh techniques as leading to death and "psychological and behavioral issues, including hallucinations, paranoia, insomnia, and attempts at self-harm and self-mutilation" (Senate Select Committee on Intelligence 2014, 114). An email sent by the CIA and discovered during the investigations argued for the necessity of keeping these programs secret, stating that head of Department of State Colin Powell "would blow his stack if he were to be briefed on what's been going on" (Human Rights Watch 2014b).

The Senate Report also revealed that detainees who were subjected to enhanced interrogation techniques were either not providing any intelligence at all, or fabricating information on critical issues, which was leading to faulty intelligence. In comparison, the findings revealed that the detainees who were not subjected to these techniques were providing significant and accurate intelligence through rapport-building (e.g., through detainee cooperation). The use of these enhanced interrogation techniques did not yield critical information, such as that needed to thwart terrorist plots or capture specific terrorists. More reliable information was provided by detainees not subjected to such techniques (Shane 2012).

The report also exposed that the CIA's enhanced interrogation program was developed, operated, and assessed by two outside psychologists, neither of whom had any firsthand experience on interrogation tactics, specialized knowledge of al-Qaeda, Middle Eastern culture and language, or academic backgrounds in terrorism studies. These psychologists, John Bruce Jessen and James Elmer Mitchell, who were previously employed

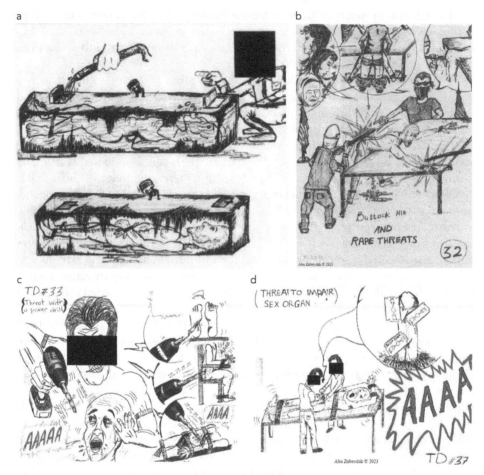

FIGURE 13.11   In a report published in 2023 titled "American Torturers: FBI and CIA Abuses at Dark Sites and Guantanamo," Abu Zubaydah, a long-time detainee at Guantanamo, shared 40 drawings with researchers. These drawings depicted the alleged CIA torture and mistreatment he and other detainees endured. The CIA stated that the original videotapes from the surveillance cameras were destroyed in 2005. *Source:* Copyright Zayn Abu Zubaydah, 2024, via Helen Duffy, Human Rights in Practice, The Hague, The Netherlands.

Figure 13.11a: *Abu Zubaydah, who was arrested by the CIA in March 2002 in Pakistan, has been detained at Guantanamo, along with other CIA "black sites," for over 20 years, without any charge or trial. What follows are Abu Zubaydah's accounts of the drawings shown in Figure 13.11. Please note that his descriptions are reproduced verbatim and thus may be slightly difficult to follow or distressing for some readers.*

"There are two methods of torture, (above) is a (drowning) method with water (water boarding). Water boarding is not only using a water and a board. In this type they put him in a wooden coffin for a long time, until he urinates on himself. Long (remaining) stay, as his hands are behind his back, he's restrained (or in the front). If he was restrained from the front, he will stay like this for days. They ask him and leave him drowned in his waste the drawing (below). If it was behind his back, he will know what they will do from an experience of what they did previously. Whereas they converse with him from a small hatch on the top of the (coffin), asking him of things that as soon as he denies or swears that he doesn't know it, another person starts strongly pouring very cold water, from another small hatch. Because the coffin is made of wood the water would leak but slowly. During this time the investigator asks him and threatens him, then leaves him, until the water reaches his nose, mouth, and then he starts to move strongly with distress while coughing off of drowning. Then the investigator will come over again and the other person stops pouring water. The water will leak from the box, but the cycle repeats again, and he'll stay terrified of drowning all day" (Denbeaux et al. 2023, 91).

Figure 13.11b: "They used to hold the prisoner on a metal table with restraints with his upper body tilted (bent over 90 degrees) for extended hours or days; as forced to relieve or defecate on himself. (They forced him to open his mouth and they would force feed him water or feed him liquids at any time they deemed appropriate, trying to force it in before the prisoner goes unconscious.) The interrogation starts by cursing and screaming then hitting the prisoner with a stick on his rear (sometimes they would hit his hands or feet). Then the interrogator started threatening to put the stick on the rectum of the prisoner until it bleeds. Then the interrogator threatened to rape him or his wife or his daughter (if he had a wife or daughter)—no matter how young she is; or rape his mother—no matter how old she is. Sometimes, I noticed that the interrogators (when he starts working) and thinks that the procedures are not appropriate and against the law; or maybe he will be ashamed of the act in the future; or he gets afraid that he will be punished for it, he would cover a part of his face with a (US flag camouflage) handkerchief" (Denbeaux et al. 2023, 120).

Figure 13.11c: "I myself was hearing the sound of the (power drill) moving very powerfully and violently, and no other sound could cover up its sound except the person who is receiving the torture (threat with a power drill). They were opening the door of my cell (which I stay locked behind 24 hours a day) only when the interrogators or torturers entered. They opened the cell door of the person that they will torture with the (power drill), so I could hear the sound of the (power drill) and the sounds of shouting, begging, and crying in 'horror' of the brother who is receiving the torture. So if they turn off the power drill after several hours, I could hear the sound of the tortured brother still shouting, begging, and crying in (horror), then I hear the sound of (the person who is doing the torture) shouting and threatening that he will use the power drill to drill the head and/or foot, and/or rear end, and/or stomach of the brother who is exposed to torture. When the power drill was stopped, the interrogator and/or person who is assigned to torture me was starting to threaten that he would do all these types of torture using the power drill with me. Then the power drill was started again and the brother started to shout, cry, and beg until his voice suddenly stopped without prior signs. Then the sound of the power drill stopped. At that time only, they closed my cell door!! Then, all the sounds which could be heard by the human ears were stopped . . . (except the sound of my troubled breath)" (Denbeaux et al. 2023, 123).

Figure 13.11d: "This drawing is self-explanatory, so I don't need to further describe. But maybe I should apologize for revealing the private parts/genitals in the drawing. This is because I need to show the ugly truth and the dirty reality which happened to the detainees" (Denbeaux et al. 2023, 127).

with the US Air Force Survival, Evasion, Resistance, and Escape (SERE) School, developed these techniques based on the psychological concept of "learned helplessness." The CIA paid them more than $80 million dollars and provided them with an indemnification agreement to protect them from legal liability that may arise from the use of the program in the future (Shane 2012, 11).

The Senate investigation concluded that the CIA's detention and interrogation program seriously damaged the public and international standing of the United States—a nation that had long been known for its global leadership on human rights (Chen 2019) These techniques violated laws and conventions and did not result in actionable intelligence or detainee cooperation. Reports revealed that personnel who tried to stop these brutal techniques (officers, medical personnel, and analysts) were repeatedly overruled by senior CIA officials.

In 2009, then-President Obama issued an executive order closing the remaining secret CIA facilities (i.e., black sites) and prohibited the use of enhanced interrogation

FIGURE 13.12   Dianne Feinstein, the former Democratic Senator from California until her death in 2023, played a significant role in releasing the Senate Intelligence Committee's report on the CIA's use of enhanced interrogation techniques or torture. Feinstein, who chaired the Senate Intelligence Committee, faced pushback and resistance from some quarters within the US government and intelligence community for her determination to make the report public. *Source:* Benjamin Dunn, CC BY-SA 2.0, via Wikimedia Commons.

techniques. However, to date no CIA officials have been prosecuted for inflicting pain and suffering on prisoners with tactics that went beyond the legal limits, or for providing inaccurate information about the effectiveness of the program to government officers, the media, and the public (Kaplan 2014).

13.3.2 Use of Anonymous Undercover Informants and Entrapment Operations Against the Domestic Population

Another controversial counterterrorism initiative that followed the 9/11 attacks was the prosecution and charging of hundreds of individuals with international terrorism-related offenses, despite the fact that the majority of these individuals did not engage in acts of violence, never left the United States, nor had any communication with anyone associated with terrorism outside of the United States. Information gathered from various sources, including the US Department of Justice, court files, press releases, and inmate data from the US Bureau of Prisons, indicates that prosecutors filed vague and nonviolent charges against these individuals such as material support, criminal conspiracy, and immigration violations. They also relied on information obtained through sting operations to justify lengthy convictions of Muslim Americans, resulting in sentences ranging from several decades to life in prison (Aaronson & Williams 2023; Miller 2021; Shortland et al. 2021).

Use of a Discredited Theory of Radicalization: Predisposition to Secure Convictions
The trend of labeling individuals, namely Muslims, who did not pose any substantial threat to the nation as terrorists began during the heated atmosphere of the post–9/11 era. Many of the charges and subsequent convictions were based on a now discredited theory of radicalization, **"susceptibility (predisposition) to terrorism,"** developed by terrorism consultant Evan F. Kohlmann, who is affiliated with a right-wing anti-Muslim think tank called the Investigative Project on Terrorism (Kundnani 2014). Kohlmann argues that because of their religious and political beliefs (and associations), Muslims have an ideological **predisposition** to violence. It was later discovered that Anders Breivik, the far-right domestic terrorist responsible for the 2012 mass murder in Oslo, Norway, drew inspiration from the Kohlmann's writings. Breivik had copied verbatim 25 pages from an ideologically driven text authored by Kohlmann in his manifesto before carrying out his massacre, resulting in the tragic deaths of almost 70 people (Gardell 2011).

Kohlmann's theory regarding susceptibility to terrorism suggests that individuals, particularly Muslims, can be predisposed to engage in acts of terrorism based on their religious and political beliefs, as well as their associations. The theory offers several indicators that Kohlmann suggests may serve as evidence that individuals are becoming terrorists, including:

FIGURE 13.13   Anders Behring Breivik, a Norwegian far-right extremist who carried out the 2011 Norway attacks, did cite various individuals and sources in his manifesto, titled "2083: A European Declaration of Independence." One of the individuals mentioned in his manifesto was Evan Kohlmann, an American terrorism analyst who specializes in the study of jihadist movements and extremism. *Source:* Ole Berg-Rusten/ POOL/EPA-EFE/Shutterstock.

1. Having extreme religious and political beliefs (e.g., Islamist extremism)
2. Choosing to travel to conflict zones
3. Engaging in online activities related to extremist content
4. Acquiring material and propaganda from the internet or elsewhere
5. Using logistical subterfuge (e.g., encrypting electronic communications or taking indirect routes to destinations)
6. Attempting to contact like-minded individuals
7. Marriage with certain individuals
8. Camouflage dressing

Many experts argue that these indicators can also apply to individuals who never engage in acts of terrorism, and that focusing solely on these factors may result in false positives and civil liberties violations. These activities in themselves are not terrorism. The theory concerns what Kohlmann argues is *susceptibility* to terrorism—persons who may display these indicators have not committed acts of terrorism. Hence, Kohlmann's theory has been widely criticized by researchers as being overly broad and failing to account for the complexity of radicalization. It has never undergone rigorous testing or received verification from independent researchers. Nevertheless, Kohlmann has been repeatedly chosen by the US government as a go-to witness for terrorism-related charges and convictions. Starting in 2004, Kohlmann served as an expert witness for the **Federal Bureau of Investigation (FBI)** in numerous trials related to radicalization and homegrown terrorist threats and assisted other federal agencies through consulting and investigatory help (Aaronson 2013; 2020). By mid-2010, Kohlmann's testimonies, rooted in his theory, had played a significant role in securing convictions for several defendants in US federal courts and military commissions at Guantanamo Bay (Yang 2010).

During several court hearings, lawyers described Kohlmann as untrustworthy as an academic expert and questioned Kohlmann's impartiality as a witness because he appeared to take the role of a government agent rather than an independent expert consultant (Aaronson 2013). Political commentator Wesley Yang interviewed Kohlmann and observed, "Kohlmann does not speak Arabic; has never been to Iraq or Afghanistan; does not hold a postgraduate degree in any related field; has no experience in military, law-enforcement, or intelligence work; and continues to submit—seven years into his career as a court-appointed expert on Al Qaeda—his undergraduate thesis on Arab muja-heddin in Afghanistan as evidence of his expertise" (Yang 2010). In Fact a 2013 court hearing, Kohlmann himself testified that neither his "indicators of terrorism" nor his methodology have been verified by any statistical analysis (Aaronson 2013).

Prodding and Inducements by the FBI Through Sting Operations

The post–9/11 era also witnessed the frequent use of sting operations, in which federal agencies employed informants in attempts to determine if persons of interest would be susceptible to terrorism (Byrnes 2015; Hussain & Ghalayini 2015). According to a 2021 estimate, the FBI was reported to have utilized over 15,000 informants. As noted in Chapter 12, while informants have played a significant role in foiling terrorist plots, in assessing their contributions to counterterrorist it is important to understand the varying roles that informants have played, as well as government definitions of terrorist plots. Of concern is the extent to which the intervention of informants creates a situation that leads a person to engage in behaviors that they would not have done without the interfer-ence of the informant.

In particular, critics have accused the FBI of engaging in **entrapment**—encouraging persons to commit crimes (or suspicious behaviors) they would probably not have com-mitted without the enticement of an informant. Many informants have prior criminal backgrounds or immigration-related issues, and for incentives including financial rewards, clemency, improved immigration status, immunity, or a combination of these benefits, contribute to the creation of criminal cases against individuals who have not engaged in illegal activities (hence plots being "foiled"). Estimates of entrapment among cases of terrorism convictions are high. Academic research published in 2016 suggests that only 5 percent of jihadi prosecutions involving informants since 2001 were actual plots of terrorism (Norris & Grol-Prokopczyk 2016). This analysis of all terrorism pros-ecutions in the US between 2001 and 2016 identified the following six key factors (among others) that suggest entrapment:

1. Defendant has no previous terrorism offenses
2. Government proposed the crime (i.e., informant provided the defendant with the idea for the crime)
3. Informant pressured or persuaded the defendant
4. Material incentive(s) were offered
5. Defendant expressed reluctance
6. The government maintained control of the crime, rather than allowing the crime to happen on its own (Norris & Grol-Prokopczyk 2016).

In the case of counterterrorism, paid FBI informants first spend months befriending the defendants, and over time create intimate relationships with them by sharing their grievances and frustrations: mostly toward the US politics, the invasion of Afghanistan and Iraq, and the widespread mistreatments of Muslims after 9/11. Eventually, the infor-mants propose to their targets the so-called terrorism plots, coaching and providing financial and logistical help (e.g., means of execution, passports, information about travel abroad, and obtaining weapons). When the targets comply, for various possible reasons (e.g., financial gain, emotional distress), their activities are considered to demonstrate involvement in a domestic terrorism plot (Aaronson 2013; Norris & Grol-Prokopczyk 2016).

As an illustration of this process, we discuss two notable cases of have raised entrapment concerns and have received considerable media attention: the Fort Dix Five and the Newburgh Four.

The Fort Dix Five: The Case of Duka Brothers

In 2009, three brothers living in New Jersey were convicted to life in prison after a lengthy sting operation (known as "Fort Dix Five") that involved the use of several paid informants to secure the convictions. The arrests of the Duka brothers and two other men in 2007 was announced to the public in a press conference, described as the foiling of a terrorist plot to attack US military personnel stationed at the Fort Dix military base in New Jersey. However, investigative reporting and analyses of court records have suggested entrapment (Hussain & Ghalayini, 2015).

The brothers gained the attention of the FBI after an employee at a Circuit City electronics store reported suspicious activity on a video brought in to be converted to a DVD. On the video, the Duka brothers and friends, all Muslim, were firing guns at a public shooting range, speaking Arabic, and shouting "Allah u Akbar" (God is great) while on vacation in the Pocono Mountains. In response, the FBI dispatched two informants to befriend the brothers and their associates and assess their susceptibility to terrorism. The first informant, Mahmoud Omar, who had several convictions for fraud and was paid over $200,000 for his work, developed a relationship with the Duka Brothers' brother-in-law, Mohamad Ibrahim Shnewer, who was also on the vacation. As their relations developed, the FBI informant began discussing politics, religion, and other topics with Shnewer, such as the US presence in the Middle East, and determined that Shnewer was open to the idea of violence. The informant taught Shnewer how to find and download Islamist propaganda videos from the internet and eventually brought up the idea of launching an armed attack on a nearby military base, Fort Dix. He then asked Schnewer to recruit others to help them. In response, Schnewer mentioned Serdar Tatar, whose father owned a pizza shop near the base, and the Duka brothers as possible conspirators.

Following his own unsuccessful attempts to involve the Duka brothers in the plot, Omar persisted in trying to convince Shnewer to arrange a meeting with them. According to wiretap recordings made by the FBI, between August and September 2006, Omar approached Shnewer approximately 200 times with the request to facilitate a meeting with the Duka brothers. Omar eventually informed the FBI that the Duka brothers seemed more focused on their family responsibilities.

At this juncture, the FBI made the decision to introduce a new informant into the situation: Besnik Bakalli, an undocumented Albanian who was incarcerated in a Philadelphia prison and facing deportation to his home country. Bakalli agreed to become an informant in exchange for the opportunity to remain in the United States. After receiving brief training from the FBI about the Duka brothers' regular activities (such as where they bought coffee and the mosque they attended), as well as techniques for approaching them, Besnik successfully befriended the brothers.

As time passed, Bakalli gradually introduced discussions about religion and the concept of jihad to the Duka brothers. The brothers, however, remained resistant to discussions of jihad with both Bakalli and Omar, so the FBI put a new plan in place. Aware that the brothers liked guns but were unable to purchase them legally due to their immigration status, Omar approached the brothers with information about a gun store in Baltimore rumored to be conducting under-the-counter sales of firearms at highly discounted prices. In May 2007, Omar orchestrated a meeting between one of the Duka brothers and a fake under-the-counter gun seller in an apartment that had been rented by the FBI for this purpose. The intention was for the Duka brother to inspect the firearms they were considering purchasing. However, shortly after the meeting began, the police entered the apartment and arrested him. Subsequently, the other two Duka brothers were arrested.

While in custody, the Duka brothers awaited charges related to the illegal possession of firearms. However, the following morning, they were unexpectedly presented with charges of conspiracy to kill US military personnel at Fort Dix. These charges were primarily based on recorded conversations between FBI informant Omar and Shnewer, where Shnewer had falsely implicated the Duka brothers by claiming that they were committed to participating in the plan to attack the military base, even though they had no prior knowledge of such a plot.

During the trial, the prosecution pursued the argument that the brothers possessed the "state of mind" to engage in terrorism, an argument based on Kohlmann's susceptibility theory—that the brothers had attempted to purchase weapons, which suggested intent. Kohlmann served as an expert witness for the prosecution. With no direct evidence linking the Duka brothers to a plot to harm soldiers, the judge convicted the brothers and sentenced them to life in prison, stating "I cannot deter this defendant, because of his belief system, from further crimes" (Hussain & Ghalayini 2015). The brothers remain incarcerated (Aaronson 2013).

The Newburgh Four

In June of 2011, four Black Muslims in Newburgh, New York, received 25-year sentences for a terror plot to fire a missile at US military aircraft and plant bombs at synagogues. The arrest was part of an FBI sting operation in which Shahed Hussain, a previous informant in terrorism cases who was known as a skilled con artist, convinced the men to plan and attempt to execute the attack.

Hussain entered the impoverished Muslim community in Newburgh, drawing attention with his flashy appearance and nice cars. He befriended James Cromitie, who was known for his anti-Semitic sentiments, and attempted to educate him about jihad. Hussain offered Cromitie $250,000 along with a BMW, free vacations, and help starting his own business. Cromitie initially tried to avoid Hussain, but when he lost his job and became desperate, he contacted him and agreed to participate. All the while, Cromitie did not seem like a typical terrorist but more like a destitute man willing to do anything for cash. When Cromitie gave him a camera for reconnaissance purposes, Cromitie sold it (Harris 2011).

At Hussain's request, Cromitie recruited three other men—David Williams, Onta Williams, and Laguerre Payen—to join them as lookouts. These men were also poor, and one showed signs of mental illness. They were each paid thousands of dollars to participate in the scheme. The men conducted surveillance of the Air National Guard base and traveled to obtain a missile system and explosive devices (which were fakes, provided by the FBI). They then placed the bombs in cars outside of Jewish targets in the Bronx and began to travel to the Stewart Air National Guard Base in Newburgh, when they were intercepted by law enforcement.

Cromitie remains in prison; however, in July of 2023, Onta Williams, David Williams, and Laguerre Payen were ordered to be released by US District Judge Colleen McMahon for "unduly harsh and unjust" sentences. The judge stated that it was "heinous" of the men to agree to participate in the fabricated plot, but in granting the request for a compassionate release he wrote, "the real lead conspirator was the United States . . . the sentence was the product of a fictitious plot to do things that these men had never remotely contemplated, and that were never going to happen" (Sisak & Peltz 2023).

Data compiled on all terrorism defendants prosecuted by the US Department of Justice since the 9/11 attacks indicate that of the 992 total defendants, 584 convicted of terrorism-related charges have since been released from custody with no supervision or ongoing surveillance. This suggests that the government no longer believes that these individuals are a threat to homeland security. The data show that informants were used in 298 FBI sting operations (Intercept 2023). The frequency with which entrapment occurs, as illustrated in the examples of the Fort Dix Five and the Newburgh Four, raises questions about the actual extent of the terrorist threat within the nation. Such cases are often touted as successful stories in thwarting planned domestic terrorist attacks.

The substantial use of informants operating under a reward-based system—such as monetary incentives or assistance with judicial, legal, or immigration matters—has resulted in an abundance of false intelligence. This has led to innocent individuals being wrongfully targeted as suspects and publicly branded as terrorists. These cases underscore the importance of scrutiny and transparency when evaluating law enforcement's handling of counterterrorism efforts, especially when informants are involved.

The FBI's Anti-Muslim Counterterrorism Training Programs

Some argue that the targeting of Muslims through sting operations is a direct result of the FBI's counterterrorism training programs, which are often mandatory for all agents. These programs have relied heavily on instructional materials that characterize average Muslims as radical and prone to violence, and suggest that the more devout a Muslim is, the more likely they are to commit a terrorist act. This implicitly encourages FBI agents to focus on Muslims in the name of counterterrorism. Revelations leaked by a concerned law enforcement official indicated that the FBI was stocking many biased, Islamophobic books in its libraries and featuring presentations that portrayed Muslims as inherently violent (Ackerman 2011). The books found within the library at the FBI Academy in Quantico, Virginia, included *Slamikaze: Manifestations of Islamic Martyrology* and *Militant Islam Reaches America*, and featured provocative, Islamophobic cover designs. An internal audit conducted by the agency in 2012 revealed that more than 700 pages of inaccurate, biased, and offensive information, such as describing Muslims as violent and sympathetic to terrorists or depicting conversion to Islam as a potential early warning sign of terrorism, had been purged from approximately 300 training presentations given to FBI agents since 9/11 (Ackerman 2012). Human rights groups express concern that the scope of this systemic anti-Muslim training material may be much larger, as the agency has

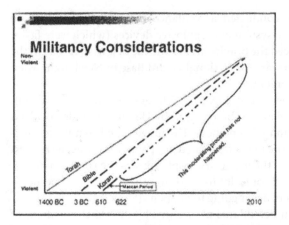

FIGURE 13.14 Training presentations crafted by FBI trainee William Gawthrop for United States security forces have sparked controversy due to their portrayal of mainstream Muslims. In these presentations, mainstream Muslims are depicted as individuals sympathetic to terrorism, prone to violence, and inherently radical. Gawthrop's presentations fail to acknowledge the vast majority of Muslims who unequivocally reject terrorism and violence, instead focusing on a narrow and distorted interpretation of Islamic teachings. By conflating mainstream Islamic beliefs with extremism, these presentations risk alienating Muslim communities and undermining efforts to build trust and cooperation between law enforcement agencies and the people they serve.

reviewed less than 1 percent of all the training documents and presentations (estimated to be over 160,000) provided to its agents.

Following the revelations, the agency's executives announced their commitment to conducting a comprehensive review of all training and reference materials. They pledged to ensure that anti-Islam documents, which include offensive, inappropriate, and insensitive content, would not be incorporated into their future counterterrorism training programs. Civil rights advocates, however, maintain that eradicating the deeply ingrained Islamophobic culture within the agency's training division, which has influenced its agents for years, will be a substantial challenge (Ackerman & Shachtman 2011).

13.4 CONCLUSION

The final chapter of this book examined the ethical and human rights dilemmas that emerged in response to various counterterrorism practices that followed the 9/11 attacks. These practices encompass a wide spectrum, including the use of drones for targeted killings, bulk data collection, and pervasive and invasive surveillance of both foreign and domestic populations, as well as long-standing controversial counterterrorism methods such as enhanced interrogation techniques, stings, entrapment operations, and indefinite detentions without trials.

A significant number of these measures has been disproportionately applied to the Muslim population, both within the United States and globally. Federal and state-level law enforcement agencies, along with military officials, have often justified these measures in the name of safeguarding the homeland from future acts of terror.

It is important to note that this book does not assert that all of these measures were applied without justification. However, it is imperative that we examine counterterrorism practices—their successes as well as their failures—in order to develop effective and ethical means of fighting terrorism. As discussed throughout this text, terrorism is an enduring challenge. Continued social scientific research is critical to furthering our understanding of its nature, causes, consequences, and prevention.

Key Lessons

Lesson 1

Controversial counterterrorism practices employed in the post–9/11 era include the use of unmanned aerial vehicles (drones), mass data collection, and enhanced interrogation techniques, among others. We know about the failures of previous efforts due to the efforts of concerned citizens, politicians, and government officials.

Lesson 2

Drone strikes have been utilized extensively in counterterrorism efforts; however, country-specific reports indicate that many are unsuccessful and cause extensive civilian death and destruction.

Lesson 3

Drone programs may potentially radicalize individuals into terrorism. Critics argue that the high level of civilian casualties caused by drone strikes can foster resentment and anger, driving individuals toward participation in terrorism or supporting violent attacks against US interests in the region.

Lesson 4

The US National Security Agency (NSA) engaged large-scale telecommunication data collection that critics contend violated Americans' 4th Amendment rights. The NSA was unable to produce evidence that its mass data collection and secret surveillance program had thwarted large-scale terrorist attacks against the United States.

Lesson 5

The Senate Intelligence Committee Report on Torture (2014) revealed that interrogations of CIA detainees were brutal and significantly worse than what the agency had presented to policymakers and others.

Lesson 6

Research indicates that the CIA's enhanced interrogation techniques largely failed to result in actionable intelligence. Most detainees subjected to the CIA's enhanced interrogation techniques either provided no intelligence at all or fabricated information on critical issues, resulting in faulty intelligence.

Lesson 7

Sting operations became common in the post–9/11 era, in which federal agencies employed informants to encourage defendants into schemes to commit terrorist acts. Critics argue that these operations often entrap individuals who had no intention of committing acts of terrorism prior to meeting the informant.

Lesson 8

Many terrorism-related convictions in the post–9/11 era relied on a now discredited theory of radicalization developed by terrorism consultant Evan F. Kohlmann. Kohlmann argued that Muslims have an ideological predisposition to violence due to their religious and political beliefs and associations.

Lesson 9

Critics argue that the increasing targeting of Muslims through sting operations in the post–9/11 era is a result of FBI counterterrorism training programs that utilized Islamophobic instructional materials.

Lesson 10

The development of future counterterrorism programs requires learning from past mistakes. Critical examination of past counterterrorism policies and programs is imperative.

Lesson 11

Future social scientific research is critical to addressing the enduring challenge of terrorism.

KEY WORDS

black sites
Central Intelligence Agency (CIA)
coercive techniques

conditioning techniques
corrective techniques
drones

dietary manipulation
entrapment operations
ethics
Federal Bureau of Investigation (FBI)
Government Communications
  Headquarters (GCHQ)
interrogation programs
mass data collection
National Security Agency (NSA)
predisposition or susceptibility theory

PRISM Program
Senate Torture Report
signals intelligence (SIGINT)
Tailored Access Operations (TAO)
targeted killing
torture memos
undercover informants
unmanned aerial vehicles (UAV)
waterboarding

RECOMMENDED SOURCES

Research Articles & Books

Aaronson, T. (2013). The terror factory: Inside the FBI's manufactured war on terrorism. New York: Ig Publishing.

International Human Rights and Conflict Resolution at Stanford Law School & Global Justice Clinic at NYU School of Law (2012). Living under drones: Death, injury, and trauma to civilians from US drone practices in Pakistan.

Kurtulus, E. N. (2012). The new counterterrorism: Contemporary counterterrorism trends in the United States and Israel. *Studies in Conflict & Terrorism, 35*(1), 37–58

Marks, J. H. (2005). What counts in counterterrorism. Colum. Hum. Rts. L. Rev., 37, 559.

Miller, S. (2021). Use of stings in counterterrorism: Entrapment and ethics. In Counterterrorism: The ethical issues (pp. 105–115). Edward Elgar Publishing.

Norris, J. J., & Grol-Prokopczyk, H. (2016). Estimating the prevalence of entrapment in post-9/11 terrorism cases. *J. Crim. L. & Criminology, 105,* 609.

Wolfendale, J. (2021). Technology as Terrorism: Police Control Technologies and Drone Warfare. Ins A. Henschke, A. Reed, S. Robbins, & S. Miller (Eds), Counter-Terrorism, Ethics and Technology: Emerging Challenges at the Frontiers of Counter-Terrorism, (pp. 1–22). Springer

News Articles & Government and Think Tank Reports

FBI counterterrorism informant spent a decade committing fraud.
    Author(s): Trevor Aaronson
    Source: The Intercept

Video: FBI trainer says forget 'irrelevant' al-Qaida, target Islam.
    Author(s): William Gawthrop
    Source: Wired

US to continue 'signature strikes' on people suspected of terrorist links.
    Author(s): Spencer Ackerman
    Source: The Guardian

Senate report: CIA misled lawmakers, public on enhanced interrogation.
    Author(s): Rebecca Kaplan
    Source: CBS News

Study of the central intelligence agency's detention and interrogation program together with foreword by chairman Feinstein and additional and minority views.
    Author(s): Dianne Feinstein
    Source: U.S. Senate

Documents reveal top NSA hacking unit.
    Author(s): Von Spiegel Staff
    Source: Spiegel International
Edward Snowden: Leaks that exposed US spy programme.
    Source: BBC News
Who, what, why: when is it legal to kill your own citizens?
    Source: BBC News
The CIA torture report: what you need to know.
    Author(s): Sarah Childress, Priyanka Boghani, & Jason M. Breslow
    Source: Frontline
Role of torture revisited in Bin Laden narrative.
    Author(s): Scott Shane
    Source: The New York Times
Secret 'kill list' proves a test of Obama's principles and will.
    Author(s): Jo Becker & Scott Shane
    Source: The New York Times
Mass surveillance exposed by Snowden 'not justified by fight against terrorism'.
    Author(s): Owen Bowcott
    Source: The Guardian
Leaked documents reveal new details about the U.S.'s lethal drone programs.
    Author(s): Lauren Walker
    Source: Newsweek
Afghanistan war logs: Task Force 373 – special forces hunting top Taliban.
    Author(s): Nick Davies
    Source: The Guardian
Judge green-lights 'kill list' lawsuit.
    Author(s): Josh Gerstein
    Source: Politico
US Senate report slams CIA torture, lies.
    Source: Human Rights Watch (HRW)

Documentaries, Videos, and Other Educational Media

National Bird
    Producer(s)/Director(s): Sonia Kennebeck & Ines Hoffmann Kanna
    Source: PBS
Snowden
    Producer(s)/Director(s): Oliver Stone
    Source: Netflix
The Newburgh Sting
    Producer(s)/Director(s): Kate Davis & David Heilbroner
The ~~Torture~~ Report
    Producer(s)/Director(s): Scott Z. Burns
Shock and Awe
    Producer(s)/Director(s): Rob Reiner
Turning Point: 9/11 and the War on Terror
    Producer(s)/Director(s): Brian Knappenberger
    Source: Netflix
The Mauritanian
    Producer(s)/Director(s): Kevin Macdonald
Moral Implications of U.S. Anti-Terrorism Policies
    Featuring: Nina Shea, J. Stephen Morrison, John Wimberly
    Source: WETA (The Greater Washington Educational Television Association)
The ethics and law of international counterterrorism: The challenges of the next 10 years
    Featuring: Gabriella Blum, Kenneth Anderson, Sarah Cleveland, Stephen Carter, John Rizzo
    Source: Harvard Law School YouTube Channel
The ethics and law of domestic counterterrorism: The challenges of the next 10 years'
    Featuring: Philip Heymann, Trevor Morrison, Ben Wizner, Gerald Neuman, Richard
    Source: Harvard Law School YouTube Channel
Is a "Kill List" of Terrorists Ethical?
    Source: Carnegie Council for Ethics in International Affairs YouTube Channel
Religion and Terrorism: A Human Rights Approach
    Featuring: David Little
    Source: Case Western Reserve University School of Law YouTube Channel
How Terrorism Ends: Understanding the Decline and Demise of Terrorist Campaigns
    Featuring: Audrey Kurth Cronin
    Source: George Mason University Television YouTube Channel
Drone wars: the gamers recruited to kill
    Featuring: Michael Haas, Missy Cummings, Chris Woods
    Source: The Guardian YouTube Channel

REFERENCES

Aaronson, T. (2013). The terror factory: Inside the FBI's manufactured war on terrorism. Ig Publishing.

Aaronson, T. (2020). FBI counterterrorism informant spent a decade committing fraud. *The Intercept.* https://theintercept.com/2020/12/29/fbi-counterterrorism-informant-wire-fraud-scam/

Aaronson, T., & Williams, M. (2023). Trial and terror. *The Intercept.* https://trial-and-terror.theintercept.com/

Ackerman, S. (2011). New evidence of anti-Islam bias underscores deep challenges for FBI's reform pledge. *Wired.* https://www.wired.com/2011/09/fbi-islam-domination

Ackerman, S. (2012). FBI purges hundreds of terrorism documents in Islamophobia probe. *Wired.* https://www.wired.com/2012/02/hundreds-fbi-documents-muslims/

Ackerman, S. (2014). 41 men target but 1,147 people killed: US drone strikes: The facts on the ground. *The Guardian.* https://www.theguardian.com/us-news/2014/nov/24/sp-us-drone-strikes-kill-1147

Ackerman, S. (2016). US to continue "signature strikes" on people suspected of terrorist links. *The Guardian.* https://www.theguardian.com/us-news/2016/jul/01/obama-continue-signature-strikes-drones-civilian-deaths

Ackerman, S., & Shachtman, N. (2011). Video: FBI trainer says forget "irrelevant" Al-Qaida, target Islam. *Wired.* https://www.wired.com/2011/09/fbi-islam-qaida-irrelevant/

Acosta, J. (2015). Obama to make new push to shift control of drones from CIA to Pentagon. CNN. https://www.cnn.com/2015/04/27/politics/drones-cia-pentagon-white-house/index.html

Appelbaum, J., Poitras, L., Rosenbach, M., Stocker, C., Schindler, J., & Stark, H. (2014). Documents reveal top NSA hacking unit. *Der Spiegel.* https://www.spiegel.de/international/world/the-nsa-uses-powerful-toolbox-in-effort-to-spy-on-global-networks-a-940969.html

Ball, J. (2013). NSA monitored calls of 35 world leaders after US official handed over contacts. *The Guardian.* https://www.theguardian.com/world/2013/oct/24/nsa-surveillance-world-leaders-calls

Ball, J., Borger, J., & Greenwald, G. (2013). Revealed: How US and UK spy agencies defeat internet privacy and security. *The Guardian.* https://www.theguardian.com/world/2013/sep/05/nsa-gchq-encryption-codes-security

Bandow, D. (2010). Terrorism: Why they want to kill us. *CATO Institute.* https://www.cato.org/commentary/terrorism-why-they-want-kill-us

BBC (2014). Edward Snowden: Leaks that exposed US spy programme. https://www.bbc.com/news/world-us-canada-23123964

Becker, J., & Shane, S. (2012). Secret "kill list" proves a test of Obama's principles and will. *New York Times.* https://www.nytimes.com/2012/05/29/world/obamas-leadership-in-war-on-al-qaeda.html?pagewanted=all

Bender, J. (2015). Former US military intel chief: The Obama administration loves the ability "to find a guy in the middle of the desert in some sh---y little village and drop a bomb on his head." *Business Insider.* https://www.businessinsider.com/former-us-military-intel-chief-the-obama-administration-loves-the-ability-to-find-a-guy-in-the-middle-of-the-desert-in-some-sh-y-little-village-and-drop-a-bomb-on-his-head-and-kill-him-2015-10

Bergen, P. (2012). Drone is Obama's weapon of choice. CNN. https://www.cnn.com/2012/09/05/opinion/bergen-obama-drone/index.html

Blankenship, B. (2023). Ten years after Snowden leaks, dangers of US spying continue. *Global Times.* https://www.globaltimes.cn/page/202305/1290958.shtml

Bowcott, O. (2014). Mass surveillance exposed by Snowden "not justified by fight against terrorism." *The Guardian.* https://www.theguardian.com/world/2014/dec/08/mass-surveillance-exposed-edward-snowden-not-justified-by-fight-against-terrorism

Bradbury, S. (2005a). Memorandum for John A. Rizzo senior deputy general counsel, central intelligence agency. US Department of Justice, Office of Legal Counsel. https://www

.herenditionproject.org.uk/pdf/PDF%20 16%20[Bradbury%20Memo%20to%20 Rizzo%20Certain%20Techniques% 2010%20May%20200.pdf

Bradbury, S. (2005b). Memorandum for John A. Rizzo senior deputy general counsel, central intelligence agency. US Department of Justice, Office of Legal Counsel. https://www.justice .gov/sites/default/files/olc/legacy/2013/10/21/ memo-bradbury2005.pdf

Bush, G. W. (2002). Humane treatment of al-Qaeda and Taliban detainees. The White House. https://nsarchive2.gwu.edu/NSAEBB/ NSAEBB127/02.02.07.pdf

Bybee, J. S. (2002a). Memorandum for Alberta R. Gonzales, Counsel to the president. US Department of Justice, Office of Legal Counsel. https://www.therenditionproject .org.uk/pdf/PDF%2019%20[Bybee%20 Memo%20to%20Gonzales%20Standards %20Interrogation%201%20Aug.pdf

Bybee, J. S. (2002b). Memorandum for John Rizzo acting general counsel of the Central Intelligence Agency. US Department of Justice, Office of Legal Counsel. https://www .therenditionproject.org.uk/pdf/PDF%20 15%20[Bybee%20Memo%20to%20CIA%20 1%20Aug%202002].pdf

Byrnes, J. (2015). FBI investigating ISIS suspects in all 50 states. The Hill. https://thehill.com/ blogs/blog-briefing-room/233832-fbi-investigating-isis-suspects-in-all-50-states/

Chen, D. (2019). Senate investigation into CIA torture hits the big screen. Friends Committee on National Legislation. https://www .fcnl.org/updates/2019-11/senate-investigation-cia-torture-hits-big-screen

Childress, S., Boghani, P., Breslow, J. M. (2014). The CIA torture report: What you need to know. PBS. https://www.pbs.org/wgbh/ frontline/article/the-cia-torture-report-what-you-need-to-know/

Crabtree, I. (2019). The real story behind Amazon's the report starring Adam Driver as Daniel J. Jones. Esquire. https://www.esquire .com/entertainment/movies/a30154297/ daniel-jones-cia-the-report-true-story/

Crawford, N. C. (2003). The slippery slope to preventive war. Ethics & International Affairs, 17(1), 30–36.

Currier, C. (2015). The kill chain. The Intercept. https://theintercept.com/drone-papers/ the-kill-chain/

Dance, G. (2013). Connected by cables. The Guardian. https://www.theguardian.com/ world/interactive/2013/nov/01/snowden-nsa-files-surveillance-revelations-decoded# section/3

Davies, N. (2010). Afghanistan war logs: Task Force 373—special forces hunting top Taliban. The Guardian. https://www.theguardian .com/world/2010/jul/25/task-force-373-secret-afghanistan-taliban

Debelak, J. (2013). Why the NSA's gathering of metadata matters. ACLU. https://www.aclu-wa.org/blog/why-nsa-s-gathering-metadata-matters

Denbeaux, M., Ghannam, D. J., & Zubaydah, A. (2023). American Torturers: FBI and CIA Abuses at Dark Sites and Guantanamo. https://papers.ssrn.com/sol3/papers.cfm? abstract_id=4443310

Der Spiegel (2013). Britain's GCHQ hacked Belgian telecoms firm. Spiegel International. https://www.spiegel.de/international/europe/ british-spy-agency-gchq-hacked-belgian-telecoms-firm-a-923406.html

Edney-Browne, A. (2019). The psychosocial effects of drone violence: Social isolation, self-objectification, and depoliticization. Political Psychology, 40(6), 1341–1356.

Elliott, J., & Meyer, T. (2013). Claim on "attacks thwarted" by NSA spreads despite lack of evidence. ProPublica. https://www.propublica .org/article/claim-on-attacks-thwarted-by-nsa-spreads-despite-lack-of-evidence

Entous, A., & Barnes, J. E. (2011). U.S. doubts intelligence that led to Yemen strike. Wall Street Journal. https://www.wsj.com/articles/ SB10001424052970203889504577126883574284126

FCNL (2021). Understanding drones. Friends Committee on National Legislation. https:// www.fcnl.org/updates/2021-10/under standing-drones#:~:text=Unmanned%20 aerial%20vehicles%2C%20commonly%20 known,and%20other%20non%2Dlethal %20operations

Gallagher, R., & Greenwald, G. (2014). How the NSA plans to infect "millions" of computers with malware. *The Intercept.* https://theintercept.com/2014/03/12/nsa-plans-infect-millions-computers-malware/

Gardell, M. (2011). Flat examination of Breivik's background. Fria Tidningen. https://www.fria.nu/artikel/89268

Gellman, B. & Poitras, L. (2013). U.S., British intelligence mining data from nine U.S. internet companies in broad secret program. *Washington Post.* https://www.washingtonpost.com/investigations/us-intelligence-mining-data-from-nine-us-internet-companies-in-broad-secret-program/2013/06/06/3a0c0da8-cebf-11e2-8845-d970ccb04497_story.html

Gerstein, J. (2018a). Judge green-lights "kill list" lawsuit. *Politico.* https://www.politico.com/blogs/under-the-radar/2018/06/13/judge-green-lights-kill-list-lawsuit-645584

Gerstein, J. (2018b). Under the radar. *Politico.* https://www.politico.com/blogs/under-the-radar/2018/06/13/judge-green-lights-kill-list-lawsuit-645584

Gettinger, D. (2018). Summary of drone spending in the fy 2019 defense budget request. Center for the Study of the Drone at Bard College. https://dronecenter.bard.edu/files/2018/04/CSD-Drone-Spending-FY19-Web-1.pdf

Gonzales, A. R. (2002). Memorandum for the president. White House, Office of Counsel. https://nsarchive2.gwu.edu/NSAEBB/NSAEBB127/02.01.25.pdf

Gordon, A. (2006). "Purity of arms," "preemptive war," and "selective targeting" in the context of terrorism: General, conceptual, and legal analyses. *Studies in Conflict & Terrorism, 29*(5), 493–508.

Greenwald, G. (2009). A Rumsfeld-era reminder about what causes Terrorism. *Salon.* https://www.salon.com/2009/10/20/terrorism_6/

Greenwald, G. (2012). Joe Klein's sociopathic defense of drone killings of children. *The Guardian.* https://www.theguardian.com/commentisfree/2012/oct/23/klein-drones-morning-joe

Greenwald, G., & MacAskill, E. (2013). NSA PRISM program taps in to user data of Apple, Google and others. *The Guardian.* https://www.theguardian.com/world/2013/jun/06/us-tech-giants-nsa-data

Hari, J. (2010). Johann Hari: Obama's robot wars endanger us all. *The Independent.* https://www.independent.co.uk/voices/commentators/johann-hari/johann-hari-obamas-robot-wars-endanger-us-all-2106931.html

Harris, L., & Monaghan, R. (2018). Ethics and human rights in counterterrorism. In A. Silke (Ed). Routledge Handbook of Terrorism and Counterterrorism (pp. 483–492). Routledge.

Harris, P. (2011). Newburgh Four: Poor, black, and jailed under FBI "entrapment" tactics. *The Guardian.* https://www.theguardian.com/world/2011/dec/12/newburgh-four-fbi-entrapment-terror

Hattem, J. (2014). Websites look to "harness the outrage." *The Hill.* https://thehill.com/policy/technology/197859-thousands-of-sites-to-protest-nsa-spying/

Human Rights Watch (2014a). A wedding that became a funeral: US drone attack on marriage procession in Yemen. https://www.hrw.org/report/2014/02/19/wedding-became-funeral/us-drone-attack-marriage-procession-yemen

Human Rights Watch (2014b). US: Senate report slams CIA torture, lies. https://www.hrw.org/news/2014/12/10/us-senate-report-slams-cia-torture-lies

Hussain, M., & Ghalayini, R. (2015). Christie's conspiracy: The real story behind the Fort Dix Five terror plot. *The Intercept.* https://theintercept.com/2015/06/25/fort-dix-five-terror-plot-the-real-story/

International Human Rights and Conflict Resolution at Stanford Law School & Global Justice Clinic at NYU School of Law (2012). Living under drones: Death, injury, and trauma to civilians from US drone practices in Pakistan.

Isikoff, M. (2013). NSA program stopped no terror attacks, says White House panel member. NBC News. https://www.nbcnews.com/news/other/nsa-program-stopped-no-terror-attacks-says-white-house-panel-f2D11783588

Kaplan, R. (2014). Senate report: CIA misled lawmakers, public on enhanced interrogation. CBS News. https://www.cbsnews.com/

news/senate-report-cia-misled-lawmakers-public-on-enhanced-interrogation/

Kundnani, A. (2014). *The Muslims are coming! Islamophobia, extremism, and the domestic war on terror.* Verso Books.

Kurtulus, E. N. (2012). The new counterterrorism: Contemporary counterterrorism trends in the United States and Israel. *Studies in Conflict & Terrorism, 35*(1), 37–58.

Lewis, N. (2002). A guide to the memos on torture. *New York Times.* https://archive.nytimes.com/www.nytimes.com/ref/international/24MEMO-GUIDE.html

Macaskill, E., & Dance, G. (2013). NSA files decoded: What the revelations mean for you. *The Guardian.* https://www.theguardian.com/world/interactive/2013/nov/01/snowden-nsa-files-surveillance-revelations-decoded#section/1

Marks, J. H. (2005). What counts in counterterrorism. *Columbia Human Rights Law Review, 37*, 559.

Mazzetti, M. (2009). U.S. says C.I.A. destroyed 92 tapes of interrogations. *New York Times.* https://www.nytimes.com/2009/03/03/washington/03web-intel.html

McLaughlin, J. (2015). U.S. mass surveillance has no record of thwarting large terror attacks, regardless of Snowden leaks. *The Intercept.* https://theintercept.com/2015/11/17/u-s-mass-surveillance-has-no-record-of-thwarting-large-terror-attacks-regardless-of-snowden-leaks/

Miller, S. (2021). Use of stings in counterterrorism: Entrapment and ethics. In S. Miller, A. Henschke, & J. Feltes (Eds.), Counterterrorism: The ethical issues (pp. 105–115). Edward Elgar Publishing.

Norris, J. J., & Grol-Prokopczyk, H. (2016). Estimating the prevalence of entrapment in post-9/11 terrorism cases. *Journal of Criminal Law and Criminology, 105*, 609.

Open Society Justice Initiative (2015). Death by drone: Civilian harm caused by U.S. targeted killings in Yemen. https://www.justiceinitiative.org/uploads/1284eb37-f380-4400-9242-936a15e4de6c/death-drones-report-eng-20150413.pdf

Pew (2012). Pakistani public opinion ever more critical of U.S. Pew Research Center. https://www.pewresearch.org/global/2012/06/27/pakistani-public-opinion-ever-more-critical-of-u-s/

Powell, C. L. (2002). Draft decision memorandum for the president on the applicability of the Geneva Convention to the conflict in Afghanistan. United States Department of State. https://nsarchive2.gwu.edu/NSAEBB/NSAEBB127/02.01.26.pdf

Prokop, A. (2014). The huge new Senate report on CIA torture, explained. *Vox.* https://www.vox.com/2014/12/9/7339753/senate-torture-report

Senate Select Committee on Intelligence (2014). Study of the central intelligence agency's detention and interrogation program together with foreword by chairman Feinstein and additional and minority views. US Senate. https://www.intelligence.senate.gov/sites/default/files/publications/CRPT-113srpt288.pdf

Shah, A. (2016). Drone blowback in Pakistan is a myth. Here's why. Carnegie Endowment for International Peace. https://carnegieendowment.org/2016/05/17/drone-blowback-in-pakistan-is-myth.-here-s-why-pub-63635

Shane, S. (2012). Role of torture revisited in Bin Laden narrative. *New York Times.* https://www.nytimes.com/2012/05/01/world/americas/senators-reject-claim-that-torture-helped-hunt-for-bin-laden.html

Shortland, N. D., Evans, N., & Colautti, J. (2021). A public health ethics model of countering violent extremism. *Terrorism and Political Violence, 33*(2), 324–337.

Singer, P. (2023). Ethics. *Encyclopedia Britannica.* https://www.britannica.com/topic/ethics-philosophy/Anthropology-and-ethics.

Sisak, M. R., & Peltz, J. (2023). Judge orders release of 3 of "Newburgh Four" and assails FBI's role in a post-9/11 terror sting. Associated Press. https://apnews.com/article/newburgh-four-terrorism-sting-fbi-compassionate-release-62065491755cf80766aaab46410cdeff

Sottek, T. C., & Kopfstein, J. (2013). Everything you need to know about PRISM. *The Verge.* https://www.theverge.com/2013/7/17/4517480/nsa-spying-PRISM-surveillance-cheat-sheet

Steele, C. (2014). The 10 most disturbing snowmen revelations. *PC Mag.* https://www

.pcmag.com/news/the-10-most-disturbing-snowden-revelations

Szoldra, P. (2016). This is everything Edward Snowden revealed in one year of unprecedented top-secret leaks. *Business Insider.* https://www.businessinsider.com/snowden-leaks-timeline-2016-9

The Intercept. (2023). Trial and terror. https://trial-and-terror.theintercept.com/

US Department of Justice (2002). Memorandum for William J. Haynes II, general counsel, department of defense. Office of Legal Counsel. https://nsarchive2.gwu.edu/NSAEBB/NSAEBB127/02.01.09.pdf

Walker, L. (2015). Leaked documents reveal new details about the U.S.'s lethal drone programs. *Newsweek.* https://www.newsweek.com/leaked-documents-reveal-new-details-about-uss-lethal-drone-programs-383949

Webster, S. C. (2014). Edward Snowden's 10 biggest revelations about the NSA. *The Progressive.* https://progressive.org/latest/edward-snowden-s-10-biggest-revelations-nsa/

West, A. (2013). 17 disturbing things Snowden has taught us (so far). *The World.* https://theworld.org/stories/2013-07-09/17-disturbing-things-snowden-has-taught-us-so-far

Wolfendale, J. (2021). Technology as terrorism: Police control technologies and drone warfare. In A. Henschke, A. Reed, S. Robbins, & S. Miller (Eds.), *Counter-terrorism, ethics and technology: Emerging challenges at the frontiers of counter-terrorism* (pp. 1–22). Springer,

Woods, C. (2012). "Drones causing mass trauma among civilians," major study finds. Bureau of Investigative Journalism. https://www.thebureauinvestigates.com/stories/2012-09-25/drones-causing-mass-trauma-among-civilians-major-study-finds

Yang, W. (2010). The terrorist search engine. *New York Magazine.* https://nymag.com/news/features/69920/

Zenko, M. (2011). Targeted killings and America's "kill lists." Council on Foreign Affairs. https://www.cfr.org/blog/targeted-killings-and-americas-kill-lists

GLOSSARY

ABU SAYYAF GROUP a militant Islamist extremist group in the Philippines with the goal of establishing an independent Muslim state.

ACTIVE SUPPORT the provision of direct financial or military support including intelligence, tactical training, and war equipment to terrorist groups.

ACTIVIST in the two-pyramids model of radicalization developed by McCauley and Moskalenko, a person engaged in legal or political action. Activists occupy the top of the action pyramid of the two-pyramids model.

ADVERTISEMENT a strategic objective of terrorism in which attacks are carried out against targets for their potential to generate maximum media attention and publicize the terrorists' cause.

AFRICAN NATIONAL CONGRESS a political party and liberation movement in South Africa known for its opposition to apartheid.

AL-KHANSAA BRIGADE an all-women morality police force of the Islamic State (IS/ISIL/ISIS) that monitors women in ISIS territories to ensure that they adhere to the groups' rules.

ALTERNATIVE RIGHT (ALT-RIGHT) loosely connected diverse groups of far-right nationalist movements that reject mainstream conservative politics and advocate for White supremacy.

AL-QAEDA a Salafist Jihadi terrorist organization founded by Osama bin Laden in the late 1980s, responsible for the terrorist attacks of September 11, 2001 in the United States.

ANARCHISM a political ideology that favors the establishment of a noncoercive society without an official governing body, characterized by opposition to the state, authority, man-made laws, and coercive forms of power.

ANIMAL LIBERATION FRONT (ALF) an international, loosely organized far-left extremist movement that fights against the abuse and exploitation of animals.

ANOMIE social instability resulting from the inability of a state to adequately regulate goal seeking behaviors and the acts of its people, as described in Merton's anomie theory of criminal behavior.

ANTI-FASCISTS (ANTIFA) an informal anti-fascist, anti-capitalist, and anti-racist political movement motivated in opposition to right-wing ideologies.

ANTI-MUSLIM ORGANIZATIONS organizations with anti-Muslim agendas, many of which claim to be objective sources for information about Middle Eastern and Muslim culture.

ANTI-TERRORISM measures that aim to prevent terrorist attacks from happening.

ANXIETY a psychological feeling of uneasiness that may accompany the experience of stress.

APOCALYPTIC TERRORISM terrorism aimed to initiate a global level catastrophe as part of a necessary divine mission to initiate end of the world and religious promises of a new beginning.

ARAB SPRING a series of pro-democracy protests, uprisings, and armed revolts in the Middle East and North Africa that began in Tunisia in 2010 and then spread to other countries in the MENA region.

ARMED ASSAULT terrorist actions with the primary motivation of killing or physically harming an adversary, using lethal weapons such as firearms, sharp instruments, and incendiary devices.

ARMY OF GOD (AOG) a Christian fundamentalist terrorist organization in the United States known for anti-abortion violence.

ASSASSINATION the murder of an important public figure, such as a head of state, government leader, political party leader, celebrity, prominent member of a social or political movement, or other senior leader, such as a high-ranking military official.

ATTRITION a strategic objective of terrorism aimed at reducing the enemy's strength.

AUM SHINRIKYO a Japanese religious movement and doomsday cult that carried out the 1995 sarin gas attack in the Tokyo subway

AVOIDANCE BEHAVIORS behavioral coping responses to stressors that involve the restriction of what one does, such as limiting travel and avoiding large events or crowded places.

BASQUE FATHERLAND AND LIBERTY (ETA) a nationalist and separatist organization that operated in a region of Spain and France known as Basque from 1959 to 2018, with the goal of creating an independent Basque state.

BEHAVIORAL COPING STRATEGIES actions that people take in attempts to prevent or deal with the harm caused by experience of stress.

BEHAVIORAL DISENGAGEMENT limiting one's activities to avoid or cope with stressful situations.

BEHEADINGS killings by decapitation; a terrorism tactic for which the Islamic State gained notoriety by publicly releasing videoed executions.

BLACK SEPTEMBER a Palestinian terrorist group known for the Munich massacre in which they took 11 members of the Israeli Olympic team hostage in during the 1972 Olympic Games in Germany.

BLACK SITES clandestine detention facilities located in extrajudicial domains in foreign countries.

BLACK WIDOWS the Russian nickname for the Islamist Chechen all-female battalion of suicide bombers.

BOMBING the use of explosives in an attack.

BURGLARY the act of illegally entering a building or other area to commit theft.

CASCADING NETWORK ACTIVATION a model developed by Robert Entman that illustrates the process by which news related to US foreign policy spreads through multiple points of influence including administration, political elites, the media, news frames, and the public.

CAUSAL FACTORS conditions that contribute to the occurrence of a particular event or result (e.g., terrorism or extremism).

CENTRAL INTELLIGENCE AGENCY (CIA) the foreign intelligence service of the US federal government, responsible for gathering, processing, and analyzing national security information.

CHARITY a nonprofit organization that provides help and raises money for those in need.

CHRISTIAN IDENTITY a religious, anti-Semitic, and racist extremist Protestant group that operates across hundreds of small churches in every region of the United States and in some other English-speaking countries including Canada, England, Ireland, Australia, and South Africa.

CITIZEN REPORTING the use of social media by citizens who are not professional journalists, to spread news.

CIVIC NATIONALISM identification with and support of one's nation based on principles of human rights and personal freedom.

CIVILIAN TARGETS places and individuals targeted in acts of terrorism that are not members of security forces, such as private citizens and civilian businesses.

COERCIVE TECHNIQUES a category of enhanced interrogation techniques used by the CIA designed to increase psychological and physical stress on the detainee.

COGNITIVE RESTRUCTURING a process by which people change the way they think.

COLD WAR a period of geopolitical tension between the United States and the Soviet Union as each engaged in the development of nuclear weapons.

COLLECTIVE BEHAVIOR group-level behavior that is purposeful, organized, and dedicated to achieving a common social goal.

COMBAT 18 a neo-Nazi terrorist group that originated in the United Kingdom in 1992 and spread throughout Europe, the United States, and Canada.

COMMUNISM an ideology and form of government that aims to eliminate socioeconomic class struggles by creating a classless society in which all means of production and products are communally owned by the people.

COMMUNIST PARTY OF THE UNITED STATES (CPUSA) a communist party established in New York in 1919 following the Russian Revolution.

COMPLIANCE terrorist targeting of places and individuals that are important to the adversary government in order to frighten them into fulfilling the demands of the group to avoid facing more severe consequences.

CONCENTRATED DISADVANTAGE   areas or neighborhoods with a high proportion of low socioeconomic status residents.

CONCERNED CHRISTIANS   an American doomsday cult and religious movement that planned to carry out violent terrorist activities to hasten the second coming of the Messiah.

CONDITIONING TECHNIQUES   a category of enhanced interrogation techniques used by the CIA designed to demonstrate to detainees that they have no control over basic human needs.

CORRECTIVE TECHNIQUES   a category of enhanced interrogation techniques used by the CIA that involves some degree of physical interaction with the detainees to correct or startle them.

COUNTERFEITING   the fraudulent imitation of a trusted brand or product to gain profit.

COUNTERING VIOLENT EXTREMISM (CVE)   terrorism prevention efforts that seek to prevent individuals from radicalizing to commit acts of violence.

COUNTERTERRORISM   political, security, or military responses to existing terrorist threats or attacks.

CRIMINALIZATION   the act of making a behavior illegal and therefore a criminal offense. In the case of terrorism, criminalization could include officially designating a group as a terrorist organization on a national list.

CRIMINOLOGY   the study of the nature, extent, and cause of crime and the control of criminal behavior.

CROWDFUNDING   funding a cause or a project by soliciting relatively small amounts of money from a large number of people via the internet.

CRYPTOCURRENCIES   digital currencies that are decentralized and encrypted to secure transactions, which are verified and recorded on a blockchain.

DELEGITIMIZATION   the act of taking away a valid status or authority. Groups that have been delegitimized are not considered to be legal actors.

DEPARTMENT OF HOMELAND SECURITY (DHS)   a stand-alone executive department that combined 22 different US federal departments and agencies, in an attempt to unify national security efforts following the terrorist attacks of September 11, 2001.

DEPERSONALIZATION   a process by which individual group members are seen only as the stereotypical group prototype and not as unique individual actors.

DEPRESSION   a mood disorder characterized by feelings of unhappiness, hopelessness, and low self-esteem, among other symptoms.

DERADICALIZATION   when one rejects the terrorist mindset or experiences changes in the values or attitudes that support terrorism.

DERADICALIZATION PROGRAMS   programs that are designed to change extremist attitudes and modify violent behavior with the goal of getting individuals to give up terrorism.

DESIGNATION   the action of assigning an official label to someone or something. This could include officially declaring a group as a terrorist organization.

DETERRENCE THEORY   a classical criminological theory that assumes people are rational actors that weigh the costs and benefits of their actions and posits that crime may be deterred with punishments that are certain, swift, and severe.

DIASPORA FUNDING   in terrorism financing, funding provided to terrorist groups by supporters who leave their homelands and settle in other countries.

DIETARY MANIPULATION   a US CIA enhanced interrogation technique in which detainees are only provided a bland unappetizing diet.

DIFFERENTIAL ASSOCIATION   in Sutherland's differential association theory of criminal behavior, interactions with others, such as family members and peers, who hold definitions, including values, perspectives, attitudes, motivations, and techniques, that support criminality.

DIGITAL TECHNOLOGY   systems and devices that process, store, and transmit information electronically.

DISCRIMINATE ATTACKS   terrorist attacks in which groups only attack enemy combatants and legitimate military targets such as military officials, installations, and police officers.

DISENGAGEMENT   when terrorist ceases their involvement in terrorist activities; disengagement requires a change in behavior.

DISENGAGEMENT PROGRAMS   countering violent extremism (CVE) programs that attempt to convince individuals to abandon involvement in a terrorist group.

DISINFORMATION   informational content that is false and deliberately intended to harm someone or something.

DISORIENTATION   a strategic objective of terrorism aimed at confusing the adversary.

DOMESTIC TERRORISM   terrorist acts against the civilian population or infrastructure of a nation committed by perpetrators, often citizens, within that nation. Also known as homegrown terrorism.

DRONES remotely operated computer-based aerial systems frequently employed for carrying out lethal counterterrorism operations and long-range surveillance on enemy targets. Also known as unmanned aerial vehicles (UAVs).

DRUG TRAFFICKING global trade including the cultivation, manufacture, distribution, and sale of illegal drugs.

EARTH LIBERATION FRONT (ELF) a far-left group that engages in economic sabotage to stop the exploitation and destruction of the environment.

EASTERN LIGHTNING a highly secretive, organized, and violent Christian movement founded in the Henan Province of China in 1990 with an apocalyptic focus.

ENHANCED INTERROGATION TECHNIQUES the term given to the systematic torture applied by the CIA and other governmental operatives on terrorism suspects and other detainees in remote detention centers, including the Guantanamo Bay detention camp.

ENTRAPMENT OPERATIONS law enforcement programs that involve the use of an informant to encourage persons to commit crimes or engage in suspicious behaviors they would probably not have done without the enticement of an informant.

ETHICS rules of conduct or moral principles arising from a society's culture, customary standards, laws, and religious teachings that help individuals to determine what is morally right and wrong or what kind of behavior is acceptable and what is not under specific conditions.

ETHNIC NATIONALISM identification with and support for one's nation based on the idea that membership in the nation is defined by ethnicity.

EXPRESSIVE TARGETS persons and places that are targeted by terrorists due to emotion-based motivations and desires.

EXTERNAL FACTORS elements that are outside of the individual, such as the economic structure and political environment.

EXTORTION the act of obtaining something by use of a threat.

EXTREMIST a person who holds radical or fanatical social, political, or religious views.

FAILED PLOT a terrorist plot that was unsuccessful because of something the would-be perpetrators did, a factor internal to the plot—either they made

a mechanical mistake or they had a change of intention.

FAR LEFT the extreme left wing of the political spectrum, characterized by anti-establishment perspectives and advocacy for social equality and egalitarianism.

FAR RIGHT the extreme right wing of the political spectrum, characterized by radical conservative, nationalist, and authoritarian perspectives.

FASCISM a political ideology or regime headed by an autocratic leader in which the government controls all aspects of a society through forceful suppression of opposition. Fascist systems are characterized by extreme nationalism, militarism, and the rule of a powerful leader over the citizens.

FEAR a basic emotion that people feel when they experience a decrease in their sense of power. Fear has survival value because it signals danger or a threat to one's self-interest or social group and encourages a fight-or-flight response.

FEAR OF OUTSIDERS a fear of individuals or groups that are different from oneself or one's social groups.

FEDERAL BUREAU OF INVESTIGATION (FBI) the US federal government agency that enforces federal law and investigates criminal activities including terrorism, cybercrime, white-collar crime, civil rights violations, and others.

FEMININITY the qualities considered to be characteristic of women or girls.

FIGHT-OR-FLIGHT a physiological reaction to a stressful situation that helps people respond by either confronting the stressor or removing oneself from the situation.

FOILED PLOT a terrorist plot that was unsuccessful because of some kind of intervention, whether from members of the public, friends or family, or by government authorities.

FORCED MARRIAGE a marriage that takes place without the consent of one or both members of the couple.

FOREIGN INTELLIGENCE SURVEILLANCE ACT (FISA) a US federal law that establishes the procedures for physical and electronic surveillance and the collection of foreign intelligence information.

FOREIGN STATE SUPPORT active or passive support provided to terrorist groups by foreign states.

FOUR-STAGE MODEL OF TERRORISM a theory that explains the emergence of a terrorist mindset through four incremental stages, beginning with the emergence of a negative event or grievance among a group.

FRAMING a process through with one (e.g., the media, politicians, political groups, social movement organizations) define an issue, diagnose its causes, make a moral assessment, and suggest remedies. Frames are worldviews that guide individual and collective behaviors.

FRAUD the use of intentional deception for material or monetary gain, frequently used as a fundraising tactic for terrorist and insurgent groups.

FREE PRESS the right of news organizations to report without government intervention.

FRENCH REVOLUTION a period of dramatic social and political change in France between 1789 and 1799. The term "terrorism" was used for the first time during the French Revolution.

FRONT COMPANIES businesses set up and controlled by another organization, such as a terrorist group, through which the group raise funds and conceals and launders proceeds obtained from legal and illegal activities.

FRUSTRATION-AGGRESSION (DRIVE) THEORY a theory of criminal behavior that argues aggression or violence stems from the frustration experienced at being prevented from achieving a goal.

FUNCTIONAL TARGETS a person or place that is targeted in an act of terrorism because its annihilation is important for the continued operation and the cause of the terrorist group.

FUNDAMENTALISM a strict adherence to a belief system and reactions to changes that threaten this belief system.

GENDER ROLES sets of behaviors and attitudes that a society deems appropriate for a particular gender, based on cultural norms and tradition.

GENERAL DETERRENCE when the general public is deterred from engaging in crime because they are aware of the punishments faced by those who do.

GENERAL STRAIN THEORY OF TERRORISM a theory of terrorism that proposes collective strains increase the likelihood of engaging in terrorist acts because they increase the negative emotions and foster the social learning of terrorism as a coping strategy.

GERMAN AUTUMN a reference to the series of high-profile terrorist attacks carried out in Germany in the autumn of 1977 by the Red Army Faction and the Popular Front for the Liberation of Palestine.

GLOBAL DEATH TOLL the number of deaths worldwide during a defined time period (e.g., one year), due to a specified cause (e.g., terrorist attacks).

GLOBAL TERRORISM DATABASE (GTD) The Global Terrorism Database (GTD) is an open-source database including information on terrorist events around the world from 1970 through 2020 (with annual updates planned for the future). Unlike many other event databases, the GTD includes systematic data on domestic as well as international terrorist incidents that have occurred during this time period and now includes more than 200,000 cases

GLOBAL WAR ON TERRORISM the global military campaign to counter and prevent terrorism initiated by the United States following the terrorist attacks on September 11, 2001, which included major wars in Afghanistan, Iraq, and Syria.

GOVERNMENT COMMUNICATIONS HEADQUARTERS (GCHQ) the security organization responsible for providing signals intelligence to the government and armed forces of the United Kingdom.

GULAG SYSTEM a Soviet system of forced labor camps in which over 1.5 million people died between the 1920s and 1950s.

GUNPOWDER PLOT a failed assassination attempt of King James of England in the sixteenth century; one of the first known examples of Christian terrorism.

GUSH EMUNIM an ultra-religious fundamentalist Zionist Jewish group, established by the followers of Rabbi Abraham Isaac Kook, the first chief Rabbi of Palestine, and organized around messianic ideas and the goal of creating Jewish settlements across Palestine.

HARD POWER the use of coercion to achieve a desired outcome.

HARD TARGETS a place or person that is guarded and protected from threats by strong physical security.

HEDONISM the pursuit of pleasure and avoidance of pain.

HEZBOLLAH a Lebanese Shia Muslim political party and militant group that is supported by Iran and opposes Israel and Western influence in the Middle East.

HIJACKING a terrorist tactic in which terrorists forcefully seize control of an aircraft, land vehicle, or ship while it is in transit.

HORSESHOE THEORY a theory that argues the political spectrum takes the shape of a horseshoe, with the middle-rounded section representing the political center and the ends of the horseshoe representing the extreme right and left. The extreme political ideologies are not portrayed as opposites, rather they resemble each other.

HOSTAGE-TAKING the military takeover of a place and the seizure of individuals present as a bargaining tool until the terrorists' demands are met.

HOT SPOTS a region of significant activity or violence. In recent years, terrorist attack hot spots have been located in Southeast Asia, the Middle East, and Northern Africa.

HUMAN SMUGGLING the provision of services such as transportation across international borders or the procurement of fraudulent documents for individuals who voluntarily want to gain illegal access into a foreign country. Also known as migrant smuggling.

HUMILIATION-REVENGE THEORY a theory of criminal behavior that argues that the experience of humiliation can result in a desire to seek revenge, often leading to violent behavior against the oppressor.

IDEOLOGY a particular set of beliefs, ideas, and principles that explain how society should be organized

ILLEGITIMATE SOURCES a reference to illegal sources of income in the financing of terrorism.

ILLICIT TRADE the illegal trade of controlled or scarce commodities such as oil, diamonds, and gold, in the black market.

INDICATED PREVENTION a terrorism prevention strategy that involves screening processes for people who already show signs of radicalization.

INDISCRIMINATE ATTACKS terrorist attacks that are random and fail to distinguish between combatants and protected individuals or objects such as civilians and civilian infrastructure.

INFORMAL VALUE TRANSFER SYSTEMS (IVTS) any system, mechanism, or network of people that receives money for the purpose of making the funds or an equivalent value payable to a third party in another geographical location.

INSURGENT TERRORISM nonstate actors that use terrorism in attempts to achieve social or political goals.

INTERGROUP PROCESSES interactions and relations between different groups.

INTERNATIONAL TERRORISM terrorist acts that extend beyond national borders or are sponsored by international terrorist organizations.

INTERROGATION PROGRAMS techniques used by security personnel to gain information or confessions related to criminal wrongdoing.

INTIMIDATION one of the common themes of terrorism. Intimidation involves inspiring fear and insecurity in a population.

INVOLUNTARY CELIBATES (INCELS) an online, gender-based, ideology-driven, anti-feminist extremist group composed of men who engage in violence against women because of their inability to find sexual partners.

IRAQ WAR LOGS the nearly 400,000 United States army field reports of the Iraq War from 2004 to 2009 that were published online in 2010 by WikiLeaks.

IRGUN ZVAI LEUMI a Jewish right-wing nationalist paramilitary organization that operated in Palestine when it was under British mandate between 1931 and 1948.

IRISH REPUBLICAN ARMY (IRA) a nationalist republican paramilitary group seeking to end British rule in Northern Ireland and to reunify the Irish territories as a fully independent sovereign state.

ISLAMIC STATE (IS/ISIL/ISIS) a transnational Salafi-jihadist group that has conducted and inspired terrorist attacks worldwide. Also known as the Islamic State or the Islamic State of Iraq and the Levant.

ITALIAN RED BRIGADES (BR) a far-left ideological terrorist group, primarily active from 1970 to 1981, known as the largest and most enduring terrorist group in Italy's history.

JACOBINS left-wing revolutionary actors during the French Revolution. The Jacobins were the first to use the term "terrorism" to refer to their use of indiscriminate violence during the French Revolution to destroy the old regime.

JAPANESE RED ARMY (JRA) an international Marxist-Leninist terrorist group, founded in 1971 with the goal of achieving a worldwide Marxist-Leninist revolution and overthrowing the Japanese government through terrorism.

JEWISH DEFENSE LEAGUE (JDL) a militant far-right religious and political organization in the United States and Canada that espouses anti-Arab Jewish nationalism.

JEWISH FIGHTING ORGANIZATION (EYAL) an extreme right-wing Jewish nationalist group that emerged in 1993, known for its role in the assassination of Israeli Prime Minister Yitzhak Rabin in 1995.

JEWISH ZEALOTS members of a violent political movement that encouraged rebellion against the Roman empire in the first century during the first Jewish-Roman War.

JOURNALISM ETHICS a reference to the professional code followed by journalists that includes (1) seek truth and report it, (2) minimize harm, (3) act independently, and (4) be accountable and transparent.

KAHANISM an ultra-religious, right-wing Jewish ideology based on the views of American-born extremist and Orthodox rabbi, Meir David Kahane.

KIDNAPPING the abduction and confinement of person against their will.

KOSOVO LIBERATION ARMY (UCK) an ethnic Albanian separatist militant group that fought for Kosovo's independence from Serbia in the 1990s.

KU KLUX KLAN the name for numerous historical and contemporary American far-right terrorist and hate groups motivated by a White supremacist agenda.

KURDISTAN WORKERS' PARTY (PKK) a Marxist-Leninist Kurdish militant political group and armed guerrilla movement primarily based in the Kurdish-majority regions of Turkey and northern Iraq.

LEFT-WING TERRORISM terrorism motivated by far-left political ideologies, often aimed at overthrowing capitalist systems in favor of communist or socialist government.

LEGITIMATE SOURCES a reference to means of obtaining funds from legal sources in the financing of terrorism.

LIBERATION FRONT OF QUEBEC (FLQ) a militant French Canadian separatist group that engaged in violence in its attempt to achieve Quebec's independence from Canada from 1963 to 1970.

LIBERATION TIGERS OF TAMIL EELAM (LTTE) a militant ethnic nationalist group in Sri Lanka that engaged in violence in attempts to establish an independent Tamil state between 1976 and 2009.

LIVESTREAMED ATTACKS terrorists' use of online media to broadcast attacks to the public in real time.

LOGISTICAL TARGETS a target of terrorism that is attacked to provide resources for a group's sustenance.

LONE ACTOR TERRORISTS individuals that carry out terrorist attacks without the support or direction of a terrorist organization.

LORD'S RESISTANCE ARMY (LRA) is a terrorist organization established in Uganda in the late 1980s with the goal of creating a new government based on Christianity's Ten Commandments.

MACRO-LEVEL STRESSORS an experience or event that causes strain or tension on whole societies.

MALINFORMATION content that is based in fact but removed from its original context and spread with the intent to cause harm.

MASS DATA COLLECTION the use of technology to collect and analyze data on large numbers of people.

MEDIA primary means of mass communication including broadcasting (e.g., television, radio), print (e.g., newspapers, magazines) and the internet (e.g., social media).

MENTAL ILLNESS a diverse range of psychological health conditions within individuals that can affect emotions, thinking, and behavior.

MILITARY TARGETS targets of terrorism that include individuals who have an official status with the security forces of the government and facilities and installations that are owned by the security forces.

MISINFORMATION information that is false or misleading but is spread without an intent to deceive.

MONEY LAUNDERING the disguising of the origins of illicit funds.

MUJAHIDEEN Islamist guerrilla fighters. The Afghan mujahideen fought against the Democratic Republic of Afghanistan and the Soviet Union.

MUSLIM TERRORIST STEREOTYPE an untrue generalized belief that Muslims are terrorists.

NATION a group of people who are bound together based on some common defining features such as history, religion, language, culture, or ethnicity.

NATIONAL LIBERATION FRONT a nationalist political party in Algeria.

NATIONAL LIBERATION FRONT OF TRIPURA (NLFT) a Baptist Christian nationalist terrorist organization that aimed to establish an independent Tripuri state in northeast India between 1989 and 2019.

NATIONAL ORGANIZATION OF CYPRIOT STRUGGLE (EOKA) a Greek Cypriot nationalist guerrilla organization that fought to end British colonial rule in Cyprus between 1955 and 1959.

NATIONAL SECURITY AGENCY (NSA) an intelligence agency of the US Department of Defense, responsible for global monitoring, collection, and processing of signal intelligence.

NATIONAL SOCIALIST UNDERGROUND (NSU) a German far-right neo-Nazi terrorist group consisting of three key members, active between 2001 and 2010.

NATIONALISTIC TERRORISM terrorism motivated by the desire to build, maintain, or promote a single national identity and unity within a state, based on some shared social characteristics such as ethnicity, language, culture, or religion.

NAZISM (NATIONAL SOCIALISM) a form of fascism that includes dictatorship, anti-Semitism, racism, and White supremacism, associated with the National Socialist German Workers' Party, which rose to power under the leadership of Adolf Hitler in 1933.

NEO-NAZIS members of militant social and political movements that seek to revive Nazi White supremacist ideology in the post–World War II era.

NEW HUMANITARIANS a reference to persons who support the repatriation of detained wives of ISIS fighters and their children into their home countries and argue that they should be regarded as victims and provided with social and psychological assistance.

NIQÁB a long garment worn by some Muslim women in public that covers their entire body and face, excluding the eyes.

NONSTATE ACTORS organizations or individuals that exert social or political influence but are not affiliated with any particular state.

ONLINE PAYMENT AND PROCESSING SYSTEMS nonbank financial institutions that offer internet-based payment and processing services to facilitate transactions among customers and merchants.

ONLINE RADICALIZATION radicalization into terrorism through online sources such as social media and online propaganda.

OUT-GROUPS a group defined as different or "other" in relation to a group to which one belongs.

PARAMILITARY a militant force that is not part of a state's official or legitimate armed forces.

PASSIVE SUPPORT indirect support provided to terrorist organizations such as providing safe haven to terrorist groups and allowing them to engage in fundraising activities.

PATRIARCHY a social system in which men are the heads of households and hold a disproportionate amount of power over women.

PATRIOTISM affective attachment and support of one's nation.

PHINEAS PRIESTHOOD an American domestic terrorist organization in which adherents follow a

religious ideology based on a story found in the Old Testament, "the Phineas action."

PHYSICAL DISENGAGEMENT refraining from terrorist activities and actions.

POLITICAL ELITES a reference to the small group of people who hold a disproportionate amount of political power in a society.

POLITICAL SPECTRUM the depiction of political ideology along an imaginary line, with extreme right and left ideologies placed at the opposite side of each end and the middle of the line indicating the political center.

POLITICS OF FEAR the construction of fear among the public to serve political interests.

POPULAR FRONT FOR LIBERATION OF PALESTINE (PFLP) a Palestinian Marxist-Leninist militant faction of the Palestine Liberation Organization that carried out numerous terrorist attacks against Israeli and Western targets, often by hijacking aircraft.

POPULAR LIBERATION MOVEMENT OF ANGOLA a Marxist-Leninist nationalist political organization in Angola that emerged to fight for Angola's independence from Portugal.

POPULATION HETEROGENEITY an aggregate of individuals that differs from each other in significant ways; population diversity.

POST-TRAUMATIC STRESS ORDER (PTSD) a mental health condition caused by a traumatic experience. Symptoms of PTSD include flashbacks, nightmares, anxiety, and trouble sleeping.

POVERTY a condition in which individuals lack the socioeconomic resources necessary to achieve a certain standard of living.

POWERLESSNESS an inability to achieve desired goals or exert influence over a situation or others.

PREDISPOSITION OR SUSCEPTIBILITY THEORY a theory developed by Evan Kohlmann, which argues that due to their religious and political beliefs and associations, Muslims have an ideological predisposition to violence.

PREJUDICE an unfair and unreasonable opinion of dislike for a person or group.

PREPLANNED TARGETS targets of terrorism that involved complex operations and advance planning prior to the attack.

PREVENTION PROGRAMS countering violent extremism (CVE) programs that seek to prevent the radicalization process from taking hold in the first place and generally target a segment of society rather than a specific individual.

PRISM PROGRAM the code name for a surveillance program by which the US National Security Agency collects internet communications from various online providers.

PROGRAM EVALUATIONS systematic studies that examine the effectiveness of intervention programs.

PROPAGANDA BY THE DEED the use of terrorist tactics to promote a political cause. The phrase referred to violence used by anarchists and revolutionary groups during the second half of the nineteenth century and early twentieth century.

PROTECTION RACKETS a scheme in which a group guarantees protection to an individual or group outside the sanction of the law.

PROTECTIVE BEHAVIORS behavioral coping responses that involve actions taken to alleviate stress associated with being a victim of crime such as installing a security system or purchasing a gun.

PROUD BOYS a North American all-male militant far-right extremist group that espouses an Islamophobic, anti-Semitic, homophobic, transphobic, misogynistic, and xenophobic ideology.

PROVOCATION the use of terrorist tactics by groups in order to encourage governments to take harsh repressive measures against the terrorist group and its supporters and sympathizers.

PSYCHOLOGICAL DISENGAGEMENT discontinuing support of terrorist ideology or ceasing cognitions that support terrorism.

PSYCHOLOGICAL DISTRESS an aversive state including negative emotions and behaviors that endanger one's well-being, experienced in response to stress.

PSYCHOLOGICAL RESEARCH investigations conducted by psychologists that involve the systematic study of human cognition, experiences, and behaviors.

PSYCHOLOGICAL SYMPTOMS negative emotions, feelings, or states of mind including sadness, anxiety, and fear that can result from exposure to stress.

PSYCHOLOGY the study of the mind and behvior, including mental processes such as thoughts, feelings, and motives.

PUBLIC REPORTING PROGRAMS terrorism prevention programs that encourage the public to look out for possible terrorism-related behaviors, often encouraging people to call a tip line with information if they observe something suspicious.

PUBLICITY attention given to someone or something by the media.

RADICALIZATION a process of escalation from non-violent to increasing violent repertoires of action that develop through a complex set of interactions unfolding over time.

RAIDS a tactic of terrorism in which armed fighters attack for a short period at an unexpected time (often overnight) in order to surprise and demoralize the adversary with heavy casualties and destruction. Also known as surprise attacks.

RATIONAL CHOICE AND DETERRENCE a theory that argues that people weigh pros (potential benefits) and cons (possible costs) when they make a decision to commit crime. Crime may be committed if an individual perceived it to create immediate benefits and limited consequences.

RED ARMY FRACTION (RAF) a West German far-left militant organization founded in the late sixties.

RED SCARE a period of public fear and anxiety over the perceived rise of communist or socialist ideologies in a noncommunist state, often used in reference to two periods in US history following each of the world wars.

REDEMPTION in reference to suicide bombings, motivation by the belief that a voluntary act of martyrdom (suicide bombing) will atone for past misdeeds or accusations.

REIGN OF TERROR a period of time during the French Revolution characterized by mass executions of people who were perceived to be enemies of the newly established French government.

REINFORCEMENT any stimulus that increases the probability that a response will occur.

RELIGIOUS DISCRIMINATION unfair treatment of a person or group because of their religious identity.

RELIGIOUS TERRORISM terrorism that is influenced by interpretations of religious texts, beliefs, or clerical authorities used to achieve political or divine goals.

REPATRIATION the return of someone to their own country.

RESOURCE MOBILIZATION the process of obtaining resources needed to reach a group's goals.

REVENGE the act of inflicting harm in pursuit of justice.

REVOLUTIONARY ARMED FORCES OF COLOMBIA (FARC) a Colombian Marxist-Leninist guerrilla group that emerged in 1964 following a decade-long civil war and fought the Colombian government through kidnapping, extortion, and drug-trafficking activities.

REVOLUTIONARY TAXES taxes extorted by terrorist groups from businesses against the threat of being attacked. Also known as protection money.

RIGHT-WING TERRORISM terrorism motivated by far-right political ideologies, often characterized by ethno-traditional nationalism, xenophobia, racism, and authoritarianism.

SABOTAGE the deliberate destruction of nonhuman targets, such as places, property, or equipment that are owned by the adversary.

SALAFISM a contemporary Sunni Islamist school of thought that emerged during the late nineteenth and early twentieth century and involves following and imitating the lived examples of the Islamic Prophet Muhammad and the first Muslims in every sphere of the life, from religious practices to daily activities such as culinary habits and outward appearance.

SECULARIZATION the process of disassociating from religious rules and concerns.

SELECTIVE PREVENTION a terrorism prevention strategy that targets specific groups of people who are perceived to be at a high risk for radicalization.

SELF-FINANCING in terrorism funding, paying for the costs of terrorism using one's own resources.

SENATE TORTURE REPORT an extensive document released in December 2014 as a result of a multi-year investigation by the United States Senate Select Committee on Intelligence into the use of enhanced interrogation techniques by the Central Intelligence Agency (CIA) in the post–9/11 era.

SEXUAL EXPLOITATION the acts of taking advantage of a person's body in a sexual manner for another's benefit, usually financial.

SICARII a subgroup of Jewish Zealots known as the most extremist Jews who engaged in assassinations and brutal terrorist acts against the ruling Romans and their Jewish sympathizers.

SIEGE the military takeover of a place, such as a school, bank, theater, or shopping mall with the aim of forcing the surrender of the adversary.

SIGNALS INTELLIGENCE (SIGINT) a type of foreign intelligence gathering that involves the interception and analysis of signals, including communications between people and systems such as radar and weapons.

SINGLE-ISSUE TERRORISM terrorism in which certain groups or individuals fight for one cause such as animal rights, environmental protection, or anti-abortion.

SITUATIONAL CRIME PREVENTION an approach to crime prevention that recognizes that criminals take advantage of opportunities in given situations and changes the environment to increase the effort needed and risks associated with committing crime.

SMUGGLING the illegal movement of people or goods into or out of a country.

SOCIAL CONTEXT the physical and social setting in which people live including their culture, institutions, and relationships with others.

SOCIAL DISORGANIZATION THEORY a theory that argues that criminal behavior stems from the social context in which people live, rather than from individual traits. Breakdowns in the social institutions of a community weaken the community's ability to provide informal social control and socialize youth, thereby leading to higher levels of crime.

SOCIAL IDENTITY THEORY a social psychological theory that proposes individuals have, as a part of their self-conceptions, group-based social identities. Through a process of social categorization, individuals come to view those sharing their social identity as the in-group and those not sharing the identity as out-groups.

SOCIAL ISOLATION a state characterized by the absence of interactions and relationships between an individual and others or society as a whole.

SOCIAL LEARNING THEORY a theory that argues criminal behavior is learned through interactions with others who have values and perspectives that support criminal behavior.

SOCIAL MEDIA websites and online applications that allow users to create and share content.

SOCIAL MOVEMENT THEORY a combination of insights from research primarily based in sociology and political science that seek to understand collective behavior that is organized and dedicated to achieving a common social goal.

SOCIAL TRUST a belief in the honesty, integrity, and reliability of others.

SOCIALIZATION the process of learning to think and behave in a way acceptable to a society or group.

SOCIOLOGY the study of social life, including the social causes and consequences of human behavior.

SOFT POWER the use of persuasion to obtain desired outcomes.

SOFT TARGETS a location, place, or a person that is vulnerable to attacks due to a lack of security measures and protections in place.

SOLDIERS OF JESUS a violent neo-Pentecostalist terrorist organization in Brazil that seized control of neighborhoods outside of Rio de Janeiro.

SPECIFIC DETERRENCE   the prediction that individuals who do engage in crime will be deterred from committing future crimes due to the punishment that they experienced.

STAIRCASE MODEL OF TERRORISM   a theory that explains radicalization into terrorism as a gradual progression of thoughts and behaviors in which fewer and fewer people ascend a metaphorical staircase to engaging in acts of terrorism.

STAMMHEIM PRISON   a maximum-security prison in Germany specifically constructed to detain the leaders of the Red Army Faction during their criminal trial.

STATE   is an association of people with its own sovereign political organization and independent government within a clearly defined territorial boundary.

STATE TERRORISM   a government's use and support of violent nonstate actors as proxies, including funding terrorist activities, providing training and arms, and protecting terrorist groups.

STEREOTYPING   attributing generalized, oversimplified, and often untrue characteristics to a person or group.

STRAIN THEORY   a theory of criminal behavior that argues that individuals may commit crime when they are unable to achieve socially prescribed goals.

STRESS   mental or physical strain that results from exposure to a stimulus (e.g., event or condition).

SUBSTITUTION EFFECT   when a potential target or tactic of terrorism is replaced with another target or tactic due to an increase in security measures associated with the original targets or tactics.

SUICIDE ATTACK   a terrorist attack in which the actor uses their body as a weapon and intentionally kills themself in the process.

SUICIDE TERRORISM   a terrorism tactic in which the attacker intentionally kills themself in the process of carrying out the attack.

SURVEILLANCE   close observation of someone or something, particularly when suspected of criminal behavior.

SYMBIONESE LIBERATION ARMY   an American militant far-left organization that aimed to create small homelands for minority groups and fought against racism, monogamy, and all institutions that sustained capitalism between 1973 and 1975.

SYMBOLIC TARGETS   a target of terrorism that is selected due to its ability to inflict heavy psychological damage on the enemy.

TACTIC   in terrorism, an act or strategy planned to achieve a desired result.

TAILORED ACCESS OPERATIONS (TAO)   an elite unit of the US National Security Agency that identifies, monitors, infiltrates, and gathers intelligence on foreign computer systems.

TARGETED KILLINGS   discriminate violence which targets only the "enemies of the people," such as government officials, politicians, judges, police officers, and elites.

TARGETS OF ATTENTION (PSYCHOLOGICAL TARGETS)   the primary audiences that the terrorists aim to influence by their attacks.

TARGETS OF OPPORTUNITY   vulnerable enemy targets that appear in an unexpected time and place when an attack has not been preplanned or arranged.

TARGETS OF VIOLENCE (PHYSICAL TARGETS)   the actual targets that terrorists aim to kill or destroy in an attack.

TAX FRAUD   intentionally committing acts to avoid paying taxes such as the falsifying of income records and obtaining tax exemption certificates to buy goods without tax and then resell them at higher prices.

TERROR BOMBINGS   the use of bombing as a tactic of terrorism.

TERRORISM   the use of violence against noncombatants to affect a larger audience and achieve some social or political goal.

TERRORISM FINANCING   the processes of raising, storing, and transferring funds acquired through various means to enable terrorist organizations to plan and execute terrorist acts and maintain the daily functioning of their organizations.

TERRORISM-RELATED DEATH   human casualties that result from terrorist attacks.

TERRORIST PROFILING   the process of identifying likely terrorist suspects by a set of characteristics thought to be common to terrorists.

THEFT   the taking of another person's or business's property or services without their consent.

THREAT ELIMINATION   terrorist attacks that are targeted toward enemy individuals and installations that pose a threat to the well-being and interests of a terrorist group and its members.

TORTURE MEMOS   a set of legal memorandums exchanged between the Department of Justice, White House, CIA, and the Department of Defense regarding the protection of US officials from being charged with war crimes for the mental and physical torture and coercion of detainees.

TOTALITARIAN relating to a government that is centralized, has almost complete control over the lives of its citizens, and does not permit political opposition.

TULSA MASSACRE an 18-hour terrorist attack in Tulsa, Oklahoma, 1921, in which mobs of White supremacists attacked and destroyed a Black neighborhood, killing approximately 300 Black residents.

TWO-PYRAMIDS MODEL OF TERRORISM a theory of radicalization that consists of two models (pyramids)—an opinion pyramid and an action pyramid—that distinguish different types of individuals that occupy different levels of the pyramids, with higher levels corresponding to greater commitment to terrorism.

UNDERCOVER INFORMANT a person who works with law enforcement to gather and provide information about criminal activities.

UNIVERSAL PREVENTION terrorism prevention efforts that target the entire population in an effort to strengthen public resilience.

UNMANNED AERIAL VEHICLES (UAV) remotely operated computer-based aerial systems frequently employed for carrying out lethal counterterrorism operations and long-range surveillance on enemy targets. Also known as drones.

USA PATRIOT ACT an act signed by President George W. Bush following the terrorist attacks of September 11, 2001, relaxed existing privacy laws to increase the intelligence gathering capabilities of the government and facilitate information sharing between law enforcement and intelligence personnel that may detect and disrupt terrorist plots.

VIGILANTE TERRORISM terrorism committed by the citizens of a country against other citizens.

VIOLENT EXTREMISM beliefs and actions that support the use of violence to achieve social, religious, or political goals.

VISUAL MEDIA the use of visual elements including videos, photographs, and illustrations to communicate information.

VULNERABILITY FACTORS motivational factors that may push an individual into terrorism, such as perceived injustice, humiliation, or a need for belonging.

VULNERABILITY PERSPECTIVE a criminological theory that argues that fear of crime is greatest among individuals who, due to their personal characteristics, are believed to face a greater risk of criminal victimization than others.

WATERBOARDING a form of torture used in interrogations in which water is poured over a cloth covering the face while a person is restrained, causing them to experience the sensation of drowning.

WEAPONS OF MASS DESTRUCTION (WMD) chemical, biological, radioactive, and nuclear weapons that have the potential for widespread psychological and physical destruction on the critical structures of society and human lives.

WEATHER UNDERGROUND an American militant far-left student-led group that emerged in opposition to US involvement in the Vietnam War and American imperialism and sought to advance communism through violent revolution.

WHITE SUPREMACY a prejudiced belief that White people constitute a superior race and therefore should dominate non-Whites.

WIKILEAKS a nonprofit whistleblowing media organization and online publisher of leaked information.

INDEX

Tables, figures, and boxes are indicated by an italic *t*, *f*, and *b* following the page number.